HANDBOOK OF
Mental Health
IN THE
Workplace

HANDBOOK OF Mental Health IN THE Workplace

Jay C. Thomas
Pacific University

Michel Hersen
Pacific University

SAGE Publications
International Educational and Professional Publisher
Thousand Oaks ▪ London ▪ New Delhi

For information:

Sage Publications, Inc.
2455 Teller Road
Thousand Oaks, California 91320
E-mail: order@sagepub.com

Sage Publications Ltd.
6 Bonhill Street
London EC2A 4PU
United Kingdom

Sage Publications India Pvt. Ltd.
M-32 Market
Greater Kailash I
New Delhi 110 048 India

Printed in the United States of America

Library of Congress Cataloging-in-Publication Data

Handbook of mental health in the workplace / edited by Jay C. Thomas
and Michel Hersen.
    p. cm.
Includes bibliographical references and index.
  ISBN 978-0-7619-2255-1
  1. Industrial psychiatry. I. Thomas, Jay C., 1951- II. Hersen,
Michel.
  RC967.5 .H355 2002
  616.89—dc211

                    2002001784

10 11 12 13 10 9 8 7 6 5 4 3 2

Acquiring Editor:	Jim Brace-Thompson
Editorial Assistant:	Karen Ehrmann
Copy Editor:	Liann Lech
Production Editor:	Claudia A. Hoffman
Typesetter:	C&M Digitals (P) Ltd., Chennai, India
Indexer:	Molly Hall
Cover Design:	Michelle Lee

Contents

PART III: EFFECTS OF PSYCHOPATHOLOGY
ON WORK

PART IV: EFFECTS OF DISRUPTIVE BEHAVIOR AT WORK

PART V: ORGANIZATIONAL PRACTICE AND MENTAL HEALTH

Preface

The *Handbook of Mental Health in the Workplace* is a unique contribution in a burgeoning new field because it combines insights, methods, and problems from multiple disciplines. The growth in interest in mental health in the workplace is fueled by two trends. First, clinicians are growing more aware that the mental health concerns of their adult clients are affected by the workplace, and that treatment without regard to what happens in the employment setting is not likely to succeed. Second, there is growing recognition of the extent of psychopathology in the workforce. Prevalence rates of mental disorders make it likely that many, if not most, employees will, at some time during their career, either experience one or more episodes themselves or know someone who does. In the past, the employer's response to mental illness was to simply discharge the employee, but over the past decade, laws regulating employment of individuals with disabilities have made this a problematic practice. In some cases, such as conditions resulting from job stress, the employer may be considered to have responsibility for the condition and may even be liable for damages. Consequently, organizations have to contend with issues related to psychopathological or disruptive behavior that, a few years ago, they would have swept under the rug. Thus, we see three audiences for this book: clinical and counseling psychologists, who need to know how work and the workplace will influence their clients' progress; industrial and organizational (I/O) psychologists and human resources managers (HRM), who need to contend with organizational environments and policies; and administrators of Employee Assistance Programs. Students in these fields will also find it useful in providing them with a distinctive perspective and information that is not readily available elsewhere.

The book is divided into five parts. Part I, General Issues, provides an overview of the problems surrounding mental health in the workplace and describes the employee and employer rights and responsibilities under the law. Part II, Working Conditions, Life Stressors, and Mental Health, presents the current thinking and research on job stress and its effects on mental and physical health; the impact of work-family conflict, a special type of stressor of particular interest to women; and organizational interventions for reducing job stress and work-family conflict. Part III, Effects of Psychopathology on Work, presents detailed descriptions of the most common forms of psychopathology that may affect the workplace. Although each of these diagnostic categories is well documented elsewhere, the unique contribution of this book is to concentrate on how the disorder affects the ability to work, precipitating factors, and recommended treatments and their likely side effects. All of this is designed to give the clinician, the I/O psychologist, and the HRM the information they need to determine the employee's fitness for work and what, if any, accommodations may be needed. Part IV, Effects of Disruptive Behavior at Work, deals with behavior that may or may not fall into standard diagnostic categories, but that has clear mental health implications. This includes the effects of anger and violence in the workplace, poor social skills, the impact of abuse, exposure to traumatic events in the workplace, passive-aggressive behavior, and the impact of grieving on work. Part V, Organizational Practice and Mental Health, describes how mental health issues need to be considered in designing organizations, designing policies related to mental health concerns, analyzing jobs to identify essential functions that may be affected by mental health, and designing accommodations for psychological disabilities. These chapters will be particularly useful in meeting the legal obligations of employers toward psychologically disabled employees.

The authors of the chapters deserve special recognition because we asked them to think about their subject in new ways. Although this led initially to some intellectual discomfort, the result was to stimulate new perspectives on established theories and to generate some practical, yet rigorous, solutions to new problems.

We also thank Carole Londerée for her immense contributions to the organization of this project and Kay Waldron for continually going above and beyond her duties in the preparation of this book. The able assistance of Alex Duncan and Angelina Marchand was invaluable. Finally, Jim Brace-Thompson and his staff at Sage Publications have been a delight to work with and have provided great assistance. Jim, in particular, has been very patient, yet a great motivator in having us complete this project.

— JAY C. THOMAS
Portland, Oregon
— MICHEL HERSEN
Forest Grove, Oregon

Part I

GENERAL ISSUES

[redacted]

CHAPTER 1

Mental Health in the Workplace: Toward an Integration Organizational and Clinical Theory, Research, and Practice

JAY C. THOMAS
JEFFREY HITE

Until recently, there has been little need for a *Handbook of Mental Health in the Workplace*. Two factors accounted for this: lack of awareness of the extent of mental disorders by those who design and manage organizations, and the ease of eliminating the problem by eliminating the affected employee. In this chapter, we present sufficient data to show that mental illness[1] is pervasive in American society as well as in economically advanced societies in general. We also argue that organizations will find it in their own interests, as well as the employee's, to attempt to accommodate the needs of an individual experiencing mental distress. Our third goal in this introduction is to outline briefly how mental health issues intersect with organizational practices. No attempt is made to be comprehensive in reviewing the literature to meet this third goal. The other chapters in this book, some of which we cite in this chapter, accomplish that. The intent is to present the issues sufficiently to demonstrate that mental health and organizational theory and practice are, indeed, bedfellows, and have been for a long time.

The stigma attached to mental illness was sufficient to cause most people to keep personal or family distress hidden whenever possible. One result of keeping mental health issues in the closet was the perception that such problems were rare, and hence of no concern to anyone except those who

AUTHORS' NOTE: The authors would like to express their appreciation for the helpful comments by Jon Frew and Paula Truax on earlier drafts of this chapter.

were afflicted and medical or psychological specialists. Mental health has come out of the closet, thanks in part to the well-publicized problems of several politicians, celebrities, and athletes. When the public learned of senators and Olympic champions coping with depression, of movie actors with personality disorders, and of innumerable well-known personages struggling with alcohol or drug addiction, not to mention the thousands of veterans with symptoms of posttraumatic stress disorder, the problems of a parent or child, or of one's self, became less shameful and were recognized as a common situation.

Mental disorders are, in fact, extremely common. Epidemiological studies cited in Milazzo-Sayre, Henderson, and Manderscheid (1997) indicate that within the United States, in a 1-year period, approximately 28% of the adult population has a mental or addictive disorder. These authors cite other evidence that indicates that nearly 3% of the adult U.S. population suffers from a "severe" mental disorder during a 1-year period. The National Institute of Mental Health (NIMH) provides data on its Web site that give an idea of the numbers of Americans with various types of mental disorders. Selected figures are presented in Table 1.1. Comorbidity—the joint appearance of two or more disorders—complicates the picture somewhat, but the total still adds up to a great many people. These numbers represent only adults, who may have jobs. There are also millions of children with mental disorders whose parents may well be employees, probably distracted ones. Finally, the prevalence of mental disorders is sufficient to gain the attention of the Surgeon General of the United States, who commissioned a major report issued in 1999 (Satcher, 1999). This report concluded that all Americans are affected either directly or indirectly by mental illness, through family, coworkers, friends, or neighbors. With all of this information, it is impossible to escape the conclusion that mental health concerns can, and probably do, appear in almost any workplace in the country.

The second factor why a handbook on mental health in the workplace is needed can be traced to the needs and responsibilities of employers. It is now clear that mental health issues are in the workplace, but these issues affect the way organizations are managed and even the profitability of enterprises. Recently, the *Wall Street Journal* acknowledged this impact by devoting most of the cover page of its Marketplace section to this topic. The lead article begins as follows:

> In a typical office of 20 people, chances are that four will suffer from a mental illness this year. Depression, one of the most common, primarily hits workers in their most productive years: the 20s through 40s. Its annual toll on U.S. businesses amounts to about $70 billion in medical expenditures, lost productivity and other costs. (Tanouye, 2001, p. B1)

Gabriel (2001) gives a somewhat more conservative estimate of the cost of depression to U.S. employers: between $30 billion and $44 billion. These totals consist of direct treatment costs, costs associated with absenteeism, lost productivity, and mortality costs due to suicide. Such costs will also occur for other mental disorders, although the weighting may change as a function of the type and severity of disorder.

Gabriel (2001) also cites interesting figures from First Chicago Corporation, which indicate that, out of 10 common medical afflictions, mental illness is second only to ischemic heart disease in total cost. Cancer is a near third. Outpatient treatment costs are comparable for all three, and both

Table 1.1   Estimated Numbers of American Adults With Various Mental Disorders

Disorder	Estimated Occurrence
Major depression	More than 19 million
Manic-depressive illness (bipolar disorder)	More than 2.3 million
Schizophrenia	More than 2 million
Anxiety disorders	
Overall	More than 16 million
Panic disorder	About 2.4 million per year
Obsessive-compulsive disorder	Approximately 3.3 million
Posttraumatic stress disorder	About 5.2 million
Social phobia	About 5.3 million

SOURCE: National Institute of Mental Health (n.d.-b).

heart disease and cancer have roughly double the inpatient cost of mental illness. However, mental illness results in far higher short-term disability costs, which ultimately result in increased expenses and lower profits. Disability is a common consequence of mental illness. Internationally, mental illness, including suicide, is second only to "all cardiovascular conditions" in disease burden (measured in DALYs—Disability Adjusted Life Years, lost years of healthy life) in established market economies (NIMH, n.d.-a). Therefore, disabilities are expensive to employers, those who are disabled, and society at large.

In the past, because mental illness was so costly, as long as sufferers were stigmatized, employers could deal with the problem easily by terminating the affected employee. Since enactment of the Americans with Disabilities Act (ADA) in 1990, it has been illegal to fire an employee solely because of a disability. "Reasonable accommodation" must be made to allow most people with disabilities to continue working, if at all possible. Many other countries have similar or more stringent laws (Gabriel & Liimatainen, 2001), so the need to work with mentally disabled employees does not end at the U.S. border.

Even if there were no legal impediments, termination has not been easy and is often costly (Miner & Brewer, 1976). Labor agreements, while allowing for termination in cases of egregious behavior, often afford an employee with protection, so that termination can be a drawn-out and expensive affair. Unless the employee has managed to alienate his or her coworkers, there are also problems of morale and perceived injustice. These may have significant, albeit hidden, costs that many employers would just as soon avoid. There is also the issue of fairness. We do not terminate an employee who has suffered a heart attack or cancer. A broken leg, not covered by ADA, may still be looked upon with some patience by an employer, although with some disappointment. Why, then, terminate an employee who is suffering a bout with depression or anxiety? Indeed, an employee with a broken leg from a skiing accident may be out of action longer than many with major depression. Finally, a employer may have a lot invested in an employee, an investment that is not easily abandoned. So, there are a number of sound business reasons to find an accommodation. Cronshaw and Kenyon (Chapter 25) and Tetrick and Toney (Chapter 26) offer insight into how such an accommodation may be found and implemented. However, the human resource professional or industrial and organizational (I/O) psychologist needs some basic knowledge about the most common disorders, including the nature of the disorder, precipitating stressors, and treatment.

ORGANIZATIONAL PRACTICE AND MENTAL HEALTH

Elton Mayo (cited in Gellerman, 1963), Chris Argyris (1957), Douglas McGregor (1960, 1966), and other mid-20th-century writers pointed out that organizational practices may affect mental health. Mayo's work inspired an extensive, but curious, form of industrial counseling, similar in some respects to Rogerian nondirective counseling, but oriented toward work (Highhouse, 1999). Although there was some anecdotal evidence of the method's effectiveness, it eventually lost favor due to an inability to show a positive impact on employees or the bottom line. In the Argyris formulation, a worker's adaptation to rigid hierarchy, autocratic management, and an unenriched job was itself an indication of retarded emotional development. The nature of the job could prevent the worker from attaining full mental health. McGregor, writing more or less contemporaneously with Argyris, believed that organizations were designed based on assumptions about the workers. His Theory X[2] consisted of management assumptions that had three basic assumptions but included several inexplicit beliefs, such as the following:

1. The average man is by nature indolent— he works as little as possible.

2. He lacks ambition, dislikes responsibility, prefers to be led.

3. He is inherently self-centered, indifferent to organizational needs.

4. He is by nature resistant to change.

5. He is gullible, not very bright, the ready dupe of the charlatan and the demagogue. (McGregor, 1966, p. 6; items renumbered from original)

Theory Y, in contrast, was based on the opposite assumptions of human nature. Of note is the Theory Y assumption that "people are not by nature passive or resistant to organizational needs. *They have become so as a result of experience in organizations* [italics added]" (McGregor, 1966, p. 15). Thus, if Theory X paints a picture of a man or woman who lacks full mental health, Theory Y holds that it is the organization for whom he or she works that is responsible. Today, we would question this last premise, realizing that to some extent, employees bring their mental disorders with them to work or develop them coincident to employment. Meaningful work is regarded as therapeutic by some psychologists, as described in some later chapters, but it seems doubtful that work alone is generally an effective therapy.

We present these classic theories in some detail because they form the foundation for the primary organizational and motivational theories up to the present. On the intellectual side, virtually everyone hopes for a world in which Theory Y is true, but our behavior often reveals little faith in that occurring. To illustrate, one of the unspoken worries about the ADA was that it would encourage malingering, the ultimate Theory X behavior. Claims of disability are often met with skepticism by management and coworkers. No one disputes that disability claims should be investigated and substantiated, but we maintain that this book will help lead to informed skepticism rather than an automatic assumption that a claimant is most likely "faking it."

The universal rejection of Theory X by organizational theorists opened the door for current conceptualizations of flat hierarchies; self-managed, team-based organizations; and expectations that employees make decisions with the organization's interests at heart. All of these concepts require an assumption that employees either can or can be easily taught to communicate openly, face situations honestly, work together with others, recognize others' priorities and adapt to them, shift priorities or tasks quickly and easily, and make and carry out decisions that may be contrary to their own interests (Cannon-Bowers, Tannenbaum, Salas, & Volpe, 1995; Wellins, Byham, & Wilson, 1991). People who are depressed, anxious, or overly stressed may have difficulty carrying out required behaviors to meet these assumptions. Individuals with personality disorders or psychotic conditions may not be able to gain or use such skills, except in extraordinary circumstances. Thus, the ultimate success of current theories of organization may depend upon the prevalence of clinical or even subclinical mental disorders in the workforce. To our knowledge, few, if any, studies have examined the robustness of these management theories to violations of the assumptions of a mentally healthy workforce.

THE IMPACT OF THE WORKPLACE ON MENTAL HEALTH

The workplace itself may contribute to distress and, ultimately, to mental disorders. This notion dates to at least the 1930s, with studies examining the presence of inhalable toxic chemicals and employee emotionality (cf. Tiffin, 1942). As we described earlier, the effect of the social organization was fundamental to Argyris's (1957) work and implicit in McGregor's (1960, 1966) writing. Today, descendants of these ideas have been validated by considerable research on the impact of stress on the worker and the work (see Sutherland and Cooper, Chapter 3, and Smith, Sulsky, and Uggerslev, Chapter 4). Too much work, poorly defined responsibilities, an unsupportive boss, a lack of control, and many other factors can constitute stressors that, in turn, under the right (or perhaps we should say wrong) conditions, can create sufficient strain such that a person becomes physically or mentally ill.

Unfortunately, stress appears to be additive because the key is the total stress under which one operates. Stressors need not be confined to one area of life. Stress from a person's non-work life can combine with work stress to create problems. Making matters worse, different aspects of life can interact to create even more stress. Work-family conflict is the classic example of this and the cause of much distress across the workforce. Hammer, Colton, Caubet, and Brockwood (Chapter 5) show how work and family life conflict can wreak havoc in one's life, and Beehr and O'Driscoll (Chapter 6) describe how organizational stress and work-family conflict can be reduced.

Current organizational theories differ from those of the mid-20th century in two important ways. First, the assumed motivational foundation for employees has shifted from needs-based theories to a complex mix of environmental, social, cognitive, learning, emotional, and personality factors. This wider vista of motivational forces eventually will lead to an even fuller understanding of behavior in the workplace by allowing a stronger connection between organizational and clinical perspectives. Newly developing organizational and clinical theories of motivation are beginning to parallel one another in unexpected ways. As one example, Nolen-Hoeksema (1993) proposed that one causal factor in the development of depression was a response style she termed "rumination." Rumination consists of focusing inward on one's emotional feelings. Nolen-Hoeksema (1993) cites examples, such as thinking about how tired one is or how much one is lacking in motivation. Rumination may also include worrying about the implications of symptoms, such as not completing important work. Ruminative responses have been tied to depth and duration of a depressive episode and to interfering with the ability to make the instrumental responses necessary to eliminate the source of the worry. In other words, ruminating over one's failure to complete an important task may well interfere with initiating the behavior necessary to complete that task. At the opposite pole from ruminators are distracters. A distracting response style consists of removing attention from the negative feelings and concentrating on something else—almost anything else. Distracters find that they are able to plan effectively and carry out problem-solving behaviors efficiently and so do not slip into a depressive cycle.

Compare Nolen-Hoeksema's (1993) theory to a theory of motivation that is beginning to attract attention within I/O psychology: Kuhl's Action-State Theory (cited in Hall, Schlauch, & Chang, 2001) and its attendant Action-State Orientation. In this theory, when people encounter an anxiety-provoking situation, they adopt a state orientation, characterized by thoughts of failure, and exhibit difficulty in taking useful actions. People with an action orientation, in the same situation, may express anxiety about failure, but they use effective coping responses to plan and execute behaviors. Hall et al. (2001) utilize this theory in an interesting attempt to explain the effects of autonomy on job satisfaction and performance. There appears to be little

difference between a rumination strategy and a state orientation or between a distraction strategy and an action orientation. Additional research testing for both of these theories is needed before they can become fully established, but we anticipate that they will prove to be useful additions to our store of knowledge. A useful rule of thumb is that when two different fields of endeavor independently develop very similar propositions, it is likely that these propositions will prove to be important and general.

A second important difference between mid-20th-century organizational theories and current ones lies in the motivation for choosing the preferred organization design. Lawler (1991) traced this development from the Human Relations school, in which participation was valued because it would result in greater employee satisfaction and commitment; to the Human Resource approach, in which an investment in people pays off because they are more valuable; and to the High Involvement Organization ideal, in which having a hand in decision making in the management of their work by even the lowest level employees makes for greater organizational effectiveness. The impetus for such effectiveness comes from the necessity of adapting to forces in the outside world: changing competition, technology, consumer preferences, and other environmental influences (Galbraith & Kazanjian, 1988; Mohrman, 1993). Being driven by the environment requires a broad perceptual focus, openness, and the ability to make realistic appraisals of opportunities and threats. It also requires the ability to translate these appraisals into changed goals and priorities and the skill to communicate this to others. Most people would find working in such an environment arousing. It is well established that arousal and performance are related to each other according to an inverted U function

(Sutherland & Cooper, Chapter 3). Move a lethargic person up the arousal continuum and performance improves. Move too far and performance deteriorates. Undoubtedly, there are individual differences in where the apex of this curve lies and even in the function relating environmental forces to the degree of arousal. Degree and type of psychopathology may well influence both. Psychotherapists and physicians sometimes recommend transfer to "a less stressful job" as an accommodation for mental disability. Such requests are often defined so poorly as to be "impossible to satisfy" (Conti & Burton, 1999, p. 331). Moreover, if they were defined clearly, such jobs may not exist in organizations relying on high-involvement strategies.

The Need for Integration of Knowledge Between Clinical and I/O Psychology and Human Resources

For many years, clinical/counseling psychologists have gone one way, and I/O psychologists and their colleagues in human resources have gone another. Tiffin's (1942) textbook on industrial psychology included explicit attention to emotional factors and, in the context of personality testing, explained the major mental disorders as they were conceived at the time. Sometime after Tiffin's text, such matters largely disappeared from I/O psychology. Such research as was conducted through 1970 was reviewed by Miner and Brewer (1976) in the first edition of Dunnette's (1976) *Handbook of Industrial and Organizational Psychology*. In their chapter on the management of ineffective performance, "stress, emotion, and emotional disturbance" comprised 2 out of 34 pages, whereas alcoholism and drug addiction together took up three pages.

Levinson's (1983) work at the Division of Industrial Mental Health at the Menninger Foundation from 1956 to 1970 was an exception to the general separation of clinical and I/O psychology. At that time, he worked primarily on the "three A's—absenteeism, alcoholism, and accidents" (Levinson, 1983, p. 8). Levinson has continued to exert an influence on the field of organizational theory, although his psychoanalytic framework has left him somewhat outside the mainstream of I/O psychology.[3]

As mentioned previously, early counseling programs in industry faded away by the late 1950s or early 1960s (Highhouse, 1999). There remained a need for the counseling of employees with emotional or mental health problems, a niche eventually filled by Employee Assistance Programs (EAPs). These programs began as a means of providing employees with many types of assistance, including financial advice and planning, but have expanded their services to include providing mental health and some wellness services. As such, EAPs are primarily the reserve of clinical/counseling psychologists, counselors, and social workers. They have developed largely independently of I/O psychology but are integrated with human resources, because that is the department that usually selects and hires the EAP provider. By the mid-1970s, work in EAPs had evolved to the point where Manuso (1983) coined the term *occupational clinical psychology*. The scope of EAP service delivery has expanded to the point that many provide organizational services (Cagney, 1999), which may be indistinguishable in name from those offered by I/O psychologists (see Ginsberg, Kilburg, & Gomes, 1999, for an example). Although I/O psychologists often complain among themselves about this development and the loss of "their" market, a reversal of this trend does not seem likely in the foreseeable future. Joining together scientists and practitioners from the clinical, I/O, and human resource disciplines will further the interests of organizational and individual clients, a theme included in Manuso's (1983) book, and enrich development of the knowledge base of these fields.

By the second edition of Dunnette's *Handbook* in the early 1990s (Dunnette & Hough, 1992), which had grown to four large volumes, a chapter appeared detailing how to utilize counseling techniques in the development of employees and to achieve behavior change in general (Hellervik, Hazucha, & Schneider, 1992). Lowman (1993, 1996) has presented an integration of clinical and I/O psychology in his work on dysfunctional employees. Similarly, symposia and posters have appeared at Society for Industrial and Organizational Psychology (SIOP) conferences concerned with alcohol and drug use, emotional behavior, use of EAPs, and other clinically related topics. Recently, one of us (JCT) attended a preconference workshop at the SIOP conference on executive coaching. The issue that brought the greatest discussion among participants was how to differentiate between a client who was "odd" or "eccentric" and one who had a mental disorder that required clinical skills to treat and that lay outside the scope of coaching. The workshop participants understood the high probability that an executive coach with a large clientele would run into this situation eventually. They also recognized the need for gaining information that may be useful in such circumstances. Thus, we see a press for greater integration of I/O and clinical psychology from the perspectives of research and practice.

Clinicians and counselors work with clients on workplace issues. Under ADA, they may make recommendations as to fitness for duty, limitations on work, and even the types of accommodations that may be necessary. It is difficult to see how this is done properly without a basic working knowledge of work and the workplace, but it is being done.

Conti and Burton's (1999) description of how to manage behavior health disability makes it clear that this knowledge is essential in creating workable solutions. In addition to ADA issues, the workplace poses various risk factors for mental health, many of which would seem to be logical targets for therapy. Kasl (1992) listed 10 dimensions of the work setting that he considered to be at least provisionally affecting worker psychological health. These included interpersonal factors, such as coworkers and leaders; work content; organizational and structural aspects; and community and social aspects, such as prestige and status of occupation. A clinician who knows how organizations operate, the roles of leaders, the impact of organizational culture and climate, the impact of discrimination and harassment, and other features of the workplace will be better placed to assist clients in decision making, recognizing cognitive or behavioral traps, and otherwise making helpful changes.

As scientists and practitioners in the field of human behavior, we need to know more about the borders of normal behavior, if for no other reason than to better understand everyday life. That is as true in the work setting as in the rest of life. Herbert Simon (1969) wrote that we gain our greatest understanding of systems when they break down. We know a good deal about how the average person responds in a large number of organizational situations, but relatively little about how people at the extremes of personality, cognitive capacity, and emotionality respond. There is a shortage of research on the workplace and mental health. An exception lies in the area of counterproductive work behaviors, most notably anger, hostility, and violence. McNulty, Bordeaux, and Hogan (Chapter 20) review this area, whereas Svyantek and Brown (Chapter 24) examine the interaction of these behaviors and organizational climate and culture. Binning and

Wagner (Chapter 23) present a review and theory of passive-aggressive behavior, the first and only mental disorder originally identified in the workplace.

Enough is known about mental health in the workplace to fill a large book, but we would be the first to admit that what we know is insufficient. Although some interest in the topic goes back many years, it is only because of legal and social changes of the past 10 or 15 years that we have created the conditions where such a book is possible. Much more research is needed. Although we have made the case that mental disorders are common in the workplace, the base rate for a particular disorder in a particular workplace is likely to be too low for commonly employed research technologies. Generating the knowledge we will need for future developments may require the development of new research techniques amenable for use with small samples, such as randomization or permutation tests (Edgington, 1995; Ludbrook & Dudley, 1998). It may also require greater acceptance of some existing, but underused, techniques. Babiak's (1995) case study of an industrial psychopath is an excellent example of the latter. His detailing of that psychopath's mode of operation provides a rich source of potential further research ideas and also gives direction for the practitioner faced with such a person in a client organization. As new research accumulates, we expect organizational, human resource, and clinical practice to evolve along with it. Integration of I/O and clinical psychology, human resources, and other disciplines in the study, prevention, and treatment of mental health issues in the workplace is an exciting development that should pay dividends for many years.

NOTES

1. We use the term *mental illness* with some reluctance, but it is the phrase used in the most current literature (e.g., Gabriel & Liimatainen, 2001).

2. Although McGregor's nomenclature of Theory X and Theory Y implies a sort of algebraic objectivity, we believe that there was a clear message to the reader of the day. In the 1940s (at least) through the early 1960s, a common advertising ploy was to compare the name brand against "Brand X." Brand X was always decidedly inferior in results. It would be difficult for a reader in 1960 to not get the connection between "Theory X" and "Brand X."

3. A brief review of the psychodynamic view of organizational behavior, inspired largely by Levinson, is provided by Cilliers and Koortzen (2000).

REFERENCES

Argyris, C. (1957). *Personality and organization.* New York: Harper & Row.

Babiak, P. (1995). When psychopaths go to work: A case study of an industrial psychopath. *Applied Psychology: An International Review, 44,* 171-188.

Cagney, T. (1999). Models of service delivery. In J. M. Oher (Ed.), *The employee assistance handbook* (pp 59-70). New York: John Wiley.

Cannon-Bowers, J. A., Tannenbaum, S.I., Salas, E., & Volpe, C. E. (1995). Defining competencies and establishing team training requirements. In

R. A. Guzzo & E. Salas (Eds.), *Team effectiveness and decision making in organizations* (pp. 333-380). San Francisco: Jossey-Bass.

Cilliers, F., & Koortzen, P. (2000). The psychodynamic view on organizational behavior. *Industrial-Organizational Psychologist, 38*(2), 58-67.

Conti, D. J., & Burton, W. N. (1999). Behavioral health disability management. In J. M. Oher (Ed.), *The employee assistance handbook* (pp. 319-336). New York: John Wiley.

Dunnette, M. (Ed.). (1976). *Handbook of industrial and organizational psychology.* Chicago: Rand McNally.

Dunnette, M. D., & Hough, L. M. (Eds.). (1992). *Handbook of industrial and organizational psychology* (2nd ed., Vols. 1-4). Palo Alto, CA: Consulting Psychologists Press.

Edgington, E. S. (1995). *Randomization tests* (3rd ed.). New York: Marcel Dekker.

Gabriel, P. (2001). *Mental health in the workplace: Situation analysis—United States.* Geneva: International Labour Office.

Gabriel, P., & Liimatainen, M.-R. (2001). *Mental health in the workplace: Introduction.* Geneva: International Labour Office.

Galbraith, J. R., & Kazanjian, R. K. (1988). Strategy, technology, and emerging organizational forms. In J. Hage (Ed.), *Futures of organizations* (pp. 29-42). Lexington, MA: Lexington Books.

Gellerman, S. (1963). *Motivation and productivity.* New York: American Management Association.

Ginsberg, M. R., Kilburg, R. R., & Gomes, P. G. (1999). Organizational counseling and the delivery of integrated services in the workplace: An evolving model for employee assistance and practice. In J. M. Oher (Ed.), *The employee assistance handbook* (pp. 439-456). New York: John Wiley.

Hall, R. J., Schlauch, C. A., & Chang, C.-H. (2001, April). *Implications of an Action Control Theory approach and Action State Orientation for the understanding of autonomy effects on satisfaction and performance.* Paper presented at the annual meeting of the Society for Industrial and Organizational Psychology, San Diego, CA.

Hellervik, L. W., Hazucha, J. F., & Schneider, R. J. (1992). Behavior change: Models, methods, and review of evidence. In M. D. Dunnette & L. M. Hough (Eds.), *Handbook of industrial and organizational psychology* (2nd ed., Vol. 3, pp. 823-895). Palo Alto, CA: Consulting Psychologists Press.

Highhouse, S. (1999, April). *Frazier in the factory: The brief history of personnel counseling in I-O.* Paper presented at the annual meeting of the Society for Industrial and Organizational Psychology, Atlanta, GA.

Kasl, S. V. (1992). Surveillance of psychological disorders in the workplace. In G. P. Keita & S. L. Sauter (Eds.), *Work and well-being: An agenda for the 1990s* (pp. 73-95). Washington, DC: American Psychological Association.

Lawler, E. E., III. (1991). *High involvement management.* San Francisco: Jossey-Bass.

Levinson, H. (1983). Clinical psychology in organizational practice. In J. S. J. Manuso (Ed.), *Occupational clinical psychology* (pp. 7-13). Westport, CT: Praeger.

Lowman, R. (1993). *Counseling and psychotherapy of work dysfunctions.* Washington, DC: American Psychological Association.

Lowman, R. (1996). Work dysfunctions and mental disorders. In K. R. Murphy (Ed.), *Individual differences and behavior in organizations* (pp. 371-415). San Francisco: Jossey-Bass.

Ludbrook, J., & Dudley, H. (1998). Why permutation tests are superior to t and F tests in biomedical research. *American Statistician, 52*, 127-132.

Manuso, J. S. J. (Ed.). (1983). *Occupational clinical psychology.* Westport, CT: Praeger.

McGregor, D. (1960). *The human side of enterprise*. New York: McGraw-Hill.

McGregor, D. (1966). The human side of enterprise. In W. G. Bennis & E. H. Schein (Eds.), *Leadership and motivation* (pp. 3-20). Cambridge: MIT Press.

Milazzo-Sayre, L. J., Henderson, M. J., & Manderscheid, R. W. (1997). Serious and severe mental illness and work: What do we know? In R. J. Bonnie & J. Monahan (Eds.), *Mental disorder, work disability, and the law* (pp. 13-24). Chicago: University of Chicago Press.

Miner, J. B., & Brewer, F. J. (1976). The management of ineffective performance. In M. D. Dunnette (Ed.), *Handbook of industrial and organizational psychology*. Chicago: Rand McNally

Mohrman, S. A. (1993). Integrating roles and structure in the lateral organization. In J. A. Galbraith, E. E. Lawler III, & Associates (Eds.), *Organizing for the future: The new logic for managing complex organizations* (pp. 109-141). San Francisco: Jossey-Bass.

National Institute of Mental Health. (n.d.-a). *The impact of mental illness on society*. Available at www.nimh.nih.gov/publicat/burden.cfm.

National Institute of Mental Health (n.d.-b). *The numbers count*. Available at www.nimh.nih.gov/publicat/numbers.cfm.

Nolen-Hoeksema, S. (1993). Sex differences in control of depression. In D. M. Wegner & J. W. Pennebaker (Eds.), *Handbook of mental control* (pp. 306-324). Englewood Cliffs, NJ: Prentice-Hall.

Satcher, D. (1999). *Mental health: A report of the Surgeon General*. Washington, DC: Government Printing Office.

Simon, H. A. (1969). *The sciences of the artificial*. Cambridge: MIT Press.

Tanouye, E. (2001, June 13). Mental illness: A rising workplace cost. *Wall Street Journal*, p. B1.

Tiffin, J. (1942). *Industrial psychology*. New York: Prentice-Hall.

Wellins, R. S., Byham, W. C., & Wilson, J. M. (1991). *Empowered teams: Creating self-directed work groups that improve quality, productivity, and participation*. San Francisco: Jossey-Bass.

CHAPTER 2

Mental Health and Disabilities, the Employer, and the Law

H. JOHN BERNARDIN
BARBARA A. LEE

Individuals with mental or emotional disorders face challenges in the workplace. Stereotypical attitudes about the behavior and abilities of workers with psychiatric disorders may lead to exclusion, discrimination, or harassment. Although workers with such disorders are protected by federal and state nondiscrimination laws, managers' and coworkers' attitudes toward individuals with psychological disorders, judicial disinclination to view such disorders as worthy of accommodation, and the stigma that clings to individuals with mental disorders exacerbate the difficulties that these workers encounter.

Most employees are protected from disability discrimination by state or federal civil rights laws (and, for many workers, by both). The Americans with Disabilities Act (ADA) of 1990, the Rehabilitation Act of 1973, and the nondiscrimination laws of each state forbid an employer from making employment decisions solely on the basis of an individual's physical or mental health. Because the ADA is most relevant to most workers, we will restrict our detailed discussion to descriptions of the ADA and the case law relevant to psychiatric disorders.

The purpose of this chapter is to describe the ADA, discuss the current state of ADA law as it applies to psychiatric disabilities, and report on a survey of attitudes and opinions regarding workers with disabilities. Based on our review of the case law and the survey results, we conclude with some recommendations for employers and workers with psychiatric disabilities.

THE AMERICANS WITH DISABILITIES ACT

The ADA provides that qualified individuals with disabilities may not be discriminated against by a private sector organization or a department or agency of a local government employing 15 or more employees, and must provide the disabled with "reasonable accommodations" that do not place an undue hardship on the business. Reasonable

[handwritten annotation:] AGAIN it is STUPID TO DISCLOSE YOUR DISABILITY to Employer

[handwritten annotation:] Sure... Who is in there needs making the desition?

accommodations are determined on a case-by-case basis and may include reassignment, part-time work, and flexible schedules. They may also include providing readers, interpreters, assistants, or attendants. No accommodation is required if an individual is not otherwise qualified for the position. Box 2.1 presents excerpts from the ADA.

According to the Equal Employment Opportunity Commission's (EEOC's) 1997 *EEOC Enforcement Guidance on the Americans with Disabilities Act and Psychiatric Disabilities* (available at http://www.eeoc.gov), the ADA rule defines "mental impairment" to include "any mental or psychological disorder, such as emotional or mental illness." Examples of "emotional or mental illness(es) include major depression, bipolar disorder, anxiety disorders (which include panic disorder, obsessive compulsive disorder, and post-traumatic stress disorder), schizophrenia, and personality disorders."

The 1999 *EEOC Policy Guidance on Reasonable Accommodation* (also available on the EEOC Web site) under ADA suggests the following process for assessing "reasonable accommodation":

1. Look at the particular job involved; determine its purpose and its *essential functions.*

2. Consult with the individual with the disability to identify potential accommodations.

3. If several accommodations are available, deference should be given to the individual's preferences.

Public facilities such as restaurants, doctor's offices, pharmacies, grocery stores, shopping centers, and hotels must be made accessible to the disabled unless "undue hardship" would occur for the business. It is not clear, however, how organizations can show undue hardship, although the law suggests that a reviewing court compare the cost of the accommodation with the employer's operating budget.

Temporary help agencies and their clients are considered employees under the ADA according to the EEOC. Temporary or contingent employees are thus protected by the ADA from disability discrimination by either the help agency or the client organization. For example, neither the help agency nor the client may ask disability-related questions or require medical or psychiatric examinations until after a job offer has been made. This is an important interpretation because people with disabilities often seek temporary employment.

The EEOC approved enforcement guidelines on preemployment disability-related inquiries and medical exams under ADA. The guidelines state that "the guiding principle is that while employers may ask applicants about the ability to perform job functions, employers may not ask about disability." For example, a lawful question would be, "Can you perform the functions of this job with or without reasonable accommodation?" But it is unlawful for an employer to ask questions related to a disability, such as "Have you ever filed for worker's compensation?" or "What prescription drugs do you take?" or "Have you ever been treated for mental illness?" After an employer has made an offer and an applicant requests accommodation, the employer may "require documentation of the individual's need for, and entitlement to, reasonable accommodations."

ADA Case Law and Psychiatric Disabilities. Many workers with psychiatric disabilities have sought protection from

Box 2.1   Excerpts From the ADA

Section 102. Discrimination

(a) General Rule. No covered entity shall discriminate against a qualified individual with a disability because of the disability of such individual.

(b) Construction. As used in subsection (a), the term "discrimination" includes:

(1) Limiting, segregating, or classifying a job applicant or employee in a way that adversely affects the opportunities or status of such applicant or employee because of . . . disability. . . .

(2) Participating in a contractual or other arrangement or relationship that has the effect of subjecting a qualified applicant or employee with a disability to the discrimination prohibited by this title. . . .

(5) Not making reasonable accommodations to the known physical or mental limitations of a qualified individual who is an applicant or employee, unless such covered entity can demonstrate that the accommodation would impose an undue hardship on the operation of the business of such covered entity, and;

(7) Using employment tests or other selection criteria that screen out or tend to screen out an individual with a disability or a class of individuals with disabilities unless the test or other selection criteria, as used by the covered entity, is shown to be job-related for the position in question and is consistent with business necessity.

(c) Medical Examinations and Inquiries

(1) In general. The prohibition against discrimination as referred to in subsection (a) shall include medical examinations and inquiries.

Section 3. Definitions

(2) Disability. The term "disability" means, with respect to an individual:

(A) A physical or mental impairment that substantially limits one or more of the major life activities of such individual;

(B) A record of such an impairment, or;

(C) Being regarded as having such impairment.

Section 101. Definitions

(7) Qualified Individual with a Disability. The term "qualified individual with a disability" means an individual with a disability who, with or without reasonable accommodation, can perform the essential functions of the employment position that such individual holds or desires.

(8) Reasonable Accommodation. The term "reasonable accommodation" may include:

(A) Making existing facilities used by employees readily accessible to and usable by individuals with disabilities, and;

(B) Job restructuring, part-time or modified work schedules, reassignment to a vacant position, acquisition or modification of equipment or devices, appropriate adjustment or modifications of examinations, training materials or policies, the provision of qualified readers or interpreters, and other similar accommodations for individuals with disabilities.

(9) (A) In general. The term "undue hardship" means an action requiring significant difficulty or expense.

(10) (B) Determination. In determining whether an accommodation would impose an undue hardship on a covered entity, factors to be considered include:

(i) the overall size of the business;

(ii) the type of operation, and;

(iii) the nature and cost of the accommodation.

Section 103. Defenses

(b) Qualification Standards. The term "qualification standards" may include a requirement that an individual with a currently contagious disease or infection shall not pose a direct threat to the health or safety of other individuals in the workplace.

Section 104. Illegal Drugs and Alcohol

(a) Qualified Individual with a Disability. For purposes of this title, the term "qualified individual with a disability" shall not include any employee or applicant who is a current user of illegal drugs. . . .

(b) Authority of Covered Entity. A covered entity:
(1) may prohibit the use of alcohol or illegal drugs at the workplace by all employees;

(2) may require that employees shall not be under the influence of alcohol or illegal drugs at the workplace;

(3) may require that employees behave in conformance with the requirements established under "The Drug-Free Workplace of 1988" (41 U.S.C. 701 et seq.) [See Chapter 16, page . . ., and;

(4) may hold an employee who is a drug user or alcoholic to the same qualification standards for employment or job performance and behavior that such entity holds other employees. . . .

(c) Drug Testing
(1) In general. For purposes of this title, a test to determine the use of illegal drugs shall not be considered a medical examination.

alleged employment discrimination under the ADA and other laws. For example, between the date the ADA became effective (July 26, 1992) and the end of the 1999 fiscal year (September 30, 1999), individuals filed 25,221 claims involving alleged employment discrimination related to some type of psychological or cognitive impairment—fully 20% of all ADA claims filed with the EEOC for that time period (EEOC, 2001). This category of disorders constitutes the largest of all categories of disorders in EEOC claims for this period of time. The proportion of EEOC claims related to mental disorders parallels their frequency of occurrence in the working population; by some estimates, approximately one out of five individuals has a diagnosed or diagnosable mental or psychiatric disorder in any particular year (Hall, 1997, p. 248).

The ADA protects workers who are discriminated against by employers because of an impairment that meets the law's definition of disability (discussed below). Workers are also protected from discrimination if they have a record of a disability (but are not presently disabled), and also if they are regarded as disabled (but are not). Therefore, the ADA provides three theories of disability discrimination under which workers can proceed.

In March 1997, the EEOC issued a document titled "Enforcement Guidance on the Americans with Disabilities Act and Psychiatric Disabilities" (EEOC, 1997). This guidance, developed in a question-and-answer format, addresses numerous issues such as coverage of mental illness by the law, how to assess whether the disorder interferes with a major life function, employers' rights to seek information on the employee's disorder, and many other issues. Reasonable accommodations for employees with psychiatric disorders are also discussed. An Addendum to the 1997 guidance

was issued in 2001 to help interpret the most recent Supreme Court rulings.

Despite what appears to be strong protection from employment discrimination for workers with disabilities, workers have found it difficult to prevail in court. Until 1999, most individuals with disabilities who filed discrimination claims with the EEOC or discrimination lawsuits in federal court under the ADA used the first "prong" of the definition of disability: an individual whose mental or physical disorder substantially limits one or more major life functions. The EEOC Interpretive Guidance to the ADA states that the mere presence of a disorder is not enough for ADA coverage; the effect of the impairment on the individual's life and ability to work must be determined. The lower federal trial and appellate courts disagreed on the interpretation of the ADA's definition of disability, particularly with respect to whether the individual's disorder should be evaluated in its unmitigated state, or whether any mitigating measures that the employee took, such as medication or the use of a prosthetic device, should be taken into consideration. Research conducted on all federal appellate court opinions published in the 6 years subsequent to the date that the ADA became effective (July 26, 1992) demonstrated that plaintiff-employees prevailed in ADA lawsuits only 4% of the time (Lee, 2001b).

A trio of opinions released by the U.S. Supreme Court in the summer of 1999 has focused the attention of claimants on the second and third prongs of the definition of disability (*Albertson's v. Kirkingburg*, 1999; *Murphy v. United Parcel Service*, 1999; *Sutton v. United Airlines*, 1999). In a group of cases called the Sutton trilogy, the Court determined that an individual's coverage by the ADA should be determined in light of whatever mitigating measures the individual had taken to minimize the effects of the disorder. Thus, these mitigating measures had to be taken into account during the determination of whether an individual was "substantially limited" and therefore could meet the Act's definition of disabled. These rulings meant that even individuals with serious conditions such as cancer, multiple sclerosis, and epilepsy could not demonstrate that they were disabled if their medication or other mitigating measure controlled the more severe effects of their disorder (Goldstein, 2001).

So, if a person has little or no difficulty performing a major life activity due to the mitigating measure (e.g., medication), then that person does not meet the ADA's first definition of disability. Readers should consult "Instructions for Field Offices: Analyzing ADA Charges After Supreme Court Decisions Addressing 'Disability' and 'Qualified,'" which can be retrieved from the EEOC Web site (http://www.eeoc.gov).

The significance of the Sutton trilogy is particularly great for individuals with mental or psychological disorders whose effects can be controlled or limited by medication. Simply obtaining a diagnosis of a mental or psychiatric disorder is insufficient under the law to entitle the employee to coverage by the ADA. He or she must either demonstrate that the medication, therapy, or other mitigating measure does not sufficiently neutralize the effects of the mental illness, or that the side effects or other reactions to the medication themselves create a substantial limitation to a major life function. For example, in *Taylor v. Phoenixville School District* (1999), the court refused to award summary judgment to the employer because the plaintiff was able to demonstrate that the medication she took for her psychiatric disorder (depression) caused nausea and impaired her ability to think clearly. Furthermore, the episodic nature of psychiatric

illnesses and the hesitancy of individuals with such illnesses to seek treatment for them compound the difficulty faced by workers with psychiatric disorders.

Even if an individual with a psychiatric disorder can meet the law's definition of a disabled individual, the ADA also requires that the employee demonstrate that he or she is "qualified"—that he or she can perform the essential functions of the position. Courts have ruled that regular attendance and appropriate workplace behavior are essential functions of every position (Lee, 2001b). Even if an individual with such a disability has the skills, education, and experience to perform the job, the side effects of medication, or the employee's decision not to take medication (an element of the underlying mental disorder), may affect the employee's attendance, job performance, or behavior at work. These difficulties for employees with mental illness are compounded by the courts' lack of sympathy for employees who are periodically absent or tardy, who have difficulty following the directions of supervisors, or who may have interpersonal problems with coworkers or customers, even if these problems are related directly to the underlying psychiatric disorder. Although not all individuals with mental illness have these problems, such performance issues are not unusual for individuals with psychiatric disorders (Zuckerman, Debenham, & Moore, 1993), and individuals with behavioral or performance problems have been very unsuccessful in pursuing ADA claims in court.

Scholars and commentators reacted to the Court's rulings in the Sutton trilogy by predicting that employees would turn to the second and third prongs of the ADA's definition of disability (a record of disability or being regarded as disabled). It appears that they have done so, but an analysis of ADA employment cases claiming discrimination on the basis of either physical or mental disabilities, decided during the first year after the Sutton trilogy opinions were released, suggests that employees are no more successful under these theories than they were using the first definition of disability. A review of federal court cases decided the first year after publication of the trilogy indicated that plaintiffs prevailed in 3.5% of cases brought under the "regarded as disabled" prong of the ADA definition, whereas plaintiffs bringing claims under that definition prior to the publication of the trilogy had not prevailed at all (Lee, 2001a). Plaintiffs were slightly more likely to be given the opportunity to take their claims to trial (summary judgments for employers were reversed in 9% of the "regarded as disabled" cases pre-Sutton and in 12% of those cases post-Sutton). Given the great difficulty faced by plaintiffs claiming mental or psychiatric disorders in prevailing prior to Sutton (Blair, 1999, p. 1391; Miller, 1997), it is unlikely that such plaintiffs will be more successful now that Sutton is binding precedent.

According to Blair (1999), cases in which courts rule against workers with psychiatric disabilities fall into six categories.

1. The employee may have engaged in disruptive behavior or other misconduct, which makes him or her unqualified because of an inability to perform essential functions of the job.

2. The employee may have a difficult relationship with a particular supervisor, but can otherwise function. Because getting along with supervisors is an essential function of the job, courts have rejected ADA claims under these circumstances.

3. The employee claims that stress from the job "caused" the disability. Courts have ruled that stress is a normal part of worklife and ability to deal with stress is an essential function of any job.

4. The employee's proffered "reasonable accommodation" may be rejected by the court as unreasonable (e.g., requiring the employer to assign a different supervisor to work with the plaintiff).

5. The employer may not have known that the employee had a psychiatric disorder and thus was not obliged under the law to accommodate the individual. Only those disabilities that have been disclosed trigger the ADA's protections.

6. In some cases, disruptive behavior by the employee has enabled the employer to claim that the individual is a "direct threat," and, thus, accommodation is unreasonable.

ATTITUDES TOWARD WORKERS WITH DISABILITIES

The case law regarding psychiatric disabilities is generally unfavorable to claims of psychiatric disability. Unfortunately, past research, albeit limited in scope, also indicates rather pervasive negative attitudes and opinions regarding workers with such disabilities (Lee, 1996). However, most of this research involved respondents who had little or no experience involving workers with psychiatric disabilities.

In order to determine contemporary attitudes and treatment of job applicants and employees with psychiatric disabilities based on actual experience, a questionnaire was administered to participants attending

[handwritten margin note: I would neve disclose that at a job Regardless of what the ADA say]

a certificate course in human resource management. Many of these individuals had personal experience in human resources (HR) in dealing with disabilities in the workplace.

In addition to inquiring as to whether respondents had any workplace experience with individuals with particular disabilities, we asked what types of accommodations had been made for the disability, what cost was incurred, judgments of the performance of workers with disabilities, and whether the accommodation had been effective. We also asked respondents to provide information as to their gender, age, employment status, industry, and organization/company size.

The questionnaire was completed at the beginning of one of the two 3-hour sessions of the seminar. Results of the survey were reported at the second session. A total of 196 questionnaires were completed and analyzed. The majority of the respondents (82%) worked in personnel and had some (or more) knowledge of ADA and ADA-related compliance activities.

Employed respondents represented the following industries: construction and agriculture (8%); finance and insurance (4%); manufacturing (28%); services (10%); trade (25%); transportation, communication, and public utilities (9%); health care organizations (12%). The balance of the respondents classified their organization as "other." Thirty-one questionnaires were completed by individuals who indicated that they were "currently unemployed" and had no previous experience involving workers with disabilities.

Approximately 72% of the respondents indicated that their organization had employed a disabled individual in the past 5 years. This figure is slightly higher than a 1992 Gallup survey of 400 businesses in which 66% of respondents indicated that they had hired a disabled worker in the past

5 years (Gallup Organization, 1992), and higher than a 1993 survey of New Jersey employers (Lee, 1996) in which 55% of respondents reported that they had hired a worker with a disability during the past 3 years.

We were particularly interested in attitudes toward psychiatric disabilities as a function of previous work experiences with various disabilities. However, we also made several comparisons among respondents who varied on other background variables. We also made comparisons to individuals who had no prior experience regarding disabled workers in the workplace.

We will report the most interesting findings on these differences as they relate to attitudes and perceptions regarding the following areas: (a) preferences for employing workers with various disabilities, (b) experience in accommodating various disabilities and cost estimates of the accommodations, (c) relative job performance of disabled employees versus others, and (d) relative difficulties in working with employees who are disabled. The majority of respondents to the survey who were presently working in HR-related jobs had firsthand experience with one or more personnel matters concerning a disabled employee. Forty-seven respondents had firsthand experience in dealing with a "mental impairment" under the ADA. Thirty-two of these respondents had first-hand experience with at least one other class of disabilities.

JOB PREFERENCES
AND DISABILITIES

Research has shown that employers generally prefer to hire employees with sensory disabilities (e.g., sight), paralysis, or developmental disabilities (e.g., retardation) over

Table 2.1   Hiring Preferences for Various Disabilities

Disability Class	Mean Rank
Sensory impairments (e.g., hearing, sight)	2.2
Mobility impairments (e.g., paralysis)	1.7
Developmental impairments (e.g., mental retardation)	2.9
Diseases (e.g., cancer, diabetes)	3.2
Psychological impairments (e.g., depression, anxiety)	3.4

other classes of psychiatric problems under study (Lee, 1996). We explored this hiring "hierarchy" with a number of questions and analysis. First, we asked the following question of all study participants:

> Think of a position in your organization that is not physically demanding. Then review the classes of disabilities below and provide a rank ordering of disabilities that you would *prefer* in workers for this position. The #1 ranked disability would be the class of disabilities that you would most prefer, #2 ranked the second most preferred class, etc. If you are not presently involved in hiring personnel, please provide your general hiring preferences for positions which are not physically demanding.

Table 2.1 presents a summary of these results. As with previous research, psychiatric disabilities were among the least preferred of all disabilities for hiring purposes, regardless of industry or job.

We also asked respondents to explain why the selected class of disabilities had been ranked first or last. Whereas psychiatric disabilities were ranked last more often than any of the other classes, they were never ranked as the most preferred disabilities. Among the most common explanations for selecting psychiatric disabilities as the least preferred for hiring were the following: (a) most difficult (or impossible)

to accommodate, (b) problems in team work settings, (c) interference with performing essential functions of the job, (d) an undue hardship on the employer, and (e) employees use these problems as excuses to get out of work or as an excuse for poor performance.

Ranking psychiatric disabilities as the least preferred disability was a robust finding that did not differ significantly as a function of previous respondent work experience with a psychiatric disability or any respondent demographic variables. There were some industry effects related to the sensory class obviously related to ability to perform the essential functions of certain jobs.

Although not statistically significant, individuals who had personal experiences in dealing with psychiatric disabilities at work expressed a somewhat more negative attitude toward this class of disabilities than did those with no such personal experience at work. Conversely, those respondents who had indicated a personal experience with a sensory impairment ranked such impairments as relatively more preferred for hiring purposes. Our results suggest that experience with issues or problems related to psychiatric disabilities at work foster relatively more negative impressions of such disabilities, whereas experience with other classes of disabilities fostered relatively more positive impressions of workers with these disabilities.

Table 2.2 Accommodations for Psychiatric Disabilities

Accommodation	Percentage Used[a]
Modified work schedule (part-time, time off)	62
Reassigning tasks to coworkers	21
Additional training and/or reassignment	10
Additional supervision	5
Modifications to work area	8
Assistant, interpreter, reader	0
Equipment adaptation	0

a. Respondents could select more than one type of accommodation.

JOB ACCOMMODATIONS

Respondents were also asked to indicate what (if any) types of accommodations were made for workers with disabilities. Table 2.2 presents a summary of the findings regarding psychiatric disabilities. For respondents describing a psychiatric disability, 62% indicated that the worker had been provided a modified work schedule (part-time, additional time off). This percentage was higher than for any other class of disability except major illness. Other accommodations that were provided for psychiatric disabilities included reassigning tasks to coworkers, additional training, and reassignment.

There was an indication that individuals who had personal experience in dealing with a psychiatric disability at work expressed a somewhat more negative attitude toward the effectiveness of accommodations for such disabilities than did those with no such personal experience at work. These respondents were more likely to indicate that whatever accommodation was provided was not successful, and that the accommodations provided were relatively more costly. More than 18% of respondents who had provided an accommodation for a psychiatric disability estimated that the cost exceeded $5,000. No other class of disabilities had more than 10% of cost

estimates exceeding $5,000. Those respondents who had indicated a personal experience with a sensory impairment indicated that accommodations were relatively simple to implement, not very costly (54% indicated the cost was less than $500), and successful.

In general, our results indicated a relatively more negative attitude toward the effectiveness of accommodating psychiatric disabilities. Again, although the sample was small, unlike other classes of disabilities, those individuals who had work experience related to dealing with a psychiatric disability indicated that the attempt to accommodate the disability was relatively less successful. For all other classes of disabilities, the mean rating of effectiveness was above the midpoint of the scale.

RELATIVE JOB PERFORMANCE OF WORKERS WITH DISABILITIES

We were also interested in perceptions of job performance among disabled workers. Again, we segregated our analysis by previous experience and asked respondents who had no previous experience with disabilities in the workplace to respond based on what they had read or heard about the disability.

Table 2.3 presents a summary of the major results related to the perceived job

Table 2.3   Perceived Job Performance as a Function of Disability Class Performance Rating[a]

	Mean	*SD*
Sensory impairments (e.g., hearing, sight)	3.1	1.1
Mobility impairments (e.g., paralysis)	3.2	1.4
Developmental impairments (e.g., mental retardation)	2.7	1.9
Diseases (e.g., cancer, diabetes)	3.1	1.8
Psychological impairments (e.g., depression, anxiety)	2.5	2.3

	Gallup	*All Disabilities*	*Psychiatric*
Performance of workers with disabilities			
Is more productive	3.13	3.05	2.52
Is more reliable	3.33	3.18	2.60
Works in a safer manner	3.11	3.01	3.06

a. A rating above 3.0 indicates performance was judged to be more effective than that of nondisabled workers; a rating below 3.0 indicates less effective.
b. Responses to Likert Scale (1 = *strongly disagree*, 5 = *strongly agree*); Gallup sample data are from Table U, 1992, p. 56.

performance of disabled workers. In general, respondents with no previous experience with disabled workers indicated that the job performance of such workers was equivalent to the performance of others doing the same work. However, when we asked these same people to speculate on job performance across the classes of disabilities, psychiatric disabilities had a lower rating of job performance than all other classes except cognitive or learning disabilities. The psychiatric class of disabilities was perceived more negatively with regard to job performance regardless of previous experience. The highest percentage of respondents also indicated that the job performance of workers with psychiatric disabilities was relatively less effective than that of nondisabled workers performing the same job (11% vs. 4% for other classes), and the lowest percentage of respondents indicated that the job performance of workers with psychiatric disabilities was relatively more effective than that of nondisabled workers performing the same job (3% vs. 9% for other disabled classes). Ratings of the

productivity and reliability of workers with psychiatric disabilities were significantly lower than were ratings of the performance of disabled workers in general from the 1992 Gallup sample using the same questions and rating scale.

These negative findings regarding psychiatric disabilities were slightly more pronounced when we focused our analysis on the respondents with previous experience with a psychiatric disability. Our small sample of individuals judged the job performance of workers with psychiatric disabilities to be relatively less effective than that of other workers in general (17%) and workers with other disabilities (17% vs. 3% for other classes of disabilities).

RELATIVE DIFFICULTIES WORKING WITH DISABLED EMPLOYEES

Table 2.4 presents a summary of perceived problems in employing workers with psychiatric disabilities. Although the majority of respondents did not agree that any of the

Table 2.4   Perceived Problems Working With Disabilities

Problem	Mean/SD	
	Psychiatric	Others
Frequent absences	2.9/1.4	2.5/1.3
Difficulty with supervision	2.8/1.4	2.6/.9
Difficulty with coworkers	2.5/1.1	2.4/1.0
Poor work attitude	2.3/1.5	2.1/1.1
Communication issues	2.7/1.6	2.4/1.5
Inexperience	2.4/1.2	2.9/1.1
Poor performance	3.3/1.6	2.8/1.3

NOTE: Responses to 5-point, Likert scale: 1 = *strongly disagree*, 5 = *strongly agree*.

problems were that serious, the most negative responses and the highest standard deviations were found when the focus was on a psychiatric disability. For example, problems of frequent absences, difficulty in supervision and getting along with others, poor worker attitude, and interference with job performance were all judged to be greater when the respondent focused on psychiatric disabilities. When the focus was on workers with sensory impairments, respondents were more likely to disagree or strongly disagree that any of these issues was a problem.

The small number of respondents who had personal work experience regarding psychiatric disabilities was more likely to agree or strongly agree that frequent absences, difficulties with supervision and co-workers, and attitudes toward work were more of a problem for workers with psychiatric disabilities relative to respondents who did not have personal experience.

SURVEY CONCLUSIONS

From the perspective of workers with psychiatric disabilities, results of our survey rival the legal review for pessimism. In general, survey respondents with firsthand experience in dealing with a psychiatric disability at work and those respondents with little or no experience in personnel matters expressed relatively more negative views toward this class of disabilities. People who had firsthand experience viewed accommodations for psychiatric disabilities as relatively more costly, more difficult, and less effective. They also considered workers with such disabilities as more difficult in a number of respects and less effective as workers. Compared to the Gallup survey data from 1992, perceptions of the job performance of workers with disabilities were more negative than were perceptions of workers with disabilities in general.

One possible explanation for such negative findings when we isolate on people with firsthand experience is that such firsthand experience may be related to either an ADA complaint or litigation. Obviously, this bias in our sample could reflect an unrepresentative view of workers with psychiatric disabilities; that is, respondents working in an HR department may not even be aware that a worker had a psychiatric disability if the problem had been resolved outside of HR by a line manager. Of course, the same argument probably could be made regarding respondents who had first-hand experience with other disabilities.

Unfortunately, we have no other data that would enable us to sort out this issue. Suffice it to say that the increased negativity reported by those respondents who had actual experience in dealing with workers with disabilities is disturbing and needs further examination.

RECOMMENDATIONS BASED ON CASE LAW AND WORKER ATTITUDES

Because the Supreme Court's 1999 Sutton trilogy is still a relatively recent precedent, it is too soon to determine whether a shift to the "regarded as disabled" definition of disability will be a successful strategy for individuals with psychiatric disorders seeking relief under the ADA. And although plaintiffs with these disorders have been quite unsuccessful in the past, this does not mean that employers can ignore the ADA or evade their responsibility to provide reasonable accommodations to workers with psychiatric disorders. Combined with the literature on attitudes toward workers with disabilities, and until the ADA is amended or until courts become more willing to extend ADA protections to these individuals, the following suggestions may be helpful.

1. Workers with psychiatric disorders need to determine whether or not to disclose the existence of their disorder. Failure to disclose excludes the individual from ADA protections. Disclosure may subject the individual to discrimination, stereotyping, negative employment actions, and limited career opportunities. This catch-22 situation is a difficult one for individuals with psychiatric disorders, and they should confer with therapists, family members, and others who can assist them with this difficult decision.

2. If an individual with a psychiatric disorder decides to disclose the diagnosis, he or she should be prepared to provide information on the underlying condition and the appropriate accommodations (if any are needed) to the HR manager. At that point, the HR manager and the individual should discuss the degree of confidentiality that the individual desires. Although the ADA requires the employer to treat information about an employee's disorder as confidential, it may be in the employee's interest, depending on the disorder and its manifestations, to disclose some information to coworkers or supervisors about the nature of the disorder.

3. Should the individual be willing to disclose limited or full information about the condition, he or she and the HR manager should discuss educating his or her supervisor and coworkers about the condition. This strategy may increase the comfort levels of the people working with the individual and give them an understanding of what the worker with the psychiatric condition is facing. Particularly if specific behavioral events may occur (such as periodic depression, fatigue, nausea, or other effects of either the condition or the medication taken to control it), advising coworkers and supervisors of this possibility in advance may increase their acceptance of the individual and reduce their fear of the unknown.

4. All individuals involved should be informed that performance expectations for the individual with the disorder will not be changed (the ADA does not require performance expectations to be reduced), and that the individual also will be held to the same behavioral standards required of others in similar jobs.

5. The individual with the psychiatric disorder should consider scheduling regular

meetings between his or her therapist or other health professional and the relevant supervisors or managers to ascertain whether accommodations are successful or whether changes need to be made.

At this point in the evolution of case law interpreting the ADA, individuals with psychiatric disorders cannot rely on the law to punish employers whose fears or bias against mental illness motivate negative employment decisions. Education of supervisors and coworkers, and collaboration among the individual, the organization's management, and the individual's health care providers, should help individuals with

psychiatric disorders be meaningfully employed and avoid the need to use the very imperfect tool of litigation under the ADA.

As one recent review concluded,

> Despite passage of the ADA—and efforts by companies to make jobs more accessible—the disabled still face an uphill struggle when it comes to finding work and earning salaries that are on par with the rest of the workforce. (Wells, 2001, p. 40)

Our evidence about case law and attitudes toward workers indicates that this struggle may be considerably steeper for people with psychiatric disabilities.

REFERENCES

Albertson's, Inc. v. Kirkingburg, 119 S. Ct. 2162 (1999).

Blair, D. A. (1999). Employees suffering from bipolar disorder or clinical depression: Fighting an uphill battle for protection under Title I of the Americans with Disabilities Act. *Seton Hall Law Review, 29,* 1347-1404.

Equal Employment Opportunity Commission (1997, March 25). *Enforcement guidance on the Americans with Disabilities Act and psychiatric disabilities.* Available at http://www.eeoc.gov/docs/psych.html.

Equal Employment Opportunity Commission. (2001). *Cumulative ADA charge data—Receipts.* Available at http://www.eeoc.gov/stats/.

Gallup Organization. (1992). *Baseline study to determine business' attitudes, awareness and reaction to the Americans with Disabilities Act.* Washington, DC: Electronic Industries Foundation.

Goldstein, R. I. (2001). Note: Mental illness in the workplace after *Sutton v. United Air Lines. Cornell Law Review, 86,* 927-973.

Hall, L. L. (1997). Making the ADA work for people with psychiatric disabilities. In R. Bonnie & J. Monahan (Eds.), *Mental disorder, work disability, and the law* (pp. 241-280). Chicago: University of Chicago Press.

Lee, B. A. (1996). Accommodation of disability in the workplace: Legal requirements and employer responses. *Human Resource Management Review, 6,* 231-251.

Lee, B. A. (2001a). *A decade of the Americans with Disabilities Act: Judicial outcomes and unresolved problems.* Working Paper, School of Management and Labor Relations, Rutgers University.

Lee, B. A. (2001b). The implications of ADA litigation for employers: A review of federal appellate court decisions. *Human Resource Management, 40,* 35-50.

Miller, S. P. (1997). Keeping the promise: The ADA and employment discrimination on the basis of psychiatric disability. *California Law Review, 85,* 701-745.

Murphy v. United Parcel Service, Inc., 119 S.Ct. 2133 (1999).

Sutton v. United Airlines, Inc., 119 S. Ct. 2139 (1999).

Taylor v. Phoenixville School District, 184 F.3d 296 (3d Cir. 1999).

Wells, S. J. (2001). Is the ADA working? *Human Resource Magazine, 46,* 38-47.

Zuckerman, D., Debenham, K., & Moore, K. (1993). *The ADA and people with mental illness: A resource manual for employers.* Washington, DC: American Bar Association; Alexandria, VA: National Mental Health Association.

Part II

WORKING CONDITIONS, LIFE STRESSORS, AND MENTAL HEALTH

CHAPTER 3

Models of Job Stress

VALERIE J. SUTHERLAND
CARY L. COOPER

It is not uncommon for stress and stress management in the workplace to be treated with apprehension, suspicion, and a certain degree of cynicism. Constant media attention and well-publicized stress litigation cases have helped to create a negative and unhelpful climate resulting in some reluctance to tackle a potentially costly workplace problem. Stress seems to have become an organizational whipping boy, blamed for all our ills and wrongs and in danger of becoming the "back pain" of the 21st century. An unhelpful and damaging view of stress as a "four-letter word" will persist unless we can eliminate the myths and nonsense that surround the concept of stress.

Certain problems arise because stress, like love and electricity, cannot be seen or touched. Most of us have experience with these concepts but find them difficult to understand and explain. In addition, many managers believe that "if you cannot see it, you cannot measure it; if you cannot measure it, you cannot manage it."

In such a negative organizational climate, the need to proactively tackle work-related problems is denied and even ignored. Thus, employees tend to hide a stress condition rather than admit that they cannot cope. The business and humanistic costs associated with this behavior are enormous, and everyone suffers in the long term.

Recent figures provided by the Health and Safety Executive (2001) suggest that stress-related illness is responsible for the loss of 6.5 million working days each year, costing British employers around £370 million (about $518 million) and British society as a whole as much as £375 billion (about $525 billion). The true impact of mismanaged stress must be viewed in terms of costs associated with poor performance and productivity, increased accidents at work, high labor turnover, forced early retirement, ill health, job dissatisfaction, and unhappiness, in addition to increased insurance premiums and compensation and stress litigation costs.

If we examine the business case and understand the real costs associated with mismanaged stress, the need to tackle work-related stress is paramount and the potential benefits are tremendous.

In this chapter, we suggest that to manage stress successfully, we must acknowledge and define what we mean by stress. We need to recognize the effects of exposure to stress and understand how and why stress is damaging in its consequences. To do this, we offer a theoretical framework by describing certain models of stress. Exploration of models of job stress and an understanding of the evolution of such models provide an explanation of the stress mechanism and how and why exposure to certain conditions and situations has an adverse impact on health, job performance, and quality of life. Most importantly, it guides action in the management of stress. At both organizational and individual levels, it is important that we know how and why exposure to the contemporary work environment might lead to poor performance, low productivity, and ill health.

By examining models of stress, we can

1. Define and clarify what we mean by the word *stress*.

2. Explain the various ways in which stress is perceived.

3. Distinguish between terms such as *stress, stress agent, stress stimulus,* and *stress response.*

4. Recognize how and why our response to stress can be behavioral, emotional, physical, and psychological.

5. Understand how models of stress have evolved to influence our thinking about the stress response and stress management strategies.

6. Understand the concept of adaptive and maladaptive stress coping.

7. Identify potential sources of stress in our environment.

8. Understand the concept of individual differences in response to stress.

A LAYPERSON MODEL OF STRESS

A common assumption is that "stress is what happens to people." This is misleading and likely to be the cause of error in our understanding about the nature of stress. Such perceptions held by employees, work colleagues, staff, customers, or clients might lead to faulty thinking, inappropriate blame, and damage to self-confidence. The organization also suffers because stress management initiatives are likely to be restricted in scope, effectiveness, and success. Thus, an essential part of any stress management initiative is to ensure that everyone involved is aware of the nature of stress and how it is damaging in its consequences.

Misinformation and faulty thinking about stress are commonly observed. Pause for a moment or two and write down the words or phrases that immediately come into your mind when you think about the word *stress* and what it means to you. If we ask a group of people to take part in this exercise, the list of words produced usually has three key characteristics.

1. Most of the words or phrases are expressed in negative terms. That is, we tend to perceive stress as something bad or unwanted. For example, words or phrases such as "depression," "feeling out of control," "overworked," "migraine or headache," "time pressure," "panic attack," "anxiety," "unable to sleep," and "tearful" typically appear on such lists to express thoughts and feelings about the concept of stress. Consistently, stress appears to be a pessimistic experience, and this reinforces the general view that stress is bad. In organizational life, the stressed employee tends to be regarded as a problem employee and as someone who is unable to cope. Thus, the negative sentiment is intensified. A culture of

blame dominates in which real problems and symptoms of stress remain concealed. The eradication of misinformation and faulty thinking about stress is essential if stress in the workplace is to be tackled successfully. Employers and staff need to understand that stress is an inevitable part of organizational life, and mismanaged stress can be harmful and damaging for everybody.

2. Our word lists are dominated by expressions or words that describe symptoms of exposure to a stressful situation. For example, stress is described as "feeling anxious," "depressed," or having a headache or panic attacks because the experience is perceived in terms of feelings and reactions rather than acknowledging the cause of symptoms or reactions. This habit can lead to an incorrect acceptance of blame and feelings of low self-worth because the individual has not understood that these feelings and symptoms are part of the normal reaction and response to a difficult situation at work.

3. Lists rarely contain words that describe the actual source of the stress. We use the words *stressor* or *stress agent* to describe the source of stress. In our example in Point 1 above, "being overworked" and "time pressures" are workplace stressors. However, these work conditions and situations need to be explained in more detail before we are able to use this information to effectively manage the perceived stressful work condition. For example, it is necessary to know if the perception of being overworked was due to having too much to do in the time available, having more to do than other colleagues engaged in the same tasks, or having to perform a task that is too difficult. Each of these situations would demand a different solution, and so accurate specification of the stressor is vital.

Although problems are inherent in the layperson view of stress, these perceptions actually form the basis of early models of stress, namely, a response-based model of job stress and a stimulus-based model of job stress. These are described below. However, such models of stress are rather simplistic and inadequate when trying to understand the complex nature of stress and the stress response. A more comprehensive model is needed for both further research into the study of stress and guidance in a practical approach to stress management.

Broad application of the stress concept to medical, social, and behavioral science research over the past 60 to 70 years has also compounded the problem of trying to find a satisfactory model of job stress. Each discipline investigated and attempted to explain stress from its own unique perspective, and early models of stress reflect this limitation. In the next sections, the historical origins and early approaches to the study of stress are outlined to illustrate how a contemporary interactive model of stress evolved. This discussion will be followed by a description of this model of job stress.

Finally, we will demonstrate how our understanding of the stress concept has been further advanced by the introduction of two additional models of job stress, the person-environment fit model and the operational model.

RESPONSE-BASED MODEL OF JOB STRESS

As we have stated, when asked to provide alternate words to the term *stress*, associations tend to be in terms of response-based meanings that take the form of strain, tension, or pressure. The layperson readily identifies with the expressions "being under

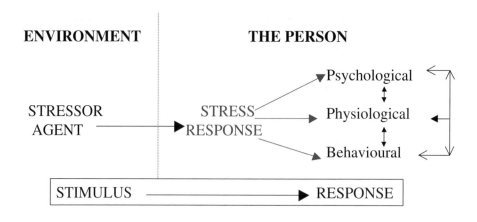

Figure 3.1   A Response-Based Model of Job Stress

stress" and "I feel very stressed," and can usually describe the manifestations of the stress response. Therefore, the response-based approach to understanding stress, in seeking to define an intangible phenomenon, views stress as the outcome. In research terminology, this is described as the *dependent variable*, where the main conceptual domain is the manifestation of stress. Figure 3.1 illustrates a response-based model of stress.

The origins of response-based definitions of stress are found in medicine and are usually viewed from a physiological perspective. This is a logical stance for a discipline trained to diagnose and treat symptoms, but not necessarily the cause of the condition. For example, John Locke, the 17th-century physician and philosopher, proposed that intellectual function, emotions, muscle movement, and the behavior of internal organs were the product of sensory experiences processed by the brain. From these early notions, the study of stress from a physiological perspective developed. Links were established between life experiences, emotions, and the importance of hormone and chemical actions in the body.

Whereas Claude Bernard proposed that emotional stress was the cause of ischemic

heart disease as early as 1860, Osler (1910) connected the high incidence of angina pectoris among Jewish businessmen with their hectic pace of life. In the 1930s, psychoanalyst Franz Alexander and physician Frances Dunbar reported on the relationship between personality patterns and constitutional tendencies to certain organic disorders. Thus, they described the psychosomatic theory of disease (Warshaw, 1979). Claude Bernard was the first person to suggest that the internal environment of a living organism must remain fairly constant despite exposure to external changes. This concept of stability or balance was later developed and called *homeostasis* by Walter Cannon (1935). In systems theory, this would become known as dynamic equilibrium, whereby the coordination of physiological processes maintains a steady state within the organism. The theory states that natural homeostatic mechanisms normally maintain a state of resistance but are not able to cope with unusually heavy demands. Under homeostatic principles, it is acknowledged that there is a finite supply to meet demand.

The earliest report of a systematic study on the relationship between life events and bodily responses is probably attributed to Wolf and Wolff (see McLean, 1979). Their observations and experiments with the patient, "Tom," provided an opportunity to observe changes in stomach activity in response to stressful situations. These researchers were able to document the changes in blood flow, motility, and secretions of the stomach, with feelings of frustration and conflict produced under experimental conditions. Sadness, self-reproach, and discouragement were found to be associated with prolonged pallor of the stomach mucosa and a hyposecretion of acid. Hostility and resentment were associated with a high increase in gastric secretion and acidity. From the results of this research, our understanding of the relationship between engorgement of the stomach lining, lowered resistance to psychological trauma, and the incidence of gastric ulcers was formed. As McLean (1979) suggested, the study of Tom inaugurated the scientific study of psychosomatic medicine.

However, it is the work of Hans Selye in the 1930s and 1940s that really marked the beginning of a response-based approach to the study of stress. In 1936, Selye introduced the concept of stress-related illness in terms of a general adaptation syndrome known as GAS. He suggested that "stress is the non-specific response of the body to any demand made upon it . . . and that all patients, whatever the disease, looked and felt sick" (Selye, 1936, p. 32). This general malaise was characterized by loss of motivation, appetite, weight, and strength. Early experimentation was with animals, and Selye was able to demonstrate internal physical degeneration and deterioration as a result of exposure to a wide variety of stimuli that he called "stress." According to Selye, stress is the lowest common denominator in the organism's reaction to every conceivable kind of stressor exposure, challenge, and demand. Selye used the word *stress* as an abstraction to mean the nonspecific

features of a reaction rather than the entire reaction. Also, Selye (1956) stated that, "The apparent specificity of diseases of adaptation is ascribed to conditioning factors such as genetic predisposition, gender, learning experiences and diet, etc." (p. 127). Therefore, the response to stress was deemed to be invariant to the nature of the stressor and followed a universal pattern. It is a biological concept described as the syndrome of "just being sick."

Three stages of response were described within the GAS (see Figure 3.2). The alarm reaction is the immediate psychophysiological response, and at this time of initial shock, our resistance to the stressor is lowered. After the initial shock phase, the countershock phase can be observed, and resistance levels begin to increase. At this time, our defense mechanisms are activated, forming the reaction known as the fight-or-flight response (Cannon, 1935).

The fight-or-flight response prepares our body to take action. Increased sympathetic activity results in the secretion of catecholamines that make the body ready to act. Internal physiological changes initiated by hormones provide energy from the metabolism of fat and glucose. This causes increased delivery of oxygen (another energy source) to muscles through an increased number of red blood cells in the circulation, increased blood flow to the muscles, and reduced blood flow through the skin and the gut. So, our breathing becomes more rapid, our heart beats faster, and our blood pressure increases. The spleen contracts, and blood supplies are redirected from the skin and viscera to provide an improved blood supply to the brain and skeletal muscles. Glucose stored as glycogen in the liver is released to provide energy for muscular action; blood coagulation processes become enhanced, and the supply of blood lymphocytes is increased to

In bell curve a "possitive" amount of stress that stay as same level (evon copy) un more thes p--de the

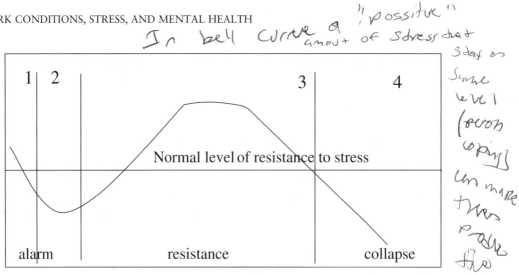

Figure 3.2   General Adaptation Syndrome (GAS)

combat the impact of injury and infection from wounds.

Table 3.1 illustrates the physiological changes experienced when we are in the alarm stage of the stress response and explains the effects we experience in response to stress. In summary, this is the result of

- The release of adrenal hormones and free fatty acids
- Lipid changes, for example, in cholesterol and triglyceride levels
- Changes in various catecholamines, such as thyroxin in urine and blood

Thus, the actions of adrenaline, noradrenaline, and cortisol combine to produce the reaction we know as the fight-or-flight stress response.

In evolutionary terms, stress and the stress response are good for us and necessary for the development of our society. Indeed, social Darwinism has been defined as the "promotion of the fittest," assuming that the individual survives the rat race in the first place (McCloy, 1995). The response to stress was meant to be both adaptive and vital for survival. In the past, we had simple choices to make. That is, either stand and fight an enemy, or run away from a threatening and potentially dangerous situation. However, in contemporary society, we face a dilemma because rarely are these options appropriate behaviors in the workplace. In the work environment, there is no opportunity to indulge in physical action and thereby dissipate the physiological effects that become dominant and can cause distress. We cannot physically fight to escape workplace stress, nor can we run from a situation without losing face. Therefore, our bodies are continually primed to take actions that we are denied. Because many of us also lead increasingly sedentary lives at work and at home, we are denied both the aggression release and the physical activity necessary to quickly remove the build up of hormone and chemical secretions. Fats released to fuel muscle actions are not used, and so we have elevated blood lipids. The fat deposits that are not used are likely to be stored on the lining of our arteries. This means that our blood pressure increases as the heart works harder to pump blood around the body through smaller capillary openings. If a clot breaks away from the lining of an artery and finds its way to the brain or heart, it will cause a stroke or heart attack (thrombosis).

Table 3.1   The Physiology of Stress and the Stress Response

Organ or Tissue Involved	*Reaction*
Lungs	Airways dilate and breathing becomes more rapid and deeper
Heart	The heart beats faster and harder; we experience palpitations and chest pains
Legs/arms	An experience of muscle tension or tingling in the arms and legs as the electrical balance of the cells in the muscles undergoes change
Liver and fat tissue	Mobilization of glucose and fats for energy to fuel muscles
Brain	Increased mental activity to be alert for quick decision making
Skin and sweat glands	Increased sweating; hands and feet (extremities) often feel cold as blood supplies are diverted to the brain and muscles; hairs stand erect and we experience "goosepimples"
Salivary glands	Decreased flow of saliva; the mouth feels dry
Gut muscles	Gut activity is slowed; blood supply is reduced and we might experience indigestion or the feeling of a knotted stomach because digestive processes stop or slow down
Spleen	Contracts and empties red blood cells into the circulation
Kidneys	Reduced urine formation
Ears	Hearing becomes acute; under extreme stress, we report feeling sensitive to noise
Eyes	Pupils dilate as an aid to keen vision; vision can become blurred if oxygenated blood is impeded in getting to the brain and if blood vessels in the neck constrict
Blood	Cortisol produces an increased ability for blood clotting; the immune system is activated to prevent infection

Therefore, coronary heart disease can be caused by indirect effects, namely, the stress-physiological consequences of sustained active distress on the increase of blood pressure, the elevation of blood lipids and blood platelets, and impaired glucose tolerance and related metabolic processes (Siegrist, 1997). Recent studies have documented associations between high levels of psychosocial stress and the prevalence of hypertension, high levels of blood lipids not attributable to diet, and high fibrinogen (a soluble protein in blood plasma that is converted to fibrin by the action of the enzyme thrombin when the blood clots).

In addition to diseases of the heart, we are also likely to suffer from ulcers, troubles with the gastrointestinal tract, asthma, colds and flu, and various skin conditions such as psoriasis, caused by exposure to mismanaged stress. These problems can be exacerbated because we often resort to using maladaptive coping strategies in response to stress rather than adaptive, positive stress management techniques (this issue will be discussed in more detail later in the chapter).

In the third phase of the GAS, we observe resistance to a continued stressor, and where the adaptation response and/or return to equilibrium replaces the alarm reaction. If the alarm reaction is elicited too intensely or too frequently over an extended period of time, the energy required for adaptation becomes depleted, and the final stage of exhaustion, collapse, or death occurs. Resistance cannot continue indefinitely, even when given sufficient energy, because, as

Selye (1983) says, "Every biological activity causes wear and tear . . . and leaves some irreversible chemical scars which accumulate to constitute signs of ageing" (p. 6). Therefore, in Selye's terms, stress is viewed as wear and tear on the body.

Although the nonspecificity concept of stress-related illness and the GAS model had far-reaching influence and a significant impact on our understanding of stress, it has been challenged. Research indicates that responses to stimuli do not always follow the same pattern. They are, in fact, stimulus-specific and dependent on the type of hormonal secretion. We now understand that differing perceptions of a stress agent result in different patterns of neuroendocrine activation. For example, a challenge that is met with feelings of being in control and enthusiasm, and is handled easily and successfully, elicits noradrenaline and an increase in levels of testosterone. However, with increasing fear or anxiety, we move from active coping to passive acceptance that is characterized by increases in adrenaline, prolactin, rennin, and free fatty acids. Cortisol is needed to sustain the response in such situations and as the degree of distress grows. Therefore, anxiety-producing situations seem to be associated with the secretion of adrenaline (e.g., waiting for an appointment with the dentist, or sitting and waiting for a written examination to commence). Response to this type of experience produces the feelings of fear and dread that make us want to just run away from the situation. In response to aggression or challenge-producing events, however, noradrenaline is released. These situations stir feelings of elation and excitement as we prepare to fight or take the plunge of the parachute skydive or bungee jump.

However, the GAS model makes no attempt to address the issue of psychological response to events, or that response to a potential threat may, in turn, become the stimulus for a different response. The framework of the GAS can explain our response to certain stressors, such as the physical effects of heat and cold, but it is not adequate to explain response to psychosocial stress (Christian & Lolas, 1985).

Kagan and Levi (1975) extended the response-based model of stress to incorporate psychosocial stimuli as causal factors in stress-related illness. Response to stress is viewed as the product of an interaction between the stimulus and the psychobiological program of the individual; that is, genetic predisposition and experience or learning. The term *interaction* is used in this instance to mean a response that follows a particular pattern. Because Kagan and Levi's model also incorporates the concept of feedback, it cannot be considered a simple stimulus-response model of stress.

An additional problem associated with a response-based model is that stress is recognized as a generic term that subsumes a large variety of manifestations (Pearlin, Lieberman, Menaghan, & Mullan, 1981). Disagreement exists about the real manifestation of stress and the level in the organism or system that most clearly reflects the response. For example, Pearlin et al. ask if the response is in the single cell, in an organ, or throughout the entire organism; is it biochemical, physiological, or emotional functioning? Is it at the endocrine, immunological, metabolic, or cardiovascular level, or in particular diseases, either physical or psychological? The answers to these questions are not simple because the findings of replication research are likely to be confounded. Individuals adapt to a potential source of stress, and so response will vary over time (e.g., in the assessment of noise on hearing and performance).

Levi (1998) suggested that in seeking to define stress, Selye actually intended to choose an analogy from engineering. The

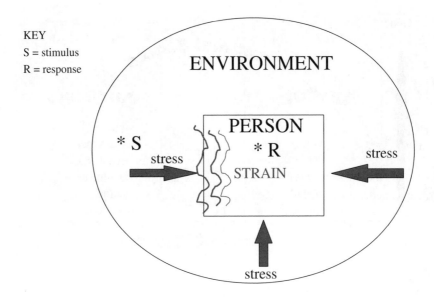

KEY
S = stimulus
R = response

ENVIRONMENT

PERSON
* S   * R
stress   STRAIN   stress

stress

Figure 3.3   A Stimulus-Based Model of Job Stress

implication was that *stress* is the force that deforms a body, and what happens in the body in question is described as *strain.* However, it is believed that Selye misinterpreted English terminology and called the observed phenomena of strain, "stress," thus causing a great deal of subsequent confusion. Nevertheless, the focus of interest for Selye was the response to a stress agent or stressor, and the engineering analogy was free to be used to describe stress in terms of a stimulus-based model.

A STIMULUS-BASED MODEL OF JOB STRESS

Historically, this approach, which links health and disease to certain conditions in the external environment, can be traced back to Hippocrates (5th century BC). Hippocratic physicians believed that the external environment conditions characteristics of health and disease (Goodell, Wolf, & Rogers, 1986). The stimulus-based psychological model of stress has its roots in physics

and engineering, the analogy being that stress can be defined as an external force that results in a demand or load reaction that causes distortion. Both organic and inorganic substances have tolerance levels that, if exceeded, result in temporary or permanent damage. Indeed, it is also suggested that the word *stress* derives from the Latin word *stringere,* which means "to bind tight."

The aphorism, "it is the straw that breaks the camel's back," is a view consistent with a stimulus-based model of stress. An individual is bombarded with stimuli in the environment, but just one more, apparently minor or innocuous event can alter the balance between the ability to cope with demand and a breakdown in coping and of the system itself. Figure 3.3 illustrates this model of stress, which treats a potential stressor as an independent variable that will cause a certain effect (i.e., an outcome or symptom).

Rapid industrialization provided an impetus for the increasing popularity of this particular model of stress. Much of the early research into blue-collar stress at work

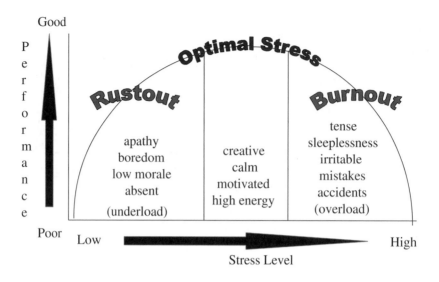

Figure 3.4   Inverted U Model of Stress—The Relationship Between Stress and Performance

adopted a stimulus-based model when seeking to identify sources of stress in the work environment. Considerable attention was paid to our actual physical working conditions and task circumstances, such as exposure to heat and cold, light levels, and social density. Thus, workload conditions, namely, overload or underload, were explored and understood within the framework of a stimulus-based model of stress.

However, it was acknowledged that the relationship between a source of stress and the outcome is not always linear. This phenomenon can be understood in terms of a simple inverted "U" model of stress and performance (see Figure 3.4). It explains how response to a stimulus cannot be viewed or measured in simple linear terms. Thus, a certain level of arousal (i.e., a stimulus) is needed for optimal performance. In an optimal state, we feel creative, calm, and highly motivated to do the job well. When the level of arousal exceeds our ability to meet the demand placed upon us, we experience feelings of burnout, exhaustion, and, ultimately, collapse. Likewise, if we do not

feel challenged or stimulated by the job, or we do not believe that our contribution is valued, we may experience apathy, boredom, a poor morale, and a lack of self-worth. This is called "rust-out" and is the opposite of burnout. Ultimately, such individuals may "vote with their feet" by staying away from work, complaining that they are sick of the job rather than physically unwell. New technology that leads to the increasing automation of industry can lead to the simplification of work. The repetitive, simple, short-cycle jobs that are a product of automation can cause qualitative underload at work. Although the hectic pace at work can create stress, work that is dull and monotonous can lead to rust-out, which is also detrimental to the individual's physical and psychological well-being if his or her job expectations are not met. This highlights a major weakness of the simple stimulus-response model of job stress, because stress needed to be defined in terms of the imbalance between the perceived demand from the environment and the individual's perceived resources to meet those demands. This is known as the person-environment fit model of job stress. It is described in detail later in the chapter.

Thus, the restricted usefulness of an engineering or physical model of stress became clear when it was realized that purely objective measures of environmental conditions were inadequate and unable to explain an observed response to stress. Individual differences, including variability in tolerance levels, personality traits, past experiences (learning and training), needs, wants, and expectations account for the fact that two individuals, exposed to exactly the same situation, might react in completely different ways. In fact, Lazarus (1966) stated that no objective criterion was good enough to describe a situation as stressful, and only the individual experiencing the event could do this. It implies that objective measure of, for example, the concept of "boring" is probably meaningless. Only the description of the job as boring as defined by the incumbent is relevant in understanding the psychological state and stress condition of that individual.

Using Simple Models of Job Stress in the Organization

Although a stimulus-based model of job stress has limitations, its use has appeal in organizations seeking to identify common stressor themes or patterns of stress that might affect the majority of the workforce. Thus, the strategy is to manage the stressor situation without taking into account the needs and differences of individual job incumbents. This means that the work environment and job conditions are designed around a notion of average conditions for the average employee. Other organizations favor a response-based model to guide a stress management program. They view the problem of stress as something inherent to

the person. This allows the organization to transfer the responsibility to the individual employee. Typically, this organization will introduce a program that, in good faith, aims to help the employee cope with the stressor situation, but usually does nothing to actually remove or eliminate the source of stress itself.

Both models have limitations and weaknesses, and these have been magnified by the changing nature of the workplace and society itself. Industrialization brought problems associated with physical and task-related sources of strain and pressure. Poor working conditions caused diseases such as tuberculosis and pneumonia, which often led to early death. Legislation regarding health and safety requirements in the workplace resolved many of these unsatisfactory conditions. However, contemporary industrialization and new technology have introduced different problems and new forms of illness and injury. These include upper body limb disorder, known as repetitive strain injury, and psychological ill-health problems, including problems associated with sick building syndrome. In addition, changing expectations of quality of life and work-life balance have brought a new meaning to the concept of health. It means not only an absence of disease or infirmity, but also a satisfactory state of physical, mental, and social well-being (WHO, 1984). This broad definition of well-being is described as a dynamic state of mind, characterized by reasonable harmony between a worker's ability, needs, expectations, environmental demands, and opportunities (Levi, 1987).

In reality, a model of job stress that seeks to explain and guide stress management practice in contemporary organizations cannot be found in the simple models of job stress already described. An interactive or transactional model of stress, which considers the stressor source, the perception of the situation or event, situational factors, and the response itself, is suggested as a more useful approach for providing guidelines for the study and management of job stress.

AN INTERACTIVE MODEL OF JOB STRESS

In the 1970s and 1980s, there was a move away from simple product models of stress toward more ecologically valid models. These ecological models attempted to account for both the external stressor and the body's response, and also to emphasize the importance of the transactional or inter-actionist dimension. Thus, an *interactive* model of stress incorporates both the response-based and the stimulus-based models of stress, and the concept of cognitive appraisal plays a central role in the stress response of the individual.

Such models suggest that sources of stress arising from workplace conditions and situations are mediated through perception, appraisal, and experience. Individual determinants of this appraisal and reaction process are described as psychobiological programming. This includes all the genetic factors and earlier environmental influences that shape personality, attitudes, customs, and values. In addition, the process is modified by interacting variables such as social support and learned coping strategies. Together, these will determine the physiological, emotional, and behavioral reaction mechanisms that, under certain circumstances, lead to precursors of disease or disease itself. Whereas predisposing interacting variables may promote this chain of events, other interacting factors will counteract potentially damaging outcomes. In simple terms, for example, we might describe this as having an adequate stress coping mechanism. Most importantly, the sequence is not

a one-way process but constitutes part of a cybernetic system with multiple and continuous feedback (Kagan & Levi, 1975). Essentially, it is a dynamic system in which stress (the stress agent) is inevitable, but distress or strain is not. Ecological models also represent the relationship between the individual and the environment as dynamic in nature, and the person is acknowledged as entering a transaction or interacting with the environment.

Cognitive appraisal and reappraisal are incorporated into a feedback circuit in an interactive model of stress. The objective is to minimize the distress experienced and to maximize any potential benefits. Davies and Underwood (2000) argue for a three-factor model of coping, namely, the management of emotional responses, problem solving, and avoidance. However, they also point out, "It should be remembered that stress is a natural process that has evolved to offer adaptive benefits. It is only when coping strategies fail to accrue benefits that we should conceive stress as detrimental to an individual" (p. 480).

Figure 3.5 provides an illustration of the way in which a situation is perceived and how a response is subsequently modified by individual differences. In summary, we can observe that five key characteristics are associated with an interactive model of job stress.

Cognitive Appraisal. Stress is regarded as a subjective experience contingent upon the perception of a situation or event. Individuals will appraise the relevance of an external event to their own situation. This is known as primary appraisal. It means that "stress is not simply out there in the environment" (Lazarus, 1966, p. 466). As Shakespeare's Hamlet says, "There is nothing either good or bad, but thinking makes it so" (Act II, scene ii). Secondary appraisal

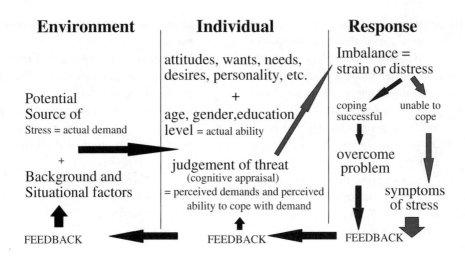

Figure 3.5   An Interactive Model of Job Stress

incorporates the coping strategies available and the evaluation of their likely efficacy. Appraisal feedback might lead to changes in the coping strategy used; this is referred to as reappraisal.

Experience. The way a situation or event is perceived depends upon familiarity with the situation, previous exposure to the event, learning, education, and training (i.e., the individual's actual ability). Related to this is the concept of success or failure in coping with the demand on previous occasions. Therefore, conditioning and reinforcement are an important part of an interactive model of stress.

Demand. Pressure or demand is the product of actual demands, perceived demands, actual ability, and perceived ability to meet that demand. Needs, desires, and the immediate level of arousal all will influence the way in which a demand is perceived.

Interpersonal Influence. A potential source of stress is not perceived in a social vacuum. The presence or absence of other people or work colleagues will influence our perception of stress. Thus, background and situational factors will influence the subjective experience of stress, our response, and the coping behavior used. The presence or absence of other people can have both a positive and a negative influence. For example, the presence of work colleagues can be a source of distraction, irritation, or unwanted arousal. Conversely, the presence of work colleagues can also provide a support network that helps to boost confidence and self-esteem, provide confirmation of values, and provide a sense of personal identity and self-worth. Through the process of vicarious learning, increased awareness and an understanding of potential consequences can also be gained.

A State of Stress. This is acknowledged as an imbalance or mismatch between the perceived demand and the perception of one's ability to meet that demand. The processes that follow are the coping process and the consequences of the coping strategy applied. Therefore, the importance of feedback at all levels is specified in this model of stress. Successful coping restores any imbalance, whereas unsuccessful coping results in the manifestation of symptoms of exposure to stress. The response may produce either short-term stress manifestations in the form of maladaptive coping strategies such as "light up another cigarette," "need alcohol," or "take a sleeping pill," or long-term effects such as heart disease, certain forms of cancer, or ulcers. Obviously, it is acknowledged that the short-term consequences of exposure to stress and maladaptive coping strategies can also be causal factors in the etiology of these long-term diseases (e.g., the link between cigarette smoking and lung cancer). Thus, a method of coping with a source of stress can ultimately become the source of stress itself.

Within this model of stress, an accident at work can be both a short-term and a long-term manifestation of exposure to stress (having both direct and indirect impact on behavior). McGrath (1976) states that a source of stress must be perceived and interpreted by the individual. However, it is also necessary to perceive that the potential consequences of successful coping are more desirable than the expected consequences of leaving a situation unaltered. For example, an individual who chooses to use palliatives as a coping strategy (perhaps as an escape from reality) views this type of short-term, immediate response as less costly or more personally desirable than trying to alter the demand. Of course, it might not be possible for the individual to actually alter the demand at a personal level. This could happen, for example, if an individual is forced to work permanent night shifts because no alternative work schedule is available to him or her.

In summary, an interactive model of stress acknowledges that situations are not inherently stressful, but are potentially stressful, and it is necessary to take account of the

- Source of stress (the stressor or stress agent)
- Mediators or moderators of the stress response (the interacting variables that predispose or protect)
- Mechanism or manifestation of stress (the stress response in physiological, behavioral, or emotional terms)

One example of an interactive model of stress is known as the person-environment fit approach to understanding stress (Cooper, 1981; French & Caplan, 1973).

PERSON-ENVIRONMENT FIT MODEL OF JOB STRESS

Contemporary theories of stress recognize the importance of both the person and the environment in understanding the consequences of exposure to a stress agent. Person constructs relevant to our understanding of the nature of stress include type A behavior (Friedman & Rosenman, 1959) and locus of control (Rotter, 1966). The impact of environment has been researched in terms of constructs such as life events (Holmes & Rahe, 1967), daily hassles (DeLongis, Coyne, Dakof, Folkman, & Lazarus, 1982), and role overload and underload (French & Caplan, 1973). However, a dual emphasis on both person and environment is characteristic of an interactive perspective in understanding the nature of stress. In this ecological model of job stress, the person is seen to interact with the environment. Implicit in this is the notion that the person and the environment determine behavior, attitudes, and well-being jointly, and that stress arises from lack of fit between the person and the environment. The person-environment (P-E) fit theory and model of job stress have been expounded and developed

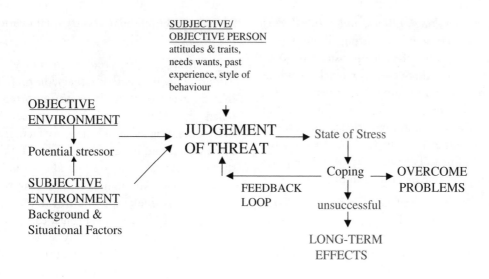

Figure 3.6   Person-Environment Fit Model of Stress

by authors such as French, Rodgers, and Cobb (1974), Harrison (1978), and Caplan (1983). In this discussion, we provide the key elements of this model of job stress illustrated in Figure 3.6.

The exponents of P-E fit theory suggest that stress does not arise from the person or the environment separately but from a lack of fit with one another. There are three key distinctions to acknowledge within the P-E fit theory of stress.

1. Person and environment are two separate entities.

2. Both person and environment are defined in *subjective* and *objective* terms.

   • Objective person refers to the attributes of the person, as they actually exist.

   • Subjective person refers to the person's perceptions of his or her attributes, such as self-identity and self-concept.

   • Objective environment refers to the physical and social situations and events, as they exist independent of the individual's perceptions.

   • Subjective environment refers to the events and situations as encountered and perceived by the individual (Edwards, Caplan, & Van Harrison, 1998).

Harrison (1978) suggests that the objective person and environment are causally related to their subjective counterparts, but these relationships are imperfect because of perceptual distortions. Limited human information-processing capabilities, denial, and repression cause perceptual distortion. Also, we need to acknowledge that an organizational structure and climate can limit access to objective information (Harrison, 1978). However, cognitive appraisal of both objective and subjective environment may be distorted by irrational beliefs and common distortions that create faulty thinking. These include the following:

• *Thinking in Black-and-White Terms.* This concept involves putting all our experiences into one of two opposite categories so that everything is either black or white, with no room for anything in between. For example, the belief that attending Meeting X is always a good experience and attending Meeting Y is always a bad experience can lead us to behave and perform inappropriately in one or both situations.

• *Overgeneralizing From One Situation to Another.* This means drawing conclusions from one or two isolated events and assuming that those same conclusions can be applied to all situations. For example, your train journey from Manchester to London always arrives on time. Making plans on the assumption that this will be the situation on a rail journey from London to Cardiff can create stress when this thinking is found to be faulty because the train arrives late and an important meeting is missed.

• *Jumping to Conclusions.* This means drawing a conclusion when there is no appropriate evidence or facts to justify it, or even when the facts suggest something totally different. For example, because it did not snow in January, you conclude that winter is over. You drain the antifreeze from the engine in your car, even though snow fell in April the previous year.

• *Ignoring Important Details.* This involves focusing on a particular detail taken out of context and ignoring the more important aspects of the situation. For example, a colleague has been promoted. Because you have both worked in the department for the same length of time, you are feeling distressed and depressed because you feel that you have been passed over for promotion. However, you have chosen to ignore the fact that the promoted colleague has attended evening classes for the past 2 years to obtain the necessary qualification for promotion.

• *Exaggerating the Importance of Things.* This means that either you pretend that an event or thing is of no importance when, in reality, it is vital, or you believe that something is vital when, in fact, it is quite trivial and insignificant. For example, the boss has asked to see you about one of your projects. Automatically assuming that everything is fine and going to the meeting unprepared to discuss the project can create problems in just the same way as assuming that you must have done something wrong and spending the day becoming more frantic, anxious, and unable to work. Both are distortions that can lead to dysfunctional behavior because stress arises from how we perceive a situation and our thoughts and feelings about it.

• *Taking Things Personally.* This is the tendency to believe that things happening around us are somehow related to us in an important way, even when there is no real evidence for this. For example, you pass a colleague in the building at work and he or she appears not to notice you. You interpret this to mean that he or she dislikes you or is avoiding you.

Likewise, cognitive appraisal of both objective and subjective person may be distorted by the perceptual distortion and irrational beliefs described above. This is described as a lack of accuracy in self-assessment. For example, your belief that the boss does not like you may cause you to accept this as the reason for your failure to be promoted. In fact, it is due to your laziness or lack of motivation, because, unlike other colleagues, you did not attempt to gain the business qualifications needed for further promotion.

3. Two types of fit are assumed in the P-E fit model of stress.

The first type of fit describes fit or misfit between the demands of the environment and the abilities of the person. Demands include, for example, role responsibilities, and qualitative and quantitative task load or underload. Abilities of the individual might include experience, level of skill, training, stamina, and dexterity. The second type of fit refers to the match or fit between the needs, wants, and desires of the person and the degree to which the environment meets these needs. It is acknowledged that needs are determined by innate biological and psychological processes and the product of learning and socialization. The environment can meet the needs of the individual by providing extrinsic and intrinsic resources and rewards such as food, shelter, money, social interaction, and the opportunity to achieve (Harrison, 1978).

Four classifications of misfit between person and environment are possible.

1. *Objective P-E fit*—the fit between the objective person and the objective environment

2. *Subjective P-E fit*—the fit between the subjective person and the subjective environment

3. *Contact with reality*—the degree to which the subjective environment is consistent with the objective environment

4. *Accuracy of self-assessment*—the match between the objective person and the subjective person

Although lack of discrepancy between person and environment fit is a requirement for good mental health, under certain conditions, disengagement from the objective aspects of a situation or the self may dampen anxiety and facilitate adaptation, thus promoting mental health (Lazarus, 1983). Indeed, present wisdom suggests that subjective P-E fit is the critical pathway to mental health and other dimensions of well-being.

Therefore, stress arises when the perceived environment does not provide adequate supplies to meet the person's perceived needs, or the perceived abilities of the person fail to meet the perceived demands of the work environment. Thus, stress is defined in terms of the degree of perceived goodness of fit between person and environment. Subjective P-E misfit leads to physical, psychological, and behavioral strain, defined as deviation from normal functioning (Harrison, 1978), whereas good fit produces positive health and well-being. Judgment of threat and lack of fit, that is, stress, leads to the employment of one or more coping strategies and provides impetus for change. Outcomes are then fed back into the perception of fit. For example, perceived work overload and having too much to do may prompt the employee to seek help in the form of assertiveness training, because the ability to be assertive and say no to increased demand in the form of more work is a way of reducing the strain between a perceived demand in the environment and the perceived ability of that person to meet that demand. This is described as adaptive coping. However, as we have noted, the individual may engage in maladaptive coping by using certain defense mechanisms such as denial, repression, or projection. This is an attempt to enhance subjective P-E fit through the process of cognitive distortion of the attributes of either the person or the environment. Denial of the experience of strain is also a way of coping with the stress associated with perceived misfit. This characteristic is typical of type A coronary-prone behavior, in which an individual is likely to deny both physical and psychological strain when working under the pressure of a high workload.

Therefore, fit is assessed in terms of the desired and actual levels of various job conditions. The main weakness of this model is that it infers some static situation; in reality, response to stress is a dynamic process. However, the model is useful when certain personality traits are relatively stable. For example, Kahn, Wolfe, Quinn, Snoek, and Rosenthal (1964) found that introverts under stress from role conflict will tend to reduce contact with other people and further irritate work colleagues by appearing to be too independent. Role senders, attempting to define the role, will increase their efforts, thereby adding to the strain. This means that the introvert's coping strategy of defensive withdrawal is, in effect, maladaptive. An understanding of such differences between introverts and extroverts can help to avoid potentially stressful interpersonal conflict situations. Kahn et al. also noted that rigid personality types tend to avoid conflict. They rely on compulsive work habits and show increased dependence on authority figures when under threat. Flexible people, however, are more likely to respond to a conflict situation by complying with work demands and seeking support from peers and subordinates. This compliance strategy can lead to work overload problems. Also, reliance on those of equal or lower status does not help to resolve the stressor situation because it is often the boss or superior who sets the work expectation that is the source of stress. Thus, the rigid and the flexible personality types create very different problems in the workplace in response to stress and ultimately may be more suited to some work environments more than others.

Other Interactive Models of Job Stress

Siegrist (1997) suggests that a theoretical concept is needed to identify the "toxic" components of stressful experiences at work. To understand the response to stress, we need to apply an interactive model of stress and consider the interaction between work characteristics and the individual. For example, the demand-control model of work stress proposed by Karasek and Theorell (1990) suggests that we can understand response to job demands only if we also take into account the individual's perceptions of control in the workplace. According to this model, the combined effect of high job demand and low job control (low decision latitude at work, low skill discretion) creates recurrent negative emotions and associated physiological stress reactions that, in the long term, affect health adversely, including the cardiovascular system (Siegrist, 1997). Social support from both work colleagues and supervisors will also moderate the impact of job demand and job control, and this has been added to the demand-control model of stress.

The effort-reward imbalance model proposed by Siegrist (1997) offers another explanation of how an individual copes with the demands of work. This concept claims that the same types of tasks may produce quite different psychological and physiological reactions depending on the person's way of coping with a demand. Two sources of high effort are defined. *Extrinsic effort* refers to demands and obligations, and *intrinsic effort* refers to the motivations of the individual. Siegrist states,

Stressful experience associated with high effort results from the absence of an appropriate reward, either in terms of esteem, money, career opportunities and job security. Having a demanding but unstable job, achieving at high level without being offered promotion prospects, or receiving an inadequate wage in comparison to one's efforts or qualifications, are examples of "toxic" psychosocial experience at work which adversely affects cardiovascular health. (p. 36)

As Siegrist suggests, it is possible to define jobs in terms of "psychomental" rather than physical demands. Psychomental overload and underload, work pressure due to rationalization, job insecurity, and forced mobility are now commonplace sources of stress at work.

A View of Stress—Implications for Managing Stress in the Workplace

As we have seen, a variety of models have been offered in an attempt to increase our understanding of the nature of stress. The most recent transactional models of stress are indicative of the complexity of the concept. In reality, models tend to over-simplify the problem to the extent that the issue of stress can seem to become trivialized. As Schuler (1980) says, "It is too all encompassing a phenomenon, too large to investigate" (p. 185). This has not deterred interest in the topic, nor has the interest always been positive. Incorrect usage of the word *stress* is common, and it is used interchangeably to refer to a state or condition, a symptom, or the cause of a state or symptom. Defining the word *stress* is problematic, if, indeed, the word even exists. In certain quarters, people ask if it should be used at all, or if it is a helpful term to describe work conditions. *Stress, pressure,* and *strain* are used interchangeably to describe feelings, emotions, or situations. The layperson seems quite able to identify with the concept of stress and has an appetite to know more. The press and media serve this need too eagerly, and without a doubt, certain individuals hope to make a quick profit from "being stressed" at work. What is really needed is action and encouragement to prevent and manage positively the strains and pressures that are an inevitable part of modern-day living and working.

So, it is vital that we apply a model of job stress that embraces the view that *not all stress is bad*. Hans Selye, the acknowledged father of stress research, said that the only person without stress was a dead person (Selye, 1983). By this, Selye meant that stress is an inevitable part of being alive and should be viewed as stimulation to growth and development. Hans Selye used the word *stress* to describe a state of arousal in the nervous system. So, it is *any* stimulus, event, or demand affecting the sensory nervous system. A state of stress exists when there is unwanted pressure. It is manifest when we feel that a situation is out of our control or when we feel unable to cope with an event. Stress is a subjective experience—it is in the eye of the beholder. An understanding of this explains why, in a given situation, one person might be highly distressed, whereas another seems to prosper and thrive.

In organizational life, it is likely that we are now denied a natural outlet and expression of the stress response yet are physiologically primed to take actions that are inappropriate. The sedentary nature of work exacerbates this situation. Although our response to stress is, in the first instance, physiological, complex emotional and behavioral reactions also take place. These can lead to potentially damaging health outcomes. Understanding the nature of stress in these terms helps us to think positively and proactively about stress instead of taking a defensive, self-blaming stance. It implies that each of us, at various times, will be vulnerable to stress. Therefore, it is essential that any model of stress embrace this notion and include the issue of coping and coping style in response to arousal. The P-E fit model of stress suggests that coping strategies are put into place to overcome a perceived threat.

The use of inappropriate coping strategies will sustain the stress response and lead to either the short- or long-term manifestations of exposure to a stress agent. Differences between adaptive and maladaptive coping are explained below. It is an important aspect of understanding the nature of stress and why it can be harmful.

Adaptive Versus Maladaptive Ways of Coping With Stress

It is essential that we manage a potentially stressful situation in an active and positive manner, without resorting to maladaptive ways of coping. Maladaptive coping strategies include

1. Excessive use of alcohol or nicotine

2. Dependence on other drugs, such as tranquilizers, sleeping pills, "pep" pills, and caffeine

3. Failure to get adequate levels of exercise or engage in fulfilling social and recreational activities

4. Indulgence in "comfort" eating because we feel sorry for ourselves, especially when we binge on those foods high in sugar and fat, which have empty calories, and foods with low or poor nutritional value

5. Procrastination, or putting off dealing with a situation because it is threatening or difficult, which usually causes the situation to escalate and leads to even larger problems to tackle

6. Anger and aggression toward oneself and other people. This is a particularly damaging strategy if we persist in bottling up anger. A quietly seething time bomb becomes dangerous and unstable with time and can cause irreparable damage when a situation

finally leads to a major eruption or explosion.

Maladaptive coping exacerbates the stress problem and can become the source of stress itself. For example, we consume alcohol because we believe it gives us confidence or aids sleep or relaxation; we drink lots of strong coffee to gain the "buzz" necessary to sustain long hours of working without a break; we smoke cigarettes to calm our nerves or take the place of meals that we skip because of time pressures; we use various pills and potions to bring sleep or to pep ourselves up; and we eat comfort foods with low or poor nutritional value. These forms of coping render us less fit to cope and, in the long term, actually become the source of stress, when addiction aggravates the problem. This explains why we insist that it is mismanaged stress that is damaging in its consequences.

An Operational Model of Job Stress

A working model of the dynamics of stress proposed by Cooper and Marshall (1978) has been used widely within organizations to guide stress management initiatives. It has become a framework for conducting a stress audit and a model for a holistic, organizational approach to the management of stress (see Figure 3.7).

Consistent with an interactive approach to stress, a successful approach to the management of stress must consider three key elements.

1. The source of stress or stress agent

2. Individual differences in response to stress

3. Outcomes or symptoms of exposure to stress for both the organization and individual

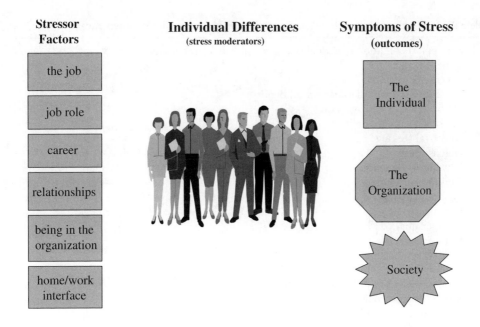

Stressor Factors

the job

job role

career

relationships

being in the organization

home/work interface

Individual Differences
(stress moderators)

Symptoms of Stress
(outcomes)

The Individual

The Organization

Society

Figure 3.7   Dynamics of Job Stress

Evidence from a significant body of research suggests that five major categories of job stress can be identified. These are illustrated in Figure 3.7. The model includes a sixth stressor classification to take account of the home-work interface of the employee. Sources of stress include the following:

1. *Stress in the job itself*—includes workload conditions, the physical work environment, hours of working, decision-making latitude, and so on

2. *Role-based stress*—includes stressors such as role conflict, role ambiguity, and job responsibility

3. *Stress due to the changing nature of relationships with other people at work*—includes relationships with managers, supervisors, subordinates, and coworkers

4. *Career stress*—associated with the lack of opportunity for career development and promotion, as well as job insecurity

5. *Stress associated with the organizational structure and climate*—includes the stressful nature of the culture and politics of the organization, the restrictions imposed on behavior, and no sense of belonging. Essentially, it is about "simply being in the organization"

6. *Stressors associated with the home and work interface*—includes conflicts of loyalty, the spillover of demands from one environment to another, life events, and life crises

To understand a response to a source of stress, it is necessary to take account of the individual and all the differences that interact to modify that response. This is known as the person factor, and included in this are the many personality traits, characteristics,

Table 3.2   Facets of Job Stress—Employee Health Domain: The Personal Facet

1. Psychological condition (personality traits and behavioral characteristics)
   Type A behavior
   Ego needs
   Need for clarity/intolerance for ambiguity
   Introversion or extroversion
   Internality or externality
   Approval seeking
   Defensiveness
   Level of intelligence
   Abilities—training
   Previous experience
   Impatience
   Intrapersonal conflicts
   Self-esteem
   Motives/goals/aspirations
   Anxiety level, emotion, neuroticism
   Perceptual style
   Values (human, religious, etc.)
   Personal work standards
   Need for perfection
   Satisfaction with job/life satisfaction

2. Physical condition
   Physical fitness
   General health condition
   Diet and eating habits
   Exercise
   Work, sleep, and relaxation patterns

3. Life stage characteristics
   Stage of personal development
   Family stage
   Career stage

4. Demographics
   Age
   Education (amount and type)
   Sex
   Race
   Socioeconomic status
   Occupation/vocation

SOURCE: Based on Beehr and Newman (1978).

and behavioral styles that are part of our inheritance or learned through the process of socialization. Thus, response to stress is mediated and influenced by needs, wants, attitudes, personal values, past experiences, life circumstances, life stage, ability, and physical condition.

The complexity of understanding stress in terms of individual differences is illustrated in Table 3.2. Beehr and Newman (1978) describe job stress and employee health in terms of a facet analysis model. This includes environmental, personal, and process facets; human and organizational consequences; an adaptive response facet; and a time facet. Table 3.2 provides details of the elements included in the personal facet.

These are the personal conditioning variables that are important to the individual's perception of the work environment. The long list explains the diversity of individual differences observed in response to a source of stress, and so individual vulnerability to stress is dependent on a large number of complex and interacting factors. Therefore, dealing with stress in the workplace is a twofold process of understanding the potential stressors that might exist to cause harm, and acknowledging the attributes of the individual that will mediate appraisal and any subsequent outcomes.

The operational model of job stress illustrated in Figure 3.7 also indicates that we need to consider both individual and organizational symptoms or outcomes of exposure to stress. Indeed, costs to society itself should not be ignored by responsible corporations.

A wide variety of individual symptoms of stress, and the use of maladaptive coping strategies, can lead to numerous physical and psychological health problems, including heart disease, certain cancers, depressive disorders, and gastrointestinal problems. In addition, we need to acknowledge the organizational and social problems associated with, for example, alcoholism, obesity, poor physical condition, psychoses, neuroses, and personality disorders. Therefore, the real bottom line for an organization must include the high business costs of absence, labor turnover, unsatisfactory industrial relations, poor job performance, and frequent and severe accidents. So, in addition to identifying sources of stress and understanding individual differences in response to stress, it is necessary to understand and measure the consequences and costs of stress to the individual and the organization. This information is essential if individuals are required to justify and rationalize the need for stress management interventions. It is also vital as part of the process of evaluation and the calculation of a cost-benefit analysis.

This model of stress can be used to guide the steps to successful stress management programs.

- Have a clear understanding of why you are implementing the program—stress management should not be a flavor-of-the-month activity. The need for clearly defined objectives and goals is paramount in gaining the commitment of the workforce.
- Recognize and measure the benefits to be gained (i.e., evaluate).
- Take time to understand staff attitudes to stress management.
- Define clearly and communicate your plan. Identify who will be involved and what will happen.
- Acknowledge that stress is a dynamic process. Stress management is not a one-off project but should be integrated into the organization.
- Stress management is everyone's responsibility—it is not an activity confined to the health and safety department or human resources personnel.
- Stress is inevitable; distress is not.

Defining Stress

As we have stated previously, the successful management of stress requires us to state and define clearly what we mean by stress in the work environment. Examination of dictionary definitions of stress reflects their origins and the schools of thought on the mechanism and nature of stress. For example, in the 17th century, stress was used to mean "hardship, straits, and adversity of affliction." By the 18th and 19th centuries, the use of the word *stress* had broadened to indicate "strain, pressure, or strong effort." This was intended to include terms to describe the laws of physics and engineering in addition to a person's organs and mental powers (Hinkle, 1973). Within the field of physics, stress was used to refer to an object's resistance to external pressure, and this model was adopted by the social sciences. However, as Cox (1985) pointed out, an engineering analogy was too simplistic. He stated, "We have to accept some intervening psychological process which does mediate the outcome. . . . Stress has to be perceived and recognized by man. A machine, however, does not have to recognize the load or stress placed upon it" (p. 15).

More recent dictionary definitions actually associate stress with disease. For example, the *Concise Oxford Dictionary* (1984), new edition, described stress as "suffered by managers, etc; subject to continual stress." Medical dictionaries include both a response-based and a stimulus-based approach to stress when providing guidance on definitions of stress. For example, *Stedman's Medical Dictionary* (1982, 24th ed.) states that stress is

> 1. Reactions of the body to forces of a deleterious nature, infections, and various abnormal states that tend to disturb its normal physiologic equilibrium. . . .
> 3. The force or pressure applied or exerted between portions of a body or bodies. . . .
> 5. A physical or psychological stimulus . . . which, when impinging upon an individual, produces psychological strain or disequilibrium.

The *Encyclopaedia and Dictionary of Medicine, Nursing and Allied Health* (1978, 2nd ed.) suggests that stress is

the sum of all the non-specific biological phenomena elicited by adverse external influences including damage and defence. Stress may be either physical or psychological, or both. Just as a bridge is structurally capable of adjusting to certain physical stresses, the human body and mind are normally able to adapt to the stresses of new situations. This ability has definite limits beyond which continued stress may cause a breakdown . . . although this limit varies from person to person. . . . For example, peptic ulcers may result from prolonged nervous tension in response to real or imagined stresses in people who have a predisposition for ulcers.

However, within our conceptualization of stress, a person-environment fit model also acknowledges that both underload and overload can be stress agents. Levi (1987) takes account of this when he describes stress as a poor fit.

> The interaction between, or misfit of, environmental opportunities and demands, and individual needs and abilities, and expectations, elicit reactions. When the fit is bad, when needs are not being met, or when abilities are over- or under-taxed, the organism reacts with various pathogenic mechanisms. These are cognitive, emotional, behavioural and/or physiological and under some conditions of intensity, frequency or duration, and in the presence or absence of certain interacting variables, they may lead to precursors of disease. (p. 9)

This definition is consistent with a contemporary, interactive approach to the study of stress. Implicit in Levi's definition is the view that stress can have both positive and negative consequences. That is, "Stress can be a motivator to growth, development and adaptation; it can be challenge and variety . . . it can be the spice of life" (Selye, 1936, p. 32).

Therefore, a distinction must be made between stressors that cause distress and those that result in "eustress" (i.e., a positive stress response), because stress is inevitable, distress is not (Quick & Quick, 1984). Beehr and Newman (1978) acknowledge this and provide our ultimate definition of job stress:

> A situation wherein job-related factors interact with a worker to change (that is, disrupt or enhance) his or her psychological and or physiological condition such that the person (that is, mind or body) is forced to deviate from normal functioning. This definition also serves to define what we mean by "employee health"; namely a person's mental and physical condition. We are referring to health in its broadest sense—the complete continuum from superb mental and physical health all the way to death. Note that we are not excluding the possibility of beneficial effects of stress on health. (p. 670)

CONCLUSION

Our review of various models of job stress has guided us in providing an adequate definition of stress, and it is clear that our understanding of stress must be in terms of transaction or interactive process models, where stress is viewed as a dynamic process in which time plays a vital role. Models of stress have been used to explain how occupational stressors arise from both the work environment and work conditions, but are mediated through perceptual appraisal and experience. Furthermore, stressor-induced physiological, psychological, and behavioral mechanisms are activated and can lead to stress-related physical and psychological diseases and a host of social and organizational problems. Therefore, a dual approach to the management of stress is advocated. It means that the organization and every employee must exercise a joint duty of care in reducing the mounting costs associated with stress in the workplace.

REFERENCES

Beehr, T. A., & Newman, J. E. (1978). Job stress, employee health and organisational effectiveness: A facet analysis model and literature review. *Personnel Psychology, 31,* 665-699.

Cannon, W. B. (1935). Stresses, strain of homeostasis. *American Journal of Medical Science, 189*(1), 1-14.

Caplan, R. D. (1983). Person-environment fit: Past, present and future. In C. L. Cooper (Ed.), *Stress research* (pp. 35-78). New York: Wiley.

Christian, P., & Lolas, F. (1985). The stress concept as problem for theoretical pathology. *Social Science and Medicine, 21*(2), 1363-1365.

Cooper, C. L. (1981). *The stress check.* Englewood Cliffs, NJ: Prentice Hall.

Cooper, C. L., & Marshall, J. (1978) *Understanding executive stress.* London: Macmillan.

Cox, T. (1985). *Stress.* London: Macmillan.

Davies, M. N., & Underwood, G. (2000). Cognition and stress. In G. Fink (Ed.), *Encyclopedia of stress* (Vol.1, pp. 478-483). San Diego, CA: Academic Press.

DeLongis, L. R., Coyne, J. C., Dakof, G., Folkman, S., & Lazarus, R. S. (1982). Relationship of daily hassles, uplifts, and major events to health status. *Health Psychology, 1,* 119-136.

Edwards, J. R., Caplan, R. D., & Van Harrison, R. (1998). Person-environment fit theory: Conceptual foundations, empirical evidence, and directions for future research. In C. L. Cooper (Ed.), *Theories of organizational stress* (pp. 28-67). Oxford, UK: Oxford University Press.

French, J. R. P., & Caplan, R. D. (1973). Organisational stress and individual strain. In A. J. Merrow (Ed.), *The failure of success* (pp. 30-66). New York: Amacon.

French, J. R. P., Jr., Rodgers, W. L., & Cobb, S. (1974). Adjustment as person-environment fit. In G. Coelho, D. Hamburg, & J. Adams (Eds.), *Coping and adaptation* (pp. 316-323). New York: Basic Books.

Friedman, M., & Rosenman, R. H. (1959). Associations of specific overt behaviour pattern with blood and cardiovascular findings, blood cholesterol level, blood clotting time, incidence of arcus senilis and clinical coronary artery disease. *Journal of the American Medical Association, 169,* 1286-1296.

Goodell, H., Wolf, S., & Rogers, F. B. (1986). Historical perspective. In S. Wolf & A. J. Finestone (Eds.), *Occupational stress: Health and performance at work* (pp. 8-23). Littleton, MA: PSG.

Harrison, R. V. (1978). Person-environment fit and job stress. In C. L. Cooper & R. Payne (Eds.), *Stress at work* (pp. 175-205). New York: Wiley.

Health and Safety Executive. (2001). *Tackling work-related stress: A manager's guide to improving and maintaining employee health and well-being* (No. HSG218). Sudbury, Suffolk, UK: HSE Books.

Hinkle, L. E. (1973). The concept of stress in the biological and social sciences. *Science, Medicine and Man, 1,* 31-48.

Holmes, T. H., & Rahe, R. H. (1967). The Social Readjustment Rating Scale. *Journal of Psychosomatic Research, 11,* 213-218.

Kagan, A. R., & Levi, L. (1975). Health and environment—Psychosocial stimuli: A review. In L. Levi (Ed.), *Society, stress and disease—Childhood and adolescence* (pp. 241-260). Oxford, UK: Oxford University Press.

Kahn, R. L., Wolfe, D. M., Quinn, R. P., Snoek, J. D., & Rosenthal, R. A. (1964). *Organisational stress: Studies in role conflict and ambiguity.* London: Wiley.

Karasek, R., & Theorell, T. (1990). *Healthy work: Stress, productivity and the reconstruction of working life.* New York: Basic Books.

Lazarus, R. S. (1966). *Psychological stress and the coping process.* New York: McGraw-Hill.

Lazarus, R. S. (1983). The costs and benefits of denial. In S. Breznitz (Ed.), *Denial of stress* (pp. 1-30). New York: International Universities Press.

Levi, L. (1987). Definitions and the conceptual aspects of health in relation to work. In R. Kalimo, M. A. El-Batawi, & C. L. Cooper (Eds.), *Psychosocial factors at work and their relation to health* (pp. 9-14). Geneva: WHO.

Levi, L. (1998). Preface: Stress in organisations—Theoretical and empirical approaches. In C. L. Cooper (Ed.), *Theories of organizational stress* (pp. v-xii). Oxford, UK: Oxford University Press.

McCloy, E. (1995, June). Stress—A clinical perspective for managers. In *Occupational stress—Causes and victims.* Conference proceedings, Civil Service Occupational Health and Safety Agency.

McGrath, J. E. (1976). Stress and behaviour in organisations. In M. D. Dunnette (Ed.), *Handbook of industrial and organisational psychology* (pp. 1351-1395). Chicago: Rand McNally.

McLean, A. A. (1979). *Mind, self and society* (pp. 508-536). Chicago: University of Chicago Press.

Osler, W. (1910). Angina pectoris. *Lancet, 1,* 839.

Pearlin, L. I., Lieberman, M. A., Menaghan, E. G., & Mullan, J. T. (1981). The stress response. *Journal of Health and Social Behaviour, 22,* 337-356.

Quick, J. C., & Quick, J. D. (1984). *Organisational stress and preventive management.* New York: McGraw-Hill.

Rotter, J. B. (1966). Generalized expectancies for internal versus external control of reinforcement. *Psychological Monographs, 80*(1, Whole No. 609).

Schuler, R. S. (1980). Definition and conceptualisation of stress in organisations. *Organisation Behaviour and Human Performance, 25,* 184-215.

Selye, H. (1936). A syndrome produced by diverse nocuous agents. *Nature, 138,* 32.

Selye, H. (1956) *The stress of life.* USA: McGraw-Hill.

Selye, H. (1983). The stress concept: Past, present and future. In C. L. Cooper (Ed.), *Stress research.* London: Wiley.

Siegrist, J. (1997, November). Working conditions and cardiovascular disease. *Safety and Health Practitioner,* pp. 35-37.

Warshaw, L. J. (1979). *Managing stress.* Reading, MA: Addison-Wesley.

WHO. (1984). *Psychosocial factors and health: Monitoring the psychosocial work environment and workers' health.* Geneva: Author.

CHAPTER 4

Effects of Job Stress on Mental and Physical Health

CARLLA S. SMITH
LORNE M. SULSKY
KRISTA L. UGGERSLEV

Most workers today will readily admit that both their work and nonwork lives are very stressful. If questioned further, they will also admit that they think the stress in their lives has negatively affected their physical and emotional health and their work effectiveness. The deleterious effects of work-related stress are increasingly cited as a key concern for both workers and their employing organizations. A new term has even been coined to identify the darker side of work stress: *desk rage*. Desk rage refers to destructive acts that employees use to vent their anger at work, such as verbal abuse and petty theft (Daw, 2001).

These concerns about stress seem to be quite valid. Beyond the widely accepted link, both direct and indirect, between stress and many illnesses (e.g., cancer and heart and gastrointestinal disorders), it has been estimated that stress-related disorders cost U.S. organizations in excess of $150 billion per year. Stress-related claims also account for more than 14% of all insurance compensation claims (Pelletier & Lutz, 1989, 1991). Other estimates indicate that U.S. industry loses about 50 million working days annually due to stress-related absenteeism (Danna & Griffin, 1999). In addition, one survey suggests that 48% of workers react to work-related stress by cutting corners, lying about sick days, and covering up incidents that should be reported (Boyd, 1997).

These and related statistics, input from organizational and government leaders, plus a plethora of personal anecdotes, all underscore the now well-accepted relationship between job stress and health problems. However, does the research literature support such strong, pervasive assumptions? The purpose of this chapter is to explore critically the relationship between job stress and mental and physical health.

First, we review major topic areas in job-related stress and health research, such as Type A and burnout. Then, we address some of the emerging areas, such as the impact of technology and the effects of corporate downsizing. In the conclusion section, we summarize and distill this research, answering our original question: What is the relationship between job-related stress and health?

Before embarking on our review, however, we present a simple stress framework to guide the discussion. Specifically, we propose that some external source of stress, or stressor (e.g., a demanding supervisor at work), provokes a stressful cognitive appraisal (Lazarus, 1966), which leads to a stress response (Cannon, 1932). This stress response has physiological (e.g., increased heart rate, respiration); psychological (e.g., fear); and behavioral (e.g., fleeing the scene) components. If the stressor continues and/or is joined by other stressors, stress outcomes, such as headaches, high blood pressure, depression, and decreased work performance, may occur. If unabated over time, the stress process can produce more serious, chronic decrements, such as heart disease, clinical depression, and alcoholism, which are collectively called strains. Variables that can effect this process are usually called stress moderators; for example, both men and women report being stressed, but women often report more psychological stress responses (e.g., depression), whereas men report more physical stress responses (e.g., backache) (Jick & Mitz, 1985). We define stress as a function of the stressor(s), cognitive appraisal, stress responses, stress outcomes, strains, and stress moderators. Any reference to stress in this chapter refers to this total process (Ganster & Schaubroeck, 1991; Smith & Sulsky, in press).

REVIEW OF THE RESEARCH: MAJOR TOPICS ON WORK STRESS AND HEALTH

We have selected five contemporary research topics on work stress and health—stressful life events and daily hassles, Type A behavior pattern, burnout, social support, and perceived control—to discuss in this chapter. Although these topics are certainly not all-inclusive, we consider them to have had a major impact on organizational stress research over the past 20 to 30 years. The empirical studies on these topics allow us to examine the impact of work stress across multiple jobs and health strains.

Stressful Life Events and Daily Hassles

Holmes and Rahe (1967) proposed one of the earlier attempts to link major life and work stressors to health problems. They examined the relationship between the number of stressful life events (SLEs) experienced by a person (e.g., "change in financial state," "divorce," "retirement," "fired at work") and the development of illness. The researchers reasoned that people repeatedly experience the stress response after exposure to multiple sources of stress or stressors over time; these accumulated stress responses, of course, can contribute to the development of disease.

More specifically, SLEs have been examined within the context of diseases such as cancer (Levenson & Bemis, 1991), coronary heart disease (Tennant, 1987), the common cold (Totman, Kiff, Reed, & Craig, 1980), and immune system dysfunction (Geiser, 1989). SLEs have also been implicated in the development of psychological disorders, such as depression (Hammen, Davila, Brown, Ellicott, & Gitlin, 1992) and schizophrenia (Rabkin, 1980).

These studies have generally reported a small but significant relationship between SLEs and disease onset.

The self-report method (e.g., the self-administered, paper-and-pencil Schedule of Recent Experiences) used to collect the occurrence (and sometimes severity) of SLEs has been criticized by other researchers (see Dohrenwend, Raphael, Schwartz, Stueve, & Skodol, 1993). The reasons include its simplicity, as well as its weak predictive validity (i.e., the small relationships between SLEs and disease) (Kasl, 1983). To address these concerns, Lazarus and his colleagues (e.g., DeLongis, Coyne, Dakof, Folkman, & Lazarus, 1982) proposed and confirmed that the annoying, minor stressors that people frequently encounter, or daily hassles, are better predictors of disease onset than SLEs. These hassles include both nonwork and work events, such as family-related obligations, investments, fellow workers, job security, and bureaucratic red tape. The researchers hypothesized that SLEs are probably too distal to predict the development of recent illness, whereas daily hassles are more proximal, expressing the immediate pressures of living.

Subsequent research has replicated these findings for psychological symptoms (Flannery, 1986), mood (Wolf, Elston, & Kissling, 1989), and physical health (Holahan & Holahan, 1987). In work settings, Ivancevich (1986) reported that hassles were significantly related to physical health and absenteeism, and were stronger predictors than SLEs. Also, Chiriboga and Bailey (1986) found similar results in a sample of more than 1,000 critical care and medical surgical nurses in six hospitals. More recently, Zohar (1999) reported that a daily record of the severity of work hassles predicted end-of-day mood and fatigue in a sample of military personnel.

Despite the fact that both SLEs and daily hassles continue to receive criticism on methodological grounds (e.g., Hahn & Smith, 1999), researchers have certainly not abandoned the constructs. Today the consensus is that SLEs and daily hassles have a small to moderate, but important, relationship with physical and mental disorders.

Type A Behavior Pattern

Type A Behavior Pattern (TABP) is an individual difference variable that has captured both public and scientific attention since the 1960s. Type A is an individual difference that moderates the stressor-strain relationship (i.e., Type A people experience stressors differently and respond differently than do non-Type As).

The notion of Type A originated in the 1950s from the clinical observations of two cardiologists, Friedman and Rosenman (1974); they noticed that patients with heart disease often behaved differently from those patients free of heart disease (coronary heart disease, or CHD). They defined TABP as

> an action-emotion complex that can be observed in any person who is aggressively involved in a chronic, incessant struggle to achieve more and more in less and less time, and if required to do so, against the opposing efforts of other things or persons. (p. 76)

More specifically, Friedman and Rosenman reported that those with CHD were distinguished by an exaggerated sense of time urgency, excessive competitiveness and achievement striving, hostility, and aggressiveness. Other descriptors include tense, preoccupied with deadlines, work-oriented, impatient, and control-oriented. The non-Type A person, or Type B, was described as the polar opposite of Type A.

Subsequent research revealed that, in addition to these behavioral characteristics, TABP is associated with several stress and health-related outcomes. Type As have higher cholesterol levels, greater blood clotting tendencies, higher triglyceride levels, and greater sympathetic nervous system arousal than Type Bs (Lovallo & Pishkin, 1980). Type As also report higher stress levels (Gamble & Matteson, 1992), increased physical health problems (Kirkcaldy & Martin, 2000), and increased smoking and decreased exercise behavior (Howard, Cunningham, & Rechnitzer, 1976) relative to Type Bs. The Type A construct has also captured the attention of organizational scientists because Type As perform better (Lee, 1992), are more job-involved (Jamal & Baba, 1991), and, unfortunately, commit more aggressive acts toward other employees (Baron, Neuman, & Geddes, 1999).

To examine Friedman and Rosenman's original prediction, several large-scale prospective (longitudinal) research projects have systematically investigated the link between TABP and the development of CHD; only a few are discussed here. The most well-known study is the Western Collaborative Group Study (Rosenman et al., 1975), which was the first to assess the relationship between CHD and TABP in men. Potential confounding factors were controlled by using a double-blind study (i.e., ensuring that the investigators had no a priori knowledge of the health status or Type A scores of the participants), and by measuring and statistically accounting for risk factors, such as obesity, smoking, and high blood pressure. The men were tracked for 8½ years and then assessed for coronary heart disease. The results showed that Type A people had a risk ratio for heart disease of more than 2 to 1, even after the risk factors were considered (Brand, 1978). Later, this study was extended in a project, the Framingham Heart Study, which examined Type A in both men and women and in a wider array of jobs (Haynes & Feinleib, 1982); these results were consistent with the original study.

Researchers also specifically attempted to replicate the Western Collaborative Study (Stamler, 1980). A similar research design was used across eight different data collection sites in the United States. Seven years later, the relationship between Type A and heart disease was assessed. Surprisingly, however, no relationship was found between Type A and heart disease (Shekelle et al., 1985). After carefully examining these disconfirming results, researchers concluded that the measurement of Type A as a global construct contributed to these null findings. More specifically, the replication study used a different type of measure, a self-report scale, to assess Type A, whereas prior studies had used a specific type of structured interview, called the Structured Interview (SI). The SI is a protocol in which the interviewee's responses and behaviors are both assessed by the interviewer.

Ganster, Schaubroeck, Sime, and Mayes (1991) pointed out that Type A is really a multidimensional, not global, construct. They found that the hostility component of Type A was a significant predictor of heart disease. Other components (e.g., achievement striving) were related to other criteria (e.g., performance) (Edwards & Baglioni, 1991). These researchers emphasized the difficulties in making global predictions about Type A because it is a multifaceted construct in which different components differentially predict select criteria. In this case, the self-report measure did not adequately tap the hostility component, whereas the SIs used in previous research had assessed hostility quite well.

So, what is the current status of Type A? After years of scientific scrutiny and debate (e.g., Barling & Charbonneau, 1992; Edwards, 1991; Lee, Ashford, & Jamieson, 1993), as well as two quantitative reviews or meta-analyses (Booth-Kewley & Friedman, 1987; Matthews, 1988), researchers agree that Type A is an independent risk factor for coronary heart disease. However, the magnitude of the risk varies depending on the type of Type A measure or dimension, the type of study design, and the type of participant population considered. Researchers also agree that the negative affect components of Type A (anger-hostility and impatience-irritability) appear to be consistently related to health status, and that the SI best captures these negative affect dimensions (Dembroski & Czajkowski, 1989).

Burnout

In recent years, the topic of burnout has been a focus of attention for the popular media and scientific researchers. Most of us have exclaimed that we are "burned out" after a series of examinations, job interviews, or any arduous experience. In a more formal sense, however, burnout has been used in reference to the stress experienced specifically by human service professionals, particularly social workers, therapists, nurses, police officers, and teachers.

Within the past three decades, the medical and psychological community began to realize that workers in the helping or service professions were at serious risk because their jobs require them to accommodate the extreme needs and dependencies of their clients, patients, or students. Such demands can prove to be emotionally and physically debilitating for workers. Maslach and her colleague (Maslach & Jackson, 1982, 1984, 1986) are often credited with the development of burnout as a scientific concept deserving of rigorous inquiry. According to

Maslach and Jackson (1981), burnout can be defined as three specific types of stress responses, usually found in workers in people-intensive jobs: (a) *emotional exhaustion,* or feelings of being drained or used up, unable to face a day's work, or totally unenthusiastic; (b) *depersonalization,* or the act of putting psychological distance between the individual and others, creating emotional detachment; and (c) *(decreased) personal accomplishment,* or the feeling of not living up to former goals and expectations, and wasted efforts. In turn, these stress responses can lead to serious health strains (e.g., depression, drug abuse, maladaptive coping) and organizational strains (e.g., poor performance, increased absenteeism, turnover).

Consistent with this definition, subsequent research determined that burnout is multidimensional (Cherniss, 1980; Leiter, 1991; Maslach, 1982). However, the emotional exhaustion component indisputably appears to be the most important of the three (e.g., Cox, Kuk, & Schur, 1991; Maslach & Jackson, 1981), such that Shirom (1989) and Leiter (1991) both argued that it is the defining component of the syndrome called burnout. Researchers have also debated the appropriate process model of the burnout process (i.e., which dimension precedes or follows the others) (see Golembiewski & Munzenrider, 1988; Leiter, 1993), but no model has garnered clear support.

Some researchers have even suggested that the defining component of burnout, emotional exhaustion, may be little more than the experience of stress, depression, or negative affect, in essence, a new label for an old concept. However, researchers believe that the development of burnout over time as a multidimensional syndrome distinguishes it from other constructs, such as stress (see Cox et al., 1991;

Maslach & Schaufeli, 1993). Empirical research has also shown that the three burnout dimensions are related to different variables, hence demonstrating discriminant validity for the syndrome (e.g., Corrigan, Holmes, & Luchins, 1995; Janssen, Schaufeli, & Houkes, 1999). For example, Firth and Britton (1989) reported that emotional exhaustion was related to increased absenteeism, and depersonalization was related to turnover. Lee and Ashforth's (1996) meta-analyses of the three burnout dimensions across 61 empirical studies provided further quantitative evidence of the discriminant validity of the dimensions.

Although early burnout research used case studies, single-item ("How burned out do you feel?) inventories, and items developed for only a single study (Maslach, 1993), multiple-item self-report measures are the norm today. The two most commonly used self-report scales are the Maslach Burnout Inventory (MBI) (Maslach & Jackson, 1986) and the Burnout Measure (BM) (Pines & Aronson, 1988). The MBI assesses the three burnout dimensions: emotional exhaustion, depersonalization, and reduced accomplishment. The BM, however, assesses a single dimension, emotional exhaustion, which is considered to be the most important component of burnout. Overall, both the BM and the MBI are reliable and valid measures. More recent measures, which expand burnout to jobs outside of human services (e.g., Schaufeli, Leiter, Maslach, & Jackson, 1996) have also been developed.

Today, the scientific concept of burnout as a specific type of stress response in human service jobs has been extended to other occupations, such as managers (Dolan, 1995; Garden, 1989), lawyers (Jackson, Turner, & Brief, 1987), and industrial workers (Demerouti, Bakker, Nachreiner, & Schaufeli, 2001). Definitions

of burnout have been expanded to include such concepts as increasing disillusionment and psychological erosion (Schaufeli & Enzmann, 1998). Researchers have examined some of the most important causes (e.g., workload, time pressure) and consequences (e.g., depression, psychosomatic complaints) of burnout in detail. They have also developed diverse theoretical models of the burnout process (e.g., burnout as a mismatch between person and job, Schaufeli & Enzmann, 1998; burnout as an outcome of job demands and lack of job resources, Demerouti et al., 2001). And, although the longitudinal studies of burnout have not been as supportive as the cross-sectional ones (Schaufeli & Enzmann, 1998), burnout researchers today agree that burnout is a viable syndrome, one that is undoubtedly more pervasive in many work settings than previously believed (Demerouti et al., 2001; Lee & Ashforth, 1996).

Social Support

Social support, defined here as "the resources provided by other persons" (Cohen & Syme, 1985, p. 4), has probably received more attention from organizational stress researchers in recent years than any other individual or group characteristic. Social support is thought to enable people to cope with life and work stress more effectively because they feel valued and are enmeshed in a network of communication and mutual obligation as a consequence of the support (House, 1981; Lazarus & Folkman, 1984). Indeed, research has largely supported this claim. Those people who indicate that they have close, supportive family members, friends, supervisors, and/or coworkers have reported lower depression (e.g., Billings & Moos, 1981; Frese, 1999), fewer physical health problems (e.g., Schmieder & Smith, 1996), and less anxiety (e.g., Barrera, 1981; Frese, 1999). They have also reported less frequent use of health services (e.g., Broadhead, Gehlbach, DeGruy, & Kaplan, 1989) and lower health care costs (e.g., Manning, Jackson, & Fusilier, 1996).

An issue that has been debated frequently in research on social support is whether it directly affects strain, regardless of the severity of the stressor in question, or whether it functions best only for highly stressed people. The first perspective, commonly called a direct or main effect of social support on strain, predicts that social support has beneficial effects on strain regardless of the degree of stress experienced (Beehr, 1976; Blau, 1981). As an example, Beehr (1976) found that workers who reported low supervisor support also reported strains, such as depression and job dissatisfaction, regardless of their stress levels. The second perspective is often referred to as a buffering or moderating effect of social support on the stressor-strain relationship (e.g., Schaubroeck & Fink, 1998; Schmieder & Smith, 1996). This moderating effect posits that the relationship between stressors and strains varies such that social support is effective primarily for those individuals experiencing high levels of stress. For example, in a sample of chemical plant employees, House and Wells (1978) found that the highly stressed workers, who also reported high levels of supervisor support, experienced few mental and physical health problems. This relationship did not exist for workers who indicated that they received lower levels of social support.

Which perspective is correct? Both are correct, but the conditions under which each occurs seem to differ. Most studies that have reported a moderating effect examined health-related strains, such as physical well-being and depression (e.g.,

Cohen & Wills, 1985; Parkes, Mendham, & von Rabenau, 1994). Studies that have found main effects examined (job) attitudes, not health (Beehr, King, & King, 1990). These assumptions seem reasonable because health and well-being should be more affected than attitudes in high-stress situations. In support of these assumptions, recent meta-analyses (Viswesvaran, Sanchez, & Fisher, 1999) suggest that social support is related to reductions in stressors and strains (main effect), and that social support also moderates the stressor-strain relationship (interactive effect).

To add to the complexity, researchers have also noted differences depending on the type of social support measure used in a study. One type of social support measure, social embeddedness, describes a person's integration in a social network (i.e., the number of friends and relatives). Another type of social support, received or enacted support, assesses what people do when they seek support from others (i.e., who they have asked for help in the past). Neither of these types of social support measures, however, has consistently demonstrated any relationships with health. The third type of measure, perceived support, or support perceived to be available but not yet received, is the most frequently used type of social support. Perceived support has shown the most consistent relationships with stress and health strains and is considered to be health-protective (House & Wells, 1978; Wethington & Kessler, 1986). Perceived support is assumed to be health-protective because, if people perceive that they have potential support from others, they are less likely to appraise a situation as stressful. Consequently, one rarely needs to deal with the negative effects of stress because the process is circumvented early.

Social support can also vary in terms of content (e.g., obtaining advice, money), as well as form. The most commonly researched content type is emotional social support, or expressions of concern or empathy for a distressed person, which may be positive, negative, non-job related (Fenlason & Beehr, 1994), or emphatic (Zellars & Perrewe, 2001). Zellars and Perrewe (2001) found that employees who sought emotional support in terms of "gripe sessions" reported greater burnout, whereas those who received empathy from coworkers and focused on the positive aspects of their jobs reported less burnout.

The evidence for the positive role of social support in the stress process is substantial. Social support appears to exert its influence in a variety of ways, and that influence is almost universally helpful in dealing with job and life stress. Because of its efficacious effects, social support has been incorporated into some major perspectives on work stress, such as the demands-control model, to which we next turn our attention.

Work Control

Psychologists have long known that feelings of personal control are important in maintaining psychological and physical health in both animals and humans (Averill, 1973; Rodin & Langer, 1977; Seligman, 1975). Furthermore, the empirical evidence is rather compelling that perceptions of personal control are related to health and lack of personal control to illness across a variety of subjects and settings (e.g., Bosma, Stansfeld, & Marmot, 1998; Folkman, 1984; Miller, 1979; Shirom, Melamed, & Nir-Dotan, 2000; Tetrick, Slack, DaSilva, & Sinclair, 2000).

From this knowledge, Robert Karasek (1979) developed, and later expanded (Karasek & Theorell, 1990), what many work psychologists call the most influential model of organizational stress in the latter part of the 20th century. The demands-control model hypothesizes that psychological strain develops from the joint effects of job demands and the decision latitude available to the worker. He defined job demands as the psychological stressors present in the work environment, primarily work overload, and decision latitude as the discretion in decision making or job control. According to the model, job strain occurs when job demands are high and job decision latitude or control is low; conversely, growth and development occur when both job demands and job decision latitude are high. However, the focus of the model is on the combination of high demands and low control. Karasek (1979) reasoned that high demands produce a state of stressful arousal that, if coupled with conditions of low control, cannot be easily managed. He tested this hypothesis on data from large national surveys of U.S. and Swedish workers and found that high demands and low control were associated with exhaustion in the U.S. data and depression in the Swedish data. In effect, these data demonstrated that a link exists between work stress and job design (i.e., job demands and control).

In subsequent research, empirical support for the model has been mixed; some studies support the model's predictions (e.g., Karasek, 1990), whereas others do not (e.g., Spector, 1987; Wall, Jackson, Mullarkey, & Parker, 1996). Based on these inconsistent results, researchers criticized Karasek's model, mostly on methodological grounds (see Ganster & Schaubroeck, 1991, for a review). The most consistent criticism was that the preponderance of the data did not support an interactive effect as predicted by the model, but only main effects for demands and control. Critics also alleged that the model was conceptually very narrow in that it contains only two constructs, demands and control, which do not capture adequately the complexity of contemporary jobs.

In answer to the latter criticism, much contemporary research on the demands-control model has focused on extensions of the model to include other theoretically relevant variables. The most promising addition is social support, which was included in Karasek and Theorell's (1990) elaboration of the original model. For example, Parkes et al. (1994) found that reports of high levels of somatic symptoms are associated with high demands-low control *only* when support is low.

Recent research has explored the boundary conditions under which the model's predictions do and do not hold up, resulting in more support for the model, especially in specific situations (see van der Doef & Maes, 1999, for a recent review). For example, de Jonge, Dollard, Dormann, Le Blanc, and Houtman (2000), using improved measures of demands and control, found that jobs characterized by high demands and low control are associated with ill health, but only in some occupational groups. Schaubroeck, Jones, and Xie (2001) discovered that job demands are positively related to ill health and decreased immune functioning among efficacious (i.e., high self-efficacy, or perceived ability to accomplish tasks) workers who perceived low control, which supports the predictions of the demands-control model. However, for inefficacious workers who perceived that they had high control, job demands are also related to ill health and decreased immune functioning. They reasoned that workers who are low in self-efficacy might find control debilitating because they cannot use it effectively to cope with demands. Therefore, following the prescriptions of the demands-control model may actually exacerbate stress and strain for some workers.

Despite the criticisms of the demands-control model, it continues to guide much contemporary research and practice (e.g., stress management programs). The model's focus on the work environment, not the worker, as the locus of stress and strain encourages the creation of healthier workplaces. However, recent research, such as Schaubroeck et al.'s (2001) study, implies that a one-size-fits-all approach to work stress is often overly simplistic and inappropriate.

REVIEW OF THE RESEARCH: CONTEMPORARY AND EMERGING TOPICS ON WORK STRESS AND HEALTH

The topics that we discuss in this section include job-related technology, downsizing and job loss, and cross-cultural work stress. These topics have emerged within the past 20 years as major areas of interest in organizational stress research. However, this list is certainly not all-inclusive but merely representative. Other topics, such as work-non-work conflict and work-related violence, are sufficiently important that other chapters in this book are devoted to them.

Job-Related Technology

One of the newest and most controversial technological innovations in contemporary workplaces is electronic performance monitoring (EPM). EPM provides management with access to workers' computer terminals through the use of computer networks. Through this access, managers can determine the pace and accuracy of their employees' online work activities (e.g., the number of keystrokes or errors within a specified time interval). Most of the workers subject to EPM are clerical workers who perform simple, repetitive office work. However, monitoring of upper-level employees is increasing, especially for electronic correspondence or e-mail (U.S. Congress, Office of Technology Assessment, 1987).

Although proponents claim that it is a more objective and fair assessment method than traditional supervisor ratings, EPM has generally been assumed to be an organizational stressor. As a consequence, some European countries currently have laws that limit its use. Indeed, the assumed link between EPM and job-related stress seems to be valid. Several studies, in both the laboratory and the field, have reported that EPM is associated with increased job-related stress (e.g., Aiello & Shao, 1993; Davidson & Henderson, 2000; Gallatin, 1989; Smith, Carayon, Sanders, Lim, & LeGrande, 1992). For example, in a survey of more than 700 telecommunications workers, Smith et al. (1992) found that monitored employees reported higher levels of tension, depression, anger, anxiety, and fatigue compared to their nonmonitored peers.

Why is EPM so stressful? A few reasons have been proposed. EPM seems to be associated with increased stress because of the changes in job design that frequently accompany advances in technology. Monitored workers have complained about increases in workload and decreases in personal control over their work activities (Smith et al., 1992). Other issues include decreased opportunities for socialization with coworkers because of close monitoring and the deskilling and simplification of work in attempting to quantify it (Amick & Smith, 1992).

Given that EPM will probably continue in some form regardless of its stressfulness, Aiello and Kolb (1995) offered a few recommendations to employers. First, to curtail the potential for adversarial worker-management relationships fostered by EPM, efforts should be directed toward creating positive worker-management relationships through open communication. Second, worker control should be increased by involving

employees in the development of EPM standards (also see Stanton & Barnes-Farrell, 1996). Aiello and Kolb (1995) suggested that the strain caused by EPM may be understood using the demands-control model discussed earlier in this chapter; specifically, EPM systems may cause jobs to be redesigned such that decision latitude decreases and productivity demands increase.

Beyond EPM, work environments have been broadly affected by new technology. One relatively new phenomenon is the blurring of barriers between traditional white- and blue-collar work. Technological advances, particularly computer technology, have eased the physical demands and increased the cognitive demands of many blue-collar or industrial jobs and therefore elevated their status. However, the computerization of white-collar jobs has often produced work tasks that are simpler (less skilled), more fractionated, and more boring (see similar discussion about EPM). Also, as a consequence of technology, fewer industrial and office jobs are often required to perform the same amount of work. The result is that many lower-level office jobs and low- to mid-level management positions, along with traditional industrial jobs, have become redundant over the past couple of decades (Kraut, 1987; Nolan & Croson, 1995). The issue of organizational downsizing and resulting job loss is our next topic.

Downsizing and Job Loss

In recent years, major organizational changes—acquisitions, mergers, technological change, and downsizing—have become increasingly common as whole industries struggle for their economic survival. The decision to downsize, or systematically reduce the workforce, may eventually result in increased profitability for the organization. However, in the short term, the repercussions of downsizing can be traumatic, especially for the terminated employee (Applebaum, Simpson, & Shapiro, 1987).

Because the effects of job loss, a major life stressor, can be so personally devastating, particularly for the more disadvantaged segment of the workforce (Hamilton, Broman, Hoffman, & Renner, 1990), the topic would seem to be a likely target for psychological research. However, until the mid-1980s, little research had dealt with job loss at the individual level, focusing instead on societal or economic trends associated with unemployment. When DeFrank and Ivancevich (1986) reviewed the scant individual-level research, they concluded (not surprisingly) that job loss has deleterious effects on physical health and on psychological and social adaptation.

In the mid-1980s, the current downsizing trend began, providing organizational researchers with increased opportunities to study job loss. Kinicki (1985) sampled recently unemployed plant workers and found that anxiety was especially high for those workers who reported that the cost of new employment was high because their new employment options were not as attractive (e.g., less pay, fewer benefits). On the other hand, prior knowledge of the plant shutdown appeared to be beneficial in reducing stressful life events, the costs associated with unemployment, and anxiety. From these results, Kinicki (1985) recommended that organizations should reduce the costs associated with reemployment by helping terminated workers find suitable new employment and by providing advance warning of plant shutdowns to allow sufficient time for planning and recovery.

Prussia, Kinicki, and Bracker (1993) demonstrated the powerful role that cognitive factors can play in job loss. They sampled manufacturing employees 1 month prior to and 1 month after termination and found that attributions for job loss influenced reemployment prospects. Specifically, those workers who believed their own efforts were generally responsible for their job loss (i.e., self-blame) had lower expectations for reemployment. A negative, self-deprecating mind-set can prevent the displaced worker from presenting him- or herself positively or even from seeking new employment.

Probably the most novel area of job loss research has focused on the organizational survivors, not the recipients, of job loss (i.e., the coworkers who survive the job cuts). Joel Brockner and his colleagues (e.g., Brockner, Davy, & Carter, 1985; Brockner, Grover, Reed, & Dewitt, 1992; Brockner, Wiesenfeld, & Martin, 1995) have been prolific contributors to organizational survivor research. They have examined survivor responses both in simulated laboratory settings (e.g., Brockner et al., 1985) and in field settings experiencing actual layoffs (e.g., Brockner et al., 1992). The laboratory simulations typically were created using a simulated work group with college students. Job survivor responses were studied by dismissing one of the group members and then measuring the effects on the survivors. In the field studies, survivors of recent organizational layoffs were usually surveyed both before and after the layoff. Regardless of the context, Brockner and his colleagues consistently found that the organizational survivors who expressed the most negative attitudes toward their employing organization were those who felt highly committed to the organization prior to the layoff. However, they felt that the organization had handled the layoff unfairly (e.g., giving no prior warning or explanation for their decisions).

More recently, Allen, Freeman, Russell, Reizenstein, and Rentz (2001) examined several survivor reactions in a longitudinal research design and discovered that the initial impact was negative, as predicted by prior research. Although some variables did not change over time, organizational commitment, job involvement, and role overload decreased from the pretest (predownsizing) to the second posttest (postdownsizing). These results indicate that some of the negative effects of downsizing may persist over time if management does not intervene.

As the previous discussion illustrates, when organizations implement change, especially downsizing, ignoring the human element can result in at least two undesirable outcomes. First, the displaced workers may internalize job loss, feeling personally demoralized, which could negatively influence their future employment prospects. Second, if the survivors of downsizing feel that management acted unfairly in handling the terminations, they may feel more negatively toward their employing organization even if they were not affected personally.

Cross-Cultural Job Stress

Modern technology is rapidly guiding nations toward a global economy. Communications between distant colleagues or clients are now almost instantaneous, enabling professional relationships to develop that would have been difficult a decade or two ago. Consequently, contemporary organizations have a real need to understand cultural differences that may influence the conduct of international business. In response to this need, organizational stress researchers have increasingly explored cultural differences in work stress over the past decade. Typically, culture is conceived to affect strain indirectly as a moderator of the stressor-strain relationship.

Although there are some exceptions (cf. Jamal, 1999), research has generally shown

that cultural differences in organizational stress do exist. For example, comparing British and German managers, Kirkcaldy and Cooper (1992) found significant differences between these two groups on home/work interface and other stressors, as well as differences in several types of coping behaviors. Peterson et al. (1995) found cross-cultural effects for middle managers across 21 countries on work role conflict, ambiguity, and overload. Across seven countries, Bhagat et al. (1994) discovered cultural differences in managers and their staff in work role variables, work overload, decision latitude, and problem- and emotion-focused coping. Finally, Kirkcaldy, Brown, and Cooper (1994) reported that senior police officers in Berlin experienced higher levels of stress and engaged in greater numbers of coping behaviors than their counterparts in Northern Ireland.

More recently, Yang, Chen, Choi, and Zou (2000) reported an interesting comparative study on work-family conflict. They hypothesized that Americans experience greater family demands, which have a greater impact on work-family conflict than do work demands; the Chinese experience greater work demands, which have a greater impact on work-family conflict than do family demands. Their rationale was guided by Hofstede's (1980) notion of individualism versus collectivism. In individualistic countries such as the United States, a career or work emphasis implies the satisfaction of personal ambition and achievement, often at the expense of personal and family life. However, in collectivist countries such as China, career and work signify sacrifice for the good of the family; that is, extra work should bring prosperity and honor to the family. The researchers collected relevant data from Chinese and U.S. industrial workers. For the most part, they confirmed their predictions, although the data did not fully support the work priority prediction in the Chinese sample.

On the surface, large cultural differences in job-related stress appear to exist. However, in many cases, these differences are accompanied by similarities (e.g., Lu, Kao, Cooper, & Spector, 2000). On a more general level, all cultures experience work-related stress in the form of common organizational stressors, such as overload and work-family conflict. All cultures respond to these stressors by using common types of coping behaviors. Continuation of these stressors and maladaptive coping behaviors will undoubtedly culminate in decreased physical and/or psychological health. So, although relative differences do exist, the stress *process* is highly similar across cultures.

CONCLUSIONS

In the beginning of this chapter, we stated that our purpose was to explore critically the relationship between job stress and mental and physical health. So, what has our review revealed? Although the majority of the data are not causal, substantial evidence indicates that job stress affects mental and physical health.

The research studies discussed in this review underscore this relationship. Specifically, the frequency and severity of stressful life events (SLEs) and daily hassles, which are composed of both work and life stressors, have a small but significant relationship with mental and physical health. Type A Behavior Pattern, an individual difference that moderates the stressor-strain relationship, frequently characterizes the competitive, achievement-oriented worker. Research has consistently demonstrated that Type A, especially its negative affect components (anger-hostility and impatience-irritability), is an independent risk factor for coronary heart disease. Burnout

has been defined in terms of three specific types of stress responses: emotional exhaustion, depersonalization, and decreased personal accomplishment. Studies have demonstrated that these stress responses, in turn, can lead to serious health strains. Decades of research have confirmed the health-protective effects of job-related and personal sources of social support. Social support appears to exert its influence directly on health, as well as indirectly as a moderator of the stressor-strain relationship. Likewise, perceptions of work control, directly and interactively (as expressed in the seminal theory of organizational stress, the demands-control model), are related to health and well-being. Lack of control, on the other hand, is associated with illness across a variety of subjects and settings.

The contemporary and emerging sources of work stress—job-related technology, organizational downsizing and job loss, and cross-cultural work stress—are all related to increased perceptions of stress and disease risk factors (e.g., anxiety, maladaptive coping). Despite fewer studies to support these relationships, the evidence clearly indicates that their impact on mental and physical health is/will be as compelling as the other topics discussed here.

The next logical question is, "Given that job stress—in its many forms—has effects on mental and physical health, what can be done?" Although a review of the work stress management literature is beyond the scope of this chapter, we will review briefly some of the approaches that have been suggested to address the topics discussed here.

Attempts to reduce work stress by decreasing the number of SLEs or hassles are uncommon. However, Evans, Johansson, and Rydstedt (1999) devised a job redesign intervention for urban bus drivers (e.g., installation of electronic information systems on buses, creation of separate bus road lanes) to decrease job-related hassles, such as passenger demands and traffic congestion. Compared to the preintervention assessment, perceived stress, heart rate, and systolic blood pressure decreased after the intervention was implemented. This study illustrates the value of using job redesign to alleviate frequent work stressors.

Because of the serious health implications, programs to manage Type A have focused primarily on the person, not his or her environment. For example, Roskies, Seraganean, and Oseasohn (1986) developed an eight-part program composed largely of self-monitoring, problem solving, relaxation exercises, and cognitive-behavioral training. Social support and social network interventions (e.g., group counseling), commonly prescribed for recovering heart attack victims, have also been used to treat Type A (Bruhn, 1996). Because the negative affect component of Type A is related directly to the development of cardiovascular disease, programs that target anger reduction (e.g., Abernethy, 1995) have also been developed for Type A management. All of these programs have proven to be effective, at least to some degree.

In contrast to Type A, programs to manage burnout have focused on both the environment and the person. For example, variations of work socialization programs or realistic job previews have been used to dispel any unrealistic job expectations of human service workers (e.g., Kramer, 1974). Work performance appraisal systems using realistic performance standards and frequent performance feedback can also be effective in alleviating the distorted sense of work performance common to burnout victims (Cherniss, 1993). Personal-level interventions, such as cognitive restructuring, have also been used to treat burnout (e.g., van Dierendonck, Schaufeli, & Buunk, 1998). Similar to the Type A interventions,

all of these burnout interventions have, to some extent, proven to be effective.

Two of the major topic areas, social support and work control, remain to be discussed. Several types of social support interventions have been routinely (and often successfully) used in many types of stress management programs (e.g., Type A; see previous discussion). Therefore, the effectiveness of such interventions is not addressed here. Organizational researchers and practitioners have long attempted (with varying degrees of success) to increase work control and subsequently increase employee morale and performance through participatory management programs, such as quality circles. A few programs have attempted to increase work control as a stress reduction technique. For example, Mikkelsen, Saksvik, and Landsbergis (2000) examined the effects of a short-term participatory intervention in the form of seminar attendance and work group participation for employees in a community health care institution. The intervention decreased work stress and psychological job demands, as hypothesized. These results indicate that participatory work programs can exert a positive influence on well-being and job stress.

Of the contemporary and emerging topics, to our knowledge, only job loss interventions have been investigated systematically. Excellent examples are the longitudinal studies by Caplan, Vinokur, and their colleagues. Caplan, Vinokur, Price, and van Ryn (1989) examined the effectiveness of a multicomponent intervention that focused on training in job seeking using a problem-solving orientation. They concluded that the program participants who received the intervention obtained higher quality reemployment than the control participants. Recently, Vinokur, Schul, Vuori, and Price (2000) published a 2-year follow-up of the effects of an intervention that was similar to the one used by Caplan et al. (1989). They found that those participants who had received the intervention had higher levels of reemployment and income, lower levels of depressive symptoms, and better emotional functioning than did the control group participants.

In closing, we believe that we have shown conclusively that the several common forms of job stress discussed in this chapter have effects on mental and physical health. We then proposed several interventions that, to some extent, have successfully alleviated these various forms of job stress. We hope that this information will be helpful to students and professionals as they encounter stress in the workplace.

REFERENCES

Abernethy, A. D. (1995). The development of an anger management training program for law enforcement personnel. In L. R. Murphy, J. J. Hurrell, Jr., S. L. Sauter, & G. P. Keita (Eds.), *Job stress interventions* (pp. 21-30). Washington, DC: American Psychological Association.

Aiello, J. R., & Kolb, K. J. (1995). Electronic performance monitoring: A risk factor for workplace stress. In S. L. Sauter & L. R. Murphy (Eds.), *Organizational risk factors for job stress.* Washington, DC: American Psychological Association.

Aiello, J. R., & Shao, Y. (1993). Electronic performance monitoring and stress: The role of feedback and goal setting. In G. Salvendy & M. Smith (Eds.), *Human computer interaction: Software and hardware interfaces.* Amsterdam: Elsevier.

Allen, T. D., Freeman, D. M., Russell, J. E. A., Reizenstein, R. C., & Rentz, J. O. (2001). Survivor reactions to organizational downsizing: Does time ease the pain? *Journal of Occupational & Organizational Psychology, 74,* 145-164.

Amick, B. C., III, & Smith, M. J. (1992). Stress, computer-based work monitoring and measurement systems: A conceptual overview. *Applied Ergonomics, 23,* 6-16.

Applebaum, S. H., Simpson, R., & Shapiro, B. T. (1987). The tough test of downsizing. *Organizational Dynamics, 16*(2), 68-79.

Averill, J. (1973). Personal control over aversive stimuli and its relationship to stress. *Psychological Bulletin, 80,* 286-303.

Barling, J., & Charbonneau, D. (1992). Disentangling the relationship between the achievement striving and impatience-irritability dimensions of Type A behavior, performance, and health. *Journal of Organizational Behavior, 13,* 369-377.

Baron, R. A., Neuman, J. H., & Geddes, D. (1999). Social and personal determinants of workplace aggression: Evidence for the impact of perceived injustice and the Type A behavior pattern. *Aggressive Behavior, 25,* 281-296.

Barrera, M., Jr. (1981). Social support in the adjustment of pregnant adolescents: Assessment issues. In B. Gottlieb (Ed.), *Social networks and social support.* Beverly Hills, CA: Sage.

Beehr, T. A. (1976). Perceived situational moderators of the relationship between subjective role ambiguity and role strain. *Journal of Applied Psychology, 61,* 35-40.

Beehr, T. A., King, L. A., & King, D. W. (1990). Social support and occupational stress: Talking to supervisors. *Journal of Vocational Medicine, 36,* 61-81.

Bhagat, R. S., O'Driscoll, M. P., Babakus, E., Frey, L., Chokkar, J., & Ninokumar, B. H., et al. (1994). Organizational stress and coping in seven national contexts:

A cross-cultural investigation. In G. P. Keita & J. J. Hurrell, Jr. (Eds.), *Job stress in a changing workforce* (pp. 93-105). Washington, DC: American Psychological Association.

Billings, A., & Moos, R. H. (1981). The role of coping responses and social resources in attenuating the stress of life events. *Journal of Behavioral Medicine, 4,* 157-189.

Blau, G. J. (1981). An empirical investigation of job stress, social support, and job strain. *Organizational Behavior and Human Performance, 27,* 279-302.

Booth-Kewley, S., & Friedman, H. S. (1987). Psychological predictors of heart disease: A quantitative review. *Psychological Bulletin, 101,* 343-362.

Bosma, H., Stansfeld, S. A., & Marmot, M. G. (1998). Job control, personal characteristics, and heart disease. *Journal of Occupational Health Psychology, 3,* 402-409.

Boyd, A. (1997). Employee traps—Corruption in the workplace. *Management Review, 86,* 9.

Brand, R. (1978). Coronary-prone behavior as an independent risk factor for coronary heart disease. In T. M. Dembroski (Ed.), *Coronary-prone behavior.* New York: Springer-Verlag.

Broadhead, W. E., Gehlbach, S. H., DeGruy, F. V., & Kaplan, B. (1989). Functional versus structural social support and health care utilization in a family medicine outpatient practice. *Medical Care, 27,* 221-223.

Brockner, J., Davy, J., & Carter, C. (1985). Layoffs, self-esteem, and survivor guilt: Motivational, affective, and attitudinal consequences. *Organizational Behavior and Human Decision Processes, 36,* 229-244.

Brockner, J., Grover, S., Reed, T. F., & Dewitt, R. L. (1992). Layoffs, job insecurity, and survivors' work effort: Evidence of an inverted-U relationship. *Academy of Management Journal, 35*(2), 413-425.

Brockner, J., Wiesenfeld, B. M., & Martin, C. L. (1995). Decision frame, procedural justice, and survivors' reactions to job layoffs. *Organizational Behavior and Human Decision Processes, 63,* 59-68.

Bruhn, J. G. (1996). Social support and heart disease. In C. L. Cooper (Ed.), *Handbook of stress, medicine, and health* (pp. 253-268). Boca Raton, FL: CRC Press.

Cannon, W. B. (1932). *The wisdom of the body.* New York: W. W. Norton.

Caplan, R. D., Vinokur, A. D., Price, R. H., & van Ryn, M. (1989). Job seeking, reemployment, and mental health: A randomized field experiment in coping with job loss. *Journal of Applied Psychology, 74,* 759-769.

Cherniss, C. (1980). *Professional burnout in human service organizations.* New York: Praeger.

Cherniss, C. (1993). Role of professional self-efficacy in the etiology and amelioration of burnout. In W. B. Schaufeli, C. Maslach, & T. Marek (Eds.), *Professional burnout: Recent developments in theory and research. Series in applied psychology: Social issues and questions* (pp. 135-149). Washington, DC: Taylor & Francis.

Chiriboga, D. A., & Bailey, J. (1986). Stress and burnout among critical care and medical surgical nurses: A comparative study. *Critical Care Quarterly, 9,* 84-92.

Cohen, S., & Syme, S. L. (1985). *Social support and health.* San Diego, CA: Academic Press.

Cohen, S., & Wills, T. A. (1985). Stress, social support and the buffering hypothesis. *Psychological Bulletin, 98*(2), 310-357.

Corrigan, P. W., Holmes, E. P., & Luchins, D. (1995). Burnout and collegial support in state psychiatric hospital staff. *Journal of Clinical Psychology, 51,* 703-710.

Cox, T., Kuk, G., & Schur, H. (1991). *The meaningfulness of work to professional burnout.* Unpublished manuscript, University of Nottingham.

Danna, K., & Griffin, R. W. (1999). Health and well-being in the workplace. *Journal of Management, 25,* 357-384.

Davidson, R., & Henderson, R. (2000). Electronic performance monitoring: A laboratory investigation of the influence of monitoring and difficulty on task performance, mood state, and self-reported stress levels. *Journal of Applied Social Psychology, 30,* 906-920.

Daw, J. (2001). Road rage, air rage, and now "desk rage." *Monitor on Psychology, 32,* 52-54.

DeFrank, R. S., & Ivancevich, J. M. (1986). Job loss: An individual level review and model. *Journal of Vocational Behavior, 28,* 1-20.

de Jonge, J., Dollard, M. F., Dormann, C., Le Blanc, P. M., & Houtman, I. L. D. (2000). The demand-control model: Specific demands, specific control, and well-defined groups. *International Journal of Stress Management, 7,* 269-287.

DeLongis, A., Coyne, J. C., Dakof, G., Folkman, S., & Lazarus, R. S. (1982). Relationship of daily hassles, uplifts, and major life events to health status. *Health Psychology, 1,* 119-136.

Dembroski, T. M., & Czajkowski, S. M. (1989). Historical and current developments in coronary-prone behavior. In T. M. Dembroski (Ed.), *In search of coronary-prone behavior: Beyond Type-A.* Hillsdale, NJ: Lawrence Erlbaum.

Demerouti, E., Bakker, A. B., Nachreiner, F., & Schaufeli, W. (2001). The job demands-resources model of burnout. *Journal of Applied Psychology, 86,* 499-512.

Dohrenwend, B. P., Raphael, K. G., Schwartz, S., Stueve, A., & Skodol, A. (1993). The structured event probe and narrative rating method for measuring stressful life events. In L. Goldberger & S. Breznitz (Eds.), *Handbook of stress: Theoretical and clinical aspects* (pp. 174-184). New York: Free Press.

Dolan, S. L. (1995). Individual, organizational, and social determinants of managerial burnout: Theoretical and empirical update. In R. Crandall & P. L. Perrewe (Eds.), *Occupational stress: A handbook* (pp. 223-238). Washington, DC: Taylor & Francis.

Edwards, J. R. (1991). The measurement of Type A Behavior Pattern: An assessment of criterion-oriented validity, content validity, and construct validity. In C. L. Cooper & R. Payne (Eds.), *Personality and stress: Individual differences in the stress process* (pp. 151-180). Chichester, UK: Wiley.

Edwards, J. R., & Baglioni, A. J. (1991). Relationship between Type A behavior pattern and mental and physical symptoms: A comparison of global and component measures. *Journal of Applied Psychology, 76,* 276-290.

Evans, G. W., Johansson, G., & Rydstedt, L. (1999). Hassles on the job: A study of a job intervention with urban bus drivers. *Journal of Organizational Behavior, 20,* 199-208.

Fenlason, K. J., & Beehr, T. A. (1994). Social support and occupational stress: Effects of talking to others. *Journal of Organizational Behavior, 15*(2), 157-175.

Firth, H., & Britton, P. (1989). Burnout, absence, and turnover amongst British nursing staff. *Journal of Occupational Psychology, 62,* 55-59.

Flannery, R. B., Jr. (1986). Major life events and daily hassles in predicting health status: Methodological inquiry. *Journal of Clinical Psychology, 42,* 485-487.

Folkman, S. (1984). Personal control and stress and coping processes: A theoretical analysis. *Journal of Personality and Social Psychology, 46,* 839-852.

Frese, M. (1999). Social support as a moderator of the relationship between work stressors and psychological dysfunctioning: A longitudinal study with objective measures. *Journal of Occupational Health Psychology, 4,* 179-192.

Friedman, M. D., & Rosenman, R. H. (1974). *Type A behavior and your heart.* New York: Knopf.

Gallatin, L. (1989). *Electronic monitoring in the workplace: Supervision or surveillance.* Boston: Massachusetts Coalition on New Office Technology.

Gamble, G. O., & Matteson, M. T. (1992). Type A behavior, job satisfaction, and stress among Black professionals. *Psychological Reports, 70,* 43-50.

Ganster, D. C., & Schaubroeck, J. (1991). Work stress and employee health. *Journal of Management, 17,* 235-271.

Ganster, D. C., Schaubroeck, J., Sime, W. E., & Mayes, B. T. (1991). The homological validity of the Type A personality among employed adults. *Journal of Applied Psychology, 76,* 276-290.

Garden, A. (1989). Burnout: The effect of psychological type on research findings. *Journal of Occupational Psychology, 62,* 223-234.

Geiser, D. S. (1989). Psychosocial influences on human immunity. *Clinical Psychology Review, 9,* 689-715.

Golembiewski, R. T., & Munzenrider, R. F. (1988). *Phases of burnout: Developments in concepts and applications.* New York: Praeger.

Hahn, S. E., & Smith, C. S. (1999). Daily hassles and chronic stressors: Conceptual and measurement issues. *Stress Medicine, 15,* 89-101.

Hamilton, V. L., Broman, C. L., Hoffman, W. S., & Renner, D. S. (1990). Hard times and vulnerable people: Initial effects of plant closing on autoworkers' mental health. *Journal of Health and Social Behavior, 31,* 123-140.

Hammen, C., Davila, J., Brown, G., Ellicott, A., & Gitlin, M. (1992). Psychiatric history and stress: Predictors of severity of unipolar depression. *Journal of Abnormal Psychology, 101,* 45-52.

Haynes, S. G., & Feinleib, M. (1982). Type A behavior and the incidence of coronary heart disease in the Framingham Heart Study. In H. Denolin (Ed.), *Psychological problems before and after myocardial infarction: Advances in cardiology* (Vol. 29). Basel: Karger.

Hofstede, G. (1980). *Cultural consequences: International differences in work-related values.* Beverly Hills, CA: Sage.

Holahan, C. K., & Holahan, C. J. (1987). Life stress, hassles, and self-efficacy in aging: A replication and extension. *Journal of Applied Social Psychology, 17,* 574-592.

Holmes, T. H., & Rahe, R. H. (1967). The Social Readjustment Rating Scale. *Journal of Psychosomatic Research, 11,* 213-218.

House, J. S. (1981). *Work stress and social support.* Reading, MA: Addison-Wesley.

House, J. S., & Wells, J. A. (1978). Occupational stress and health. In *Reducing occupational stress: Proceedings of a conference.* Cincinnati, OH: National Institute for Occupational Safety and Health.

Howard, J. H., Cunningham, D. A., & Rechnitzer, P. A. (1976). Health patterns associated with type A behavior: A managerial population. *Journal of Human Stress, 2,* 24-28.

Ivancevich, J. M. (1986). Life events and hassles as predictors of health symptoms, job performance, and absenteeism. *Journal of Occupational Behavior, 7,* 39-51.

Jackson, S. E., Turner, J. A., & Brief, A. P. (1987). Correlates of burnout among public service lawyers. *Journal of Occupational Behavior, 8,* 339-349.

Jamal, M. (1999). Job stress, type-A behavior, and well-being: A cross-cultural examination. *International Journal of Stress Management, 6,* 57-67.

Jamal, M., & Baba, V. V. (1991). Type A behavior, its prevalence and consequences among women nurses: An empirical examination. *Human Relations, 44,* 1213-1228.

Janssen, P. M., Schaufeli, W. B., & Houkes, I. (1999). Work-related and individual determinants of three burnout dimensions. *Work and Stress, 13,* 74-86.

Jick, T. D., & Mitz, L. F. (1985). Sex differences in work stress. *Academy of Management Review, 10,* 408-420.

Karasek, R. A., Jr. (1979). Job demands, job decision latitude, and mental strain: Implications for job redesign. *Administrative Science Quarterly, 24,* 285-308.

Karasek, R. (1990). Lower health risk with increased job control among white collar workers. *Journal of Organizational Behaviour, 11,* 171-185.

Karasek, R., & Theorell, T. (1990). *Healthy work: Stress, productivity, and the reconstruction of working life.* New York: Basic Books.

Kasl, S. V. (1983). Pursuing the link between stressful life experiences and disease: A time for reappraisal. In C. L. Cooper (Ed.), *Stress research: Issues for the eighties* (pp. 79-102). Chichester, UK: Wiley.

Kinicki, A. J. (1985). Personal consequences of plant closings: A model and preliminary test. *Human Relations, 38*(3), 197-212.

Kirkcaldy, B. D., Brown, J., & Cooper, C. L. (1994). Occupational stress profiles of senior police managers: Cross-cultural study of officers from Berlin and Northern Ireland. *Stress Medicine, 10,* 127-130.

Kirkcaldy, B. D., & Cooper, C. L. (1992). Cross-cultural differences in occupational stress among British and German managers. *Work and Stress, 6*(2), 177-190.

Kirkcaldy, B. D., & Martin, T. (2000). Job stress and satisfaction among nurses: Individual differences. *Stress Medicine, 16,* 77-89.

Kramer, M. (1974). *Reality shock: Why nurses leave nursing.* St. Louis, MO: Mosby.

Kraut, R. E. (1987). Social issues and white-collar technology. In R. E. Kraut (Ed.), *Technology and the transformation of white-collar work.* Hillsdale, NJ: Lawrence Erlbaum.

Lazarus, R. S. (1966). *Psychological stress and the coping process.* New York: McGraw-Hill.

Lazarus, R. S., & Folkman, S. (1984). *Stress, appraisal, and coping.* New York: Springer.

Lee, C. (1992). The relations of personality and cognitive styles on job and class performance. *Journal of Organizational Behavior, 13,* 175-185.

Lee, C., Ashford, S. J., & Jamieson, L. F. (1993). The effects of Type A behavior dimensions and optimism on coping strategy, health, and performance. *Journal of Organizational Behavior, 14,* 143-157.

Lee, R. T., & Ashforth, B. E. (1996). A meta-analytic examination of the correlates of the three dimensions of job burnout. *Journal of Applied Psychology, 81,* 123-133.

Leiter, M. (1991). Coping patterns as predictors of burnout: The function of control and escapist coping behavior. *Journal of Organizational Behavior, 12,* 123-144.

Leiter, M. (1993). Burnout as a developmental process: Consideration of models. In W. B. Schaufeli, C. Maslach, & T. Marek (Eds.), *Professional burnout: Recent developments in theory and research. Series in applied psychology: Social issues and questions* (pp. 237-250). Washington, DC: Taylor & Francis.

Levenson, J. L., & Bemis, C. (1991). The role of psychological factors in cancer onset and progression. *Psychosomatics, 32*(2), 124-132.

Lovallo, W. R., & Pishkin, V. (1980). Type A behavior, self-involvement, autonomic activity, and the traits of neuroticism and extraversion. *Psychosomatic Medicine, 42,* 329-334.

Lu, L., Kao, S.-F., Cooper, C. L., & Spector, P. E. (2000). Managerial stress, locus of control, and job strain in Taiwan and UK: A comparative study. *International Journal of Stress Management, 7,* 209-226.

Manning, M. R., Jackson, C. N., & Fusilier, M. R. (1996). Occupational stress, social support, and the costs of health care. *Academy of Management Journal, 39*, 738-750.

Maslach, C. (1982). *Burnout: The cost of caring.* Englewood Cliffs, NJ: Prentice Hall.

Maslach, C. (1993). Burnout: A multidimensional perspective. In W. B. Schaufeli, C. Maslach, & T. Marek (Eds.), *Professional burnout: Recent developments in theory and research. Series in applied psychology: Social issues and questions* (pp. 19-32). Washington, DC: Taylor & Francis.

Maslach, C., & Jackson, S. E. (1981). The measurement of experienced burnout. *Journal of Occupational Behavior, 2*, 99-113.

Maslach, C., & Jackson, S. E. (1982). Burnout in health professions: A social psychological analysis. In G. Sanders & J. Suls (Eds.), *Social psychology of health and illness* (pp. 227-251). Hillsdale, NJ: Lawrence Erlbaum.

Maslach, C., & Jackson, S. E. (1984). Patterns of burnout among a national sample of public contact workers. *Journal of Health and Human Resources Administration, 7*, 189-212.

Maslach, C., & Jackson, S. E. (1986). *The Maslach Burnout Inventory: Manual* (2nd ed.). Palo Alto, CA: Consulting Psychologists Press.

Maslach, C., & Schaufeli, W. B. (1993). Historical and conceptual development of burnout. In W. B. Schaufeli, C. Maslach, & T. Marek (Eds.), *Professional burnout: Recent developments in theory and research. Series in applied psychology: Social issues and questions* (pp. 1-16). Washington, DC: Taylor & Francis.

Matthews, K. A. (1988). Coronary heart disease and type A behaviors: Update on an alternative to the Booth-Kewley and Friedman (1987) quantitative review. *Psychological Bulletin, 104*, 373-380.

Mikkelsen, A., Saksvik, P.O., & Landsbergis, P. (2000). The impact of a participatory organizational intervention on job stress in community health care institutions. *Work & Stress, 14*, 156-170.

Miller, S. M. (1979). Controllability and human stress: Method, evidence, and theory. *Behavior Research and Therapy, 17*, 287-304.

Nolan, R. L., & Croson, D. C. (1995). *Creative destruction: A six-stage process for transforming the organization.* Boston: Harvard Business School Press.

Parkes, K. R., Mendham, C. A., & von Rabenau, C. (1994). Social support and the demand-discretion model of job stress: Tests of additive and interactive effects in two samples. *Journal of Vocational Behavior, 44*, 91-113.

Pelletier, K. R., & Lutz, R. (1989). Mindbody goes to work: A critical review of stress management programs in the workplace. *Advances, Institute for the Advancement of Health, 6*, 28-34.

Pelletier, K. R., & Lutz, R. W. (1991). Healthy people—Healthy business: A critical review of stress management programs in the workplace. In S. M. Weiss, J. E. Fielding, & A. Baum (Eds.), *Perspectives in behavioral medicine: Health at work* (pp. 189-204). Hillsdale, NJ: Lawrence Erlbaum.

Peterson, M. F., Smith, P. B., Akande, A., Ayestaran, S., Bochner, S., Callan, V., et al. (1995). Role conflict, amibiguity, and overload: A 21-nation study. *Academy of Management Journal, 38*, 429-452.

Pines, A., & Aronson, E. (1988). *Career burnout: Causes and cures* (2nd ed.). New York: Free Press.

Prussia, G. E., Kinicki, A. J., & Bracker, J. S. (1993). Psychological and behavioral consequences of job loss: A covariance structure analysis using Weiner's (1985) attribution model. *Journal of Applied Psychology, 78*, 382-394.

Rabkin, J. G. (1980). Stressful life events and schizophrenia: A review of the research literature. *Psychological Bulletin, 87*, 408-425.

Rodin, J., & Langer, E. (1977). Long term effects of control-relevant interventions with institutionalized aged. *Journal of Personality and Social Psychology, 35,* 897-902.

Rosenman, R. H., Brand, R. J., Jenkins, D., Friedman, M., Straus, R., & Wurm, M. (1975). Coronary heart disease in the Western Collaborative Group study: Final follow-up experience of 8½ years. *Journal of the American Medical Association, 233,* 872-877.

Roskies, E., Seraganean, P., & Oseasohn, R. (1986). The Montreal Type A intervention project: Major findings. *Health Psychology, 5,* 45-69.

Schaubroeck, J., & Fink, L. S. (1998). Facilitating and inhibiting effects of job control and social support on stress outcomes and role behavior: A contingency model. *Journal of Organizational Behavior, 19,* 167-195.

Schaubroeck, J., Jones, J. R., & Xie, J. L. (2001). Individual differences in utilizing control to cope with job demands: Effects on susceptibility to infectious disease. *Journal of Applied Psychology, 86,* 265-278.

Schaufeli, W. B., & Enzmann, D. (1998). *The burnout companion to study and practice: A critical analysis.* London: Taylor & Francis.

Schaufeli, W. B., Leiter, M. P., Maslach, C., & Jackson, S. E. (1996). The Maslach Burnout Inventory—General Survey. In C. Maslach, S. E. Jackson, & M. P. Leiter, *Maslach Burnout Inventory manual* (3rd ed.). Palo Alto, CA: Consulting Psychologists Press.

Schmieder, R. A., & Smith, C. S. (1996). Moderating effects of social support in shiftworking and non-shiftworking nurses. *Work and Stress, 10,* 128-140.

Seligman, M. E. P. (1975). *Helplessness: On depression, development, and death.* San Francisco: W. H. Freeman.

Shekelle, R. B., Hulley, S. B., Neaton, J. D., Billings, H., Borhani, N. O., Gerace, T. A., Jacobs, D. R., Lasser, N. L., Mittlemark, M. B., & Stamler, J. (1985). The MRFIT behavior pattern study: II. Type A behavior and incidence of coronary heart disease. *American Journal of Epidemiology, 122,* 559-570.

Shirom, A. (1989). Burnout in work organizations. In C. L. Cooper & I. Robertson (Eds.), *International review of industrial and organizational psychology* (pp. 25-48). Chichester, UK: Wiley.

Shirom, A., Melamed, S., & Nir-Dotan, M. (2000). The relationships among objective and subjective environmental stress levels and serum uric acid: The moderating effect of perceived control. *Journal of Occupational Health Psychology, 5,* 374-385.

Smith, M. J., Carayon, P., Sanders, K. J., Lim, S.-Y., & LeGrande, D. (1992). Employee stress and health complaints in jobs with and without electronic performance monitoring. *Applied Ergonomics, 23,* 17-27.

Smith, C. S., & Sulsky, L. M. (in press). *Work stress.* Belmont, CA: Wadsworth/ Thomson Learning.

Spector, P. (1987). Interactive effects of perceived control and job stressors on affective reactions and health outcomes for clerical workers. *Work and Stress, 1,* 155-162.

Stamler, J. (1980). Type A behavior pattern: An established major risk for coronary heart disease? In E. Rappaport (Ed.), *Current controversies in cardiovascular disease.* Philadelphia: W. B. Saunders.

Stanton, J. M., & Barnes-Farrell, J. L. (1996). Effects of electronic performance monitoring on personal control, task satisfaction, and task performance. *Journal of Applied Psychology, 81,* 738-745.

Tennant, C. C. (1987). Stress and coronary heart disease. *Australian and New Zealand Journal of Psychiatry, 21,* 276-282.

Tetrick, L. E., Slack, K. J., DaSilva, N., & Sinclair, R. R. (2000). A comparison of the stress-strain process for business owners and nonowners: Differences in job demands, emotional exhaustion, satisfaction, and social support. *Journal of Occupational Health Psychology, 5,* 464-476.

Totman, R., Kiff, J., Reed, S. E., & Craig, J. W. (1980). Predicting experimental colds in volunteers from different measures of recent life stress. *Journal of Psychosomatic Research, 24,* 155-163.

U.S. Congress, Office of Technology Assessment. (1987). *The electronic supervisor: New technology, new tensions.* Washington, DC: Government Printing Office.

van der Doef, M., & Maes, S. (1999). The Leiden Quality of Work Questionnaire: Its construction, factor structure, and psychometric qualities. *Psychological Reports, 85,* 954-962.

van Dierendonck, D., Schaufeli, W. B., & Buunk, B. P. (1998). The evaluation of an individual burnout intervention program: The role of inequity and social support. *Journal of Applied Psychology, 83,* 392-407.

Vinokur, A. D., Schul, Y., Vuori, J., & Price, R. H. (2000). Two years after a job loss: Long-term impact of the JOBS program on reemployment and mental health. *Journal of Occupational Health Psychology, 5,* 32-47.

Viswesvaran, C., Sanchez, J. I., & Fisher, J. (1999). The role of social support in the process of stress: A meta-analysis. *Journal of Vocational Behavior, 54,* 314-334.

Wall, T. D., Jackson, P. J., Mullarkey, S., & Parker, S. K. (1996). The demands-control model of job strain: A more specific test. *Journal of Occupational & Organizational Psychology, 69,* 153-166.

Wethington, E., & Kessler, R. C. (1986). Perceived support, received support, and adjustment to stressful life events. *Journal of Health & Social Behavior, 27*(1), 78-89.

Wolf, T. H., Elston, R. C., & Kissling, G. E. (1989). Relationship of hassles, uplifts, and life events to psychological well-being of freshman medical students. *Behavioral Medicine, 15,* 37-45.

Yang, N., Chen, C. C., Choi, J., & Zou, Y. (2000). Sources of work-family conflict: A Sino-U.S. comparison of the effects of work and family demands. *Academy of Management Journal, 43,* 113-123.

Zellers, K. L., & Perrewe, P. L. (2001). Affective personality and the content of emotional social support: Coping in organizations. *Journal of Applied Psychology, 86,* 459-467.

Zohar, D. (1999). When things go wrong: The effect of daily work hassles on effort, exertion and negative mood. *Journal of Occupational and Organizational Psychology, 72,* 265-283.

CHAPTER 5

The Unbalanced Life: Work and Family Conflict

Leslie B. Hammer
Cari L. Colton
Suzanne L. Caubet
Krista J. Brockwood

The integration of work and nonwork has been a concern among scholars for more than 100 years (Wilensky, 1960). For example, early work by Engels in the 1800s focused on how the demoralization and alienation of the worker led to limited leisure and family time (Wilensky, 1960). More recently, several trends that have occurred over the past 30 years have contributed to the focus on work and family issues by both researchers and practitioners. These include, but are not limited to, increased labor force participation by women, aging of the American workforce and the accompanying increase in the proportion of workers caring for aging parents (in addition to children), changes in the nature and place of work, and decreases in the available labor pool. The implications of these trends are reviewed below.

First, women now constitute more than 50% of the workforce, compared to about 37% in 1970. This increase of women in the paid labor force has led to a number of changes in the family, including a redistribution of traditional gender role responsibilities and an increase in the interdependency between work and family (e.g., Barnett, 1998). Although this movement into the workforce has had significant beneficial effects on women's overall physical and mental health, increases in the difficulties of managing multiple work and family role demands have been observed among both women and men.

Second, the median age of the workforce is rising and will continue to do so, contributing to an increased probability that workers will be faced with parent care demands in addition to their responsibilities for dependent children (Rosenthal, Martin-Matthews, & Matthews, 1996). Bureau of Labor Statistics data indicate that the median age of the labor force was 35.3 years in 1986, 38.2 years in 1996, and is projected to be 40.6 years in 2006 (Fullerton, 1997). Adults who provide help to their frail or disabled parents and who also have responsibility for dependent children have been dubbed the "sandwich generation" (Fernandez, 1990), in that they are sandwiched between the needs of their children and their parents, and often, their jobs. Nichols and Junk (1997) surveyed individuals between the ages of 40 and 65 and found 15% to have responsibilities for aging parents and financially dependent children. Furthermore, based on their national study of sandwich generation employees, Neal, Hammer, Rickard, Isgrigg, and Brockwood (1999) estimated that between 9% and 13% of the dual-earner American households with heads between 30 and 60 years of age were sandwiched between caring for their children and caring for their frail or disabled parents or parents-in-law.

Third, recent changes in the nature of work, including the growing reliance on contract and temporary workers, who tend to have increased flexibility in the timing and place of work (Belous, 1989), have contributed to a greater focus among employers and employees on work-family issues. Furthermore, changes in the U.S. economy from manufacturing to service-based industries have led to changes not only in the way that work is done, but also changes in the schedules and location of work. These changes in the nature of work can affect employees' ability to combine work with their family caregiving roles in both positive and negative ways.

Fourth, the available trained labor force is projected to increase by only 11% between 1996-2006, compared to a 14% increase in the previous 10 years (Fullerton, 1997). An organizational implication of the reduced growth in the labor pool, coupled with low unemployment rates, is that managers need to work harder to attract and retain highly skilled and experienced employees. Providing family-friendly organizational supports may be one way of attracting and retaining qualified employees who might otherwise go elsewhere (Friedman & Galinsky, 1992). Thus, organizations may play a larger role in assisting employees with their multiple work and family care demands.

Therefore, these trends have all contributed to more research on work and family issues, as well as increases in the need for organizations to offer more family-friendly workplace supports (e.g., on-site child or parent care) to not only help attract quality employees, but also help employees better manage their work and multiple family care demands (Kossek & Ozeki, 1999). Thus, researchers and practitioners have placed more attention on identifying ways to increase employee well-being and decrease negative mental and physical health outcomes as a result of work and family imbalance.

The traditional framework for studying the effects of work and family role responsibilities has been to focus on work-family conflict, a form of interrole conflict in which participation in one role makes it difficult to participate in the other role. More recently, researchers have also begun to examine the positive effects of combining work and family. This chapter will focus on both the negative and positive effects of engaging in multiple work and family roles.

The purpose of this chapter is to provide an overview of work and family issues from both researcher and practitioner perspectives. Theory and research on work-family conflict, positive work-family spillover, and multiple role occupation are reviewed. This is followed by a summary of various organizational responses to work-family demands, and finally, a discussion of systems theory as a framework for understanding the integration of work and family and its application to the new field of occupational health psychology.

WORK-FAMILY CONFLICT

Theoretical Perspective

According to Kahn, Wolfe, Quinn, Snoek, and Rosenthal (1964), role theory provides a basis for identifying sources of organizational stress. Roles are the result of expectations of others about appropriate behavior in a particular position, and role conflict is described as the psychological tension that is aroused by conflicting role pressures. Role theory suggests that conflict occurs when individuals engage in multiple roles that are incompatible (Katz & Kahn, 1978). Interrole conflict occurs when pressures associated with one role are incompatible with pressures associated with another role, and work-family conflict is a type of interrole conflict in which the role demands stemming from one domain (work or family) are incompatible with role demands stemming from the other domain (family or work) (Kahn et al., 1964).

Work-family conflict consists of two dimensions: work-to-family conflict (i.e., work interfering with family) and family-to-work conflict (i.e., family interfering with work). These dimensions have been identified as distinct, reciprocal constructs that have independent antecedents and outcomes (Frone, Russell, & Cooper, 1992; Frone, Yardley, & Markel, 1997). Therefore, the recent trend in research that examines work-family conflict has been to model these dimensions separately.

Work-family conflict can be time-based, strain-based, or behavior-based (Greenhaus & Beutell, 1985). Time-based conflict occurs when role pressures stemming from the two different domains compete for the individual's time. Strain-based conflict occurs when the strain experienced from occupying a role in one domain interferes with effective performance of role behaviors in the other domain. Behavior-based conflict is described as conflict stemming from incompatible behaviors demanded by competing work and family roles. Time-based conflict, the most common type of work-family conflict, is based on the scarcity hypothesis. This hypothesis suggests that multiple roles inevitably create strain (Goode, 1960) and work-family conflict, and has been the basic premise behind most of the work and family literature (e.g., Beutell & Greenhaus, 1982; Chapman, Ingersoll-Dayton, & Neal, 1994; Frone et al., 1992; Goff, Mount, & Jamison, 1990; Hammer, Allen, & Grigsby, 1997; Loerch, Russell, & Rush, 1989).

Research on Work-Family Conflict

As mentioned earlier, consistent with the idea that they are separate dimensions, work-to-family and family-to-work conflict have been found to have different antecedents and outcomes. For example, some research has demonstrated that work-to-family conflict is primarily caused by work-related stressors and characteristics, and that it predicts family-related affective and behavioral outcomes, whereas family-to-work conflict is caused by family-related stressors and characteristics and predicts work-related outcomes (e.g., Frone et al., 1997). The underlying assumption is that high levels of interference from one role to a second role makes meeting the demands of the second role more difficult (Frone et al., 1992). In their integrative model of the work-family interface, Frone et al. (1997) suggest that these two types of work-family conflict reciprocally affect one another indirectly through role overload and distress. Even though recent research has identified the two-dimensional nature of work-family conflict, it should be noted that this construct was traditionally assessed using an overall global measure. What follows is a selected review of the vast literature on the antecedents and outcomes of work-family conflict.

Antecedents. Pleck (1977) hypothesized that the work and family domains were asymmetrically permeable, with work interfering with family more frequently for men and family interfering with work more frequently for women. Gender is one of the most frequently studied personal characteristics related to work-family conflict, but the findings are generally mixed. For example, some research demonstrates that women experience higher levels of work-family conflict than do men (e.g., Carlson, Kacmar, & Williams, 2000; Hammer et al., 1997), and other research has failed to find gender differences (e.g., Frone et al., 1992; Grandey & Cropanzano, 1999). In addition to gender, other individual characteristics, such as lower levels of perceived control (Duxbury, Higgins, & Lee, 1994) and Type A personality (Carlson, 1999), have been linked to higher levels of work-family conflict.

Family characteristics, such as age and number of dependents, have been positively related to work-family conflict with regard to care of children (Beutell & Greenhaus, 1982; Goff et al., 1990; Hammer et al., 1997; Pleck, Staines, & Lang, 1980) and care of elderly relatives (Neal, Chapman, Ingersoll-Dayton, & Emlen, 1993; Scharlach, 1994). Family type, in terms of single- or dual-parent households, has also been found to influence levels of work-family conflict, with single mothers experiencing higher levels of work and family conflict (Duxbury et al., 1994; Eagle, Icenogle, Maes, & Miles, 1998). Finally, household income was found to be negatively related to difficulties in managing work and family by Neal et al. (1993).

Personal and family stressors, such as stress due to being a parent or a spouse, have contributed to family-to-work conflict (Frone et al., 1992; Frone et al., 1997). Similarly, stress due to being a caregiver to an adult is related to increased difficulty combining work and family (Neal et al., 1993). In addition, the level of work-family conflict of one's spouse/partner (Hammer et al., 1997) and the number of hours spent in the family role (Gutek, Searle, & Klepa, 1991) have been related to work-family conflict and family-to-work conflict, respectively. Research has also demonstrated that general measures of family stressors and family involvement were positively related to increased overall work-family conflict and family-to-work conflict (e.g., Frone et al., 1992; Frone et al., 1997; Loerch et al., 1989).

Work-related antecedents tend to be more significantly related to work-to-family conflict than family-to-work conflict. Although a number of studies have demonstrated positive effects of alternative types of work schedules in helping people to better balance their work and family demands (e.g., Pierce & Newstrom, 1983), the findings are somewhat inconsistent (Christensen & Staines, 1990). One reason for this inconsistency is that schedules may vary with respect to the amount of flexibility a person feels he or she has in meeting his or her work and family needs (Christensen & Staines, 1990;), with perceived flexibility in work schedule being negatively related to work-family conflict (Hammer et al., 1997). Perceived flexibility may buffer the negative effects of nonstandard work schedules for women more so than for men (Staines & Pleck, 1986). Also, the number of hours that a person works predicted work-to-family and overall work-family conflict in studies by Gutek et al. (1991) and Shamir (1983).

The frequency of family intrusions at work has also been shown to predict conflict experienced between work and family roles (Loerch et al., 1989; MacEwen & Barling, 1994).

Job stress predicted work-to-family conflict and work-family conflict in a number of studies (e.g., Burke, 1988; Frone et al., 1992) and was the strongest predictor of work-family conflict among Hispanics in a study by Amaro, Russo, and Johnson (1987). Work role ambiguity has also been found to be a significant predictor of work-family conflict (Bedian, Burke, & Moffett, 1988; Greenhaus, Parasuraman, Granrose, Rabinowitz, & Beutell, 1989), and psychological work involvement was found to be significantly, positively related to work-family conflict and work-to-family conflict in a number of studies (e.g., Adams, King, & King, 1996; Frone et al., 1992; Frone et al., 1997; Greenhaus et al., 1989; Hammer et al., 1997). It has been suggested that people with high levels of psychological involvement in their work role may devote an excessive amount of energy to their work role at the expense of the family role, resulting in overall work-family conflict and work-to-family conflict (e.g., Greenhaus et al., 1989).

Outcomes. One frequently studied outcome of work-family conflict has been absenteeism, with work-family conflict and family-to-work conflict being positively related to missing work (Barling, MacEwen, Kelloway, & Higginbottom, 1994; Goff et al., 1990; Hepburn & Barling, 1996; Kossek, 1990; Kossek & Nichol, 1992; MacEwen & Barling, 1994; Thomas & Ganster, 1995). Overall work-family conflict and family-to-work conflict have also been positively related to intentions to leave work (Aryee, 1992; Burke, 1988) and negatively related to job satisfaction (Aryee, 1992; Bedian et al., 1988; Boles, Johnston, & Hair,

Outcomes

1997; Burke, 1988; Kossek & Ozeki, 1998; Thomas & Ganster, 1995; Wiley, 1987). Likewise, work-family conflict and work-to-family conflict have been negatively related to family satisfaction (Higgins, Duxbury, & Irving, 1992) and life satisfaction (Bedian et al., 1988; Kossek & Ozeki, 1998; Pleck et al., 1980). Additionally, negative mental and physical health outcomes have been related to high levels of work-family conflict and work-to-family conflict (Barnett & Rivers, 1996; Boles et al., 1997; Frone, 2000; Frone et al., 1992; Frone et al., 1997; Thomas & Ganster, 1995).

WORK-FAMILY POSITIVE SPILLOVER

Positive Work-fam "Spillover"

Although work-family conflict has garnered the majority of the attention from researchers, the media, and the public, there is increasing awareness of the positive side of work and family. Thus, we feel it is important to highlight the growing body of research that examines the *benefits* of combining work and family, in addition to the costs. Theorists have recognized for some time these potential benefits. For example, both Marks (1977) and Sieber (1974) argued that the benefits of occupying multiple roles outweigh the costs. Acknowledging that combining work and family roles can have beneficial effects, as well as the negative effects associated with conflict, helps to expand theoretical perspectives of the work-family interface. These ideas are also consistent with recent work by Barnett and Hyde (2001), emphasizing the importance of role quality in work-family research.

Self identity beomly important to needs of people, sep from fam

Theoretical Perspective

Spillover theory suggests a positive correlation, or relationship, between two roles

(Staines, 1980). Therefore, psychological states (either positive or negative) experienced in one role affect psychological states (either positive or negative) experienced in another role, and vice versa (Lambert, 1990; Staines, 1980; Zedeck & Mosier, 1990). Positive spillover between work and family roles refers to the occupation of one role resulting in perceived gains in the other role (Stephens, Franks, & Atienza, 1997) and is associated with positive health, well-being, and work outcomes (e.g., Kirchmeyer, 1992).

Positive work-to-family spillover refers to the work role having a positive impact on the family role, whereas positive family-to-work spillover refers to the positive impact of the family role on the work role (Edwards & Rothbard, 1999; Grzywacz & Marks, 2000b; Stephens et al., 1997). Recently, work-family researchers have begun to examine the beneficial effects, in addition to the negative effects, of holding both work and family roles (e.g., Baruch & Barnett, 1986; Ingersoll-Dayton, Neal, & Hammer, 2001; Kirchmeyer, 1992, 1993; Marshall & Barnett, 1993; Pavalko & Woodbury, 2000).

Research on Positive Spillover

Antecedents. At present, little is known about the antecedents of positive spillover. This is due partially to its conceptualization as a moderator, or buffer, between negative events and stress. Two studies by Kirchmeyer (1992, 1993) examined positive spillover from nonwork roles, including parenting, community work, and recreation, to the role of employee. The first study found that psychological parental involvement was positively related to positive spillover between parenting and work roles, whereas actual time spent parenting was negatively related to positive spillover. In the 1993 study, Kirchmeyer also found that individuals who used certain coping strategies, such as role redefinition, reported higher levels of positive spillover. These two studies examined spillover from nonwork to work and had measures of role-specific types of spillover, such as leisure-to-work or parenting-to-work. Other research has examined positive work-family spillover in a sample of women who were caregivers to aging parents (Stephens et al., 1997). Although a majority of the sample experienced high levels of positive spillover, caregiver satisfaction was not significantly related to positive spillover in either direction.

A recent study by Grzywacz and Marks (2000b) provides a comprehensive examination of positive spillover antecedents. Using data from the National Survey of Midlife Development in the United States (MIDUS), with a sample of 1,986 employed adults, the researchers examined the relationships of work and family antecedents to positive spillover, both work-to-family and family-to-work. The researchers found that the family-related antecedents of support from one's spouse and support from other family members were related to positive spillover from family-to-work only, but that the work-related antecedents of increased decision latitude and decreased pressure at work were related to both work-to-family and family-to-work positive spillover.

Outcomes. Although limited research exists on the outcomes of positive spillover, additional analyses conducted with the MIDUS data have revealed that positive work-to-family spillover resulted in better physical and mental health, whereas positive family-to-work spillover was related to fewer chronic conditions, better overall well-being (Grzywacz, 2000), and decreased likelihood of problem drinking (Grzywacz & Marks, 2000a). Thus, more research is clearly needed on the effects of positive spillover between work and family roles on both individual and organizational outcomes.

MULTIPLE ROLE OCCUPATION

Theoretical Perspective

The idea that positive spillover may result from multiple roles also relates to role accumulation theory (Sieber, 1974; Thoits, 1983) and expansion theory (Marks, 1977; Marks & MacDermid, 1996), suggesting that the benefits of role accumulation tend to outweigh any stress that additional roles may create. Expansion theory and role accumulation theory are consistent with the idea that occupying more roles may lead to increased energy. Sieber (1974) further claimed that multiple roles might compensate for role conflicts by providing numerous buffers and support against failures in other roles. Stoller and Pugliesi (1989) concluded that work and family role accumulation enhances social networks and resources that are instrumental to balancing work and family commitments.

As stated previously, many role theorists traditionally have viewed human energy as a limited resource, so that the more roles in which one was engaged, the more opportunity for conflict (Goode, 1960). This scarcity hypothesis has been used both implicitly and explicitly in much of the research on work-family conflict. Not only is lack of energy an important factor for conflict, but lack of time is as well (see Greenhaus & Beutell, 1985). In contrast, the enhancement hypothesis argues that the more roles one occupies, the more resources one has and the more opportunity for energy to be recharged through enhanced self-esteem (Marks, 1977).

Research on Multiple Role Occupation

Empirical research has found that many employed men and women report rewards and benefits of multiple role participation (Piotrkowski, 1979; Yogev, 1981). Some of these benefits include decreased psychological distress (Pietromonaco, Manis, & Frohardt-Lane, 1986; Thoits, 1983), increased job satisfaction (Pietromonaco et al., 1986), and increased physical well-being (Cooke & Rousseau, 1984) and health (Collijn, Appels, & Nijhuis, 1996). Another study of individuals with various caregiving responsibilities, however, found more support for the scarcity hypothesis, in that having more caregiving responsibilities (e.g., for children, adults, and/or elders) was associated with increased absenteeism and stress (Chapman et al., 1994). The researchers noted that the disparate findings might be a function of the outcome variables examined, in that research on enhancement tends to focus on outcomes such as happiness and well-being, instead of negative outcomes such as stress. In fact, research has found that these two hypotheses are not mutually exclusive, and that both stressors and rewards spill over from one role to another (e.g., Marshall & Barnett, 1993). Based on their study of a sample of business professionals, Friedman and Greenhaus (2000) concluded that work and family are both "allies" and "enemies," in that resources and emotions can be shared across domains, but they can also be depleted by an overly demanding role.

One shortcoming of the multiple role literature has been the failure to consider role quality as a factor in the relationship between role occupation and outcomes (for exceptions, see Barnett & Hyde, 2001; Stephens & Townsend, 1997). In a review of multiple role occupation and health, Froberg, Gjerdingen, and Preston (1986) argued that the quality of a role will influence the outcomes of role participation. Research has demonstrated that poor role quality at home and at work is linked to increased psychological distress (Barnett, Marshall, Raudenbush, & Brennan, 1993). In addition, decreases in both job and marital role quality were related to decreases over time in distress (Barnett, Raudenbush, Brennan, Pleck, & Marshall, 1995). In order to gain a better understanding of the dynamics of the work and family roles, role quality measures should be considered more fully in future research.

ORGANIZATIONAL RESPONSES TO WORK-FAMILY ISSUES

Although positive effects have been observed when individuals combine work and family roles, the stress from multiple role demands can have detrimental effects on individuals' mental and physical well-being. In response to the increased awareness of work-family issues, organizations have implemented a variety of "family-responsive" programs or policies to enhance the positive and decrease the negative effects of combining work and family roles. These "formal" workplace supports include child care and elder care services (e.g., information and referral, financial assistance with care, and off-site or on-site care centers); alternative work scheduling (e.g., flextime, compressed work weeks, job sharing, part-time work); telecommuting; and parental leave (Friedman & Galinsky, 1992; Zedeck & Mosier, 1990). Although increased awareness of work and family struggles has led to organizational responses, it has been suggested that formal family-supportive benefits are often underutilized and may not always have their intended effects or

outcomes for individuals or organizations (Kossek & Ozeki, 1999).

Effects of Formal Workplace Supports or Policies

The effects of these family-responsive programs or policies are not well-established, and research results regarding the outcomes of using these benefits or policies are often mixed (viz. Galinsky, Friedman, & Hernandez, 1991; Kossek & Ozeki, 1999). Research on flexible work scheduling has linked this type of alternative work schedule with a variety of outcomes (see Baltes, Briggs, Huff, Wright, & Neuman, 1999; Hammer & Barbera, 1997, for reviews). For example, certain forms of flextime have been shown to be related to increased performance (e.g., Kossek & Ozeki, 1999), increased job satisfaction (e.g., Marshall & Barnett, 1994; Scandura & Lankau, 1997), and reduced work-family conflict (e.g., Christensen & Staines, 1990). However, the use of flextime has been demonstrated to be unrelated to family satisfaction (e.g., Shinn, Wong, Simko, & Ortiz-Torres, 1989) and has shown mixed results with regard to turnover intentions (e.g., Grover & Crooker, 1995; Kossek & Ozeki, 1999), absenteeism (e.g., Kossek & Ozeki, 1999; Thomas & Ganster, 1995), and organizational commitment (e.g., Grover & Crooker, 1995; Kossek & Ozeki, 1999; Scandura & Lankau, 1997). Although there has been very little research on telecommuting, one notable study by Hill, Miller, Weiner, and Colihan (1998) found that telecommuting was related to perceived positive effects on flexibility and productivity; however, the effects on morale and work-life balance were mixed.

Research on the effects of dependent care assistance has also produced mixed results. Access to dependent care benefits may reduce intentions to turnover and increase organizational commitment (e.g., Grover & Crooker, 1995). Rothausen, Gonzalez, Clarke, and O'Dell (1998) found the use of on-site child care to be related to increased satisfaction with organizational support, but unrelated to job satisfaction, turnover intentions, and actual turnover. The use of on-site child care centers has not been shown to reduce absenteeism directly (e.g., Goff et al., 1990; Kossek & Nichol, 1992) or to improve job performance (e.g., Kossek & Nichol, 1992). Furthermore, the availability of information and referral services has not been related to absenteeism or job satisfaction (e.g., Thomas & Ganster, 1995), whereas utilization of such services was associated with increased absenteeism (e.g., Wagner & Hunt, 1994). This later finding may be explained by the fact that people who are absent more (possibly due to high levels of caregiving demands) may be more likely to use information and referral services.

Simply offering family-responsive benefits and formal policies may not be sufficient to reduce work-family conflict and produce positive outcomes (Galinsky, Bond, & Friedman, 1996; Starrels, 1992). Other informal workplace characteristics, such as the general supportiveness of the organizational work-family culture, may influence the use of, and effects associated with, these formal policies.

Informal Organizational Support

A distinction between formal organizational support (e.g., family-supportive policies or programs) and informal organizational support (e.g., supportive workplace culture, supervisors, and coworkers) for work and family has been made by a number of researchers (e.g., Kossek & Ozeki, 1999; Raabe, 1990; Starrels, 1992). Raabe (1990) contends that

"unsupportive supervisors and organizational cultures can counteract formal policies" (p. 483).

A variety of researchers have indicated the importance of the role of organizational culture in work and family issues. According to Starrels (1992), "Corporate culture may either advance or thwart the development and effectiveness of work-family programs" (p. 261). Friedman (1990) emphasizes the need for a supportive organizational work-family culture, contending that policies or programs "are not going to have their desired effects if they are implemented in a culture hostile to families" (p. 86). Although Grover and Crooker (1995) found family-responsive policies to be related to increased organizational attachment, they emphasize the importance of the organizational culture, asserting that positive outcomes will not result if the organizational culture does not support employees making use of the policies. Frankel (1998) identifies an "antagonistic" organizational work-family culture as an obstacle to the adoption of family-supportive programs or policies by employers and as a barrier to the use of such policies by employees. Thompson, Thomas, and Maier (1992) also assert that corporate culture may affect the use of programs. Perlow (1995) emphasizes the importance of addressing underlying assumptions about work that serve as barriers to the use and success of family-responsive policies or programs.

Unfortunately, only a small amount of empirical work has investigated work-family culture (i.e., Clark, 2001; Galinsky, Bond, & Friedman, 1993; Litchfield & Pitt-Catsouphes, 1999; Orthner & Pittman, 1986; Thompson, Beauvais, & Lyness, 1999; Warren & Johnson, 1995). This research has indicated that perceptions of organizational support for work and family (i.e., perceptions of a positive work-family culture) were related to increased job commitment, decreased burnout, higher organizational commitment, increased job satisfaction, higher levels of quality of work life, and increased work-family balance.

Supervisor support is another aspect of informal workplace support. Supervisor support has been related to such work-family outcomes as increased career satisfaction; decreased work distress or dissatisfaction, work overload, and role strain; lower levels of work-family conflict; increased employee citizenship and had indirect effects on decreasing depression (Aryee & Luk, 1996; Bowen, 1998; Clark, 2001; Frone et al., 1997; Goff et al., 1990; Greenberger, Goldberg, Hamill, O'Neil, & Payne, 1989; Thomas & Ganster, 1995). Thus, supervisor support has demonstrated positive effects on individual and organizational outcomes.

Taken together, these findings suggest that provision and utilization of formal workplace supports may be related to higher levels of organizational attachment and lower levels of work-family conflict, but the findings are somewhat inconclusive. One reason that these findings on formal workplace supports may be inconsistent is that informal supports, such as work-family culture and supervisor support, may be important factors in determining whether or not individuals make use of formal work-family supports (e.g., benefits or policies) and whether use of these formal supports has the intended positive effects. Future research on this issue is needed.

FUTURE ISSUES TO CONSIDER: SYSTEMS THEORY AND OCCUPATIONAL HEALTH PSYCHOLOGY

Unfortunately, the work-family literature has been notoriously void of a coherent theoretical framework to guide its research (Westman & Piotrkowski, 1999; Zedeck, 1992). Furthermore, a shortcoming of much of the work-family literature has been the lack of attention paid to the spouse or partner in a dyad, as data are typically gathered and analyzed at the individual level. Even less attention has been given to the effects of work on other family members' well-being (for an exception, see Crouter, Bumpus, Maguire, & McHale, 1999). On the other hand, some researchers have broadened the context to include societal-level influences and historical trends (Shellenberger & Hoffman, 1995). Therefore, it has been suggested that work-family researchers should consider the broader family system by, at a minimum, using the couple as the unit of analysis (Hammer et al., 1997; Zedeck & Mosier, 1990). Systems theory provides a framework for directing such future research.

Systems theory will be reviewed below. This will be followed by a discussion of occupational health psychology, a new discipline that applies systems concepts to the prevention of occupational injuries and illnesses, improving mental and physical health in the workplace.

Systems Theory

General systems theory is a framework that can be used for understanding the dynamic relationships between work and family (Bronfenbrenner, 1977; Piotrkowski, 1979). This is an approach used most recently in the study of work and family by Shellenberger and Hoffman (1995), Grzywacz and Marks (2000b), and Westman (2001), but it warrants further elaboration. Furthermore, family systems theory, based in general systems theory, provides a basis for elucidating the effects of work and family within the context of the family or dual-earner couple.

A system can be defined as "any two or more parts that are related, such that change in any one part changes all parts" (Hanson, 1995, p. 27). As stated in this definition, when a change is made in one part of a system, all other components of that system, as well as other neighboring and connected systems, are also affected. These changes create a ripple effect throughout the system and return to the point of origin, continuing the cycle. For example, consider a woman who is returning to work after taking time off to be a full-time mother. This change affects the entire family, both physically and psychologically, eliciting certain behaviors in the family that, in turn, affect the woman's attitudes and behaviors both at work and at home. The patterns and processes that emerge from these continuing changes and feedback loops are an essential quality of the systems perspective.

When considering work-family issues in light of systems theory, we can examine systems on two conceptual levels. At the first level, we can focus on both the work system and the family system as subsystems of a larger life system. The work and family systems are interrelated and interacting subsystems that can have strong effects on one another. At the second level, we can consider either the work system or the family system, focusing on the subsystems that comprise them. For example, in studying the work system, it may be informative to consider the supervisor-employee dyad or employee-coworker relationships as important subsystems. Likewise, in studying the family system, we may examine the marital dyad and parent-child or sibling relationships.

Family Systems Theory

Family systems theory, a subset of general systems theory, calls for examination of how complex interactions among family members affect individual behavior (Day, 1995). The primary focus of this theory is that we learn more about the family if we study the interactions among family members than if we simply study each family member individually. The key to examining family systems is to identify "patterns in the processes" as individuals behave (Day, 1995, p. 94).

Although family systems theory was developed for clinical use in couples' and family counseling, many of its tenets, grounded in general systems theory, can be adopted for use in nonclinical, or applied, research settings. One of the most central of these tenets is the importance of context, that behavior can be understood only within the context of the multiple systems in which it occurs. For instance, in family systems counseling, the behavioral problems of children are not examined in isolation from the rest of the family, but rather by observing the patterns of interactions among family members. Taking this one step further, it is argued that the behavior of one family member cannot be completely understood without considering the behavior of other family members, and that our family roles affect these interactions (Day, 1995). Using a family systems approach involves including a broader contextual base (e.g., the family, the couple) for understanding the dynamic relationships between attitudes and behaviors of members within a family, and how these family members can affect each others' work systems, providing a useful framework for work-family researchers.

Family systems researchers have noted the complexities involved in studying the family system because of the interactional and reciprocal effects of stress, strain, and psychopathology of one family member on another (Cook, 1994; Hayden et al., 1998). Furthermore, research has demonstrated that the attitudes and behaviors of individuals within a family have effects on other family members' attitudes and behaviors (e.g., Hammer et al., 1997; Hayden et al., 1998; Westman & Vinokur, 1998). For example, recent research on these effects, also referred to as "crossover effects" in the stress literature, have demonstrated that the work and family experiences of one member of a dyad are significant predictors of the work and family experiences of the other member (Hammer et al., 1997; Westman, 2001; Westman & Etzion, 1995). Thus, interventions such as family-friendly workplace supports that are expected to improve job attitudes and decrease work-family conflict for one member of a couple may have similar effects on the other member. Taking a family systems perspective when studying work-family issues, including examining the interactive relationship between attitudes and behaviors of both members of dual-earner couples, should enhance understanding of these two important spheres of our lives.

Occupational Health Psychology

Occupational health psychology (OHP) is a new discipline that focuses on the individual, work, and the work-family interface in the prevention of injuries, stress, and illness in the workplace (Quick, Quick, Nelson, & Hurrell, 1997). Taking a systems perspective, OHP merges the disciplines of health, organizational, and clinical psychology to improve health in the workplace (Quick, 1999). With its origins in preventive medicine and the public health model, OHP focuses on prevention, rather than treatment. Such prevention approaches include work and job redesign, monitoring of stress and distress in the workplace, education and training, and the provision of mental health services such as employee

assistance programs (Quick et al., 1997). With organizational interventions focused on the prevention of stress and illness in the workplace, OHP emphasizes the importance of promoting a positive work-family interface among organizational researchers and practitioners.

CONCLUSION

This chapter has provided an overview of the research on the interaction of work and family roles, focusing on both work-family conflict and work-family positive spillover. We have discussed some of the theoretical perspectives that have guided past work-family research, and we have proposed systems theory as a viable theoretical framework to guide future research on work and family.

In summary, work-family conflict and work-family positive spillover are important issues for employees and organizations alike. Employees who experience work-family conflict may have increased absenteeism, increased health problems, decreased job satisfaction, decreased family satisfaction, and decreased life satisfaction, and they are more likely to experience mental and physical health problems. Clearly, these outcomes are important for organizations as well, because they can have significant and costly organizational implications. On the other hand, there may also be positive effects of occupying work and family roles. As discussed, implementing formal family-responsive benefits or programs may result in some positive outcomes, but it is also critical that organizations examine and improve the informal support for work and family (e.g., by creating a family-friendly workplace culture). This will lead to improved health and well-being of both employees and the organization.

OH

have
Benifits & Programs that Support
employee + their family

REFERENCES

Adams, G. A., King, L. A., & King, D. W. (1996). Relationships of job and family involvement, family social support, and work-family conflict with job and life satisfaction. *Journal of Applied Psychology, 81,* 411-420.

Amaro, H., Russo, N. F., & Johnson, J. (1987). Family and work predictors of psychological well-being among Hispanic women professionals. *Psychology of Women Quarterly, 11,* 505-521.

Aryee, S. (1992). Antecedents and outcomes of work-family conflict among married professional women: Evidence from Singapore. *Human Relations, 45,* 816-837.

Aryee, S., & Luk, V. (1996). Work and nonwork influences on the career satisfaction of dual-earner couples. *Journal of Vocational Behavior, 49,* 38-52.

Baltes, B. B., Briggs, T. E., Huff, J. W., Wright, J. A., & Neuman, G. A. (1999). Flexible and compressed workweek schedules: A meta-analysis of their effects on work-related criteria. *Journal of Applied Psychology, 84,* 496-513.

Barling, J., MacEwen, K. E., Kelloway, E. K., & Higginbottom, S. F. (1994). Predictors and outcomes of elder-care-based interrole conflict. *Psychology and Aging, 9,* 391-397.

Barnett, R. C. (1998). Toward a review and reconceptualization of the work/family literature. *Genetic, Social, & General Psychology Monographs, 124*(2), 125-182.

Barnett, R. C., & Hyde, J. S. (2001). Women, men, work, and family. *American Psychologist, 56,* 781-796.

Barnett, R. C., Marshall, N. L., Raudenbush, S. W., & Brennan, R. T. (1993). Gender and the relationship between job experiences and psychological distress: A study of dual-earner couples. *Journal of Personality and Social Psychology, 64,* 794-806.

Barnett, R. C., Raudenbush, S. W., Brennan, R. T., Pleck, J. H., & Marshall, N. L. (1995). Change in job and marital experiences and change in psychological distress: A longitudinal study of dual-earner couples. *Journal of Personality and Social Psychology, 69,* 839-850.

Barnett, R. C., & Rivers, C. (1996). *She works/he works: How two-income families are happier, healthier, and better-off.* New York: HarperCollins.

Baruch, G. K., & Barnett, R. C. (1986). Consequences of fathers' participation in family work: Parents' role strain and well-being. *Journal of Personality and Social Psychology, 51,* 983-992.

Bedian, A. G., Burke, B. G., & Moffett, R. G. (1988). Outcomes of work-family conflict among married male and female professionals. *Journal of Management, 14,* 475-491.

Belous, R. S. (1989). *The contingent economy: The growth of the temporary, part-time and subcontracted workforce.* Washington, DC: National Planning Association.

Beutell, N. J., & Greenhaus, J. H. (1982). Interrole conflict among married women: The influence of husband and wife characteristics on conflict and coping behavior. *Journal of Vocational Behavior, 21,* 99-110.

Boles, J. S., Johnston, M. W., & Hair, J. F. (1997). Role stress, work-family conflict and emotional exhaustion: Inter-relationships and effects on some work-related consequences. *Journal of Personal Selling & Sales Management, 1,* 17-28.

Bowen, G. L. (1998). Effects of leader support in the work unit on the relationship between work spillover and family adaptation. *Journal of Family and Economic Issues, 19,* 25-52.

Bronfenbrenner, U. (1977, July). Toward an experimental ecology of human development. *American Psychologist,* pp. 513-531.

Burke, R. J. (1988). Some antecedents and consequences of work-family conflict. *Journal of Social Behavior and Personality, 3*(4), 287-302.

Carlson, D. S. (1999). Personality and role variables as predictors of three forms of work-family conflict. *Journal of Vocational Behavior, 55,* 236-253.

Carlson, D. S., Kacmar, K. M., & Williams, L. J. (2000). Construction and initial validation of a multidimensional measure of work-family conflict. *Journal of Vocational Behavior, 56,* 249-276.

Chapman, N. J., Ingersoll-Dayton, B., & Neal, M. B. (1994). Balancing the multiple roles of work and caregiving for children, adults, and elders. In C. P. Keita & J. J. Hurrell, Jr. (Eds.), *Job stress in a changing workforce* (pp. 283-300). Washington, DC: American Psychological Association.

Christensen, K. E., & Staines, G. L. (1990). Flextime: A viable solution to work/family conflict? *Journal of Family Issues, 11,* 455-476.

Clark, S. C. (2001). Work cultures and work/family balance. *Journal of Vocational Behavior, 58,* 348-365.

Collijn, D. H., Appels, A., & Nijhuis, F. (1996). Are multiple roles a risk factor for myocardial infarction for women? *Journal of Psychosomatic Research, 40,* 271-279.

Cook, W. L. (1994). A structural equation model of dyadic relationships within the family system. *Journal of Consulting and Clinical Psychology, 62,* 500-509.

Cooke, R. A., & Rousseau, D. M. (1984). Stress and strain from family roles and work-role expectations. *Journal of Applied Psychology, 69,* 252-260.

Crouter, A. C., Bumpus, M. F., Maguire, M. C., & McHale, S. M. (1999). Linking parents' work pressure and adolescents' well-being: Insights into dynamics in dual-earner families. *Developmental Psychology, 35,* 1453-1461.

Day, R. D. (1995). Family-systems theory. In R. D. Day, K. R. Gilbert, B. H. Settles, & W. R. Burr (Eds.) *Research and theory in family science* (pp. 91-101). Pacific Grove, CA: Brooks/Cole.

Duxbury, L., Higgins, C., & Lee, C. (1994). Work-family conflict: A comparison by gender, family type, and perceived control. *Journal of Family Issues, 15,* 449-466.

Eagle, B. W., Icenogle, M. L., Maes, J. D., & Miles, E. W. (1998). The importance of employee demographic profiles for understanding experiences of work-family interrole conflicts. *Journal of Social Psychology, 138,* 690-709.

Edwards, J. R., & Rothbard, N. P. (1999). Work and family stress and well-being: An examination of person-environment fit in the work and family domains. *Organizational Behavior and Human Decision Processes, 77,* 85-129.

Fernandez, J. P. (1990). *The politics and reality of family care in corporate America.* Lexington, MA: D. C. Heath.

Frankel, M. (1998). Creating the family friendly workplace: Barriers and solutions. In S. Klarreich (Ed.), *Handbook of organizational health psychology: Programs to make the workplace healthier* (pp. 79-100). Madison, WI: Psychosocial Press.

Friedman, D. E. (1990). Work and family: The new strategic plan. *Human Resource Planning, 13,* 78-89.

Friedman, D. E., & Galinsky, E. (1992). Work and family issues: A legitimate business concern. In S. Zedeck (Ed.), *Work, families, and organizations* (pp. 168-207). San Francisco: Jossey-Bass.

Friedman, S. D., & Greenhaus, J. H. (2000). *Work and family—Allies or enemies? What happens when business professionals confront life choices.* New York: Oxford University Press.

Froberg, D., Gjerdingen, D., & Preston, M. (1986). Multiple roles and women's mental health: What have we learned? *Women and Health Review, 11,* 79-96.

Frone, M. R. (2000). Work-family conflict and employee psychiatric disorders: The national comorbidity survey. *Journal of Applied Psychology, 85,* 888-895.

Frone, M. R., Russell, M., & Cooper, M. L. (1992). Antecedents and outcomes of work-family conflict: Testing a model of the work-family interface. *Journal of Applied Psychology, 77,* 65-78.

Frone, M. R., Yardley, J. K., & Markel, K. S. (1997). Developing and testing an integrative model of the work-family interface. *Journal of Vocational Behavior, 50,* 145-167.

Fullerton, H. N., Jr. (1997, November). Labor force 2006: Slowing down and changing composition. *Monthly Labor Review Online, 120*(11). Retrieved from http://stats.bls.gov/opub/mlr/1997/11/art3esc.htm

Galinsky, E., Bond, J. T., & Friedman, D. E. (1993). *The changing workforce: Highlights of the national study.* New York: Families and Work Institute.

Galinsky, E., Bond, J. T., & Friedman, D. E. (1996). The role of employers in addressing the needs of employed parents. *Journal of Social Issues, 52,* 111-136.

Galinsky, E., Friedman, D. E., & Hernandez, C. A. (1991). *The corporate reference guide to work-family programs.* New York: Families and Work Institute.

Goff, S. J., Mount, M. K., & Jamison, R. L. (1990). Employer supported child care: Work/family conflict and absenteeism: A field study. *Personnel Psychology, 43,* 793-809.

Goode, W. J. (1960). A theory of role strain. *American Sociological Review, 25,* 483-496.

Grandey, A., & Cropanzano, R. (1999). The conservation of resources model and work-family conflict and strain. *Journal of Vocational Behavior, 54,* 350-370.

Greenberger, E., Goldberg, W. A., Hamill, S., O'Neil, R., & Payne, C. K. (1989). Contributions of a supportive work environment to parents' well-being and orientation to work. *American Journal of Community Psychology, 17,* 755-783.

Greenhaus, J. H., & Beutell, N. J. (1985). Sources of conflict between work and family roles. *Academy of Management Review, 10,* 76-88.

Greenhaus, J. H., Parasuraman, S., Granrose, C. S., Rabinowitz, S., & Beutell, N. J. (1989). Sources of work-family conflict among two-career couples. *Journal of Vocational Behavior, 34,* 133-153.

Grover, S. L., & Crooker, K. J. (1995). Who appreciates family-responsive human resource policies: The impact of family-friendly policies on the organizational attachment of parents and nonparents. *Personnel Psychology, 48,* 271-288.

Grzywacz, J. G. (2000). Work-family spillover and health during midlife: Is managing conflict everything? *American Journal of Health Promotion, 14,* 236-243.

Grzywacz, J. G., & Marks, N. F. (2000a). Family, work, work-family spillover and problem drinking during midlife. *Journal of Marriage and the Family, 62,* 336-348.

Grzywacz, J. G., & Marks, N. F. (2000b). Reconceptualizing the work-family interface: An ecological perspective on the correlates of positive and negative spillover between work and family. *Journal of Occupational Health Psychology, 5,* 111-126.

Gutek, B. A., Searle, S., & Klepa, L. (1991). Rational versus gender role explanations for work-family conflict. *Journal of Applied Psychology, 76,* 560-568.

Hammer, L. B., Allen, E., & Grigsby, T. (1997). Work-family conflict in dual-earner couples: Within-individual and crossover effects of work and family. *Journal of Vocational Behavior, 50,* 185-203.

Hammer, L. B., & Barbera, K. M. (1997). Toward an integration of alternative work schedules and human resource systems. *Human Resource Planning, 20*(2), 28-36.

Hanson, B. G. (1995). *General systems theory beginning with wholes.* Washington, DC: Taylor & Francis.

Hayden, L. C., Schiller, M., Dickstein, S., Seifer, R., Sameroff, A. J., Miller, I., Keitner, G., & Rasmussen, S. (1998). Levels of family assessment: I. Family, marital, and parent-child interaction. *Journal of Family Psychology, 12,* 7-22.

Hepburn, C. G., & Barling, J. (1996). Eldercare responsibilities, interrole conflict, and employee absence: A daily study. *Journal of Occupational Health Psychology, 1,* 311-318.

Higgins, C. A., Duxbury, L. E., & Irving, R. H. (1992). Work-family conflict in the dual-career family. *Organizational Behavior and Human Decision Processes, 51,* 51-75.

Hill, E. J., Miller, B. C., Weiner, S. P., & Colihan, J. (1998). Influences of the virtual office on aspects of work and work/life balance. *Personnel Psychology, 51,* 667-682.

Ingersoll-Dayton, B., Neal, M. B., & Hammer, L. B. (2001). Aging parents helping adult children: The experience of the sandwiched generation. *Family Relations, 50,* 262-271.

Kahn, R. L., Wolfe, D. M., Quinn, R., Snoek, J. D., & Rosenthal, R. A. (1964). *Organizational stress.* New York: Wiley.

Katz, D., & Kahn, R. (1978). *The social psychology of organizations* (2nd ed.). New York: Wiley.

Kirchmeyer, C. (1992). Perceptions of nonwork-to-work spillover: Challenging the common view of conflict-ridden relationships. *Basic and Applied Social Psychology, 13,* 231-249.

Kirchmeyer, C. (1993). Nonwork-to-work spillover: A more balanced view of the experiences and coping of professional women and men. *Sex Roles, 28,* 531-552.

Kossek, E. E. (1990). Diversity in child care assistance needs: Employee problems, preferences, and work-related outcomes. *Personnel Psychology, 43*(4), 769-791.

Kossek, E. E., & Nichol, V. (1992). The effects of on-site child care on employee attitudes and performance. *Personnel Psychology, 45,* 485-509.

Kossek, E. E., & Ozeki, C. (1998). Work-family conflict, policies, and the job-life satisfaction relationship: A review and directions for organizational behavior-human resources research. *Journal of Applied Psychology, 83,* 139-149.

Kossek, E. E., & Ozeki, C. (1999). Bridging the work-family policy and productivity gap: A literature review. *Community, Work and Family, 2,* 7-32.

Lambert, S. J. (1990). Processes linking work and family: A critical review and research agenda. *Human Relations, 43,* 239-257.

Litchfield, L., & Pitt-Catsouphes, M. (1999). Culture and work/life balance: Findings from the *Business Week* study. Boston College Study for Work and Family. Research Highlights Series.

Loerch, K. J., Russell, J. E., & Rush, M. C. (1989). The relationships among family domain variables and work-family conflict for men and women. *Journal of Vocational Behavior, 35,* 288-308.

MacEwen, K. E., & Barling, J. (1994). Daily consequences of work interference with family and family interference with work. *Work and Stress, 8,* 244-254.

Marks, S. R. (1977). Multiple roles and role strain: Some notes on human energy, time, and commitment. *American Sociological Review, 42,* 921-936.

Marks, S. R., & MacDermid, S. M. (1996). Multiple roles and the self: A theory of role balance. *Journal of Marriage and the Family, 58,* 417-432.

Marshall, N. L., & Barnett, R. C. (1993). Work-family strains and gains among two-earner couples. *Journal of Community Psychology, 21,* 64-78.

Marshall, N. L., & Barnett, R. C. (1994). Family friendly workplaces, work-family interface, and worker health. In G. P. Keita & J. J. Hurrell (Eds.), *Job stress in a* changing workforce: *Investigating gender, diversity, and family issues* (pp. 253-264). Washington, DC: American Psychological Association.

Neal, M. B., Chapman, N. J., Ingersoll-Dayton, B., & Emlen, A. C. (1993). *Balancing work and caregiving for children, adults, and elders.* Newbury Park, CA: Sage.

Neal, M. B., Hammer, L. B., Rickard, A., Isgrigg, J., & Brockwood, K. (1999, November). *Dual-earner couples in the sandwiched generation: Who they are, what they do, how they manage.* Paper session presented at the Annual Scientific Meeting of the Gerontological Society of America, San Francisco.

Nichols, L. S., & Junk, V. W. (1997). The sandwich generation: Dependency, proximity, and task assistance needs of parents. *Journal of Family and Economic Issues, 18,* 299-326.

Orthner, D. K., & Pittman, J. F. (1986). Family contributions to work commitment. *Journal of Marriage and the Family, 48,* 573-581.

Pavalko, E. K., & Woodbury, S. (2000). Social roles as process: Caregiving careers and women's health. *Journal of Health and Social Behavior, 41,* 91-100.

Perlow, L. A. (1995). Putting the work back into work/family. *Group & Organization Management, 20,* 227-239.

Pierce, J. L., & Newstrom, J. W. (1983). The design of flexible work schedules and employee responses: Relationships and process. *Journal of Occupational Behavior, 4,* 247-262.

Pietromonaco, P. R., Manis, J., & Frohardt-Lane, K. (1986). Psychological consequences of multiple social roles. *Psychology of Women Quarterly, 10,* 373-382.

Piotrkowski, C. S. (1979). *Work and the family system: A naturalistic study of working class and lower-middle-class families.* New York: Free Press.

Pleck, J. H. (1977). The work-family role system. *Social Problems, 24,* 417-427.

Pleck, J. H., Staines, G., & Lang, L. (1980). Conflicts between work and family life. *Monthly Labor Review, 103,* 29-32.

Quick, J. C. (1999). Occupational health psychology: The convergence of health and clinical psychology with public health and preventative medicine in an organizational context. *Professional Psychology: Research and Practice, 30,* 123-128.

Quick, J. C., Quick, J. D., Nelson, D. L., & Hurrell, J. J., Jr. (1997). *Preventative stress management in organizations.* Washington, DC: American Psychological Association.

Raabe, P. H. (1990). The organizational effects of workplace family policies: Past weaknesses and recent progress toward improved research. *Journal of Family Issues, 11,* 477-491.

Rosenthal, C. J., Martin-Matthews, A., & Matthews, S. H. (1996). Caught in the middle? Occupancy in the middle roles and help to parents in a national probability sample of Canadian adults. *Journal of Gerontology: Social Sciences, 51B,* S274-S283.

Rothausen, T. J., Gonzalez, J. A., Clarke, N. E., & O'Dell, L. L. (1998). Family friendly backlash—fact or fiction? The case of organizations' on-site child care centers. *Personnel Psychology, 51,* 685-706.

Scandura, T. A., & Lankau, M. J. (1997). Relationships of gender, family responsibility and flexible work hours to organizational commitment and job satisfaction. *Journal of Organizational Behavior, 18,* 377-391.

Scharlach, A. (1994). Caregiving and employment: Competing or complementary roles? *Gerontologist, 34,* 378-385.

Shamir, B. (1983). Some antecedents of work-nonwork conflict. *Journal of Vocational Behavior, 23,* 98-111.

Shellenberger, S., & Hoffman, S. S. (1995). The changing family-work system. In R. H. Mikesell & D. D. Lusterman (Eds.), *Integrating family therapy: Handbook of family psychology and systems theory.* Washington, DC: American Psychological Association.

Shinn, M., Wong, N. W., Simko, P. A., & Ortiz-Torres, B. (1989). Promoting the well-being of working parents: Coping, social support, and flexible job schedules. *American Journal of Community Psychology, 17,* 31-55.

Sieber, S. D. (1974). Toward a theory of role accumulation. *American Sociological Review, 39,* 467-478.

Staines, G. L. (1980). Spillover versus compensation: A review of the literature on the relationship between work and nonwork. *Human Resources, 33,* 111-129.

Staines, G. L., & Pleck, J. H. (1986). Work schedule flexibility and family life. *Journal of Occupational Behavior, 7,* 147-153.

Starrels, M. E. (1992). The evolution of workplace family policy research. *Journal of Family Issues, 13,* 259-278.

Stephens, M. A. P., Franks, M. M., & Atienza, A. A. (1997). Where two roles intersect: Spillover between parent care and employment. *Psychology and Aging, 12,* 30-37.

Stephens, M. A. P., & Townsend, A. L. (1997). Stress of parent care: Positive and negative effects on women's other roles. *Psychology and Aging, 12,* 376-386.

Stoller, E. P., & Pugliesi, K. L. (1989). Other roles of caregivers: Competing responsibilities or supportive resources. *Journal of Gerontology: Social Sciences, 44,* S231-S238.

Thoits, P. A. (1983). Multiple identities and psychological well-being: A reformulation and test of the social isolation hypothesis. *American Sociological Review, 48,* 147-187.

Thomas, L. T., & Ganster, D. C. (1995). Impact of family-supportive work variables on work-family conflict and strain: A control perspective. *Journal of Applied Psychology, 80,* 6-15.

Thompson, C. A., Beauvais, L. L., & Lyness, K. S. (1999). When work-family benefits are not enough: The influence of work-family culture on benefit utilization, organizational attachment, and work-family conflict. *Journal of Vocational Behavior, 54,* 392-415.

Thompson, C. A., Thomas, C. C., & Maier, M. (1992). Work-family conflict: Reassessing corporate policies and initiatives. In U. Sekaran & F. T. Leong (Eds.), *Womanpower: Managing in times of demographic turbulence* (pp. 59-84). Newbury Park, CA: Sage.

Wagner, D. L., & Hunt, G. G. (1994). The use of workplace eldercare programs by employed caregivers. *Research on Aging, 16,* 69-84.

Warren, J. A., & Johnson, P. J. (1995). The impact of workplace support on work-family role strain. *Family Relations, 44,* 163-169.

Westman, M. (2001). Stress and strain crossover. *Human Relations, 54,* 557-591.

Westman, M., & Etzion, D. (1995). Crossover of stress, strain and resources from one spouse to another. *Journal of Organizational Behavior, 16,* 169-181.

Westman, M., & Piotrkowski, C. S. (1999). Introduction to the special issue: Work-family research in occupational health psychology. *Journal of Occupational Health Psychology, 4,* 310-316.

Westman, M., & Vinokur, A. D. (1998). Unraveling the relationship of distress levels within couples: Common stressors, empathic reactions, or crossover via social interaction? *Human Relations, 51,* 137-156.

Wilensky, H. L. (1960). Work, careers, and social integration. *International Social Science Journal, 12,* 543-560.

Wiley, D. L. (1987). The relationship between work/nonwork role conflict and job-related outcomes: Some unanticipated findings. *Journal of Management, 13,* 467-472.

Yogev, S. (1981). Do professional women have egalitarian marital relationships? *Journal of Marriage and the Family, 43,* 865-871.

Zedeck, S. (1992). Introduction: Exploring the domain of work and family concerns. In S. Zedeck (Ed.), *Work, families, and organizations.* San Francisco: Jossey-Bass.

Zedeck, S., & Mosier, K. L. (1990). Work and family and employing organization. *American Psychologist, 45,* 240-251.

CHAPTER 6

Organizationally Targeted Interventions Aimed at Reducing Workplace Stress

Terry A. Beehr
Michael P. O'Driscoll

"Alice, Alice, Alice . . . companies are designed to maximize stockholder value, not employee happiness," said Catbert, the Evil Human Resources Director.

Adams (1998), p. 52

Work-related stress is recognized as having significant implications for organizations and their members. International data demonstrate the substantial financial and other costs of stress-related illness and disability (DeFrank & Ivancevich, 1998; Murphy, 1995). In Britain, for instance, as many as 2 million people have reported that they suffer from a work-caused illness (Altman, 2000), and it is estimated that 60% of all absences are stress-related (Cartwright, 2000). In the United States, according to the American Heart Association, about $100 billion was lost in productivity due to cardiovascular disease in 1997 alone (Wright & Wright, 2000). These statistics illustrate that stress can have a major impact on both individual employees and employers, and that effective stress management interventions are essential to deal with the increasingly pervasive effects of workplace stress (Cooper, Dewe, & O'Driscoll, 2001).

The present chapter is concerned with occupational stress interventions that are targeted primarily at the organization, rather than at the individual (Beehr, 1995; Newman & Beehr, 1979). Because the expression *organizational intervention* can have a variety of meanings and connote different kinds of "treatment," it is as important to clarify what is *not* included in this category of intervention as it is to understand which approaches are included. First, we do not label an intervention as organizationally focused simply because it is undertaken by or with the consent of the organization or one of its components (e.g., a department within the organization). Hence, implementation of an Employee Assistance Program by a single department or even by a whole organization does not automatically qualify the intervention for inclusion in this category. Second, and related to the first issue, promotion or financial support for a stress management intervention by the organization does not necessarily indicate that the intervention itself is focused at the organization level. Finally, the relative timing of a treatment in relation to stress effects also does not demonstrate whether it is an organizationally targeted treatment. That is, a stress management intervention could be implemented either before or after any effect on employees' health has occurred. The issue is the target of the intervention, not its timing.

Hence, for an intervention to be classified as organizationally targeted, it must focus on work environment or organizational stressors, that is, situations or events within the workplace that are stress-inducing for organizational members. For example, many organizational interventions address organizational structures, policies, and practices, as well as the behaviors of members (e.g., managers or supervisors) that affect subordinate employees. Although the ultimate goal is to relieve strain in the person, an organizationally targeted treatment strategy does this indirectly by altering elements of the environment that are or could be stressors. This often means changing the design of the organization (or some part of it) in order to reduce stress. As Catbert would tell us, however, organization design or redesign is usually done for other purposes, not for stress reduction.

This is probably a major reason why organizationally targeted stress interventions are undertaken less often than those addressing occupational stress problems at the individual level. Organizational researchers have noted repeatedly that little is known about the effectiveness of these

interventions, and that this is probably due to the fact that these types of treatments are rarely implemented (e.g., Beehr, Jex, & Ghosh, 2001; Ganster, Mayes, Sime, & Tharp, 1982; Ivancevich & Matteson, 1987; Kahn & Byosiere, 1992; Kompier, Geurts, Gründemann, Vink, & Smulders, 1998; MacLennan, 1992; Murphy, 1984; Newman & Beehr, 1979; Quick, Quick, & Nelson, 1998). Nor does there appear to be any trend toward greater usage of organizational relative to individual interventions to alleviate occupational stress (Houtman & Kompier, 1995). Furthermore, when such interventions have been conducted, only a subset of them has been evaluated in a methodologically rigorous way. In the present chapter, we describe several evaluations of organizationally targeted stress treatments, an indication that this approach is being applied gradually in some organizations.

By contrast, individually targeted treatments for occupational stress have been implemented far more frequently. These interventions focus primarily on individuals' perceptions (of stressors) and their responses to stressors (coping behaviors), with the aim of enhancing the person's ability to deal effectively with perceived threats to his or her well-being. For strains such as anxiety or hypertension, for example, individually targeted interventions might include anxiety treatments from clinical psychology or psychiatry, such as systematic desensitization, relaxation training, or even medication. Some of the more psychologically oriented of these treatments have been examined in rigorous studies, but researchers have concluded that their effects tend to be small and/or temporary (e.g., Beehr, 1998; Burke, 1993; Ganster et al., 1982). Because of this, and because some workplace stressors cannot be alleviated effectively by individual coping responses alone, it is often recommended that organizational interventions be attempted. The argument goes that it would make more sense to fix the cause (stressor), rather than leaving the cause alone and simply endeavoring to address its impact (strain). If the stressors were reduced, the resulting strains would be lessened. Without attempting organizationally targeted treatments and evaluating them appropriately, however, their effectiveness is unknown.

A problem with most individually targeted treatments of occupational stress is that there is usually no strong reason to believe that they are occupational stress treatments at all (Beehr, 1995, 1998). Just because an employee has hypertension or is depressed does not mean that these illnesses were caused by stressors in the organizational or workplace setting. Illnesses can have many causes, and it is often not possible to attribute the cause of these illnesses to a specific factor in the employee's job or off-the-job life. This simple fact is surprisingly ignored in much of the occupational stress intervention literature. For many examples labeled occupational stress treatments, there is no evidence that there ever was any significant organizational cause (stressor) to begin with. Instead, there is a report of illness among employed people and a treatment of the illness. Without some minimal evidence that occupational stressors could be at least partially causing the illness, there is no compelling reason to consider such efforts to be treatments of occupational stress.

This is more than a philosophical issue when we focus on organizational stress management interventions. When implementing an individually targeted approach to stress reduction, one needs to know only

that there is an illness (or might be if action is not taken). For an organizationally targeted intervention, however, one needs to know not only that there is an illness (or might be one if action is not taken), but also what environmental event or situation is contributing to the illness.

In other words, organizational treatments for stress usually require a diagnosis of the situation to identify stressors or potential stressors (Beehr, 1995, 1998; Briner & Reynolds, 1999). Otherwise, one does not know what part of the organization might need changing, that is, what stressors to try to remove or reduce. When this problem is solved, the problem still exists of getting permission from those in power to alter some aspect of the organization. Because most organizations are designed to enhance the goals of productivity, efficiency, and effectiveness, more than the goal of employee health, endeavoring to enhance employee well-being by reducing stressors may conflict with primary organizational values. Therefore, considerable effort may be required to persuade managers and organizational stakeholders of the benefits of implementing an organizationally targeted stress management program.

This review of relatively rigorously evaluated work stress treatments is organized around two questions. First, what kinds of organizationally targeted interventions of stress are being undertaken? Given the preceding discussion, it is apparent that there is a proclivity to focus on individually targeted treatments, but when organizationally targeted treatments occur, what is their nature? Second, when these treatments are undertaken, how effective are they? The next section reviews the types of interventions that have been reported. The evaluation of their effectiveness is saved for a subsequent section of the chapter.

WHAT ARE THE TYPES OF ORGANIZATIONALLY TARGETED STRESS INTERVENTIONS?

Although organizational stress management interventions are less common than individually targeted programs, the logic for implementing organizationally targeted treatments in order to eliminate or reduce stressors (thereby alleviating employee strains) has been accepted for some time. We searched computerized databases (primarily PsycINFO), other reviews of related topics, and recent issues of relevant journals. Then, we obtained further references cited in those that were thus identified. We looked for reports of interventions that (a) were clearly organizationally targeted and (b) had employed research designs that were rigorous enough to permit relatively strong causal inference. This search uncovered 14 empirical investigations of the effectiveness of organizational stress management interventions. A straightforward approach to organizational interventions would include a diagnosis in which potential stressors would be identified, the strength of their link to strains would be estimated, and then the stressors would be reduced by altering the work environment. Another organizationally targeted treatment strategy would be to improve the work situation in some way that would include changing moderator variables. That is, if stressors interact with other organizational (moderator) variables, those other variables could be improved in order to reduce the effect of the stressors on personal strains. For instance, if social support moderates the relationship between certain work-related stressors and strains, increasing the extent of social support available in the workplace should serve to alleviate the negative impact of those stressors on the individual.

Early reviews specifically of organizationally targeted interventions (Ivancevich & Matteson, 1987; Newman & Beehr, 1979) were hard-pressed to find any published evaluations to report. For the present review, we found several studies that met the criteria of (a) having at least an important part of the intervention focused on changing the organizational environment and (b) having at least a quasi-experimental design. Six general types of interventions were found: participative decision making, changes in organizational structure, ergonomic changes, role-based interventions, increasing social support, and the provision of information about environmental stressors involving uncertainty. Illustrations of each of these intervention types are presented below.

Participation in Decision Making

Some organizationally targeted stress treatments include employee participation in decision making as an organizational change. Such changes encompass increased control, autonomy, or influence by people in the organization. In practice, in a typical hierarchical organization, this usually means increased influence by people relatively low in the hierarchy. Participative decision making has been advocated for reasons other than stress management, including being a more effective leadership style in some situations (e.g., Vroom & Jago, 1988) and, more generally, a decentralization of power within the organization (e.g., Beehr, 1996). It has also been recommended for treatment of occupational stress (e.g., Harrison, 1985), often on the grounds that such participation might make people feel more positive about themselves in general and that people can make decisions that will result in less stressful situations for themselves. In some theories, control itself is thought to alleviate negative effects of stress (e.g., Karasek, 1979).

An early reported example of the effects of participative decision making on job-related strain was a dissertation by Douglas Campbell (1973) at the University of Michigan. At NASA's Goddard space flight center, an intervention was developed that included participation and survey feedback focusing on information relating to person-environment fit (based on the Person-Environment fit [P-E fit] theory of occupational stress) (e.g., Caplan, 1983). The intervention comprised 10 weekly meetings aimed at examining stressors in the workplace, and it was aimed at increasing participative decision making, but also any (unknown) changes that were undertaken as a result of the meetings. This early intervention really did not "take," however, as it was never clear that the groups in the study became more participative or increased their level of P-E fit. This is a problem for organizationally targeted interventions—actually changing the organization can be very difficult.

Another frequently cited participative decision-making intervention examined for stress effects was reported by Jackson (1983, 1984). At a university hospital, she was able to take advantage of the naturally occurring intervention of an increase in number of staff meetings, accompanied by a 2-day training session for unit heads on how to conduct such meetings. The immediate aim was to increase participation in decision making, and Jackson was able to get the hospital to introduce the change to randomly selected groups (with delayed treatment to the control groups) and to measure stress-type variables before and after the intervention.

Wall and his colleagues reported two projects in which participation was increased in an attempt to reduce psychological strains. In the first study (Wall & Clegg, 1981), an action research program of sociotechnical changes in jobs increased workers' autonomy at the group level; in the second (Wall, Kemp, Jackson, & Clegg, 1986), confectionary workers were given increased autonomy in decisions about job allocation, production targets, solutions for production problems, record keeping, ordering, and some selection.

Due to problems relating to absenteeism in a public agency concerned with housing in the United Kingdom, Reynolds (1997) conducted a study testing both individually and organizationally targeted stress treatments. Managers were taught skills in coaching, counseling, and employee development, and they held meetings with their subordinates to agree on developmental plans and provide feedback. The general aim of the intervention was to increase participation and control and to clarify the situation. This study was well designed, in that it included the implementation of individual and organizational interventions to different (although not randomly chosen) groups and contained a no-intervention comparison group.

Overall, it is apparent that some stress-related organizational interventions focusing explicitly on increasing participation have been undertaken, although few recent evaluations of the effectiveness of these interventions exist (only one was published in the past 10 years). Many other interventions reviewed, although not classified here as participation interventions, probably also have some element of increasing participation.

Structural Changes

It may be possible to alter the amount of stress on employees by changing the organization's structure—the pattern of relationships among its component parts. Maes, Verhoeven, Kittle, and Schoten (1998) reported both a lifestyle and an organizationally targeted change program guided by a wellness committee in a Dutch manufacturing organization. The organizational change included moving from a product-oriented to a functional structure while simultaneously laying off foremen and increasing a group focus in terms of performance appraisals and rewards. In addition, more group autonomy was introduced for production workers. Clearly, this was a large-scale change in the organization, and it was accompanied by individual lifestyle interventions. Another relevant structural intervention entailed the reorganization of the engineering divisions of an aircraft manufacturer (Joyce, 1986). The organization changed from a relatively traditional functional structure to a matrix organization. Although not undertaken primarily for stress purposes, some stress-type measures were taken before and after the intervention in the changed divisions and at a nonequivalent control site.

A specific type of stress-related intervention that can be considered at least partly structural is the creation of a new subunit to focus on making organizationally targeted changes to reduce stress. The development of a subunit is a structural change in itself, but it is not in itself an organizationally targeted stress reduction strategy. Many examples of the implementation of a wellness unit or a department running an Employee Assistance Program create a new structure, but they end up focusing on individually targeted interventions such as counseling, exercise, or other individual treatments. Also, some of these units, perhaps those resembling more temporary task forces, seem to have focused more on environmental stressors. In one such project, recommendations from committees in two divisions of a manufacturing company included a daily newsletter, problem-solving training for team leaders, and the creation of problem-solving teams that could propose organizational changes (Heany et al., 1993). It should be noted, however, that management and the union often did not agree to implement the suggestions of these teams.

In another project (Landisbergis & Vivona-Vaughan, 1995), in a public agency and using a matched control group, the agency elected a problem-solving committee that analyzed stressors and made recommendations to management for changing the organization. Some of the recommendations involved improving group processes. As in the Heany et al. (1993) research, not all of the committee's recommendations for change were implemented by management. This may show a management reluctance to make changes in the organization for the sake of reducing stress, a phenomenon that bodes ill for the possibility of organizationally targeted interventions. An important vehicle for designing and implementing organizationally targeted changes, however, is the development of a *stress audit* unit whose purpose is to diagnose or discover potential stressors in the organization and to determine the most appropriate ways to counteract these stressors.

Ergonomic Approaches

Kompier et al. (1998) reported 10 cases of stress management interventions that were (at least in part) ergonomically oriented. Two of these, in Dutch organizations, employed relatively strong research designs, including the use of control groups. One was a ministry department that was believed to have too much time pressure and also poor ergonomics, based on self-reports about employees' workstations and mental workload. Both organizational interventions (reorganizing the work) and an individual training approach were used. The department head took responsibility for reorganizing and implementing the change, which is probably necessary for a successful organizationally targeted intervention. The other example reported by Kompier et al. concerned a hospital experiencing high sickness and absenteeism rates and difficulty in recruiting personnel. The diagnosis incorporated self-reports and records of sickness, along with assessment of six potential stressors. Line management implemented work reorganization, although some participation was also apparently involved. The interventions included changing work schedules, technology, physical workloads, and enriching jobs. Individually targeted treatments involving health and stress management were also undertaken. Not all of these changes are specifically ergonomic. In addition, there was some participation in decision making in these approaches, either directly in the diagnosis phase or through committees that guided the projects.

Role-Based Interventions

Much of the early research on organizational stress, probably spurred by a book by Kahn, Wolfe, Quinn, Snoek, and Rosenthal (1964), focused on stressors derived conceptually from role theory. Each employee's job can be conceived as a role in a social network that is an organization. The job or role is defined by the expectations and demands of others in the network. Role ambiguity, role conflict (conflicting expectations and demands placed on the person), and role overload are three organizational stressors derived directly from role theory, and it is easy to conceive of interventions that would have at least face validity for reducing these stressors. Traditional management theory and recommendations would usually recognize these situations as poor management. Employees are supposed

to know what is expected of them (little role ambiguity), they are not supposed to have conflicting demands (little role conflict), and their job is supposed to have an amount of work that is appropriate for them to handle (little role overload).

Examples of role-based stress interventions would include role clarification, or making expectations clear; reduction in role conflict (e.g., by reducing competing demands on a person's time and energy); and reduction in overall workloads. In an intervention designed to improve role clarity (Schaubroeck, Ganster, Sime, & Ditman, 1993), a 2-hour role clarification session was presented for employees in the business services division of a major university. Employees were assigned randomly to treatment and control groups. Both groups received some preliminary "responsibility charting" procedures, however, which could mean that both received at least a little clarification of their job roles. In another project (Quick, 1979), supervisors and subordinates in an insurance company attended an 8-hour session composed of lectures, writing descriptions of the tasks for their own jobs, and supervisor-subordinate role plays to develop goal-setting skills. These activities should be directly related to role clarification. There was no control group, but 1-month and 14-month follow-up measures were taken for comparison with a pretest.

Increasing Social Support

Social support has long been assumed to alleviate the effects of occupational stress, but the exact manner in which it does this is unclear (e.g., Beehr, 1995). The dominant social support hypothesis for many years was that it interacted with stressors to reduce the strength of their effects on strains (Ganster, Fusilier, & Mayes, 1986). This is sometimes referred to as the *stress-buffering* hypothesis. It is not clear, however, whether there is such an effect, or whether the effect of social support on strains is more direct.

Confusion over the exact meaning of social support has further complicated debate on the role of this variable in moderating stressor-strain relationships. For instance, Vaux (1988) noted that "people assist each other in an astonishing variety of ways" (p. 17), and most of these ways can be considered social support. Nevertheless, there is agreement that social support, in one form or another, can have a beneficial effect on well-being by reducing the level of strain that people experience, and many interventions are based on the provision of social support for employees experiencing strain. However, relatively little has been done to implement social support specifically for dealing with workplace stress, although the broad definition of social support might argue that almost every intervention has a social support component.

Theorell, Orth-Gomer, Moser, Unden, and Eriksson (1995) reported an intervention in Swedish government enterprises and agencies that had both individually and organizationally targeted treatments. There were three experimental sites and one control site. The organizationally targeted interventions included reduced work pace, feedback from supervisors, and employee discussions of stressors and ways to increase social support. Considering all the support groups that exist for other purposes (which could be interpreted generally as off-the-job stressors), it is perhaps surprising that this type of intervention has not occurred more in the context of workplace stress. There is a great deal of published research on social support and job stress, but typically it is nonexperimental field research. That is, this body of research measures social support (usually perceived support) as it exists in the workplace rather than introducing it as an intervention.

Provision of Information

House (1981) argued that some kinds of social support can be conceived as information, and Cobb (1976) focused on information as an important element of social support. The type of information usually is related to one's status as a person who is valued by others. Information may serve to clarify the important elements of a stressful situation and perhaps even allow more of a sense of control. Therefore, during stressful times, information may be useful and help to reduce strains. It can decrease uncertainty, which (as noted above) has been demonstrated to be a major contributor to occupational strain (e.g., Beehr & Bhagat, 1985; O'Driscoll & Beehr, 1994).

With the trend toward downsizing in the last part of the 20th century, many employees are likely to experience the strain of uncertainty during potential takeovers, mergers, and so forth. A system of providing information to employees about the status of such changes might help (Davy, Kinicki, Kilroy, & Scheck, 1988). In one such intervention (Schweiger & DeNisi, 1991), the provision of information about an impending merger included a letter from the CEO, information about how the merger might affect specific employees, a merger newsletter, a telephone hotline, bulletin board notices, and weekly meetings held by the plant manager over a 7-week period. The study had no comparison group, but it included two pretests and two posttests. The use of information had in it an implicit diagnosis—that the merger was a stressor and that information about it would help to alleviate the stress.

Other Organizationally Targeted Interventions

The six types of organizationally focused interventions described above were reported and evaluated in only one or two studies each, and hence there are still very few evaluations of such interventions. Furthermore, in many cases, the organizational intervention was only part of a larger set of interventions, usually including individually targeted interventions as well. It might make sense from a practical point of view to make the changes as many and as big as possible if there is a stress problem in the organization. This would increase the chance of having an effect. From a research and knowledge point of view, however, this "shotgun" approach makes it very difficult or even impossible to determine the separate effects of any one intervention.

Furthermore, in addition to the six intervention types overviewed here, several other types of organizational stress management interventions are possible. In 1978, Beehr and Newman listed 13 interventions that could be considered organizationally targeted (see Box 6.1). Although all of the interventions in this table are targeted at changing the environment within the organization, it should be noted that they could be carried out by the organization itself, by the individual, or by third parties (e.g., by consultants or legislated by government bodies). This emphasizes the fact that the agent of change need not be the same as the target of the change. It does seem, however, that the organization as agent might be in the most powerful position to make the change (more potential changes exist in this category than in the agent category). Almost none of these interventions had been attempted, rigorously evaluated, and reported in the literature in 1979. Now,

however, as noted in this chapter, several of these interventions have been implemented and evaluated.

HOW EFFECTIVE ARE ORGANIZATIONALLY TARGETED STRESS MANAGEMENT INTERVENTIONS?

Earlier, we noted that individually targeted interventions for reducing stress problems have been found to be, at best, modest in their effectiveness, and there are suggestions that organizationally focused approaches may be required. However, considerable concerns still exist regarding the effectiveness of organizational stress management interventions. In order for organizationally targeted interventions to be effective, they must change one or more elements of the work or organizational environment that has been inducing strain among workers. To date, there is mixed evidence that interventions at this level are effective in bringing about significant environmental changes, although some interventions (such as participative decision making) would appear to hold promise in terms of reducing the amount of strain experienced by organizational members.

In early research on job stress, lack of participation itself was sometimes studied as a stressor (e.g., Beehr, Walsh, & Taber, 1976; French & Caplan, 1973), but this issue has been given less attention in more recent research. Another approach is to consider that lack of participation may cause other stressors, which in turn lead to higher strain. For instance, Jackson (1983, 1984) found that participation in decision making reduced role ambiguity and role conflict, two well-known stressors. She did not, however, measure any strains as

---

Box 6.1   Organizationally Targeted Interventions

Adaptive responses by the organization

- Job redesign
- Alteration of organizational structure
- Changes in evaluation, reward systems
- Changes in work schedules
- Provision of feedback to employees aimed at role clarification
- Refinement of selection and placement procedures, inclusion of job stress as a validation criterion
- Provision of human relations training
- Clarification of career paths and promotion criteria
- Improvement in communication

Adaptive responses by the individual

- Mastery of the environment (including stressors)
- Search for sympathy or social support (if at work)
- Search for more suitable job

Adaptive responses by third parties

- Legislation regarding quality of work life, mandatory retirement

SOURCE: Adapted from Beehr and Newman (1978).

---

dependent variables in her study, so it is not clear whether strains were reduced by the intervention. Similarly, Wall et al. (1986) found that the introduction of autonomous work groups, which should have increased participation, had no clear effect on psychological strains (although some types of satisfaction might have increased). On the other hand, Wall and Clegg (1981) found that increasing job autonomy (similar to participation) did have a marked effect in terms of alleviating psychological strain. Finally, Reynolds (1997) reported an intervention that was largely participative in which some physical strains seemed to get worse. Psychological strains also worsened according to that article's text, but an accompanying figure in the article showed the opposite. Overall, the direct effects of participation in decision making on stressors and strains appear to be inconsistent.

Turning now to other kinds of interventions, health complaints were reduced by an ergonomic approach in research reported by Kompier et al. (1998), and one project focusing on the provision of information about a stressful situation had no effect early but appeared to reduce strains after a period of months (Schweiger & DeNisi, 1991). Some studies have reported small or inconsistent effects on strain indicators, including one with interventions using structural change (Landisbergis & Vivona-Vaughan, 1995; and a subset of people in Heany et al., 1993), and one with a social support intervention (Theorell et al., 1995). No noticeable effect on strains was found in other research on a structural intervention (Maes et al., 1998) or a role-based intervention (Schaubroeck et al., 1993).

From an organizational perspective, reducing absenteeism is sometimes a motive for stress management interventions, and evidence exists that these interventions can influence stress-related absences. However, not all absenteeism is due to stress-related illnesses, and therefore, the effects of organizationally targeted stress interventions on absenteeism are unclear. Although one ergonomic approach (Kompier et al., 1998) and one structural intervention (Maes et al., 1998) appeared to reduce absenteeism, other research on ergonomic intervention (Kompier et al., 1998), participative decision making (Reynolds, 1997), and changes in role demands (Quick, 1979) were not found to affect absenteeism.

In addition to effects of interventions on outcomes such as strains and absenteeism, it is also relevant to ask about the effectiveness of organizationally targeted stress interventions for reducing stressors themselves. These interventions are usually aimed at changing stress-inducing characteristics of a work environment, which is a necessary precondition for organizational interventions to affect strain-related outcomes. A few studies have explored the direct impact of interventions on stressors. For instance, Jackson's (1983, 1984) participative decision-making intervention and Quick's (1979) role-based interventions appeared to have reduced levels of both role ambiguity and role conflict, and Schaubroeck et al.'s (1993) role demands intervention also reduced role ambiguity. In addition, it is relevant that a structural intervention that was not actually undertaken with stress in mind found that changing to a matrix organization structure may have increased role ambiguity, but probably not role conflict (Joyce, 1986). Overall, it appears that some organizational interventions can influence role-based stressors.

In sum, based on the research to date, the effects of organizationally targeted interventions appear modest. It is apparent, however, that there is still relatively little good research on which to make this judgment. One problem is that few of these interventions have been studied more than once; therefore, any results need to be replicated. A second problem is that the full sequence and dynamics of the stress process need to be examined empirically. That is, we still need to determine whether the nature of the stressor(s) in a given organizational situation can be diagnosed, so that interventions can be designed to work specifically on those stressors. This would be followed by an assessment of the effectiveness of reducing the appropriate stressors, which in turn would reduce the strains of the organization members. In brief, determining which environmental stressors are empirically linked with strains in a given organization is a crucial first step in the development of appropriately targeted interventions.

LOGIC AND METHOD OF DESIGNING ORGANIZATIONALLY TARGETED STRESS INTERVENTIONS

Elsewhere, we have discussed and illustrated methods for evaluating interventions aimed at alleviating stressful situations at work (e.g., Beehr & O'Hara, 1987; Cooper et al., 2001). These general methods include experimental and quasi-experimental designs (e.g., Cook, Campbell, & Peracchio, 1990). A stress treatment can be conceptualized as an experimental manipulation, but the designs are often only quasi-experimental because of the difficulty in randomly assigning people to treatment conditions and controlling non-individual difference variables.

Figure 6.1 indicates that a diagnosis needs to be a first step in these interventions.

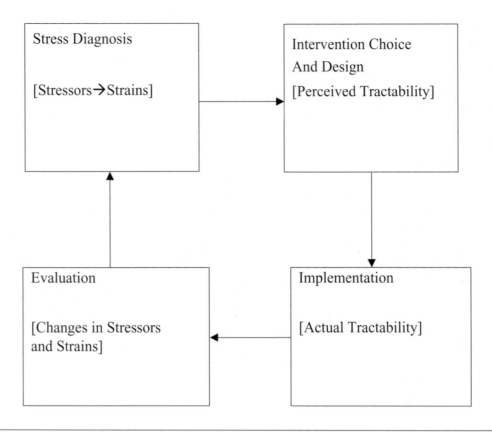

Figure 6.1   Logic and Method of Designing Organizationally Targeted Interventions

This diagnosis is an evaluation of the situation to determine the extent to which a tractable environmental stressor is likely to be causing individual strains. The typical logic of using organizationally targeted interventions depends on (a) identifying one or more stressors that are causing strains, and (b) being able to alter those stressors for the better. The need for this diagnosis has been ignored sometimes in attempts to implement organizational stress management interventions, but without systematic diagnosis, it is difficult to know whether the results, especially failed results, are due to such interventions in general not working, or to inappropriate application in a given situation. Organizationally targeted stress interventions are inherently situational, which is often not the case for individually targeted interventions. Although provision of medication or relaxation training may help individuals alleviate strains and strain-like symptoms due to a variety of causes, organizational interventions must be tailored to the stressors that are causing the problems. For example, role ambiguity as a stressor implies the need for role clarification, whereas interpersonal conflict as a stressor implies the need for conflict resolution as an intervention. There is little reason to believe that switching the treatments between these two conditions would be effective.

It is usually impossible to conclude definitively that potential stressors in an organization are, in fact, causing strains, because experimental methods are unlikely to be used in the diagnosis stage of the intervention. Instead, diagnoses of stressors and strains tend to rely on correlational analyses. Due to research in the past few decades, we now have fairly clear depictions of typical occupational stressors. The list is long and includes role-based stressors, task-based stressors, interpersonal stressors, and technology stressors, among others. Many specific examples can be found in the various chapters of this book. A diagnosis might determine, for example, that role conflict is (a) strongly related to strains and (b) very strong or prevalent in a given organization. This might call for a role-based intervention aimed at reducing role conflict. However, if, in a particular organization, role conflict is not substantially correlated with the existence of physical or psychological strains, there is little reason to believe it could be causing the strains, and even less reason to prescribe an intervention aimed at reducing role conflict. If role conflict is already low (e.g., compared to norms or data from other organizations), one might wonder whether it is actually possible to reduce conflict even further, which might discourage the use of an intervention aimed at further reducing this role stressor.

Therefore, the diagnosis leads to the choice of intervention type (Figure 6.1). Furthermore, the intervention must be one that the organization, its members, and its decision makers will accept. Campbell (1973) reported a study in which the intervention was really never carried out as intended. Increased participation and P-E fit were not achieved. When this happens, implementation of the chosen intervention has failed. Such failures might be quite common, considering the difficulty in implementing many other organizational change projects.

The final stage of the process in Figure 6.1 is evaluation, but of course, evaluation is best planned in the beginning of the intervention. Which variables to measure as outcomes and when to measure them are decisions that need to be made at the outset. Pretests, posttests, and long-term follow-up tests measuring strains make sense for organizationally targeted stress interventions. In addition, the implementation of the intervention should also be assessed, because it is important to know the extent to which a given stressor is actually reduced as intended by the intervention.

CONCLUDING THOUGHTS

Some organizationally focused interventions have now been undertaken with the aim of reducing or alleviating occupational stress, but they are still few in number. When evaluated rigorously, these interventions appear to have only weak effects at best, although it should be noted that this is also a frequent criticism of individually targeted interventions.

We might speculate about why organizational stress management interventions are undertaken disproportionately less than individually targeted stress interventions (which are typically focused on enhancing individuals' stress-coping skills and behaviors). Several reasons seem plausible. One is that organizational interventions are perceived to not work as well as individually targeted interventions. Evidence reported to date, and summarized above, suggests that organizational interventions are not a panacea and might have only small successes, although more evaluative work needs to be done.

A second possibility is that they are difficult to accomplish, for at least two reasons. First, it may be difficult to get organizations to try them, and second, it may be difficult to make intended changes in the organization even if permission is granted. Organizations may not want to undertake organizational changes for the purpose of reducing stress. Instead, they are more concerned with changes that are aimed at improving productivity and/or profits (consistent with Catbert's statement at the beginning of this chapter). Although one may argue that reducing stress improves productivity, the argument is made through a series of assumptions about causal linkages that may or may not be accurate and may not appear immediately obvious to managers.

Third, suggesting that employee strains are due to stressors within the work environment may be seen by managers as tantamount to saying the organization is causing ill health in the employee, which is not something managers have a vested interest in believing. At the extreme, it might even suggest legal liability, but short of that, some blame might fall on a manager's shoulders. After all, the responsibility for the organization's practices, structure, and policies typically rests at the top of the organization. In addition, organizationally targeted changes require more management commitment and involvement, as well as a greater investment of their time and energy. On the other hand, individually targeted changes might imply that individuals are responsible for both the causes and effects of their own well-being.

Fourth and finally, some large industries are focused on developing and implementing individually targeted interventions, such as medicine, psychiatry, clinical and counseling psychology, and social work. Furthermore, third parties (e.g., insurance companies) will sometimes pay for individually targeted treatments. Thus, there are social, organizational, legal, and financial forces leading us to choose individually targeted over organizationally targeted treatments for work stress regardless of the relative effectiveness of each.

Because of the above issues, organizationally targeted interventions (as well as any other intervention in an organization) must be viewed in a favorable light by the organization's decision makers if they are to be undertaken. Many interventions are presented to management as improving productivity, but, as noted earlier, this is not clearly and obviously true of stress management interventions. A more direct argument is that interventions save costs (e.g., absenteeism due to sickness, turnover, and health insurance costs) and improve employee-management relations. This is not to suggest that managers are uncaring about the welfare of their employees—indeed, many managers exhibit strong concerns for employee well-being and health. However, stress management interventions, especially those that may entail considerable financial and other costs for the organization, must be seen by managers as cost-effective and as ultimately contributing to overall organizational productivity. As noted by Cooper et al. (2001), the "challenge is to persuade employers and managers of the long-term benefits of this approach to stress management, for their employees [and] for the organization as a whole" (p. 208).

Ballance?

REFERENCES

Adams, S. (1998). *Journey to Cubeville*. Kansas City, MO: Andrews.

Altman, W. (2000). Health and Safety Commission Chair Bill Callaghan on "good health is good business." *Academy of Management Executive, 14*(2), 8-11.

Beehr, T. A. (1995). *Psychological stress in the workplace*. London: Routledge.

Beehr, T. A. (1996). *Basic organizational psychology*. Boston: Allyn & Bacon.

Beehr, T. A. (1998). An organizational psychology meta-model of occupational stress. In C. L. Cooper (Ed.), *Theories of organizational stress* (pp. 6-27). Oxford, UK: Oxford University Press.

Beehr, T. A., & Bhagat, R. S. (1985). Introduction to human stress and cognition in organizations. In T. A. Beehr & R. S. Bhagat (Eds.), *Human stress and cognition in organizations: An integrated perspective* (pp. 3-19). New York: Wiley.

Beehr, T. A., Jex, S. M., & Ghosh, P. (2001). The management of occupational stress. In C. M. Johnson, W. K. Redmon, & T. C. Mawhinney (Eds.), *Handbook of organizational performance: Behavior analysis and management* (pp. 228-254). Binghamton, NY: Haworth.

Beehr, T. A., & O'Hara, K. (1987). Methodological designs for the evaluation of occupational stress interventions. In S. Kasl & C. L. Cooper (Eds.), *Stress and health: Issues in research methodology* (pp. 79-112). New York: Wiley.

Beehr, T. A., Walsh, J. T., & Taber, T. D. (1976). Relationship of stress to individually and organizationally valued states: Higher-order needs as a moderator. *Journal of Applied Psychology, 61,* 41-47.

Briner, R. B., & Reynolds, S. (1999). The costs, benefits, and limitations of organizational level stress interventions. *Journal of Organizational Behavior, 20,* 647-664.

Burke, R. (1993). Organizational-level interventions to reduce occupational stressors. *Work and Stress, 7,* 77-87.

Campbell, D. (1973). *A program to reduce coronary heart disease risk by altering job stresses*. Unpublished doctoral dissertation, University of Michigan, Ann Arbor.

Caplan, R. D. (1983). Person-environment fit: Past, present and future. In C. L. Cooper (Ed.), *Stress research: Where do we go from here?* (pp. 35-77). London: Wiley.

Cartwright, S. (2000). Taking the pulse of executive health in the U.K. *Academy of Management Executive, 14*(2), 16-23.

Cobb, S. (1976). Social support as a moderator of life stress. *Psychosomatic Medicine, 38,* 300-314.

Cook, T. D., Campbell, D. T., & Peracchio, L. (1990). Quasi-experimentation. In M. D. Dunnette & L. M. Hough (Eds.), *Handbook of industrial and organizational psychology* (Vol. 1, 2nd ed., pp. 491-576). Palo Alto, CA: Consulting Psychologists Press.

Cooper, C. L., Dewe, P., & O'Driscoll, M. P. (2001). *Organizational stress: A review and critique of theory, research, and applications*. Thousand Oaks, CA: Sage.

Davy, J., Kinicki, A., Kilroy, J., & Scheck, C. (1988). After the merger: Dealing with people's uncertainty. *Training and Development Journal, 42,* 56-61.

DeFrank, R., & Ivancevich, J. (1998). Stress on the job: An executive update. *Academy of Management Executive, 12*(3), 55-66.

French, J. R. P., Jr., & Caplan, R. D. (1973). Organizational stress and individual strain. In A. J. Marrow (Ed.), *The failure of success*. New York: AMACOM.

Ganster, D. C., Fusilier, M. R., & Mayes, B. T. (1986). Role of social support in the experience of stress at work. *Journal of Applied Psychology, 71*, 102-110.

Ganster, D. C., Mayes, B. T., Sime, W. E., & Tharp, G. D. (1982). Managing organizational stress: A field experiment. *Journal of Applied Psychology, 67*, 533-542.

Harrison, R. V. (1985). The person-environment fit model and the study of job stress. In T. A. Beehr & R. S. Bhagat (Eds.), *Human stress and cognition in organizations* (pp. 23-55). New York: Wiley.

Heany, C. A., Israel, B. A., Schurman, S. J., Baker, E. A., House, J. S., & Hugentobler, M. (1993). Industrial relations, worksite stress reduction, and employee well-being: A participatory action research investigation. *Journal of Organizational Behavior, 14*, 495-510.

House, J. S. (1981). *Work stress and social support.* Reading, MA: Addison-Wesley.

Houtman, I. L. D., & Kompier, M. A. J. (1995). Courses on work stress: A growing market, but what about their quality? In L. R. Murphy, J. J. Hurrell, S. L. Sauter, & G. P. Keita (Eds.), *Job stress interventions* (pp. 337-349). Washington, DC: American Psychological Association.

Ivancevich, J. M., & Matteson, M. T. (1987). Organizational level stress management interventions: A review and recommendations. In J. M. Ivancevich & D. C. Ganster (Eds.), *Job stress: From theory to suggestion* (pp. 229-248). New York: Haworth.

Jackson, S. E. (1983). Participation in decision making as a strategy for reducing job-related strain. *Journal of Applied Psychology, 68*, 3-19.

Jackson, S. E. (1984). Correction to "Participation in decision making as a strategy for reducing job-related strain." *Journal of Applied Psychology, 69*, 546-547.

Joyce, W. F. (1986). Matrix organization: A social experiment. *Academy of Management Journal, 29*, 356-361.

Kahn, R. L., & Byosiere, D. (1992). Stress in organizations. In M. Dunnette & L. Hough (Eds.), *Handbook of industrial and organizational psychology* (Vol. 3, 2nd ed., pp. 571-660). Palo Alto, CA: Consulting Psychologists Press.

Kahn, R. L., Wolfe, D. M., Quinn, R., Snoek, J. D., & Rosenthal, R. A. (1964). *Organizational stress.* New York: Wiley.

Karasek, R. A. (1979). Job demands, job decision latitude, and mental strain: Implications for job design. *Administrative Science Quarterly, 24*, 285-308.

Kompier, M. A. J., Geurts, S. A. E., Gründemann, R. W. M., Vink, P., & Smulders, P. G. W. (1998). Cases in stress prevention: The success of a participative and stepwise approach. *Stress Medicine, 14,*155-168.

Landisbergis, P. A., & Vivona-Vaughan, E. (1995). Evaluation of an occupational stress intervention in a public agency. *Journal of Organizational Behavior, 16*, 29-48.

MacLennan, B. W. (1992). Stressor reduction: An organizational alternative to individual stress management. In J. C. Quick, L. R. Murphy, & J. J. Hurrell, Jr. (Eds.), *Stress and well-being at work: Assessments and interventions for occupational mental health* (pp. 79-95). Washington, DC: American Psychological Association.

Maes, S., Verhoeven, C., Kittle, F., & Schoten, H. (1998). Effects of a Dutch work-site wellness-health program: The Barabantia project. *American Journal of Public Health, 88*, 1037-1041.

Murphy, L. (1984). Occupational stress management: A review. *Journal of Occupational Psychology, 57*, 1-15.

Murphy, L. (1995). Occupational stress management: Current status and future directions. In C. Cooper & D. Rousseau (Eds.), *Trends in organizational behavior* (Vol. 2, pp. 1-14). Chichester, UK: Wiley.

Newman, J. E., & Beehr, T. A. (1979). Personal and organizational strategies for handling job stress: A review of research and opinion. *Personnel Psychology, 32,* 1-43.

O'Driscoll, M. P., & Beehr, T. A. (1994). Supervisor behaviors, role stressors, and uncertainty as predictors of personal outcomes for subordinates. *Journal of Organizational Behavior, 15,* 141-155.

Quick, J. C. (1979). Dyadic goal setting and role stress: A field study. *Academy of Management Journal, 22,* 241-252.

Quick, J. D., Quick, J. C., & Nelson, D. L. (1998). The theory of preventive stress management in organizations. In C. L. Cooper (Ed.), *Theories of organizational stress* (pp. 246-268). Oxford, UK: Oxford University Press.

Reynolds, S. (1997). Psychological well-being at work: Is prevention better than cure? *Journal of Psychosomatic Research, 43,* 93-102.

Schaubroeck, J., Ganster, D. C., Sime, W. E., & Ditman, D. (1993). A field experiment testing supervisory role clarification. *Personnel Psychology, 46,* 1-25.

Schweiger, D. M., & DeNisi, A. S. (1991). Communication with employees following a merger: A longitudinal field experiment. *Academy of Management Journal, 34,* 110-135.

Theorell, T., Orth-Gomer, K., Moser, V., Unden, A., & Eriksson, I. (1995). Endocrine markers during a job intervention. *Work & Stress, 9,* 67-76.

Vaux, A. (1988). *Social support: Theory, research, and intervention.* New York: Praeger.

Vroom, V. H., & Jago, A. G. (1988). *The new leadership: Managing participation in organizations.* Englewood Cliffs, NJ: Prentice-Hall.

Wall, T., & Clegg, C. (1981). A longitudinal study of work group design. *Journal of Occupational Behavior, 2,* 31-49.

Wall, T., Kemp, N. J., Jackson, P. R., & Clegg, C. W. (1986). Outcomes of autonomous workgroups: A long-term field experiment. *Academy of Management Journal, 29,* 280-304.

Wright, T. D., & Wright, V. P. (2000). How our "values" influence the manner in which organizational research is framed and interpreted. *Journal of Organizational Behavior, 21,* 603-607.

Part III

EFFECTS OF PSYCHOPATHOLOGY ON WORK

CHAPTER 7

Depression in the Workplace

PAULA TRUAX
TRACY MCDONALD

Depression represents one of the most common, most debilitating, and most expensive mental health disorders, contributing to unemployment and work impairment in a large number of adults. Depression diagnoses, such as Major Depressive Disorder (MDD) and Dysthymic Disorder (DD) represent a large proportion of the mental health diagnoses. The American Psychiatric Association (APA, 1994) indicates that 10% to 25% of women and 5% to 12% of men will suffer from MDD at some point in their lifetime. In addition to individuals meeting full criteria for depressive diagnoses, a high percentage of people are known to have subclinical levels of depression (Broadhead, Blazer, George, & Tse, 1990). In a study by Broadhead et al. (1990), 8% of their sample experienced minor depression with mood disturbance, and 35% experienced minor depression without mood disturbance. Additionally, roughly 50% to 60% of those individuals with a single MDD episode can be expected to experience a second episode (APA, 1994). These numbers are even more daunting when combined with the fact that the functional impairment of depressed patients has been shown to be similar to or more severe than that of eight major medical conditions, such as hypertension, diabetes, angina, arthritis, back problems, lung problems, and gastrointestinal disorders. The only chronic medical condition with levels of impairment similar to those of depression is a current heart condition (Wells, Stewart, et al., 1989). Furthermore, one of the primary areas likely to be affected by depression is work performance (Wells, Golding, & Burnam, 1989).

Studies addressing the economic impact of depression have also increased awareness of the effect of depression on work performance (e.g., Conti & Burton, 1994; Greenberg, Stiglin, Finkelstein, & Berndt, 1993; Stoudemire, Frank, Hedemark, Kamlet, & Blazer, 1986). In 1990, it was estimated that the yearly cost of depression was approximately $43.7 billion. Of this total cost, 55% was due to effects of depression in the workplace. Specifically, $11.7 billion was lost because of reduced productivity from work absenteeism, and $12.1 million was lost because of a reduction in productive work capacity while at work (Greenberg et al., 1993). These estimates were based on those with diagnosable depressive conditions. Broadhead et al. (1990) suggested that those with subclinical levels of depression might be responsible for up to 51% more disability days than those with MDD. Given the prevalence, functional impairment, and cost of depression in the workplace, it is imperative that employers and those who provide services to employees can identify, understand, and treat it effectively.

This chapter will address a comprehensive range of issues related to depression in the workplace. MDD, DD, and subclinical depression will be defined in the context of their diagnostic criteria. The epidemiology of depression, including information relevant to the workplace, will also be explored. Assessment techniques for depression and work performance will subsequently be addressed. To give a more practical understanding of depression in the workplace, a case example of how depression may appear in a work environment will be offered, including a description of functional impairments and how they may be evidenced. More important, the various levels of interaction between depression and work environment will be presented, including an examination of workplace and nonworkplace stressors. Finally, with an understanding of depression and how it affects the workplace, prognosis and course, databased treatments, and relapse prevention will be addressed.

DESCRIPTION OF THE DISORDER

Depression can manifest itself in many ways. The *Diagnostic and Statistical Manual for Mental Disorders, Fourth Edition (DSM-IV)* (APA, 1994) presents several categories of unipolar depression: MDD, DD, adjustment disorder with depressed mood, substance-induced depressive disorder, and depression due to a general medical condition. As mentioned previously, even depression at a subclinical level can cause functional difficulties. Although all of these categories are likely to affect the work environment, the primary focus of this chapter will be MDD. Milder conditions, such as DD and subclinical depression, will be addressed secondarily, as relevant.

Diagnosis

To meet criteria for MDD and DD diagnoses, an individual must evidence a constellation of emotional, physical, behavioral, and cognitive symptoms that meet certain duration and severity criteria. MDD criteria require an individual to display symptoms that demonstrate a significant and distressing change in level of functioning most of the day, nearly every day, for at least a 2-week period of time. The individual must display five of nine symptoms, at least one of which is depressed mood or anhedonia. The other three or four symptoms can include weight or appetite change, insomnia or hypersomnia, psychomotor retardation or agitation, fatigue or loss of energy, feelings of worthlessness or inappropriate guilt, decreased ability to concentrate or make decisions, and recurrent suicidal ideation (See Table 7.1). For DD, the symptoms must be present and represent a noticeable change from previous functioning for more than half the day, more days than not, for a minimum of 2 years, with no more than 2 months free of symptoms during that time. DD involves the primary symptom of depressed mood in addition to two or more of the following symptoms: poor appetite or overeating, insomnia or hypersomnia, low energy or fatigue, low self-esteem, poor concentration or difficulty with decisions, and feelings of hopelessness. For both disorders, the criteria for a manic, mixed, or hypomanic episode must never have been met, nor can

Table 7.1   *DSM-IV* Diagnostic Criteria for Major Depressive Disorder

A. Five (or more) of the following symptoms have been present during the same 2-week period and represent a change from previous functioning. At least one of the five is #1 or #2.

   1. Depressed mood *most of the day nearly every day*

   2. Markedly decreased interest or pleasure *most of the day nearly every day*

   3. Significant increase or decrease in weight *or* appetite *nearly every day*

   4. Insomnia or hypersomnia *nearly every day*

   5. Psychomotor agitation or retardation *observable by others nearly every day*

   6. Fatigue or loss of energy *nearly every day*

   7. Feelings of worthlessness or excessive guilt *nearly every day*

   8. Difficulty concentrating or making decisions *nearly every day*

   9. Recurrent thoughts of death or suicide

B. The symptoms do not meet criteria for a Mixed Episode (significant manic symptoms).

C. The symptoms cause clinically significant distress or impairment in social occupational or other important areas of functioning.

D. The symptoms are not due to a substance or general medical condition.

E. The symptoms are not better accounted for by bereavement.

the disorder be better explained by another *DSM-IV* or physical disorder. Common Axis I disorders that should be ruled out are bipolar disorder, bereavement, posttraumatic stress disorder, and generalized anxiety disorder (APA, 1994). It must also be clear that the symptoms are not due to the direct physiological effects of a substance or a general medical problem. A referral to a physician may also be necessary to rule out any possible medical problems that may precipitate depression, such as thyroid problems, infections, vitamin or mineral deficiencies, or cancer or liver disease (Morrison, 1995).

Effect of Depression in the Workplace

These various constellations of symptoms may have a significant impact on both work absenteeism and work performance. Clinical levels of depression are likely to result in an increased risk of disability days for up to 1 year, and, although less clear, subclinical depression also involves an increased risk (Broadhead et al., 1990). In addition, performance and productivity while at work may be impaired by depressive symptoms (Motowidlo, Packard, & Manning, 1986). Some possible explanations include fatigue or low energy either related directly to depression or as sequelae of depressive sleep disturbance; difficulty concentrating on the task at hand, making decisions, or remembering instructions; lack of interest in tasks; insecurities or negative evaluations of one's own work to the point that it interferes with production; or increased sensitivity to criticism such that feedback is not elicited or clarification is not sought. Whereas the individual impact for any one employer dealing with depression in any one employee may be profound, the collective effects of depression, given its prevalence, are even more sobering.

EPIDEMIOLOGY

Recent studies investigating the epidemiology of depression have estimated that the lifetime prevalence of MDD for men and women combined is approximately 5% to 14%, with 3% to 9% experiencing MDD in any one year (Kaelber, Moul, & Farmer, 1995). Women, however, are nearly twice as likely to experience depression, with lifetime prevalences ranging from 10% to 25% (APA, 1994). Although addressed less often in the literature, subclinical depression also appears to be quite common. In the Epidemiology Catchment Area Study (ECA) (Weissman, Bruce, Leaf, Florio, & Holzer, 1991), a representative sample of more than 20,000 people from the general population was interviewed regarding a variety of mental health conditions, including people's experience of individual depression symptoms for at least a 2-week period of time. The authors found that the lifetime prevalence of symptoms ranged from 5.2% of people having experienced a loss of interest to 29.9% having reported feelings of dysphoria. Other lifetime prevalence rates of common symptoms likely to interfere with work were sleep change (22.9%), fatigue (15.9%), and diminished concentration (13.9%) (Weissman et al., 1991). Given the significant prevalence and impact of depression, it is not surprising that depression is one of the top three reasons why people seek psychotherapy; the other two reasons—anxiety and relational problems—are closely related to depression and may coexist with it (Kelleher, Talcott, Haddock, & Freeman, 1996).

Among the mental health diagnoses, depression has one of the highest rates of comorbidity with other psychological (Kessler et al., 1994) and physical (McCracken & Gatchel, 2000) conditions. According to the National Comorbidity Study, 56% of those individuals identified as having at least one clinical depression diagnosis had two or more mental health disorders (Kessler et al., 1994). Diagnoses

such as anxiety and substance use disorders, which are especially likely to co-occur with depression, involve significant impairment of their own (cf. Wittchen, Carter, Pfister, Montgomery, & Kessler, 2000). When depression is coupled with the disability of these comorbid conditions, overall functional impairment increases significantly (Bakish, 1999; Roy-Byrne et al., 2000), as does occupational disability (Wittchen, Nelson, & Lachner, 1998).

Perhaps the greatest of all potential costs of depression is the risk of suicide. Suicide is the eighth leading cause of death in the United States (APA, 1994; National Institute of Mental Health [NIMH], 1999). It is estimated that more than 30,000 people commit suicide each year, and that approximately 90% of those people were depressed (U.S. Bureau of Health and Human Services, 1991). Additionally, 15% of depressed people will commit suicide (APA, 1994; NIMH, 1999). Attempted suicide is also costly in both dollars and human suffering. For every one completed suicide, there are between 8 and 25 attempted suicides. Depression is one of the strongest risk factors for attempted suicide, along with alcohol abuse, cocaine use, and separation or divorce (NIMH, 1999).

Along with demographic and symptom-related data, a body of epidemiological data exists that addresses the impact of depression on unemployment and workplace disability. According to the ECA study data mentioned above, the 1-year prevalence of MDD is 2.2% among employed people and 3.4% among unemployed people. Similarly, the percentage of individuals with MDD who were unemployed for under 6 months in the past 5 years was 2.0%, whereas the percentage of depressed individuals who were unemployed for 6 months or more was 6.1% (Kaelber et al., 1995). These figures suggest that people with depression comprise a larger proportion of the unemployed population relative to the employed population.

The discrepancy between depressed individuals who maintain employment and those who do not may be explained, in part, by the resultant disability. According to a Web site maintained by the International Labor Organization (ILO, 2000), more than 6 million Americans have a status of "work disabled," and more than 15 million Americans are considered "functionally disabled." Of those considered work disabled, 30% have mental health disabilities; of those considered functionally disabled, more than 64% have mental health disabilities. Broadhead et al. (1990) suggest that many of the disability days accounted for by mental health disabilities are due to depression. During any 90-day period, people with MDD may account for 5.6% of disability days, and subclinical depression with and without depressed mood may account for an additional 8.5% and 16% of disability days, respectively. People with MDD were 4.36 times more likely to have disability than were people who had no symptoms of depression (Broadhead et al., 1990). Conti and Burton (1994) found that, between 1989 and 1992, 3% of the short-term disability days at First Chicago were due to diagnosable depressive disorders. Given the prevalence of subthreshold depression symptoms and their detrimental impact on functional capacity (Broadhead et al., 1990), this number is likely to be an underestimate of the imprint depression leaves on the workplace.

Greater attention to the impact of depression on functional capacity to work has spurred some companies to assess depression in their organizations. Westinghouse, for example, found that 17% of female employees and 9% of male employees met criteria for MDD (ILO, 2000). Similarly, Wells Fargo found rates of clinical depression

to be between 12% and 15% among its employees. In addition, Wells Fargo found that 30% to 35% of its employees were affected negatively by subclinical depression (ILO, 2000). The high prevalence rates of depression, coupled with the substantial disability, work absenteeism, and reduced work performance, point to the need for accurate identification of depression symptoms to facilitate treatment and timely return to full work capacity.

ASSESSMENT

Interviews

There are a number of assessment methods for depression. The most commonly employed method is the clinical interview. A therapist conducting such an interview must be sure to have adequate knowledge about the constellations of symptoms, the duration and severity criteria, and the possible differential diagnoses that may appear similar to depressive disorders such as generalized anxiety disorder, posttraumatic stress disorder, bereavement, or adjustment disorder. In addition to the specific depressive symptoms, it is important that a clinical interview gather information about history, education, time line of depression, family history of depression or bipolar disorder, medical history, substance use, and mental status. Although unstructured clinical interviews are the most common interview format, they tend to have variable reliability.

Semistructured interviews, such as the Structured Clinical Interview for the *DSM-IV*—Clinician's Version (SCID-CV) (First, Spitzer, Gibbon, & Williams, 1997), are less commonly used but may enhance substantially the reliability of the diagnostic determinations (First et al., 1997). Because the SCID-CV is divided into modules

(Mood Episodes, Psychotic Symptoms, Psychotic Disorders, Mood Disorders, Substance Use Disorders, Anxiety and Other Disorders), depressive disorders can be assessed independently or as part of a comprehensive diagnostic interview. Although the entire SCID-CV may take 1½ hours to administer, the Mood Episodes and Disorders sections take as little as 20 minutes. Other structured interviews for MDD include the Diagnostic Interview Schedule (DIS) (Robins, Helzer, Croughan, & Ratcliff, 1981) and the Schedule for Affective Disorders and Schizophrenia (SADS) (Endicott & Spitzer, 1978).

Self-Report Questionnaires

Self-report measurement is another common way to assess depression symptoms. Measures should be practical, relevant, commonly used, reliable, and valid. Some frequently used self-report measures that meet these criteria are the Beck Depression Inventory (BDI) (Beck & Steer, 1993), which focuses on cognitive symptoms; the Hamilton Depression Inventory (HDI) (Reynolds & Kobak, 1995), which focuses on physical symptoms; and the Center for Epidemiological Studies Depression Scale (CESD) (Radloff, 1977), which was designed as a screening tool to identify depressed people in the population. Among those mentioned, the BDI is probably the most commonly used in both clinical and research settings. It measures depression severity with a series of 21 questions congruent with the *DSM-IV* symptoms of depression. Respondents rate each item from 0 to 3 according to the severity of that item for the preceding 2 weeks (e.g., Item 1: 0 = "I do not feel sad"; 1 = "I feel sad much of the time"; 2 = "I am sad all of the time"; 3 = "I am so sad or unhappy that I can't stand it"). The BDI score is the sum

of all the items with total scores ranging from 0 to 63. Scores correspond to depression severity as follows: 0-9 = minimal depression; 10-16 = mild depression; 17-29 = moderate depression; and 30-63 = severe depression (Beck & Steer, 1993). The BDI has sound psychometric properties with internal consistency alpha of .86 in a meta-analysis with nine psychiatric populations (Beck, Steer, & Garbin, 1988).

Both the BDI and the HDI have one item addressing work functioning. The item on the BDI asks clients to pick from the following options about how they have felt in the past 2 weeks: 0 = "I can work about as well as before"; 1 = "It takes an extra effort to get started at doing something"; 2 = "I have to push myself very hard to do anything"; 3 = "I cannot do any work at all" (Beck & Steer, 1993). The HDI asks clients to choose from the following options related to work: 0 = *no difficulty*; 1 = *thoughts and feelings of incapacity, fatigue, or weakness related to activities*; 2 = *loss of interest in activity*; 3 = *decrease in actual time spent/decrease in productivity*; 4 = *stopped working because of present illness* (Hamilton, 1960). Although these single questions provide some information about work functioning, their validity for assessing work-related dysfunction has not been tested.

Few measures have been developed for the purpose of addressing the impact of depression on work performance. One instrument, however, does evaluate work performance as part of the construct of social adjustment (The Social Adjustment Scale—Self Report, or SAS-SR) (Weissman & Bothwell, 1976). The SAS-SR is designed to measure instrumental and expressive role performance in work activities, as well as social and leisure activities, relationships in the extended family, marriage, parental activities, and relationships in the family unit. This measure assesses four major categories of each of these role areas: performance at expected tasks, amount of friction with others, finer aspects of interpersonal relationships, and inner feelings and satisfactions (Weissman, Prousoff, Thompson, Harding, & Myers, 1978). For work, there are functional and affective items. The three functional items are indicators of absenteeism, performance problems, interpersonal problems, poor overall functioning, and unemployment (Mintz, Mintz, Robertson, Liberman, & Glynn, 1996). The affective items are indicators of subjective adequacy, distress, and interest level (Mintz et al., 1996).

The Endicott Work Productivity Scale (EWPS) (Endicott & Nee, 1997) is one of the few self-report measures designed specifically to evaluate the effect of psychological problems on work productivity and efficiency. There are 25 items, each rated on a 5-point scale. A total score of 0 is the best possible score, and a score of 100 is the worst possible score. This total represents the extent to which psychological symptoms, such as depression, are affecting work performance. The EWPS has been shown to have adequate test-retest and internal consistency reliability (interclass correlation coefficient .92 and alpha internal consistency coefficient .93, respectively) (Endicott & Nee, 1997). Although the EWPS can discriminate between depressed and nondepressed subject groups, it is more sensitive to functional differences in patients over time.

In combination, use of these instruments may clarify the clinical picture for therapists or employers. One example of the interaction between depression and the work environment is presented below.

CLINICAL PICTURE

Kelly is a 29-year-old recently divorced mother of a 3-year-old daughter. Her daughter spends the days at day care. She has worked for several years as a bookkeeper at a local law firm. She has always prided herself on working hard and "producing perfectly balanced books on schedule, every time." Although, in the past, she was fond of this fast-paced and fairly stressful job, a recent addition of customer service to her already substantial job responsibilities left Kelly feeling overworked, frustrated, and burned out. She responded to this additional stress by frequently staying up nights at home to catch up. As her job stress increased, her relationships with coworkers deteriorated, and she felt unsupported by her employers. She frequently arrived late, and she took long breaks to nap in her car. She had gotten into verbal fights with customers regarding their bills and was often tardy in submitting the reports for which she was responsible. She frequently broke down in tears at work and sometimes left early after an emotional episode. During this time, she made several critical errors in the finances, costing the firm significant revenue. As a result, she was put on involuntary unpaid leave. Her employers are investigating the possibility of foul play on her part.

Since the time of her leave, she has stayed in bed most of the day. Despite significant financial hardship because of the recent divorce and job layoff, she continues to take her daughter to day care because she feels she does not have the energy to attend to an active child. Currently, she has frequent thoughts of killing herself, but when she considers the possible means, she becomes overwhelmed and cries uncontrollably. She has lost 15 pounds in the past 4 months and has not been dieting. Every day, she feels down and hopeless, constantly attending to her negative aspects. She also finds herself being quite critical of others and pessimistic about the future.

On two occasions, her boss referred her to the Employee Assistance Program (EAP). The first time, she considered it but decided not to go because she feared that her employer might have access to her records. The second time she was referred, her return to work was contingent on her seeking therapy services, so she chose to go for an assessment.

Her initial interview at the EAP included an unstructured clinical interview and a more structured SCID-CV. The clinical interview revealed that Kelly had recently sought medical assistance for her symptoms of fatigue, but no identifiable medical problems were found. Her BDI score was 35, which indicated severe depression. Her score of 40 on the EWPS was in the range of scores often seen in people with depressed mood. She answered "almost always" to items regarding reduced productivity, forgetting to respond to requests, having difficulty concentrating, and slowed work pace. She responded with "often" to questions about arriving late or leaving early, taking longer lunch or coffee breaks, and becoming annoyed with others at work. The case illustration is just one example of how depression may be evidenced in the workplace. Although this case represents a fairly typical presentation of depression in the workplace, it should be noted that depression could present in a variety of ways. Additionally, several factors mentioned in this case illustration could be the possible precipitants to Kelly's episode of depression.

PRECIPITATING CONDITIONS

There are many possible causal explanations for depression. Factors such as personality characteristics (e.g., Akiskal, Hirschfeld, & Yerevanian, 1983); learned helplessness and depressive attributional styles (e.g., Peterson & Seligman, 1984; Seligman, Abramson, Semmel, & von Baeyer, 1979); life stresses, resources, and coping styles (e.g., Billings & Moos, 1984; Monroe, Bellack, Hersen, & Himmelhoch, 1983; Paykel et al., 1969; Swindle, Cronkite, & Moos, 1989); and biological processes (e.g., Thase & Howland, 1995) have all been implicated as possible precipitants for depression. Many workplace factors have also been identified as salient catalysts for depression. Workplace stress, for example, has been shown to have an impact on affective well-being in terms of depression (Cooper & Marshall, 1976; Kandel, Davies, & Raveis, 1985; Motowidlo et al., 1986), physical health (Cooper & Marshall, 1976), and somatic complaints (Kandel et al., 1985; Shirom, Westman, & Melamed, 1999). An important caveat to the ensuing discussion is that the directionality of causal factors is difficult to pinpoint. It is often unclear whether difficulties at work are the result or the cause of depression. Instead, they may be synergistically exacerbating each other (Mintz et al., 1996). Furthermore, individual characteristics may interact with the nonworkplace circumstances and the work environment and lead to even more complications.

Although the reciprocal relationship of person and environment is acknowledged, the stressors and precipitating conditions that contribute to the functional limitations seen in depression will be the focus of the next section. Specifically, the intersection between depression and the work environment will be conceptualized in terms of two categories: workplace stressors and nonworkplace stressors. First, the literature examining workplace stressors that have been shown to be a risk factor for depression will be explored, with attention to the effects on job satisfaction and performance.

Next, stressors other than those in the workplace will be examined, with attention to the individual and social mediating factors of depression.

Workplace Stressors

Workplace stress is a vague construct that has come to mean a number of things. For the purposes of this chapter, it is defined as "characteristics of the job environment which make demands on (tax or exceed) the abilities or resources of people for meeting the demands or which may otherwise threaten attainment of people's needs" (Abramis, 1994, p. 548). Within this definition, several levels of stress in a work environment may increase an employee's risk for mental health problems. In Kasl's (1973) literature review on the effects of work stress on employee job satisfaction and mental health, low job satisfaction was found to be associated with conditions at work, job content, circumstances around relationships at work, circumstances around supervision, circumstances around work organization, and wages and promotions. These same categories of circumstances, with the exception of relationships and the addition of shift work, were found to be associated with mental health. Consistent with the definition of workplace stress offered earlier, these workplace stressors will be divided into two categories: those making physical demands on physical needs and those making psychological demands. Although not all can be covered, the literature related to the unpleasant working conditions, role stress, stresses related to career development and security, and stresses related to relationship and organizational issues at work will be examined. These stressors will be related to depression, and, when possible, each will be examined in terms of its effect on job satisfaction and performance.

Workplace Stressors Causing Physical Demands

The work environment is where most adults spend the majority of their time, so unpleasant working conditions have a potentially significant impact. These unpleasant conditions may create challenges to the maintenance of basic physical needs such as sleep, safety, financial security, and physical health. Conditions that may produce these challenges are inconvenient working schedules (e.g., shift work), difficult physical requirements, pay systems that threaten income stability, or monotony. Each of these is an occupational stressor that may increase physical demands and increase the risk for depression (Cooper & Marshall, 1976).

Shift Work. The effects of shift work on employees have received substantial attention in recent years (e.g., Healy, Minors, & Waterhouse, 1993; Healy & Waterhouse, 1991; Scott, 1994). Generally, shift work is considered a less-than-desirable working condition. It is often marked by complaints of disturbed appetite, sleep, and concentration as well as fatigue and apathy (Healy et al., 1993). Perhaps the most salient of these difficulties associated with shift work, as it relates to depression, is the negative effect on sleep. Studies examining the effects of sleep loss and sustained work have found that work environments that require these conditions cause a significant amount of occupational stress on employees. In an examination of the chronobiological considerations of shift work, Scott (1994) reviewed several studies that found that not only were shift workers chronically, partially sleep deprived, but also the quality of their sleep was disturbed.

There seems to be a reciprocal relationship between problems with sleep due to depression and jobs that require nontraditional sleep patterns. Not only is it likely that changes in sleep patterns related to job requirements will affect one's mood, but it is also likely that difficulties with sleep, when related to a depressive disorder, will have an effect on job performance (Pilcher & Huffcutt, 1996), job satisfaction, and emotional well-being (Healy et al., 1993). Pilcher and Huffcutt (1996) conducted a meta-analysis of primary studies on the effects of sleep deprivation and found that the level of functioning of those who were sleep deprived was only at the ninth percentile of those who were not deprived of sleep. Sleep loss appears to decrease cognitive, perceptual, and attentional performance (Krueger, 1989). This drop in level of functioning could lead to potentially dangerous circumstances. Additionally, the affect on mood appears to be even more pronounced than that on objective performance (Krueger, 1989; Pilcher & Huffcutt, 1996).

The effect of shift work on sleep is an important consideration in the discussion of depression. Sleep disturbance is both a common symptom of depression and a possible precipitant for recurrent episodes of depression (Morin & Ware, 1996). A review by Morin and Ware (1996) suggests that there is an important link between disturbances of sleep and psychopathology. Most psychological problems, especially mood and anxiety disorders, are associated with sleep impairments. Inversely, of patients entering treatment complaining primarily of insomnia, between 35% and 44% were found to have coexisting psychopathology. Length of sleep difficulty also seemed to be related to the associated psychological problems, with acute sleep disturbance being associated with stress and anxiety, and chronic insomnia being associated with depressive symptoms (Morin & Ware, 1996). This evidence suggests that the chronic difficulties in sleep

experienced by workers participating in a night shift schedule might increase the risk for a depressive disorder.

A study of nurses undertaking shift work for the first time showed that they experienced neurovegetative symptoms even when they previously had been healthy. The neurovegetative symptoms, such as changes in sleep, appetite, energy, interest, and concentration, were similar to those seen in depressed patients (Healy et al., 1993). Thus, it may be concluded that shift work, in particular, may have a unique impact on sleep and wake cycles that may increase vulnerability to depression.

Pay Systems. In addition to work conditions involving shift work, a relationship has been found between pay systems and employee emotional distress. Although there have been few studies in this area, most of the studies on pay systems have used somatic complaints and anxiety as measures of emotional distress. Shirom et al. (1999) looked at employees paid based on time worked versus those paid based on performance on measures of depression as well as anxiety and somatic complaints. Employees paid based on performance, specifically when wages were a function of individual job performance or output, had more complaints of depression and somatic problems than did those paid based on time. A possible explanation for this discrepancy is that performance-based pay systems may involve a higher proportion of repetitive work, either because management set up the job that way or because employees organized their work in a repetitive way to increase their wage (Shirom et al., 1999). Consistent with this explanation, type of pay system has been found to partially mediate an employee's experience of subjective job task monotony. In other words, when employee wages are contingent on performance, employees tend to report a higher degree of subjective monotony. In turn, these perceptions that work is monotonous may precipitate feelings of boredom, worthlessness, or hopelessness, which may contribute to depression.

Workplace Stressors
Causing Psychological Demands

Like physical demands, psychological demands that exceed the individual's resources may lead to a reduction in mental health functioning. Psychological conditions associated with work environments include predictability, controllability, understanding, and support (e.g., Caplan & Jones, 1975; Cooper & Marshall, 1976; Kelloway & Barling, 1991). A deficit in any of these psychological areas may increase the risk of depression. Common work-related problems that may overtax an individual's psychological skills include role ambiguity or role conflict, emotional exhaustion or burnout, job stability, and conflicted relationships.

Role Ambiguity and Role Conflict. The extent to which employees are able to understand the parameters of their job roles while balancing job tasks may be associated with depression risk. Role ambiguity, which refers to a lack of clarity about one's role in a working environment, has been associated with increased depressed mood (Caplan & Jones, 1975; Margolis, Kroes, & Quinn, 1974). This lack of clarity may stem from inadequate information about objectives, expectations, or responsibilities (Cooper & Marshall, 1976). For example, although Kelly's primary job responsibility was bookkeeping, the recent addition of customer service duties may have caused her to experience role ambiguity. Role conflict, on the other hand, involves the presence of conflicting demands or multiple tasks that are either not desirable or part of the job specifications (Cooper & Marshall, 1976). Here, Kelly may have experienced role conflict when her customer service responsibilities interfered with her completion of her assigned bookkeeping tasks, causing her to make uncharacteristic errors. Hence, the cumulative effect of adding customer service to Kelly's job duties may have increased her feelings of helplessness, leading to the initial development of depression; the ensuing disciplinary action may have then exacerbated her depression.

Research on role congruence suggests that as role ambiguity and conflict increase, so does depression. In a study examining the relationship of job stressors to job performance, researchers found that depression was significantly correlated with role conflict, along with role ambiguity, job insecurity, and job dissatisfaction (Abramis, 1994). Similarly, the presence of role ambiguity or conflict has also been shown to have a negative impact on occupational performance and satisfaction. Furthermore, a study of nurses found role ambiguity to be related not only to occupational stress, but also to job satisfaction. Occupational stress, in turn, was related to symptoms of depression (Revicki & May, 1989). To compound the potential impact of role ambiguity or conflict, these difficulties are often associated with job burnout (Firth & Britton, 1989). Additional information on stress may be found in Chapters 3 and 4 in this volume.

Job Burnout. Job burnout also appears to be related to depression. Burnout is typically described as emotional exhaustion, depersonalization, and lack of performance accomplishment (Jackson, Schwab, & Schuler, 1986). Each of these components is associated with symptoms closely related to depression, such as low energy; feelings of lack of control and helplessness; lowered motivation to engage in work; and negative attitudes toward the self, work, and others (Glass, McKnight, & Valdimarsdottir, 1993). Burnout has been most evident in people with significant responsibility for other people, such as management, health professionals, or mental health professionals. In a study that examined burnout and its relationship to family relations, child welfare workers with high scores on burnout scales were likely to report high levels of anxiety, depression, irritation, and somatic complaints; low levels of job satisfaction; and lower levels of marital satisfaction (Jayaratne, Chess, & Kunkel, 1986). Similarly, a study of caregivers working with AIDS patients found depression to be among the personal characteristics of the caregivers likely to predict burnout (Bellani & Furlani, 1996). Although some may argue that the premorbid depression may be a significant cause of job burnout, findings in a 2-year longitudinal study of nurses by McKnight and Glass (1995) suggest that burnout actually tended to precede depressive symptoms. Taken together, these findings suggest that work environments that contribute to employees feeling emotionally exhausted; unable to relate to their customers, clients, or patients; or experiencing little sense of personal accomplishment may be increasing depression risk.

Unemployment. In addition to stresses related to roles or burnout at work, the ever-changing labor market can increase the risk of depression. Lack of job security, for example, may tax an individual's psychosocial needs significantly and be related to the development of depression (Cooper & Marshall, 1976).

Although a good body of correlational literature supports a link between depression and unemployment, the directionality

of the relationship is less clear. Some theorists have posed that this is a bidirectional relationship. That is, people with affective disorders are more likely to have problems at work and therefore become unemployed, and those who are unemployed are more likely to develop affective disorders (Weissman et al., 1991). Kelly's depression is a good example of the potential reciprocal relationship between depression and the workplace. The work environment contributed to the development and exacerbation of her depression symptoms; at the same time, her depression affected her work performance negatively, leading to errors, relationship problems, and absences. These problems then led to her being fired, which further exacerbated her depression.

There is evidence to support both sides of this argument. A number of longitudinal studies indicate that unemployment can affect depression symptoms. Vinokur, Price, and Caplan (1996), for example, studied 815 unemployed individuals and their partners or spouses over a period of 6 months to assess the impact of unemployment and economic hardship on relationship satisfaction and depression. Their results suggested a cascading effect with financial strain directly affecting depression symptoms in both partners. This, then, led to a reduction in relationship satisfaction that further increased the depressive symptoms. Similarly, a 2- to 3-year longitudinal study with young people suggested that those who were unemployed over the full 3-year period showed significantly higher levels of depressed mood and negative thinking, lower self-esteem, and a more external locus of control than did those who had obtained employment (Winefield & Tiggemann, 1990). Brown, Beck, Steer, and Grisham (2000) also found that for psychiatric outpatients, unemployment was a significant predictor of subsequent suicide. In addition to this evidence to support a causal relationship between unemployment and depression, a well-documented relationship also exists between reemployment after a period of being unemployed and a reduction in depression symptoms (Hamilton, Hoffman, Broman, & Rauma, 1993; Isaksson, 1990; Winefield & Tiggemann, 1990). In the reverse direction, some researchers have found that depression influences employment status. In a 2-year prospective study of General Motors employees in closing and nonclosing plants, Hamilton et al. (1993) found that preexisting depression negatively affected the future potential for employment. Caplan, Vinokur, Price, and Van Ryn (1989) also found that unemployed individuals who found reemployment demonstrated a lower posttest level of mental health problems, such as depression and anxiety, than did those who did not find reemployment. In summarizing the findings on depression and unemployment, it appears that depression is both a risk and a result of unemployment.

Work Relationships. Relationships with superiors, inferiors, and equals; the structural makeup of the organization; and the experience of being a part of that structure can influence a person's access to certain psychological needs such as control, support, and understanding (Cooper & Marshall, 1976).

Colloquially, people often say, "If I like the people I work with, I can stand any job." Conversely, many people feel that no job is worth tolerating poor work relationships. Thus, it is no surprise that when people are in work situations with unpleasant or oppressive interpersonal relationships, they may be prone to developing depression. Kelly, presented earlier, found that her work relationships deteriorated as she became more depressed. In turn, the reduction in the quality of these relationships also contributed to her job dissatisfaction and depression. Indeed, research on the association between work relationships and job stress points to the negative psychological effects of poor working relationships. One study of stressful work situations for nurses by Motowidlo et al. (1986) found that the most frequently noted stressors involved difficulties with physicians, uncooperative patients, criticism, negligent coworkers, and work overload. The subjective stress, anxiety, and fear of negative evaluation, as well as the frequency and intensity of stressors such as these interpersonal events, were then found to correlate significantly with depression scores. Similar to other potential precipitating factors, depression has also been identified as a possible causal factor in poor work relationships. In another study of nurses, for example, depression negatively influenced performance at work and led the nurses to react to stress in a more hostile interpersonal manner (Motowidlo et al., 1986).

Although work relationships that are generally negative may increase the risk of depression, some research suggests that certain types of negative relationships may make employees particularly vulnerable to depression. Coworker relationships, for example, may be particularly important to depression risk. Frone (2000) found that conflict with coworkers is more detrimental to psychological health than is conflict with supervisors. Furthermore, in a study of 288 African American social workers, undermining coworker relationships were found to contribute uniquely to depression vulnerability (Gant et al., 1993). On the flip side, when employees are faced with stressful working conditions, positive relationships with coworkers may actually provide a protective factor against depression (Revicki, Whitley, & Gallery, 1993). On an even grander level, individuals' relationships with their organizations may be related to depression. The extent to which employees understand their organizations and feel understood may be pivotal in mood and job satisfaction. In a study of Norwegian shift workers at a petroleum refinery, one of the most problematic elements for the workers surveyed was how the organizational structure affected them (Vaernes et al., 1988). Specifically, relationships with superiors and lack of communication and cooperation within the organization stood out as being significantly correlated with depression and anxiety. Similarly, organizational climate has been shown to be related to job satisfaction (Revicki & May, 1989), which, in turn, may contribute to depression.

In summary, workers tend to be negatively affected by conditions that interfere with their basic needs, such as confusion or conflict about job roles, job insecurity, and relationships with the organization as well as others at work. These factors—individually or in combination—may increase depression risk.

Nonworkplace Stressors

Although workplace stressors can be important precipitants to depression, depression that affects the work environment may also be caused by factors external to the workplace, such as personal characteristics or nonworkplace stressors. A review of all the non-work-related precipitating factors of depression is beyond the scope of this chapter; however, broad categories of common depression precipitants will be discussed. At the most general level, precipitants of depression may be categorized as either intrinsic or extrinsic to the individual. Intrinsic characteristics are those characteristics that are a function of an individual's personality or style. Extrinsic factors, on the other hand, are those circumstances that arise not out of personal characteristics, but out of an individual's environment or situation. Intrinsic factors commonly related to depression include Type A behavior, attributional and coping styles, and gender. Extrinsic characteristics that increase risk for depression include family/marital problems, life events, and loss.

Intrinsic Factors. Type A behavior has often been examined as it relates to work-related variables. As a general concept, Type A behavior is marked by the exhibition of competitive, achievement-oriented, urgent, restless, and impatient behavior similar to Kelly's perfectionism and impatience with customers and coworkers in the case presented above. This type of behavior has been shown to be the beginning of a causal chain that leads to increases in subjective workload, followed by workload dissatisfaction, and finally depression (Brief, Rude, & Rabinowitz, 1983). Research suggests that nurses with Type A behavior patterns are more likely to feel stressed and to have more feelings of anxiety and depression regardless of the intensity or frequency of stressful events (Motowidlo et al., 1986). Additionally, a workplace study by Bluen, Barling, and Burns (1990) found that the Type A dimensions of achievement striving and impatience-irritability predicted depression differentially. Achievement striving was shown to be related to sales performance and job satisfaction, but not to depression. The impatience-irritability component was significantly related to depression, negatively related to job satisfaction, and unrelated to sales performance. Although Type A behavior patterns traditionally are considered to be personality characteristics, cognitive theorists have posed that what differentiates Type A personalities from other personality types is their beliefs about themselves, others, and the world (cf. Martin, Kuiper, & Westra, 1989).

Research on depression has often focused on the cognitive characteristics that cause or perpetuate depression (Seligman et al., 1979). Recently, this research was extended to suggest ways by which cognitive characteristics and an employee's style of coping may influence mood, ability to deal with stress at work, and work performance (Ostell & Divers, 1987; Parkes, 1990). Namely, people who are depressed are more likely to attribute bad events to internal, stable, and global factors, whereas good events are attributed to external and unstable factors (Peterson & Seligman, 1984; Seligman et al., 1979). So, for Kelly, the fact that her daughter is doing well (good event) may be attributed to good day care (external) and luck (unstable), whereas the fact that she has had difficulty at work (bad event) may be attributed to internal, stable, global factors such as innate incompetence or ineptitude. The presence of this depressive cognitive style tends to be the most detrimental to mood when the bad outcome is either anticipated or actually occurs and global, stable, and internal factors are attributed (Seligman et al., 1979). Employment-related studies of depression have supported this connection between attributional style and depression. One study of unemployed managers showed that individuals who have an attributional style in which the cause of negative events is attributed to their characters (e.g., stupidity, incompetence, unworthiness) versus their actions (e.g., making a mistake, being tired, being too busy) were more likely to have poorer mental health (Ostell & Divers, 1987). This attributional style and the ensuing depression may then reciprocally affect the perceptions of functioning as well as actual functioning (Parkes, 1990).

A close cousin to the concept of attributional style is an individual's response style to depressed mood. Although most individuals experience feelings of sadness and even depression at times, the way an individual responds to this depressed mood may influence whether he or she actually develops a full-blown depressive disorder. Specifically, a good body of literature suggests that people who respond to increases in depressed mood by ruminating are particularly vulnerable to developing more severe depression (Nolen-Hoeksema, Parker, & Larson, 1994) of longer duration (Nolen-Hoeksema, Morrow, & Fredrickson, 1993). In contrast, those who respond to depressed mood by distraction are less apt to develop a full major depressive diagnosis (Nolen-Hoeksema et al., 1993). According to Nolen-Hoeksema and her colleagues (1993), a ruminative response style is characterized by thoughts and behaviors, which lend attention to the symptoms and consequences associated with depressed mood. A distractive response style involves thoughts and behaviors that focus attention away from the depressed mood and toward more neutral or pleasant events (Nolen-Hoeksema et al., 1993). Similarly, coping responses that involve emotional discharge instead of problem solving or attempts to manage mood are associated with greater levels of depression (Billings & Moos, 1984). Additionally, Billings and Moos (1984) found that depressed people's way of coping and level of social resources may be less effective at buffering the effects of life stress. Research addressing coping and stress in working environments has linked the research on coping styles to occupational and emotional well-being. A study by Parkes (1990), for example, found individual styles of coping to be relevant in minimizing the strain of work stressors.

Although different, on many levels, from the intrinsic precipitants of depression, gender is also an important risk factor for depression. In a review of the research on sex difference in unipolar depression, Nolen-Hoeksema (1987) examined the empirical research behind several biological and psychosocial explanations for the greater prevalence of depression in women. One explanation suggests that the higher number of depressed women is actually an artifact of income or reporting bias. Additional explanations have suggested that women are at an increased risk for depression because of different levels of hormones or biochemicals for mood, differences in psychosexual development, differences in sex roles, or greater exposure to circumstances that perpetuate learned helplessness (Nolen-Hoeksema, 1987). However, none of these explanations is well supported by research. Although it is obvious that more women than men are depressed, it is not clear why. The increase of women in the workplace has led to an awareness of the demands involved in the interaction between work and individual or social variables. Much like for men, job distress has been found to be a predictor of depression, anxiety, and physical symptoms for women (O'Neill & Zeichner, 1985). Additionally, working women may be faced with additional role stressors that may increase risk of depression. A large body of research suggests that working women in dual-earner marriages assume a greater responsibility for household and child-rearing tasks than their husbands, even when the hours on the job are similar (Biernat & Wortman, 1991). Likewise, women are particularly likely to experience role strain in response to juggling home and work responsibilities (Loerch, Russell, & Rush, 1989), which has been associated with an increased risk of depression for women (Galambos & Walters, 1992). Working single mothers and lower-income women may be particularly taxed by the multiple responsibilities

of work, parenting, and home (Jackson, 1993), putting them at an even greater risk of depression than women who are married with greater income potentials (Wallace, 1999). Although being female in an occupational setting may synergistically increase the depression risk, some research suggests that stresses related to marital and household roles have a more significant impact on women's mental health than do work-related stressors. Specifically, depression has been shown to be significantly affected, especially when the role stress is related to household roles (Kandel et al., 1985).

Extrinsic Factors. Although it is nearly impossible to clearly separate depression causes that originate within the individual from environmental causes, some elements of precipitants appear to exist outside the individual. For example, a preponderance of stressful life events appears to increase depression risk. Specific stressors such as family/marital problems, financial problems, and loss appear to further predispose individuals to depression.

The frequency of life events, in general, is likely to have a negative effect on emotional well-being for all employees. In an important study by Paykel et al. (1969), the effects of life events on depression were explored. First, in comparison to nondepressed people, depressed people reported three times as many stressful life events out of a list of 33 events (e.g., move, pregnancy, court appearance). These findings were corroborated later by Billings, Cronkite, and Moos (1983), who found that depressed people are also more likely to report more severe life strains than are nondepressed controls. When Paykel and colleagues (1969) attempted to group these life events according to themes, it appeared that depressed individuals were more likely than nondepressed individuals to report events that were undesirable or involved significant loss. More specifically, Paykel et al. (1969) found that several particular types of events were reported significantly more often by the depressed sample than by the control group: increased arguments with spouse, marital separation, starting a new type of work, death of immediate family member, departure of family member from home, serious personal physical illness, and change in work conditions. Thus, it appears that the occurrence of stressful life events at home and at work may be associated with depression. Of the events most commonly reported by depressed individuals, more than half of them involve family events.

Although many variables can affect depression risk in working adults, perhaps the most influential factor is relationships with family members. In a longitudinal study of 267 employed parents on work-family conflict, family stress that led to work stress was related to higher levels of depression 4 years later (Frone, Russell, & Cooper, 1997). Conversely, although work stress that led to family conflict was more likely to be associated with heavy alcohol use, it was less likely to have a consistent effect on health or depression (Frone et al., 1997).

More specifically, stress due to either parenting or the marital relationship may be an important factor in depression. Windle and Levent (1997), for example, found that the combination of difficulties associated with parental social roles and occupational stress was associated with higher levels of depression for both the men and women of dual-earning couples. Similarly, marital distress frequently has been identified as a risk factor for depression (Basco, Prager, Pita, Tamir, & Stephens, 1992; Paykel et al., 1969). Marital distress may also increase the risk of relapse in people who initially respond to depression treatment (Hooley & Teasdale, 1989). Likewise, separation or

divorce may increase the risk of future depression (Aseltine & Kessler, 1993). Specific maritally distressing events such as a spouse's infidelity or threats to dissolve the marriage may further increase the likelihood of developing depression. In a recent study by Cano and O'Leary (2000), depression rates for 25 women who had experienced recent humiliating marital events were compared with those of 25 similarly maritally distressed women without recent humiliating events. The results suggested that the women who had experienced humiliating marital events were six times more likely to be depressed than the control group, even when depressive history was controlled for. Both parental and spousal stressors such as these may be important concomitants to depressed mood. Additional stressors, such as financial hardship, may further exacerbate an individual's load of risk factors.

A couple dealing with financial difficulties may be at an increased risk of depression in at least one of the members; however, the determinants of the depression are likely to be different for men than for women (Ross & Huber, 1985). According to Ross and Huber (1985), men tend to become more depressed as a direct effect of perceived economic hardship and their own lack of earning, whereas wives' depression tended to be a result of level of education, age, and the presence of young children. This result may be evidence of psychological effects of perceived failure at traditional male and female social roles (Ross & Huber, 1985). Also, coping with financial difficulty as a function of job loss has been found to be related to depressive symptoms in both the person looking for another job and his or her partner. In addition to depression as a result of financial strain, depression in turn created a higher likelihood of negative interactions and conflicts within the marriage, which also perpetuated depression (Vinokur et al., 1996).

Many of these life events and stressors are interrelated and may tend to have an additive effect. Perhaps the most difficult life events are those that involve loss. As has been discussed indirectly early in the chapter and recently above, loss is a significant component to the manifestation of depression. The loss of a job, for example, has been linked to depressive symptoms not only in the former employee, but in his or her partner as well (Vinokur et al., 1996). Losses external to the work environment may also be important in perpetuating depressive symptoms. In a study by Finlay-Jones and Brown (1981) on stressful events and the onset of depression and anxiety, severe loss in the past 3 months was significantly related to the onset of depression. Compared to those individuals with anxiety, those with depression were more likely to report a significant loss. Fateful loss events that are considered events outside of the person's control have also been reported 2.5 times more frequently among depressed individuals as compared to nondepressed controls (Shrout et al., 1989). On the flip side, positive events that involve hope are associated with recovery from depression (Brown, 1993). The case of Kelly presented earlier includes many of the possible depression precipitants, such as financial difficulties, recent loss of a spouse, and job loss.

Both workplace stressors and non-workplace precipitants of depression affect an employee's well-being and ability to function effectively in the work environment. This overview has demonstrated the various levels of stressors impinging on the employee's well-being and gives some hint as to how to deal with these issues. There is also evidence that some of these factors mentioned above affect the course and prognosis of depressive disorders. These issues will be addressed in the next section.

COURSE AND PROGNOSIS

Depression is a serious condition that is often chronic or recurrent with its course, sometimes beginning before the symptoms are actually evident. First-degree relatives of those suffering from MDD are 1½ to 3 times more likely to develop MDD, and are more likely to have DD, than are those relatives of nondepressed individuals (APA, 1994). A standard age of onset has not been found in the literature, but it is usually in the mid-20s (APA, 1994). After onset of a first major depressive episode, about 50% to 60% of those people will have a second episode. People who have a second episode then have a 70% chance of having a third episode, and there is a 90% chance that those having a third will go on to have a fourth. Studies have provided evidence that 1 year after the diagnosis of MDD, 40% of people still meet full criteria, 20% meet criteria for MDD in partial remission, and 40% no longer meet criteria for a mood disorder (APA, 1994). Although milder in severity, DD typically follows a more chronic course often beginning in childhood, adolescence, or early adulthood. Among these variants of depression, DD has been shown to have the poorest prognosis (Wells, Burnam, Rogers, Hays, & Camp, 1992). This prognosis is further exacerbated by a superimposition of MDD on the DD diagnosis (Wells et al., 1992).

Although each successive episode of depression increases the risk of a future episode, the severity and length of the current episode, as well as the amplitude and frequency of future episodes, may be diminished with effective treatment. In a study of working individuals who sought depression treatment of any kind, between 41% and 55% experienced full symptom remission (Mintz, Mintz, Arruda, & Hwang, 1992; Simon et al., 2000). An additional 47%

demonstrated symptom improvement without full remission (Simon et al., 2000). It is encouraging to note that as symptoms remitted, level of work functioning was also likely to improve (Simon et al., 2000). In fact, those whose symptoms remitted were three times more likely to regain work capacity than were those who continued to experience symptoms (Mintz et al., 1992). More important, however, the amelioration of symptoms may precede the increase in work capacity. Mintz and colleagues (1992) suggest that the improvement of work capacity may be 4 to 6 weeks behind the symptom improvement. Although employers may be discouraged by this seemingly slow return to full work functioning, it is important to note that at least one study suggested that the cost of depression treatment was fully offset by the savings in lost workdays due to depression (Zhang, Rost, Fortney, & Smith, 1999).

Despite the potential positive impact of depression treatment, only about one in three people who suffer from depression seek out treatment (Dew, Bromet, Schulberg, Parkinson, & Curtis, 1991). Of those who do initiate treatment, they wait an average of 12 weeks before seeking professional help (Benazzi, 1998). This failure to self-refer, coupled with a delay in seeking care, may reduce the probability of a quick recovery. Kupfer, Frank, and Perel (1989) found, for example, that those treated early for a second episode of depression experienced episodes 4 to 5 months shorter than did those who were not treated early.

Together, these findings highlight the importance of recognizing and referring employees for treatment. Information on depression and its effect on employees and the workplace may help raise the awareness of depressive disorders and lead to quicker intervention. Additionally, ongoing self-screenings may aid in the identification of depressed employees. These measures may address issues of job satisfaction, confidence, enjoyment, and depressive symptoms (Mintz et al., 1996). Collaboration with the company Employee Assistance Program (EAP) may also facilitate these trainings and referrals. In order for any employer-facilitated screening and referral program to be effective, however, the employees must have confidence that their information will be kept confidential and that the admission of emotional concerns will not have detrimental effects on current working conditions or future opportunities. One way that employers may aid in referring clients to services while allowing them a maximum of privacy is for the employer to give self-screenings simultaneously to a group or unit of employees. The employees would be given guidelines for completing, scoring, and interpreting the questionnaires. Employees would be instructed about scores that suggest that treatment is indicated and be encouraged to self-refer to services. With this screening method, employees would not need to share these personal issues with their employers.

In sum, it is imperative that individuals suffering from depression be confidentially identified, encouraged, and supported in seeking an effective intervention to reduce current symptoms and potential future episodes so that they may improve their well-being and return to full work functioning.

RECOMMENDED DATA-BASED TREATMENTS

To maximize the chances that afflicted employees will benefit from treatment, it is important that they participate in empirically supported interventions. A number of both psychotherapeutic and pharmacotherapeutic interventions have ample data to support their effectiveness in treating depression. Within each category, there are a number of treatment options. Although the effectiveness of individual treatment options varies somewhat across individuals, group studies suggest that initial recovery rates, according to the BDI, range from 25% to 69% for antidepressant medication and 50% to 88% for psychotherapy (Craighead, Craighead, & Ilardi, 1998). Even though these statistics suggest that a significant minority of individuals are not helped by treatment, these rates are significantly better than the meager 12% to 20% of individuals who remit without treatment over a 12- to 20-week period (typical length of psychotherapy or medication trial). Furthermore, a meta-analysis of cognitive psychotherapies by Dobson (1989) suggests that treated individuals are less depressed than 98% of those who do not receive treatment at therapy posttest.

Although immediate outcomes for medication and psychotherapy have been largely comparable, each has unique advantages and disadvantages. Medications tend to lead to a quicker symptom reduction (Watkins, Leber, Imber, & Collins, 1986), a faster return to full work capacity (Mintz et al., 1992), and more effective treatment response with severe depression (Elkin et al., 1989). On the other hand, psychotherapy may be almost twice as durable as medication in the long term (Evans et al., 1992; Fava, Rafanelli, Grandi, Conti, & Belluardo, 1998; Hollon, Shelton, & Loosen, 1991; Paykel et al., 1999; Shea et al., 1992) and does not lead to some of the annoying, and sometimes serious, side effects of medication (Antonuccio, Danton, & DeNelsky, 1995).

Although combined treatments may appear to be the best of both worlds for resolving depression, there is little evidence to support the notion that combination treatments outperform monotherapies (Antonuccio et al., 1995; Evans et al., 1992), at least for mild, moderate, and nonchronic depression (Thase et al., 1997). More severe and/or chronic depression may respond more favorably to combined therapies, however (Keller et al., 2000; Thase et al., 1997). In a recent comparison of a version of cognitive-behavioral therapy only, nefazodone only, or combined interventions for subjects with chronic depression, approximately half of the subjects in the monotherapy conditions recovered, whereas 85% of those in the combined condition remitted (Keller et al., 2000).

Among the psychotherapy interventions, those that have the most consistent empirical support include cognitive-behavioral therapy, interpersonal therapy, and behavioral marital therapy. For medications, several classes of antidepressants have empirical support for resolving depression; these include tricyclics, selective serotonin re-uptake inhibitors (SSRIs), and monoaminoxidase inhibitors (MAOIs). Each of these interventions and considerations for employers will be discussed below.

Empirically Supported Psychotherapies

Cognitive-Behavioral Therapy. Cognitive-behavioral therapy (CBT) is the most frequently researched and supported psychotherapy for depression (Craighead et al., 1998). It typically involves 12 to 20 weeks of directive, structured, action-oriented group or individual therapy focused on helping clients identify and modify their thinking (cognitions) and behavior patterns that are causing and maintaining their depression. The initial cognitive goal is to increase clients' awareness of self-defeating thoughts about themselves, others, and the world through regular homework assignments in which they are instructed to write down what they are thinking in response to difficult daily events. Individuals who are depressed tend to make characteristic thinking errors, such as overgeneralization (e.g., "Because I got a bad work report, it means I am a failure as a human being!"); minimization of the positive (e.g., "Even though I made a successful sale this morning, that was just good luck!"); and inflexible expectations (e.g., "I must be liked by all my managers and coworkers at all times!"). The second cognitive goal is to help clients develop more realistic alternatives to their extreme beliefs (e.g., "I don't like getting a bad work report, but I can tolerate it and learn from it"; "I did a number of things that led to a successful sale this morning, and I can apply similar strategies in the future"; and "I would prefer to have everyone like me, but I can tolerate having people mad at me"). The behavioral component of CBT involves teaching clients to identify and set reasonable goals to accomplish "antidepressant" activities that are pleasurable and lead to a feeling of accomplishment. In combination, these interventions are designed to reduce depression through increasing realistic thinking and positive activity level in a collaborative therapeutic relationship. In a meta-analysis comparing CBT with control groups and other psychotherapies, CBT was found to outperform no treatment and alternative therapies (Dobson, 1989).

Interpersonal Therapy. A rival, empirically supported, short-term therapeutic depression treatment is interpersonal therapy (IPT) (Klerman, Weissman, Rounsaville, & Chevron, 1995). Although IPT shares some characteristics with CBT (i.e., 12 to 20 sessions, collaborative, structured, action-oriented), it focuses more on types of relationship difficulties that may be responsible for causing or maintaining the depression than an individual's thoughts or behaviors. In this approach, a particular area of relationship difficulty is targeted (i.e., grief, role dispute, role transition, or interpersonal skills deficit) in the first few sessions. The remaining sessions focus on raising the clients' awareness about the role of the relationship difficulties in their depression and developing skills for improving these relationships. According to a large-scale, multisite study comparing CBT, IPT, imipramine, and placebo medication, IPT performed as well as CBT for the mildly and moderately depressed subjects (Elkin et al., 1989). For those with more severe depression, IPT and imipramine showed a slight advantage over CBT. Although this large-scale study has been widely criticized for inconsistencies in the quality of therapy across sites (cf. Jacobson & Hollon, 1996), these findings provide tentative support for the efficacy of IPT for treating depression, especially with more severely depressed clients. Although IPT addresses how depressed individuals may change their behavior with others, it does not directly target the behavior of important others in clients' environments.

Behavioral Marital Therapy. Behavioral marital therapy (BMT) (Jacobson & Margolin, 1979), another empirically supported intervention for depression, has widened its focus from the depressed individual to the marital relationship. Because depression and marital distress often coexist and exacerbate one another (Whisman & Bruce, 1999), an intervention that addresses both simultaneously may increase the chances of recovery and maintenance for depressed individuals. The purpose of BMT is to increase positive relationship behaviors and improve communication skills between spouses in a 20-session intervention. The initial goals of BMT are thorough assessment followed by enlisting a "collaborative set" in which spouses agree to change their own behaviors to improve the relationship, without waiting for the other to change. Once both spouses have committed to the collaborative set, the next goals are for both members to increase their partner's marital satisfaction by increasing their positive behaviors toward their partner. Then, the couple learns how to increase their communication skills (e.g., using "I" statements rather than "you" statements) and apply problem-solving skills to their relationship problems. Recent research by Jacobson and his colleagues (Jacobson, Dobson, Fruzzetti, Schmaling, & Salusky, 1991) comparing BMT, individual CBT, and combined BMT/individual CBT for depressed married women found that for maritally distressed subjects, BMT was as effective as CBT in relieving depression and more effective at relieving marital distress. For happily married couples, CBT was the most effective at relieving depression, whereas the combined condition had the most positive impact on marital satisfaction. These findings suggest that individuals with comorbid depression and marital distress may benefit from interventions targeted at the couple rather than the depressed individual.

Considerations for Employers. One of the primary advantages of psychotherapeutic treatments is that there are no physiological side effects. One of the main disadvantages is that psychotherapies may be relatively time-consuming, especially during the early phases. Even though it is unlikely that employers will observe any negative consequences of employees participating in psychotherapy, they may need to allow extra time for employees to attend one or two weekly appointments of 1 to 2 hours in duration. In the therapies listed above, treatment usually lasts less than 6 months, and the frequency of sessions typically does not exceed one appointment per week after the second month of therapy. In addition to the time spent in the therapy sessions, most empirically supported psychotherapies operate under the assumption that the skills learned in therapy would best generalize to the individual's daily life through practicing the skills outside of the session. Often, this involves daily or weekly homework assignments, such as tracking daily mood, thoughts, or reactions. Because depressed individuals are sometimes asked to keep track of thoughts or moods, either while they are actually occurring or soon after, employees occasionally may need to make brief notations on tracking sheets while at work. Typically, these interruptions are brief and are unlikely to affect work performance.

Additionally, behavioral therapies often emphasize having the client set goals for engaging in both mastery and pleasurable activities. Clients are taught to set goals that are measurable, observable, attainable, and meaningful. This mirrors the goal-setting practices at the heart of one of the best supported and most widely used employee motivational techniques (cf. Latham & Locke, 1991). Thus, a happy result for an employer who has an employee involved in such therapy is that the employee may be better skilled at this fundamental motivational technique within the workplace. On the other hand, therapists may attempt to imbue the client with assertiveness skills, particularly if the depression is related to work overload, ambiguity, or powerlessness. Employers and coworkers may see the previously depressed individual begin to refuse extra assignments or responsibility and, perhaps, be less willing to take the blame when things go wrong.

Empirically Supported Psychotropic Medications

As either an adjunct to psychotherapy or as a treatment in its own right, psychotropic medication is one of the most common treatments for depression (Antonuccio et al., 1995), and it has a significant body of research supporting its efficacy (Nemeroff & Schatzberg, 1998). Although a comprehensive review of antidepressant medication is beyond the scope of this chapter, the basic groups of antidepressants will be introduced, and the factors that may affect an individual's work performance will be addressed.

Antidepressant medications may be divided into three broad categories: tricyclics, SSRIs, and MAOIs. The tricyclics are the oldest of the antidepressants and are often referred to by brand names such as Elavil, Tofranil, Norpramin, and Pamelor. Relative to other antidepressants, they are less expensive and may be preferred for individuals with low appetite, weight loss, and insomnia. The primary downside to the tricyclics is their significant side effects, such as drowsiness, dry mouth, constipation, and blurred vision, especially when first beginning the medication. The SSRIs, in contrast, are relatively expensive but have few side effects. These are commonly known by names such as Prozac, Zoloft, Paxil, and Luvox. Although the MAOIs may be effective when other antidepressants have failed, they are prescribed relatively infrequently because of the potential for dangerous, and even fatal, hypertensive crises due to interactions with other drugs or certain foods (e.g., red wine, chocolate, aged cheeses). With careful monitoring of diet and drug use, MAOIs may be the treatment of choice for depression characterized by overeating, oversleeping, and/or anxiety.

Considerations for Employers. Therapeutic responses as well as side effects vary widely across individuals, antidepressants, and dosages. Thus, an employer should not assume that the employee will have a particular reaction to any of the medications listed. Instead, communication between the employee, employer, and physician (with the appropriate written release of information) will allow all parties to make decisions about appropriate accommodations when antidepressant medications are involved. Safety, of course, is a priority concern. Any time employees' symptoms or medication side effects may jeopardize the safety of themselves or others, duties should be changed to accommodate current functioning. Examples of accommodations may include a change in schedule or duties for employees who experience significant drowsiness; allowing employees with dry mouth to have a water bottle while on shift; helping employees who are experiencing blurred vision to revise duties so they are not spending long hours looking at a computer screen or reading small print; or helping employees plan meal times so that medication can be taken with food (if so directed). With adequate time and effective treatment, it is likely that the depression will improve and the side effects will diminish. Thus, the workplace accommodations typically will be temporary.

Maintenance of Gains/Relapse Prevention

The treatments mentioned above are designed to influence depression directly through professional interventions. Preventive measures should also be taken by organizations and individuals that not only improve the work environment and employee well-being, but may also prevent depression relapse. Sauter, Murphy, and Hurrell (1990) and the National Institute for Occupational Safety and Health (NIOSH) offered some broad categories of methods that can prevent work-related psychological disorders: improve work conditions and the general psychological well-being of employees; improve the monitoring of depression on a national, state, and organizational level; and enhance dissemination of information, education, and training about mental health.

One of the most important ways that the workplace can counteract the development, exacerbation, and/or relapse of depression is through improving work conditions that might be likely to precipitate depression. Examples of such improvements would involve ensuring that an employee's demands and capacities are balanced and ensuring that his or her work schedule is appropriate given the employee's demands outside of work. Work roles should be well-defined, and employees should be informed of job security and job opportunity issues. Consistent with research suggesting that social support has a negative relationship with anxiety and depression (Holahan & Moos, 1981), there should be social support and opportunities for social interaction at work. The content of the job should be such that employees have the opportunity to use their developed skills, and they should be given some input on decisions and actions that concern them. Regular individual or group meetings with employees in which feedback is invited regarding each of these issues may facilitate the employer's ability to identify and correct such problems.

In terms of monitoring depression, some large studies in recent years have suggested that depression is a very prevalent mental health disorder (Kaelber et al., 1995). Additionally, studies specific to the impact of depression on the workplace have shown it to be a significant factor (Broadhead et al., 1990; Conti & Burton, 1994; Kessler et al., 1999). Continuations of these types of studies are important to keep national and state agencies, as well as organizations, aware of the prevalence and effect of depression on the workplace. In addition to larger scale surveillance, it is also important that the psychological well-being of employees is monitored. For example, depression should be questioned as a part of all routine health examinations. Additionally, risk factors for depression or other mental health issues should be included in the assessment of workplace safety and industrial hygiene (Sauter et al., 1990).

There are several ways to improve awareness of depression, not only in the general public, but also in the work environment. The NIMH Depression Awareness, Recognition, and Treatment Program was intended to increase public awareness, change public attitudes, and motivate changes in the treatment of depression (Regier et al., 1988). A study of this program indicated that the goals of this program are being met, and that these aims are important for the improvement of awareness, detection, and treatment of depression (O'Hara, Gorman, & Wright, 1996). NIOSH suggests that workers need to be educated about mental health disorders. Specifically, they need an understanding of the symptoms and indicators of specific disorders, such as depression. This consciousness raising may be included as an adjunct to agendas that are already in place, such as during meetings or in newsletters. With the increase in awareness and understanding of mental health problems such as depression, it is important that some procedures are in place to improve the psychological functioning among employees. NIOSH suggests that services for mental health care and occupational health be integrated. This may entail both workers and management planning the services, having the services be ongoing, having formal policies, maintaining confidentiality, offering specialized training, including mental health coverage in benefit packages, and making mental health programs available to all employees (Sauter et al., 1990).

SUMMARY

Employment is central to the experience of adulthood for the majority of Americans. Problems in getting or maintaining a job, as well as the actual qualities of the job, have important implications for mood. Likewise, salient events and experiences external to the workplace may increase the risk for mood-related disorders. Whether depression is a result of workplace stressors, factors unrelated to the job, or a combination of both, it will almost certainly affect work functioning negatively. This decrease in functioning leads to a multitude of complex costs for the employer as well as a reduction in self-esteem and a further worsening of depression for the individual. Early detection is vital, and effective treatment may significantly reduce the severity, duration, and recurrence of depression. Similarly, improvements in workplace conditions, identification of depressive symptoms, and availability of effective treatments may prevent additional hardship to the organization and the individual.

REFERENCES

Abramis, D. J. (1994). Relationship of job stressors to job performance: Linear or an inverted-u. *Psychological Reports, 75,* 547-558.

Akiskal, H. S., Hirschfeld, R. M., & Yerevanian, B. I. (1983). The relationship of personality to affective disorders. *Archives of General Psychiatry, 40*(7), 801-810.

American Psychiatric Association. (1994). *The diagnostic and statistical manual for mental disorders* (4th ed.). Washington, DC: Author.

Antonuccio, D. O., Danton, W. G., & DeNelsky, G. Y. (1995). Psychotherapy versus medication for depression: Challenging the conventional wisdom with data. *Professional Psychology: Research and Practice, 26,* 574-585.

Aseltine, R. H., & Kessler, R. C. (1993). Marital disruption and depression in a community sample. *Journal of Health and Social Behavior, 34,* 237-251.

Bakish, D. (1999). The patient with comorbid depression and anxiety: The unmet need. *Journal of Clinical Psychiatry, 60*(Suppl. 6), S20-S24.

Basco, M. R., Prager, K. J., Pita, J. M., Tamir, L. M., & Stephens, J. J. (1992). Communication and intimacy in the marriages of depressed patients. *Journal of Family Psychology, 6,* 184-194.

Beck, A. T., & Steer, R. A. (1993). *Beck Depression Inventory: Manual.* San Antonio, TX: The Psychological Corporation.

Beck, A. T., Steer, R. A., & Garbin, M. (1988). Psychometric properties of the Beck Depression Inventory: Twenty-five years of evaluation. *Clinical Psychology Review, 8,* 77-100.

Bellani, M. L., & Furlani, F. (1996). Burnout and related factors among HIV/AIDS health care workers. *AIDS Care, 8*(2), 207-221.

Benazzi, F. (1998). Bipolar II depressed outpatients seek treatment more quickly than do unipolar outpatients. *Canadian Journal of Psychiatry, 43*(6), 647.

Biernat, M., & Wortman, C. B. (1991). Sharing of home responsibilities between professionally employed women and their husbands. *Journal of Personality & Social Psychology, 60*(6), 844-860.

Billings, A. G., Cronkite, R. C., & Moos, R. H. (1983). Social-environmental factors in unipolar depression: Comparisons of depressed patients and non-depressed controls. *Journal of Abnormal Psychology, 92*(2), 119-133.

Billings, A. G., & Moos, R. H. (1984). Coping, stress, and social resources among adults with unipolar depression. *Journal of Personality and Social Psychology, 46*(4), 877-891.

Bluen, S. D., Barling, J., & Burns, W. (1990). Predicting sales performance, job satisfaction, and depression by using the achievement strivings and impatience-irritability dimensions of type A behavior. *Journal of Applied Psychology, 75*(2), 212-216.

Brief, A. P., Rude, D. E., & Rabinowitz, S. (1983). The impact of type A behavior pattern on subjective workload and depression. *Journal of Occupational Behavior, 4*, 157-164.

Broadhead, W. E., Blazer, D. G., George, L. K., & Tse, D. K. (1990). Depression, disability days, and days lost from work in a prospective epidemiologic survey. *Journal of the American Medical Association, 264*(19), 2524-2528.

Brown, G. K., Beck, A. T., Steer, R. A., & Grisham, J. R. (2000). Risk factors for suicide in psychiatric outpatients: A 20-year prospective study. *Journal of Consulting & Clinical Psychology, 68*(3), 371-377.

Brown, G. W. (1993). Life events and affective disorder: Replications and limitations. *Psychosomatic Medicine, 55*(3), 248-259.

Cano, A., & O'Leary, K. D. (2000). Infidelity and separations precipitate major depressive episodes and symptoms of non-specific depression and anxiety. *Journal of Consulting and Clinical Psychology, 68*, 774-781.

Caplan, R. D., & Jones, K. W. (1975). Effects of work load, role ambiguity, and type A personality on anxiety, depression, and heart rate. *Journal of Applied Psychology, 60*(6), 713-719.

Caplan, R. D., Vinokur, A. D., Price, R. H., & van Ryn, M. (1989). Job seeking, reemployment, and mental health: A randomized field experiment coping with job loss. *Journal of Applied Psychology, 74*, 759-769.

Conti, D. J., & Burton, W. N. (1994). The economic impact of depression in a workplace. *Journal of Occupational and Environmental Medicine, 36*(9), 983-988.

Cooper, C. L., & Marshall, J. (1976). Occupational sources of stress: A review of the literature relating to coronary heart disease and mental ill health. *Journal of Occupational Psychology, 49*, 11-28.

Craighead, W. E., Craighead, L. W., & Ilardi, S. S. (1998). Psychosocial treatments for major depressive disorder. In P. E. Nathan & J. M. Gorman (Eds.), *A guide to treatments that work*. New York: Guilford.

Dew, M. A., Bromet, E. J., Schulberg, H. C., Parkinson, D. K., & Curtis, E. C. (1991). Factors affecting service utilization for depression in a white collar population. *Social Psychiatry & Psychiatric Epidemiology, 26*(5), 230-237.

Dobson, K. S. (1989). A meta-analysis of the efficacy of cognitive therapy for depression. *Journal of Consulting & Clinical Psychology, 57*(3), 414-419.

Elkin, I., Shea, T., Watkins, J. T., Imber, S. D., Sotsky, S. M., Collins, J. F., Glass, D. R., Pilkonis, P. A., Leber, W. R., Docherty, J. P., Fiester, S. J., & Parloff, M. B. (1989). National Institute of Mental Health Treatment of Depression Collaborative Research Program. *Archives of General Psychiatry, 46*, 971-982.

Endicott, J., & Nee, J. (1997). Endicott Work Productivity Scale (EWPS): A new measure to assess treatment effects. *Psychopharmacology Bulletin, 33*(1), 13-16.

Endicott, J., & Spitzer, R. (1978). A diagnostic interview: The Schedule for Affective Disorders and Schizophrenia. *Archives of General Psychiatry, 35*, 98-103.

Evans, M. D., Hollon, S. D., DeRubeis, R. J., Piasecki, J. M., Grove, W. M., Garvey, M. J., & Tuason, V. B. (1992). Differential relapse following cognitive therapy and pharmacotherapy for depression. *Archives of General Psychiatry, 49,* 802-808.

Fava, G. A., Rafanelli, C., Grandi, S., Conti, S., & Belluardo, P. (1998). Prevention of recurrent depression with cognitive behavioral therapy. *Archives of General Psychiatry, 55,* 816-820.

Finlay-Jones, R., & Brown, G. W. (1981). Types of stressful life event and the onset of anxiety and depressive disorders. *Psychological Medicine, 11,* 803-815.

First, M. B., Spitzer, R. L., Gibbon, M., & Williams, J. B. W. (1997). *User's guide for the Structured Clinical Interview for* DSM-IV *Axis I Disorders—Clinician Version (SCID—CV).* Washington, DC: American Psychiatric Press.

Firth, H., & Britton, P. (1989). "Burnout," absence and turnover amongst British nursing staff. *Journal of Occupational Psychology, 62,* 55-59.

Frone, M. R. (2000). Interpersonal conflict at work and psychological outcomes: Testing a model among young workers. *Journal of Occupational Health Psychology, 5*(2), 246-255.

Frone, M. R., Russell, M., & Cooper, M. L. (1997). Relation of work-family conflict to health outcomes: A four-year longitudinal study of employed parents. *Journal of Occupational & Organizational Psychology, 70*(4), 325-335.

Galambos, N. L., & Walters, B. J. (1992). Work hours, schedule inflexibility, and stress in dual-earner spouses. *Canadian Journal of Behavioural Science, 24*(3), 290-302.

Gant, L. M., Nagda, B. A., Brabson, H. V., Jayaratne, S., Chess, W. A., & Singh, A. (1993). Effects of social support and undermining on African American workers' perceptions of coworker and supervisor relationships and psychological well-being. *Social Work, 38*(2), 158-164.

Glass, D. C., McKnight, J. D., & Valdimarsdottir, H. (1993). Depression, burnout, and perceptions of control in hospital nurses. *Journal of Consulting and Clinical Psychology, 68,* 147-155.

Greenberg, P. E., Stiglin, L. E., Finkelstein, S. N., & Berndt, E. R. (1993). The economic burden of depression in 1990. *Journal of Clinical Psychiatry, 54*(11), 405-418.

Hamilton, M. (1960). A rating scale for depression. *Journal of Neurology, Neurosurgery & Psychiatry, 23,* 56-61.

Hamilton, V. L., Hoffman, W. S., Broman, C. L., & Rauma, D. (1993). Unemployment, distress, and coping: A panel study of autoworkers. *Journal of Personality & Social Psychology, 65*(2), 234-247.

Healy, D., Minors, D. S., & Waterhouse, J. M. (1993). Shiftwork, helplessness and depression. *Journal of Affective Disorders, 29*(1), 17-25.

Healy, D., & Waterhouse, J. M. (1991). Reactive rhythms and endogenous clocks. *Psychological Medicine, 21*(3), 557-564.

Holahan, C. J., & Moos, R. H. (1981). Social support and psychological distress: A longitudinal analysis. *Journal of Abnormal Psychology, 49,* 365-370.

Hollon, S. D., Shelton, R. C., & Loosen, P. T. (1991). Cognitive therapy and pharmacotherapy for depression. *Journal of Consulting and Clinical Psychology, 59,* 88-99.

Hooley, J. M., & Teasdale, J. D. (1989). Predictors of relapse in unipolar depressives: Expressed emotion, marital distress, and perceived criticism. *Journal of Abnormal Psychology, 98*(3), 229-235.

International Labour Organization. (2000). *Mental health in the workplace* [On-line]. Retrieved from http://www.ilo.org/public/english/employment/skills/targets/disability/papers/execsumcontents.htm

Isaksson, K. (1990). A longitudinal study of the relationship between frequent job change and psychological well being. *Journal of Occupational Psychology, 63,* 297-308.

Jackson, A. P. (1993). Black, single, working mothers in poverty: Preferences for employment, well-being, and perceptions of preschool-age children. *Social Work, 38*(1), 26-34.

Jackson, S. E., Schwab, R. L., & Schuler, R. S. (1986). Toward an understanding of the burnout phenomena. *Journal of Applied Psychology, 71,* 630-640.

Jacobson, N. S., Dobson, K., Fruzzetti, A. E., Schmaling, K. B., & Salusky, S. (1991). Marital therapy as a treatment for depression. *Journal of Consulting & Clinical Psychology, 59*(4), 547-557.

Jacobson, N. S., & Hollon, S. D. (1996). Cognitive-behavior therapy versus pharmacotherapy: Now that the jury's returned its verdict, it's time to present the rest of the evidence. *Journal of Consulting and Clinical Psychology, 64,* 74-80.

Jacobson, N. S., & Margolin, G. (1979). *Marital therapy: Strategies based on social learning and behavior exchange principles.* New York: Brunner Mazel.

Jayaratne, S., Chess, W. A., & Kunkel, D. A. (1986). Burnout: Its impact on child welfare workers and their spouses. *Social Work, 31*(1), 53-59.

Kaelber, C. T., Moul, D. E., & Farmer, M. E. (1995). Epidemiology of depression. In E. E. Beckman & W. R. Leber (Eds.), *Handbook of depression* (2nd ed.). New York: Guilford.

Kandel, D. B., Davies, M., & Raveis, V. H. (1985). The stressfulness of daily social roles for women: Marital, occupational, and household roles. *Journal of Health and Social Behavior, 26,* 64-78.

Kasl, S. V. (1973). Mental health and the work environment: An examination of the evidence. *Journal of Occupational Medicine, 15*(6), 509-518.

Kelleher, W. J., Talcott, G. W., Haddock, C. K., & Freeman, R. K. (1996). Military psychology in the age of managed care: The Wilford Hall model. *Applied & Preventive Psychology, 5*(2), 101-110.

Keller, M. B., McCullough, J. P., Klien, D. N., Arnow, B., Dunner, D. L., Gelenberg, A. J., Markowitz, J. C., Nemeroff, C. B., Russell, J. M., Thase, M. E., Trivedi, M. H., & Zajecka, J. (2000). A comparison of nefazodone, the cognitive behavioral-analysis system of psychotherapy, and their combination for the treatment of chronic depression. *New England Journal of Medicine, 342*(20), 1462-1470.

Kelloway, E. K., & Barling, J. (1991). Job characteristics, role stress and mental health. *Journal of Occupational Psychology, 64,* 291-304.

Kessler, R., Barber, C., Birnbaum, H. G., Frank, R. G., Greenberg, P. E., Rose, R. M., Simon, G. E., & Wang, P. (1999). Depression in the workplace: Effects on short-term disability. *Health Affairs, 18*(5), 163-171.

Kessler, R. C., McGonagle, K. A., Zhao, S., Nelson, C. B., Hughes, M., Shleman, S., Wittchen, H. U., & Kendler, K. S. (1994). Lifetime and 12-month prevalence of *DSM-III-R* psychiatric disorder in the United States. *Archives of General Psychiatry, 51,* 8-19.

Klerman, G. L., Weissman, M. M., Rounsaville, B., & Chevron, E. S. (1995). Interpersonal psychotherapy for depression. *Journal of Psychotherapy Practice and Research, 4*(4), 342-351.

Krueger, G. P. (1989). Sustained work, fatigue, sleep loss and performance: A review of the issues. *Work & Stress, 3*(2), 129-141.

Kupfer, D. J., Frank, E., & Perel, J. M. (1989). The advantage of early treatment intervention in recurrent depression. *Archives of General Psychiatry, 46,* 771-775.

Latham, G. P., & Locke, E. A. (1991). Self-regulation through goal setting. *Organizational Behavior & Human Decision Processes, 50*(2), 212-247.

Loerch, K. J., Russell, J. E., & Rush, M. C. (1989). The relationships among family domain variables and work-family conflict for men and women. *Journal of Vocational Behavior, 35*(3), 288-308.

Margolis, B. L., Kroes, W. H., & Quinn, R. P. (1974). Job stress: An unlisted occupational hazard. *Journal of Occupational Medicine, 16*(10), 654-661.

Martin, R. A., Kuiper, N. A., & Westra, H. A. (1989). Cognitive and affective components of the Type A behavior pattern: Preliminary evidence for a self-worth contingency model. *Personality and Individual Differences, 10*(7), 771-784.

McCracken, L. M., & Gatchel, R. J. (2000). The magnification of psychopathology sequelae associated with multiple chronic medical conditions. *Journal of Applied Biobehavioral Research, 5*(1), 92-99.

McKnight, J. D., & Glass, D. C. (1995). Perceptions of control, burnout, and depressive symptomatology: A replication and extension. *Journal of Consulting & Clinical Psychology, 63*(3), 490-494.

Mintz, J., Mintz, L. I., Arruda, M. J., & Hwang, S. S. (1992). Treatments of depression and the functional capacity to work. *Archives of General Psychiatry, 49,* 761-768.

Mintz, J., Mintz, L. I., Robertson, M. J., Liberman, R. P., & Glynn, S. M. (1996). Treatment of depression and the restoration of work capacity. In *The Hatherleigh guide to managing depression: Vol. 3. The Hatherleigh guides series* (1st ed., pp. 199-223). New York: Hatherleigh Press.

Monroe, S. M., Bellack, A. S., Hersen, M., & Himmelhoch, J. M. (1983). Life events, symptom course, and treatment outcome in unipolar depressed women. *Journal of Consulting and Clinical Psychology, 51*(4), 604-615.

Morin, C. M., & Ware, J. C. (1996). Sleep and psychopathology. *Applied & Preventive Psychology, 5,* 211-224.

Morrison, J. (1995). DSM-IV *made easy: The clinician's guide to diagnosis.* New York: Guilford.

Motowidlo, S. J., Packard, J. S., & Manning, M. R. (1986). Occupational stress: Its causes and consequences for job performance. *Journal of Applied Psychology, 71*(4), 618-629.

National Institute of Mental Health. (1999). Suicide facts [On-line]. Retrieved from http://www.nimh.mih.gov/research/suifact.htm.

Nemeroff, C. B., & Schatzberg, A. F. (1998). Pharmacological treatment of unipolar depression. In P. E. Nathan & J. M. Gorman (Eds.), *A guide to treatments that work.* New York: Guilford.

Nolen-Hoeksema, S. (1987). Sex differences in unipolar depression: Evidence and theory. *Psychological Bulletin, 101,* 259-282.

Nolen-Hoeksema, S., Morrow, J., & Fredrickson, B. L. (1993). Response styles and the duration of episodes of depressed mood. *Journal of Abnormal Psychology, 102,* 20-28.

Nolen-Hoeksema, S., Parker, L. E., & Larson, J. (1994). Ruminative coping with depressed mood following loss. *Journal of Personality & Social Psychology, 67*(1), 92-104.

O'Hara, M. W., Gorman, L. L., & Wright, E. J. (1996). Descriptions and evaluation of the Iowa Depression Awareness, Recognition, and Treatment Program. *American Journal of Psychiatry, 153*(5), 645-649.

O'Neill, C. P., & Zeichner, A. (1985). Working women: A study of relationships between stress, coping and health. *Journal of Psychosomatic Obstetrics & Gynecology, 4*(2), 105-116.

Ostell, A., & Divers, P. (1987). Attributional style, unemployment and mental health. *Journal of Occupational Psychology, 60,* 333-337.

Parkes, K. R. (1990). Coping, negative affectivity, and the work environment: Additive and interactive predictors of mental health. *Journal of Applied Psychology, 75*(4), 399-409.

Paykel, E. S., Myers, J. K., Dienelt, M. N., Klerman, G. L., Lindenthal, J. J., & Pepper, M. P. (1969). Life events and depression: A controlled study. *Archives of General Psychiatry, 21,* 753-760.

Paykel, E. S., Scott, J., Teasdale, J. C., Johnson, A. L., Garland, A., Moore, R., Jenaway, A., Cornwall, P. L., Hayhurst, H., Abbott, R., & Pope, M. (1999). Prevention of relapse in residual depression by cognitive therapy. *Archives of General Psychiatry, 56,* 829-835.

Peterson, C., & Seligman, M. E. (1984). Causal explanations as a risk factor for depression: Theory and evidence. *Psychological Review, 91*(3), 347-374.

Pilcher, J. J., & Huffcutt, A. J. (1996). Effects of sleep deprivation on performance: A meta-analysis. *Sleep, 19*(4), 318-326.

Radloff, L. S. (1977). The CES-D Scale: A self-report depression scale for research in the general population. *Applied Psychological Measurement, 1,* 385-401.

Regier, D. A., Hirschfelk, R. M. A., Goodwin, F. K., Burke, J. D., Lazar, J. B., & Judd, L. L. (1988). The NIMH Depression Awareness, Recognition, and Treatment Program: Structure, aims, and scientific basis. *American Journal of Psychiatry, 145,* 1351-1357.

Revicki, D. A., & May, H. J. (1989). Organizational characteristics, occupational stress, and mental health in nurses. *Behavioral Medicine, 15*(1), 30-36.

Revicki, D. A., Whitley, T. W., & Gallery, M. E. (1993). Organizational characteristics, perceived work stress, and depression in emergency medicine residents. *Behavioral Medicine, 19*(2), 74-81.

Reynolds, W. M., & Kobak, K. A. (1995). Reliability and validity of the Hamilton Depression Inventory: A paper-and-pencil version of the Hamilton Depression Rating Scale Clinical Interview. *Psychological Assessment, 7*(4), 472-483.

Robins, L. N., Helzer, J. E., Croughan, J., & Ratcliff, K. S. (1981). National Institute of Mental Health Diagnostic Interview Schedule: Its history, characteristics and validity. *Archives of General Psychiatry, 38,* 381-389.

Ross, C. E., & Huber, J. (1985). Hardship and depression. *Journal of Health and Social Behavior, 26,* 312-327.

Roy-Byrne, P. P., Stang, P., Wittchen, H., Ustun, B., Walters, E. E., & Kessler, R. C. (2000). Lifetime panic-depression comorbidity in the National Comorbidity Survey: Association with symptoms, impairment, course and help-seeking. *British Journal of Psychiatry, 176,* 229-235.

Sauter, S. L., Murphy, L. R., & Hurrell, J. J. (1990). Prevention of work-related psychological disorders: A national strategy proposed by the National Institute for Occupational Safety and Health (NIOSH). *American Psychologist, 45*(10), 1146-1158.

Scott, A. J. (1994). Chronobiological considerations in shiftworker sleep and performance and shiftwork scheduling. *Human Performance, 7*(3), 207-233.

Seligman, M. E., Abramson, L. Y., Semmel, A., & von Baeyer, C. (1979). Depressive attributional style. *Journal of Abnormal Psychology, 88,* 242-247.

Shea, M. T., Elkin, I., Imber, S. D., Sotsky, S. M., Watkins, J. T., Collins, J. F., Pilkonis, P. A., Beckham, E., Glass, D. R., Dolan, R. T., & Parloff, M. B. (1992). Course of depressive symptoms over follow-up: Findings from the National Institute of Mental Health Treatment of Depression Collaborative Research Program. *Archives of General Psychiatry, 49,* 782-787.

Shirom, A., Westman, M., & Melamed, S. (1999). The effects of pay systems on blue-collar employees' emotional distress: The mediating effects of objective and subjective work monotony. *Human Relations, 52*(8), 1077-1097.

Shrout, P. E., Link, B. G., Dohrenwend, B. P., Skodol, A. E., Stueve, A., & Mirotznik, J. (1989). Characterizing life events as risk factors for depression: The role of fateful loss events. *Journal of Abnormal Psychology, 98*(4), 460-467.

Simon, G. E., Revicki, D., Heiligenstein, J., Grothaus, L., VonDroff, M., Katon, W. J., & Hylan, T. R. (2000). Recovery from depression, work productivity, and health care costs among primary care patients. *General Hospital Psychiatry, 22,* 153-162.

Stoudemire, A., Frank, R., Hedemark, N., Kamlet, M., & Blazer, D. (1986). The economic burden of depression. *General Hospital and Psychiatry, 8,* 387-394.

Swindle, R. W., Jr., Cronkite, R. C., & Moos, R. H. (1989). Life stressors, social resources, coping, and the 4-year course of unipolar depression. *Journal of Abnormal Psychology, 98*(4), 468-477.

Thase, M. E., Greenhouse, J. B., Frank, E., Reynolds, C. F., III, Pilkonis, P. A., Hurley, K., Grochocinski, B., & Kupfer, D. J. (1997). Treatment of major depression with psychotherapy or psychotherapy-pharmacotherapy combinations. *Archives of General Psychiatry, 54*(11), 1009-1015.

Thase, M. E., & Howland, R. H. (1995). Biological processes in depression: An updated review and integration In E. E. Beckman & W. R. Leber (Eds.), *Handbook of depression* (2nd ed.). New York: Guilford.

U.S. Bureau of Health and Human Services, National Center for Health Statistics. (1991). Death rates for 72 selected causes by 5 year age groups, race, and sex: U.S. 1988 (Vol. 2, Part A, "Mortality," Tables 1-9, p. 51). *Vital statistics of the United States.* Washington, DC: GPO.

Vaernes, R. J., Knardahl, S., Romsing, J., Aakvaag, A., Tonder, O., Walther, B., & Ursin, H. (1988). Relations between environment problems, psychology and health among shift-workers in the Norwegian process industry. *Work & Stress, 2*(1), 7-15.

Vinokur, A. D., Price, R. H., & Caplan, R. D. (1996). Hard times and hurtful partners: How financial strain affects depression and relationship satisfaction of unemployed persons and their spouses. *Journal of Personality and Social Psychology, 71,* 166-179.

Wallace, J. E. (1999). Work-to-nonwork conflict among married male and female lawyers. *Journal of Organizational Behavior, 20*(6), 797-816.

Watkins, J. T., Leber, W. R., Imber, S. D., & Collins, J. F. (1986, May). *NIMH Treatment of Depression Collaborative Research Program: Temporal course of symptomatic change.* Paper presented at the annual meeting of the American Psychiatric Association, Washington, DC.

Weissman, M. M., & Bothwell, S. (1976). Assessment of social adjustment by patient self-report. *Archives of General Psychiatry, 33,* 1111-1115.

Weissman, M. M., Bruce, M. L., Leaf, P. H., Florio, L. P., & Holzer, C. (1991). Affective disorders. In L. N. Robins & D. A. Regier (Eds.), *Psychiatric disorders in America: The Epidemiologic Catchment Area Study* (pp. 53-80). New York: Free Press.

Weissman, M. M., Prousoff, B. A., Thompson, W. D., Harding, P. S., & Myers, J. K. (1978). Social adjustment by self-report in a community sample and in psychiatric outpatients. *Journal of Nervous and Mental Disease, 166*(5), 317-326.

Wells, K. B., Burnam, M. A., Rogers, W., Hays, R., & Camp, P. (1992). The course of depression in adult outpatients: Results from the medical outcome study. *Archives of General Psychiatry, 49,* 788-794.

Wells, K. B., Golding, J. M., & Burnam, M. A. (1989). Chronic medical conditions in a sample of the general population with anxiety, affective, and substance use disorders. *American Journal of Psychiatry, 146*(11), 1440-1446.

Wells, K. B., Stewart, A., Hays, R. D., Burnam, M. A., Rogers, W., Daniels, M., Berry, S., Greenfield, S., & Ware, J. (1989). The functioning and well-being of depressed patients: Results of the medical outcomes study. *Journal of the American Medical Association, 262*(7), 914-919.

Whisman, M. A., & Bruce, M. L. (1999). Marital dissatisfaction and incidence of major depressive episode in a community sample. *Journal of Abnormal Psychology, 108*(4), 674-678.

Windle, M., & Levent, D. (1997). Parental and occupational stress as predictors of depressive symptoms among dual income couples: A multilevel modeling approach. *Journal of Marriage & the Family, 59*(3), 625-634.

Winefield, A. H., & Tiggemann, M. (1990). Employment status and psychological well-being: A longitudinal study. *Journal of Applied Psychology, 75,* 455-459.

Wittchen, H., Carter, R. M., Pfister, H., Montgomery, S. A., & Kessler, R. C. (2000). Disabilities and quality of life in pure and comorbid generalized anxiety disorder and major depression in a national survey. *International Clinical Psychopharmacology, 15*(6), 319-328.

Wittchen, H., Nelson, C. B., & Lachner, G. (1998). Prevalence of mental disorders and psychosocial impairments in adolescents and young adults. *Psychological Medicine, 28*(1), 109-126.

Zhang, M., Rost, K. M., Fortney, J. C., & Smith, G. R. (1999). A community study of depression treatment and employment earnings. *Psychiatric Services, 50,* 1209-1213.

CHAPTER 8

Bipolar Disorders

EDWARD S. FRIEDMAN
ANDREA FAGIOLINI
MICHAEL E. THASE

Bipolar disorder, known historically as manic depression, is a debilitating mental disorder on one hand, and on the other hand, it is a condition that encompasses traits we associate with the finest human qualities—creativity and genius. Such is the concept of manic-depressive illness as described by the pioneer European psychiatrist Emil Kraepelin (1921). Kraepelin brought an order to the process of symptom categorization that had been a predominant concern of European psychiatry at the end of the 19th century. In his nosology, which continues to be applied in modern descriptive psychiatry, Kraepelin divided the major psychiatric illnesses into two major categories: manic-depressive illness and dementia praecox (schizophrenia). Kraepelin's careful observation of the course, outcome, and pattern of symptoms of patients with depressive and manic moods led him to describe the illness as a continuum or spectrum of symptoms of fluctuations in moods, energy patterns, and behaviors. Kraepelin based his categories of mental disorders upon similarities in characteristic symptoms, family history, and patterns of recurrence. The Kraepelinian model relied on a concept of cycling—between depressive periods and euthymic periods, between manic periods and euthymic periods, and the various combinations of these states—in its definition of manic-depressive illness.

However defined, bipolar disorders have a large impact on the individual and society. Wyatt and Henter (1995) estimated the societal costs of bipolar disorder to the United States in the early 1990s at $45 billion annually. One sixth, or $7 billion, goes to treatment costs; $38 billion is estimated for the loss of productivity in the workplace. As well, the costs of care in an insured population for bipolar patients are equal to that of other serious chronic medical illnesses, such as diabetes, and are almost 2½ times the health care costs of control individuals (Simon & Unützer, 1999) (see Figure 8.1).

CLINICAL DESCRIPTION AND DIAGNOSIS

Bipolar disorders are diagnostically categorized in the *Diagnostic and Statistical*

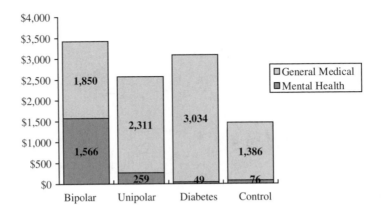

Figure 8.1   Comparison of Health Care Costs in an HMO for Patients With BPD, Unipolar Depression, Diabetes, and General Medical Outpatients

Manual of Mental Disorders, Fourth Edition (DSM-IV) (American Psychiatric Association [APA], 1994) by the severity, duration, and quality of the patient's presenting manic symptoms. Those patients who have experienced a manic episode are described diagnostically as Bipolar I Disorder. Patients who experience milder symptoms of mania and/or symptoms of briefer duration (hypomania) are described as having Bipolar II Disorder. The pattern of mild alterations in elevated and depressed mood episodes is referred to as Cyclothymia Disorder. A final category, Bipolar Disorder Not Otherwise Specified, defines patients with some symptoms of mania that are of insufficient intensity or duration to qualify for one of the other diagnostic categories, but for whom there appears to be a strong likelihood they are suffering from a bipolar illness. Although these distinctions are based upon the manic symptomatology, patients with bipolar disorders experience more depressions than manic episodes (Angst, 1978; Goodwin & Jamison, 1990). In fact, 90% of patients who reported experiencing manic episodes also suffer from depressive episodes (Sachs & Thase, 2000). The criteria for defining depressive episodes are the same regardless of whether the patient carries a diagnosis of unipolar or bipolar depression. (Major depression is discussed at length in Chapter 7; therefore, we will only briefly state the criteria for a depressive episode here). To fit the category of a depressive episode, the patient must display five depressive symptoms, including one or both of either a dysphoric (sad) or an anhedonic (unable to experience pleasure) mood. The remaining symptoms of depression are sleep disturbance; appetite or weight disturbance; diminished concentration; decreased energy; feelings of worthlessness, guilt, or low self-esteem; psychomotor agitation or retardation; and suicidal ideation.

Manic Episode

A Manic Episode is defined in *DSM-IV* (APA, 1994) by several criteria. First, it is defined by a distinct period of time in which a person experiences an abnormally and persistently elevated, expansive, or irritable mood. The period of abnormal mood must last 1 week (or less if the person is hospitalized) (Criterion A). The elevated and/or expansive mood must be accompanied by at least three of the following seven cardinal symptoms of mania: inflated self-esteem or grandiosity, decreased need for sleep, pressure of speech, flight of ideas, distractibility, increased involvement in goal-directed activities or psychomotor agitation, and excessive involvement in pleasurable activities with a high potential for painful consequences. Criterion B states that if the mood is irritable rather than elevated or expansive, at least four of the seven symptoms must be present. Criterion C requires that the symptoms must not also satisfy the criteria for a major depressive episode for a 1-week period; that is a week-long period in which the person experiences simultaneously a combination of manic and depressive symptoms. Such an episode is termed a *mixed episode*. Criterion D states that the disturbance must be sufficiently severe to cause (a) marked impairment in social or occupational functioning; (b) hospitalization to prevent harm to self or others; or (c) presence during the episode of symptoms of psychosis, such as paranoid ideation, hallucinations, ideas of reference, or bizarre or delusional beliefs. Criterion E specifies that the episode is not due to direct physiological effects attributable to another cause. Some variables that may cause manic-like symptoms include drugs of abuse; medications; other somatic treatments for depression, such as electroconvulsive therapy or light therapy; toxin exposure; or the direct physiological effects of a general medical condition (neurological disorders, brain tumors, or endocrine disorders). This is an extremely important differential diagnosis, because ignorance of an underlying medical illness will lead to not treating the cause of the illness and the attribution of the symptoms to a behavioral disorder.

The elevated mood of a manic episode is described as euphoric, unusually good, too cheerful, or high. The person experiencing a manic episode may feel wonderful, creative, and productive, but such moods are often recognized as excessive and atypical by people who know the individual well. The expansive quality of a manic mood is characterized by unceasing and indiscriminate enthusiasm for interpersonal, sexual, or occupational interaction. The person may be intrusive in social situations, indiscriminate in conversation and actions, and unmindful of the negative consequences of pleasurable activities. Although an elated mood is prototypical of a manic episode, an irritable mood is as common a presentation. Often, the individual experiences alterations between irritability and euphoria, especially during interpersonal conflict or experiences that elicit frustration of their efforts.

A common characteristic of mania is the presence of inflated self-esteem. Manic individuals may be uncritically self-confident; markedly grandiose; and, at the extreme, suffering from delusional beliefs. Grandiose delusions are common and frequently have hyperreligious, pop cultural, or political themes (e.g., the wholehearted belief that the person is Jesus, Mick Jagger, or the President of the United States). Frequently, such patients will undertake an activity for which they are not truly prepared, make a life change, or suffer substantial financial losses as a consequence of their poor judgment and lack of insight. For example, decision making in social, occupational, and financial areas is often impaired and goes unrecognized by the individual in the midst of a manic episode, leading to significant consequences.

Sleep is most often disturbed during a manic episode. Typically, patients experience a decreased need for sleep while maintaining excessive energy and drive. They may suffer from difficulty in falling asleep, midcycle sleep awakenings, and/or early-morning awakening that characterizes disruptions of the normal sleep cycle. In the most severe manifestation of manic insomnia, the person may not sleep for several days on end and not experience any subjective sense of tiredness and fatigue. Such sleeplessness frequently is associated with a quality of psychomotor agitation, restlessness, or hyperactivity that is also characteristic of manic episodes.

Manic episodes are also characterized by changes in the individual's usual speech rate and tone of speech. Manic speech is characteristically pressured, loud, and rapid, and manic individuals may be difficult to interrupt. This pressure to speak leads people to talk excessively; for example, they may talk on the telephone for hours, accruing bills they can ill afford to pay. They dominate conversations, making it difficult to communicate. Often, their thought processes are loose and their thoughts are tangential or circumstantial, leading to long, winding narratives that are difficult to comprehend or to follow. When extremely elated, the manic individual may behave in a dramatic and theatrical manner, and his or her speech may become sing-song, rhyming, or dominated by sound associations (i.e., clanging). When the individual is elated and euphoric, manic speech is often jocular and full of puns, associations, and idiosyncratic meanings. When manic individuals are experiencing a more irritable than euphoric mood, their speech may be characterized by shouting; a loud, argumentative style; and an angry, hostile tone.

Associated with the pressured speech characteristic of mania is a rapid thought process that is described as "racing." People describe the sensation of multiple thoughts competing for their diminished concentration and limited attention, which produces a rapid succession of jumbled and incomplete thoughts. Another characteristic of the manic thought process is described as flights of ideas. This describes the increased rate of thought process where one idea leads to an association that leads to another line of thought. The individual is preoccupied with thoughts that lack cohesion or logic to an interlocutor.

The manic individual often has difficulty with attention and focus. There is a deficiency in the mind's ability to screen out irrelevant stimuli that is referred to as *distractibility*. Along with this tendency to shift focus rapidly and frequently is an increase in goal-directed activities. These may include increased sexual drive, increased sexual fantasies, and indiscriminate sexual behaviors. During the manic episode, individuals may initiate new business ventures in an unprepared and unrealistic manner, mindless of the consequences of their rash and often outlandish decisions. They may be more sociable than is typical of their normal personality, but they also may be domineering, demanding, and socially inappropriate. The effusion of thoughts and flights of ideas lead to marathon telephone or Internet conversations with friends, old and new acquaintances, and even strangers. They may be imbued with a motor restlessness or agitation that manifests in hyperactivity.

When the elation of mood, grandiose and expansive thoughts, unbridled optimism, poor judgment, and desire for pleasurable activities happen simultaneously, the person may experience negative, unanticipated, and long-lasting consequences of his or her activities. To qualify for the diagnosis of mania, there must be marked impairment in function, or the individual must require hospitalization as protection from the negative consequences of his or her actions. By definition, the presence of psychotic symptoms—such as auditory or visual hallucinations, delusional beliefs, and/or paranoid ideation—during a manic episode constitutes marked impairment and thereby fulfills the severity criteria necessary to make a diagnosis of mania. As we shall see, other diagnoses associated with the bipolar disorders are made if the severity criteria for a manic episode are not met. Most frequently, manic episodes begin with a sudden onset and a rapid escalation of symptoms over days to weeks. Often, a manic episode is preceded by a biopsychosocial stressor, such as a loss, an interpersonal conflict, or even work shift changes. Manic episodes generally last from a few weeks to several months. They are typically briefer than major depressive episodes and end more abruptly. Some people have typical patterns of cycling between depressive and manic moods, and others may have intervening episodes of euthymic mood.

Goodwin and Jamison (1990) have reviewed 14 studies of mood symptoms during mania and have calculated frequencies of symptoms per manic episode. They determined that 80% of patients reported irritable mood, 72% reported depression, 71% reported euphoria, 69% reported mood liability, and 60% reported expansive mood. The most common cognitive symptoms experienced by patients during manic episodes were grandiosity (78%), racing thoughts and/or flight of ideas (71%), poor concentration or distractibility (71%), and confusion (25%) (see Box 8.1).

Hypomanic Episode

A Hypomanic Episode (APA, 1994, p. 335) is defined as a distinct period during which there is an abnormally and persistently elevated, expansive, or irritable mood of at least 4 days' duration (Criterion A). This period of abnormal mood must be accompanied by at least three additional symptoms associated with manic episodes. These symptoms include inflated self-esteem or grandiosity (nondelusional), decreased need for sleep, pressure of speech, flight of ideas, distractibility, increased involvement in goal-directed activities, increased psychomotor agitation, and excessive involvement in pleasurable activities that have a high potential for painful consequences (Criterion B). If the mood state is irritable rather than elevated or expansive, then four of the symptoms must be present. This list of symptoms is similar to the list that defines a manic episode.

It is the briefer duration and lesser severity of symptoms that differentiates hypomanic from manic episodes. Another distinction between these two diagnoses is that the presence of delusions or psychotic symptoms is pathognomonic of a manic episode. Criterion C describes a particular characteristic of the hypomanic mood state, that the mood must be clearly different from the individual's usual nondepressed mood, and there must be a clear change in functioning that is not characteristic of the individual's usual functioning. This change in mood or functioning must be observable to others (Criterion D). For many individuals, this change in function may take the form of a marked increase in efficiency, accomplishments, or creativity. On the other hand, a hypomanic mood episode may cause other individuals emotional, social, or occupational impairment (see Box 8.2).

Individuals in a hypomanic mood are often euphoric, and they appear to be unusually and unflappably cheerful, or on a "high." They may become socially outgoing, jocular and playful, and much fun to be around, but most people who know them

Box 8.1   Criteria for Manic Episode

A. A distinct period of abnormally and persistently elevated, expansive, or irritable mood, lasting at least 1 week (or any duration if hospitalization is necessary).

B. During the period of mood disturbance, three (or more) of the following symptoms have persisted (four if the mood is only irritable) and have been present to a significant degree:
    1. Inflated self-esteem or grandiosity
    2. Decreased need for sleep (e.g., feels rested after only 3 hours of sleep)
    3. More talkative than usual or pressure to keep talking
    4. Flight of ideas or subjective experience that thoughts are racing
    5. Distractibility (i.e., attention too easily drawn to unimportant or irrelevant external stimuli)
    6. Increase in goal-directed activity (either socially, at work or school, or sexually) or psychomotor agitation
    7. Excessive involvement in pleasurable activities that have a high potential for painful consequences (e.g., engaging in unrestrained buying sprees, sexual indiscretions, or foolish business investments)

C. The symptoms do not meet criteria for a Mixed Episode.

D. The mood disturbance is sufficiently severe to cause marked impairment in occupational functioning or in usual social activities or relationships with others, or to necessitate hospitalization to prevent harm to self or others, or there are psychotic features.

E. The symptoms are not due to the direct physiological effects of a substance (e.g., a drug of abuse, a medication, or other treatment) or a general medical condition (e.g., hyperthyroidism).

NOTE: Manic-like episodes that are clearly caused by somatic antidepressant treatment (e.g., medication, electroconvulsive therapy, light therapy) should not count toward a diagnosis of Bipolar I Disorder.

would agree that this quality of mood is not their normal mood. Although this is the classic description of hypomanic mood, some individuals experience an irritable mood period or alternating periods of euphoric and irritable moods. Often, as opposed to the marked grandiosity of manic episodes, those in a hypomanic mood may seem overly self-confident and seemingly unaware of the negative aspects or consequences of their plans and schemes. The speech of people who are hypomanic is often loud and mildly pressured; however, unlike the manic person's speech, hypomanic people typically can be understood. They often require little sleep, eat less food, and yet seem hyperactive and full of energy. The person experiencing hypomania may be overly distractible and responsive to extraneous stimuli. They may become preoccupied

---

Box 8.2   Criteria for Hypomanic Episode

A. A distinct period of persistently elevated, expansive, or irritable mood, lasting throughout at least 4 days, that is clearly different from the usual nondepressed mood.

B. During the period of mood disturbance, three (or more) of the following symptoms have persisted (four if the mood is only irritable) and have been present to a significant degree:
    1. Inflated self-esteem or grandiosity

    2. Decreased need for sleep (e.g., feels rested after only 3 hours of sleep)

    3. More talkative than usual or pressure to keep talking

    4. Flight of ideas or subjective experience that thoughts are racing

    5. Distractibility (i.e., attention too easily drawn to unimportant or irrelevant external stimuli)

    6. Increase in goal-directed activity (either socially, at work or school, or sexually) or psychomotor agitation

    7. Excessive involvement in pleasurable activities that have a high potential for painful consequences (e.g., the person engages in unrestrained buying sprees, sexual indiscretions, or foolish business investments)

C. The episode is associated with an unequivocal change in functioning that is uncharacteristic of the person when not symptomatic.

D. The disturbance in mood and the change in functioning are observable by others.

E. The episode is not severe enough to cause marked impairment in social or occupational functioning, or to necessitate hospitalization, and there are no psychotic features.

F. The symptoms are not due to direct physiological effects of a substance (e.g., a drug of abuse, a medication, or other treatment) or a general medical condition (e.g., hyperthyroidism).

NOTE: Hypomanic-like episodes that are clearly caused by somatic antidepressant treatment (e.g., medication, electroconvulsive therapy, light therapy) should not count toward a diagnosis of Bipolar II Disorder.

---

in planning and participating in multiple activities, and often, these activities are creative and productive pursuits. A person in a hypomanic mood may engage in increased sexual activity, impulsive buying sprees, or foolish business ventures, but these behaviors do not produce serious impairment or severe functional consequences that are

characteristic of the activities and behaviors of manic episodes.

The course of hypomanic episodes typically involves a rapid, often sudden, onset. The symptoms tend to escalate over 1 to 2 days, and they may last for several weeks to months. Generally, these episodes are briefer than major depressive episodes and are often preceded or followed by them. An interesting study by Coryell et al. (1995) that examined the 5-year course of illness in patients with affective disorders found that those with the Bipolar II condition rarely progressed to Bipolar I disorder.

Mixed Episodes

A Mixed Episode describes a distinct mood state that is characterized by a period of at least 1 week during which the individual experiences, simultaneously, symptoms that fulfill the criteria for both a manic episode and a major depressive episode. The individual experiences rapidly alternating moods—between sadness, irritability, and euphoria. He or she must experience three or more of the eight criteria characteristic of a manic episode if in a euphoric mood, and four if the mood is irritable, and five of eight criteria of a major depressive episode. Individuals experiencing a mixed episode frequently present with severe agitation; insomnia; altered appetite; psychotic symptoms (e.g., paranoid ideation, bizarre delusional beliefs, auditory or visual hallucinations); and suicidal ideation. Severity criteria require that the mood disturbance must be sufficiently severe to cause marked impairment in social or occupational functioning, require hospitalization, or be characterized by the presence of psychotic features (Criterion B).

Mixed episodes can evolve out of either manic or depressive episodes, or they may arise spontaneously. They generally last from weeks to months and may remit to a euthymic or depressive episode, and less commonly to a manic episode. Mixed episodes occur in up to 40% of bipolar patients over the course of a lifetime (Akiskal et al., 2000) (see Box 8.3).

One caveat to making any of the bipolar disorder diagnoses is the necessity of distinguishing bipolar episodes from mood episodes due to the direct physiological effects of a substance (e.g., drugs of abuse; a medication; or other treatment, such as phototherapy) or a general medical condition (e.g., hyperthyroidism). Manic, hypomanic, and mixed episodes can all result from the direct effect of antidepressant medications, electroconvulsive therapy, phototherapy, or other medications prescribed for other disorders (such as corticosteroids). *DSM-IV* (APA, 1994) prefers that people experiencing symptoms typical of a bipolar disorder under the influence of another agent be diagnosed as suffering from a Substance-Induced Mood disorder. There is some evidence to suggest that such individuals may demonstrate a "diathesis" toward bipolar disorder, and that such individuals may have an increased risk of developing the disorder in the future (Akiskal, 1983; Akiskal et al., 2000).

Cyclothymia

Cyclothymia describes a chronic, fluctuating mood disturbance involving numerous episodes of hypomanic symptoms and numerous episodes of depressive symptoms (Criterion A). However, neither the hypomanic nor the depressive symptoms are of sufficient severity, number, pervasiveness, or duration to qualify for a diagnosis of Major Depressive Episode or Manic Episode. To qualify for this diagnosis, the individual must also experience the disorder for at least an initial 2-year period during which no symptom-free period of longer than 2 months occurs (Criterion B). Criterion C requires that the diagnosis of Cyclothymic Disorder be made only if the initial 2-year period of cyclothymic symptoms is present in the absence of a major depressive, manic, or mixed bipolar episode. After the initial 2-year period, other bipolar diagnoses can be added to the

---

Box 8.3   Criteria for Mixed Episode

A. The criteria are met both for a Manic Episode and for a Major Depressive Episode (except for duration) nearly every day during at least a 1-week period.

B. The mood disturbance is sufficiently severe to cause marked impairment in occupational functioning or in usual social activities or relationships with others, or to necessitate hospitalization to prevent harm to self or others, or there are psychotic features.

C. The symptoms are not due to the direct physiological effects of a substance (e.g., a drug of abuse, a medication, or other treatment) or a general medical condition (e.g., hyperthyroidism).

NOTE: Mixed-like episodes that are clearly caused by somatic antidepressant treatment (e.g., medication, electroconvulsive therapy, light therapy) should not count toward a diagnosis of Bipolar I Disorder.

---

cyclothymia diagnosis, and both diagnoses would be appropriate. As with the other bipolar diagnoses, Criterion D states that the disorder cannot be described better by other Axis I diagnoses (e.g., Schizophrenia, Delusional Disorder, etc.), nor can the symptoms be better accounted for due to the direct physiologic effect of a substance, a medication, or another medical illness (Criterion E). Furthermore, the diagnosis requires that the disorder produce a clinically significant distress to the individual or an impairment in social, occupational, or other important area of function as a result of the mood disturbance (Criterion F).

Additional Course Specifiers

Individuals who are diagnosed with bipolar disorders can be categorized further by severity, presence of psychotic features, and remission status specifiers. Severity is generally noted as mild, moderate, or severe depending on the number of criteria symptoms that are endorsed, severity of the symptoms, the functional disability that is the result of the episode, and the need for supervision. The presence of psychotic features—primarily delusions or hallucinations—denotes a severe episode. Other specifiers describe other variants of the disorder:

- Chronic features—The presence of the disorder at the syndromal level for a period greater than 2 years' duration
- Catatonic features—A clinical picture that includes two of the following features: cataplexy or stupor, excessive motor activity, extreme negativism, peculiar posturing, and the presence of echolalia or echopraxia
- Melancholic features—Occuring during the depressive phase of a Bipolar I or II Disorder when the person experiences either a total loss of ability to experience pleasure or a lack of reactivity to normal pleasurable stimuli, and three of the following: depressed mood, depression worse in the morning, early-morning awakening, marked psychomotor agitation or retardation, significant anorexia or weight loss, or excessive and inappropriate guilt

- Atypical features—The appropriate brightening of mood termed mood reactivity and two of the following features: significant weight gain or hyperphagia, hypersomnia, heaviness in limbs, leaden paralysis, and a long-standing pattern of rejection sensitivity in interpersonal situations
- Postpartum onset

Longitudinal specifiers include whether or not the individual experiences full or partial interepisodal recovery. Finally, the Seasonal Pattern specifier describes the clinical pattern of a regular onset and offset of the mood episodes that are related temporally to the changes in the seasons. Rapid cycling describes a pattern of bipolar illness where the individual experiences four or more alterations between depressive and manic episodes in the course of 1 year. Rapid cycling episodes are more frequent in individuals with a Bipolar II Disorder at baseline rather than Bipolar I Disorder.

EPIDEMIOLOGY

Prevalence rate for Bipolar I Disorder is 1% of the general population. Emerging data suggest a prevalence rate of up to 5% of the general population and 10% to 15% of all individuals with mood disorders, if broader definitions of the disorder are included, as demonstrated by the European literature (Akiskal et al., 2000; Regier et al., 1988; Weissman et al., 1996). The mean age of onset for the first manic episode is the early 20s, but some people experience their first episode in adolescence or in their 50s (APA, 1994).

Approximately 5% to 15% of individuals with hypomania develop manic episodes (APA, 1994). Individuals who experience hypomanic episodes are described as having

Bipolar II Disorder. This disorder was first characterized by Dunner, Gershon, and Goodwin (1976), who argued for this distinction. The course and diagnosis of Bipolar II Disorder is often complicated by the presence of comorbid conditions, such as substance abuse or other medical conditions (Vieta et al., 2000). Individuals with Bipolar II Disorder are recognized to be at greater risk for suicide (Rihmer & Pestality, 1999). Thus, treatment for such individuals is crucial (Akiskal et al., 2000). Recent studies suggest that Bipolar II Disorder may be the most common presentation among the bipolar disorders, and that 30% to 55% of all patients with major depressions may have some variant or components of Bipolar II Disorder. This may not be so startling a statistic if we consider the common association of mild excitement, anxiety, and irritability with depressive illnesses (Akiskal et al., 2000). Table 8.1 reviews common Axis I comorbidities associated with bipolar depressive disorders.

Cyclothymia often begins early in life and is sometimes considered to reflect a temperamental predisposition to bipolar disorders. Cyclothymia is equally distributed by sex in community samples. Lifetime prevalence is 0.4% to 1%, and the prevalence in mood clinics ranges from 3% to 5% of patients. Cyclothymia usually begins in adolescence or early adult life (APA, 1994). Some authors argue that rapid cycling is a transient complication for up to 20% of bipolar patients in the course of their lifetimes and frequently may be a consequence of antidepressant use (Akiskal et al., 2000; Perugi et al., 2000).

ASSESSMENT

The psychiatric assessment of mood disorders is based upon a generally accepted

Table 8.1   BPD and Axis I Comorbidity: 12-month Prevalence Rates (in percentages)

Diagnosis	Population[a] (n = 7,076)	BD[b] (n = 78)	Odds[b]
Panic Disorder	2.2	14.4	8.3
Agoraphobia	1.6	17.6	15.9
Simple Phobia	7.1	31.6	6.4
Social Phobia	4.8	38.1	13.8
Generalized Anxiety Disorder	1.2	27.8	17.5
Obsessive-Compulsive Disorder	0.5	7.2	21.5
Alcohol Abuse	4.6	9.2	2.1
Alcohol Dependence	3.7	11.3	3.4
Drug Abuse	0.5	N < 5	N < 5
Drug Dependence	0.8	14.4	25.7

a. Data from Bijl, Ravelli, and van Zessen (1998).
b. Data from William Nolan, MD, oral communication.

psychiatric evaluation process, which, in turn, is based upon a patient interview (that also includes a medical component). The patient provides data about the history of present illness, past psychiatric history, social history, developmental history, medical history, medication history, family history of medical and psychiatric illnesses, current stressors and stressor severity, lethality issues (including evaluation of suicidal and homicidal ideation), and an assessment of the patient's biopsychosocial strengths. In addition, there is a laboratory examination to rule out hematologic, metabolic, endocrine, hepatic, renal, or other medical illnesses that can present as mania or depression. If possible, historical data provided by the patient are corroborated, or expanded upon, by spouses, children, parents, siblings, or others. In addition, it is beneficial to also obtain old medical records to help establish the patient's history. This overall process of data collection is critical because incorrect information may lead to incorrect diagnoses and treatment.

With this information, the psychiatric diagnosis is made according to procedures described in the *DSM-IV* (APA, 1994), a product of expert consensus under the aegis of the American Psychiatric Association. *DSM-IV* defines Mood Disorders as disorders that have a disturbance in mood as the predominant feature. *DSM-IV* makes a conceptual distinction between Mood Disorders and Mood Episodes (e.g., depressive, manic, mixed, and hypomanic episodes). A mood episode is described in terms of symptom severity, duration, and quality. Mood Episodes are not diagnosed as separate entities; rather, they are the components for making longitudinal mood disorder diagnoses. Mood Disorders are generally divided into depressive disorders ("unipolar depression") and bipolar disorders. The major distinction between the depressive and bipolar disorders is the presence or absence of a lifetime history of the individual having experienced a manic, mixed, or hypomanic episode. The bipolar disorders—Bipolar I Disorder, Bipolar II Disorder, Cyclothymia Disorder, and Bipolar Disorder Not Otherwise Specified—represent the categories of bipolar illness as defined by symptomology, severity, duration, and cyclicity. Some experts continue to argue in favor of a broader understanding of bipolar illness, hypothesizing a spectrum of bipolar disorders that would include conditions considered below the syndromal threshold required by *DSM-IV* criteria (Akiskal, 1996; Akiskal et al., 2000; Akiskal & Pinto, 1999; Goodwin & Jamison, 1990; Manning, Connor, & Sahai, 1998; Marneros, 2001).

CLINICAL PICTURE

Mrs. D. is a 32-year-old married female. She has always been a creative person who grew up in a household that valued culture and achievement. Her family psychiatric history is positive for a brother diagnosed with Schizophrenia. She attended college, studied and later practiced architecture, and married in her 20s. She had a past psychiatric history of mild depressive episodes and at other times of heightened energy and "intuition." She had been successful in her career and was working for a large architectural firm until 2 years ago, when she began experiencing racing thoughts and grandiose and unrealistic ideas. She began socializing with colleagues more in the workplace and even flirting with some male colleagues. Her manic symptoms progressed to severe insomnia, hyperactivity, and increasingly inappropriate and impulsive behaviors. She reached a point where she was distracting other colleagues and interfering with their work. Soon, people were questioning her unusual behavior, and many people were avoiding her. Appropriately, she was referred to her company's Employee Assistance Program (EAP), which lead to a psychiatric referral, hospitalization, and medication. After discharge, she resumed her previous lifestyle. She returned to work, but her concentration was poor, she was easily distractible, and she could not complete tasks as easily as she had

previously. Her mood did not fully recover, and she continued to experience bouts of mild to moderate depression. After 6 months, she and her husband decided to try and conceive a child, and at the patient's insistence, she was tapered off of her medications. After 3 weeks off medication, she experienced a relapse of manic symptoms. She has not been able to return to work as an architect, and she is applying for Social Security Disability Insurance.

As this example shows, bipolar illnesses can lead to loss of occupation, loss of social position and status, and severe interpersonal problems in private life and in the workplace—a reduction in overall functional capacity. This case is typical of severe cases of bipolar illness. Many individuals with milder forms of the illness may have brief severe episodes but then return to their previous level of functioning. Some individuals with a mild form of the disorder function well in the workplace and are extremely productive due to their increased baseline high levels of creativity, energy, and activity, and their decreased need for sleep.

PRECIPITATING CONDITIONS

The Stress Diathesis model of illness (Zubin, Magaziner, & Steinhauer, 1983) hypothesizes that with increased levels of stress, there is an increased likelihood of the expression of a mood disorder. This is true for the bipolar disorders. Certainly, interpersonal stress from workplace social interactions and the pressures of high workload demands can precipitate mood episodes. Existence of comorbid conditions, such as medical conditions, reactions to prescribed medications, and other substances of abuse, can trigger bipolar episodes.

Bipolar disorders are thought to be genetically determined based on studies of the incidence of the disorder in twins studies, adoption studies, and family studies. Numerous studies over the course of 50 years have shown that the concordance rate in identical twins is higher than in fraternal twins, which strongly argues for heritability (Goodwin & Jamison, 1990, p. 376). A high degree of genetic loading may predispose an individual to bipolar illness in the presence of a significant stress. Precipitants of the illness most prominently include family, workplace, and environmental stressors. Workplace interpersonal conflicts, disputes, and job-related failures all impose stress upon the individual. Some examples of environmental stressors include changes or other rapid shifts in circadian rhythms (e.g., jet lag), changes in work shifts, seasonal variations, and exposures to chemicals and toxins.

COURSE AND PROGNOSIS

An important characteristic of the bipolar disorders is the cyclical and recurrent nature of the disorder. Predictors of poorer response include having a highly loaded family history, especially in first-degree relatives; early age of onset; severity of the illness; a history of past suicide attempts; a chronic course; and a rapid-cycling course. A patient's prognosis becomes poorer when more of these predictors of poor response describe his or her course of illness. Typically, such individuals experience episodes that become more frequent, severe, and unstable.

Bipolar disorders represent a broad spectrum of illness severity and functional capability. Most patients with cyclothymia or hypomania do not seek treatment (Sachs, 2001). Appearance of functionally impairing symptoms of depression or mania require rapid evaluation and treatment. The referral process to a company's EAP or other health program should facilitate a referral to a psychiatrist for assessment, evaluation, and treatment (medication and psychotherapy). Often, a treatment team for the patient is comprised of a psychiatrist and a social worker or psychologist. A patient could also be referred to a specialty program for acute, continuation, and maintenance treatment.

Because bipolar disorders are recurrent and cycling, the best strategy after acute stabilization of symptoms is prevention of relapse. Most often, psychiatric medication management and psychotherapy are continued in a team approach as during the acute phase of the illness (some psychiatrists do provide both services). Continuing the effective acute phase treatments is essential for relapse prevention. When stability of the illness is achieved, a maintenance medication and psychotherapy program is recommended to enhance the period of wellness. Such maintenance therapy might focus on current family, workplace, or other stressors in the psychotherapy, and medications are modified with respect to side effects and the desired goals of treatment. The psychosocial consequences of bipolar disorder include lower socioeconomic status, unemployment, dropping out of school, financial problems, job loss, divorce and/or marital problems, alcohol or substance abuse, injury to self or others, excessive gambling, minor crime, and multiple hospitalizations (Bowden, Marcotte, Katzelnick, & Hussain, 2001; Lish, Dime-Meenhan, Whybrow, Price, & Hirschfeld, 1994).

In summary, prognosis is multifactored and depends upon the phase, symptom severity, level of functional impairment, and degree of treatment response and return to premorbid state. Bipolar disorders display a spectrum of responses ranging from excellent with little impairment to severe with profound impairment.

TREATMENT

The goal of the treatment of bipolar disorder is to decrease the severity and duration of manic and depressive episodes; manage the mood liability or instability during the acute, continuation (early stability) phase; and reduce the risk of recurrence during the maintenance or prophylactic treatment phase. Mood stabilizers are, by definition, medications that serve all these functions, but their efficacy in some of these areas is not completely satisfactory, and the use of other medications (e.g., antidepressants) and of specific psychotherapeutic interventions is often necessary. The classic mood stabilizers are lithium carbonate, divalproex sodium (Valproate), and carbamazepine. Second-choice potential mood stabilizers are the newer anticonvulsants topiramate, gabapentin, and lamotrigine (see Table 8.2).

Lithium carbonate is a first-line treatment for classic euphoric mania, if no medical contraindications (e.g., significant renal or cardiovascular disease, severe debilitation, or dehydration or sodium depletion) exist for its use. Lithium's efficacy in the treatment of mania is well-established in placebo-controlled trials (Goodwin, Murphey, & Bunney, 1969; Price & Heninger, 1994; Schou, Juel-Nielsen, Stromgren, & Voldby, 1954; Stokes, Shamoian, Stoll, & Patton, 1971). Lithium blood levels must be monitored carefully, and lithium plasma levels determine the most effective dose. Lithium levels must be checked 12 hours from last dose, and specific arrangements should be made for helping the patients being compliant with this need. Diarrhea, vomiting, drowsiness, muscular weakness, and lack of coordination may be early signs of toxicity. Late signs include blurred vision, giddiness, tinnitus, polyuria, and ataxia. Toxicity can be precipitated by reduced intake of fluids or food, change in dietary habits, excessive sweating, coadministration of medication like diuretics or NSAIDs, infections, fever, nausea, vomiting, or diarrhea. Increased thirst and urination, fine hand tremor, salty taste, and mild diarrhea are common side effects that may occur during initial therapy and, in the absence of lithium toxicity, may persist throughout treatment. Generally, side effects are more severe during the onset of treatment and contribute to work impairment during the acute phase of the illness. Goiter, hypothyroidism, and nephrogenic diabetes insipidus can be induced by lithium therapy. Specific laboratory investigations are required before and after starting lithium.

Valproate sodium is an effective alternative to lithium for the treatment of euphoric mania. Valproate is a first-choice mood stabilizer in the presence of rapid cycling, mixed episodes, or a predominantly irritable or dysphoric mood. In general, valproate is well tolerated, but divalproex (Depakote), the enteric-coated derivative, is better tolerated than valproic acid. Side effects of valproate and divalproex include tremor, sedation, hair loss, weight gain, headache, nausea, vomiting, diarrhea, dyspepsia, and thrombocytopenia. As is the case with lithium, some of the side effects can cause work impairment, especially in the acute phase of treatment. The side effect that most commonly will cause work impairment in patients taking valproate is sedation. Rare but more serious adverse events include hepatotoxicity and pancreatitis. Hepatotoxicity may be preceded by symptoms such as malaise, lethargy, weakness, anorexia, nausea, vomiting, and lethargy. Pancreatitis often presents itself with worsening abdominal pain, nausea, vomiting, and anorexia.

Carbamazepine is an anticonvulsant and an analgesic for trigeminal neuralgia that has been shown to have comparable

Table 8.2   FDA Approval Status for Drugs in the Treatment of BPD

Drug	*FDA-Approved*	*Off-Label Use[a]*
Carbamazepine	✓	
Clozapine	✓	
Gabapentin	✓	
Lamotrigine	✓	
Lithium	✓	
Olanzapine	✓	
Quetiapine	✓	
Risperidone	✓	
Topiramate	✓	
Valproate	✓	

SOURCE: Bowden et al. (2001).

a. These drugs are used in patient care and are also the subject of ongoing clinical investigations.

efficacy to lithium in treating mania, although prospective, placebo-controlled studies are still lacking. Carbamazepine is structurally similar to the antidepressant imipramine, but its antidepressant properties are still questioned. Side effects of carbamazepine include skin rash, urinary frequency, drowsiness, dizziness, headache, nausea, diarrhea, constipation, diplopia, blurred vision, fatigue, and so on. Rare but serious side effects include toxic epidermal necrolysis (Lyell's syndrome), Steven-Johnson syndrome, aplastic anemia, agranulocytosis, and pancreatitis.

Gabapentin, lamotrigine, and topiramate are anticonvulsants with potential mood-stabilizing properties. They have a side-effect profile that is generally better than the classic mood stabilizers, and therefore, they are usually better tolerated. However, controlled studies have not been able to show the efficacy of gabapentin in the treatment of depression or mania (Frye et al., 2000; Ghaemi & Gaughan, 2000). The antimanic properties of topiramate have been suggested by a small number of studies, and further research is definitely needed before the mood-stabilizing efficacy of this medication can be established (Ghaemi & Gaughan, 2000). Lamotrigine is the most promising of the newer anticonvulsants (Calabrese et al., 1999; Ghaemi & Gaughan, 2000, Ichim, Berk, & Brook, 2000). This medication, however, carries the risk of a severe, potentially fatal skin rash that occurs in approximately 3 of every 1,000 adults and in as many as 1 in 100 pediatric patients. Occurrence of a nonsevere, benign rash is much more common, but, given that it is not possible to predict reliably which rashes will prove to be life threatening, lamotrigine should be discontinued at the first sign of rash. The risk of rash is increased by coadministration of valproate, higher-than-recommended initial doses, or faster-than-recommended dose escalation.

Antipsychotic agents are sometimes used in the treatment of mania. The efficacy of the atypical antipsychotic agents olanzapine, risperidone, and ziprasidone has been demonstrated in randomized controlled trials (Keck & Ice, 2000; Sachs & the Risperidone Bipolar Study Group, 1999; Tohen, Jacobs, Grundy, et al., 2000). Some studies have suggested that the addition of olanzapine (Tohen, Jacobs, Meyers, et al., 2000) or risperidone (Sachs, Thase, et al., 2000) to lithium or valproate yields significantly greater improvement compared to monotherapy in manic patients (Watson & Young, 2001). Open trials have suggested a potential usefulness of clozapine in acute mania (Licht, 1998). The typical side effects of the antipsychotics, such as sedation or dizziness, contribute to the elevated work impairment of the patients on these medications.

Although most of the guidelines recommend mood stabilizers as first-choice treatment for bipolar depression (Moller & Grunze, 2000), the antidepressant efficacy of the mood stabilizers is far from being sufficiently proven. An increasing consensus among experts is that it is possible to begin an antidepressant in conjunction with a mood stabilizer at the start of acute phase treatment for bipolar depressive episodes (Sachs, Printz, Kahn, Carpenter, & Docherty, 2000). When bipolar depressive episodes are treated with antidepressants, a close monitoring is indicated to assess for acceleration of hypomania or mania and the possible induction of rapid cycling or mixed states. Buproprion hydrochloride, venlafaxine, or a serotonin reuptake inhibitor are first-line choices (Sachs, Printz, et al., 2000). Tricyclic antidepressants can be useful, but they are likely to accelerate expansive moods and complicate treatment.

Efficacy of mood stabilizers in preventing recurrence in bipolar mood disorders has been evaluated, and many studies suggest a prophylactic benefit in moderate to severe illness (Sharma et al., 1997). However, a subgroup of patients may not benefit from prophylactic treatment, especially if their disorder is mild. There is no consensus on how this subgroup can be identified.

Although pharmacologic treatment remains the mainstay in the therapy of bipolar disorder, there are clear indications for the use of adjunctive psychosocial interventions to address features that respond poorly to pharmacotherapy alone, such as non-compliance, social and occupational dysfunction, and management of life stresses (Miklowitz & Frank, 1999). Various psychosocial treatments, including family-focused treatment, interpersonal and social rhythm therapy, and cognitive behavioral therapy, have been developed and are being tested for individuals with bipolar disorder.

Family-focused treatment consists of a manual-based approach whose goal is to improve family functioning through a combination of communication, problem-solving and coping training, illness psychoeducation, and relapse rehearsal. The treatment is based on the premise that bipolar illness is associated with bidirectional stresses that influence the ability of the family to cope with the illness, as well as the severity of symptoms and the risk of relapse (Miklowitz & Goldstein, 1997). Interpersonal and social rhythm therapy (IPSRT) is a modification of the interpersonal psychotherapy for depression originally developed by Klerman and colleagues (Frank et al., 1994). IPSRT focuses on the interactions between the patient with bipolar disorder and his or her psychosocial environment. The therapy is based on the postulate that stressful life events affect the course of the disorder by disrupting daily routines, patterns of social interactions, sleep-wake cycles, and other circadian rhythms. A key focus of IPSRT is the tracking of social rhythms, or identification of environmental factors that trigger disruptions in these patients. Cognitive-behavioral therapy (CBT) for bipolar disorder (Basco & Rush, 1996) is a manual-based treatment that expands upon the cognitive therapy for depression (Beck, Rush, Shaw, & Emery, 1979) for the treatment of unipolar depression. CBT was adapted for the treatment of bipolar disorder, and it places greater emphasis on the role of medication, treatment adherence, and the importance of symptom monitoring. Interpersonal problems are defined as errors in communication based on incorrect assumptions and misattributions. In the CBT approach, the therapist is invited to play "the communication games" by assuming the role of coach while the "player" demonstrates the behavior. The therapist watches the patient role-play and gives feedback on ways to improve his or her skills. The patients are taught strategies to cope with depression and hypomania; recognize signs of the return of symptoms; improve self-management through homework assignments; and identify and modify their negative automatic thoughts and underlying maladaptive assumptions and compensatory behaviors.

Understanding the goals of psychiatric treatment of bipolar affective disorders helps to conceptualize the necessary workplace accommodations that may be necessary for patients with this illness. The goal of the stabilization phase of medication management may require accommodation of the patient's schedule to include weekly doctor visits, and also EAP and psychotherapy visits. Accommodation for psychiatrist and psychotherapist appointments in the continuation and maintenance phases of treatment may help medication compliance and adherence, which in turn promotes a return to health. In addition, workplace accommodations may need to be made because of adverse medication effects such as oversedation and the induction of lethargy, cognitive impairment, and physical problems (e.g., a tremor of the hands that may impair an employee's ability to perform tasks requiring a high degree of manual dexterity).

We have described the negative influence of stress upon the vulnerable patient and the goals of the psychotherapies to help the patient better cope with stressors in his or her life. Often, a workplace accommodation that can reduce temporarily the level of stress experienced by the patient can be instituted. If necessary, a temporary medical leave of absence can be helpful in the acute phase of treatment. If the patient has not achieved an adequate remission of symptoms, a short-term disability of 3 to 6 months may be appropriate. Inability to achieve an adequate response to treatment after that time may indicate a need for long-term disability.

We have reviewed the symptoms of the depressive and manic phases of bipolar affective illness. Certainly, the presence of active or residual symptoms of depression and mania may require workplace accommodation. By and large, manic patients are not able to maintain their level of premorbid occupational function and appropriate workplace demeanor. Depressed patients may be able to do their usual tasks if accommodation is made to allow them to take longer and work more slowly. However, when symptoms attain a moderate or greater level of severity, it is most common for the patient to take a medical leave of absence.

SUMMARY

Bipolar disorder is an illness characterized by alterations in moods between manic and depressive episodes. The *DSM-IV* (APA, 1994) categorizes the predominant types of bipolar disorder as Bipolar I Disorder, Bipolar II Disorder, Cyclothymia Disorder, and Mixed Episodes. These types describe the severity, pervasiveness, duration, and rhythm of depressive, hypomanic, and/or manic episodes that are described syndromally. The prevalence of bipolar disorders is between 1% and 5% of the population.

→ Too costly to Accomidate

The assessment of the bipolar disorders is made using the psychiatric clinical examination, including workplace stress and medical and laboratory examinations. Genetic predisposition, coupled with precipitating stressors, appears to trigger mood episodes in bipolar patients. Treatment consists of medication and focused psychotherapies.

REFERENCES

Akiskal, H. S. (1983). The bipolar spectrum: New concepts in classification and diagnosis. In L. Grinspoon (Ed.), *Psychiatry update: The American Psychiatric Association annual review, Vol. II* (pp. 271-291). Washington, DC: American Psychiatric Press.

Akiskal, H. S. (1996). The prevalent clinical spectrum of bipolar disorders: Beyond *DSM-IV. Journal of Clinical Psychopharmacology, 1,* 4S-14S.

Akiskal, H. S., Bourgeois, M. L., Angst, J., Post, R., Moker, H. J., & Hirschfeld, R. (2000). Re-evaluating the prevalence of and diagnostic composition within the broad clinical spectrum of bipolar disorders. *Journal of Affective Disorders, 59*(Suppl. 1), 5-30.

Akiskal, H. S., & Pinto, O. (1999). The evolving bipolar spectrum: Prototypes I, II, III, IV. *Psychiatric Clinics of North America, 3,* 517-534, VII Review.

American Psychiatric Association. (1994). *Diagnostic and statistical manual of mental disorders* (4th ed.). Washington, DC: Author.

Angst, J. (1978). The course of affective disorders: II. Typology of bipolar manic-depressive illness. *Archiv für Psychiatrie Nervenkrankheiten, 226*(1), 65-73.

Beck, A. T., Rush, A. J., Shaw, B. F., & Emery, G. (1979). *Cognitive therapy of depression.* New York: Guilford.

Basco, M. R., & Rush, A. J. (1996). *Cognitive behavioral therapy for bipolar disorder.* New York: Guilford.

Bijl, R.V., Ravelli, A., & van Zessen, G. (1998). Prevalence of psychiatric disorder in the general population: Results of The Netherlands Mental Health Survey and Incidence Study (NEMESIS). *Social Psychiatry and Psychiatric Epidemiology, 33,* 587-595.

Bowden, D., Marcotte, D., Katzelnick, D., & Hussain, M. Z. (2001). New advances in bipolar disorder. *Clinical Courier, 19*(3), 1-22.

Calabrese, J. R., Bowden, C. L., Sachs, G. S., Asher, J. A., Monaghan, E., & Rudd, G. D. (1999). A double blind placebo controlled study of lamotrigine monotherapy in outpatients with bipolar I depression. *Journal of Clinical Psychiatry, 60*(2), 79-88.

Coryell, W., Endicott, J., Maser, J. D., Keller, M. B., Leon, A. C., & Akiskal, H. S. (1995). Long-term stability of polarity distinctions in affective disorders. *American Journal of Psychiatry, 152*(3), 385-390.

Dunner, D. L., Gershon, E. S., & Goodwin, F. K. (1976). Heritable factors in the severity of affective illness. *Biological Psychiatry, 11,* 31-42.

Frank, E., Kupfer, D. J., Ehlers, C. L., Monk, T. H., Cornes, C., Carter, S., & Frankel, D. (1994). Interpersonal and social rhythm therapy for bipolar disorder: Integrating interpersonal and behavioral approaches. *Behavioral Research Therapy, 17,* 43-149.

Frye, M. A., Ketter, T. A., Mimbrell, T. A., Dunn, R. T., Speer, A. M., & Osuch, E. A. (2000). A placebo controlled study of lamotrigine and gabapentin monotherapy in refractory mood disorders. *Journal of Clinical Psychopharmacology, 20*(6), 607-614.

Ghaemi, S. N., & Gaughan, S. (2000). Novel anticonvulsants: A new generation of mood stabilizers? *Harvard Review of Psychiatry, 8,* 1-7.

Goodwin, F. K., & Jamison, K. R. (1990). *Manic-depressive illness.* New York: Oxford University Press.

Goodwin, F. K., Murphy, D. L., & Bunney, W. E., Jr. (1969). Lithium-carbonate treatment in depression and mania: A longitudinal double-blind study. *Archives of General Psychiatry, 21,* 486-496.

Ichim, L., Berk, M., & Brook, S. (2000). Lamotrigine compared to lithium in mania: A double blind randomized controlled trial. *Annals of Clinical Psychiatry, 12*(1), 5-10.

Keck, P. J., & Ice, K. (2000). *A three week, double blind, randomized trial of ziprasidone in the acute treatment of mania.* The American Psychiatric Association Annual Meeting New Research Program and Abstracts.

Kraepelin, E. (1921). *Manic-depressive insanity and paranoia.* Edinburgh, UK: E & S Livingstone.

Licht, R. W. (1998). Drug treatment of mania: A critical review. *ACTA Psychiatrica Scandinavica, 97*(6), 387-397.

Lish, J. D., Dime-Meenhan, S., Whybrow, P. C., Price, R. A., & Hirschfeld, R. M. A. (1994). The National Depressive and Manic-Depressive Association (N.D.M.D.A.) survey of bipolar members. *Journal of Affective Disorders, 31,* 281-294.

Manning, J. S., Connor, P. D., & Sahai, A. (1998). The bipolar spectrum: A review of current concepts and implications for the management of depression in primary care. *Archives of Family Medicine, 7*(1), 63-71.

Marneros, A. (2001). Expanding the group of bipolar disorders. *Journal of Affective Disorders, 62*(1-2), 39-44.

Miklowitz, D. J., & Frank, E. (1999). New psychotherapies for bipolar disorder. In *Bipolar disorders: Clinical course and outcome.* Washington, DC: American Psychiatric Press.

Miklowitz, D. J., & Goldstein, M. J. (1997). *Bipolar disorder: A family-focused treatment approach.* New York: Guilford.

Moller, H. J., & Grunze, H. (2000). Have some guidelines for the treatment of acute bipolar depression gone too far in the restriction of antidepressants? *European Archives of Psychiatry and Neurological Sciences, 250,* 57-68.

Perugi, G., Micheli, C., Akiskal, H. S., Madaro, D., Socci, C., & Quilici, C. (2000). Polarity of the first episode, clinical characteristics, and course of manic depressive illness: A systematic retrospective investigation of 320 bipolar I patients. *Comprehensive Psychiatry, 41,* 13-18.

Price, L. H., & Heninger, G. R. (1994). Drug therapy: Lithium in the treatment of mood disorders. *New England Journal of Medicine, 331*(9), 591-598.

Regier, D. A., Boyd, J. H., Burke, J. D., Jr., Rae, D. S., Myers, J. K., & Kramer, M. (1988). One-month prevalence of mental disorders in the United States: Based on five epidemiologic catchment area sites. *Archives of General Psychiatry, 45,* 977-986.

Rihmer, Z., & Pestality, P. (1999). Bipolar II disorder and suicidal behavior. *Psychiatric Clinics of North America, 22,* 667-673.

Sachs, G. (2001, June). *Design and promise of NIMH multicenter effectiveness trials.* Fourth International Conference on Bipolar Disorder, Pittsburgh, PA.

Sachs, G., Printz, D. J., Kahn, D. A., Carpenter, D., & Docherty, J. P. (2000, April). The expert consensus guideline series: Medication treatment of bipolar disorder 2000. *Postgraduate Medicine* (Special Report), 1-104.

Sachs, G., & the Risperidone Bipolar Study Group. (1999, December). *Safety and efficacy of risperidone vs. placebo as add-on therapy to mood stabilizers in the treatment of manic phase of bipolar disorder*. Presented at the 38th annual meeting of the American College of Neuropsychopharmacology, Acapulco, Mexico.

Sachs, G., & Thase, M. E. (2000). *Bipolar disorder: A systematic approach to treatment*. London: Martin Dumitz.

Sachs, G., Thase, M. E., Wisniewski, S., Leahy, L. F., Conley, J., Nierenberg, A. A., Lavori, P., & Allen, M. H. (2000). *The systematic treatment enhancement program for bipolar disorder*. Poster presented at the 154th annual meeting of the American Psychiatric Association, Chicago.

Schou, M., Juel-Nielsen, N., Stromgren, E., & Voldby, H. (1954). The treatment of manic psychoses by the administration of lithium salts. *Journal of Neurology, Neurosurgery and Psychiatry, 17*, 250-260.

Sharma, V., Lakshmi, N.Y., Haslam, D. R. S., Silverstone, P. H., Sagar, V. P., Matte, R., Kutcher, S. P., & Kusumakar, V. (1997). Continuation and prophylactic treatment of bipolar disorder. *Canadian Journal of Psychiatry—Revue Canadienne de Psychiatrie, 42*(Suppl. 2), 92S-100S.

Simon, E., & Unützer, J. (1999). Health care utilization and costs among patients treated for bipolar disorder in an insured population. *Psychiatric Services, 50*, 1303-1308.

Stokes, P. E., Shamoian, C. A., Stoll, P. M., & Patton, M. J. (1971). Efficacy of lithium as acute treatment of manic-depressive illness. *Lancet, 1*, 1319-1325.

Tohen, M., Jacobs, T. G., Grundy, S. L., McElroy, S. L., Banov, M. C., Janicak, P. G., Sanger, T., Risser, R., Zhang, F., Toma, V., Franeis, J., Tolleison, G. D., & Breier, A. (2000). Efficacy of olanzapine in acute bipolar mania: A double-blind, placebo-controlled study. The olanzipine HGGW study group. *Archives of General Psychiatry, 57*, 841-849.

Tohen, M., Jacobs, T., Meyers T., et al. (2000). Efficacy of olanzapine combined with mood stabilizers in the treatment of bipolar disorder. *International Journal of Neuropsychopharmacology, 3*, S335.

Vieta, E., Colom, F., Martinez-Aran, A., Benabarre, A., Reinares, M., & Gasto, C. (2000). Bipolar II disorder and comorbidity. *Comprehensive Psychiatry, 41*(5), 339-343.

Watson, S., & Young, A. H. (2001). The place of lithium salts in psychiatric practice 50 years on. *Current Opinion in Psychiatry, 14*(1), 57-63.

Weissman, M. M., Bland, R. C., Canino, G. J., Faravelli, C., Greenwald, S., Hwu, H., Joyce, P. R., Karam, E. G., Lee, C., Lellouch, J., Lepine, J., Newman, S. C., Rubio-Stipec, M., Wells, J. E., Wickramaratne, P. J., Wittchen, H., & Yeh, E. (1996). Cross-national epidemiology of major depression and bipolar disorder. *Journal of American Medical Association, 276*, 293-299.

Wyatt, R. J., & Henter, I. (1995). An economic evaluation of manic-depressive illness—1991. *Social Psychiatry and Psychiatric Epidemiology, 30*, 213-219.

Zubin, J., Magaziner, J., & Steinhauer, S. R. (1983). The metamorphosis of schizophrenia: From chronicity to vulnerability. *Psychological Medicine, 13*, 551-571.

CHAPTER 9

Generalized Anxiety Disorder

ERIN L. SCOTT
DAVID M. FRESCO
RICHARD G. HEIMBERG

DESCRIPTION OF THE DISORDER

Worry is an experience familiar to most people. However, persistent and excessive worry may be indicative of the chronic and debilitating anxiety disorder called generalized anxiety disorder (GAD). Worry in GAD, compared to normal worry, is characterized by intensity, duration, and frequency that are often far out of proportion to the actual likelihood or impact of the circumstances of concern. In addition, individuals with GAD report great difficulty controlling their worry. That is, they seem unable to terminate worry about a topic once it has begun. Individuals with GAD tend to worry about matters that trouble most individuals (e.g., finances, day-to-day responsibilities, work or school obligations, illness in oneself or significant others), but they may also worry excessively about minor matters. They may find it nearly impossible to keep worrisome thoughts from interfering with everyday activities, such as school, work, or social events.

Although not represented in the current diagnostic criteria (summarized below), considerable evidence suggests that GAD is also characterized by long-standing interpersonal difficulties (Newman, Castonguay, Borkovec, & Molnar, in press). Roemer, Molina, and Borkovec (1997) found that interpersonal concerns were the most frequently reported topics of worry in a sample of patients with GAD. Similarly, when compared to individuals with panic disorder, the thoughts of people with GAD are dominated by concerns about interpersonal conflict (Breitholtz, Westling, & Öst, 1998). Moreover, Sanderson, Wetzler, Beck, and Betz (1994) found that approximately half of the GAD patients in their sample also met criteria for one or more personality disorders, which are often indicative of interpersonal difficulties. Not only do individuals with GAD worry about interpersonal difficulties, but recent research also suggests that they may contribute to their interpersonal problems by interacting with others in a manner that imposes stress upon their interpersonal environment (Newman et al., in press).

The problems facing individuals with GAD in the workplace are multifaceted and impairing. With respect to worry, individuals with GAD may find it difficult to maintain concentration on job-related tasks because they may be distracted by worrisome thoughts about personal concerns. In addition, worries may focus specifically on work-related activities (e.g., worries about one's ability to meet deadlines or to complete tasks adequately) and may interfere with an individual's ability to complete tasks efficiently. Individuals with GAD may also miss work frequently because of their worry. For example, a man who worries excessively about the health of his child may miss work frequently because he feels he must take the child to unnecessary doctor's appointments or be home to monitor the child if he or she is home from school. Given the tendency for individuals with GAD to experience interpersonal difficulties, these individuals may also be prone to conflicts and misunderstandings with coworkers, which may, in turn, become a source of worry and distraction for the individual with GAD. The fatigue and sleep disturbance that are common to GAD (see below) may also contribute to reduced efficiency in the workplace. More than 60% of people seeking treatment for GAD report that they experience limitations in work functioning as a result of their disorder, and they report significantly less satisfaction with their work lives than do people without an Axis I disorder (Turk, Mennin, Fresco, & Heimberg, 2000).

Diagnostic Criteria

The *Diagnostic and Statistical Manual of Mental Disorders, Fourth Edition* (*DSM-IV*) (American Psychiatric Association [APA],

1994) states that GAD is characterized by "excessive anxiety and worry, occurring more days than not for a period of at least 6 months, about a number of events or activities" (p. 432). Individuals with GAD experience worry that is difficult to control and associated with at least three of the following symptoms: restlessness or feeling keyed up or on edge; fatigue; concentration difficulties; irritability; muscle tension; and sleep disturbance (including difficulty falling or staying asleep, or restless, unsatisfying sleep). The worry experienced by individuals with GAD must cause clinically significant distress or impairment in social, occupational, or other important areas of functioning. GAD is not diagnosed if the anxiety and worry are confined to concerns related to another Axis I disorder (e.g., worry about being embarrassed in public in an individual with social anxiety disorder); the worry occurs exclusively during the course of a mood disorder, psychotic disorder, or pervasive developmental disorder; or the worry is the direct result of the physiological effects of a substance or general medical condition.

The current criteria for GAD have changed from previous editions of the *DSM*. In general, the diagnostic criteria have become progressively more specific. To meet criteria for GAD according to *DSM-III* (APA, 1980), an individual must have experienced a continuously anxious mood for at least 1 month, associated with motor tension, autonomic hyperactivity, and vigilance and scanning. In *DSM-III-R* (APA, 1987), the required duration was increased to 6 months, and 6 of 18 symptoms (from the same three categories as above) were required to receive a diagnosis. As described earlier, GAD as currently diagnosed in *DSM-IV* (APA, 1994) includes the 6-month duration requirement, the inability to control worry, and the experience of three of six symptoms that have been found to be associated specifically with GAD.

EPIDEMIOLOGY

Prevalence rates of *DSM-IV* (APA, 1994) diagnoses have not yet been examined in a large-scale epidemiological investigation. As well, changes in the diagnostic criteria for GAD over the years limit our ability to estimate precisely from older studies the current prevalence of GAD in the general population. However, two large-scale epidemiological studies conducted using earlier versions of diagnostic criteria provide some suggestion of current prevalence.

The Epidemiologic Catchment Area (ECA) study examined the prevalence of *DSM-III* GAD at three sites (Durham, NC; St. Louis, MO; and Los Angeles) (Blazer, Hughes, George, Swartz, & Boyer, 1991). Data from these sites were used to estimate the prevalence of GAD in the United States as a whole. The 1-year prevalence of GAD was reported as 3.8%; if only pure cases of GAD (i.e., those without any other Axis I diagnosis) were included, the 1-year prevalence was 1.7%. Across the three sites, the lifetime prevalence of GAD ranged from 4.1% to 6.6%. Similar prevalence estimates were made using data from the National Comorbidity Survey (NCS), which employed *DSM-III-R* criteria for GAD. The point prevalence of GAD in the U.S. population was estimated at 1.6% (Wittchen, Zhao, Kessler, & Eaton, 1994). This estimate grew to 3.1% for the 12-month prevalence of GAD and 5.1% when lifetime rates were examined. These data suggest that GAD is a prevalent disorder, affecting more than 5% of the U.S. population at some point during their lives.

Both major epidemiological surveys have documented a higher prevalence of GAD in women, with the NCS reporting rates of GAD in women nearly double that for men (Blazer et al., 1991; Wittchen et al., 1994). GAD can occur across the lifespan; however, epidemiological estimates suggest that the onset of GAD is relatively rare in adolescence and early adulthood, and more common in adulthood (Wittchen et al., 1994).

Epidemiological studies have also documented a high degree of role impairment associated with GAD. In the NCS, 82% of individuals who have suffered from GAD at some point in their lives reported either seeking professional help or taking medication for GAD, or significant interference with their life and activities as a result of their disorder (Wittchen et al., 1994). Individuals with GAD, compared to those without GAD, reported significantly poorer perceived mental health, greater social role impairment, and a greater number of missed workdays in the past month (Kessler, DuPont, Berglund, & Wittchen, 1999). These data support the picture of workplace impairment and reduced life satisfaction reported among people seeking treatment for GAD (Turk et al., 2000).

In addition, GAD is frequently associated with other mental disorders. In the ECA study, 58% to 65% of individuals who met criteria for GAD at some point in their lifetimes reported suffering from at least one other mental disorder (Blazer et al., 1991). This number was even greater in the NCS, with a lifetime comorbidity rate of 90.4% among individuals with a history of GAD. Specifically, in the NCS, approximately 80% of individuals with lifetime GAD also suffered from a mood disorder at some time in their lives (Judd et al., 1998); 12-month comorbidity between GAD and major depression was estimated at 58.1% (Kessler et al., 1999). Comorbidity with other disorders is associated with greater disability, as evidenced by increased health care utilization and reported life interference compared to pure GAD (Judd et al., 1998).

GAD may also be a vulnerability factor for depression (Kessler, 2000; Kessler, Walters, & Wittchen, in press). In a secondary analysis of NCS data, Kessler and colleagues (Kessler et al., 1996) found that major depression was more frequently comorbid with GAD than with any other diagnosis assessed in the NCS. Furthermore, the likelihood of having one's first major depressive episode increased by a factor of 62 in the first year after the onset of GAD compared to the likelihood that individuals with no Axis I disorder would have their first major depressive episode. After this first year, individuals with GAD remained 2.9 times more likely to have a first episode of major depression than did individuals with no Axis I disorder (Kessler et al., 1996). These high rates of overlap with unipolar depression and the tendency for anxiety to be temporally primary to depression have led researchers to surmise that anxiety disorders, especially GAD, may represent vulnerabilities for future depression (Kessler, 2000; Kessler et al., in press).

ASSESSMENT

The most common method of clinical assessment in research settings is the semistructured diagnostic interview. Semistructured interviews guide the clinician through the systematic evaluation of diagnostic criteria while allowing the flexibility to follow up on patients' primary areas of concern. One of the most frequently used semistructured interviews for the diagnosis of GAD is the Structured Clinical Interview for *DSM-IV* Axis I Disorders—Patient Edition (SCID I/P) (First, Spitzer, Gibbon, & Williams, 1996). The SCID is a relatively time-efficient,

broad-ranging interview that covers all Axis I disorders, allowing for ease in making differential diagnoses. The SCID employs multiple screening questions that allow the clinician to "skip out" at many points throughout the interview if specific diagnostic criteria are not met. Although this method provides for faster administration and more efficient collection of diagnosis-relevant information, the information collected may lack the depth necessary for treatment planning.

The Anxiety Disorders Interview Schedule for *DSM-IV* (ADIS-IV) (Brown, DiNardo, & Barlow, 1994) and the ADIS-IV-Lifetime Version (ADIS-IV-L) (DiNardo, Brown, & Barlow, 1994) are semistructured interviews designed to assess the diagnostic criteria for anxiety disorders; the ADIS-IV assesses current diagnoses, whereas the ADIS-IV-L assesses both current and lifetime diagnoses. In addition, the interviews contain modules for other disorders that commonly co-occur or overlap with anxiety disorders, including mood disorders, substance use disorders, and somatoform disorders, as well as screening questions for other major disorders (e.g., psychoses). In addition to examining the presence of specific facets of the various anxiety disorders, the ADIS-IV and the ADIS-IV-L collect information on situational and cognitive cues for anxiety, making them particularly useful in cognitive-behavioral treatment settings. In contrast to the SCID, the ADIS-IV and the ADIS-IV-L collect extensive information on anxiety symptoms from all individuals, including those who do not meet full diagnostic criteria. ADIS-IV interviews can be quite lengthy, although they are more time-efficient when only information on current diagnoses is required.

A useful measure for the identification of individuals with generalized anxiety disorder is the Generalized Anxiety Disorder Questionnaire for *DSM-IV* (GAD-Q-IV) (Newman, Zuellig, Kachin, Constantino, & Cashman, 2001). The GAD-Q-IV is a self-report measure designed to identify individuals suffering from GAD and has been used typically as a screening measure in studies of anxiety and worry in normal populations. However, there is some evidence that this measure may be useful in screening treatment-seeking individuals as well. The questionnaire reflects *DSM-IV* criteria for GAD and assesses whether individuals experience excessive worry across a number of domains, the degree to which the worry is experienced as uncontrollable, the degree to which an individual is bothered by worry, the degree to which worry interferes in one's life, and the presence of the criterion physical symptoms of GAD. The GAD-Q-IV maps well onto the diagnosis of GAD by structured interview using the ADIS-IV-L. Newman and colleagues (Newman et al., 2001) administered the GAD-Q-IV to undergraduates and demonstrated a specificity of 97% and a sensitivity of 69%. In another study of treatment-seeking individuals with GAD and community controls, the GAD-Q-IV demonstrated a specificity of 100% and a sensitivity of 74% (Luterek, Turk, Heimberg, Fresco, & Mennin, 2001).

Additional self-report questionnaires can also be helpful for obtaining a relatively quick assessment of the intensity, frequency, and pervasiveness of worry associated with GAD. The Penn State Worry Questionnaire (PSWQ) (Meyer, Miller, Metzger, & Borkovec, 1990) is a 16-item questionnaire designed to assess the excessiveness, duration, and uncontrollability of worry. Items describe characteristics of pathological worry (e.g., "I am always worrying about something") but do not refer to specific content areas of worry. The PSWQ is a highly reliable and valid measure of worry in individuals with GAD and has the ability to distinguish individuals with GAD from those with other anxiety disorders (Brown, Antony, & Barlow, 1992; Meyer et al., 1990). A recent study found that a cut-off score of 53 correctly classified 96% of treatment-seeking GAD patients and 98% of community controls; a score of 65 correctly classified 68% of GAD patients and 65% of social anxiety disorder patients in another comparison (Fresco, Mennin, Heimberg, & Turk, 2001).

The PSWQ focuses exclusively on the pathological characteristics of worry without regard for the degree of worry about specific circumstances. In contrast, the Worry Domains Questionnaire (WDQ) (Tallis, Eysenck, & Mathews, 1992) assesses the presence and degree of worry across various domains. The measure was designed originally to measure nonpathological worry, that is, worry in nonclinical populations. Nevertheless, the WDQ has been used in both clinical GAD and nonclinical populations to assess the intensity of worry in multiple domains. Individuals are asked to rate the degree to which they worry about specific areas that can be divided into five domains: Relationships (e.g., "that I will lose close friends"), Lack of Confidence (e.g., "that I feel insecure"), Aimless Future (e.g., "that I'll never achieve my ambitions"), Work Incompetence (e.g., "that I make mistakes at work") and Financial (e.g., "that my money will run out"). The WDQ has also demonstrated adequate reliability and validity (Joormann & Stöber, 1997; Stöber, 1998).

Further information about measures for the assessment of GAD, worry, and related constructs can be found in a paper by Turk, Mennin, and Heimberg (in press).

CLINICAL PICTURE

Case Illustration

A thorough description of an individual suffering from GAD will provide a fuller understanding of the specific features of the disorder. "Gary" is a 35-year-old, single, white male who presented for treatment because of chronic, uncontrollable worry that was beginning to affect "every facet of [his] life." Although Gary described himself as a worrier from early childhood, he reported that more recent pressures to settle on a career and get married had increased his distress substantially. Consistent with *DSM-IV* criteria, Gary experienced uncontrollable worry across multiple domains; his most severe worries were focused on the security of his job and his satisfaction with it, his relationships with supervisors and coworkers, and difficulties with an ongoing romantic relationship. Gary reported that he spent nearly 70% of his waking hours worrying about these issues. In conjunction with his worry, Gary experienced four of the physiological symptoms typically associated with GAD: frequent difficulty falling asleep, muscle aches and tension, irritability both at work and at home, and a persistent feeling of being keyed up and on edge. Gary felt that worry and its associated symptoms interfered significantly with both his work life (e.g., occasional loss of jobs, frequent conflict with his coworkers and supervisors) and his personal life (e.g., conflict with his girlfriend, difficulty making and keeping friends).

Gary's worries about work-related activities and relationships significantly disrupted his ability to perform his job. Gary described a pattern of difficulties at work characterized by feeling alienated from coworkers and feeling that he lacked the respect of his supervisors. Typically, Gary started a new job with great enthusiasm; however, he quickly became consumed by worries about the impression he was making on both coworkers and supervisors, as well as concerns about his job security. In his current position, Gary worried frequently about his company's somewhat shaky financial situation, leading him to push (often prematurely and sometimes too aggressively) his ideas for reshaping the company on both supervisors and coworkers; his frequent suggestions tended to frustrate and anger those around him.

In addition, Gary worried about his status in the company and the opinions of his supervisors. At the start of a new job, Gary believed he needed to "wow" his new employers; he worried that if he was unable to make a great first impression, he would either lose his job or fail to be promoted. Although he was a salaried employee, Gary worked long hours to win the respect of his supervisors. Gary also felt unable to delegate work to others for fear that they would not complete the job correctly. Therefore, he often missed deadlines as he obsessed over every detail before turning the project over to his supervisor. When Gary realized he might miss a deadline, he often worried that his supervisor would fire him for being incompetent. As a result, he avoided talking with the supervisor about the potential problem, only making the problem worse. In one instance, Gary avoided speaking to the supervisor for several weeks about the likelihood that he would miss a deadline because it was "too painful to admit to [himself] and to [his supervisor] that [he] had let the company down." When he finally did speak to the supervisor, the supervisor expressed great anger and frustration over Gary's behavior. As is evident in this example, Gary's efforts to manage perceived stress in his life were often unsuccessful and frequently counterproductive. Gary's supervisors rarely took note of his extra hours but reprimanded him for missed deadlines; therefore, it is not surprising that his relationship with his supervisors suffered.

Gary also worried about his relationships with coworkers. He felt that others did not take his ideas seriously and that they were not interested in socializing with him. In reaction to these worries, Gary became increasingly aggressive in his attempts to get his opinions across and to make friends with them. However, these attempts frequently led his coworkers to view him as arrogant and overly intrusive. Furthermore, they frequently expressed that they were upset that he was obsequious toward supervisors and that he did not trust them (recall that he would not delegate work to others).

Gary's worries about personal relationships affected not only those relationships but also his ability to keep his mind on work-related tasks. Gary's romantic relationships were also troubled by his constant worries. He was overwhelmed by concerns about losing his partner and often asked for reassurance about her feelings for him. He called her frequently, trying to schedule many dates and asking her repeatedly to make the relationship exclusive. His girlfriend complained that she felt smothered by his constant attention and expressions of affection. Although Gary understood the effect of his actions, he persisted because he feared that he would otherwise communicate disinterest. Gary's worry about losing his relationship also led him to avoid dealing with relationship difficulties as they arose. For example, Gary's girlfriend had recently canceled a planned dinner date. Instead of voicing his disappointment, Gary said nothing because he was afraid that she would break up with him. Nevertheless, he continued to feel frustrated by this and other incidents in their relationship. Relationship issues were a constant source of worry, interfering with his concentration on work-related tasks and contributing to his seemingly perpetual state of tension at home. Gary provides a vivid example of how excessive worry and attempts to reduce this worry can interfere with all aspects of one's life.

PRECIPITATING CONDITIONS AND WORKPLACE STRESSORS

There has been little empirical study of the conditions that contribute to the onset and development of GAD. However, GAD appears to be associated with early attachment difficulties that may lead to problematic interpersonal styles later in life (Cassidy, 1995; Zuellig, Newman, Kachin, & Constantino, 1997). Specifically, adults with GAD are more likely to report enmeshed or role-reversed relationships with their primary caregiver during childhood than are adults without GAD (Zuellig et al., 1997). Unlike other children, individuals with GAD often had to take care of their parents; therefore, they were required to anticipate potential dangers both to themselves and to other family members. It is perhaps not surprising that children with these experiences frequently develop into adults who are hypervigilant to potential danger to both themselves and others and believe that they are the only ones who can provide protection. Consequently, adults with GAD often become overly concerned about and involved with the affairs of friends, loved ones, coworkers, and customers. A preliminary cluster analysis of the Inventory of Interpersonal Problems (Horowitz, Alden, Wiggins, & Pincus, 2000) suggested that 62.1% of GAD patients could be characterized as overly nurturant and intrusive, 24.3% as cold and vindictive, and 13.5% as socially avoidant and nonassertive in their present relationships (Pincus & Borkovec, 1994).

"Eduardo" provides an excellent example of how role reversal in childhood may relate to an overly nurturant style in adulthood. Eduardo is an attorney who, prior to treatment, worried constantly about his clients. Had he litigated competently for them? Had he held out for the best possible settlement? His worry about clients occurred both at work and at home and often interfered with his ability to sleep. Eduardo attributed his tendency to become overly involved in the affairs of others to the environment in his childhood home. In a particularly poignant example, when he was a child, Eduardo fell and sustained a compound fracture to his leg. Eduardo's mother became so upset that she was unable to care for her son. In fact, Eduardo had to calm his mother and call for his own medical help. Clearly, he learned at a very young age that his parents could not care adequately for him.

Gary also reported role reversal in his childhood. At a family gathering to celebrate his parents' wedding anniversary, his father jokingly recounted stories of his children getting into trouble when they were young. When he came to Gary, his father said, "I guess I have nothing to say because you were always so obedient and we often turned to you because you were so responsible."

Onset and maintenance of GAD also may be associated with the experience of trauma. Beck and Emery (1985) suggest that the experience of early life trauma may represent a pathway to chronic worry by teaching the individual that the world is, in fact, a dangerous place, and that there is legitimate reason to be fearful in the future. Consistent with this hypothesis, both undergraduates with self-reported GAD and treatment-seeking GAD patients report significantly more past traumatic events than do individuals without GAD (Roemer, Molina, Litz, & Borkovec, 1996/1997). Specifically, 52% to

53% of GAD participants indicated that they had experienced a potentially traumatic event, compared to 21% to 30% of nonanxious participants. It also appears that certain types of trauma may differentiate those with self-reported GAD from those without (Molina, Roemer, Borkovec, & Posa, 1992). Specifically, participants with self-reported GAD were four to six times more likely than non-GAD participants to have experienced traumas characterized by physical or emotional assault and 1.5 times more likely than non-GADs to have experienced traumas involving death, illness, or injury. Similarly, Torgersen (1986) reported that individuals with GAD were more likely than control participants to experience the death of a parent before age 16. The nature of these traumatic events stands in stark contrast to the mundane worries that occupy the day-to-day lives of people with GAD, suggesting that worry may serve as a strategy by which people with GAD avoid confrontation with more disturbing events (Borkovec, Alcaine, & Behar, in press).

COURSE AND PROGNOSIS

Epidemiological studies indicate that anxiety disorders often follow a chronic or recurrent course (Angst & Vollrath, 1991) with low spontaneous recovery rates after 1 year (Bland, Newman, & Orn, 1988). The course and prognosis for GAD in particular is chronic, typically with fluctuations in severity related to the presence of current life stressors (Brown, Barlow, & Liebowitz, 1994). A large percentage of patients with GAD (between 60% and 80%) describe having been worriers for their entire lives (Barlow, 1988; Rapee, 1991). Individuals with GAD do not tend to experience remission of their symptoms in the absence of treatment (Yonkers, Warshaw, Massion, &

Keller, 1996). Finally, Beck, Stanley, and Zebb (1996) reported that elderly people also suffer from debilitating generalized anxiety, suggesting that GAD may persist into late adulthood. Gary demonstrates the persistence of GAD. He recalled worrying about the well-being and financial security of his family as a young child; however, he reported an increase in the severity of his worries in adulthood as he faced increased levels of stress.

Although this topic will be addressed more fully in the section on treatment strategies, several treatments have demonstrated considerable efficacy in the treatment of GAD. Both cognitive-behavioral therapy and several medication treatments significantly reduce GAD symptomatology (Borkovec & Ruscio, 2001; Gould, Otto, Pollack, & Yap, 1997). A recent review of cognitive-behavioral treatments for GAD suggests that up to two thirds of patients show significant response to treatment, and about half achieve high endstate functioning (Mennin, Turk, Heimberg, & Carmin, in press).

TREATMENTS FOR GAD

Cognitive-Behavioral Therapy

A growing body of literature has examined the efficacy of cognitive-behavioral therapies (CBT) and their components in the treatment of GAD. The most recent meta-analysis (Borkovec & Ruscio, 2001) examined 13 published controlled studies of CBT. The meta-analysis demonstrated that CBT was superior to no-treatment control groups in all included studies, to nonspecific or alternative treatments in 82% of comparisons, and to treatments containing only behavioral or cognitive components in 20% to 43% of comparisons. These data are consistent with an earlier meta-analysis

conducted by Gould and colleagues (Gould et al., 1997), which demonstrated significant efficacy for cognitive and behavioral interventions alone and in combination in controlled studies. Overall, CBT was more effective in reducing anxiety than control treatments. In addition, Gould and colleagues found no overall differences in efficacy between CBT and medication treatments. Although the mean effect size for CBT was somewhat higher than that for medication treatments, this finding is moderated by the fact that most CBT treatments used waitlist or attention placebo controls that have been found to be less powerful than the pill placebo controls used in medication studies.

Treatment gains achieved in CBT are durable as assessed over a several-month follow-up period. After examining six studies that provided sufficient data for analysis, Gould and colleagues (Gould et al., 1997) reported that reductions in anxiety following CBT were typically maintained through the follow-up period. Although studies usually do not provide data on control conditions at follow-up because of the ethical issue of maintaining a nonresponding patient in a control condition, Borkovec and Ruscio (2001) provided data suggesting that CBT outperforms single-component therapies to an even greater degree at follow-up than immediately posttreatment.

Brief Description

Although CBT varies in its implementation in both research and clinical settings, the typical approach contains several components that are reviewed in the following sections.

Self-Monitoring of Anxiety. All CBT techniques involve training in self-monitoring. Patients are instructed from the start of therapy to increase their attention to their anxiety responses; for individuals with GAD, their attention is drawn specifically to their worry episodes. Patients are asked to identify the components of their anxiety response, including thoughts, physical sensations, and behaviors. In addition, patients are taught to identify internal and external triggers of anxiety and worry. These precipitants may include situational factors (e.g., being in a doctor's office, provoking worry about one's health) or internal cues (e.g., an increased heart rate, triggering a rush of anxiety). Throughout therapy, patients are taught to identify cues early in the chain of anxiety- or worry-evoking events so that they will be able to initiate coping responses earlier in the anxious cycle. Daily diaries and other forms of written records are often used as tools for self-monitoring of anxiety responses.

Relaxation Training. Muscle tension is so common among patients with GAD that it was included as one of the criteria for the disorder in *DSM-IV*. Therefore, it is not surprising that relaxation strategies have been a common element in many treatments for GAD. Progressive muscle relaxation, diaphragmatic breathing, relaxing imagery, and meditation have been key elements in treatment for GAD, and these techniques have also shown a degree of success as stand-alone treatments for GAD (Borkovec & Costello, 1993). Patients are taught to practice relaxation techniques on a regular basis. In addition, they learn to apply their relaxation skills in the presence of cues that typically evoke anxiety, as well as before, during, and after stressful events. Newman and Borkovec (in press) advocate the teaching of multiple relaxation strategies for two main reasons—first, so that patients can learn to use the relaxation strategy that is best suited for the situation they must currently

confront, and second, so that the patient does not become overly reliant on a specific technique as another way to avoid the experience of anxiety or other negative emotions. At the heart of current approaches to the etiology and treatment of GAD is the belief that individuals with GAD use worry as a means to dampen or avoid the emotionally evocative aspects of stressful situations. It would not be prudent to teach patients to use relaxation techniques in this same way. Such an approach would represent replacing one control strategy (worry) for another (relaxation).

Cognitive Therapy. Because worry is a cognitive process and generally involves the misperception or catastrophization of future threat, techniques that help patients to reevaluate their thoughts and develop rational alternatives have been studied as potential interventions for GAD. Most cognitive therapy for GAD is based on the methods of Beck and Emery (1985). An essential aspect of cognitive therapy is to learn the connection between thoughts, images, and daily emotional experience. Patients are taught to identify irrational, anxiety-provoking thinking; analyze the validity of these thoughts using logic, probability, and evidence; generate alternative, more accurate ways of viewing the situation; and apply these alternative ways of viewing the situation when anxiety or worry first appears. Individuals with GAD may find it difficult to develop rational alternatives in the heat of an anxious moment or during a worry episode; therefore, practice of these techniques during the therapy session is essential. During therapy, patients may be asked to imagine anxiety-provoking situations or the cues that frequently precede anxiety. The patient can then engage actively in the cognitive coping techniques learned in session with the assistance of the therapist, if necessary.

Time Element

When compared to medication treatments, CBT typically takes longer before significant improvements are noted. However, these gains are usually maintained after treatment is discontinued (Borkovec & Ruscio, 2001), whereas improvements on medication are frequently lost when the medication treatment is stopped (Dubovsky, 1990). Therapy sessions typically take place once or twice weekly and last from 1 to 1½ hours. The number of sessions has varied greatly in studies of the treatment of GAD, with one study reporting success with some patients with as few as four sessions (Power, Jerrom, Simpson, Mitchell, & Swanson, 1989) and others using 15 or more sessions (Barlow, Rapee, & Brown, 1992).

Side Effects

Psychotherapy is not typically associated with side effects. However, CBT involves confronting feared thoughts and situations while applying new skills. Therefore, an individual in CBT for GAD may experience an initial increase in anxiety as he or she begins to approach situations and think about topics that previously had been avoided.

Workplace Accommodations

Most importantly, patients receiving CBT for GAD need flexibility in scheduling in order to allow them to make regular therapy appointments. As mentioned earlier, therapy typically takes place once or twice a week for 1 to 1½ hours each session. Frequently, these sessions must be scheduled during the typical workday because therapists may have limited evening and weekend availability.

Pharmacotherapy

Brief Description

Gould and colleagues (Gould et al., 1997) examined the efficacy of pharmacotherapy interventions for GAD using meta-analytic techniques. The majority of controlled trials examined the efficacy of benzodiazepines and buspirone; the authors reported no significant differences between types of medication, although these comparisons are limited by the small number of studies that had been conducted at that time. Across studies, medication treatments performed consistently better than pill placebo in reducing anxiety in patients with GAD. As mentioned in the previous section, on average, medication treatments performed as well as cognitive-behavioral therapy in the treatment of GAD.

Numerous studies have demonstrated the efficacy of benzodiazepines in the treatment of anxiety (Shader & Greenblatt, 1993). In an early review, Barlow (1988) reported an average reduction in anxiety (as measured by the Hamilton Rating Scale for Anxiety) (Hamilton, 1959) of 48% following benzodiazepine treatment as compared to the average reduction of 30% with pill placebo. Benzodiazepines may be particularly indicated for individuals with GAD experiencing intense distress and in need of rapid anxiety reduction. However, benzodiazepines may be contraindicated for individuals with a history of substance abuse or medical conditions in which sedation should be avoided.

Buspirone has also demonstrated efficacy for GAD. In controlled comparisons, buspirone has demonstrated efficacy comparable to many benzodiazepines, including diazepam (Feighner, Merideth, & Hendrickson, 1982), alprazolam (Enkelmann, 1991), and oxazepam (Strand et al., 1990). Compared to benzodiazepines, the onset of therapeutic effects is considerably slower; however, the side effects associated with buspirone are milder, and abuse is less likely.

The efficacy of antidepressants in the treatment of GAD has been suggested, although not widely studied. Two studies suggest that imipramine, a tricyclic antidepressant, may be more effective than benzodiazepines for treating the psychological symptoms associated with GAD (e.g., interpersonal sensitivity, anticipatory anxiety, worry), whereas benzodiazepines may have a greater effect on somatic symptoms (Hoehn-Saric, McLeod, & Zimmerli, 1988; Rickels, Downing, Schweizer, & Hassman, 1993).

Selective serotonin reuptake inhibitors (SSRIs) have only recently begun to be examined for GAD; however, given their mild side effect profile and their wide-ranging efficacy for anxiety disorders, the SSRIs are frequently used in the treatment of GAD. In one study, paroxetine demonstrated equivalent efficacy to imipramine along with a greater effect on psychological symptoms, such as worry, when compared to a benzodiazepine (Rocca, Fonzo, Scotta, Zanalda, & Ravizza, 1998). In a multisite study, Pollack and colleagues (Pollack et al., 2001) reported that individuals with GAD treated with paroxetine for 8 weeks demonstrated significantly greater anxiety reduction than did individuals treated with a placebo.

Finally, support has also been garnered for the use of the antidepressant venlafaxine, which has effects on both serotonin and norepinephrine reuptake, in the treatment of GAD (Sheehan, 1999). Davidson, DuPont, Hedges, and Haskins (1999) reported significantly greater reductions in anxiety in individuals with GAD following treatment with venlafaxine extended release (XR) compared to a placebo. These reductions were not significantly different from the reductions reported by individuals treated with buspirone in the same study.

Time Element

Medications with demonstrated efficacy for GAD vary considerably in the speed with which they produce symptomatic relief. Benzodiazepines are known for their rapid onset, often inducing nearly immediate anxiety reduction. Other medications, however, may take significantly longer before change is evident. Buspirone and most antidepressants typically take 2 to 4 weeks before significant anxiety reduction is achieved.

Side Effects

Common side effects vary across medication classes as well as across individuals. Benzodiazepine use has been limited by an array of side effects, including impaired cognitive performance and sedation, and the risk of physical dependence with long-term use and withdrawal symptoms and/or relapse following discontinuation (Shader & Greenblatt, 1993). For example, Dubovsky (1990) reported that 63% to 81% of individuals with GAD relapsed following discontinuation of benzodiazepine medication. The side effects of benzodiazepines may significantly affect an individual's ability to perform in the workplace. For example, sedation and impaired cognitive performance may be particularly dangerous for an employee who must operate heavy machinery or drive a vehicle as part of his or her job. However, the most severe side effects typically appear early in treatment and dissipate after several weeks.

Tricyclic antidepressants are typically associated with prominent anticholinergic side effects, such as dry mouth and constipation, that frequently are maintained throughout treatment (Rickels et al., 1993; Rocca et al., 1998). In contrast, buspirone, the SSRIs, and venlafaxine have a fairly mild side effect profile that includes headache, nausea, dizziness, and restlessness, and none of these is associated with physical dependence or discontinuation difficulties (Davidson et al., 1999; Rickels, Schweizer, Csanalosi, Case, & Chung, 1988; Rocca et al., 1998). Therefore, buspirone, the SSRIs, and venlafaxine may be particularly useful for patients with GAD with a history of substance abuse.

Workplace Accommodations

Employers will need to allow time for individuals to make regular doctor's appointments. Although this accommodation may be weekly early in treatment, sessions are typically brief (under 30 minutes) and, as treatment progresses, may occur once a month or less. In addition, accommodations may be necessary early in treatment for those patients who experience severe side effects. For example, an employee who experiences drowsiness at the start of benzodiazepine treatment may need a temporary reprieve from duties in which sedation could endanger the employee or those around him or her.

MAINTENANCE OF GAINS AND RELAPSE PREVENTION

Maintenance of gains from treatment will vary depending on the type of treatment received. As noted earlier, a large portion of individuals treated with medication will be vulnerable to relapse when the medication is discontinued. Therefore, medication discontinuation should be considered carefully, and follow-up evaluation should be provided to prevent relapse.

For individuals treated with psychotherapy, follow-up also may be essential to the maintenance of treatment gains. Although relapse following the end of therapy is less frequent than that following medication discontinuation, booster therapy sessions or follow-up visits may help to ensure that skills learned during therapy are maintained and continue to be used.

SUMMARY

GAD is characterized by persistent and excessive worry that is difficult to control. The disorder is common and associated with significant distress and impairment in multiple domains. Gary provides a clear example of the degree to which GAD can interfere in both the social and work arenas. Effective treatments for GAD include both cognitive-behavioral therapy and medication (e.g., buspirone, benzodiazepines, SSRIs, venlafaxine).

REFERENCES

American Psychiatric Association. (1980). *Diagnostic and statistical manual of mental disorders* (3rd ed.). Washington, DC: Author.

American Psychiatric Association. (1987). *Diagnostic and statistical manual of mental disorders* (3rd ed., rev.). Washington, DC: Author.

American Psychiatric Association. (1994). *Diagnostic and statistical manual of mental disorders* (4th ed.). Washington, DC: Author.

Angst, J., & Vollrath, M. (1991). The natural history of anxiety disorders. *Acta Psychiatrica Scandinavica, 84,* 446-452.

Barlow, D. H. (1988). *Anxiety and its disorders: The nature and treatment of anxiety and panic.* New York: Guilford.

Barlow, D. H., Rapee, R. M., & Brown, T. A. (1992). Behavioral treatment of generalized anxiety disorder. *Behavior Therapy, 23,* 551-570.

Beck, A. T., & Emery, G. (1985). *Anxiety disorders and phobias: A cognitive perspective.* New York: Basic Books.

Beck, J. G., Stanley, M. A., & Zebb, B. J. (1996). Characteristics of generalized anxiety disorder in older adults: A descriptive study. *Behaviour Research and Therapy, 34,* 225-234.

Bland, R. C., Newman, S. C., & Orn, H. (1988). Age of onset of psychiatric disorders. *Acta Psychiatrica Scandinavica, 77,* 43-49.

Blazer, D. G., Hughes, D., George, L. K., Swartz, M., & Boyer, R. (1991). Generalized anxiety disorder. In L. N. Robins & D. A. Regier (Eds.), *Psychiatric disorders in America: The Epidemiologic Catchment Area Study* (pp. 180-203). New York: Free Press.

Borkovec, T. D., Alcaine, O., & Behar, E. (in press). Avoidance theory of worry and generalized anxiety disorder. In R. G. Heimberg, C. L. Turk, & D. S. Mennin (Eds.), *Generalized anxiety disorder: Advances in research and practice.* New York: Guilford.

Borkovec, T. D., & Costello, E. (1993). Efficacy of applied relaxation and cognitive-behavioral therapy in the treatment of generalized anxiety disorder. *Journal of Consulting and Clinical Psychology, 61,* 611-619.

Borkovec, T. D., & Ruscio, A. M. (2001). Psychotherapy for generalized anxiety disorder. *Journal of Clinical Psychiatry, 62*(Suppl. 11), S37-S45.

Breitholtz, E., Westling, B. E., & Öst, L.-G. (1998). Cognitions in generalized anxiety disorder and panic disorder patients. *Journal of Anxiety Disorders, 12,* 567-577.

Brown, T. A., Antony, M. M., & Barlow, D. H. (1992). Psychometric properties of the Penn State Worry Questionnaire in a clinical anxiety disorders sample. *Behaviour Research and Therapy, 30,* 33-37.

Brown, T. A., Barlow, D. H., & Liebowitz, M. R. (1994). The empirical basis of generalized anxiety disorder. *American Journal of Psychiatry, 151,* 1272-1280.

Brown, T. A., DiNardo, P. A., & Barlow, D. H. (1994). *Anxiety Disorders Interview Schedule for DSM-IV (ADIS-IV).* San Antonio, TX: The Psychological Corporation.

Cassidy, J. (1995). Attachment and generalized anxiety disorder. In D. Cicchetti & S. L. Toth (Eds.), *Emotion, cognition, and representation: Rochester symposium on developmental psychopathology* (Vol. 6, pp. 343-370). Rochester, NY: University of Rochester Press.

Davidson, J. R. T., DuPont, R. L., Hedges, D., & Haskins, J. T. (1999). Efficacy, safety, and tolerability of venlafaxine extended release and buspirone in outpatients with generalized anxiety disorder. *Journal of Clinical Psychiatry, 60,* 528-535.

DiNardo, P. A., Brown, T. A., & Barlow, D. H. (1994) *Anxiety Disorders Interview Schedule for DSM-IV: Lifetime version (ADIS-IV-L).* San Antonio, TX: The Psychological Corporation.

Dubovsky, S. L. (1990). Generalized anxiety disorder: New concepts and psychopharmacologic therapies. *Journal of Clinical Psychiatry, 51,* 3-10.

Enkelmann, R. (1991). Alprazolam versus buspirone in the treatment of outpatients with generalized anxiety disorder. *Psychopharmacology, 105,* 428-432.

Feighner, J. P., Merideth, C. H., & Hendrickson, G. A. (1982). A double-blind comparison of buspirone and diazepam in outpatients with generalized anxiety disorder. *Journal of Clinical Psychiatry, 43,* 103-107.

First, M. B., Spitzer, R. L., Gibbon, M., & Williams, J. (1996) *Structured Clinical Interview for DSM-IV Axis I Disorders - Patient Edition* (SCID-I/P, Version 2.0). New York: New York State Psychiatric Institute.

Fresco, D. M., Mennin, D. S., Heimberg, R. G., & Turk, C. L. (2001). *Using the Penn State Worry Questionnaire to identify individuals with generalized anxiety disorder: A receiver operating characteristic analysis.* Manuscript submitted for publication.

Gould, R. A., Otto, M. W., Pollack, M. H., & Yap, L. (1997). Cognitive behavioral and pharmacological treatment of generalized anxiety disorder: A preliminary meta-analysis. *Behavior Therapy, 28,* 285-305.

Hamilton, M. (1959). The assessment of anxiety states by rating. *British Journal of Medical Psychology, 32,* 50-55.

Hoehn-Saric, R., McLeod, D. R., & Zimmerli, W. D. (1988). Differential effects of alprazolam and imipramine in generalized anxiety disorder: Somatic versus psychic symptoms. *Journal of Clinical Psychiatry, 49,* 293-301.

Horowitz, L. M., Alden, L. E., Wiggins, J. S., & Pincus, A. L. (2000). *Inventory of Interpersonal Problems: Manual.* San Antonio, TX: The Psychological Corporation.

Joormann, J., & Stöber, J. (1997). Measuring facets of worry: A LISREL analysis of the Worry Domains Questionnaire. *Personality and Individual Differences, 23,* 827-837.

Judd, L. L., Kessler, R. C., Paulus, M. P., Zeller, P. V., Wittchen, H.-U., & Kunovac, J. L. (1998). Comorbidity as a fundamental feature of generalized anxiety disorders: Results from the National Comorbidity Study (NCS). *Acta Psychiatrica Scandinavica, 98*(Suppl. 393), S6-S11.

Kessler, R. C. (2000, March). *The age of anxiety.* Paper presented at the annual meeting of the Anxiety Disorders Association of America, Washington, DC.

Kessler, R. C., DuPont, R. L., Berglund, P., & Wittchen, H.-U. (1999). Impairment in pure and comorbid generalized anxiety disorder and major depression at 12 months in two national surveys. *American Journal of Psychiatry, 156,* 1915-1923.

Kessler, R. C., Nelson, C. B., McGonagle, K. A., Liu, J., Swartz, M., & Blazer, D. G. (1996). Comorbidity of *DSM-III-R* major depressive disorder in the general population: Results from the U.S. National Comorbidity Survey. *British Journal of Psychiatry, 168*(Suppl. 30), S17-S30.

Kessler, R. C., Walters, E. E., & Wittchen, H.-U. (in press). Epidemiology of generalized anxiety disorder. In R. G. Heimberg, C. L. Turk, & D. S. Mennin (Eds.), *Generalized anxiety disorder: Advances in research and practice.* New York: Guilford.

Luterek, J. A., Turk, C. L., Heimberg, R. G., Fresco, D. M., & Mennin, D. S. (2001, November). *Psychometric properties of the GAD-Q-IV among individuals with clinician-assessed generalized anxiety disorder.* Paper presented at the annual meeting of the Association for Advancement of Behavior Therapy, Philadelphia, PA.

Mennin, D. S., Turk, C. L., Heimberg, R. G., & Carmin, C. (in press). Focusing on emotion: A new direction for conceptualizing and treating generalized anxiety disorder. In M. A. Reinecke & D. A. Clark (Eds.), *Cognitive therapy over the lifespan: Theory, research and practice.* Oxford, UK: Oxford University Press.

Meyer, T. J., Miller, M. L., Metzger, R. L., & Borkovec, T. D. (1990). Development and validation of the Penn State Worry Questionnaire. *Behaviour Research and Therapy, 28,* 487-495.

Molina, S., Roemer, L., Borkovec, M., & Posa, S. (1992, November). *Generalized anxiety disorder in an analog population: Types of past trauma.* Paper presented at the annual meeting of the Association for the Advancement of Behavior Therapy, Boston.

Newman, M. G., & Borkovec, T. D. (in press). Cognitive behavior therapy for worry and generalized anxiety disorder. In G. Simos (Ed.), *Cognitive behavior therapy: A guide for the practicing clinician.* London: Psychology Press.

Newman, M. G., Castonguay, L. G., Borkovec, T. D., & Molnar, C. (in press). Integrative therapy for generalized anxiety disorder. In R. G. Heimberg, C. L. Turk, & D. S. Mennin (Eds.), *Generalized anxiety disorder: Advances in research and practice*. New York: Guilford.

Newman, M. G., Zuellig, A. R., Kachin, K. E., Constantino, M. J., & Cashman, L. (2001). *The reliability and validity of the GAD-Q-IV: A revised self-report diagnostic measure of generalized anxiety disorder*. Manuscript submitted for publication.

Pincus, A. L., & Borkovec, T. D. (1994, June). *Interpersonal problems in generalized anxiety disorder: Preliminary clustering of patients' interpersonal dysfunction*. Paper presented at the annual meeting of the American Psychological Society, New York.

Pollack, M. H., Zainelli, R., Goddard, A., McCafferty, J. P., Bellew, K. M., Burnham, D. B., & Iyengar, M. K. (2001). Paroxetine in the treatment of generalized anxiety disorder: Results of a placebo-controlled, flexible-dosage trial. *Journal of Clinical Psychiatry, 62,* 350-357.

Power, K. G., Jerrom, D. W. A., Simpson, R. J., Mitchell, M. J., & Swanson, V. (1989). A controlled comparison of cognitive-behaviour therapy, diazepam and placebo in the management of generalized anxiety. *Behavioural Psychotherapy, 17,* 1-14.

Rapee, R. M. (1991). Generalized anxiety disorder: A review of clinical features and theoretical concepts. *Clinical Psychology Review, 11,* 419-440.

Rickels, K., Downing, R., Schweizer, E., & Hassman, H. (1993). Antidepressants for the treatment of generalized anxiety disorder. *Archives of General Psychiatry, 50,* 884-895.

Rickels, K., Schweizer, E., Csanalosi, I., Case, G., & Chung, H. (1988). Long-term treatment of anxiety and risk of withdrawal. *Archives of General Psychiatry, 45,* 444-450.

Rocca, P., Fonzo, V., Scotta, M., Zanalda, E., & Ravizza, L. (1998). Paroxetine efficacy in the treatment of generalized anxiety disorder. *Acta Psychiatrica Scandinavica, 95,* 444-450.

Roemer, L., Molina, S., & Borkovec, T. D. (1997). An investigation of worry content among generally anxious individuals. *Journal of Nervous and Mental Disease, 185,* 314-319.

Roemer, L., Molina, S., Litz, B. T., & Borkovec, T. D. (1996/1997). Preliminary investigation of the role of previous exposure to potentially traumatizing events in generalized anxiety disorder. *Depression and Anxiety, 4,* 134-138.

Sanderson, W. C., Wetzler, S., Beck, A. T., & Betz, F. (1994). Prevalence of personality disorders among patients with anxiety disorders. *Psychiatry Research, 51,* 167-174.

Shader, R. I., & Greenblatt, D. J. (1993). Use of benzodiazepines in anxiety disorders. *New England Journal of Medicine, 328,* 1398-1405.

Sheehan, D. V. (1999). Venlafaxine extended release (XR) in the treatment of generalized anxiety disorder. *Journal of Clinical Psychiatry, 60*(Suppl. 22), S23-S28.

Stöber, J. (1998). Reliability and validity of two widely-used worry questionnaires: Self-report and self-peer convergence. *Personality and Individual Differences, 24,* 887-890.

Strand, M., Hetta, J., Rosen, A., Sorensen, S., Malmstrom, R., Fabian, C., Marits, K., Vetterskog, K., Liljestrand, A.-G., & Hegen, C. (1990). A double-blind, controlled trial in primary care patients with generalized anxiety: A comparison between buspirone and oxazepam. *Journal of Clinical Psychiatry, 51*(Suppl. 9), S40-S45.

Tallis, F., Eysenck, M., & Mathews, A. (1992). A questionnaire for the measurement of nonpathological worry. *Personality and Individual Differences, 13,* 161-168.

Torgersen, S. (1986). Childhood and family characteristics in panic and generalized anxiety disorders. *American Journal of Psychiatry, 143,* 630-632.

Turk, C. L., Mennin, D. S., Fresco, D. M., & Heimberg, R. G. (2000, November). *Impairment and quality of life among individuals with generalized anxiety disorder.* Poster presented at the annual meeting of the Association for Advancement of Behavior Therapy, New Orleans.

Turk, C. L., Mennin, D. S., & Heimberg, R. G. (in press). Assessment of worry and generalized anxiety disorder. In R. G. Heimberg, C. L. Turk, & D. S. Mennin (Eds.), *Generalized anxiety disorder: Advances in research and practice.* New York: Guilford.

Wittchen, H.-U., Zhao, S., Kessler, R. C., & Eaton, W. W. (1994). *DSM-III-R* generalized anxiety disorder in the National Comorbidity Survey. *Archives of General Psychiatry, 51,* 355-364.

Yonkers, K. A., Warshaw, M. G., Massion, A. O., & Keller, M. B. (1996). Phenomenology and course of generalised anxiety disorder. *British Journal of Psychiatry, 168,* 308-313.

Zuellig, A. R., Newman, M. G., Kachin, K. E., & Constantino, M. J. (1997, November). *Differences in parental attachment profiles in adults diagnosed with generalized anxiety disorder, panic disorder, or non-disordered.* Paper presented at the annual conference of the Association for Advancement of Behavior Therapy, Miami.

CHAPTER 10

Social Anxiety Disorder, Specific Phobias, and Panic Disorder

DEBORAH A. ROTH
BRIAN P. MARX
SCOTT F. COFFEY

DESCRIPTION OF THE DISORDERS

According to Greenberg and colleagues (Greenberg et al., 1999), the annual economic burden of anxiety disorders is more than $42 billion a year, costing workplaces $256 per year for each affected worker, almost solely because of lost productivity. Greenberg et al. reported that all anxiety disorders, with the exception of simple phobias, were associated with "substantial impairment in workplace performance" (p. 431). In this chapter, the impact of social anxiety disorder and panic disorder on workplace functioning will be discussed. Although specific phobias might not cause *substantial* impairment in the workplace, ways in which this disorder can influence functioning will also be discussed.

Social Anxiety Disorder

Social anxiety disorder (also known as social phobia) is characterized by "a marked or persistent fear of social or performance situations" (American Psychiatric Association [APA], 1994, p. 411). People with the disorder worry that they will do or say something in such situations that will elicit negative evaluation from others. Another concern held by people with social anxiety disorder is that they will exhibit physical symptoms (e.g., blushing, shaking, sweating, etc.) when they are in social or performance situations that will lead others to assume that they are extremely anxious, to the exclusion of other, more benign interpretations (Roth, Antony, & Swinson, 2001). Because of these fears, people with social anxiety disorder experience a great deal of distress in social situations and often use avoidance tactics as a means of dealing with their anxiety. Avoidance can be either overt (e.g., choosing not to take a job that involves public speaking) or covert (e.g., taking the job, but having a few drinks before public speaking engagements). The distress and avoidance associated with social anxiety disorder leads to impairment in social, educational, and occupational functioning (e.g., Antony, Roth, Swinson, Huta, & Devins, 1998; Schneier et al., 1994).

By considering the situations that are problematic for people with social anxiety disorder, it is not difficult to see the ways in which the disorder can have a negative impact on workplace functioning. For instance, a fear of formal speaking seems to be ubiquitous in people with social anxiety disorder (Holt, Heimberg, Hope, & Liebowitz, 1992). Other feared situations include giving a report to a group, speaking up at meetings, and participating in small groups. Not only are these situations extremely common in the workplace, but they are also common in educational settings, through which people may need to progress in order to attain their career goals. In fact, the National Comorbidity Survey (NCS) demonstrated that a diagnosis of social anxiety disorder was negatively related to educational attainment and income (Magee, Eaton, Wittchen, McGonagle, & Kessler, 1996), and that rates of social anxiety disorder were significantly higher in people who, at the time of the study, were not working or in school (Magee et al., 1996). More anecdotally, many clinicians who work with this population notice that their clients are grossly underemployed given their intelligence and abilities.

Holt et al. (1992) report that people with social anxiety disorder also fear informal speaking and interaction, assertive interaction, and being observed—all common situations in the workplace. Many people with social anxiety disorder find casual interactions in the workplace, such as having lunch with coworkers or going to the annual holiday party, to be very distressing. Assertive interactions with supervisors and coworkers can also be difficult for people

with social anxiety disorder. As such, people with the disorder may be given undesirable work tasks or may work under undesirable conditions (e.g., long hours, low pay) without ever addressing these issues with supervisors. People with social anxiety disorder are sometimes hesitant to be observed as they work, while they write, or while they speak on the telephone. These difficulties may be relevant if the socially anxious person is asked to train a new coworker or if part of a job evaluation is to have one's work observed. It may also be a problem in today's open work environment, where people rarely have their own private offices.

Although the workplace is fraught with all sorts of difficult situations for people with social anxiety disorder, another source of distress for people with the disorder is actually securing a job. Job interviews typically entail casual conversation, answering structured questions, and sometimes can involve demonstrating a particular skill or doing public speaking (e.g., teaching a "mock" class, playing an instrument for a seat in an orchestra). Given the fear associated with these types of situations, people with social anxiety disorder may choose to be unemployed or to stay in a job that is unsatisfying in order to avoid the process of finding a new job.

Specific Phobias

According to the *DSM-IV* (APA, 1994), a specific phobia is "a marked or persistent fear of clearly discernible, circumscribed objects or situations" (p. 405). Furthermore, the *DSM-IV* states that the fear associated with these objects or situations is "excessive or unreasonable" (p. 410). Most people have a fear of some object or situation. Yet a simple fear is distinguished from a phobia in terms of both the intensity of the fear and the degree to which the fear causes distress and/or impairment. People with specific phobias almost always react to their feared stimuli with an anxiety response, typically in the form of a panic attack. Because of this response, people with a specific phobia either avoid their feared stimuli or endure them with great distress. Furthermore, this pattern of avoidance and/or distress leads to impairment in functioning. Although one does not naturally associate specific phobias with impairment in the workplace, the NCS study demonstrated that specific phobias are significantly elevated among people who were not employed at the time of the study (Magee et al., 1996).

Specific phobias are likely to have less of an impact on occupational functioning than social anxiety disorder or panic disorder because career choices may be naturally tailored to avoid feared objects or situations. For example, a person with a specific phobia of dogs would be unlikely to even want to be a veterinarian, and a person with a fear of water or storms would be unlikely to join the Navy or the Coast Guard.

However, specific phobias can stand in the way of people pursuing their career goals. People who fear blood, injections, and injuries, or who fear contracting an illness, may be unable to enter the medical professions, despite a real desire to do so. People with specific phobias of flying or driving may avoid jobs that they want, but that would require making use of these modes of transportation. Greco (1989) reported that the majority of patients in his cognitive-behavioral treatment program for fear of flying were motivated to seek treatment because of career considerations. Other situational-type phobias can also lead people to avoid taking certain jobs, including fears of heights, bridges, elevators, and small rooms. People with such fears may have problems getting to meetings or working in specific

environments. Particularly in big cities, it is very difficult to avoid these situations.

Not all people with specific phobias completely avoid their feared objects or situations; some endure them with distress. Although being able to endure these situations may be advantageous in terms of pursuing career goals, the distress associated with specific phobias can interfere with career functioning. If a person who is afraid of heights is distracted by anxious thoughts during a meeting on the top floor of a building, he or she may be less able to pay attention to the meeting and may not perform up to expectations. Similarly, a person who is afraid of flying, but who often needs to fly to business meetings, may drink alcohol on the plane or take antianxiety medication as a means of coping. Yet use of these substances may lead to cognitive impairments, interfering in performance once the individual actually arrives at his or her meeting.

Panic Disorder

The defining feature of panic disorder is the presence of recurrent, unexpected panic attacks (APA, 1994). The diagnostic criteria for panic attacks specify that the attack must develop abruptly and reach its peak within 10 minutes. Commonly experienced panic symptoms include racing heart, sweating, shaking, and dizziness. Panic attacks are also associated with cognitive symptoms such as fear of dying and fear of losing control or going crazy.

Although panic attacks are common to several of the anxiety disorders, two features distinguish the panic attacks that occur in the context of panic disorder. One feature is that panic disorder is characterized by the presence of at least some uncued or "out of the blue" panic attacks; in the other anxiety disorders, attacks are cued by anticipation of, or exposure to, feared stimuli (e.g., making a speech, seeing a dog). Furthermore, the diagnostic criteria for panic disorder specify that panic attacks are followed by at least 1 month of worry about having additional attacks; the consequences of having an attack (e.g., having a heart attack, losing control); or significant changes in behavior because of the attacks. In other words, panic disorder is characterized by fear of physical symptoms, rather than by fear of some specific object or situation.

because they occur!!

This distinction makes differential diagnosis across the anxiety disorders particularly important. When a client reports being afraid of a specific object or situation, the clinician must ask what it is that the client specifically fears. A client may be afraid of flying for fear of having a panic attack in the plane and not being able to escape (panic disorder), or he or she may be afraid of flying for fear that the plane will crash (specific phobia of flying). With regard to the differential diagnoses of social anxiety disorder and panic disorder, it is important to keep in mind that people who have panic disorder might fear negative evaluation from others, but only when they are having a panic attack (they fear that others will notice their physical symptoms of anxiety and therefore judge them negatively). In contrast, people with social anxiety disorder experience more far-reaching concerns about negative evaluation from others.

About one third to one half of community samples with panic disorder also meet criteria for agoraphobia (panic disorder with agoraphobia [PDA]); this number is far higher in clinical samples (APA, 1994). Agoraphobia is defined in the *DSM-IV* as "anxiety about being in places or situations from which escape might be difficult (or embarrassing) or in which help may not be available in the event of having a panic attack" (p. 396). Agoraphobia typically begins within the first year of experiencing persistent panic attacks (APA, 1994). Commonly feared situations for individuals with PDA include traveling on buses, trains, and airplanes; crossing bridges; being in crowds; taking walks alone; being in small rooms; going out of town; and being in movie theaters, arenas, or classrooms. Agoraphobic avoidance is associated with a great deal of distress and impairment in social, educational, and occupational functioning (see Magee et al., 1996). Ettigi, Meyerhoff, Chirban, Jacobs, and Wilson (1997) reported that 25% of their sample of clients with panic disorder were unemployed, and only 57% were employed full-time.

EPIDEMIOLOGY

Anxiety disorders are the most prevalent mental disorders affecting people in the United States. According to the NCS, which used *DSM-III-R* criteria, the lifetime prevalence rate for social anxiety disorder is about 13% (Kessler et al., 1994). Specific phobias are slightly less common, affecting about 11% of the population (Kessler et al., 1994), and the prevalence of panic disorder is even lower, affecting about 3.5% of the population (Eaton, Kessler, Wittchen, & Magee, 1994). Eaton et al. (1994) reported that panic disorder with agoraphobia has a lifetime prevalence of about 1.5%.

Although panic disorder, specific phobias, and social anxiety disorder are all more common in women than in men, this sex difference is less striking in the case of social anxiety disorder (Kessler et al., 1994), with some research in clinic samples actually showing almost equal rates of the disorder in women and men (see Mannuzza, Fyer, Liebowitz, & Klein, 1990). Age of onset for the anxiety disorders vary. Although social anxiety disorder often emerges out of shyness in childhood, the age of onset for the

PDA → panic disorder w/ agoraphi...

disorder is typically in midadolescence, when increased importance is placed on social life and when speaking up in class becomes more important. Age of onset varies according to subtype of specific phobia, but many have onset in childhood. The mean age of onset for panic disorder is quite a bit later than for social anxiety disorder or specific phobias—around age 30 (Kenardy, Oei, & Evans, 1990).

ASSESSMENT

There are three primary strategies for assessing social anxiety disorder, specific phobias, and panic disorder: clinical interviews, self-report measures, and behavior tests. All three of these strategies should include explorations into the thoughts, feelings, and behaviors that the individual experiences when exposed to his or her feared objects or situations.

Clinical Interviews

Clinical interviews for clients with phobias should focus on determining the content and nature of the fears and the ways in which these fears are affecting the client's life. Although some clinicians prefer to use an unstructured interview format, structured clinical interviews such as the Structured Clinical Interview for *DSM-IV* (SCID-IV) (First, Spitzer, Gibbon, & Williams, 1997) or the Anxiety Disorders Interview Schedule for *DSM-IV* (ADIS-IV) (Brown, DiNardo, & Barlow, 1994) can be very helpful guides for the assessment process.

In the interview process, it is not sufficient to simply find out what a client fears (e.g., flying); rather, it is important to gain a deeper understanding of what the nature of the fear is (the plane crashing, having a panic attack, being forced to sit and speak

with a stranger) and which variables affect the intensity of the fear. For example, a person who fears flying may find short flights easier than long flights, may prefer larger planes to smaller planes, and may prefer to fly accompanied rather than alone. Gathering this sort of information increases the likelihood of making a proper diagnosis, aids in treatment planning, and helps to build rapport with the client.

It is also important to get a sense of how the fear is affecting clients' lives. They should be asked about both overt avoidance (e.g., not flying at all, refusing to do public speaking or go to parties) and more subtle forms of avoidance, such as only going places with a "safe" person or using alcohol or medications to calm anxiety in anticipation of stressful situations. Clinicians should also ask about impairment in a more global sense, tapping into clients' abilities to work, attend school, and have interpersonal relationships.

Self-Report Measures

Self-Report Measures for Social Anxiety Disorder

There are many self-report measures for assessing social anxiety disorder (see McNeil, Ries, & Turk, 1995, for an excellent review). Mattick and Clarke (1998) have developed two measures—the Social Phobia Scale (SPS) and the Social Interaction Anxiety Scale (SIAS)—that are extremely useful and have been shown to have good reliability and validity by both the authors themselves and other researchers in the field (e.g., Heimberg, Mueller, Holt, Hope, & Liebowitz, 1992). The SPS focuses on the anxiety that people experience in situations where they might be observed by others (e.g., "I feel self-conscious if I have to enter a room where others are already seated"); the SIAS focuses on the cognitive, affective, and behavioral responses that people experience when they interact with others ("I get nervous when I have to speak with someone in authority [teacher, boss]").

An important component of social anxiety disorder is fear of negative evaluation by others. The Fear of Negative Evaluation Scale (FNE), developed by Watson and Friend (1969), has been used to assess this concern. A brief version of the FNE has been developed by Leary (1983) and has been found to correlate strongly with Watson and Friend's original scale. As such, Leary's scale is an efficient way to assess fear of negative evaluation, and, given its brevity, it can also be a useful tool for tracking progress weekly over the course of treatment.

Other commonly used self-report measures for social anxiety disorder include the Social Phobia Anxiety Inventory (Turner, Beidel, Dancu, & Stanley, 1989) and the Social Phobia Inventory (Davidson, 1998).

Self-Report Measures for Specific Phobias

Compared to social anxiety disorder, there are far fewer well-established measures for the assessment of specific phobias. Although some general fear survey schedules have been developed (Geer, 1965; Wolpe & Lang, 1964), these measures are not considered to be ideal for assessment of specific phobias (Antony & Swinson, 2000) given that they often assess for feared situations that are considered indicative of other disorders (e.g., social anxiety disorder, panic disorder). Furthermore, existing fear survey schedules typically ask clients about specific objects and situations that are not commonly the focus of concern for people with specific phobias (e.g., fear of the sound of vacuum cleaners, fear of nude people). Antony and Swinson (2000) provide a detailed list of scales that can be

used when assessing particular specific phobias (e.g., dental phobia, claustrophobia, etc.), but also suggest that an updated fear survey schedule should be developed that is broader and more in keeping with the current diagnostic criteria for specific phobias.

Clinicians may also find Antony, Craske, and Barlow's (1995) specific phobia treatment manual to be useful in the assessment of specific phobias. The manual includes numerous "Fearful Thoughts Questionnaires" in which clients are asked to rate the extent to which they believe a series of statements about their particular feared object or situation (e.g., driving, going to the dentist, etc.). The authors also present lists of variables that may affect people's fears (e.g., a driving phobia may be influenced by speed of traffic, highway vs. city driving, etc.) that can be very useful in the course of assessment and treatment planning.

Self-Report Measures for Panic Disorder and Agoraphobia

Numerous measures are available for assessing panic disorder and agoraphobia (see Antony & Swinson, 2000, for assessment guidelines and a more detailed review of measures). The Panic Frequency Questionnaire (PFQ) (Antony & Swinson, 2000) is useful for assessing panic frequency and the range of symptoms experienced during panic attacks. The scale asks clients about the number of cued and uncued attacks they have had in the past month. It also asks clients about the degree to which they worried about having more attacks in the past month, the degree to which they were concerned about the consequence of having attacks, and the degree to which they changed their behavior over the past month because of their panic attacks. Furthermore, the scale asks clients to indicate the symptoms that they experience during a typical panic attack. At this time, the psychometric properties of the scale have not been established, but the PFQ provides useful information to aid with diagnosis, treatment planning, and tracking progress over the course of treatment.

It is also useful to gather information about anxiety sensitivity, which has been defined by Taylor and Cox (1998) as "the fear of anxiety-related bodily sensations, said to arise from beliefs that these sensations have harmful somatic, social or psychological consequences" (p. 464). The Anxiety Sensitivity Index (ASI) (Peterson & Reiss, 1993) and the revised version of the ASI (ASI-R) (Taylor & Cox, 1998) have been designed to assess this construct. Items on the ASI-R include "When I feel like I'm not getting enough air, I get scared that I might suffocate" and "When I feel dizzy, I worry there is something wrong with my brain."

A useful measure for assessing the thoughts that people with panic disorder experience is the Agoraphobic Cognitions Questionnaire (ACQ) (Chambless, Caputo, Bright, & Gallagher, 1984). Individuals are asked to report how frequently they experience specific thoughts when they are anxious, such as "I am going to go crazy" and "I will be paralyzed by fear." Finally, clinicians may want to use the Mobility Inventory (MI) (Chambless, Caputo, Jasin, Gracely, & Williams, 1985) as a means for assessing degree of agoraphobic avoidance. On the MI, clients are asked the degree to which they avoid 26 situations (e.g., going to the theater, getting in elevators, standing in lines) while they are alone and while they are accompanied by others. HA BEAT

It should be noted that Marks and Mathews's (1979) Fear Questionnaire (FQ) can also be useful in the assessment of panic disorder, social anxiety disorder, and specific phobia. This measure assesses agoraphobic fear; social anxiety; and fear of

stimuli related to blood, injections, and injuries.

Behavior Tests

During clinical interviews and when completing self-report measures, many clients have difficulty reporting on the thoughts, behaviors, and feelings that they experience when they are faced with their feared object or situations. Other clients avoid their feared object or situation to such an extent that they may not have a clear recollection of how they reacted in the past when they actually did expose themselves to these feared stimuli. As such, having clients undergo a behavior test in the presence of the assessing clinician can provide valuable information for diagnosis and treatment planning.

Behavior tests can involve having clients engage in a single behavior, such as asking a client with a fear of public speaking to give a speech in front of an audience of strangers. Behavior tests can also involve assessing how far a client can progress through a series of actions leading up to a feared behavior. For instance, a person with agoraphobia who can no longer go to work may be asked to progress as far along his or her route to work as possible (e.g., leaving the house, getting in the car, driving through traffic, arriving at the office, etc.). The major variable of interest in this type of behavior test is to what step along the fear hierarchy the client can progress; this can also be used as a good measure of treatment outcome. Anxiety ratings, records of clients' thoughts, and psychophysiological measures (e.g., heart rate) collected before, during, and after behavior tests can also provide important information.

Case Description

M.M. was a 35-year-old woman who worked for a nonprofit organization in a

I fear going crazy
us MI mobilit Invantor

big city. She was diagnosed with social anxiety disorder and had no comorbid conditions. M.M. experienced relatively mild anxiety when interacting with close friends and family. She reported that she could go out to dinner with her husband and their friends and feel quite relaxed. She had slight concerns about looking anxious or saying something foolish, but these concerns would never preclude her from going out and being sociable.

M.M. experienced a great deal more anxiety in the workplace, where she supervised a large team of employees. M.M. loved the nature of her work and was happy spending hours alone in her office planning projects for the organization. Meeting one-on-one with a single member of her team was also comfortable for her. She had great difficulty, however, with weekly staff meetings. At these meetings, she was required to stand up in front of the entire organization and report on the progress of her team that week. M.M.'s anxiety was so intense during these meetings that she tried to speak for as brief a time as possible, one day even faking a coughing fit to allow her to leave a meeting that was making her extremely anxious. These brief presentations were frowned upon by her supervisors, who could not understand why her presentations were not representative of the excellent work that she did for the organization. Whenever possible, M.M. would ask a coworker to give the team report, but this was also frowned upon by her superiors, given her supervisory position in the organization.

M.M. had numerous concerns during these weekly meetings. She was very fearful that she would open her mouth and that no words would come out—in fact, this had happened to her once, and she viewed that experience as the point at which her anxiety

began to cause her significantly more distress and impairment. She also worried about *what* she was going to say and was quite convinced that she would come across as stupid, incompetent, and undeserving of her job. Her greatest concern, however, was that people would notice her physical symptoms of anxiety. She worried that people would hear her voice quiver, see her hands shake, and notice her blush. Blushing was a major concern for her; being quite fair, her neck and face did blush quite easily. Yet M.M. was so concerned about people noticing this symptom, and judging her negatively because of it, that she took to wearing turtlenecks all year round, even in the height of summer.

Despite feeling quite calm about casual socializing outside of work, chatting with coworkers or her supervisors also provoked anxiety in M.M. As in the more formal setting of weekly staff meetings, M.M. worried that people would find her stupid and incompetent. She also worried that if she spoke to people in close proximity, her anxiety symptoms (particularly the blushing) would be even more noticeable than at staff meetings, and that people would glean from these symptoms that she was anxious, incompetent, and mentally ill.

A few weeks into cognitive-behavioral therapy for social anxiety disorder, the client's supervisors asked her if she would be willing to go to Washington and testify to a Senate subcommittee on behalf of their organization. The client came into her session after being asked to do this and reported that she was seriously considering quitting her job. After a few additional sessions with her therapist, the client indeed went to Washington and testified successfully. She expressed to the therapist, though, that had she not been in therapy, she would have quit her job to avoid this situation.

PRECIPITATING CONDITIONS, INCLUDING WORKPLACE STRESSORS

Multiple factors—including genetics, other biological factors, personality factors, family factors, and other early life experiences—can play a role in the development of social anxiety disorder, specific phobias, and panic disorder. A detailed discussion of these issues is beyond the scope of this chapter (readers may find Mennin, Heimberg, & Holt, 2000, to be a helpful overview).

Rachman (1976, 1977) proposed three pathways to the development of phobias that are helpful in thinking about how social anxiety disorder and specific phobias develop. The first pathway is through traumatic conditioning, whereby a person develops a fear of a specific object or situation after a traumatic experience involving that object or situation. For example, a person may develop a fear of elevators after having been in an elevator that suddenly dropped a number of floors in a tall office building. Similarly, traumatic social events could contribute to the development of social anxiety disorder. People who may have been slightly shy all of their lives might develop a clinically significant problem with social anxiety after getting up to give a speech and finding that they could not speak or after having a job review in which they received negative feedback from their boss.

Many people who have phobias cannot recall a specific event that led to the development of their fears. Similarly, not all people who have traumatic experiences with specific objects or situations develop clinically significant phobias. With this in mind, Rachman proposed two other pathways to the development of fears: vicarious conditioning (also known as observational learning) and informational transmission.

Vicarious conditioning refers to the fact that people can learn to be afraid of something by watching someone else react to a specific object or situation in a fearful way. For example, watching a coworker forget what he was supposed to say during a presentation could contribute to the development of social anxiety disorder. Similarly, seeing a coworker get pricked accidentally by a used needle during a medical procedure and subsequently go through tests for HIV and other diseases could lead an individual to develop a specific phobia of contracting an illness.

People can also learn to be afraid of objects or situations by hearing from others that they should be afraid. Such information can be gleaned from family, friends, and coworkers, or from the media. Very few people have been in plane crashes or know others who have, but many people have come to fear flying based on all the media coverage when a plane does crash. Although the possible influence of friends, coworkers, and the media has not been explored in terms of the development of social fears, research has shown that people with social anxiety disorder are more likely to have grown up with parents who are themselves socially reticent than are people without the disorder (e.g., Bruch, Heimberg, Berger, & Collins, 1989; Caster, Inderbitzen, & Hope, 1999).

The precipitating factors underlying the development of panic disorder have been viewed differently from those underlying the development of phobias. Panic disorder seems to have quite a strong biological basis, with neurotransmitter alterations, anatomical abnormalities, and altered respiratory physiology all thought to play a role (see Silberman, 1999). Although biological factors are undoubtedly important to the development of panic disorder, psychological models have also been proposed that conceptualize why the experience of a panic attack can be so troubling to some individuals, as well as why panic disorder is maintained over time. Clark's (1986, 1988) model focuses on the cognitive appraisals that people make for physical symptoms. Specifically, Clark posits that panic disorder is associated with catastrophic misinterpretations of seemingly benign physical symptoms. For example, individuals with panic disorder often interpret a racing heart as a sign that they are having a heart attack.

Barlow (1988; Antony & Barlow, 1996) has developed a model that takes into account both biological and psychological factors that can lead to development of panic disorder. He suggests that problems with panic can begin when a person experiences panic symptoms during times of stress. Whereas some people might be predisposed biologically to develop ulcers or migraines when they are stressed, other people experience panic symptoms. Barlow refers to this panic reaction as a false alarm, given that the symptoms that people experience are very similar to those experienced during truly dangerous situations (e.g., being chased by a bear). Because of biological and psychological vulnerabilities, some people fear these symptoms and go on to develop anxious apprehension about having additional attacks. In the future, physical symptoms are associated with the original false alarm, and through classical conditioning, learned alarms develop such that benign physical symptoms are associated with danger and fear. Once this association is established, panic attacks can be triggered by a variety of factors, including hypervigilance to bodily sensations, exposure to situations where attacks have happened in the past, and other cognitive cues. Not surprisingly, avoidance of situations where attacks have taken place in the past and of physical sensations (e.g., not drinking coffee, not exercising) often develops, serving to maintain the disorder.

COURSE AND PROGNOSIS

Panic disorder (Ehlers, 1995; Faravelli, Paterniti, & Scarpato, 1995) and social anxiety disorder (Rapee, 1995) are generally associated with a chronic course in the absence of appropriate treatment. Specific phobias can be quite transitory in childhood (although they must persist for at least 6 months to garner a diagnosis), but those that persist into adulthood or that emerge in adulthood also tend to have a chronic course in the absence of treatment (APA, 1994). It is believed that these disorders are maintained by the client's continued avoidance of feared stimuli over time, resulting in lost opportunities to learn that one can, in fact, cope with the situation. As such, treatment that encourages clients to face their fears is the most suitable strategy for people with phobias and panic disorder.

RECOMMENDED TREATMENTS

Brief Description

Although both pharmacotherapy and psychotherapy (specifically, cognitive-behavioral therapy [CBT]) are the preferred treatments for social anxiety disorder and panic disorder, medication is rarely prescribed for the treatment of specific phobias, with the focus instead placed on psychotherapy.

Cognitive-Behavioral Approaches

Cognitive-behavioral approaches to the treatment of social anxiety disorder, specific phobias, and panic disorder have received considerable empirical support in the treatment literature. The underlying premise of CBT is that people with these disorders exhibit maladaptive cognitions and behaviors. As such, these disorders can be treated by making changes to thoughts, behaviors, or both.

CBT programs often begin with a psychoeducational component in which the CB model of the disorder is presented and the treatment rationale is explained. Little emphasis is placed on the origins of the client's problems, with the focus placed instead on how cognitions and behaviors serve to maintain the disorder over time. Self-monitoring is an important component of CBT that is introduced early in treatment. Clients are asked to keep records of the situations in which they experience anxiety, paying close attention to their thoughts and to variables that influence the experiences that they have in these situations. The information gathered through self-monitoring is essential to structuring both the cognitive and behavioral aspects of treatment.

The cognitive aspect of CBT involves identifying, examining, and restructuring negative automatic thoughts. Although general types of negative automatic thoughts (Beck, Rush, Shaw, & Emery, 1979; Beck, 1995) are seen across a broad spectrum of psychological disorders (e.g., anxiety disorders, mood disorders, eating disorders, etc.), some types of thoughts seem to be closely associated with specific disorders. In social anxiety disorder, "common" thinking errors include mind-reading errors (clients tend to assume that they know exactly what others think of them), discounting the positive (clients tend to attribute successes to external factors such as luck or the kindness of others), and mental filter (clients tend to focus on one negative detail of an event/interaction rather than taking a more global perspective) (see Hope, Heimberg, Juster, & Turk, 2000). The goal of CBT for social

anxiety disorder is not to get clients to see the world as a place filled with benevolent and accepting people, but rather to take a more balanced view of how they are judged by others and how important these judgments are.

In the case of specific phobias, two main types of thinking errors occur often (Antony et al., 1995). The first is "overestimation," which refers to the tendency to view negative events as much more likely to occur than they actually are. For example, a person with a specific phobia of flying might feel 100% convinced that the plane is going to crash each time he takes a flight. The second type of thinking error most common to specific phobias is "catastrophizing," which refers to the tendency to view events as dangerous and unbearable. For example, a person with a phobia of snakes might report to the therapist that if she saw a snake, she would just die, or if a snake came near her, it would bite her with its horrible fangs. The goal of cognitive restructuring in the treatment of specific phobias is to reframe these thoughts to be more rational and adaptive. For example, patients may be encouraged to seek out information (e.g., the probability of actually being in a plane crash) to disconfirm irrational or overstated beliefs.

Because panic disorder is essentially viewed as a fear of physical symptoms, a major aspect of cognitive work involves "correcting misappraisals of bodily sensations as threatening" (Craske & Barlow, 1993, p. 16). For example, it is helpful to remind clients of times when they experienced the same physical symptoms that they experience during panic attacks, but did not perceive the symptoms as threatening (e.g., drinking too much coffee, exercising, etc.).

Cognitive therapy for all three disorders is typically applied in conjunction with behavioral work. This entails exposing clients to situations that they have previously feared or avoided, with the goal being fear reduction. Exposure exercises are best structured through the use of a fear and avoidance hierarchy. Clients rate their feared situations from least anxiety-provoking to most anxiety-provoking and gradually expose themselves to the items on the hierarchy in a systematic way. By beginning to work on items lower on the hierarchy, clients will be more likely to have success experiences, thereby increasing their self-efficacy and leading them to feel more confident about subsequent exposures.

In vivo exposures tend to be more effective than imaginary exposures (Antony et al., 1995), although the latter is sometimes indicated early in treatment for people who are too fearful to actually face their feared stimuli (e.g., imagining a snake before being exposed to a real one), or in situations where setting up repeated exposures is difficult (e.g., exposure to thunderstorms or hurricanes) or expensive (e.g., exposure to flying). Behavioral exercises can be integrated into therapy sessions, but CBT is most effective when clients also commit time to doing exposures between sessions. It is important for clients to learn that the successes they experience in the safe therapy environment can also be experienced in real life. Another important aspect of behavioral work in CBT is that clients evaluate the success of exposures based on what they have *done* and not on how they *feel*. For a client who has not done public speaking in years, simply doing it is seen as a success, rather than if they were able to do it without experiencing anxiety.

Exposure exercises can take on many forms and depend, of course, on the concerns of the client. In the treatment of social anxiety disorder, common exposure exercises include public speaking; initiating and maintaining conversations; job interviews;

making phone calls; and doing things in front of other people, such as eating, writing, or working (see Hope et al., 2000). In the treatment of specific phobias, exposures can range from confronting feared animals/insects, to taking an airplane flight, to going to the dentist (see Antony et al., 1995).

Many types of behavioral exercises can be helpful for clients with panic disorder (see Craske & Barlow, 2000). In interoceptive exposure, the client is exposed to the physical sensations that are similar to those experienced during a panic attack. Exercises such as breathing through a straw, spinning around in a chair, or holding one's breath are undertaken as a means of bringing on these sensations (see Antony & Swinson, 2000). The purpose of these exercises is to teach clients that although feared symptoms such as breathlessness, smothering sensations, and dizziness might be uncomfortable, they are not indicative of impending disaster. More traditional exposure exercises can also be used to expose the client both to the symptoms of panic attacks (e.g., seeing a scary movie, going for a run) and to the situations that the client fears will bring on attacks (e.g., riding the subway, going for a walk alone).

A final component of CBT for anxiety disorders that is often employed is relaxation strategies, such as breathing retraining and progressive muscle relaxation. These techniques are introduced to clients as additional strategies that they can use when they experience stress or anxiety in their lives.

Pharmacotherapy

As noted above, pharmacotherapy generally is not indicated in the treatment of specific phobias. Medications are, however, effective for the treatment of both social anxiety disorder and panic disorder.

Tricyclic Antidepressants. Although tricyclic antidepressants like imipramine have not been found to be particularly useful for the treatment of social anxiety disorder, they have been used effectively for many years to treat panic disorder. It has been suggested that imipramine works by first reducing panic symptoms, leading subsequently to decreased agoraphobic avoidance (e.g., see Klein, Ross, & Cohen, 1987). Typically, a reduction in panic symptoms is observed about 2 to 4 weeks after starting medication, and, according to Silberman (1999), about 78% of people with panic disorder improve substantially when taking imipramine. A difficulty inherent with using tricyclics for the treatment of panic disorder is that some clients do not tolerate the side effects well, particularly those that mimic symptoms of panic, such as shakiness and palpitations. Furthermore, the long-term efficacy of tricyclics following discontinuation is unclear (see Silberman, 1999).

Selective Serotonin Reuptake Inhibitors (SSRIs). SSRIs, despite their relatively short history, show much promise in the treatment of anxiety (and other) disorders. As compared to the older tricyclics, SSRIs tend to have fewer side effects and are also less lethal when taken in overdose. As such, clinicians may feel more comfortable prescribing SSRIs to individuals with suicidal ideation—an issue that certainly comes up when working with clients with diagnoses of panic disorder and social anxiety disorder.

The Food and Drug Administration (FDA) has approved particular SSRIs for the treatment of panic disorder and social anxiety disorder. Paroxetine, fluvoxamine, and sertraline have all received indications for panic disorder. Paroxetine (Ballenger, Wheadon, Steiner, Bushnell, & Gergel, 1998; Oehrberg et al., 1995), fluvoxamine (Bakish et al., 1996; Black, Wesner,

Bowers, & Gabel, 1993), and sertraline (Londborg et al., 1998; Pohl, Wolkow, & Clary, 1998; Pollack, Otto, Worthington, Manfro, & Wolkow, 1998), as well as other SSRIs that do not have specific indications for panic disorder (e.g., fluoxetine) (see Michelson et al., 1998), have all been shown to be more effective than placebo in the treatment of panic. Whereas a meta-analytic study suggested that the SSRIs are more effective than imipramine for the treatment of panic disorder (Boyer, 1994), other studies have shown them to be equally effective (Bakish et al., 1996), or have shown imipramine to be more effective (Nair et al., 1996).

At the current time, only paroxetine has received an indication from the FDA for the treatment of social anxiety disorder. Paroxetine has been shown to be more effective than placebo for this disorder (e.g., Allgulander, 1999; Stein et al., 1998), as have other SSRIs, including fluvoxamine (Stein, Fyer, Davidson, Pollack, & Wiita, 1999) and sertraline (Katzelnick et al., 1995).

Despite their promise, SSRIs are difficult for some people to tolerate. Silberman (1999) points out that in some studies on the treatment of panic, upwards of 25% of clients were unable to tolerate a 20 mg dose of fluoxetine. SSRIs can lead to an initial *increase* in anxiety, which can be (not surprisingly) quite distressing to anxious individuals. It is advantageous to begin patients at a very low dose of these medications, gradually increasing the dosage to a more therapeutic range. In addition to this cautious dosing, clinicians should inform their clients that they may experience this side effect and should assure them that, with time, it will dissipate.

Another relatively common side effect for individuals taking SSRIs is sexual dysfunction—and unlike many other side effects of SSRIs, this does not tend to abate over time. This is an unfortunate side effect, because an indicator of improvement for both panic disorder and social anxiety disorder may be an interest in engaging in sexual interactions. People with panic disorder may avoid sex because they fear the physical sensations associated with it, given that many mimic the symptoms experienced during panic attacks. People with social anxiety disorder may fear intimacy of sexual interactions, but perhaps even more relevant, many may not find themselves in relationships where intimacy is even possible given their avoidance of dating. As patients begin to deal with these issues, they may feel ready to have a sexual relationship.

Monoamine Oxidase Inhibitors (MAOIs). The efficacy of MAOIs in the treatment of panic disorder has been explored, but findings have been difficult to interpret because of methodological problems (Silberman, 1999). However, it does seem that MAOIs may be effective in the treatment of panic disorder, with one study (Sheehan, Ballenger, & Jacobsen, 1980) suggesting that the MAOI phenelzine was slightly more effective than imipramine on some treatment outcome measures. Phenelzine is used more commonly in the treatment of social anxiety disorder and is effective in about two thirds of clients (Gelernter et al., 1991; Liebowitz et al., 1992; Versiani et al., 1992). The major disadvantage in using MAOIs is that clients must avoid food, beverages, and medications containing tyramine. Failure to follow these dietary restrictions can result in dangerous hypertensive crises that can be fatal. As such, MAOIs are rarely used as a first line of treatment, but might be considered if other medications, such as the SSRIs, are not effective.

Benzodiazepines. Another commonly used class of drugs for the treatment of panic disorder is the benzodiazepines, like alprazolam. These drugs have demonstrated efficacy in reducing panic attacks and are also helpful for anticipatory anxiety. Benzodiazepines have also garnered some support as an effective treatment for social anxiety disorder. A clear advantage of benzodiazepines (as compared to the medications already discussed) is that they work soon after initiation of treatment, usually within 1 week (Silberman, 1999).

Benzodiazepines are not without problems, however. People can become dependent on them, and withdrawal can be difficult, particularly if they are discontinued suddenly. Furthermore, side effects of the benzodiazepines, including drowsiness and cognitive impairment, can interfere with functioning in the workplace. These side effects may be particularly distressing to people with social anxiety disorder, given their concerns about what they are going to say or how they are going to perform in the presence of others.

The decision to prescribe benzodiazepines to individuals with anxiety disorders should be balanced against the potential danger of mixing these medications with alcohol. Both panic disorder and social anxiety disorder are associated with an increase in the odds of being diagnosed with an alcohol use disorder (Kushner, Abrams, & Borchardt, 2000; Kushner, Sher, & Beitman, 1990). Prescribing benzodiazepines to clients who drink regularly or who have had difficulties with other drugs or with alcohol in the past should be considered only after other medication options have been ruled out. If physicians do decide to prescribe benzodiazepines to this population, it should be done on a strictly time-limited basis.

Comparative Studies

Large-scale studies have compared the efficacy of pharmacotherapy to that of

CBT, with some studies also exploring the potential for increasing efficacy through the use of combined treatments. Clark and his colleagues (Clark et al., 1994) compared outcomes in individuals with panic disorder who received either 12 weeks of CBT, 12 weeks of applied relaxation, or 6 months of imipramine. At the end of 3 months, the CBT group showed an advantage over the other two groups in terms of the percentage of clients who showed high end-state functioning and the percentage of clients who had become panic-free. At the end of 6 months, clients in the CBT and medication groups did not differ, with both doing better than clients in the relaxation group. At the 15-month follow-up, once all treatments had been discontinued, the CBT group again showed an advantage over the imipramine group and the relaxation group. The results of this study suggest that CBT and imipramine are both effective in the treatment of panic disorder, but that once treatment is withdrawn, the effects of CBT are maintained whereas imipramine loses its effectiveness.

A study by Barlow, Gorman, Shear, and Woods (2000) looked at the effect of combining CBT with imipramine in the treatment of panic. In terms of acute effects, both CBT and imipramine were found to be superior to a placebo. However, consistent with the Clark et al. (1994) study, Barlow and colleagues found that CBT was a more effective treatment in the long run, as indicated by an extremely low relapse rate. In fact, the group that received both imipramine and CBT actually experienced the highest relapse rate of any of the other groups at the time of the follow-up assessment. The authors concluded that the "addition of imipramine appeared to reduce the long-term durability of CBT" (p. 2535).

Heimberg, Liebowitz, and their colleagues (Heimberg et al., 1998; Liebowitz et al., 1999) have compared the efficacy of cognitive-behavioral group therapy (CBGT) to that of the MAOI phenelzine for treating social anxiety disorder. Both CBGT and phenelzine were found to be more effective than either a pill placebo or a psychotherapy "attention placebo." Although phenelzine worked more quickly than CBGT, clients who received CBGT did better in the long run than did clients who had received medication. Once treatment had been withdrawn, clients who had received phenelzine were much more likely to relapse than were clients who had participated in CBGT. Currently, this same group is exploring the efficacy of combining CBGT and phenelzine for the treatment of social anxiety disorder.

Time Element

A major advantage of currently available treatments for phobias is that they are short term and tend to work quickly. Some specific phobias can be treated in just a few hours. Many treatment studies for social anxiety disorder and panic disorder involve approximately 12 sessions (typically one session per week) of treatment, and studies of this duration have shown impressive success rates (e.g., Barlow et al., 2000; Heimberg et al., 1998; Liebowitz et al., 1999). Medications for these disorders also work quickly and typically involve minor time commitments in terms of doctor visits. In other words, clients can take part in treatment programs for phobias without making major, long-term adjustments in work or family responsibilities.

Side Effects of Treatment and How They Affect Work

Few side effects are associated with CBT for phobic disorders, although it is expected that clients will experience an increase in anxiety at the beginning of treatment. After all, clients are asked to put themselves in situations that they may have avoided for years and to significantly modify their thoughts. It is important early in therapy to alert clients to this and to encourage them to "invest anxiety in a calmer future" (Hope et al., 2000, p. 9). It is also important that employers understand and are sensitive to this potential effect when employees enter treatment.

Side effects are clearly more of an issue with medication and have been discussed in part already. However, a few issues deserve special mention with respect to workplace functioning. First, many of the medications used to treat anxiety disorders are associated with initial *increases* in anxiety symptoms. As such, clients' symptoms might get slightly worse before they start to get better. Clinicians should be sensitive to these difficulties by making clients aware that this may happen and by helping them to "stick it out" until the side effects abate. Caution in the workplace should be exercised if benzodiazepines are used because they often result in drowsiness and cognitive impairment. These side effects can be relevant to performance in any work environment, but may be particularly relevant for clients who must drive as part of their work or who operate machinery.

Workplace Accommodations

Many workplaces offer internal and/or external Employee Assistance Programs that can clearly benefit employees who are having psychological difficulties. Such programs are most effective when employees are reassured about confidentiality, clearly a concern in the workplace. The National Institute for Occupational Safety and Health (NIOSH) and the American Psychological Association (APA) have been working together to develop additional strategies to help workplaces protect the mental health of their employees. In addition to improving mental health service delivery for employees, these organizations have proposed that workplaces should create well-designed jobs (e.g., taking into account the needs of the aging workforce and of women and minorities), develop surveillance systems to detect psychological disorders and underlying risk factors, and educate workers about psychological disorders (Sauter, 1992). All of these suggestions are well founded, yet it is unclear to what extent organizations will actually implement them.

Taking a more individualistic perspective, employers should be sensitive to an employee's need to commit time to treatment. Despite the fact that currently available treatments are relatively short term, they do take time. Often, clinicians cannot see clients in the evenings or on weekends, which necessitates absences from work. Workplaces should be sensitive to these needs, knowing that a few missed hours in the short term will result in a more productive employee in the long term.

An issue that may come up in therapy is whether or not clients *should* tell their supervisors about the difficulties that they are having. This is, of course, up to the individual client and is probably dependent on the relationship that clients have with their supervisors. Open communication about psychological difficulties, however, may make it easier for clients to get the time off for treatment that they need. Furthermore, sharing problems with others can serve as a useful way for clients to challenge their beliefs about suffering from a "mental illness." There are aspects of anxiety disorders with which all of us can identify (e.g., few people experience *no* fear when doing formal public speaking), and it is often reassuring for clients to see that others do not react as extremely as they had expected, and that they might, in fact, be quite sympathetic because of their own experiences or the experiences of someone that they know well. It is our impression that any other workplace accommodations beyond giving time off for doctor visits could facilitate a client's avoidance.

MAINTENANCE OF GAINS/RELAPSE PREVENTION

The most important strategy for maintenance of treatment gains and relapse prevention following treatment for a phobic disorder is to "avoid avoidance." In other words, once treatment ends, it is important for clients to continue to enter previously feared situations and to not avoid new situations that come up that may cause anxiety. Clients should also be encouraged to continue to use cognitive strategies for dealing with the anxiety that will inevitably come up from time to time, even for those who have done very well in treatment. Inherent in this is ensuring that, prior to the end of treatment, clients have reasonable expectations for the future. The goal of treatment is not to cure people of ever experiencing anxiety again, but rather to help them deal more effectively with stressful situations once they come up.

Workplace Strategies for Maintenance of Gains/Relapse Prevention

The workplace can facilitate maintenance of gains by being sensitive to employees' needs for time to continue working on their treatment. It is common for clients to feel a resurgence of anxiety when they are under stress and also when they must face a new situation that they might not have tackled during therapy. Often, one or two booster sessions with a therapist will set clients back on the right track by reminding them of the arsenal of strategies that they now have to cope with feared situations that they might not have had previously.

SUMMARY

Social anxiety disorder, panic disorder, and, perhaps to a lesser extent, specific phobias can all have a profound impact on people's abilities to function in the workplace. These disorders have an impact not only on a personal level in terms of financial attainment, job satisfaction, and self-esteem, but also on a larger scale in terms of lost productivity. Given the chronic course of these disorders, treatment is typically necessary. To get time off from work for treatment, employees often have to reveal to their employers that they are having difficulties, and herein lies the paradox—individuals are often afraid to reveal this information (particularly in the case of socially anxious people, who often fear making requests and sharing personal information) for fear of suffering from discrimination. The reluctance to ask for time off to seek treatment can serve to maintain the disorder. Given the immense cost of anxiety disorders, it seems prudent for employers to be sensitive to such needs. Giving an employee a few hours off per week for just a few months could result in benefits to both employee and employer.

REFERENCES

Allgulander, C. (1999). Paroxetine in social anxiety disorder: A randomized placebo-controlled study. *Acta Psychiatrica Scandinavica, 100,* 193-198.

American Psychiatric Association. (1994). *Diagnostic and statistical manual of mental disorders* (4th ed.). Washington, DC: Author.

Antony, M. M., & Barlow, D. H. (1996). Emotion theory as a framework for explaining panic attacks and panic disorder. In R. M. Rapee (Ed.), *Current controversies in the anxiety disorders* (pp. 55-76). New York: Guilford.

Antony, M. M., Craske, M. G., & Barlow, D. H. (1995). *Mastery of your specific phobia: Client manual.* San Antonio, TX: The Psychological Corporation.

Antony, M. M., Roth, D., Swinson, R. P., Huta, V., & Devins, G. M. (1998). Illness intrusiveness in individuals with panic disorder, obsessive-compulsive disorder, or social phobia. *Journal of Nervous and Mental Disease, 186,* 311-315.

Antony, M. M., & Swinson, R. P. (2000). *Phobic disorders and panic in adults: A guide to assessment and treatment.* Washington, DC: American Psychological Association.

Bakish, D., Hooper, C. L., Filteau, M.-J., Charbonneau, Y., Fraser, G., West, D. L., Thibaudeau, C., & Raine, D. (1996). A double-blind placebo-controlled trial comparing fluvoxamine and imipramine in the treatment of panic disorder with or without agoraphobia. *Psychopharmacology Bulletin, 32,* 135-141.

Ballenger, J. C., Wheadon, D. E., Steiner, M., Bushnell, W., & Gergel, I. P. (1998). Double-blind, fixed-dose, placebo-controlled study of paroxetine in the treatment of panic disorder. *American Journal of Psychiatry, 155,* 36-42.

Barlow, D. (1988). *Anxiety and its disorders.* New York: Guilford.

Barlow, D. H., Gorman, J. M., Shear, M. K., & Woods, S. W. (2000). A randomized controlled trial of cognitive-behavioral treatment vs. imipramine and their combination for panic disorder: Primary outcome results. *Journal of the American Medical Association, 283,* 2529-2536.

Beck, A. T., Rush, J., Shaw, B. F., & Emery, G. (1979). *Cognitive therapy of depression.* New York: Guilford.

Beck, J. S. (1995). *Cognitive therapy: Basics and beyond.* New York: Guilford.

Black, D. W., Wesner, R., Bowers, W., & Gabel, J. (1993). A comparison of fluvoxamine, cognitive therapy, and placebo in the treatment of panic disorder. *Archives of General Psychiatry, 50,* 44-50.

Boyer, W. (1994). Serotonin reuptake inhibitors are superior to imipramine in alleviating panic attacks: A meta-analysis. In G. Darcourt, J. Mendlewicz, & N. Brunello (Eds.), *Current therapeutic approaches to panic and other anxiety disorders* (Vol. 8, pp. 55-60). Basel, Switzerland: Kargar.

Brown, T. A., DiNardo, P. A., & Barlow, D. H. (1994). *Anxiety Disorders Interview Schedule for DSM-IV, Lifetime Version.* San Antonio, TX: The Psychological Corporation.

Bruch, M. A., Heimberg, R. G., Berger, P., & Collins, T. M. (1989). Social phobia and perceptions of early parental and personal characteristics. *Anxiety Research, 2,* 57-65.

Caster, J. B., Inderbitzen, H. M., & Hope, D. (1999). Relationship between youth and parent perceptions of family environment and social anxiety. *Journal of Anxiety Disorders, 13,* 237-251.

Chambless, D. L., Caputo, G. C., Bright, P., & Gallagher, R. (1984). Assessment of "fear of fear" in agoraphobics: The Body Sensations Questionnaire and the Agoraphobic Cognitions Questionnaire. *Journal of Consulting and Clinical Psychology, 52,* 1090-1097.

Chambless, D. L., Caputo, G. C., Jasin, S. E., Gracely, E. J., & Williams, C. (1985). The Mobility Inventory for agoraphobia. *Behaviour Research and Therapy, 23,* 35-44.

Clark, D. M. (1986). A cognitive approach to panic. *Behaviour Research and Therapy, 24,* 461-470.

Clark, D. M. (1988). A cognitive model of panic attacks. In S. Rachman & J. D. Maser (Eds.), *Panic: Psychological perspectives* (pp. 71-89). Hillsdale, NJ: Lawrence Erlbaum.

Clark, D. M., Salkovskis, P. M., Hackmann, A., Middleton, H., Anastasiades, P., & Gelder, M. (1994). A comparison of cognitive therapy, applied relaxation, and imipramine in the treatment of panic disorder. *British Journal of Psychiatry, 164,* 759-769.

Craske, M. G., & Barlow, D. H. (1993). Panic disorder and agoraphobia. In D. H. Barlow (Ed.), *Clinical handbook of psychological disorders* (2nd ed., pp. 1-47). New York: Guilford.

Craske, M. G., & Barlow, D. H. (2000). *Mastery of your anxiety and panic—Third edition (MAP-3).* San Antonio, TX: The Psychological Corporation.

Davidson, J. R. T. (1998). *Social Phobia Inventory (SPIN).* Unpublished scale, Duke University Medical School, Durham, NC.

Eaton, W. W., Kessler, R. C., Wittchen, H.-U., & Magee, W. J. (1994). Panic and panic disorder in the United States. *American Journal of Psychiatry, 151,* 413-420.

Ehlers, A. (1995). A one-year prospective study of panic attacks: Clinical course and factors associated with maintenance. *Journal of Abnormal Psychology, 104,* 164-172.

Ettigi, P., Meyerhoff, A. S., Chirban, J. T., Jacobs, R. J., & Wilson, R. R. (1997). The quality of life and employment in panic disorder. *Journal of Nervous and Mental Disease, 185,* 368-372.

Faravelli, C., Paterniti, S., & Scarpato, A. (1995). 5-year prospective, naturalistic follow-up study of panic disorder. *Comprehensive Psychiatry, 36,* 271-277.

First, M. B., Spitzer, R. L., Gibbon, M., & Williams, J. B. W. (1997). *Structured Clinical Interview for DSM-IV, Axis I Disorders (SCID-I), Clinician Version.* Washington, DC: American Psychiatric Publishing.

Geer, J. H. (1965). The development of a scale to measure fear. *Behaviour Research and Therapy, 3,* 45-53.

Gelernter, C. S., Uhde, T. W., Cimbolic, P., Arnkoff, D. B., Vittone, B. J., & Tancer, M. E. (1991). Cognitive-behavioral approaches and pharmacological treatments of social phobia: A controlled study. *Archives of General Psychiatry, 48,* 938-945.

Greco, T. A. (1989). A cognitive-behavioral approach to fear of flying: A practitioner's guide. *Phobia Practice and Research Journal, 2,* 3-15.

Greenberg, P. E., Sisitsky, T., Kessler, R. C., Finkelstein, S. N., Berndt, E. R., Davidson, J. R. T., Ballenger, J. C., & Fyer, A. J. (1999). The economic burden of anxiety disorders in the 1990s. *Journal of Clinical Psychiatry, 60,* 427-435.

Heimberg, R. G., Liebowitz, M. R., Hope, D. A., Schneier, F. R., Holt, C. S., Welkowitz, L. A., Juster, H. R., Campeas, R., Bruch, M. A., Cloitre, M., Fallon, B., & Klein, D. F. (1998). Cognitive-behavioral group treatment versus phenelzine in social phobia: 12 week outcome. *Archives of General Psychiatry, 55,* 1133-1141.

Heimberg, R. G., Mueller, G. P., Holt, C. S., Hope, D. A., & Liebowitz, M. R. (1992). Assessment of anxiety in social interaction and being observed by others: The Social Interaction Anxiety Scale and the Social Phobia Scale. *Behavior Therapy, 23,* 53-73.

Holt, C. S., Heimberg, R. G., Hope, D. A., & Liebowitz, M. R. (1992). Situational domains of social phobia. *Journal of Anxiety Disorders, 6,* 63-77.

Hope, D. A., Heimberg, R. G., Juster, H., & Turk, C. L. (2000). *Managing social anxiety: A cognitive-behavioral therapy approach* (Client workbook). San Antonio, TX: The Psychological Corporation.

Katzelnick, D. J., Kobak, K. A., Greist, J. H., Jefferson, J. W., Mantle, J. M., & Serlin, R. C. (1995). Sertraline in social phobia: A double-blind, placebo-controlled crossover study. *American Journal of Psychiatry, 152,* 1368-1371.

Kenardy, J., Oei, T. P., & Evans, L. (1990). Neuroticism and age of onset agoraphobia with panic attacks. *Journal of Behavior Therapy and Experimental Psychiatry, 21,* 193-197.

Kessler, R. C., McGonagle, K. A., Zhao, S., Nelson, C. B., Hughes, M., Eshleman, S., Wittchen, H.-U., & Kendler, K. S. (1994). Lifetime and 12-month prevalence of *DSM-III-R* psychiatric disorders in the United States: Results from the National Comorbidity Survey. *Archives of General Psychiatry, 51,* 8-19.

Klein, D. F., Ross, D. C., & Cohen, P. (1987). Panic and avoidance in agoraphobia: Application of path analysis and treatment studies. *Archives of General Psychiatry, 44,* 377-385.

Kushner, M. G., Abrams, K., & Borchardt, C. (2000). The relationship between anxiety disorders and alcohol use disorders: A review of major perspective and findings. *Clinical Psychology Review, 20,* 149-171.

Kushner, M. G., Sher, K. J., & Beitman, B. D. (1990). The relations between alcohol problems and the anxiety disorders. *American Journal of Psychiatry, 147,* 685-695.

Leary, M. R. (1983). A brief version of the Fear of Negative Evaluation Scale. *Personality and Social Psychology Bulletin, 9,* 371-375.

Liebowitz, M. R., Heimberg, R. G., Schneier, F. R., Hope, D. A., Davies, S., Holt, C. S., Goetz, D., Juster, H. R., Lin, S.-H., Bruch, M. A., Marshall, R. D., & Klein, D. F. (1999). Cognitive-behavioral group therapy versus phenelzine in social phobia: Long term outcome. *Depression and Anxiety, 10,* 89-98.

Liebowitz, M. R., Schneier, F., Campeas, R., Hollander, E., Hatterer, J., & Fyer, A. J. (1992). Phenelzine vs. atenolol in social phobia: A placebo-controlled comparison. *Archives of General Psychiatry, 49,* 290-300.

Londborg, P. D., Wolkow, R., Smith, W. T., DuBoff, E., England, D., Ferguson, J., Rosenthal, M., & Weise, C. (1998). Sertraline in the treatment of panic disorder. *British Journal of Psychiatry, 173,* 54-60.

Magee, W. J., Eaton, W. W., Wittchen, H.-U., McGonagle, K. A., & Kessler, R. C. (1996). Agoraphobia, simple phobia, and social phobia in the National Comorbidity Survey. *Archives of General Psychiatry, 53,* 159-168.

Mannuzza, S., Fyer, A. J., Liebowitz, M. R., & Klein, D. F. (1990). Delineating the boundaries of social phobia: Its relationship to panic disorder and agoraphobia. *Journal of Anxiety Disorders, 4,* 41-59.

Marks, I. M., & Mathews, A. M. (1979). Brief standard self-rating for phobic clients. *Behaviour Research and Therapy, 17,* 263-267.

Mattick, R. P., & Clarke, J. C. (1998). Development and validation of measures of social phobia scrutiny fear and social interaction anxiety. *Behaviour Research and Therapy, 36,* 455-470.

McNeil, D. W., Ries, B. J., & Turk, C. L. (1995). Behavioral assessment: Self-report, physiology, and overt behavior. In R. G. Heimberg, M. R. Liebowitz, D. A. Hope, & F. R. Schneier (Eds.), *Social phobia: Diagnosis, assessment, and treatment* (pp. 202-231). New York: Guilford.

Mennin, D. S., Heimberg, R. G., & Holt, C. S. (2000). Panic, agoraphobia, phobias and generalized anxiety disorder. In M. Hersen & A. Bellack (Eds.), *Psychopathology in adulthood* (pp. 169-207). Boston: Allyn & Bacon.

Michelson, D., Lydiard, R. B., Ollack, M. H., Tamura, R. N., Hoog, S. L., Tepner, R., Demitrack, M. A., & Tollefson, G. D. (1998). Outcome assessment and clinical improvement in panic disorder: Evidence from a randomized controlled trial of fluoxetine and placebo: The Fluoxetine Panic Disorder Study Group. *American Journal of Psychiatry, 155,* 1570-1577.

Nair, N. P., Bakish, D., Saxena, B., Amin, M., Schwartz, G., & West, T. E. G. (1996). Comparison of fluvoxamine, imipramine, and placebo in the treatment of outpatients with panic disorder. *Anxiety, 2,* 192-198.

Oehrberg, S., Christiansen, P. E., Behnke, K., Borup, A. L., Severin, B., Soegaard, J., Calberg, H., Judge, R., Ohrstrom, J. K., & Manniche, P. M. (1995). Paroxetine in the treatment of panic disorder: A randomised, double-blind, placebo-controlled study. *British Journal of Psychiatry, 167,* 374-379.

Peterson, R. A., & Reiss, S. (1993). *Anxiety Sensitivity Index revised test manual.* Worthington, OH: IDS.

Pohl, R. B., Wolkow, R. M., & Clary, C. M. (1998). Sertraline in the treatment of panic disorder: A double-blind multicenter trial. *American Journal of Psychiatry, 155,* 1189-1195.

Pollack, M. H., Otto, M. W., Worthington, J. J., Manfro, G. G., & Wolkow, R. (1998). Sertraline in the treatment of panic disorder. *Archives of General Psychiatry, 55,* 1010-1016.

Rachman, S. (1976). The passing of the two-stage theory of fear and avoidance: Fresh possibilities. *Behaviour Research and Therapy, 14,* 125-131.

Rachman, S. (1977). The conditioning theory of fear acquisition: A critical examination. *Behaviour Research and Therapy, 15,* 375-387.

Rapee, R. M. (1995). Descriptive psychopathology of social phobia. In R. G. Heimberg, M. R. Liebowitz, D. A. Hope, & F. R. Schneier (Eds.), *Social phobia: Diagnosis, assessment, and treatment* (pp. 41-66). New York: Guilford.

Roth, D. A., Antony, M. M., & Swinson, R. P. (2001). Interpretations for anxiety symptoms in social phobia. *Behaviour Research and Therapy, 39,* 129-138.

Sauter, S. L. (1992). Introduction to the NIOSH proposed national strategy. In G. P. Keita & S. L. Sauter (Eds.), *Work and well-being: An agenda for the 1990s* (pp. 11-16). Washington, DC: American Psychological Association.

Schneier, F. R., Heckelman, L. R., Garfinkel, R., Campeas, R., Fallon, B. A., Gitow, A., Street, L., Del Bene, D., & Liebowitz, M. R. (1994). Functional impairment in social phobia. *Journal of Clinical Psychiatry, 55,* 322-331.

Sheehan, D. V., Ballenger, J., & Jacobsen, G. (1980). Treatment of endogenous anxiety with phobic, hysterical and hypochondriacal symptoms. *Archives of General Psychiatry, 37,* 51-59.

Silberman, E. K. (1999). Pharmacotherapy. In M. Hersen & A. S. Bellack (Eds.), *Comparative interventions for adult disorders* (2nd ed., pp. 256-283). New York: Wiley.

Stein, M. B., Fyer, A. J., Davidson, J. R. T., Pollack, M. H., & Wiita, B. (1999). Fluvoxamine treatment of social phobia (social anxiety disorder): A double-blind, placebo-controlled study. *American Journal of Psychiatry, 156,* 756-760.

Stein, M. B., Liebowitz, M. R., Lydiard, R. B., Pitts, C. D., Bushnell, W., & Gergel, I. (1998). Paroxetine treatment of generalized social phobia (social anxiety disorder): A randomized controlled trial. *Journal of the American Medical Association, 280,* 708-713.

Taylor, S., & Cox, B. J. (1998). An expanded Anxiety Sensitivity Index: Evidence for a hierarchical structure in a clinical sample. *Journal of Anxiety Disorders, 12,* 463-483.

Turner, S. M., Beidel, D. C., Dancu, C. V., & Stanley, M. A. (1989). An empirically derived inventory to measure social fears and anxiety: The Social Phobia and Anxiety Inventory. *Psychological Assessment, 1,* 35-40.

Versiani, M., Nardi, A. E., Mundim, F. D., Alves, A. A., Liebowitz, M. R., & Amrein, R. (1992). Pharmacotherapy of social phobia: A controlled study of moclobemide and phenelzine. *British Journal of Psychiatry, 161,* 353-360.

Watson, D., & Friend, R. (1969). Measurement of social-evaluative anxiety. *Journal of Consulting and Clinical Psychology, 33,* 448-457.

Wolpe, J., & Lang, P. J. (1964). A fear survey schedule for use in behavior therapy. *Behaviour Research and Therapy, 2,* 27-30.

CHAPTER 11

PTSD *in the* Workplace

WALTER PENK
CHARLES DREBING
RUSSELL SCHUTT

DESCRIPTION OF THE DISORDER

One out of every two Americans will be exposed, sometime during his or her lifetime, to a kind of traumatic event known to produce stress reactions. Between 7% and 9%, or perhaps 25,300,000 people, will persist in their reactions to trauma to the extent that they could be classified as meeting diagnostic criteria for posttraumatic stress disorder (PTSD) (Kessler, Sonnega, Bromet, Hughes, & Nelson, 1995). What we do not know is what proportion of the American workforce is symptomatic for PTSD. Because work tends to be more stressful than other domains of living, we can only conclude that more than 9% of the American workforce is, at any one time, symptomatic for PTSD. We can infer that unacknowledged and untreated PTSD is a hidden disorder in the American workforce

that affects productivity negatively. Unfortunately, many questions about PTSD in the workplace, with exceptions as noted in this chapter, have not been addressed in any rigorous and scientific way. However, acknowledging that we know little, we must now be about our business of creating work environments that improve not just the physical safety, but also the psychological safety, of workers, both employees and employers. The possibility of terrorist attacks and anthrax scares underscore the need for clinicians to do more in the workplace. This chapter specifies how PTSD can be confronted and resolved in the workplace.

PTSD is classified as a form of Anxiety Disorder that results from exposure to life-threatening events. It is diagnosed when six criteria are met (See Box 11.1, from *DSM-IV*, American Psychiatric Association [APA], 1994):[1]

AUTHORS' NOTE: The authors wish to thank Judith Bradley, Psychology/CWT Services (116B), for her extensive and valued participation in the preparation of this manuscript.

Box 11.1   *DSM-IV* Posttraumatic Stress Disorder Criteria

Criterion A. Exposure to a life-threatening event. The stress posed by this event must be extreme and personal. It must involve actual or threatened death or serious injury, or the threat to the physical integrity of self or other person, or learning about unexpected or violent death, serious harm, or threat of death or injury, experienced by a family member or other close associate.

Criterion B. Traumatic event is re-experienced in at least one of the following ways:

1. Recurrent distressing dreams of the event;
2. Reliving the event;
3. Intense distress experienced during exposure to internal or external cues associated with the traumatic event;
4. Physiological reactivity to these cues.

Criterion C. A persistent pattern of trying to avoid stimuli associated with the trauma, and/or numbing of responsiveness, including:

1. Efforts to avoid thoughts, feelings, or people that arouse recollections of the trauma
2. Efforts to avoid activities, places, or people that arouse recollections of the trauma
3. Inability to recall an important aspect of the trauma
4. Markedly diminished interest or participation in significant activities
5. Emotional detachment or estrangement from others
6. Restricted affect
7. Sense of foreshortened future

Criterion D. A pattern of persistent symptoms of increased arousal which began after the trauma, including:

1. Sleep disturbance
2. Irritability, angry outbursts
3. Difficulty concentrating
4. Hypervigilance
5. Exaggerated startle response.

Criterion E. Criteria B, C, and D last more than one month. The onset of symptoms under criteria B, C, and D are acute if they persist for less than three months; are chronic, if they last more than three months; and onset is called delayed if symptoms appear more than six months after original trauma.

Criterion F. Criteria B, C, and D impair functioning.

PTSD in the *DSM-IV* (APA, 1994) differs significantly from the classification of PTSD in the *DSM-III* (APA, 1980) in that a new criterion, F, is added: "The disturbance causes clinically significant distress or impairment in social, occupational, or other important areas of functioning" (APA, 1994, p. 429).

The addition of this new criterion for classifying PTSD, highlighting the functional impact of PTSD in the workplace, emphasizes that PTSD is associated not merely with distress; in addition, it interferes with functioning and adjustment, not just among family and friends, but also where the traumatized person works.

Need for a Psychology of PTSD in the Workplace

Although PTSD appears much later in the *DSMs* than, for example, Major Depressive Disorder or Schizophrenia—both of which present in *DSM-I* and *DSM-II* of the 1950s and 1960s—nevertheless, rapid strides have been made in understanding PTSD since the formulation of its diagnostic criteria in 1980. Psychometrically sound measures of PTSD have been written and tested for clinical utility (see Assessment section below) (Wilson & Keane, 1997). Some randomized clinical trials of treatments are reported, and many treatment effectiveness studies are under way, providing an empirically validated body of best practices (Foa, Keane, & Friedman, 2000).

Despite this progress, many questions remain unanswered about this relatively new disorder in the *DSM*. Most research on PTSD assessment and treatment has centered on PTSD as residuals of life-threatening experiences in combat, crimes, accidents, domestic abuse, and natural disasters, without attention to causes and effects in the workplace. However, with inclusion of occupational dysfunction in the latest *DSM-IV* formulation of PTSD, the workplace is identified as a setting where symptoms of PTSD may be manifested, exacerbated, or even caused. Moreover, as explained later in more detail, work may also be among the cures for PTSD. What is needed now is a psychology of PTSD in the workplace, one that orients clinicians and managers to workplace and worker interactions, and that highlights ways in which work and workers interact to cause, exacerbate, or resolve PTSD.

Need to Develop Mental Health Services for Work and Workers

Work environments are important places where mental health workers can deliver needed services. There is a need for practices that identify employees who require treatment for nonwork traumas that workers bring from home to the workplace, such as domestic violence or childhood physical or sexual abuse. Also needed are practices that respond to the residuals of trauma that occur at work, such as violence between employees, terrorist attacks, or exposure to biological toxins. Mental health services must address the unique problems of employees when the work they are doing increases the risk of stress and trauma, such as through exposure to toxins and industrial accidents, or when dangers are experienced in the line of duty (e.g., police, firefighters, mental health workers). And finally, workplaces need to be prepared for those unfortunate times when natural and human disasters strike the workplace and the workforce. One of the many unanticipated consequences resulting from the terrorist attacks on New York City and the Pentagon on September 11, 2001, as well as the subsequent anthrax scare and deaths, is the necessity for clinicians to rethink their approaches in the workplace for coping with trauma. So, the workplace is becoming an important environment in which residuals of traumatic events, however experienced, can be addressed and assuaged.

It Is Good Business to Prepare for and Cope With Trauma

Why should employers be concerned about untreated trauma and possibilities of exposure to trauma in the workplace? The basic answer is that "caring" work environments, those that invest in human capital, are associated with higher productivity. Conversely, work environments that do not care about the adjustment of employees are associated with dysfunctional circumstances that interfere with productivity. Simply put, it is important to prepare for and treat trauma so that the workforce remains physically and psychologically healthy, allowing workers to achieve the mission of the organization. Not providing a safe and secure work environment leads to distress in the employee, which, in turn, may lead to poorer productivity (Flannery, 1995, 2001; Van den Bos & Bulatao, 1996).

There is also a darker side to PTSD, notably, an undetermined incidence of "false memories" about traumatic events, even faking PTSD, in hopes of obtaining benefits and pensions due to alleged work-related injuries and/or claimed exposure to work-related threats to life (e.g., Flannery, 1995). Erroneous cases of worker compensation settled on behalf of clients should be warning enough to employers that it is essential to assess employees accurately about alleged, current work-related injuries or stresses. Work environments that fail to undertake routine psychological assessment of employees, particularly in those corporations and businesses in high-risk industries, run the risk of worker compensation cases occurring well above industry averages (e.g., Burgess, Hibler, Keegan, & Everly, 1996). Potential for worker compensation litigation requires that managers plan to address trauma in the workplace by creating a caring organization that copes with life-threatening events that affect workers.

EPIDEMIOLOGY

Prevalence of PTSD, considered across the workplace in general, is unknown. However, one may infer workplace rates from prevalence of PTSD in the general population. Studies show that PTSD in the general population ranges from 1% to 14% (APA, 1994; Breslau & Davis, 1992; Breslau, Davis, & Andreski, 1995; Davidson & Fairbank, 1993; Davidson, Hughes, Blazer, & George, 1991; Fairbank, Jordan, & Schlenger, 1996; Fairbank, Schlenger, Saigh, & Davidson, 1995; Kulka & Schlenger, 1993). The best estimates of lifetime rates of PTSD in the general population are 10% to 12% for women, 6% to 8% for men, and 7% to 9% for the general population (Kessler et al., 1995). These totals are much higher than originally estimated in the earliest national surveys about the prevalence of mental illness in the United States, such as the Epidemiological Catchment Area (ECA) surveys in the 1980s (e.g., Helzer, Robins, & McEvoy, 1987). Recent stratified sampling studies are much closer to what Keane and Penk (1988) predicted 15 years ago about the prevalence of PTSD when they argued that PTSD had been underestimated by the ECA.

Because of added stresses associated with demands of work, particularly when occupations at risk for violence are factored in, it is likely that prevalence of PTSD in the workplace is higher than these general population estimates. When work-specific sites are sampled, rates of lifetime and current PTSD are found to be higher, as seen in studies of police, firefighters, and emergency room medical workers. (See McFarlane & de Girolamo, 1996, for a discussion of methodological issues in the epidemiology of PTSD; also Breslau et al., 1995; Norris, 1992; Resnick, Kilpatrick, Dansky, Saunders, & Best, 1993; Wilson & Keane, 1997.) For those who have been injured at work, symptoms of PTSD are widespread: Among a sample of workers' compensation patients, one third had three or more symptoms of PTSD, and more than 75% had at least one symptom (Burgess et al., 1996). PTSD symptoms were even more common in a sample of patients in treatment after workplace assaults and holdups (De Mol, 1998).

PTSD expressed in the workplace may differ from symptoms registered when seeking treatment in clinics. For example, the most common symptoms reported among a sample of traumatized workers' compensation applicants were difficulty sleeping (75%), loss of a sense of future (68%), diminished interest or pleasure (64%), and anger (57%). Nearly a third reported persistence of three or more symptoms. At least 20% wanted to seek professional help for problems continuing after exposure to trauma (Burgess et al., 1996).

But PTSD does not inevitably result when trauma is experienced (Finlay-Jones, 1981). In fact, trauma occurs more frequently than does PTSD: The National Comorbidity Survey reports that 61% of men and 51% of women say they have experienced trauma in their lifetime, compared with 6% to 12% who claim they meet PTSD criteria currently. Moreover, trauma may produce disorders in addition to, or other than, PTSD. Depression and substance abuse frequently co-occur with PTSD, as do other kinds of anxiety disorders and phobias. The age at which trauma is experienced may also influence the likelihood of developing PTSD, although the direction of and causal mechanism for any such effect are uncertain. Some research suggests that childhood traumas are more likely to result in a different form of PTSD—Complex PTSD, or "Disorders of Extreme Stress"—that shares only some symptoms, which some authors refer to as Simple PTSD (e.g., Herman, 1991; Pelcovitz et al., 1997). Other studies indicate that traumatic events early in life result in higher rates of PTSD than when they occur later in life. (See McFarlane, 1996, for a discussion of resilience, vulnerability, and course of PTSD as a disorder.)

Such methodological difficulties in estimating accurately the prevalence of PTSD, along with problems in determining Lifetime versus Current PTSD or Simple versus Complex PTSD distinctions, should not distract from the fundamental point: PTSD is a reality. PTSD is found in the workplace. Events in the workplace can cause PTSD. Workplace events can exacerbate PTSD. Prevalence of workplace PTSD is likely to be higher than for the general population. So, PTSD is a reality for which management and clinicians should prepare. All work environments must prepare for trauma, a point underscored most recently by the events of September 11 and subsequent anthrax scares resulting in workplace-related deaths. Failure to create a work environment that cares and treats leads to an impaired workforce, increasing the potential for lower productivity and poor functioning in the workplace.

ASSESSMENT

Several clinical tools have been developed for research and clinical purposes in assessing PTSD. All such measures were crafted in medical settings to test for residuals of combat trauma, early childhood physical and sexual assaults, and other forms of trauma outside the work environment. More recent assessment techniques were developed for victims of crime and survivors of natural disasters. Assessment instruments may be divided into groups based on what they assess: those that document the experience of a traumatic event (Criterion A) and those that document the reaction to and impact of that event (Criteria B, C, and D). These measures range widely in format, purpose, and empirical support. We will discuss some general issues for each group and highlight a few instruments that may be of particular interest or value for assessing PTSD in the workplace. (See Wilson & Keane, 1997, for a more comprehensive review of assessment tools.)

This brief review will not teach the mental health provider all that he or she must know to match the needs of the workplace assessment situation with the available instruments that will be clinically useful (see Clark, Crawford, Giles, & Nash, 1987). Most instruments fail to identify the workplace as a potential site of traumatic stress or as an environment that exacerbates preexisting or co-occurring nonworksite traumas. Nevertheless, mental health practitioners providing services in occupational settings will need to adapt existing instruments to the workplace. That is, clinicians must find ways to explicitly link Criteria B, C, and D symptoms to workplace traumas and stressors of Criterion A.

So, in adapting any existing measures of PTSD, clinicians assessing workplace trauma must take special care to link any statement about symptoms to whether or not the trauma in question was experienced at the workplace or outside of the workplace. One excellent example of this approach, which serves as an exception to the many trauma measures that fail to refer to the workplace, is Horowitz, Wilner, and Alvarez's (1979) Impact of Event scale. This measure starts with an open-ended question about the type of trauma and where it occurred, and then proceeds by linking personal reactions, such as intrusiveness of memories and avoidance of reminders to trauma, to the trauma listed originally. John Wilson's and Terence Keane's recent book, *Assessing Psychological Trauma and PTSD* (1997), provides specific steps that mental

health providers can take to develop an assessment approach tailored to the differing needs of various workplaces (e.g., Weiss & Marmar, 1997).

Instruments That Assess Criterion A: The Traumatic Event

A number of instruments are available, ranging from those targeting only one type of trauma, such as natural disasters (Norris, 1992), to those covering a broad menu of possible trauma. We will focus on the instruments that cover an array of trauma, with a special focus on those that address trauma with a potential link to work settings. In general, measures tapping the broadest array of trauma include more items addressing types of trauma that can occur at work. Most of the scales include items related to physical or sexual assault, natural disasters, and combat, but only a few include items such as industrial accidents, toxin exposures, or handling of bodies or accident victims. Items about terrorist attacks in workplaces undoubtedly now will begin to appear, along with items about biochemical warfare in the workplace.

The Traumatic Events Questionnaire (TEQ) assesses 11 specific traumatic events, a number of which can occur in work settings (see Table 11.1). There are sufficient empirical data to suggest that the measure is adequately reliable (Lauterbach & Vrana, 1996). Endorsement rates of TEQ items were relatively high in the initial validity study done with college students, raising questions about an overendorsement bias.

The Traumatic History Questionnaire (THQ) is the longest of the published measures of traumatic events, with 24 items addressing a wide range of traumatic experiences, some of which do not qualify for the diagnosis of PTSD. A number of items are relevant to trauma that can occur at work,

Table 11.1   Assessing Criterion A of PTSD

Scale	Reference	# of Items	Items Related to Work Trauma
Traumatic Events Questionnaire (TEQ)	Lauterbach and Vrana (1996)	11	Fires/explosions Industrial and farm accidents Witnessing injury or death of other Violent crime Other life-threatening situation
Traumatic History Questionnaire (THQ)	Green (1993)	24	Serious accident at work Toxin exposure Handling bodies Present at a crime Other serious injury
Traumatic Stress Schedule (TSS)	Norris (1990)	10	Crime involving force or threat Motor vehicle accident and injury Other terrifying or shocking experience

including an item called "Serious Accident at Work," as well as toxin exposures and handling of bodies. There have not been any published data on reliability and validity, although the author has unpublished data addressing the issue (Green, 1993; Norris, 1992). In general, the THQ is a face-valid instrument that is particularly useful because of the large number of items, but it will need additional study to fully support its psychometric soundness.

The Traumatic Stress Schedule (TSS) was developed as a short screening instrument for use with the general population. The range of items is somewhat brief but focuses on the most common severe traumatic events. Reliability and validity data have been generally supportive of its use (Norris, 1992), although some of the items may be too limited to pick up other forms of common trauma. In general, the instrument is brief and has more validity data than others, but it may be limited for use with the type of trauma that may occur at work. The events of September 11 and the subsequent anthrax scare most certainly will expand the range of types of trauma that will be assessed in the workplace.

Instruments Measuring
Criteria B, C, and D:
Impact of Trauma

These tools are designed to measure the symptoms of intrusion of the experience into current experience (Criterion B), avoidance of stimuli related to the trauma (Criterion C), and autonomic hyperarousal (Criterion D). A large number of scales have been offered for this task (Norris & Riad, 1997), with a wide variation in length, format, and validation research. The range of instruments allows a clinician or researcher to select one that will meet the specific needs of the target population and situation. There are reviews of the range of instruments elsewhere. We will offer a few of the most common, well-researched instruments suitable to different settings.

The PTSD Symptom Scale (PSS) was developed for research into the impact of rape, but it can be used with the range of trauma (see Table 11.2). It has 17 items drawn from the description of PTSD in the *DSM-III-R*. Four items focus on Criterion B

Table 11.2   Measures of Criteria B, C, and D

Scale	Reference	# of Items	Format
PTSD Symptom Scale (PSS)	Foa et al. (1993) #10	17	Interview and self-report
MMPI-PTSD Scale	Lyons and Keane (1992) #11	46	Subscale of the MMPI-2
Revised Civilian Mississippi Scale	Norris (1996) #14	30	Self-report, Spanish and English versions
PTSD Interview	Watson et al. (1991) #15	100	Interview; French, Spanish and English versions

symptoms, seven items focus on Criterion C, and six items focus on Criterion D. It can be administered in an interview or self-report format. The PSS is particularly strong with respect to published evidence of its reliability and validity (Foa, Riggs, Dancu, & Rothbaum, 1993).

In some settings, the PTSD scale of the MMPI-2 will be particularly useful. The MMPI-2 is a long but widely used measure of psychopathology. A subscale has been developed for measuring PTSD symptomatology (Keane, Malloy, & Fairbank, 1984). The advantage of this instrument is its solid reliability and validity, as documented by a number of published studies (Lyons & Keane, 1992; Watson, Juba, Maniford, Kucala, & Anderson, 1991). In addition, inclusion of the rest of the MMPI-2 offers other data that are often valuable, including those regarding response biases. Impression management, such as "faking good" and "faking bad," is important to measure. The disadvantage is its length of 46 PTSD items and the fact that most of the validity studies have been done with combat veteran populations. It is probably most appropriate for use in settings where the MMPI-2 has already been administered or where the full data provided by the MMPI-2 would be of value.

The Revised Civilian Mississippi Scale (Keane, Wolfe, & Taylor, 1987; Norris & Riad, 1997) is a medium-length self-report scale that has some important advantages relative to other scales. Items are distributed evenly between Criteria B, C, and D. Most are tied directly to the traumatic event, providing some protection against confusing general symptoms of distress with those related to the trauma. The reliability and validity of the scale has been supported empirically, including the validity of a Spanish as well as English version.

Similar to the PSS, the PTSD Interview is tied closely to the diagnostic criteria for PTSD. It is a brief interview that can be administered by nonclinicians. Its reliability and validity have been well-established in studies of veteran populations, and it is in wide use today.

It is essential to note that no measures exist for assessing Criterion F, that set of indicators that evaluates the impact of PTSD on occupational and social functioning. Neither are there measures for the phasic quality of PTSD, as well as Lifetime versus Current differentiations—except for the Structured Clinical Interview for *DSM-IV* (SCID), Diagnostic Interview Schedule (DIS), and the Composite International Diagnostic Interview (CIDI). Reliability and validity of these measures, with references, are presented in Weiss (1997). Such lacks represent opportunities for further development when PTSD researchers focus on the workplace as a site for study.

The number of instruments measuring PTSD is now proliferating. The PILOTS Database User's Guide is the gold-standard resource for deciding which instruments are most suitable for one's specific situation. PILOTS is updated at the National Center for Post-Traumatic Stress Disorder (VA Medical Center, 116D, White River Junction, VT, 05009). For more information, and to obtain a copy of the user's guide, call Fred Lerner, DLS, at (802) 296-5132. PILOTS may be accessed free of charge, without an account or password, at http://www.ncptsd.org.

A final note: Developing measures of PTSD in the workplace—whether caused by traumatic events at work or whether stresses in the workplace exacerbate past, non-work-incurred traumas—is a challenge for the next generation of PTSD researchers. Why has assessment of workplace trauma and work as exacerbation of non-work trauma been underdeveloped? Perhaps it is due to convenience, because most mental health providers deliver services in treatment centers. However, as mental health practitioners increasingly provide services in the workplace, opportunities will arise to develop measures of PTSD specific to work environments.

CLINICAL PICTURE

For most people, work provides a setting for activities from one third to one half of one's waking hours. This simple fact means that experiences during this portion of the day can play an important role in the generation, continuation, and resolution of psychiatric disorders. The potential for influence of PTSD in the workplace is heightened by the nature of PTSD symptoms. Although occupational dysfunction due to PTSD is now a part of its operational definition (i.e.,

Criterion F), the nature of the primary symptoms help to explain why this dysfunction occurs. Those with PTSD reexperience at least some aspects of the traumatic event. Such a propensity means that many features of the workplace may have a psychoactive element. In addition, reexperiencing through dreams or reliving the event may increase feelings of anxiety that interfere with optimal work performance.

Avoidance is also a symptom that can directly cause problems at work. Efforts that ensue from this symptom to avoid thoughts, people, activities, and places that arouse traumatic recollections can interfere with carrying out a full range of workplace duties in a reliable manner. The emotional detachment from others, which is another form of avoidance, can also interfere with the maintenance of productive relationships with coworkers. Symptoms of increased arousal that accompany PTSD may have a more insidious effect on work performance. Disturbed sleep, difficulty concentrating, hypervigilance, and irritability each can diminish work performance in a way that is likely to be misperceived as evidence of inadequate ability or motivation.

In spite of these common elements in the diagnosis of PTSD, symptoms of PTSD—as well as the type and amount of risk for PTSD—vary substantially across different work settings and between different people. Such variation must be taken into account by managers who seek to minimize the potential workplace impact of those suffering from PTSD. Timing of PTSD symptoms in relation to the precipitating traumatic event(s) must also be taken into account: Acute PTSD, with symptoms that last for no more than 3 months, is a much more common response to trauma than chronic PTSD and may require only temporary adjustments in workplace procedures and expectations. On the other hand, delayed-onset PTSD may create problems at work that are almost impossible to anticipate and unlikely to be diagnosed properly.

The following two case studies illustrate some of these differences in the ways that PTSD can influence different employees and the places in which they work. They are selected from our clinical practice to highlight the themes about PTSD described here: The signs of PTSD appear at work, fellow workers have a responsibility to create a caring environment, work itself may be used to assuage symptoms, untreated PTSD may lead to lower productivity, and management must develop mechanisms to treat trauma in the workplace.

Case Example 1

The first case focuses on a manager who experienced traumatic events in the Vietnam War and is still haunted by these memories. He has been an effective worker, but his work style is shaped by his ongoing struggle with symptoms of PTSD. This coping strategy failed him when an unusual event, an invitation to a Memorial Day ceremony, created a crisis.

In many ways, Tom Livingston (pseudonym) was a model employee. He was devoted to his work as a manager in an aerospace corporation. He came to work early and left late. He seemed to want the company to succeed more than most other employees—even more than some of his bosses. This made some people uncomfortable, but generally resulted in a great deal of praise and success for Tom. Everyone knew Tom as a "go-getter"— someone who could get the job done. That is why his manager was particularly concerned when Tom's wife called to say that he was in the hospital for a week.

His manager had imagined a heart attack might be in Tom's future, given how hard he pushed himself. But she was shocked to find out that Tom was in a psychiatric hospital. Their long friendship made it easier for her to find out some of the details. She called Tom's wife at home at the end of the week to check on how Tom was doing, hoping that his wife would let her know more than she had the right to request. She did.

His wife did not seem surprised that Tom was in the hospital. She described his "problem" as a long-standing one. "It is always the worst around Memorial Day. He gets so tense and irritable, I just try to stay away from him. But this year, he got an invitation to a special awards ceremony at our Town Hall to receive an award for decorated war veterans. They wanted him to wear his uniform and his medals. That would make most people so happy, but not him. It put him over the edge."

Ever since his involvement in the Vietnam War, Tom has carried an emotional burden. His memories from the war haunt him at night. He has dreams about combat and the deaths of his friends several nights each week. He rarely sleeps more than 6 hours. His wife and children do not know what the traumatic experiences were; he refuses to talk about them. They just know that he seems somewhat distant as a husband and a father. And they know that they should not ask too many questions if they want to avoid tension.

Coworkers see him as irritable, with the potential for angry outbursts. His subordinates respect his hard work but are afraid of displeasing him. He has burned out several administrative assistants, who could not keep up with his demands. Some staff call him the "Tasmanian devil," more for his energy level than for his potential for destructiveness. He is on the move at all times, always pushing himself and others toward work goals. It is not surprising that he has garnered a great deal of praise and respect, but those who work closely with him know that he needs to keep pushing even when his efforts are not tied to clear company objectives.

Tom uses his work to help him cope with his PTSD. When he is immersed in his efforts at work, he is able to focus entirely on what is before him. That gives him a temporary reprieve from the intrusive memories and underlying anxiety that are so central to PTSD. His focus on work helps him avoid the thoughts and feelings that could arouse recollections of the trauma. Not surprisingly, he does not take vacations often. Free time can be filled with anxiety for someone with PTSD. Retirement is actually a key time of risk for worsening of symptoms because the relief provided by work is lost.

There is a downside for his work, although it is not often noticed because of the amount he accomplishes. At times, his anxiety makes it difficult for him to focus. He makes decisions that reflect such lack of focus—decisions that do not incorporate new information or careful planning. His hard driving style causes strain in some work relationships. Some good employees who have been transferred to his supervision have subsequently left the company. And then there is his drinking, which has never been a clear problem, but has left some people wondering. Overall, however, Tom's investment in work is so high that these problems are overlooked by those around him.

Up to this point, work had allowed Tom to maintain a tenuous grasp on his PTSD symptoms. The invitation to the Memorial Day ceremony pushed him over the edge. The anxiety was too much, and he had to enter the hospital for crisis management. This crisis presents an opportunity for him to get real treatment for PTSD, which could give him relief from his anxiety. There is also the chance that he will have difficulty recovering from this drop in his functioning. Further hospitalizations could occur, as well as further losses in work.

Case Example 2

The second case illustrates problems resulting from PTSD generated by traumatic experiences at work. After these experiences, the employee's work performance declined gradually as her anxiety about traumatic experiences and reminders of them increased. Finally, she was classified as disabled and left work.

Michelle Barnes (pseudonym) always wanted to work as a policewoman or as a female firefighter. She wanted to be where "the action is." When she began training for Emergency Medical Technician certification, she could tell that this type of work was a perfect match for her.

Her first 5 years working for a private ambulance company in downtown Baltimore were impressive. She performed well and was well liked and respected by coworkers and supervisors. On at least two occasions, she had performed well in dangerous situations. In one particularly difficult situation, she was fired upon and almost killed while saving an attempted murder victim.

Surprisingly, Michelle's work performance has declined over the past 12 months. She has taken a lot of sick leave and has appeared less energetic at work. Her direct supervisor feels that she is slower to respond to calls.

Michelle's job, like many jobs, involves significant risk of traumatization, whether through being in situations that are dangerous to the employee or working directly with victims of trauma. There has probably been a cumulative effect of all the work for Michelle, but the incident in which she was almost killed has become the focus for the present symptoms of PTSD. Like most adults who are traumatized by incidents at work, the tendency to avoid stimuli associated with the trauma results in a decline in work performance. Michelle gets anxious whenever she hears a radio call. She is particularly anxious when she must drive in the neighborhood in which she was nearly shot or when the call is for a response to a victim of a shooting. While working, she often feels like the prior incident is just about to happen again. She knows this is illogical, but she cannot avoid the feeling. Unfortunately, she does not feel comfortable talking about her anxiety with her coworkers or supervisors. Her professional confidence is declining, and she acts less and less invested in her work.

Michelle's employer had not taken appropriate steps to deal with employees who suffer trauma, particularly in the workplace. Employee training for trauma and PTSD was inadequate, so Michelle did not understand her symptoms and did not know what response to make. Her supervisor was not well trained in how to monitor employees who had suffered trauma, so he did not know what to look for or how to respond effectively. There was no regular screening or prevention plan in place. In the end, Michelle was lost to the company. After 2 years of declining performance, she filed for disability due to depression and anxiety, which were eventually diagnosed accurately as symptoms of PTSD.

PRECIPITATING CONDITIONS

In the case of PTSD, as described at length earlier, anytime a person experiences, witnesses, and confronts an event or events that involve actual or threatened death or serious injury, or a threat to the physical integrity of the person and/or others, that person has been exposed to a precipitating condition that potentially may be associated with the development of PTSD. (See Criterion A above and the discussion of measures of traumatic events.) Additionally, the person must have made a response to such an event or events that indicates

intense fear, helplessness to do anything to avoid dying, or horror. This additional element brings in a psychological dimension to the operational definitions of *precipitating condition* and *workplace stressor*.

Precipitants of PTSD in the workplace may include being attacked; being sexually assaulted or raped; being in a fire or flood or other form of natural or manmade disaster, including exposure to chemicals and toxins; being in a bad accident or in an industrial accident; experiencing combat; being threatened with a weapon or being intimidated or sexually harassed by fellow employees; or seeing someone being badly injured or killed in the workplace. Threats to one's employment, which in turn threatens one's physical and psychological integrity, can also be experienced as a form of trauma; such precipitants vary over time with larger economic factors, as well as between workplaces.

Although many of these precipitating conditions may be experienced in any workplace, the likelihood of such experiences varies widely between occupations and workplaces (McFarlane & de Girolamo, 1996). The greatest risks for trauma occur for employees who work in settings where they may witness injuries to fellow workers and/or experience actual injuries themselves, even seeing death or causing death (e.g., Feinstein & Dolan, 1991; Flannery, Hanson, & Penk, 1994; Flannery, Hanson, Penk, & Flannery, 1994; Gleser, Green, & Winget, 1981; Green, 1993; Holen, 1993; Resnick, Falsetti, Kilpatrick, & Freedy, 1996; Resnick et al., 1993; Shalev, Peri, Schreiber, & Caneti, 1996; Weisaeth, 1989, 1993, 1994; Weisaeth & Eitinger, 1993). People who work as police officers and firefighters are frequently placed in life-threatening situations (Fullerton & Ursano, in press; Gersons & Carlier, 1994). Other employees, such as emergency workers and members of disaster response teams, are also frequently in situations where they witness death (Bartone, Ursano, Saczynski, & Ingraham, 1989; Hodgkinson & Shepherd, 1994). Other types of traumatic experiences, such as attacks on staff, may occur in institutional settings such as psychiatric facilities, prisons, and juvenile homes (e.g., Flannery, 1995; Lanza, 1996). And, as the events of September 11 and the subsequent anthrax scare have sensitized us, attacks by terrorists from outside and from within our nation have now heightened the sense of threat and danger in the workplace.

Lower exposure to trauma occurs in work environments in which employees are merely aware of destruction and loss (e.g., Baum, Gatchel, & Schaeffer, 1983; Green, 1993; Kaltrieder, Gracie, & LeBreck, 1992; Karlehagen et al., 1993; Marmar, Weiss, Metzler, Ronfeldt, & Foreman, 1996; Paton, 1990). Other work environments are characterized by higher exposure, such as when employees observe that they were vulnerable to but did not actually experience injury (Alexander, 1993; Fullerton, McCarroll, Ursano, & Wright, 1992; McCarroll, Ursano, Fullerton, & Lundy, 1995; McCarroll et al., 1993).

The potential for workplace-based generation of PTSD in settings where traumatic events are less common should not be underestimated, because systematic training and preparation for trauma can lessen the likelihood that traumatic experiences result in PTSD symptoms (Freeman, 2000). A serious accident or shooting may take a far greater toll on those who have not anticipated the event than on those for whom traumatic experience is expected (van der Kolk, McFarlane, & van der Hart, 1996).

There is also potential for the workplace to generate PTSD through an indirect rather than a direct route, when the workplace stimulates other maladies that themselves increase the risk of PTSD. Perhaps the most common such indirect pathway is substance abuse. Occupations that facilitate or even encourage drinking tend to have higher rates of substance abuse. In turn, substance abusers are more likely to experience traumatic events and so have substantially elevated rates of PTSD (Cottler, Compton, Mager, Spitznagel, & Janca, 1992). Health care professions that increase exposure to psychoactive drugs may have elevated rates of PTSD as a result of a similar indirect causal process.

None of these risks can be understood fully without attention to the backgrounds and preexisting vulnerabilities that employees bring with them into the workplace. Risk factors for PTSD have not been researched as well as those for other anxiety disorders, and evidence is inconclusive about the importance of pretrauma background in the etiology of PTSD. In fact, debate is heated concerning the relative role of the traumatic experience itself (e.g., van der Kolk, McFarlane, & van der Hart, 1996). Nevertheless, it is clear that the composition of the workforce is consequential. Limited research suggests a genetic link: In a study of Vietnam-era veterans who were twins, genetic factors were estimated to account for about 30% of the variance in risk to develop PTSD symptoms (e.g., van der Kolk, McFarlane, & van der Hart, 1996). Employees who have experienced psychiatric disorders are more likely to have been diagnosed with PTSD, to react with PTSD symptoms to workplace trauma, and to continue to evidence PTSD symptoms throughout their work experience (Breslau & Davis, 1992). The link is not only in susceptibility to developing PTSD symptoms in response to a trauma, but also in the likelihood of being exposed to trauma, with the underlying factor probably being shared personality traits associated with behaviors that expose people to trauma.

So, even though a work environment may rate low in exposure to trauma, employees could rate high in their history of experiences of life-threatening events. And even so-called safe work environments might contain cues reminding workers with PTSD about traumas experienced away from the workplace. Each workplace is a complex environment. Some workplaces can actually lead to traumatic events that result in PTSD. Other workplaces may inadvertently provide reminders about non-work-incurred traumas, exacerbating symptoms of prework traumas. Still other workplaces, by the nature of the intensity of the work, may attract risk takers, whereas other workplaces, because of lower stress levels, may attract highly traumatized people seeking presumably safe working environments.

Variability in susceptibility to PTSD serves as an important limiting factor in assessing the relative risk that a workplace poses for PTSD. In fact, the National Comorbidity Survey showed that the prevalence of Current PTSD approached 10% in the general population and identified fully 50% as having experienced or witnessed trauma.

COURSE AND PROGNOSIS

Course of PTSD

PTSD can occur at any age, and its course can be variable. Symptoms may begin appearing several months after experiencing trauma, but in some instances, the course of the disorder may be delayed and may not appear for many years. Delayed appearance is illustrated by the frequent observation that many World War II veterans did not evidence PTSD publicly until they retired from work or underwent a challenging physical examination for a medical condition much later in life. The term *acute* is applied to the disorder when symptoms persist for less than 3 months; *chronic* refers to symptoms appearing more than 6 months after the trauma; and *delayed* onset is classified any time PTSD symptoms appear more than 6 months after experiencing trauma.

There is evidence that PTSD is a phasic disorder, that is, it is not as salient when a person's life situation is controllable, but it recurs intensely when there are physical and psychological weaknesses or difficulties in handling the daily hassles of living or when positive supports and reinforcers are withdrawn. The disorder is noted as having a time-related, phasic quality associated with reminders about the initial traumatic event or events—an "anniversary" reaction, as illustrated earlier in the first case example with the resurgence of memories around Memorial Day or around the date when the trauma occurred originally.

Features of the workplace can also affect the course and expression of PTSD symptoms. Whether PTSD has its roots in the workplace or has been brought into work from outside, the perceptions, feelings, and vulnerabilities resulting from PTSD will influence interactions with coworkers as well as reactions to many aspects of the work experience. In fact, McFarlane's (1989) study of firefighters in a disaster indicates that posttrauma life events—including what happens at work—may themselves have more impact on the continuing experience of PTSD symptoms than the trauma itself after 2 years. Individuals with PTSD also tend to be more prone to anger, which is then likely to result in more workplace problems (Frueh, Henning, Pellegrin, & Chobot, 1997).

Moos's (1994) conceptualization of workplace social climate identifies workplace features that are likely to be of particular salience to employees suffering from PTSD. Moos's scheme has three areas—relationship, personal growth, and system maintenance—each of which is composed of three or four specific dimensions (see also Karasek & Theorell, 1990). Two of the relationship dimensions are of particular relevance to those suffering from PTSD. The extent of coworker cohesion and supervisor support in the workplace are likely to be of special salience to employees who have been unable to maintain adequate caring attachments due to PTSD (Flannery, 1992). A cohesive, supportive workplace can serve as an antidote to the generalized interpersonal mistrust that often accompanies PTSD, whereas a fractured, unsupportive environment can exacerbate this feeling.

The reduced sense of mastery, even helplessness, that often accompanies PTSD is likely to be worse in an environment that allows little employee autonomy and maintains a high level of work pressure (Moos's "personal growth" area). Concerns with personal safety, high levels of anxiety, social withdrawal, and a tendency to negative self-evaluations often accompany PTSD (Fogarty & Beck, 1995). These concerns are likely to be heightened in workplaces that do not provide basic levels of clear procedures and physical comfort (Moos's "system maintenance" area). In general, to the extent that the workplace fails to provide social supports, modulated affect, and a protected environment, the potential for exacerbation of PTSD symptoms is heightened and the risk for continuation of the disorder prolonged.

Prognosis for PTSD

With regard to the prognosis and treatment of PTSD, there is the proverbial good news and bad news.

The good news is that clinicians have an empirical basis for concluding that PTSD is a treatable disorder. This conclusion is empirically validated, not just by clinical practice and clinical observations, but by well-designed clinical studies based upon randomized, well-controlled clinical trials. A summary of these findings appears in Foa et al. (2000). This is a landmark volume in the treatment of PTSD, assessing the state of the science and the art of treatment. The section below on recommended data-based treatment is based on information from the International Society for Traumatic Stress Studies (ISTSS) Task Force, which produced practice guidelines for treating PTSD.

There is bad news, however. Evaluations of various techniques for treating PTSD are still in their infancy. Studies that empirically validate PTSD treatment effectiveness are still rudimentary and evolving. Techniques have not been tested for the generalizability of their findings across populations. Comparisons between types of treatment, to determine which are more effective for whom, have not been done. Results do not, as yet, yield the kind of findings by which clinicians can select, with confidence, which type of treatment to offer for what kind of trauma, for what kind of person, at what level of stage in recovery. And, most important, most of the treatment studies have been conducted with treatment-seeking samples in clinical settings. Few treatment studies have been completed on work-related and/or work-exacerbating trauma. Randomized clinical trials are needed to determine which of the empirically validated PTSD treatments are most effective for trauma experienced in work environments and/or for the residuals of trauma brought to the work environment.

But even the bad news is not really that bad. It is bad only in the sense that a mere 20 years have passed since PTSD was clearly formulated as a diagnostic disorder, and that most PTSD studies completed to date have centered on perfecting measurement. The positive view of the current status is that the next 20 years are likely to see a growth in randomized, clinical trials, comparing types of treatment. Future research now has a wealth of validated instruments both to classify PTSD with confidence as well as to measure changes across time in adjustment (see Keane, Weathers, & Foa, 2000).

Toward Developing Referral Strategies for PTSD

Referral strategies can be readily imported to worksites from agencies that have already developed practice guidelines for PTSD treatment, such as the Veterans Health Administration (see VHA, 1997, 1999). However, the most comprehensive is the aforementioned guidelines commissioned by the ISTSS (see Foa et al., 2000). Both VHA and ISTSS sources guide the treatment section in this chapter on the impact of PTSD in the workplace.

PTSD treatment should be tailored to fit each person's individual circumstances. No one treatment is suitable for all traumatized people. Individual differences in PTSD vary so enormously that clinicians have but one recourse; that is, to proceed on the basis that if you have seen one case of PTSD, you have seen one case of PTSD. No two cases are going to be alike. No two cases are going to need the same kind of treatment.

Factors accounting for individual differences are many and varied and include some of the following: age at which trauma occurred (the earlier the trauma, the more complex the presentation is likely to be); type of trauma; time when treatment is initiated relative to the traumatic event; comorbidities (either those caused by the trauma or already existing at the time trauma occurred, mainly depression and substance use disorders); interactions

between current work environment and past traumas; conflicts persisting at work, if and when trauma occurred at work; conflicts between work environment and current trauma away from the worksite, as in cases of domestic violence.

All of these factors, as well as others, have been demonstrated as contributing to variations in PTSD and as meriting an individually tailored treatment plan.

Preventing PTSD: Creating a Caring Environment

We believe that mental health professionals must work with management and with employees to create a caring work environment aimed at the prevention of PTSD. Clinicians, whether employed by management or working directly for clients, have, as their primary objective, to promote the human welfare. Thus, decisions about treating PTSD are centered on improving the well-being and productivity of the worker who has been traumatized at work or whose symptoms appear at, or are exacerbated in, the worksite.

The recent establishment of the Office for Homeland Security, currently under the leadership of the former governor of Pennsylvania, Thomas Ridge, may help sensitize all employers and employees to the importance of creating safe working environments. Although the motivation for the creation of the Office for Homeland Security derives from the events of September 11 and the anthrax scare, another possible effect will be to generalize our efforts on behalf of workplace safety to all kinds of threats and traumas, no matter what their source.

First steps in referral strategies include ensuring patient safety and then establishing a therapeutic alliance and trust. Unfortunately, traumatic events experienced in the workplace are not the best circumstances under which to foster a therapeutic alliance. Traumatized employees may blame management for traumas that have occurred in the workplace, believing that management was responsible for ensuring a safe and supported work environment. Employees may be reluctant to report certain forms of trauma for fear that work status may be jeopardized; because of shame; or for fear that as a "victim," the employee will be blamed for what went wrong. Other employees may be so angry with management that they seek compensation for real or imagined traumas.

Management, with or without mental health providers, needs to conceptualize any treatment within a relationship that ensures employee safety and elicits employee trust, even though such objectives may be difficult to attain. As a consequence, the first step in treating PTSD is prevention, and deploying those intervention techniques that are demonstrated as effective in prevention.

Thus, it is necessary to think about treatment in terms of a caring organization that formalizes, in advance, structures targeted to cope with employees who have been traumatized—structures that are formalized around referrals, peer support, professional help, and follow-up. We conclude that the first step in referral strategies for management is to invest resources into the individuals who form the company's or agency's human capital. Management must create a work environment that cares—not just for the physical but also for the psychological well-being of workers. As mentioned earlier, Moos (1994) has developed measures for determining the health status of the social climate of businesses and agencies, and we suggest that management test the psychological health of the work environment regularly and routinely.

Treatment goals for those suffering from PTSD include reducing psychological arousal, restoring a reasonable sense of mastery over the environment, maintaining caring attachments, and encouraging a meaningful purpose for life (Flannery, 1992). Clinicians should help employees suffering from PTSD, particularly those returning to work after PTSD-induced absences, to review possible stressors in the work environment and to develop tailored coping strategies (Fogarty & Beck, 1995). In the early stages of recovery, work environments that pose threats to personal safety and do not offer caring attachments should be avoided. When this is not possible, ongoing support outside the workplace, whether through familial or therapeutic relationships or self-help groups, are particularly important (Jackson-Malik, 1987). In later stages of recovery, for those suffering from chronic PTSD, a workplace that also offers some degree of job autonomy and meaningful work will facilitate the recovery process. Because the needs of people in recovery from PTSD or other disorders change over time (Creamer, Burgess, & Pattison, 1992), some mobility between jobs or changes in existing jobs may be required.

Managers who seek to lessen the adverse impact of PTSD can benefit from programs focused directly on helping employees deal with stress, whatever its source. Programmatic efforts such as Flannery's (1990, 1992) SMART self-help approach to becoming stress resistant can reduce the frequency and magnitude of PTSD symptoms. Companies that invest in techniques to increase stress resistance find that gains far outweigh costs (e.g., Flannery, 1998).

Managers of working environments are also advised to prepare their workforce for the possibilities of trauma occurring in the workplace. Programmatic interventions preparing to deal with traumas in the workplace have been developed by many mental health organizations. One empirically validated model is the Assaulted Staff Action Program (ASAP), developed by Raymond B. Flannery (1998) for mental health facilities. The ASAP model uses principles of intervention learned for treating PTSD in combat— the principles of immediacy, proximity, and expectation. That is, ASAP begins by training the workforce on what to do in case of trauma—mainly for occasions of trauma caused by patient-staff violence, but also for any source of trauma. ASAP team members begin to deploy their resources as soon as a mandated trauma reporting system is activated in the workplace. Peer support is immediate, occurring as soon as possible after the trauma has occurred. Peer support is proximal, occurring as close as is practical to the actual place where trauma was experienced. And peer support is delivered with the expectation that the person traumatized will return to work as soon as it is medically and physically possible. Flannery's ASAP model incorporates the time-honored principles of treating stress disorders under battlefield conditions.

ASAP also embodies principles of Critical Incident Stress Debriefing (Freeman, 2000; Mitchell, 1983; Mitchell & Everly, 1995). Reviews of such psychological debriefing techniques are mixed, and outcome data are meager. However, Bisson, McFarlane, and Rose (2000) conclude in their review that, when offered as part of a comprehensive management program by experienced mental health clinicians, psychological debriefing interventions are indeed valuable—as prevention, as preparation, and as necessary when any form of trauma occurs in the workplace.

DATA-BASED TREATMENTS

Reviews of the literature on PTSD treatment (e.g., Foa et al., 2000) suggest that

management has the responsibility to provide resources for determining if and when specialized interventions are needed, either as follow-up after trauma has occurred in the workplace or when workplace stressors exacerbate residuals of trauma previously experienced. Prevention techniques and worker preparation can go only so far. Specialized services to treat residuals of trauma are needed. Models of referrals for such specialized services include Employee Assistance Programs (EAPs) and Human Resources units within the workplace that refer traumatized workers to consulting mental health specialists.

A range of empirically validated treatments is available. Effectiveness of these techniques has been established, at least at the Level C criteria developed by the Agency of Health Care Policy and Research (AHCPR) for determining treatment effectiveness, where Level C refers to evidence based upon either clinical observations by qualified mental health workers or naturalistic studies without placebo controls or other comparison groups. Although some of these specialized treatments have been studied under well-controlled clinical trials with random assignment conditions, there is very little research determining which treatment works better than another treatment at different stages of recovery.

Cognitive-behavioral therapies (Rothbaum, Meadows, Resick, & Foy, 2000) have received the most attention; to date, at least eight clinical trials with random assignment to experimental and control conditions have been published in peer-reviewed journals. Results justify use of such techniques, including those involved with exposure approaches coupled with systematic desensitization, cognitive processing therapy, relaxation, and assertiveness training combined.

Pharmacotherapies are not necessarily considered the first line of treatment, in lieu of the above-mentioned success of cognitive-behavioral therapies. However, treatment with medication should always be evaluated in treatment planning. (See Friedman, Davidson, Mellman, & Southwick, 2000, for one of the more recent, up-to-date summaries of evidence for the efficacy of drugs in the treatment of PTSD.) Clinical trials are showing positive results, particularly for associated disorders. Selective serotonin reuptake inhibitors have been demonstrated as effective in reducing some forms of impulsivity and mood lability. Antiadrenergic drugs have been shown to reduce arousal behaviors and dissociation symptoms associated with PTSD. Results are sufficiently promising that consultation is essential with a physician about the role of pharmacotherapies in treatment planning.

Eye Movement Desensitization and Reprocessing (EMDR) has yielded promising results (Chemtob, Tolin, van der Kolk, & Pitman, 2000). EMDR emerges as particularly effective in cases of simple PTSD (i.e., single-event, civilian trauma) and less so for cases of complex PTSD with multiple trauma and a history of treatment resistance.

Group therapy effectiveness is substantiated at the level of clinical observation and naturalistic studies, but the results of only two randomized clinical trials have been published (Foy et al., 2000). In general, the findings are positive, but further research is needed. Group therapies range widely in type, from supported group therapy, to psychodynamic group therapy, to cognitive-behavioral group therapy. Treatment manuals are under development and are being evaluated for their treatment effectiveness.

A number of treatment techniques have been empirically validated to address other kinds of psychological disorders. Clinicians have begun to explore the usefulness of these techniques in the treatment of PTSD. For example, only one study of *hypnosis*, along with other therapies, has been reported in the PTSD literature, and findings were favorable (Cardena, Maldonado, van der Hart, & Spiegel, 2000). Reviewers of this literature report an eight-stage process model of PTSD that has not yet been subjected to empirical validation. The authors also present important exclusion criteria for the use of hypnosis.

Riggs (2000) presents a compelling argument why *marital and family therapies* might prove effective in the treatment of PTSD. Finding marital and family therapies useful in addressing other disorders, he reasons that resolving the problems of social avoidance and poor communication should reduce marital and family distress that is associated with PTSD. The treatment rationale is persuasive. Techniques such as emotion-focused marital therapy and supportive therapy for families of trauma survivors have been developed. The empirical validation has not yet been carried out.

Likewise, *psychodynamic therapies* are procedurally well developed for the treatment of PTSD, but their effectiveness awaits formal evaluation under conditions of randomized, clinical trials (Kudler, Blank, & Krupnick, 2000). Techniques vary, from psychoanalysis, to psychodynamic psychotherapy, to brief psychodynamic psychotherapy, to supportive psychotherapy. Most clinicians agree that comparatively well-adjusted clients are better candidates for such therapies, specifically those individuals judged as ready and capable of forming therapeutic alliances. Cases of complex PTSD may require this form of long-term treatment.

Inpatient PTSD treatment is offered primarily through the Veterans Health Administration. At least 16 outcome studies have been completed, in the form of naturalistic evaluations. Results suggest that high-intensity options are needed, particularly in cases of continual exposure to trauma, as occurs under combat conditions, and that findings of specialized inpatient treatment units are favorable (Courtois & Bloom, 2000). Descriptions of inpatient programs are given in the VHA's (1999) *Mental Health Program Guide,* as well as in the review article by Courtois and Bloom (2000).

Finally, *psychosocial rehabilitation techniques* are recommended; their effectiveness remains to be validated (Penk & Flannery, 2000). Psychosocial rehabilitation consists of a range of techniques, from case management that links traumatized people to appropriate services, to self-help and family psychoeducational approaches that teach survivors how to cope with the residuals of trauma.

For trauma in the workplace, however, mental health providers should consider adapting principles of treating trauma for the workplace itself (Penk, 2001). Work is regarded as therapeutic, as Sigmund Freud (1929) suggested when he wrote, "No other technique for the conduct of life attaches the individual so firmly to reality as laying emphasis on work; for work at least gives one a secure place in a portion of reality, in the human community" (p. 59).

Unfortunately, clinical tests of the hypothesis that work itself is effective in the treatment of PTSD are just under way. Benefits of work are frequently noted during the course of delivering clinical services, as illustrated in the case of Tom Livingston, but work as therapy has not been studied extensively. Nevertheless, naturalistic studies and clinical observations are sufficiently compelling that attention is merited. Vocational rehabilitation services are used by many adults with psychiatric disorders to assist in their efforts to return to work. By comparing groups of adults who participate in vocational rehabilitation, it is possible to understand how best to serve them (see Box 11.2).

As illustrated by outcome data cited in Box 11.2, but also in the case of Tom Livingston, who overcompensated for his symptoms of PTSD by losing himself in his work, compensated work therapy suggests that work itself may be beneficial in the treatment of PTSD. How can work be beneficial in treating PTSD? Work certainly addresses a core symptom of PTSD—the learned helplessness that is a feature of being traumatized, of not being in control, of not being able to do anything to save your life (Fogarty & Beck, 1995). Work restores a sense of mastery and helps reassure individuals that they can recover the capacity to control their lives, a capacity that is threatened by trauma. Furthermore, work provides social contacts in most instances, thereby reducing social isolation that is a hallmark of the avoidance maneuvers used to cope with memories of trauma. Sense of loss of attachments that is associated with trauma may be assuaged by reintegration into the workforce. Moreover, work often provides a sense of purpose, in contrast to trauma, which may destroy a person's beliefs in reasons for living. Work can be a concrete, active form of expressing that a person has goals in living. Finally, work—as distinguished from its opposite, the unemployment commonly found among psychiatric patients with histories of trauma—helps tie a person to reality, as Freud explained so long ago.

Time Element of PTSD Treatments

Work environments differ in referral mechanisms for diagnosing and assessing PTSD. Most employers have no way to refer clients other than supervisors or coworkers sensing that something is awry and eventually building up the courage to confront

Box 11.2   A Study of Vocational Rehabilitation and PTSD

Within the Veterans Health Administration, vocational rehabilitation services are offered under the rubric of Compensated Work Therapy (CWT). This program is fairly consistent across sites in its format, using a mixed model of rehabilitation that includes sheltered workshops, transitional employment and job placement (Losardo, 1999; Seibyl & Rosenheck, 2000). The stated goal of CWT is to help maximize participant levels of functioning while preparing as many veterans as possible for a successful return to competitive employment (Losardo, 1999).

The client population is predominantly male, middle-aged veterans, virtually all of whom have a psychiatric and/or substance abuse problem, with many having additional medical problems. About 15% to 25% carry a diagnosis of PTSD, depending on the program. Although this diagnosis is often related to the trauma of combat, many other forms of trauma have been experienced (Lawson, Drebing, Short, Vincellette, & Penk, 1998). The majority of participants have a history of vocational difficulties over many years (Losardo, 1999). Limited evaluation data available on this program suggest that participation by the average veteran in CWT is associated with reduced drug and alcohol use, and fewer episodes of homelessness and incarceration, but with no clear benefit in terms of psychiatric symptoms or stability (Kashner et al., 2001).

Data Collection

Data used in the current study include information about individuals entering the CWT program at the Bedford VA Medical Center between 1998 and 1999. The data concerning CWT participants have been collected routinely for administrative purposes since 1994 by the Northeast Program Evaluation Center, which monitors all CWT programs in the Veterans Health Administration (VHA). At Bedford, additional data are collected to document why participants are having difficulty with work, what they hope to gain by participating in CWT, and other aspects of their participation.

Results

Six hundred and forty participants entered CWT during that time, with 150, or 23%, having a diagnosis of posttraumatic stress disorder. Participants diagnosed with PTSD were not significantly different from other participants in terms of age, education, or other demographic variables. They were more likely to carry a comorbid diagnosis of an additional anxiety disorder or bipolar disorder. They were not more likely to have a comorbid substance abuse problem.

Prior to admission, a majority of both groups have been working competitively. The participants with PTSD are almost twice as likely as other participants with psychiatric problems to blame their current unemployment on those psychiatric problems. Similarly, they are much more likely to state that the reason they are entering rehabilitation is to work in a setting that enables them to cope with their psychiatric problems.

(Continued)

Box 11.2, Continued

Part of the challenge of working is balancing treatment and work demands. Participants with PTSD are more likely to say that they are not working competitively because of difficulty in balancing work and treatment demands. This is not surprising, as the mean number of appointments they attended in the prior month for psychiatric treatment is 30% higher than for other participants with psychiatric disorders.

Once they enter vocational rehabilitation, the PTSD group members participated as well as other diagnostic group members. On average, they stayed as long and achieved roughly equivalent "successful discharge" rates as the other groups. They were significantly more likely than others to participate in the most demanding parts of the program, where they were placed in jobs in the community, working alongside nonparticipants. In a prior study we completed with a larger sample of CWT participants from a range of programs, we found that the participants with PTSD actually were employed at a higher rate at discharge than were other participants with psychiatric disorders.

Conclusions

These data confirm that adults with PTSD make up a significant portion of the population of adults seeking vocational rehabilitation because of psychiatric problems. Compared to participants with other psychiatric disorders, those with PTSD attribute their work problems more to their psychiatric problems and to the difficulty of staying in treatment and working. Despite this, they participate in vocational rehabilitation for the same length of time and tend to be involved in the more demanding parts of rehabilitation. This may account for the slight advantage seen elsewhere in their outcome from CWT, in terms of competitive employment.

their colleague and make a referral to an individual practitioner. Knowing that PTSD is highly prevalent in workplaces should be sufficient reason for management to create referral mechanisms within the scope of the corporate culture.

Several years ago, the VHA developed screening instruments for use in assessing all patients referred to its medical centers. See Attachment A from the VHA's (1997) guidelines, which contains the screening instrument along with an algorithm for deciding when and how to refer people who may need treatment for PTSD. The VHA algorithm also provides a summary of the time elements needed in making decisions about PTSD treatments.

For larger organizations, like VHA medical centers, both management and unions require that departments be created to assist employees. As a consequence, Human Resources are established by public law in VA medical centers, as well as adaptations of the Employee Assistance Programs. The VHA system of health care is not the only organization that is mandated to be a caring environment for its employees; many businesses and corporations have their counterparts to what federal services and military agencies have been implementing throughout most of the 20th century.

Those who score positively on the PTSD screening instrument should be referred to a practitioner with experience in treating people with PTSD for purposes of conducting a more detailed evaluation. Among the first questions such a practitioner should ask is whether or not the person confirmed to meet PTSD criteria requires inpatient treatment. Criteria for hospitalization include lacking the capacity to cooperate with outpatient treatment, being at risk for suicide and/or homicide, lacking psychological and requisite social supports, having other complicating medical and/or psychiatric conditions that render outpatient treatment unsafe, and/or having a history of nonresponsiveness to outpatient treatment.

Once needs for treatment are established and needs for inpatient hospitalization have been ruled out, then the mental health professional, together with the client, can begin to develop a treatment plan that fits in with the patient's current adjustment.

Dynamic psychotherapies (see summary of treatments above) are recommended for avoidance and numbing symptoms of PTSD. Group therapy is recommended for social alienation, as well as avoidance and numbing symptoms. Cognitive therapies and dynamic psychotherapy are recommended for distorted beliefs associated with PTSD.

Cognitive-behavioral therapies and psychoeducational methods of anger management are highly recommended when affective dysregulation and dissociation—indicators of Complex PTSD—are present (see Herman, 1991; van der Kolk, McFarlane, & Weisaeth, 1996).

When anxiety is prominent in the clinical picture, particularly physiological arousal and concurrent anxiety disorder symptoms, behavioral interventions to address sleep disturbances, including nightmares, are essential. Direct therapeutic exposure is highly recommended for reducing anxiety and physiological arousal, particularly for cooperative patients with strong support groups and capacities to form therapeutic alliances. Traditional cognitive and behavioral treatments are recommended when panic attacks are co-occurring. For Simple PTSD and single traumas, EMDR is recommended. Questions about medication should be deferred until the symptom picture is well-established.

A fundamental problem when planning treatment for PTSD for workers in the workplace is that principles of level of care/rehabilitation have not been developed; these principles guide clinicians in deciding the appropriate level of treatment intensity and requisite involvement of medical intervention. In other words, nothing equivalent to the American Society of Addiction Medicine criteria exist, as adapted for level of care determination for substance abuse. The concepts that guide developing and empirically validating level of care determination for substance abuse are now well-documented, but no such empirically guided decision-making process is available for any other disorders, much less PTSD. The field of level of care/rehabilitation determination is wide open for mental health professionals to design and implement for PTSD in the world of work. The time element for treating PTSD cannot be specified until clinical guidelines are developed, relative to low and high levels of intensity of treatment in inpatient versus outpatient settings.

Side Effects of PTSD Treatments and Impact on Work

Side effects of PTSD treatments are discussed in detail in Foa et al. (2000) by types of treatments offered, and they need not be detailed here other than to note a few obvious risks. Each of the treatments offered will have some side effects, the psychosocial rehabilitation treatments as much as pharmacotherapy approaches. Friedman et al. (2000) highlight the importance of using as few medications as possible (see

Fogarty & Beck, 1995). They note sleep disturbances, and the resultant fatigue, as a major side effect that could have unique implications in the workplace. That is, physicians need to take into account and warn workers who are medicated about pharmacotherapeutic hazards in operating or working around dangerous machinery and/or operating motor vehicles.

Similarly, trauma-focused treatments based on individual and group approaches may provide reminders about trauma that are emotionally disturbing to clients. The act of remembering traumas that one strives to forget is likely to produce a period of emotional distress that, in turn, may be played out in the workplace when the everyday hassles of employment could become exaggerated or overemphasized. Mental health professionals are advised to develop treatment plans in which both the workers who are receiving services and supervisors are informed—to the extent that personal privacy permits, and only with the agreement of those receiving services. Use of support groups and implementation of employee-to-employee process groups, such as the aforementioned ASAP teams (Flannery, 1998), provide a model for assisting those receiving services in coping with side effects of PTSD treatments. In addition, mental health professionals who are treating trauma survivors also must provide support groups for themselves, because treating trauma may be hazardous to the provider.

Workplace Accommodations for PTSD Treatments

Workplace accommodations for PTSD, as well as other disorders (such as the high comorbidity of substance abuse treatment) are mandated by public laws, such as the Americans with Disabilities Act of 1990, and by management-union agreements, as well as in company memoranda of understanding with employees. Such accommodations follow blueprints established long ago (e.g., Roman, 1988), which have seven basic points:

1. Supervisors, along with workers, are trained to implement a "performance only" identification strategy. That is, interventions are activated only when job performance problems, such as higher-than-average rates of job absence and lower-than-expected job performance, are documented as occurring.

2. Employers should provide consultation from experts—mental health as well as business professionals who are experienced in creating caring environments that increase job performance and productivity, and who are knowledgeable about job stresses and traumas in the workplace.

3. Employers should develop and then follow techniques of "constructive confrontation." That is, management, unions, and representatives of employees must develop guidelines and memoranda of understanding on steps to follow when performance problems are identified in the workplace.

4. Efficient ways of referring should be developed between (a) individual workers evidencing performance problems and (b) treatment services in the community.

5. Workplace programs should have organizational linkages between workplaces and service providers, including a monitoring system, so that the employer understands the effectiveness of its responses to employee needs as well as stresses produced in the workplace.

6. Managers in the workplace should communicate to their workers that human capital is responsible for the success of the workplace, and that the workplace is a caring environment that will provide constructive assistance for dealing with stress and trauma.

7. Workplaces should invest resources into a program coordinator who reports to management, as an organizational expert, about the effectiveness of management's investments in its human capital and on how the human welfare of its employees has been nurtured.

As summarized from Roman (1988), we conclude that the most productive contribution that mental health professionals can provide to the workplace is the creation of worker-to-worker and management-to-worker programs that are activated at times of stress and trauma, and at times when performance interferences are demonstrated and are identified at work. Managers should develop plans for dealing with trauma of any kind before disaster strikes, and these plans should be reviewed periodically with staff as routinely as management conducts its fire drills (Freeman, 2000). Requirements are stated in greater detail in other source documents, such as the standards from the National Institute of Occupational Safety and Health (NIOSH) and the Occupational Safety and Health Administration (OSHA). (See, for example, *Guidelines for Preventing Workplace Violence for Health Care Workers,* 1996, in which "threat assessment" teams conduct security analyses; survey employees on potential for violent episodes; monitor trends for job-related injuries; and review medical, safety, workers' compensation, and insurance records for incidents.)

MAINTENANCE OF GAINS/RELAPSE PREVENTION

Workplace Strategies for Treating PTSD

The guarantee of safety in the workplace is not just a matter of good business—it is also mandated by law. Both federal laws—such as the Occupational Safety and Health Act of 1970, the American Disabilities Act of 1991, the National Labor Relations Acts—and state laws—such as the workers' compensation acts—specify workplace strategies for treating PTSD and, by implication, ways to maintain gains and prevent relapse after treatment. Such federal and state laws mandate that employers have a general duty to provide a workplace that is free from recognized hazards that may cause death or serious physical harm—events associated with PTSD. Employers can be cited if they violate the general duty clause that is central to all of the federal and state legislation guaranteeing workplace safety—a general duty clause that holds employers responsible for preventing and eliminating threats and hazards in the workplace.

Both NIOSH and OSHA have written guidelines to prevent and eliminate hazards in the workplace. Although not always mandatory, such guidelines include strategies for dealing with the aftermath of trauma. OSHA mandates are not promulgated to interfere with responsibilities of the states to deal with workers' compensation systems that provide for job-related injuries and illnesses. Workers' compensation rules and regulations are left up to state legislatures and state courts. But both state and federal guidelines have been developed to address residuals of work trauma in terms of lost production, lost wages, medical expenses, and disability compensation payments.

Gains from treating trauma in the workplace will be achieved when the caring work environment maintains a monitoring system focusing on how physical and psychological hazards produce stress and trauma at the worksite. Employers are advised to assess productivity in terms of how untreated hazards impair productivity, as indicated by the aforementioned lost production, lost wages, medical expenses, and disability compensation payments. An accurate accounting system linking the effects of trauma to lost production is the best guarantee that management will take steps to prevent trauma in the workplace.

Beyond a trauma/lost production system of monitoring, there are four other techniques by which management can prevent and treat the effects of trauma (see OSHA, 1996):

1. Management commitment and employee involvement in ensuring a safe and health-promoting work environment, including zero tolerance of violence with no reprisals against employees who report workplace violence and disasters

2. Continual and frequent worksite analyses as well as employee analyses to find existing or potential hazards or potentials for workplace violence and disasters (this includes the aforementioned "threat assessment" along with records for monitoring injuries, accidents, and episodes of violence)

3. Setting up engineering and administrative work practices to prevent hazards and workplace violence, such as security devices, alarm systems, panic buttons, cellular phones for employees, restrictions on working alone in isolated worksites, and so on

4. Instituting postincidence reporting systems, based upon employers and employees working together to create a caring environment for workers who have been traumatized (see Flannery's ASAP model as a blueprint for dealing with trauma) (Flannery, 1998)

Mental health workers are well-trained and experienced in developing such strategies for employers and employees. In addition to having the skills necessary to create caring environments, many mental health workers, such as psychologists, have been trained in statistics and experimental design to conduct the cost-for-gain reckoning needed for ensuring that health-promoting services are offsetting the costs of lost productivity.

SUMMARY

PTSD is a hidden problem in the workplace—hidden because its primary symptom is avoidance of reminders about the traumas that caused PTSD; hidden because co-occurring disorders, such as depression and substance abuse, obscure its importance as a reason that workers decline in productivity; and hidden because many employers tacitly collude with trauma survivors to not discuss the life-threatening events that workers have experienced either in the workplace or elsewhere.

Untreated PTSD will be evident in the workplace in many forms of lost productivity: not doing the work, not performing the work to standard, not being present to work, and expressing conflicts with supervisors and coworkers. Outlined here are steps that mental health providers, working for the goals of the organization and for the welfare of employers and employees alike, can take to maintain and improve productivity. Two stages are proposed: (a) prevention by creating a caring work environment, and (b) specialized treatment of traumatized employees by professionals. At the heart of prevention is an employee-to-employee approach, and Flannery's (1998) Assaulted Staff Action Program in health care facilities is one tried-and-true model that can be generalized to many work settings. It is an approach in which management makes a commitment to employee safety and implements a program for preventing and coping with trauma. Prevention approaches like ASAP also provide decision-making rules for determining when referrals need to be made to specialists, the second stage of treating trauma in the workplace. Algorithms for deciding when to refer to specialists have been developed in such organizations as the VHA, as have guidelines for selecting among a rich variety of empirically validated treatments.

The good news about treating PTSD in the workplace is that objective, standardized measures have been developed to identify PTSD, and treatments are proving to be effective. Limitations in both the current state of the art of assessment and treatment are noted, particularly that most PTSD measures and treatment techniques have been developed for traumas other than those experienced at work, and treatments are designed for clinics and hospitals rather than for work.

Based on the time-honored principles of immediacy, proximity, and expectancy, we conclude that assessment and treatment of PTSD in the workplace should be done in the workplace; that treatment should be done immediately with follow-up care, involving peers wherever and whenever possible; that treatment should be close to the actual work environment where trauma occurred; and that treatment should be delivered with the expectation that the traumatized employee will return to work as soon as physical and psychological health permit.

As our nation re-orients itself to the workplaces that have been the target of terrorist attacks, clinicians now may reconsider how to devise and adapt new ways for diagnosing and treating survivors of trauma that are specific to the workplace, whatever the cause of trauma.

NOTE

1. Detailed descriptions of the diagnostic features of PTSD are given in the *Diagnostic and Statistical Manual of Mental Disorders, Fourth Edition* (APA, 1994, Code 309.81, pp. 424-429).

REFERENCES

Alexander, D. A. (1993). Stress among police body handlers: A long-term follow-up. *British Journal of Psychiatry, 163,* 806-808.

American Psychiatric Association. (1980). *Diagnostic and statistical manual of mental disorders* (3rd ed.). Washington, DC: Author.

American Psychiatric Association. (1994). *Diagnostic and statistical manual of mental disorders* (4th ed.). Washington, DC: Author.

Bartone, P., Ursano, R. J., Saczynski, K., & Ingraham, L. H. (1989). The impact of a military air disaster on the health of assistance workers: A prospective study. *Journal of Nervous and Mental Disease, 177,* 317-327.

Baum, A. B., Gatchel, R. J., & Schaeffer, M. A. (1983). Emotional, behavioral, and physiological effects of chronic stress at Three Mile Island. *Journal of Consulting and Clinical Psychology, 51,* 565-572.

Bisson, J. I., McFarlane, A. C., & Rose, S. (2000) Psychological debriefing. In E. B. Foa, T. M. Keane, & M. J. Friedman (Eds.), *Effective treatments for PTSD* (pp. 39-59). New York: Guilford.

Breslau, N., & Davis, G. C. (1992). Posttraumatic stress disorder in an urban population of young adults: Risk factors for chronicity. *American Journal of Psychiatry, 149,* 671-675.

Breslau, N., Davis, G. C., & Andreski, P. (1995). Risk factors for PTSD related traumatic events: A prospective analysis. *American Journal of Psychiatry, 152,* 529-535.

Burgess, E. S., Hibler, R., Keegan, D., & Everly, G. S., Jr. (1996). Symptoms of post-traumatic stress disorder in worker's compensation patients attending a work rehabilitation program. *International Journal of Rehabilitation & Health, 2,* 29-39.

Cardena, E., Maldonado, J., van der Hart, O., & Spiegel, D. (2000). Hypnosis. In E. B. Foa, T. M. Keane, & M. J. Friedman (Eds.), *Effective treatments for PTSD* (pp. 247-279). New York: Guilford.

Chemtob, C. M., Tolin, D. F., van der Kolk, B. A., & Pitman, R. K. (2000). Eye movement desensitization and reprocessing. In E. B. Foa, T. M. Keane, & M. J. Friedman (Eds.), *Effective treatments for PTSD* (pp. 139-154). New York: Guilford.

Clark, W. G. , Crawford, J. E., Giles, S. L., & Nash, D. L. (1987). The Vietnam veteran in the 80s: A guide to assessment & intervention for the occupational health nurse. *AAOHN Journal, 35,* 79-85.

Cottler, L. B., Compton, W. M., III, Mager, D., Spitznagel, E. L., & Janca, A. (1992). Posttraumatic stress disorder among substance users from the general population. *American Journal of Psychiatry, 149*(5), 664-670.

Courtois, C. A., & Bloom, S. L. (2000). Inpatient treatment. In E. B. Foa, T. M. Keane, & M. J. Friedman (Eds,), *Effective treatments for PTSD* (pp. 199-223). New York: Guilford.

Creamer, M., Burgess, P., & Pattison, P. (1992). Reaction to trauma: A cognitive processing model. *Journal of Abnormal Psychology, 101,* 452-459.

Davidson, J. R. T., & Fairbank, J. A. (1993). The epidemiology of posttraumatic stress disorder. In J. R. T. Davidson & E. B. Foa (Eds.), *Posttraumatic stress disorder: DSM-IV and beyond* (pp. 147-169). Washington, DC: American Psychiatric Press.

Davidson, J. R. T., Hughes, D., Blazer, D. G., & George, L. K. (1991). Post-traumatic stress disorder in the community: An epidemiological study. *Psychological Medicine, 21,* 713-721.

De Mol, J. (1998). Post-aggression stress disorders: Psychosocial and work reper-cussions. *International Medical Journal, 54,* 277-282.

Fairbank, J. A., Jordan, B. K., & Schlenger, W. E. (1996). Designing and imple-menting epidemiologic studies. In E. G. Carlson (Ed.), *Trauma research method-ology.* Lutherville, MD: Sidran.

Fairbank, J. A., Schlenger, W. E., Saigh, P. A., & Davidson, J. R. T. (1995). An epidemiologic profile of post-traumatic stress disorder: Prevalence, comorbidity, and risk factors. In M. J. Friedman, D. S. Charney, & A. Y. Deutch (Eds.),

Neurobiological and clinical consequences of stress: From normal adaptation to PTSD. New York: Raven.

Feinstein, A., & Dolan, R. (1991). Predictors of post-traumatic stress disorder following physical trauma: An examination of the stressor criterion. *Psychological Medicine, 21,* 85-91.

Finlay-Jones, R. (1981). Types of stressful life events and the onset of anxiety and depression disorders. *Psychological Medicine, 11,* 803-815.

Flannery, R. B., Jr. (1990). *Becoming stress-resistant through the Project SMART program.* New York: Continuum.

Flannery, R. B., Jr. (1992). *Post-traumatic stress disorder: The victim's guide to healing and recovery.* New York: Crossroad.

Flannery, R. B., Jr. (1995). *Violence in the workplace.* New York: Crossroad.

Flannery, R. B., Jr. (1998). *The Assaulted Staff Action Program (ASAP): Coping with the psychological aftermath of violence.* Ellicott City, MD: Chevron.

Flannery, R. B., Jr. (2001, November). *The Assaulted Staff Action Program (ASAP): Ten year empirical support for critical incident stress management (CISM).* Paper presented at the Sixth World Congress on Stress Trauma and Coping, Baltimore, MD.

Flannery, R. B., Jr, Hanson, M. A., Penk, W. E., & Flannery, G. J. (1994). Violence against women: Psychiatric patient assaults on female staff. *Professional Psychology: Research and Practice, 25,* 182-184.

Flannery, R. B., Jr., Hanson, M. A., & Penk, W. E. (1994). Risk factors for psychiatric inpatient assaults on staff. *Journal of Mental Health Administration, 21,* 24-31.

Foa, E. B., Keane, T. M., & Friedman, M. J. (Eds.). (2000). *Effective treatments for PTSD: Practice guidelines from the International Society for Traumatic Stress Studies (ISTSS).* New York: Guilford.

Foa, E. B., Riggs, D. S., Dancu, C. V., & Rothbaum, B. O. (1993). Reliability and validity of a brief instrument for assessing post-traumatic stress disorder. *Journal of Traumatic Stress, 6,* 459-473.

Fogarty, C. A., & Beck, R. J. (1995). Work adjustment for individuals with PTSD. *Vocational Evaluation & Work Adjustment Bulletin, 28,* 76-80.

Foy, D. W., Glynn, S. M., Schnurr, P. P., Jankowski, M. K., Wattenberg, M. S., Weiss, D. S., Marmar, C. R., & Gusman, F. D. (2000). Group therapy. In E. B. Foa, T. M. Keane, & M. J. Friedman (Eds.), *Effective treatments for PTSD* (pp. 155-175). New York: Guilford.

Freeman, D. B. (2000). Return to work: Posttraumatic stress disorder and the injured worker: Part II. *Case Manager, 11,* 45-49.

Friedman, M. J., Davidson, J. R. T., Mellman, T. A., & Southwick, S. M. (2000). Pharmacotherapy. In E. B. Foa, T. M. Keane, & M. J. Friedman (Eds.), *Effective treatments for PTSD* (pp. 84-105). New York: Guilford.

Freud, S. (1929). *Civilization and its discontents.* New York: Norton.

Frueh, B., Henning, K. R., Pellegrin, K. L., & Chobot, K. (1997). Relationship between scores on anger measures and PTSD symptomatology, employment, and compensation-seeking status in combat veterans. *Journal of Clinical Psychology, 53,* 871-878.

Fullerton, C. S., McCarroll, J. E., Ursano, R. J., & Wright, K. M. (1992). Psychological responses of rescue workers: Fire fighters and trauma. *American Journal of Orthopsychiatry, 62,* 371-378.

Gersons, B. P. R., & Carlier, I. V. E. (1994). Treatment of work related trauma in police officers: Post-traumatic stress disorder and post-traumatic decline. In M. B. Williams & J. F. Sommer (Eds.), *Handbook of post-trauma therapy* (pp. 325-336). Westport, CT: Greenwood.

Gleser, G. C., Green, B. L., & Winget, C. N. (1981). *Prolonged psychosocial effects of disaster: A study of Buffalo Creek*. New York: Academic Press.

Green, B. L. (1993). Identifying survivors at risk: Trauma and stressors across events. In J. P. Wilson & B. Raphael (Eds.), *International handbook of traumatic stress syndromes* (pp. 135-144). New York: Plenum.

Helzer, J. E., Robins, L. N., & McEvoy, L. (1987). Post-traumatic stress disorder in the general population: Findings of the Epidemiologic Catchment Area Survey. *New England Journal of Medicine, 317*, 1630-1634.

Herman, J. (1991). *Trauma and recovery*. New York: Basic Books.

Hodgkinson, P. E., & Shepherd, M. A. (1994). The impact of disaster support work. *Journal of Traumatic Stress, 7*(4), 587-600.

Holen, A. (1993). The North Sea oil rig disaster. In J. P. Wilson & B. Raphael (Eds.), *International handbook of traumatic stress syndromes*. New York: Plenum.

Horowitz, M., Wilner, N., & Alvarez, W. (1979). Impact of Event Scale: A measure of subjective stress. *Psychosomatic Medicine, 41*, 209-218.

Jackson-Malik, P. (1987). The Vietnam veteran in the workplace: A formidable challenge to management. *AAOHN Journal, 35*, 77-78.

Kaltrieder, N. B., Gracie, C., & LeBreck, D. (1992). The psychological impact of the Bay Area earthquake on health professionals. *Journal of the American Medical Women's Association, 47*, 21-24.

Karasek, R., & Theorell, T. (1990). Health work. New York: Basic Books.

Karlehagen, S., Malt, U., Hoff, H., Tibell, E., Herrstromer, U., & Hildingson, K. (1993). The effect of major railway accidents on the psychological health of train drivers: II. A longitudinal study of the one-year outcome after the accident. *Journal of Psychosomatic Research, 37*, 807-817.

Kashner, T. M., Rosenheck, R., Campinell, A. B., Crandall, R., Garfield, N. J., Lapuc, P., Pyrcz, K., Soyka, T., Surls, A., & Widker, A. (2001). *Impact of work on health status: Application of the immediate-effects model*. Manuscript submitted for publication.

Keane, T. M., Malloy, P. E., & Fairbank, J. A. (1984). Empirical development of an MMPI subscale for the assessment of combat-related posttraumatic stress disorder. *Journal of Consulting and Clinical Psychology, 52*, 888-891.

Keane, T. M., & Penk, W. E. (1988). Letter on prevalence of post traumatic stress disorder (PTSD). *New England Journal of Medicine, 316*, 1152.

Keane, T. M., Wolfe, J., & Taylor, K. L. (1987). Posttraumatic stress disorder: Evidence for diagnostic validity and methods of psychological assessment. *Journal of Clinical Psychology, 43*, 32-43.

Keane, T. M., Weathers, F. W., & Foa, E. B. (2000). Diagnosis and assessment. In E. B. Foa, T. M. Keane, & M. J. Friedman (Eds.), *Effective treatments for PTSD* (pp. 18-36). New York: Guilford.

Kessler, R. C., Sonnega, A., Bromet, E., Hughes, M., & Nelson, C. B. (1995). Posttraumatic stress disorder in the National Comorbidity Survey. *Archives of General Psychiatry, 52*, 1048-1060.

Kudler, H. S., Blank, A. S., Jr., & Krupnick, J. L. (2000). Psychodynamic therapy. In E. B. Foa, T. M. Keane, & M. J. Friedman (Eds.), *Effective treatments for PTSD* (pp. 176-198). New York: Guilford.

Kulka, R. A., & Schlenger, W. E. (1993). Survey research and field designs for the study of posttraumatic stress disorder. In J. P. Wilson & B. Raphael (Eds.), *International handbook of traumatic stress syndromes*. New York: Plenum.

Lawson, R., Drebing, C., Short, G., Vincellette, A., & Penk, W. (1998). The long-term effect of child abuse on religious behavior and spirituality in men. *Child Abuse & Neglect, 22*, 369-380.

Lanza, M. L. (1996). Violence against nurses in hospitals. In G. VandenBos & E. Bulatao (Eds.), *Violence on the job: Identifying risks and developing solutions* (pp. 189-198). Washington, DC: American Psychological Association.

Lauterbach, D., & Vrana, S. (1996). Three studies on the reliability and validity of a self-report measure of posttraumatic stress disorder. *Assessment, 3,* 17-25.

Losardo, M. L. (1999). *Veterans in need of services: The history and development of the Edith Nourse Rogers Memorial VA Hospital Compensated Work Therapy Program.* Boston: University of Massachusetts at Boston.

Lyons, J., & Keane, T. (1992). PTSD Scale: MMPI and MMPI-2 update. *Journal of Traumatic Stress, 5,* 111-117.

Marmar, C. R., Weiss, D. S., Metzler, T., Ronfeldt, H., & Foreman, C. (1996). Stress responses of emergency services personnel to the Loma Prieta earthquake Interstate 880 freeway collapse and control traumatic incidents. *Journal of Traumatic Stress, 9,* 63-85.

McCarroll, J. E., Ursano, R. J., Fullerton, C. S., & Lundy, A. C. (1995). Anticipatory stress of handling human remains from the Persian Gulf War: Predictors of intrusion and avoidance. *Journal of Nervous and Mental Disease, 183,* 700-705.

McCarroll, J. E., Ursano, R. J., Ventis, W. L., Fullerton, C. S., Oates, G. L., Friedman, H., Shean, G. L., & Wright, K. M. (1993). Anticipation of handling the dead: Effects of gender and experience. *British Journal of Clinical Psychology, 32,* 466-468.

McFarlane, A. C. (1989). The etiology of post-traumatic morbidity: Predisposing, precipitating and perpetuating factors. *British Journal of Psychiatry, 154,* 221-228.

McFarlane, A. C. (1996). Resilience, vulnerability, and the course of posttraumatic reactions. In B. van der Kolk, A. McFarlane, & L. Weisaeth (Eds.), *Traumatic stress* (pp. 155-181). New York: Guilford.

McFarlane, A. C., & de Girolamo, G. (1996). The nature of traumatic stressors and the epidemiology of posttraumatic reactions. In B. van der Kolk, A. McFarlane, & L. Weisaeth (Eds.), *Traumatic stress* (pp. 129-154). New York: Guilford.

Mitchell, J. T. (1983). When disaster strikes. *Journal of Emergency Medical Services, 8,* 36-39.

Mitchell, J. T., & Everly, G. (1995). *Critical incident stress debriefing: An operations manual for the prevention of traumatic stress among emergency and disaster workers.* Ellicott City, MD: Chevron.

Moos, R. (1994). *The Social Climate Scales: A user's guide.* Palo Alto, CA: Consulting Psychologists Press.

Norris, F. H. (1990). Screening for traumatic stress: A scale for use in the general population. *Journal of Applied Social Psychology, 20,* 1704-1718.

Norris, F. H. (1992). Epidemiology of trauma: Frequency and impact of different potentially traumatic events on different demographic subgroups. *Journal of Consulting and Clinical Psychology, 60,* 409-418.

Norris, F. H., & Riad, J. K. (1997). Standardized self-report measures of civilian trauma and posttraumatic stress disorder. In J. P. Wilson & T. M. Keane (Eds.), *Assessing psychological trauma and PTSD.* New York: Guilford.

Occupational Safety and Health Administration. (1996). *Guidelines for preventing workplace violence for health care workers.* Washington, DC: Author.

Paton, D. (1990). Assessing the impact of disasters on helpers. *Counseling Psychology Quarterly, 3,* 149-152.

Pelcovitz, D., van der Kolk, B., Roth, S., Mandel, F., Kaplan, S., & Resick, P. (1997). Development of a criteria set and a structured interview for disorders of extreme stress (SIDES). *Journal of Traumatic Stress, 10,* 3-16.

Penk, W., & Flannery, R. B., Jr. (2000). Psychosocial rehabilitation techniques. In E. B. Foa, T. M. Keane, & M. J. Friedman (Eds.), *Effective treatments for PTSD* (pp. 224-246). New York: Guilford.

Penk, W. (2001). Designing work experiences for persons with serious mental disorders. In F. Frese & R. Lamb (Eds.), *New directions for mental health services: Psychologists and persons diagnosed with psychosis.* San Francisco: Jossey-Bass.

Resnick, H. S., Falsetti, S. A., Kilpatrick, D. G., & Freedy, J. R. (1996). Assessment of rape and other civilian trauma-related post-traumatic stress disorder: Emphasis on assessment of potentially traumatic events. In T. W. Miller (Ed.), *Stressful life events* (2nd ed.). New York: International Universities Press.

Resnick, H. S., Kilpatrick, D. G., Dansky, B. S., Saunders, B. E., & Best, C. L. (1993). Prevalence of civilian trauma and posttraumatic stress disorder in a representative sample of women. *Journal of Consulting and Clinical Psychology, 61,* 984-991.

Riggs, D. S. (2000). Marital and family therapy. In E. B. Foa, T. M. Keane, & M. J. Friedman (Eds.), *Effective treatments for PTSD* (pp. 280-301). New York: Guilford.

Roman, P. (1988). Growth and transformation in workplace alcoholism programming. In M. Galanter (Ed.), *Recent developments in alcoholism.* New York: Plenum.

Rothbaum, B. O., Meadows, E. A., Resick, P., & Foy, D. W. (2000). Cognitive-behavioral therapy. In E. B. Foa, T. M. Keane, & M. J. Friedman (Eds.), *Effective treatments for PTSD* (pp. 60-83). New York: Guilford.

Seibyl, C. L., & Rosenheck, R. (2000). *Third progress report on the Compensated Work Therapy (CWT)/Veterans Industries (VI) Program.* West Haven, CT: VA Medical Center, North East Program Evaluation Center.

Shalev, A., Peri, T., Schreiber, S., & Caneti, L. (1996). Predictors of PTSD in injured trauma survivors: A prospective study. *American Journal of Psychiatry, 153,* 219-225.

Van den Bos, G. R., & Bulatao, E. Q. (Eds.), (1996). *Violence on the job: Identifying risks and developing solutions.* Washington, DC: American Psychological Association.

van der Kolk, B.A., McFarlane, A. C., & van der Hart, O. (1996). A general approach to treatment of posttraumatic stress disorder. In B. A. van der Kolk, A. C. McFarlane, & L. Weisaeth (Eds.), *Traumatic stress* (pp. 417-440). New York: Guilford.

van der Kolk, B. A., McFarlane, A. C., & Weisaeth, L. (Eds.). (1996). *Traumatic stress.* New York: Guilford.

Veterans Health Administration. (1997). *Clinical guidelines for the management of persons with major depression disorder, PTSD, and substance abuse.* Washington, DC: Author.

Veterans Health Administration. (1999). *VHA mental health program guide 1103.* Washington, DC: Author.

Watson, D., Juba, M., Maniford, V., Kucala, T., & Anderson, P. (1991). The PTSD interview: Rationale, description, reliability and concurrent validity of a *DSM-III* based technique. *Journal of Clinical Psychology, 47,* 179-185.

Weisaeth, L. (1989). The stressors and the post-traumatic stress syndrome after an industrial disaster. *Acta Psychiatrica Scandinavica, 80,* 25-37.

Weisaeth, L. (1993). Torture of a Norwegian ship's crew: Stress reaction, coping, and psychiatric aftereffects. In J. P. Wilson & B. Raphael (Eds.), *International handbook of traumatic stress syndromes* (pp. 743-750). New York: Plenum.

Weisaeth, L. (1994). Psychological and psychiatric aspects of technological disasters. In R. J. Ursano, C. S. McCaugley, & C. Fullerton (Eds.), *Individual and community response to trauma and disaster: The structure of human chaos* (pp. 72-102). Cambridge, UK: Cambridge University Press.

Weisaeth, L., & Eitinger, L. (1993). Posttraumatic stress phenomena: Common themes across wars, disasters and traumatic events. In J. P. Wilson & B. Raphael (Eds.), *International handbook of traumatic stress syndromes* (pp. 69-77). New York: Plenum.

Weiss, D. S. (1997). Structured clinical interview techniques. In J. P. Wilson & T. M. Keane (Eds.), *Assessing psychological trauma and PTSD* (pp. 493-511). New York: Guilford.

Weiss, D. S., & Marmar, C. R. (1997). The Impact of Event Scale—Revised. In J. P. Wilson & T. M. Keane (Eds.), *Assessing psychological trauma and PTSD* (pp. 399-411). New York: Guilford.

Wilson, J. P., & Keane, T. M. (Eds.). (1997). *Assessing psychological trauma and PTSD*. New York: Guilford.

CHAPTER 12

Schizophrenia

Kim T. Mueser
Deborah R. Becker

DESCRIPTION OF THE DISORDER

Schizophrenia is a severe psychiatric disorder that has a broad impact on all aspects of personal, social, and vocational functioning. Because of the disabling nature of schizophrenia, it can have a major effect on the ability to work, including the ability to secure and sustain long-term employment, and to manage social relationships at the workplace. In this chapter, we provide an introduction to schizophrenia and related disorders, and we consider implications of the illness for employers, employees with the illness, their coworkers, and the workplace environment. We discuss the broad treatment needs of individuals with schizophrenia and address principles for assessing these needs in the context of work. We describe an approach to helping clients with schizophrenia succeed in competitive jobs in the community, the Individual Placement and Support model of supported employment; review the research supporting this model; and address common workplace accommodations for people with this disorder. We conclude by discussing strategies for maintaining successful employment in clients with schizophrenia, and for minimizing the relapses or the negative effects of relapses.

Schizophrenia is a major mental illness that can affect all aspects of functioning. The psychopathology of schizophrenia is characterized by three clusters of symptoms (Liddle, 1987; Mueser, Curran, & McHugo, 1997): positive symptoms, negative symptoms, and cognitive impairment. *Positive symptoms* (or *psychotic symptoms*) refer to hallucinations (i.e., false perceptions, such as hearing voices when no one is around); delusions (i.e., false beliefs, such as believing that your coworkers are plotting against you); and bizarre behavior (e.g., collecting odd scraps of paper). *Negative symptoms* are symptoms characterized by deficits in emotional experience, behavioral expressiveness, and energy level. Common negative symptoms include *anhedonia* (diminished experience of pleasure), *asociality* (reduced social drive), *anergia* (decreased ability to initiate and follow through with plans), *alogia* (poverty of speech or content of speech), and *blunted affect* (diminished emotional expressiveness). *Cognitive impairments* span the range of different cognitive functions, including speed of information processing, attention and concentration, memory, abstract reasoning, and planning ability.

The diagnostic criteria for schizophrenia emphasize the presence of positive and negative symptoms (American Psychiatric Association, 1994), although there is growing evidence that cognitive impairment is extremely common (Green & Nuechterlein, 1999). Typically, the positive symptoms of schizophrenia are episodic, with severity fluctuating over time, although 25% to 40% of clients experience these symptoms persistently (Carpenter & Buchanan, 1994; Silverstein & Harrow, 1978). Negative symptoms, in contrast, tend to be more stable and more pervasive, and few clients experience full remission of these symptoms between episodes of psychosis (Mueser, Douglas, Bellack, & Morrison, 1991). The cognitive symptoms in schizophrenia tend to persist throughout the course of the illness, although their severity also increases during exacerbation of positive symptoms.

In addition to the characteristic symptoms of schizophrenia, diagnostic criteria also require impairment in psychosocial functioning in major role functioning (worker, student, parent, spouse); maintenance of good interpersonal relationships; care of oneself; and enjoyment of leisure activities. In addition to the characteristic symptoms and impairments, the diagnosis of schizophrenia requires a 6-month period of impaired functioning. Therefore, at least some chronicity is incorporated into the definition of the disorder. Because some impairment in functioning is required for the diagnosis of schizophrenia, it is tautological to say that the disorder affects functioning. However, it should also be noted that for many clients, problems in role

functioning long preceded the onset of the illness (Zigler & Glick, 1986), which then exacerbated a preexisting impairment.

Schizophrenia is closely related to three other disorders: schizoaffective disorder, schizopheniform disorder, and schizotypal personality disorder. Based on studies of mental illness in families and response to treatment, these disorders are grouped together as *schizophrenia-spectrum disorders* and are treated following the same principles. Individuals who meet the symptom and impaired functioning criteria for the disorder, but whose impairment is less than 6 months' duration (or who experience a full remission of symptoms with episodes lasting less than 6 months), meet diagnostic criteria for *schizopheniform disorder*. Individuals who meet criteria for schizophrenia during periods when their mood is normal, but who also have significant episodes of depression or mania, meet diagnostic criteria for *schizoaffective disorder*. *Schizotypal personality disorder* resembles schizophrenia in many ways, although the severity of symptoms tends to be lower, and its course is less episodic and marked by less flagrant positive symptoms.

Because schizophrenia affects so many different areas of functioning, it is not surprising that many other comorbid disorders and problems are associated with the illness. Substance abuse and dependence are very common in clients with schizophrenia, with lifetime rates of approximately 50% and recent rates of abuse or dependence of 25% to 35%; these rates are in considerable excess of the rate of lifetime substance use disorder of approximately 16% in the general population (Mueser, Bennett, & Kushner, 1995; Regier et al., 1990). Depression is a very common symptom in schizophrenia, with most clients experiencing at least some symptoms of depression over the course of their illness, and a lifetime suicide rate of approximately 10%

(Drake, Gates, Whitaker, & Cotton, 1985; Roy, 1986). Problems with anxiety are high, including increased rates of trauma (Hiday, Swartz, Swanson, Borum, & Wagner, 1999), posttraumatic stress disorder (Mueser, Rosenberg, Goodman, & Trumbetta, 2002), obsessive-compulsive disorder (Tibbo, Kroetsch, Chue, & Warneke, 2000), social anxiety (Penn, Hope, Spaulding, & Kucera, 1994), and panic disorder (Argyle, 1990). These associated symptoms of schizophrenia can be as debilitating or more so than the characteristic symptoms of schizophrenia, and they can have a major impact on quality of life and the ability to sustain full-time employment.

Many clients are eligible for and receive entitlements, such as subsidized income, insurance, and housing, but the symptoms and impairments that characterize schizophrenia result in a variety of problems not solved by these subsidies. Because of the poverty, social and employment difficulties, and lack of awareness associated with the illness, many clients live in substandard housing or are intermittently homeless (Drake, Wallach, & Hoffman, 1989), and they suffer from chronic medical conditions resulting in premature mortality (Tsuang & Woolson, 1978). Furthermore, with the high rates of substance abuse and impaired social judgment, a disproportionate number of clients are jailed or imprisoned (Hodgins & Côté, 1993; Teplin, 1983). Finally, because of the episodic nature of psychotic symptoms, which may impose a threat to self or others, clients are frequently in and out of psychiatric hospitals for the treatment of acute exacerbations.

EPIDEMIOLOGY

Prevalence of schizophrenia is approximately 1% in the general population, with relatively stable rates across different nations. Whereas race and cultural group do not appear to be related to schizophrenia, socioeconomic status is, with higher rates of the disorder found in people living in poverty (Hollingshead & Redlich, 1958; Keith, Regier, & Rae, 1991). Historically, two theories have been advanced to account for this association. The *social drift* hypothesis postulates that the debilitating effects of schizophrenia on capacity to work result in a lowering of socioeconomic means, and, hence, poverty (Aro, Aro, & Keskimäki, 1995). The *environmental stress* hypothesis proposes that high levels of stress associated with poverty precipitate schizophrenia in some individuals who would not otherwise develop the illness (Bruce, Takeuchi, & Leaf, 1991). Both of these explanations may be partly true, and longitudinal research on changes in socioeconomic class status and schizophrenia provide conflicting results. For example, Fox (1990) reanalyzed data from several longitudinal studies and found that after controlling for initial levels of socioeconomic class, downward drift was not evident. However, Dohrenwend et al. (1992) did find evidence for social drift, even after controlling for socioeconomic class. Thus, poverty is associated with schizophrenia, with evidence suggesting both increased vulnerability to schizophrenia among people living in poverty, as well as declining economic standing in people who develop the illness.

ASSESSMENT

Because schizophrenia affects so many different areas of functioning, assessment is necessarily broad-based and must cover both basic psychopathology and associated impairments, as well as other common comorbid conditions. Assessment of diagnosis and symptoms is conducted most reliably with semistructured interviews that incorporate standardized probe questions and rating criteria. The "gold standard" for establishing a diagnosis of schizophrenia is the Structured Clinical Interview for *DSM-IV* (First, Spitzer, Gibbon, & Williams, 1996). The most widely used scales for assessing severity of symptoms in schizophrenia include the Brief Psychiatric Rating Scale (Lukoff, Nuechterlein, & Ventura, 1986), the Positive and Negative Syndrome Scale (Kay, Opler, & Fiszbein, 1987), and the Scale for the Assessment of Negative Symptoms (Mueser, Sayers, Schooler, Mance, & Haas, 1994).

A wide range of measures exists for evaluating functioning in clients with schizophrenia (Scott & Lehman, 1998). These instruments evaluate clients' ability to meet role expectations in a variety of different areas, including work, school, and parenting, as well as the quality of social relationships, self-care and independent living skills, and leisure and recreational activities. Assessment of functioning is most accurate when it incorporates multiple perspectives (e.g., client, clinician, and family) and when standardized measures are employed. Furthermore, the most valuable assessment information is often obtained when it is conducted in the setting in which the skills are to be used. For example, successful employment interventions incorporate assessment on the job on an ongoing basis rather than extensive prevocational testing batteries that do not generalize to real-world settings (Bond, 1998; Drake & Becker, 1996).

A great deal of research has been carried out on the functional assessment of social skills in people with schizophrenia. Social skills refer to the individual behavioral components, such as eye contact, voice loudness, and the specific choice of words, which, in combination, are necessary for effective communication with others (Mueser & Bellack, 1998). Although not all problems in social and vocational functioning are the consequence of poor social skill, many impairments appear to be related to skill deficits (Bellack, Morrison, Wixted, & Mueser, 1990). A number of different strategies can be used to assess social skill, including those related to adjustment in the workplace. Direct interviews with clients can be a good starting place for identifying broad areas of social dysfunction; additional information can be obtained through role-play tests, naturalistic observations, and significant others, including employers.

In addition to assessing symptoms and characteristic impairments of schizophrenia, routine assessment also needs to take into account several common comorbid problems that can have an impact on functioning in the workplace: substance abuse, depression, and posttraumatic stress disorder. Substance abuse is the most common comorbid disorder in schizophrenia, with approximately 50% of clients having a lifetime substance use disorder (abuse or dependence) and 25% to 35% having an active substance use disorder (Cuffel, 1996; Regier et al., 1990). Reliable evaluations of recent substance abuse can be accomplished by employing the Alcohol Use Scale and the Drug Use Scale, which are clinical rating scales that summarize clients' use of substances over the past 6 months on 5-point ratings scales: 1 = *no use*, 2 = *use without impairment*, 3 = *abuse*, 4 = *dependence*, and 5 = *severe dependence with institutionalization* (Mueser, Drake, et al., 1995).

Depression is a very common problem in people with schizophrenia (Bartels & Drake, 1989), and suicide occurs in approximately 10% of clients (Caldwell & Gottesman, 1990; Roy, 1986). Assessment of depression and suicidality can be conducted with standardized psychiatric rating scales (described above), supplemented by scales that tap specific areas (Beck, Steer, & Garbin, 1988; Stanley, Traskman-Bendz, & Stanely, 1986). There is some evidence that positive effects of work, including modest benefits in self-esteem, may alleviate depression in people with schizophrenia and other severe mental illnesses (Mueser, Becker, et al., 1997).

Clients with schizophrenia are more likely to be exposed to traumatic life events, in both childhood and adulthood, than are people in the general population (Goodman, Rosenberg, Mueser, & Drake, 1997). These high rates of trauma are associated with correspondingly high rates of posttraumatic stress disorder (PTSD), with most estimates of current PTSD in schizophrenia ranging between 25% and 35% (Rosenberg et al., 2001). Reliable assessments of trauma history and PTSD can be obtained from clients with schizophrenia (Mueser et al., 2001) by using rating scales developed for the general population, including the Trauma History Questionnaire (Green, 1996), the Revised Conflict Tactics Scales (Straus, Hamby, Boney-McCoy, & Sugarman, 1996), the PTSD Checklist (Blanchard, Jones-Alexander, Buckley, & Forneris, 1996), and the Clinician Administered PTSD Scale (Blake et al., 1990).

IMPACT OF SCHIZOPHRENIA AT THE WORKPLACE

Schizophrenia can have a major impact on the ability of people to work, their performance at work, and their relationships with coworkers. In this section, we describe how common symptoms, impairments, and related problems can influence behavior and performance in the workplace. Although we describe possible effects of symptoms on work functioning, it should also be noted that many clients with these symptoms and impairments are capable of excellent performance on the job, and that work itself may actually have beneficial effects on reducing symptom severity (Bell, Lysaker, & Milstein, 1996). Thus, presence of symptoms or associated problems should not be interpreted as a suggestion that specific problems in work are necessarily likely.

Negative symptoms of schizophrenia, including anhedonia, apathy, and anergia, are commonly reflected in the workplace by a lower level of energy, decreased stamina, and, at times, a lower motivation to succeed. Although some people with schizophrenia work full-time, part-time work is more suitable for many clients because the overall effort required is less taxing. Another negative symptom that can lead to misunderstandings at the workplace is blunted affect. People with schizophrenia often lack emotional expressiveness in their interactions with others, and frequently, they have flattened facial expressions and minimal vocal inflection. These behaviors, which are common symptoms of schizophrenia, may give the false impression of not being interested, concerned, or responsive to what others have to say, and it can make interacting with such individuals less rewarding. Despite their muted expressiveness, clients with schizophrenia often report the same emotions as others, leading to misunderstandings in communication (Blanchard, Mueser, & Bellack, 1998). Clients with blunted affect may benefit from learning how to communicate their interest and feelings to others through verbal means in order to compensate for their diminished nonverbal and vocal expressiveness.

Cognitive impairment in schizophrenia may affect work performance in a variety of ways, depending on the tasks required and the specific nature of the deficits. A common problem is reduced speed of information processing and slower reaction time. This may be reflected in social interactions with the client, in which the pace of conversation seems unnaturally slow and strained (Mueser, Bellack, Douglas, & Morrison, 1991). Jobs that require extensive interaction with others, including customers, or that require a rapid reaction time may be ill-suited for clients with schizophrenia. Other common cognitive problems include worse memory, difficulties in concept formation and abstract reasoning, and reduced planning ability. These limitations have several implications in the workplace. Clients may require longer periods of time to learn how to perform a job, and the task may need to be broken down into small steps to simplify the learning process. Jobs that involve learning a large amount of information may need to be adapted to overcome limits on memory. Work involving abstract concepts and rapid, creative decision making may be difficult or impossible for clients to perform.

Positive symptoms, including delusions and hallucinations, occur less frequently, but when they do, they can easily disrupt behavior at the workplace. With respect to delusions, clients may believe that others are talking about them or plotting against them, leading to suspicious behavior or avoidance, resulting in disruptions in relationships with coworkers and employers. Hallucinations can be problematic when clients respond to them publicly, such as talking back to voices.

Impairments in social skill can have a significant effect on functioning in the workplace. Clients may be awkward when interacting casually with coworkers, responding to customers, seeking assistance in problem situations, responding to criticism and negative feedback from supervisors, or speaking assertively with others (Mueser, Foy, & Carter, 1986). These problems can interfere with a good working milieu and, when the job involves direct customer interactions, job performance. Social skill impairments at the workplace are magnified when clients have difficulty getting help for difficult social situations, because their problem-solving skills also may be limited (Bellack, Sayers, Mueser, & Bennett, 1994).

The common problem of substance abuse in schizophrenia can affect work functioning in a similar fashion as in the general population. Substance abuse can contribute to unexplained absences, reduced job performance because of the effects of substances or withdrawal, erratic behavior, and theft. Jobs in which alcohol consumption is normative socializing behavior among coworkers after work may be especially problematic for clients, because evidence indicates that people with schizophrenia are more sensitive to experiencing negative consequences from relatively moderate alcohol use (Drake & Wallach, 1993; Mueser, Drake, & Wallach, 1998).

Case Vignette. Alex (a pseudonym; details of the case have been altered) was a 38-year-old man with a diagnosis of schizophrenia. He had a history of abusing alcohol and drugs. Alex's work history included mostly chef positions in gourmet restaurants. Although Alex was a skillful chef, working in a restaurant setting was problematic because it provided him with ready access to alcohol, frequently contributing to relapses of alcohol abuse. Alex lost several of his jobs because he used alcohol at work and became argumentative with restaurant staff. His attendance was often erratic during heavy periods of abuse. Alex was strongly motivated to work. He stated that he felt "useless" when he did not have anything structured to do with his time, and he liked to spend money on new clothes.

Alex met with an employment specialist at the mental health center where he was receiving psychiatric services. Drawing from Alex's past work experiences, they developed a plan to help him return to stable employment. They attempted to identify a job that was based on his interests and was in a work environment that would support sobriety. Within a few weeks, he obtained a position working at the ticket counter of a theater company. Alex chose not to tell his work supervisor about his psychiatric disorder. He agreed to talk two times a week with the employment specialist from the supported employment program and to abstain from alcohol and other drugs on his workdays. He also signed up for a dual disorders group at the mental health center to support him in his efforts of decreasing his alcohol and drug use (Mueser & Noordsy, 1996). Alex identified his living arrangement as problematic because he used alcohol and marijuana with his neighbors. The employment specialist encouraged Alex to contact his case manager for assistance in finding a residence away from his drug-using friends.

The employment specialist's work with Alex enabled him to develop a vocational plan that supported a sober work life. Over the course of Alex's employment, he had a relapse of his substance abuse that contributed to several absences. Through support and discussion with his employment specialist, and ongoing contact between the employment specialist and the leaders of the dual disorder group, Alex recognized the threat that his substance abuse posed to his continued work, and he decided to stop using substances. However, because of several unexplained absences, Alex was placed on probation in his job by his employer. After further discussions with the employment specialist, Alex agreed to allow her to contact the employer directly so they could all work together to help Alex succeed in his job.

The employment specialist approached the employer to explain the nature of Alex's psychiatric disability and to describe Alex's motivation to maintain his job and become a dependable worker again. The employer appreciated the employment specialist's involvement with Alex and stated that he valued Alex as a worker and wanted to retain him as an employee. They agreed to meet weekly while Alex was on probation to review Alex's performance and to identify any areas of concern, including any possible signs of a relapse of his substance abuse. These follow-up meetings provided Alex with direct feedback about his work, bolstered his self-esteem that he was a good worker, and reduced some of the stress Alex felt while at work. Alex passed his probationary period without incident. The employment specialist stopped meeting regularly with the employer, but remained available to him, having approximately monthly contact. The employment specialist continued to see Alex regularly, with contacts averaging weekly to biweekly.

PRECIPITATING CONDITIONS

Schizophrenia is widely considered to be a biological disorder whose onset and outcome can be influenced by the environment, the client's personal coping ability, medications, and commonly abused substances. A useful model for conceptualizing the interactions between biological factors, the environment (including close relationships), and the course of schizophrenia is the *stress-vulnerability model* (Liberman et al., 1986; Zubin & Spring, 1977). According to this model, the course and severity of schizophrenia are determined by the dynamic interplay between biological vulnerability, environmental stress, and coping skills. *Biological vulnerability* is assumed to be determined early in life by a combination of genetic and perinatal factors. Such biological vulnerability is critical to the development of schizophrenia, and without it, the illness will not develop. When an individual has a biological vulnerability to schizophrenia, that vulnerability can be triggered by *environmental stress*, leading to the emergence of symptoms and characteristic impairments. Common examples of stress include major life events (moving away from home, starting a challenging job, death of a loved one); tense and critical relationships with significant others; and lack of meaningful structure. After the onset of schizophrenia, exposure to stress can precipitate symptom exacerbations and further impair psychosocial functioning. Finally, the more effective *coping skills* the client has, the less susceptible he or she will be to stress-induced relapses, because successful coping can either eliminate the sources of stress or minimize their negative effects.

The stress-vulnerability model has several implications for understanding possible factors in the workplace that could contribute to symptom relapses and a deterioration in functioning for people with schizophrenia. Clients with schizophrenia who work at very demanding jobs, with substantial expectations on productivity, time pressure, and rapid change to accommodate new opportunities, may find the pace and requirements of the job stressful, which could increase their risk of relapse. Jobs requiring flexible work hours, especially overtime work, extended hours, or work on little sleep, may induce similar stress in clients. In addition, if the work environment is socially stressful, such as high levels of criticism from supervisors or tension among coworkers, clients may be at increased risk of relapse. The problem of social stress is of particular importance because clients with schizophrenia often

have poor social perception skills (e.g., recognizing facial expressions, taking hints, interpreting others' motives), resulting in, or exacerbating, social problems (Penn, Corrigan, Bentall, Racenstein, & Newman, 1997). Finally, it is possible that stress in the workplace could contribute to substance abuse in clients with schizophrenia, although research documenting such an effect is lacking.

Although the stress-vulnerability model suggests that stress in the workplace could contribute to symptom relapses in schizophrenia, it also indicates that the experience of working in a positive environment may also confer protection against relapses. Research indicates that meaningful structure is associated with reduced levels of psychotic behavior (Rosen, Sussman, Mueser, Lyons, & Davis, 1981), and social support has been well-established as a protective factor against relapses (Buchanan, 1995; Veiel, 1985). Work that provides meaning and structure to clients may help to create a sense of purpose, thereby reducing stress. Positive and supportive social relationships at the workplace may result in similar benefits.

COURSE AND PROGNOSIS

Onset of schizophrenia typically occurs between the ages of 16 and 30, with onset after the age of 35 being relatively rare (Almeida, Howard, Levy, & David, 1995). Because schizophrenia usually occurs during early adulthood, many developmental tasks are disrupted, including formation of close interpersonal or dating relationships, pursuit of higher education, career development, separation from parents, and identity formation. It is extremely rare for the first onset of schizophrenia to occur before adolescence (e.g., before the age of 12), with most diagnostic systems considering childhood-onset schizophrenia to be a different disorder from adolescent or adult onset (American Psychiatric Association, 1994). More common than childhood schizophrenia, but nevertheless rare in the total population of people with schizophrenia, are individuals who develop the illness later in life, such as after the age of 45 (Cohen, 1990). Late-onset schizophrenia is characterized by positive symptoms, but is less likely to involve formal thought disorder and negative symptoms (Bartels, Mueser, & Miles, 1998). Late-onset schizophrenia is further complicated by the lack of clear-cut, distinguishing characteristics that differentiates this disorder from a variety of other disorders that develop later in old age (Howard, Almeida, & Levy, 1994).

Prior to the onset of schizophrenia, some, but not all, people have impairments in their premorbid social functioning (Zigler & Glick, 1986). For example, some people who later develop schizophrenia were more socially isolated, passed fewer social-sexual developmental milestones, and had fewer friends in childhood and adolescence. Aside from problems in social functioning, prior to developing schizophrenia, some individuals in childhood display a maladaptive pattern of behaviors, including disruptive behavior, problems in school, and impulsivity (Baum & Walker, 1995; Hans, Marcus, Henson, Auerbach, & Mirsky, 1992). Similarly, symptoms of conduct disorder in childhood, such as repeated fighting, truancy, and lying, have been found to be predictive of the later development of schizophrenia (Neumann, Grimes, Walker, & Baum, 1995; Robins, 1966). However, other clients display no unusual characteristics in their premorbid functioning.

A second mediating factor related to the prognosis of schizophrenia is gender. Women tend to have later age of onset of the illness, spend less time in hospitals, and demonstrate better social competence and social functioning than do men (Angermeyer, Kuhn, & Goldstein, 1990; Haas & Garratt, 1998). The benefits experienced by women do not appear to be explained by societal differences in tolerance for deviant behavior.

In general, onset of schizophrenia can be described as either gradual or acute. The gradual onset of schizophrenia can take place over many months, and it may be difficult for family members and others to clearly distinguish onset of the illness. In cases of acute onset, symptoms develop rapidly over a period of a few weeks, with dramatic and easily observed changes occurring over this time. People with acute onset of schizophrenia have a somewhat better prognosis than do those with a more insidious illness (Fenton & McGlashan, 1991; Kay & Lindenmayer, 1987).

Although schizophrenia is a long-term and severe psychiatric illness, there is considerable interindividual variability in the course of illness (Marango, 1994). Generally, though, once schizophrenia has developed, the illness usually continues to be present at varying degrees of severity throughout most of the person's life. Schizophrenia is usually an episodic illness with periods of acute symptom severity requiring more intensive, often inpatient, treatment interspersed by periods of higher functioning between episodes. Despite the fact that most clients with schizophrenia live in the community, it is comparatively rare, at least in the short-term, for clients to return to their premorbid levels of functioning between episodes.

Some general predictors of the course and outcome of schizophrenia have been identified, such as premorbid functioning, but overall, the ability to predict outcome is rather poor (Avison & Speechley, 1987; Tsuang, 1986). The primary reason for this is that, as suggested by the stress-vulnerability model, symptom severity and functioning are determined by the dynamic interplay between biological vulnerability, environmental factors, and coping skills (Liberman et al., 1986; Nuechterlein & Dawson, 1984). Factors such as compliance with medication (Weiden, Mott, & Curcio, 1995), substance abuse (Swartz et al., 1998), and exposure to a hostile or critical environment (Butzlaff & Hooley, 1998) are all environmental factors that, in combination, play a large role in determining outcome. Over the lifetime, there are reasons to be optimistic about long-term outcome because the symptoms of schizophrenia tend to improve gradually, with significant numbers of clients achieving sustained remissions (Harding & Keller, 1998).

RECOMMENDED DATA-BASED TREATMENTS

Brief Description

Comprehensive treatment is needed for most clients with schizophrenia to attend to a wide range of their needs. The most common elements of treatment include case management, pharmacological treatment, and psychosocial rehabilitation.

The role of case management is to identify client needs, link clients to interventions, monitor outcomes, and advocate for clients, including obtaining entitlements (Mueser, Bond, Drake, & Resnick, 1998). Although most clients with schizophrenia benefit from case management, one model of more intensive case management is appropriate for clients with a recent history of multiple hospitalizations and poor psychosocial functioning: the Assertive Community Treatment (ACT) model (Allness & Knoedler, 1998; Stein & Santos, 1998). The ACT model is distinguished from standard case management by the lower clinician-to-case management ratio (1:10 in ACT vs. 1:30 or more in standard case management), shared caseloads across clinicians (rather than individual caseloads), services provided in the community rather than the clinic, 24-hour coverage, and services given directly by the team (rather than brokered to other providers). ACT has been found to reduce rehospitalizations and symptom severity, and to improve housing stability in multiple studies (Bond, Drake, Mueser, & Latimer, 2001).

Pharmacological treatment with antipsychotic medications, especially the newer atypical antipsychotics (Jibson & Tandon, 1998), is the mainstay of treatment for schizophrenia. Some clients also benefit from adjunctive medications, such as antidepressants or mood stabilizers (Rush et al., 1999). The vast majority of clients with schizophrenia experience at least some benefit from medication.

With respect to psychosocial treatment, several interventions have been shown to be effective at improving outcomes in people with schizophrenia. *Family psychoeducation* is appropriate for clients in regular contact with relatives and is aimed at developing a collaborative relationship between the treatment team and family, reducing stress, improving communication and problem solving, and helping members achieve personal and shared goals (Mueser & Glynn, 1999). Extensive research shows that family psychoeducation, when provided over an extended period of time (usually at least 9 months), is effective at reducing relapses and rehospitalizations, and at improving the family environment (Pitschel-Walz, Leucht, Bäuml, Kissling, & Engel, 2001).

Social skills training involves teaching new interpersonal skills, based on the principles of social learning theory, for improving social relationships and getting basic needs met (Bellack, Mueser, Gingerich, & Agresta, 1997). Multiple studies have shown that skills training is effective, especially when provided over long periods of time (e.g., more than 6 months) (Heinssen, Liberman, & Kopelowicz, 2000). Skills training that targets specific work-related situations may be effective at improving interactions with coworkers, supervisors, and customers (Mueser et al., 1986; Wallace, Tauber, & Wilde, 1999).

Integrated treatment of dual disorders (mental illness and substance use disorders) involves the use of outreach to engage clients in treatment; motivational strategies; nonconfrontational approaches; and group, individual, and family approaches to treat both disorders (Mueser, Drake, & Noordsy, 1998). Integrated treatment of both disorders is superior to separate treatment because it ensures that each disorder is addressed, and it minimizes possible inconsistencies between different groups of treatment providers. Research shows that integrated dual disorder treatment is effective at reducing substance abuse in clients with schizophrenia (Drake et al., 2001).

Cognitive-behavioral therapy for psychosis involves helping clients evaluate the evidence supporting delusional beliefs, as well as developing more realistic and more adaptive ways of thinking (Fowler, Garety, & Kuipers, 1995). Cognitive-behavioral therapy is most appropriate for clients with persistent psychotic symptoms resulting in behavioral disruption or significant subjective distress. Research on cognitive therapy indicates that it reduces the severity of psychosis, and, in some studies, it lowers the risk of relapses and rehospitalizations (Gould, Mueser, Bolton, Mays, & Goff, 2001).

Training in *illness management* involves providing clients with basic information about their psychiatric illness and

principles of treatment, developing strategies for taking medication as prescribed, teaching relapse prevention skills, and helping clients develop more effective ways of coping with persistent symptoms. Research on illness management training supports each of these core components of treatment (Mueser, Corrigan, et al., in press).

Supported employment is a vocational rehabilitation intervention used to assist people with schizophrenia and other psychiatric disorders to improve their work functioning (Becker & Drake, 1993; Bond, Becker, et al., 2001). Employment specialists work one-on-one with individuals who desire assistance in obtaining employment or, for those employed, in developing the skills and strategies for maintaining employment. Traditional vocational rehabilitation interventions emphasized prevocational assessment and training to prepare people with severe mental illness for employment. Supported employment, which helps people find employment directly, has shown higher rates of employment when compared to traditional vocational approaches such as prevocational work units and skills training, transitional employment, and sheltered work (Bond, Drake, Mueser, & Becker, 1997; Drake, Becker, Clark, & Mueser, 1999).

In supported employment, employment specialists assist people in identifying a good job match based on the person's preferences, skills, strengths, and unique challenges. The employment specialist may advocate directly with potential employers if the client is willing to disclose his or her psychiatric status to employers. In some cases, when the employment specialist introduces him- or herself, just the name of the specialist's employer reveals that the client is receiving mental health services. When contacting employers, the employment specialist is sometimes better able to advocate for a client because of the social skills deficits inherent in schizophrenia. For example, the employment specialist can address with the employer a client's apparent lack of enthusiasm in the job interview that is caused by flat affect from the illness.

The most common barrier to employment for people with schizophrenia is fear of losing governmental benefits such as Social Security income, Social Security disability insurance, and Medicaid. The employment specialist helps the client obtain accurate information about how his or her particular package of benefits will be affected by working. Many people work part-time so that they do not lose their health insurance. The client and/or the employment specialist negotiate the desired number of hours with the employer.

Employment specialists work closely with other treatment providers to ensure that services are integrated at the level of client delivery. The treatment providers form a team, meeting at least weekly, to share information, develop plans, and increase collaboration to support clients in different aspects of their lives, including employment.

The client is provided individualized, time-unlimited support to maintain employment. The type of support varies according to the needs of the individual. Most support is provided away from the job site. People with schizophrenia often feel stigmatized when the employment specialist is present at the job site. Furthermore, clients usually have little difficulty performing job duties if the job match is good. People with schizophrenia want to be treated like others without mental illness at the work site. In most cases, the employment specialist meets regularly with the client away from the job site to review his or her work progress. If the client permits the employment specialist to speak with the employer, the employment specialist makes contact periodically to find out if the client is performing satisfactorily at the job.

Time Element

Overall, treatment for schizophrenia, including case management and pharmacological treatment, needs to be long-term. The provision of supported employment services should also be long-term, although the intensity of support may decrease over time as clients become increasingly able to handle the demands of work on their own.

Specific interventions often can be delivered on a time-limited basis. Family psychoeducational programs typically last between 9 months and 2 years, although families (including clients) may also benefit from continued participation in support groups. Social skills training is usually provided in programs lasting between 3 or 4 months to more than a year. Cognitive-behavioral treatment for psychotic symptoms and illness management programs generally last between 6 and 12 months, although some programs last even longer. Finally, integrated programs for dual disorders are usually relatively long-term, lasting several years, with the duration of participation depending on when individual clients achieve stable remission of their substance use disorders.

Side Effects of Treatment

With the exception of pharmacological treatments, other interventions for schizophrenia do not have significant side effects. As newer medications for schizophrenia have been developed, severity of side effects has decreased. Nevertheless, side effects do occur, and recognition and management of them can prevent them from interfering with work functioning. The most common side effects of newer generation antipsychotic medications include sedation and akathisia. Sedation can slow down work performance and interfere with attention to the task at hand. The effects of medication on sedation can be minimized if clients take their medication in the evening, rather than in the morning. Akathisia is a side effect characterized by an inner feeling of restlessness, often accompanied by pacing. It can influence work performance if it is manifested by restlessness, pacing, and other signs of motor activation. Medication adjustment, or side effect medication, may be helpful in addressing this side effect. Isometric exercises and regularly scheduled breaks may also minimize the effects of akathisia on work.

Other side effects of medications used to treat schizophrenia can also be present. Some of the more common ones include increased weight gain, dizziness, dry mouth, and tremor. These side effects may have some minor effects on work performance, depending on the nature of the task. Accurate detection of medication side effects can lead to effective management of them, such as reducing dosage levels or trying alternative medications.

Workplace Accommodations

Accommodations at the workplace are identified to help a client manage consequences of the illness and still work. The Americans with Disabilities Act (ADA) requires employers with more than 15 employees to make reasonable accommodations to employ people with disabilities who would otherwise be qualified for the job. The types of accommodations requested by people with schizophrenia typically are low cost to the employer. An example of an accommodation is flexible work hours, such as adjusting the work schedule for appointments and medical leaves, providing more frequent breaks, and arranging time off without pay. Modification of the work space and job tasks include minimizing distractions and noise, providing space to work alone, gradual introduction of tasks, and modification of job tasks. Crisis intervention includes procedures for emergency situations, telephone calls to employment specialists, and private space. The employment specialist, the client, and the employer meet to draw up an individualized plan for the necessary workplace accommodations.

MAINTENANCE OF GAINS/RELAPSE PREVENTION

Because schizophrenia is generally accepted to be a disorder that persists throughout much of the lifetime, gains made during treatment and rehabilitation are most likely to be maintained if adequate social supports are available to the client, and if he or she has ongoing contact with the treatment team. For most clients, pharmacological treatment, supported employment, and case management are the core ingredients that need to be in place in order to maintain competitive employment. Other services may be required on a time-limited basis, such as social skills training, individual counseling, and family psychoeducation.

Relapses in schizophrenia typically involve increases in psychotic symptoms, which are often accompanied by cognitive disorganization and mood instability. Whereas severe relapses may prevent the client from fulfilling job responsibilities altogether, and possibly require hospitalization, minor relapses often can be treated effectively, resulting in minimal disruption to work performance and preventing major relapses. The key to preventing major relapses, and thereby maintaining steady and good job performance, is good monitoring of the client's psychiatric functioning, and rapid action when changes are noted. This monitoring can be especially effective when it involves several people, including the case manager, supported employment specialist, the employer (when feasible), and family members.

Relapses tend to occur slowly over time, with small changes in mood, cognitive functioning, and energy preceding the emergence or worsening of psychotic symptoms. These changes, or early warning signs of relapse, are unique to each client, but they are often stable across episodes within a given client. Identifying the early warning signs of relapse, monitoring these signs, and taking steps to address them when they emerge (e.g., providing additional medication) can be effective at preventing full-blown episodes and maintaining functional capacity (Herz, Glazer, Mirza, Mostert, & Hafez, 1989; Herz et al., 2000).

SUMMARY

Schizophrenia is a complex mental illness characterized by reduced functioning in the areas of vocational adjustment, social relationships, and self-care, and a wide range of symptoms, including hallucinations and delusions, reduced social drive, and cognitive impairment. Effective pharmacological and psychosocial treatments exist for schizophrenia that can minimize symptoms and impairments, and facilitate the ability of clients to work. Of particular relevance to successful vocational functioning for clients with schizophrenia is the availability of supported employment services. Supported employment involves assistance from an employment specialist in identifying and obtaining jobs in areas related to clients' interests, providing ongoing supports to successfully manage job demands and the social environment of the workplace, availability to employers to discuss job-related issues concerning the client, and negotiating reasonable accommodations with employers. Of particular importance, supported employment services are most effective when they are integrated with other aspects of treatment, and when employment specialists function as members of clients' treatment teams. Although schizophrenia is a serious mental illness, comprehensive treatment, access to supported employment services, and a supportive work environment make many clients capable of being consistent and valued employees.

REFERENCES

Allness, D. J., & Knoedler, W. H. (1998). *The PACT model of community-based treatment for persons with severe and persistent mental illness: A manual for PACT start-up*. Arlington, VA: National Alliance for the Mentally Ill.

Almeida, O. P., Howard, R. J., Levy, R., & David, A. S. (1995). Psychotic states arising in late life (late paraphrenia): The role of risk factors. *British Journal of Psychiatry, 166,* 215-228.

American Psychiatric Association. (1994). *Diagnostic and statistical manual of mental disorders* (4th ed.). Washington, DC: Author.

Angermeyer, M. C., Kuhn, L., & Goldstein, J. M. (1990). Gender and the course of schizophrenia: Differences in treated outcome. *Schizophrenia Bulletin, 16,* 293-307.

Argyle, N. (1990). Panic attacks in chronic schizophrenia. *British Journal of Psychiatry, 157,* 430-433.

Aro, S., Aro, H., & Keskimäki, I. (1995). Socio-economic mobility among patients with schizophrenia or major affective disorder: A 17-year retrospective follow-up. *British Journal of Psychiatry, 166,* 759-767.

Avison, W. R., & Speechley, K. N. (1987). The discharged psychiatric patient: A review of social, social-psychological, and psychiatric correlates of outcome. *American Journal of Psychiatry, 144,* 10-18.

Bartels, S. J., & Drake, R. E. (1989). Depression in schizophrenia: Current guidelines to treatment. *Psychiatric Quarterly, 60,* 333-345.

Bartels, S. J., Mueser, K. T., & Miles, K. M. (1998). Schizophrenia in older adults: Towards a comprehensive model of assessment and treatment. In M. Hersen & V. B. Van Hasselt (Eds.), *Handbook of clinical geriatric geropsychology* (pp. 173-194). New York: Plenum.

Baum, K. M., & Walker, E. F. (1995). Childhood behavioral precursors of adult symptom dimensions in schizophrenia. *Schizophrenia Research, 16,* 111-120.

Beck, A. T., Steer, R. A., & Garbin, M. G. (1988). Psychometric properties of the Beck Depression Inventory: Twenty-five years of evaluation. *Clinical Psychology Review, 8,* 77-100.

Becker, D. R., & Drake, R. E. (1993). *A working life: The Individual Placement and Support (IPS) program.* Concord, NH: New Hampshire-Dartmouth Psychiatric Research Center.

Bell, M. D., Lysaker, P. H., & Milstein, R. M. (1996). Clinical benefits of paid work activity in schizophrenia. *Schizophrenia Bulletin, 22,* 51-67.

Bellack, A. S., Morrison, R. L., Wixted, J. T., & Mueser, K. T. (1990). An analysis of social competence in schizophrenia. *British Journal of Psychiatry, 156,* 809-818.

Bellack, A. S., Mueser, K. T., Gingerich, S., & Agresta, J. (1997). *Social skills training for schizophrenia: A step-by-step guide.* New York: Guilford.

Bellack, A. S., Sayers, M., Mueser, K. T., & Bennett, M. (1994). An evaluation of social problem solving in schizophrenia. *Journal of Abnormal Psychology, 103,* 371-378.

Blake, D. D., Weathers, F. W., Nagy, L. M., Kaloupek, D. G., Klauminzer, G., Charney, D. S., & Keane, T. M. (1990). A clinician rating scale for assessing current and lifetime PTSD: The CAPS-1. *Behavior Therapist, 13,* 187-188.

Blanchard, E. P., Jones-Alexander, J., Buckley, T. C., & Forneris, C. A. (1996). Psychometric properties of the PTSD Checklist. *Behavior Therapy, 34,* 669-673.

Blanchard, J. J., Mueser, K. T., & Bellack, A. S. (1998). Anhedonia, positive and negative affect, and social functioning in schizophrenia. *Schizophrenia Bulletin, 24,* 413-424.

Bond, G. R. (1998). Principles of the Individual Placement and Support model: Empirical support. *Psychiatric Rehabilitation Journal, 22,* 11-23.

Bond, G. R., Becker, D. R., Drake, R. E., Rapp, C. A., Meisler, N., Lehman, A. F., Bell, M. D., & Blyler, C. R. (2001). Implementing supported employment as an evidence-based practice. *Psychiatric Services, 52,* 313-322.

Bond, G. R., Drake, R. E., Mueser, K. T., & Becker, D. R. (1997). An update on supported employment for people with severe mental illness. *Psychiatric Services, 48*(3), 335-346.

Bond, G. R., Drake, R. E., Mueser, K. T., & Latimer, E. (2001). Assertive community treatment for people with severe mental illness: Critical ingredients and impact on clients. *Disease Management and Health Outcomes, 9,* 141-159.

Bruce, M. L., Takeuchi, D. T., & Leaf, P. J. (1991). Poverty and psychiatric status: Longitudinal evidence from the New Haven Epidemiologic Catchment Area Study. *Archives of General Psychiatry, 48,* 470-474.

Buchanan, J. (1995). Social support and schizophrenia: A review of the literature. *Archives of Psychiatric Nursing, 9,* 68-76.

Butzlaff, R. L., & Hooley, J. M. (1998). Expressed emotion and psychiatric relapse. *Archives of General Psychiatry, 55,* 547-552.

Caldwell, C. B., & Gottesman, I. I. (1990). Schizophrenics kill themselves too: A review of risk factors for suicide. *Schizophrenia Bulletin, 16,* 571-589.

Carpenter, W. T., Jr., & Buchanan, R. W. (1994). Schizophrenia. *New England Journal of Medicine, 330,* 681-690.

Cohen, C. I. (1990). Outcome of schizophrenia in later life. *Gerontologist, 30,* 790-796.

Cuffel, B. J. (1996). Comorbid substance use disorder: Prevalence, patterns of use, and course. In R. E. Drake & K. T. Mueser (Eds.), *Dual diagnosis of major mental illness and substance use disorder II: Recent research and clinical implications* (Vol. 70, pp. 93-105). San Francisco: Jossey-Bass.

Dohrenwend, B. R., Levav, I., Shrout, P. E., Schwartz, S., Naveh, G., Link, B. G., Skodol, A. E., & Stueve, A. (1992). Socioeconomic status and psychiatric disorders: The causation-selection issue. *Science, 255,* 946-952.

Drake, R. E., & Becker, D. R. (1996). The Individual Placement and Support model of supported employment. *Psychiatric Services, 47,* 473-475.

Drake, R. E., Becker, D. R., Clark, R. E., & Mueser, K. T. (1999). Research on the Individual Placement and Support model of supported employment. *Psychiatric Quarterly, 70,* 627-633.

Drake, R. E., Essock, S. M., Shaner, A., Carey, K. B., Minkoff, K., Kola, L., Lynde, D., Osher, F. C., Clark, R. E., & Rickards, L. (2001). Implementing dual diagnosis services for clients with severe mental illness. *Psychiatric Services, 52,* 469-476.

Drake, R. E., Gates, C., Whitaker, A., & Cotton, P. G. (1985). Suicide among schizophrenics: A review. *Comprehensive Psychiatry, 26*(1), 90-100.

Drake, R. E., & Wallach, M. A. (1993). Moderate drinking among people with severe mental illness. *Hospital and Community Psychiatry, 44,* 780-782.

Drake, R. E., Wallach, M. A., & Hoffman, J. S. (1989). Housing instability and homelessness among aftercare patients of an urban state hospital. *Hospital and Community Psychiatry, 40,* 46-51.

Fenton, W. S., & McGlashan, T. H. (1991). Natural history of schizophrenia subtypes: II. Positive and negative symptoms and long term course. *Archives of General Psychiatry, 48,* 978-986.

First, M. B., Spitzer, R. L., Gibbon, M., & Williams, J. B. W. (1996). *Structured Clinical Interview for* DSM-IV *Axis-I Disorders—Patient Edition* (SCID-I/P, Version 2.0). New York: Biometrics Research Department.

Fowler, D., Garety, P., & Kuipers, E. (1995). *Cognitive behaviour therapy for psychosis: Theory and practice.* Chichester, UK: Wiley.

Fox, J. W. (1990). Social class, mental illness, and social mobility: The social selection-drift hypothesis for serious mental illness. *Journal of Health and Social Behavior, 31,* 344-353.

Goodman, L. A., Rosenberg, S. D., Mueser, K. T., & Drake, R. E. (1997). Physical and sexual assault history in women with serious mental illness: Prevalence, correlates, treatment, and future research directions. *Schizophrenia Bulletin, 23*(4), 685-696.

Gould, R. A., Mueser, K. T., Bolton, E., Mays, V., & Goff, D. (2001). Cognitive therapy for psychosis in schizophrenia: A preliminary meta-analysis. *Schizophrenia Research, 48,* 335-342.

Green, B. L. (1996). Trauma History Questionnaire. In B. H. Stamm (Ed.), *Measurement of stress, self-report trauma, and adaptation* (pp. 366-368). Lutherville, MD: Sidran.

Green, M. F., & Nuechterlein, K. H. (1999). Should schizophrenia be treated as a neurocognitive disorder? *Schizophrenia Bulletin, 25*(2), 309-318.

Haas, G. L., & Garratt, L. S. (1998). Gender differences in social functioning. In K. T. Mueser & N. Tarrier (Eds.), *Handbook of social functioning in schizophrenia* (pp. 149-180). Boston: Allyn & Bacon.

Hans, S. L., Marcus, J., Henson, L., Auerbach, J. G., & Mirsky, A. F. (1992). Interpersonal behavior of children at risk for schizophrenia. *Psychiatry, 55,* 314-335.

Harding, C. M., & Keller, A. B. (1998). Long-term outcome of social functioning. In K. T. Mueser & N. Tarrier (Eds.), *Handbook of social functioning in schizophrenia* (pp. 134-148). Boston: Allyn & Bacon.

Heinssen, R. K., Liberman, R. P., & Kopelowicz, A. (2000). Psychosocial skills training for schizophrenia: Lessons from the laboratory. *Schizophrenia Bulletin, 26*(1), 21-46.

Herz, M. I., Glazer, W., Mirza, M., Mostert, M. A., & Hafez, H. (1989). Treating prodromal episodes to prevent relapse in schizophrenia. *British Journal of Psychiatry, 155*(Suppl. 5), S123-S127.

Herz, M. I., Lamberti, J. S., Mintz, J., Scott, R., O'Dell, S. P., McCartan, L., & Nix, G. (2000). A program for relapse prevention in schizophrenia: A controlled study. *Archives of General Psychiatry, 57,* 277-283.

Hiday, V. A., Swartz, M. S., Swanson, J. W., Borum, R., & Wagner, H. R. (1999). Criminal victimization of persons with severe mental illness. *Psychiatric Services, 50,* 62-68.

Hodgins, S., & Côté, G. (1993). The criminality of mentally disordered offenders. *Criminal Justice and Behavior, 28,* 115-129.

Hollingshead, A. B., & Redlich, F. C. (1958). *Social class and mental illness: A community study.* New York: Wiley.

Howard, R., Almeida, O., & Levy, R. (1994). Phenomenology, demography and diagnosis in late paraphrenia. *Psychological Medicine, 24,* 397-410.

Jibson, M. D., & Tandon, R. (1998). New atypical antipsychotic medications. *Journal of Psychiatric Research, 32*(3-4), 215-228.

Kay, S. R., & Lindenmayer, J. (1987). Outcome predictors in acute schizophrenia: Prospective significance of background and clinical dimensions. *Journal of Nervous and Mental Disease, 175,* 152-160.

Kay, S. R., Opler, L. A., & Fiszbein, A. (1987). The Positive and Negative Syndrome Scale (PANSS) for schizophrenia. *Schizophrenia Bulletin, 13,* 261-276.

Keith, S. J., Regier, D. A., & Rae, D. S. (1991). Schizophrenic disorders. In L. N. Robins & D. A. Regier (Eds.), *Psychiatric disorders in America: The Epidemiologic Catchment Area Study* (pp. 33-52). New York: Free Press.

Liberman, R. P., Mueser, K. T., Wallace, C. J., Jacobs, H. E., Eckman, T., & Massel, H. K. (1986). Training skills in the psychiatrically disabled: Learning coping and competence. *Schizophrenia Bulletin, 12,* 631-647.

Liddle, P. F. (1987). The symptoms of chronic schizophrenia: A re-examination of the positive-negative dichotomy. *British Journal of Psychiatry, 151,* 145-151.

Lukoff, D., Nuechterlein, K. H., & Ventura, J. (1986). Manual for the expanded Brief Psychiatric Rating Scale (BPRS). *Schizophrenia Bulletin, 12,* 594-602.

Marango, J. (1994). Classifying the courses of schizophrenia. *Schizophrenia Bulletin, 20,* 519-536.

Mueser, K. T., Drake, R., & Wallach, M. (1998). Dual diagnosis: A review of etiological theories. *Addictive Behaviors, 23*(6), 717-734.

Mueser, K. T., Bennett, M., & Kushner, M. (1995). Substance abuse disorders among persons with chronic mental illness. In A. Lehman & L. Dixon (Eds.), *Double jeopardy: Chronic mental illness and substance abuse.* Chur, Switzerland: Harwood.

Mueser, K. T., Becker, D. R., Torrey, W. C., Xie, H., Bond, G. R., Drake, R. E., & Dain, B. J. (1997). Work and nonvocational domains of functioning in persons with severe mental illness: A longitudinal analysis. *Journal of Nervous and Mental Disease, 185*(7), 419-426.

Mueser, K. T., & Bellack, A. S. (1998). Social skills and social functioning. In K. T. Mueser & N. Tarrier (Eds.), *Handbook of social functioning in schizophrenia* (pp. 79-96). Needham Heights, MA: Allyn & Bacon.

Mueser, K. T., Bellack, A. S., Douglas, M. S., & Morrison, R. L. (1991). Prevalence and stability of social skill deficits in schizophrenia. *Schizophrenia Research, 5,* 167-176.

Mueser, K. T., Bond, G. R., Drake, R. E., & Resnick, S. G. (1998). Models of community care for severe mental illness: A review of research on case management. *Schizophrenia Bulletin, 24,* 37-74.

Mueser, K. T., Corrigan, P. W., Hilton, D., Tanzman, B., Schaub, A., Gingerich, S., Copeland, M. E., Essock, S. M., Tarrier, N., Morey, B., Vogel-Scibilia, S., & Herz, M. I. (in press). Illness management and recovery for severe mental illness: A review of the research. *Psychiatric Services.*

Mueser, K. T., Curran, P. J., & McHugo, G. J. (1997). Factor structure of the Brief Psychiatric Rating Scale in schizophrenia. *Psychological Assessment, 9,* 196-204.

Mueser, K. T., Douglas, M. S., Bellack, A. S., & Morrison, R. L. (1991). Assessment of enduring deficit and negative symptom subtypes in schizophrenia. *Schizophrenia Bulletin, 17,* 565-582.

Mueser, K. T., Drake, R. E., Clark, R. E., McHugo, G. J., Mercer-McFadden, C., & Ackerson, T. (1995). *Toolkit for evaluating substance abuse in persons with severe mental illness.* Cambridge, MA: Evaluation Center at HSRI.

Mueser, K. T., Drake, R. E., & Noordsy, D. L. (1998). Integrated mental health and substance abuse treatment for severe psychiatric disorders. *Practical Psychiatry and Behavioral Health, 4*(3), 129-139.

Mueser, K. T., Foy, D. W., & Carter, M. J. (1986). Social skills training for job maintenance in a psychiatric patient. *Journal of Counseling Psychology, 33,* 360-362.

Mueser, K. T., & Glynn, S. M. (1999). *Behavioral family therapy for psychiatric disorders* (2nd ed.). Oakland, CA: New Harbinger.

Mueser, K. T., & Noordsy, D. L. (1996). Group treatment for dually diagnosed clients. In R. E. Drake & K. T. Mueser (Eds.), *Dual diagnosis of major mental illness and substance abuse disorder II: Recent research and clinical implications: New directions for mental health services* (Vol. 70, pp. 33-51). San Francisco: Jossey-Bass.

Mueser, K. T., Rosenberg, S. D., Goodman, L. A., & Trumbetta, S. L. (in press). Trauma, PTSD, and the course of severe mental illness: An interactive model. *Schizophrenia Research.*

Mueser, K. T., Salyers, M. P., Rosenberg, S. D., Ford, J. D., Fox, L., & Cardy, P. (2001). A psychometric evaluation of trauma and PTSD assessments in persons with severe mental illness. *Psychological Assessment, 13,* 110-117.

Mueser, K. T., Sayers, S. L., Schooler, N. R., Mance, R. M., & Haas, G. L. (1994). A multisite investigation of the reliability of the Scale for the Assessment of Negative Symptoms. *American Journal of Psychiatry, 151,* 1453-1462.

Neumann, C. S., Grimes, K., Walker, E., & Baum, K. (1995). Developmental pathways to schizophrenia: Behavioral subtypes. *Journal of Abnormal Psychology, 104,* 558-566.

Nuechterlein, K. H., & Dawson, M. E. (1984). Information processing and attentional functioning in the developmental course of schizophrenic disorders. *Schizophrenia Bulletin, 10,* 160-203.

Penn, D. L., Corrigan, P. W., Bentall, R. P., Racenstein, J. M., & Newman, L. (1997). Social cognition in schizophrenia. *Psychological Bulletin, 121*(1), 114-132.

Penn, D. L., Hope, D. A., Spaulding, W., & Kucera, J. (1994). Social anxiety in schizophrenia. *Schizophrenia Research, 11*, 277-284.

Pitschel-Walz, G., Leucht, S., Bäuml, J., Kissling, W., & Engel, R. R. (2001). The effect of family interventions on relapse and rehospitalization in schizophrenia— A meta-analysis. *Schizophrenia Bulletin, 27*, 73-92.

Regier, D. A., Farmer, M. E., Rae, D. S., Locke, B. Z., Keith, S. J., Judd, L. L., & Goodwin, F. K. (1990). Comorbidity of mental disorders with alcohol and other drug abuse: Results from the Epidemiologic Catchment Area (ECA) study. *Journal of the American Medical Association, 264*, 2511-2518.

Robins, L. N. (1966). *Deviant children grown up.* Huntington, NY: Krieger.

Rosen, A. J., Sussman, S., Mueser, K. T., Lyons, J. S., & Davis, J. M. (1981). Behavioral assessment of psychiatric inpatients and normal controls across different environmental contexts. *Journal of Behavioral Assessment, 3*, 25-36.

Rosenberg, S. D., Mueser, K. T., Friedman, M. J., Gorman, P. G., Drake, R. E., Vidaver, R. M., Torrey, W. C., & Jankowski, M. K. (2001). Developing effective treatments for post-traumatic disorders: A review and proposal. *Psychiatric Services, 52*, 1453-1461.

Roy, A. (Ed.). (1986). *Suicide in schizophrenia.* Baltimore: Williams & Wilkins.

Rush, A. J., Rago, W. V., Crismon, M. L., Toprac, M. G., Shon, S. P., Suppes, T., Miller, A. L., Trivedi, M. H., Swann, A. C., Biggs, M. M., Shores-Wilson, K., Kashner, T. M., Pigott, T., Chiles, J. A., Gilbert, D. A., & Altshuler, K. Z. (1999). Medication treatment for the severely and persistently mentally ill: The Texas Medication Algorithm Project. *Journal of Clinical Psychiatry, 60*(5), 284-291.

Scott, J. E., & Lehman, A. F. (1998). Social functioning in the community. In K. T. Mueser & N. Tarrier (Eds.), *Handbook of social functioning in schizophrenia* (pp. 1-19). Boston: Allyn & Bacon.

Silverstein, M. L., & Harrow, M. (1978). First rank symptoms in the post acute schizophrenic: A follow-up study. *American Journal of Psychiatry, 135*, 1418-1426.

Stanley, B., Traskman-Bendz, L., & Stanely, M. (1986). The Suicide Assessment Scale: A scale evaluating change in suicidal behavior. *Psychopharmacology Bulletin, 11*, 200-205.

Stein, L. I., & Santos, A. B. (1998). *Assertive community treatment of persons with severe mental illness.* New York: Norton.

Straus, M. A., Hamby, S. L., Boney-McCoy, S., & Sugarman, D. B. (1996). The Revised Conflict Tactics Scales (CTS2): Development and preliminary psychometric data. *Journal of Family Issues, 17*, 283-316.

Swartz, M. S., Swanson, J. W., Hiday, V. A., Borum, R., Wagner, H. R., & Burns, B. J. (1998). Violence and mental illness: The effects of substance abuse and nonadherence to medication. *American Journal of Psychiatry, 155*, 226-231.

Teplin, L. A. (1983). The criminalization of the mentally ill: Speculation in search of data. *Psychological Bulletin, 94*, 54-67.

Tibbo, P., Kroetsch, M., Chue, P., & Warneke, L. (2000). Obsessive-compulsive disorder in schizophrenia. *Journal of Psychiatric Research, 34*, 139-146.

Tsuang, M. T. (1986). Predictors of poor and good outcome in schizophrenia. In L. Erlenmeyer-Kimling & N. E. Miller (Eds.), *Life-span research on the prediction of psychopathology.* Hillsdale, NJ: Lawrence Erlbaum.

Tsuang, M. T., & Woolson, R. F. (1978). Excess mortality in schizophrenia and affective disorders. *Archives of General Psychiatry, 35*, 1181-1185.

Veiel, H. O. F. (1985). Dimensions of social support: A conceptual framework for research. *Social Psychiatry, 20*, 156-162.

Wallace, C. J., Tauber, R., & Wilde, J. (1999). Teaching fundamental workplace skills to persons with serious mental illness. *Psychiatric Services, 50,* 1147-1153.

Weiden, P. J., Mott, T., & Curcio, N. (1995). Recognition and management of neuroleptic noncompliance. In C. L. Shriqui & H. A. Nasrallah (Eds.), *Contempory issues in the treatment of schizophrenia* (pp. 411-433). Washington, DC: American Psychiatric Press.

Zigler, E., & Glick, M. (1986). *A developmental approach to adult psychopathology.* New York: Wiley.

Zubin, J., & Spring, B. (1977). Vulnerability: A new view of schizophrenia. *Journal of Abnormal Psychology, 86,* 103-126.

CHAPTER 13

Antisocial Personality Disorder

KIRSTEN N. BARR
BRIAN P. O'CONNOR

Saddam Hussein. Josef Stalin. Idi Amin. Slobodan Milosevic. Ted Bundy. Gary Gilmore. Bonnie and Clyde. Hannibal Lecter. Most people have some familiarity with real or fictitious antisocial personalities. They are infamous in human history and regular villains in books and films. Less murderous, less dramatic, but still harmful versions of these characters might well be found at your workplace. Michael Douglas's character in the film *Wall Street* is a useful, albeit still dramatic, workplace example (he played a physically nonviolent but nevertheless vicious and remorseless tycoon who believed that "greed is good"). "Psychopathy," "sociopathy," and "moral insanity" are just some of the terms used to describe what is officially known as the antisocial personality disorder (APD). Although the terminology varies, the APD phenomenon has a long history in the professional literature, and it is the most reliably diagnosed personality disorder.

Antisocial behavior in the workplace is a relatively broad phenomenon, covering blackmail, bribery, discrimination, espionage, extortion, fraud, violence, kickbacks, lawsuits, lying, sabotage, sexual harassment, theft, violations of confidentiality—the list goes on (Giacalone & Greenberg, 1997). These individual, potentially isolated, and occasional antisocial behaviors can be displayed by people who do not have APD. The focus of the present chapter is not on specific antisocial behaviors but on the constellation of psychological traits and behaviors that sometimes coalesce to form the APD pattern in particular individuals. Unfortunately for employers and other workers, individuals with APD are likely to display a wide assortment of antisocial behaviors in their workplaces.

DESCRIPTION OF THE DISORDER

A personality disorder (PD) is defined in the *DSM-IV* as

> an enduring pattern of inner experience and behavior that deviates markedly from the expectations of the individual's culture, is pervasive and inflexible, has an onset in adolescence or early adulthood, is stable over time, and leads to distress or impairment. (American Psychiatric Association [APA], 1994, p. 629)

Ten PDs are described in the *DSM-IV*, and APD falls under "Cluster B," pertaining to dramatic, emotional, or erratic behavior. (Cluster A involves withdrawn, suspicious, odd, or eccentric behavior, and Cluster C involves anxiety and fearfulness.) APD is characterized by "a pervasive pattern of disregard for, and violation of, the rights of others that begins in childhood or early adolescence and continues into adulthood" (APA, 1994, p. 645). The deviation from cultural expectations occurs in the context of moral or sociolegal norms. In the *DSM-IV*, PDs are categorical, you-have-it-or-you-don't phenomena. Although many researchers now suspect that most PDs are, instead, continua on which different people have different scores, APD may be a distinct clinical entity or taxon, as originally believed (Harris, Rice, & Quinsey, 1994). People do not suddenly become "ill" with APD and seek help. The disorder is not disturbing to the individuals "suffering" from it, and the individuals are typically brought to the attention of mental health professionals by family members or friends (who suffer from their contact with APD individuals), or by the criminal justice system.

Antisocial individuals present as emotionally shallow, cold, narcissistic, lacking in empathy, deceitful, manipulative, and immoral. Behavioral hallmarks include truancy, fire-setting, vandalism, frequent lying (in childhood), theft, fighting, early substance abuse, early promiscuous behavior (in adolescence), numerous short-term relationships, chronic substance abuse, fraud or embezzlement, and more serious property and violent offenses (in adulthood). Individuals with APD tend to be criminal generalists (i.e., committing a large number of different crimes) as opposed to specialists (i.e., committing the same or similar crimes repeatedly). There is repeated lying for personal gain, impulsiveness, irritability, aggressiveness, disregard for safety, inconsistent work behavior, failure to honor financial and interpersonal commitments, and lack of remorse for harmful actions.

Antisocial personalities can be superficially charming and ingratiating. They may have relationships, but they seem unable to maintain stable, mutually satisfying, intimate relationships. They are irresponsible and exploitative even with their spouses and children. Their inner lives are flat and emotionally empty. The social world is hostile and self-serving in their eyes, and other people are objects to be used and abused. They rarely feel shame or empathy, and their expressions of emotion do not seem genuine.

Although usually of average intelligence, antisocial personalities fail to plan ahead, disregard the truth, lack insight, and fail to learn from past problems. They are impulsive, reckless, and act as if codes of conduct do not apply to them. Harmful and criminal behaviors are performed for thrills and not just personal gain. They often die prematurely and violently, by suicide, homicide, or accidents (Hare, 1998, 1999; Hart & Hare, 1997; O'Connor & Dyce, 2001). Interested readers are referred to Fishbein (2000); Gacono (2000); Hare (1999); Millon, Simonsen, Birket-Smith, and Davis (1998); and Stoff, Breiling, and Maser (1997) for excellent, state-of-the-art textbook reviews of APD and psychopathy. For broad reviews of all 10 official *DSM-IV* PDs, see O'Connor and Dyce (2001) and Widiger and Sanderson (1997).

EPIDEMIOLOGY

The *DSM-IV* (APA, 1994) estimates the prevalence of APD in the general population at 3% for men and 1% for women, while noting that the prevalence can be as high as 30% in clinical or forensic settings. Hare's estimates (1998, 1999; Hart & Hare, 1997) are slightly lower: 1% for the general population and 15% to 25% for prison populations. Two large epidemiological studies, the Epidemiologic Catchment Area (Robins & Regier, 1991) and the National Comorbidity Survey (Kessler et al., 1994), reported APD prevalences of 2.6% (4.5% for men and 0.8% for women) and 3.5% (5.8% for men and 1.2% for women), respectively. Although high concentrations of APD occur in forensic populations, it is widely suspected that this PD may be overdiagnosed in these groups and underdiagnosed in nonclinical samples. APD is more common in urban and low socioeconomic status environments, and among people with less education (Cloninger, Bayon, & Przybeck, 1997). However, it can be found in all occupations and segments of society, including among business executives, lawyers, physicians, politicians, college professors, and evangelists. There are no consistent racial or ethnic differences in rates of diagnoses. The condition has been documented in a range of societies and for different points in historical time (Cleckley, 1976; Mealey, 1995), although it may be more prevalent in competitive, individualistic cultures (Cooke, 1998).

Comorbid conditions are common in APD (Cloninger et al., 1997; Dahl, 1998). In the ECA study, the lifetime prevalence of definite alcoholism among individuals with APD was 39%, with an additional 12% for possible alcoholism. In contrast, the lifetime prevalence of alcoholism in the general population was much lower, at 14.1% (Robins & Regier, 1991). Somatization was also common, with 12% of individuals with APD reporting multiple bodily pains. Depression and anxiety are frequent concomitants of psychiatric disorders, but they are less common in APD (8% for depression, and 0% to 4% for anxiety) than they are in other PDs (46% to 54% for depression, and 4% to 8% for anxiety).

Assessment

There are two main approaches to identifying APD or psychopathy in North America: (a) the formal diagnostic criteria outlined in the *DSM-IV,* which are typically used in clinical work, and (b) checklist, interview, and questionnaire measures of psychopathy, which are used in both clinical work and research. The *DSM-IV* criteria for APD are as follows:

A. There is a pervasive pattern of disregard for and violation of the rights of others occurring since age 15 years, as indicated by three (or more) of the following:

(1) failure to conform to social norms with respect to lawful behaviors as indicated by repeatedly performing acts that are grounds for arrest

(2) deceitfulness, as indicated by repeated lying, use of aliases, or conning others for personal profit or pleasure

(3) impulsivity or failure to plan ahead

(4) irritability and aggressiveness, as indicated by repeated physical fights or assaults

(5) reckless disregard for safety of self or others

(6) consistent irresponsibility, as indicated by repeated failure to sustain consistent work behavior or honor financial obligations

(7) lack of remorse, as indicated by being indifferent to or rationalizing having hurt, mistreated, or stolen from another

B. The individual is at least age 18 years.

C. There is evidence of Conduct Disorder (see p. 90) with onset before age 15 years.

D. The occurrence of antisocial behavior is not exclusively during the occurrence of Schizophrenia or a Manic Episode. (APA, 1994, pp. 649-650)

These *DSM-IV* criteria are largely behavioral, which is good for interrater reliability but not for validity. The criteria have been criticized for focusing on destructive and criminal activity rather than personality. It is difficult to diagnose APD in individuals who do not have a criminal record, and the behavioral criteria diagnose too many people with criminal records as having APD, overextending the boundaries of the construct (Lilienfeld, Purcell, & Jones-Alexander, 1997). The criteria also rely heavily on reports of specific behaviors in childhood.

The most popular, reliable, and valid measure is the Revised Psychopathy Checklist (PCL-R) (Hare, 1998, 1999; Hart & Hare, 1997; see also Gacono, 2000). Clinicians and researchers using the PCL-R provide ratings on 20 dimensions that were selected based on their close parallels with Cleckley's (1976) influential theoretical description of psychopathy, and on the basis of their usefulness in discriminating prototypical psychopaths from normals. The PCL-R involves both a clinical interview, which can take up to 2 hours, and a review of file or collateral information. The interview covers educational, occupational, family, marital, and criminal history, and provides an opportunity to observe the individual's interactional style. The type of collateral information reviewed in PCL-R assessments depends on the setting. Ample information is available in correctional settings, whereas psychiatric files, medical assessments, and interviews with family members and police may be necessary in other environments.

Dimensional analyses have revealed that the PCL-R consists of two well-replicated, separable but related factors. The first, Emotional/Interpersonal factor is defined by superficial charm, grandiose sense of self-worth, pathological lying, manipulativeness, lack of remorse, shallow affect, callousness, and lack of empathy. The second, Social Deviance factor is related more closely to the *DSM* diagnostic criteria and is defined by need for stimulation, parasitic lifestyle, poor behavioral controls, early behavioral problems, lack of realistic long-term goals, impulsivity, irresponsibility, revocation of conditional release, and juvenile delinquency (or adolescent antisocial behavior). Scores on the PCL-R predict future violent and criminal offenses. Scores on the Emotional/Interpersonal factor are unrelated to intelligence, whereas scores on the Social Deviance factor are negatively associated with intelligence, at least among criminals.

A distinction is often made between psychopathy and APD. Psychopathy is the broader construct because of its focus on affective and interpersonal characteristics in addition to behavioral characteristics. It also envelops the extensive research descriptions and findings better than does the more narrow, psychiatric, and primarily North American *DSM* criteria for APD. Nevertheless, the *DSM-IV* mentions that the APD pattern "has also been referred to as psychopathy" (APA, 1994, p. 645), and *DSM-IV* and PCL-R assessments identify many of the same individuals. Much of our current research-based knowledge of the APD construct, including many findings described in the present chapter, derives from work on psychopathy.

Hare (1998, 1999; Hart & Hare, 1997) states that the vast majority of psychopaths would be diagnosed with APD, but that not all individuals with APD would be considered psychopaths. Prison inmates meet the behavioral criteria for APD more often than they meet the additional interpersonal and affective criteria for psychopathy. There is also much variation in the psychological makeup of the people who meet the behavioral criteria for APD. The behavioral criteria necessary for a diagnosis of APD may also exclude a substantial number of people who meet the interpersonal and affective criteria for psychopathy but who have managed to avoid trouble with the law. "Successful" or "white-collar" psychopaths may not come to the attention of clinicians and others who rely solely on the formal diagnostic criteria for APD. In Hare's (1991) words,

> Paradoxically, the criteria for APD appear to define a diagnostic category that is at once too broad, encompassing criminals and antisocial persons who are psychologically heterogeneous, and too narrow, excluding those who have the personality structure of the psychopath but have not exhibited some of the specific antisocial behaviors listed for APD. (p. 393)

He also maintains that the Emotional/Interpersonal factor in the PCL-R helps differentiate true psychopaths from career criminals.

In addition to the full PCL-R, an abbreviated screening version that takes less time to administer and requires less collateral information has been used with nonforensic populations (Hart, Cox, & Hare, 1995). Also promising is the P-SCAN (Hare & Hervé, 1999), which is a 90-item checklist that can be used by nonpsychologists (e.g., therapists, social workers, correctional service employees, law enforcement officers, prosecutors) to assess the interpersonal, affective, and lifestyle aspects of psychopathy.

Several semistructured interviews have been developed to facilitate PD assessments (see Lilienfeld et al., 1997, and Van Velzen & Emmelkamp, 1996, for reviews). Some of the assessment tools consist of questions that match *DSM* criteria precisely, whereas others focus on thematic content areas (e.g., work, social relations). Recent and promising self-report measures of psychopathy were developed by Blackburn and Fawcett (1999) and Lilienfeld and Andrews (1996). Hogan and Hogan (1989) developed a personality measure of employee unreliability and organizational delinquency that is associated with a wide range of antisocial behaviors in the workplace, including absenteeism, warning and suspension letters, grievances, discharges, workers' compensation claims, and supervisor ratings. Psychopaths are likely to score high on this measure.

PDs are, by definition, broad patterns that involve a wider domain of behavior than is the case for other psychiatric disorders. Selected antisocial traits or behaviors may not seem particularly problematic or serious when viewed in isolation, but their overall constellations can be maladaptive (O'Connor & Dyce, 2001). Clinicians or personnel managers in organizations must somehow identify the broad constellations and then determine whether the characteristics are stable across time and situations. Single interviews and single sources of information are not likely to be sufficient, yet there is often little time for the necessary in-depth assessments. Once a working diagnosis of APD has been formulated, the challenge then is to deal with clients or employees who are typically unwilling to see their personalities as disordered and who minimize problems and deflect blame.

Other behavioral and personality features besides those in standardized assessment instruments can serve as possible indicators of psychopathy. Antisocial individuals exhibit high levels of Machiavellianism (Mealey, 1995), which is a willingness to exploit others and flout societal rules to gain influence or rewards. Individuals high in Machiavellianism espouse attitudes such as "It's a dog-eat-dog world," "I have to look out for number one first," and "Suckers get what's coming to them." Babiak (1995a, 1995b) described how "industrial psychopaths" manipulate and exploit other employees. They will befriend and flatter employees who seem useful to them, and undermine and sabotage those who do not. APDs are consistently willing to lie and deceive, and an early red flag may be that different employees in the workplace have very discrepant views of, and have heard wildly different stories from, the psychopath. Another red flag is consternation and confusion surrounding the actions of an employee. Psychopaths are fluent and facile liars, and so it is best to seek information about questionable employees from several sources, especially in cases where official corroboration is possible (e.g., for educational or employment history).

Some employers use integrity tests during the preemployment screening process to identify potentially deviant or antisocial individuals (Ones & Viswesvaran, 1998). Several personality-based measures have been developed that purport to measure broad constructs that are relevant to antisociality. However, unlike most psychological tests, these are often developed by private corporations for profit, and their scoring keys are proprietary. Comparatively little independent research has been conducted on these instruments, although they generally appear reliable and valid. However, failure rate on the tests is often between 30% and 60%, thus requiring employers to turn away many applicants. The tests are also not substitutes for the proper corroboration and verification of information provided by applicants. An applicant's past behavior is probably the best predictor of the applicant's future behavior. Employers can help themselves by learning as much as possible about past behavior.

It is also important to distinguish APD from other psychiatric disorders with sometimes similar symptoms. Individuals with the narcissistic PD can exhibit glib and superficial charm, a grandiose sense of self-worth, shallow affect, and a lack of empathy. Individuals with the borderline PD often have a need for stimulation, exhibit poor behavioral control and impulsivity, and have numerous and unstable romantic or sexual relationships. Individuals with the histrionic PD are often impulsive, promiscuous, and sensation seeking. The main difference between these PDs and APD is the long history of antisocial behavior in APD, contraventions of social mores, exploitation of others, callousness, lack of empathy and remorse, and a tendency toward aggressive or violent behavior. Furthermore, as is the case for all PDs, the symptoms of APD must not occur exclusively during acute flare-ups of Axis I disorders (such as bipolar disorder or psychotic disorders), and they should not be due to an underlying medical condition, such as head injury, medication, or substance abuse. Although there is considerable comorbidity between APD and substance abuse, the behavioral indexes of APD should have been evident before the onset of the substance abuse in order for there to be a diagnosis of APD or psychopathy. See the *DSM-IV* (APA, 1994), O'Connor and Dyce (2001), and Widiger and Sanderson (1997) for more information on the differential diagnosis of APD.

CLINICAL PICTURE

Psychopaths in the Workplace

Case studies of individuals with APD typically describe violent, remorseless, life-long criminals who are now in prison or in the forensic units of mental health settings. The APD prototype in these settings is familiar and clear after years of extensive research and clinical observation. In contrast, the clinical picture of APD in the workplace is not as focused or detailed because research and clinical observation have begun only recently. The wealth of information from forensic settings is due in part to the fact that individuals with APD in these settings are easily recognized by their long and varied criminal histories. In employment settings, the signs are less obvious because such information is typically not available, and because psychopaths mask their antisocial traits and present themselves in socially desirable ways. Nevertheless, an interesting clinical picture of psychopathy in the workplace is beginning to emerge based on the hard lessons learned by employers and their workers (Babiak, 1995a, 1995b, 2000; Hare, 1999).

"To find psychopaths in the workplace, look for the commotion and disruption around them" (V. L. Quinsey, personal communication, September 19, 2000). Unfortunately, such after-the-fact identification of psychopaths is common because of both the skills of psychopaths and the fact that those responsible for personnel selection often do not have experience or training in recognizing the disorder. During initial interviews, psychopaths may appear charming, gregarious, enthusiastic, intelligent, and dynamic, and they can seem like perfect candidates for leadership or management positions. Their willingness to lie and

deceive can result in apparently excellent educational and vocational histories. They may also be attracted to fast-growing, dynamic organizations in which they can do their damage without being recognized (Babiak, 1995b).

Babiak (1995a, 1995b, 2000) described the typical series of events that occurs once psychopaths enter an organization. After Organizational Entry, psychopaths go through a period of Assessment. They typically make good initial impressions on most or all fellow workers. During this grace period, psychopaths evaluate other employees in terms of their utility and their power or influence within the organization. Individuals judged to be sufficiently powerful are chosen for the formation of a positive relationship: They will be courted, flattered, and befriended. Patrons are befriended individuals of higher rank, whereas Pawns are befriended individuals of equal or lower rank who are exploited for their access to resources and ability to manipulate the rules for the psychopath's benefit. Patrons and Pawns often persist with their positive impressions of psychopathic employees, even after the eventual disruptions, in which case they are referred to as Supporters.

Staff members judged to be of low utility to psychopaths are often quicker to see the troublesome people behind the personas. Psychopaths will often undermine these individuals—spreading rumors and gossip, taking credit for their work, and sabotaging their work or their relationships—and psychopaths may be hostile or aggressive toward them when confronted or questioned. They may lodge complaints about these employees, describing their interactions accurately except with their roles reversed, to preempt complaints that could be filed against them. Detractors are workers with unfavorable opinions of psychopaths, and they fall into two categories. Patsies actively dislike the psychopaths after having seen their true patterns. Patsies can be former Patrons or Pawns who lost their utility for the psychopath and thus were dropped. Organizational members who have a policing role (e.g., security personnel, accountants, auditors) often see through the psychopaths' attempts to charm and manipulate. However, they often do not have the influence to change the attitudes of upper management regarding problem employees (Babiak, 1995a).

During the Manipulation phase, psychopaths skillfully exploit, cheat, sabotage, plagiarize, gossip about, spread rumors about, and disparage others. These behaviors further their own careers and damage relationships among other employees, thus making it less likely that they will band together and realize what is being done to them behind their backs. In the final Confrontation phase, at least some employees realize what has been going on (especially if they have been demoted from Patron or Pawn to Patsy), and the opinions of staff members begin to diverge until the Supporters and Detractors are polarized. Because the Detractors have already been undermined by the psychopaths' insidious networking, any complaints they may lodge have already been neutralized. Their own credibility may be damaged in the eyes of the Supporters with whom the psychopaths have established alliances. If they personally confront the psychopaths, they may become victims of harassment or verbal and physical aggression. The lowered organizational morale, chaos, and confusion can be further manipulated by psychopaths to bring about reorganization and self-promotion. Throughout these phases, psychopaths are willing and likely to betray fellow employees, regardless of their past relationships, in order to achieve personal success within the organization (Babiak, 1995b, 2000).

Case Description

Ms. T. was a 28-year-old technician hired by Dr. W. to work in a university biomedical research laboratory. Her educational background consisted of 1 year of undergraduate studies in science, after which she held a series of menial jobs. She later entered a 2-year certificate program to become a laboratory technician. She was hired by Dr. W. when he first started his research laboratory, and she was placed in charge of running the lab. Dr. W. trained her in the specific protocols used in his lab. Her job also included orienting new graduate students, training them on the protocols she had learned, assisting them with research, maintaining the equipment, caring for the research animals, and keeping the lab stocked with supplies.

When the lab was small, Ms. T. could work independently, supervised only by Dr. W., and she made herself indispensable to him. As more graduate students and postdoctoral fellows came to the lab, there were more people observing her work, and she began having to report to more than one person. Ms. T. had enjoyed being high in the pecking order and resented having to give up her exalted status as the only person who knew how to keep the lab running. Not only did the graduate students become able to work independently of her, but more people were around to notice inconsistencies in her behavior and stories. As she became resentful, the inconsistencies became more obvious.

Ms. E. was a graduate student who later started working with Dr. W. Initially, Ms. T. was welcoming and friendly, familiarizing her with laboratory procedures, sharing inside information on which faculty and students to watch out for, and on Dr. W.'s habits. Ms. T. expressed dim views of the competence of workers in other labs with which Dr. W. collaborated and of the one other graduate student he had at that time. Ms. T. projected an image of busy competence and efficiency, but also insinuated that she was underappreciated. When the lab started to expand, her competent worker image began to unravel.

Ms. E. began realizing that the technician was telling lies about her own actions and those of others. For example, Ms. T. claimed that a professor with whom Ms. E. sometimes worked stole supplies from her and had contaminated the lab space. When Ms. E. threatened to confront the professor, Ms. T. tried to prevent her, even to the point of physically blocking the exit. Ms. E. realized the story had been fabricated and began questioning the truthfulness of Ms. T.'s other stories. When she compared her experiences and information with those of others, she realized that the technician had lied consistently about both important and trivial matters.

Ms. T.'s lies were pathologically common and of three types: concealing, protective, and destructive. Concealing lies were told to cover up a lack of knowledge, sometimes even causing students to make mistakes in their lab work. She then lied about these incidents. When caught diluting solutions, she claimed the student using them told her to. When caught writing down fraudulent numbers for data, she claimed the numbers were correct but that she had forgotten to note a changed concentration. When caught tampering with equipment while experiments were under way, she falsely claimed a pressure reading was too high. Destructive lies were told about staff or students to cause strain or damage to their working relationships. She told a graduate student that a professor had stolen her

supplies. She told Dr. W. that his students made serious experimental errors that were, in fact, her own errors. To maintain control over aspects of running the lab, she told students that Dr. W. requested that only she be allowed to order supplies, but then delayed ordering the supplies to hold students up. She told students that she was solely responsible for creating preparations, but then did not always make them properly. Protective lies were often more elaborate stories she told when she was caught lying. She even told blatant, risky lies with apparently little concern about getting caught. A meeting with Dr. W., Ms. E., and one other researcher was held to discuss the many problems that were emerging. Ms. T. steadfastly refused to accept responsibility for her actions. When she felt outnumbered, she refused to talk altogether, sitting sullenly in her chair with her eyes down and her arms crossed in resentment. The next day, she filed a written report with the Human Resources department stating that Ms. E. had threatened to kill her.

Ms. E. realized that Ms. T. had often manipulated people with her lies, creating ill will between coworkers. Ms. T. confided to Ms. E. that some researchers and students had spread malicious rumors about her and had harmed her experiments. She interfered in experiments in which she was not involved. She was caught by Ms. E. taking apart machinery, changing equipment settings, taking needed supplies home with her the night before an experiment for which they were needed, and engaging in other acts of sabotage. She also interfered in more subtle ways, such as "mistakenly" ordering the wrong supplies, or claiming she had ordered necessary supplies when she hadn't, refusing to take or pass on telephone messages, and continuously moving supplies and equipment so that students could not find them during experiments. Whenever

Ms. E. confronted her about these matters, she became angry, vehemently denied wrongdoing, blamed others, and stepped up the harassment. Ms. T. created an atmosphere of fear and secrecy in the lab. Students were forced to hide solutions or equipment that they were using in ongoing experiments to prevent her from tampering with them. Ms. T.'s organizational tactics eventually led coworkers to become suspicious of one another, and reduce their discussions and collaborations.

Ms. E. realized that Ms.T.'s behavior was seriously harming the laboratory's research and possibly rendering their findings invalid. She tried discussing matters with other workers. A postdoctoral fellow was willing to discuss incidents she had experienced or witnessed, but others expressed varying degrees of reluctance to become involved. Some said, in confidence, that they were afraid of what the technician would do if they were found out. In spite of the worries and mixed support, Ms. E. and her postdoctoral colleague tried to apprise Dr. W. of the situation, but with only partial success. Dr. W. was a busy Patron who had been taken in early on by Ms. T.'s glibness and superficial charm. He was not sure what to believe and hoped the friction represented minor tiffs between coworkers that would eventually evaporate. He kept saying he would look into the problems if they persisted, but he never did.

Dr. W. was useful to Ms. T., and so she consistently went out of her way to make herself necessary to him by taking on additional responsibilities. She often presented her experimental results and work to him with an overly positive slant. Dr. W. consistently downplayed the destructiveness of Ms. T.'s actions, giving her the benefit of the doubt. Ms. T. often counteracted Ms. E.'s complaints about her behavior with complaints of her own. Although Dr. W. was aware that these were exaggerated, Ms. T. was a union member and previously implied that she would not hesitate to bring the union into any disagreements. Ms. T. also created an alliance with another researcher in the lab, Dr. J., for whom she did considerable tedious research work. Dr. J. supported Ms. T. in situations that involved her word against others. Dr. W. still held positive views of Ms. T., for he had no firsthand knowledge of her harmful actions and was busy, confused by the mixed reports, and reluctant to apply formal sanctions.

Case Overview and Workplace Impact

Ms. T.'s behavior and the sequence of events in her work group are in accordance with Babiak's (1995a, 1995b, 2000) portrait of successful, subcriminal industrial psychopaths. The work group was initially dynamic and fast-growing, and the Assessment, Manipulation, and Confrontation phases unfolded as predicted. The cast included a psychopath (Ms. T.), a Patron (Dr. W.), a Detractor (Ms. E.), a Supporter (Dr. J.), a few Patsies (sadder but wiser graduate students), although no Pawn. The overall workplace effects included mutual suspiciousness, withdrawal, and conflict among coworkers; job stress and serious distractions for coworkers; bad work habits and sabotage; unnecessary expenses; possibly invalid research results; and a group of bright minds eventually failing to thrive. The mess that emerged was difficult to sort out because of factions among employees, one person's word against another's, and the threatened quasi-legal actions that would be taken against attempts to remedy the situation. The psychopath maintained undeserved status in the organization and benefited from the troubles she created, she confirmed her views of the world as consisting of dupes and hostile competitors, and she converted at least some of her coworkers into believing that people cannot be trusted.

The case illustrates how employers should attend to subtle differences between psychopathy and the official criteria for APD. Ms. T. did display many prototypical features of APD, including a pervasive pattern of disregard for the rights of others, a failure to conform to social norms with respect to lawful behaviors (but not obviously to the point of providing grounds for arrest), deceitfulness, impulsivity, irritability, verbal aggressiveness, consistent irresponsibility, and lack of remorse. Ms. T. did not have a long criminal record or a history of physical violence. Dr. W. or other officials would have had difficulty documenting and confirming the occurrence of behaviors that meet the strict *DSM-IV* criteria for APD. A diagnosis of APD was unlikely, despite the fact that Ms. T.'s psychological makeup was otherwise highly similar to that of the prototypical APD and psychopath. However, Ms. T. would certainly have scored high on a measure of psychopathy, especially on the Interpersonal/Affective factor of the PCL-R. She caused serious trouble for other employees and her organization. Her psychopathic influences should not be trivialized merely because she did not assault a fellow employee or end up in jail. Violent psychopaths with criminal records are identified more easily by employers, and they are presumably either not hired or quickly terminated. Nonviolent, subcriminal, successful psychopaths are more likely to be hired, are much harder to identify once they are hired, and may cause as much, if not more, damage to organizations than their more blatantly criminal and violent counterparts (Hare, 1999). They are like malignant cancers whose pernicious operation remains undetected because of the lack of open sores.

A more careful investigation of Ms. T.'s background when she first applied for the job could have produced red flags. She had enrolled in a technician's certificate program, but did not tell Dr. W. that she never finished the program. She was previously employed only periodically, and there were disruptions in her other workplaces. Dr. W. initially contacted two of her references; one was positive (a previous Patron), and one vague (a former victim like himself who did not know what to think or say). Asking previous employers questions from Hare and Hervé's (1999) P-SCAN may have produced more red flags and more unambiguous information about the prospective employee. Unfortunately, some aspects of Ms. T.'s past would have been difficult to uncover even if more careful background checks had been conducted. She had intermittent problems with alcohol. She was accused of stealing from a former employer, and she had filed countercharges against him. This was, of course, never mentioned in her job interview. She was twice divorced, and in both cases, messy and complicated legal battles occurred over children and property, and with unfounded claims of psychiatric disturbance and abuse on the part of her ex-husbands.

In hindsight, it seems obvious that when problems were first brought to Dr. W.'s attention, he should have corroborated the information independently, documented all complaints, and run the previously neglected background checks. However, Dr. W. had been charmed by Ms. T. and was afraid of her reactions to his attempts to address the problems (he was officially obliged to discuss with her any negative information that went into her file). He was a busy scientist with little experience and interest in human resources issues. He was also reluctant to go through the fuss of preparing the case for dismissal and hiring and training another technician. Tiffs between employees are common, and Dr. W.'s wait-and-see, hope-it-all-blows-over approach to workplace problems might have worked well in many other cases, but not with a psychopath in the mix. The time, resources, vigilance, and checks and balances required to weed out psychopaths might seem extraordinary to employers, insulting to many employees, and unnecessary given the statistical rarity of psychopaths in the population. However, the disruptions caused by psychopaths have presumably left many employers wishing they had been more vigilant.

PRECIPITATING CONDITIONS

APD is not a periodic illness that suddenly afflicts people. It emerges in childhood or adolescence, and there are no obvious precipitating conditions in the immediate environments of adults with APD. Indeed, presence of precipitating conditions, such as brain trauma, medication, or stressful life events, would disqualify a PD diagnosis. There has been much speculation and research on the biological and brain conditions that are believed to be responsible, at least in part, for APD, and the primary theories will be described briefly.

Biological Precipitating Conditions

Some believe that APD is inherited and perhaps even an evolutionarily stable and adaptive strategy. The criminal records of adopted children separated from their biological parents early in life are more similar to the criminal records of their biological parents than they are to the records of their adopted parents. The concordance rate for

criminal behavior is approximately 50% in identical twins, but only 20% in fraternal twins. Heritability estimates for delinquent behavior in children and criminal behavior in adults are in the 30% to 50% range (Carey & Goldman, 1997; McGuffin & Thapar, 1998), which is the same range as the heritability coefficients that have emerged for most normal and abnormal personality traits. Thus, genes are an important part of the picture. There may also be variability among psychopaths in the strength of the genetic basis of their disorders. Mealey (1995) claimed that there are "primary psychopaths" whose ancestors developed certain behavioral adaptations that allowed them to manipulate, exploit, and cheat others in interpersonal interactions, thus increasing their reproductive or inclusive fitness. This psychopathy subtype is largely heritable and impervious to environmental influences. In contrast, "secondary psychopaths" are individuals with some biological risk factors who were exposed to environments that encouraged antisocial behavior and made it a profitable behavioral strategy.

Psychopaths and persistently violent criminals differ from nonpsychopathic offenders and nonoffender controls on psychophysiological indexes, including electroencephalograms (more slow wave activity, combined with more positive spikes in the temporal area of the brain), and less reactive skin conductance in aversive situations (Raine, 1997; Siever, 1998). One explanation is that they suffer from general underarousal that is aversive to them. Chronic underarousal early in life may result in disinhibited temperaments and a preference for novel, stimulating situations that eventually lead to impulsive, antisocial, and violent behaviors in adolescence and adulthood. An alternative explanation is that underarousal in psychopaths impairs learning from punishment and the acquisition of fears of events that are aversive to normal people. Fearlessness, based on underarousal, allows psychopaths to engage in behaviors that have frightening negative consequences that would otherwise inhibit people.

APD may also be rooted in brain chemistry. Serotonin is an inhibitory neurotransmitter that plays a role in the regulation of sexual behavior, analgesia, appetite, sleep, mood, and aggression. There are inverse relationships between antisocial behavior and measures of serotonergic activity, suggesting that serotonin normally acts to inhibit antisocial impulses (Berman, Kavoussi, & Coccaro, 1997; Coccaro, Kavoussi, & McNamee, 2000; Siever, 1998). These relationships have been observed in animals; personality-disordered men; abstinent alcoholics; intimate partner murderers; impulsive violent offenders; and children with attention-deficit hyperactivity disorder, oppositional defiant disorder, and conduct disorder.

Another popular theory, based on the large discrepancy between men and women in antisocial behavior and aggression, is that psychopaths have excessive amounts of testosterone. However, the relationships between testosterone and antisocial behavior in children, adolescents, and adults are mixed and often weak (Brain & Susman, 1997). Hormones may be important to psychopathy, but apparently, they are only a small part of the picture.

Neuropsychological function associated with the frontal lobe of the brain may also be impaired in psychopathy (Giancola, 2000; Siever, 1998). In both incarcerated and nonincarcerated samples, there is a link between verbal deficits, executive function deficits, and antisocial behavior. The relationships remain significant after socioeconomic status, race, and academic achievement are statistically controlled. The neuropsychological deficits emerge before the development of antisocial behavior, and they are especially predictive of antisocial behavior and criminal recidivism in individuals with a history of attention-deficit hyperactivity disorder. The effect sizes for these relationships are in the small-to-medium range.

Opportunities to Exploit

The genetic, psychophysiological, neurotransmitter, hormonal, and neuropsychological features of APD together may encourage one to believe that the disorder exists rigidly and full-time. Therefore, psychopaths should be easy to spot, given that so many things are different about them. However, whereas the psychopathic personality structure is stable and persistent, the display of psychopathic behavior is potentially more intermittent and variable. Psychopaths can turn on the charm and blend with the crowd when it suits them. They scan their social environments for opportunities to exploit others, and they take action when such opportunities arise. Therefore, opportunities to exploit can be viewed as precipitating conditions for the display of psychopathic behavior. Unfortunately, little is known about the range and nature of such precipitating conditions. They are presumably ubiquitous, given that so much of the daily social contract involves trusting other people. Workplaces that provide few opportunities to exploit others are almost certainly very rare. (Psychopaths might even be risky lighthouse keepers!)

Babiak (1995a, 1995b, 2000) described how new and rapidly developing organizations, as well as organizations undergoing change (e.g., due to mergers, acquisitions, or downsizing), may be particularly appealing to psychopaths seeking to climb the corporate ladder. They have more room to maneuver and exploit in organizational structures that are fluid and chaotic. In these contexts, communication and information sharing often deteriorate to the point that the actions of psychopathic employees are not quickly recognized. The less rigid and less bureaucratic structures of the modern business world provide flexibility and enhance competitiveness, but they also provide attractive opportunities for antisocial personalities (Babiak, 2000, p. 305). Employers and managers who carefully identify and monitor sensitive positions within their organizations and who are concerned with exploitation by psychopaths also face a peculiar challenge when problems arise. The commotion surrounding an employee may be due to psychopathy in the employee in question, or the employee may be an innocent victim of a smear campaign orchestrated by a psychopath seeking power, prestige, or resources. Psychopaths can be charming, righteous, deceitful, self-serving whistle-blowers.

COURSE AND PROGNOSIS

APD and psychopathy, or at least their precursors, are evident early in life. Fledgling psychopaths throw frequent temper tantrums and test parental limits as infants and toddlers; they are truant and defiant of teachers' authority in elementary school; and there are often deception, fire-setting, cruelty to animals, vandalism, physical confrontations, and property crimes in adolescence. Moffitt (1993) claimed that two groups of children engage in antisocial behavior: those who begin early and persist in their misbehavior into and throughout adulthood ("life-course-persistent antisociality"), and those who begin when they are somewhat older, misbehave for a few years, then desist in late adolescence ("adolescence-limited antisociality"). Numerous longitudinal studies have found that age of onset is a reliable predictor of the seriousness and persistence of antisocial behavior. Children who begin antisocial behavior earlier, and who are oppositional, defiant, and hostile toward authority figures, tend to have more lengthy and variable antisocial careers (Lynam, 1996).

Retrospective and prospective studies indicate that parental behaviors are also important predictors (Loeber & Farrington, 1997). Parents who provide little or poor supervision, who show little involvement in their children's lives, who are rejecting, and who use harsh and inconsistent discipline are more likely to have children who become antisocial (Loeber & Farrington, 1997; Shaw & Winslow, 1997). The parents tend to alternate between hostility and neglect. Researchers have also noted that children with difficult temperaments often evoke negative reactions from their parents, sometimes within a few weeks of birth. Child-to-parent effects and parent-to-child effects may both take place, and the magnitudes of the two effects have yet to be disentangled. Reciprocal causation is also likely: Difficult temperaments may prompt inconsistent or harsh discipline, which in turn exacerbates temperamental problems and increases the chances of conduct disorder (Moffit, 1993).

Physical, sexual, and psychological abuse are also common in the histories of persistently antisocial individuals, perhaps providing formative models and training for future psychopathy. However, the majority of abused children do not grow up to be antisocial or psychopathic. There are likely complex interactions between being a victim of abuse or witnessing abuse, individual difference factors such as resilience and coping skills, and protective factors such as exposure to prosocial role models (Widom, 1997). Parental divorce, alcoholism, depression, and stress are common, as are large families, frequent family moves, and poorly regulated schooling. Antisocial peers also increase risk, and environmental factors such as neighborhood quality and socioeconomic status exhibit indirect influences via their effects on family behavior (Thornberry & Krohn, 1997). This collection of adverse childhood experiences, combined with insufficient social skills for obtaining normative reinforcements and a growing history of poor behavioral choices (e.g., dropping out of school, problems with drugs and the law), can become ensnaring and seriously limit one's options (Moffitt, 1993). Although much of the research on conduct problems has focused on males, a recent review concluded that the experiences and trajectories described above also apply to females (Pajer, 1998).

Lynam (1996) described a path that may be particularly risky for the development of adult psychopathy: A dual diagnosis of hyperactivity-impulsivity-attention problems (HIAP) and conduct problems (CP) provides a double hazard. Either diagnosis on its own merely increases the risk of negative interactions with parents and teachers, rejection by peers, academic difficulties, or mild antisocial behavior. Children with both kinds of problems are on a developmental pathway that may culminate in adult psychopathy. The neuropsychological and psychophysiological phenomena described above as characteristic of psychopathic offenders have also been observed in children with HIAP-CP. Lynam claims that these children are responsible for the observed associations between childhood and adult antisocial behavior.

By definition, PDs begin early and last long. The prognosis for psychopathic individuals is generally the same (poor) across the lifespan. Psychopaths sometimes burn out of their criminal careers around age 50 (Hare, 1998, 1999; Hart & Hare, 1997). However, although older psychopaths may be less confrontational, impulsive, and violent, they may continue to engage in more subtle, less visible crimes such as domestic violence, embezzlement, and fraud. Behaviors that are problematic for the workplace may not abate. Psychopaths may also be continually learning how to manipulate other people and their emotions. Thematic continuity underlies changes in the specifics of their antisocial behaviors across the lifespan. The emotional and interpersonal aspects of psychopathy are more stable than the social deviance aspects.

RECOMMENDED DATA-BASED TREATMENTS

PDs are notoriously difficult to treat, and APD is the most difficult. APD begins early, lasts long, affects many aspects of an individual's life, and has a number of roots in genes, brain function, and family experiences. Psychopaths rarely seek treatment unless they are encouraged by attractive incentives (e.g., avoiding responsibilities) or unattractive potential consequences (e.g., a prison term). They consider themselves sane, they do not believe they are disordered or in distress, they value their antisocial traits, and they blame others for their difficulties (Hare, 1998, 1999; Hart & Hare, 1997). Intervention programs thus face formidable challenges, and treatment objectives should be modest, focusing on symptom reduction and management rather than cure (Gacono, 2000). Personality change is not a realistic goal.

Most of the research on the treatment of APD has focused on programs implemented in correctional settings. Very little is known about the effectiveness of treatments that are implemented in other environments. Furthermore, the goals of treatment programs in correctional systems are not always the same as the treatment goals in private practice or workplace organizations. A major objective of correctional treatment programs is a reduction in the commission of new crimes after release from prison. Correctional programs often focus more on such concrete behavioral objectives than on personality change or increasing insight into affective states or cognitive processes.

Psychotherapy

Whereas reviews of correctional psychotherapy programs indicate positive effects for some approaches, the findings are not as encouraging for APD or psychopathic offenders (Rice & Harris, 1997). Most evaluation studies have not specified the percentages of treated offenders who were psychopathic or APD. Studies that have focused more specifically on psychopaths or APD have found that psychotherapy is either ineffective or results in worse outcomes. Outpatient programs generally do not work, and psychopaths can be manipulative, exploitative, and abusive in inpatient programs (Widiger & Sanderson, 1997). Insight-oriented therapies and those focusing on affective functioning or self-esteem tend to result in poor outcomes (e.g., Ogloff, Wong, & Greenwood, 1990; Rice & Harris, 1997). They may provide psychopaths with more sophisticated understandings of the psychological workings of others, which are subsequently used to further manipulate and exploit others. Hare (1999) claimed that there are no proven effective treatment programs for psychopaths. This does not mean that psychopaths cannot be changed, only that currently available programs have not been empirically proven to change them. Researchers and reviewers of the literature are generally more pessimistic than therapists in the field, who tend to believe (hope) that at least some psychopaths are treatable.

Psychotherapy with psychopaths has many unique features (Sperry, 1995). Therapy generally works best when strong working alliances are formed with clients, yet psychopaths are deficient in forming genuine close relationships, and therapists often dislike psychopathic clients. Psychopaths crave attention, and clinicians sometimes stimulate discussion by encouraging them to talk about their accomplishments while being careful not to approve of their exploits. Therapists should avoid appearing judgmental and accusatory, should avoid power struggles, and should present themselves as nonmanipulative allies. They should beware that psychopathic self-disclosures are likely to be replete with distortions and fabrications. Psychopaths attempt to manipulate their therapists, they exploit unstructured programs, and they mask their resistance with charm and verbal skills. They become angry and critical when therapists resist their manipulations. They are seldom remorseful about their treatment of others, and it can be difficult to focus their attention on their impulsivity and on the negative consequences of their actions. However, they can be made to realize that things are going poorly for them. Therapy requires firm structure and close supervision. Intense confrontation by peers, almost on a daily basis, has been recommended, especially for countering the persistent rationalization of irresponsibility and the manipulation of others. Understanding, sympathetic peers and self-help groups may be more effective than personal therapists, who are likely to trigger memories of harsh and untrustworthy parental figures.

The most effective treatment programs for psychopaths target specific features of their behavior, such as anger, aggressiveness, impulsivity, and substance abuse, while trying to enhance social skills, empathy, problem solving, and moral reasoning (Rice & Harris, 1997). Learning is facilitated when there are incentives such as money or other concrete and attractive reinforcers. Punishment by itself tends to be ineffective. It was previously believed that psychopaths do not learn from punishment, whereas it now appears that there is no general deficit in avoidance learning and that most punishments are simply not meaningful to them.

Bandura (1986) provided an intuitively appealing description of the circumstances that should be effective in reducing many antisocial behaviors. Reinforcements for antisocial behavior are withdrawn and punishments implemented. The clients are then exposed to individuals who model desirable behavior, and a system of rewards for such behavior is put in place. Finally, extrinsic rewards for desirable behavior are gradually withdrawn as the behavior becomes increasingly internalized and self-regulated. These procedures may be effective in reducing isolated antisocial behaviors, especially in youngsters, but little internalization may take place in adult psychopaths. They would likely just play along with the program while contemplating how to exploit the new arrangements.

Beck and Freeman (1990) described cognitive treatments for PDs, including APD. Social and moral behavior are improved by effecting changes in beliefs and cognitive function. Common, self-serving, dysfunctional beliefs include the belief that merely wanting something justifies one's actions, the belief that one always makes good choices, the belief that the views of others are irrelevant to one's decisions, and the belief that undesirable consequences will not occur. Psychopaths also tend to think of themselves as strong, independent loners who must look out for number one and manipulate others. Guided discussions, structured cognitive exercises, and behavioral experiments are used to identify flaws with these beliefs and to replace them with prosocial and adaptive beliefs. Cognitive therapy begins by targeting specific behaviors for change, and it focuses on automatic thoughts and underlying schemas when clients become more comfortable with self-disclosures. As the end of treatment approaches, the focus shifts to the pressures for antisocial behavior that clients should expect to face. Relapse prevention focuses on sensitizing clients to the people and situations that are potential triggers for antisocial behavior (Sperry, 1995). Although enthusiastic case studies suggest that cognitive therapy may be effective for APD, controlled experimental trials have not yet been conducted.

Pharmacotherapy

Numerous drugs have been suggested and tested in the treatment of antisocial behavior, but the findings are mixed, weak, and not encouraging (Karper & Krystal, 1997; Von Knorring & Ekselius, 1998). Stimulants can reduce cortical underarousal and sometimes alleviate specific behavioral symptoms, but they cannot be used for prolonged periods. Antianxiety medication is sometimes effective in reducing hostility. Drugs used to treat bipolar disorder, such as lithium and carbazemine, are sometimes effective in reducing aggressive-impulsive behavior in violent criminals, although the side effects are difficult to tolerate. Decreased serotonin function may play a role in impulsivity and aggression, as mentioned above. Therefore, some researchers believe that drugs that inhibit the reuptake of serotonin in the synapse (SSRIs), such as Prozac and Zoloft, could be effective in the management of disorders involving aggression and impulsivity. The SSRIs have relatively few side effects, are tolerated well by most patients, and they are not toxic in overdose. Their antidepressant effects generally take several weeks to commence, and it is not known if the time line for effects on impulsive or aggressive behaviors is different. Typical side effects include nausea, occasional diarrhea, insomnia, tremor, headache, and dizziness. However, these are generally mild and may desist after several weeks of treatment. The major problem is that none of these drugs has a substantial, enduring impact on APD as a whole, only on specific symptoms or behaviors. Other biological treatments, such as electroconvulsive therapy and psychosurgery, have not proven effective either.

MAINTENANCE OF GAINS/RELAPSE PREVENTION

The very modest effectiveness of treatment programs and the psychopath's resistance to change suggest that treatments, if they are to work at all, will take longer than treatments for other disorders. Periodic booster sessions are probably necessary to maintain gains. Compliance with therapeutic recommendations is likely to be low because psychopaths do not believe they have problems. They are likely to feel cynical and annoyed, and they will have high dropout rates. The mere suggestion that they seek help for personality problems may make them angry and resentful. If they do agree to counseling, employers should be wary of their expressed commitment and compliance. Commitment to treatment typically lasts only as long as external pressure for treatment is exerted. Furthermore, behavioral changes are often temporary. Change may occur only as long as the client is confined and closely supervised, and the changes may not generalize to other settings.

The fact that psychopathy may be an evolutionarily stable strategy does not mean that psychopaths are programmed like robots to always be antisocial. Remorseless exploitation of others is merely a viable option when opportunities arise or when they can be created. Thus, the manifestation of psychopathic behavior perhaps can be reduced by the removal or reduction of such opportunities. According to Mealey (1995), "to reduce antisocial behavior, a society must establish and enforce a reputation for high rates of detection of deception and identification of cheaters, and a willingness to retaliate" (p. 537).

Recent research on antisocial behavior in organizations, although not focusing on APD per se, has revealed that such behaviors are less common when (a) employers treat employees with dignity and respect, pay them fairly, and model integrity; (b) there is a formal antitheft policy that is known to employees; (c) employers have a known record of punishing antisocial behavior; (d) group norms are such that there is a perceived threat of sanctions from coworkers for antisocial behaviors; and (e) security measures (such as guards and cameras) are in place to monitor problem behavior (Boye & Jones, 1997). The controls required to identify and snuff out antisocial behavior resemble those of a police state. The controls may be insulting to the much larger number of non-APD employees, and they may stifle creativity, initiative, and commitment to the organization. Nevertheless, the potential damage caused by workers with APD is considerable, and employers must somehow try to strike the right balance and hope for the best.

SUMMARY

APD is "a pervasive pattern of disregard for, and violation of, the rights of others that begins in childhood or early adolescence and continues into adulthood" (APA, 1994, p. 629). In the workplace, APD may give rise to blackmail, bribery, discrimination, espionage, extortion, fraud, violence, kickbacks, lawsuits, lying, sabotage, sexual harassment, theft, and violations of confidentiality. APD occurs in 1% to 3% of the population, and it is more common among males and criminal offenders. The official diagnostic criteria for APD are largely behavioral. However, the predominant focus of research and clinical work has been on the closely related, broader construct of psychopathy, which incorporates additional, distinctive emotional and interpersonal characteristics of the disorder and for which reliable and valid assessment procedures are available. A model of the prototypical manifestation of APD in the workplace was presented, along with a case illustration. There are no precipitating conditions for APD in the immediate environment, although certain enduring biological, neuropsychological, and psychosocial factors have been noted. APD begins early in life and has a chronic course and poor prognosis. Psychological and pharmacological treatments generally are not effective. Workplace environments that discourage antisocial behavior can be designed, but these environments may insult and frustrate nonpsychopathic employees. Employers caught with a psychopath in their midst should consult with their legal and accounting departments.

REFERENCES

American Psychiatric Association. (1994). *Diagnostic and statistical manual of mental disorders* (4th ed.). Washington, DC: Author.

Babiak, P. (1995a). Psychopathic manipulation in organizations: Pawns, patrons, and patsies. *Issues in Criminological and Legal Psychology, 24,* 12-17.

Babiak, P. (1995b). When psychopaths go to work: A case study of an industrial psychopath. *Applied Psychology: An International Review, 44,* 171-188.

Babiak, P. (2000). Psychopathic manipulation at work. In C. B. Gacono (Ed.), *The clinical and forensic assessment of psychopathy: A practitioner's guide* (pp. 287-311). Mahwah, NJ: Lawrence Erlbaum.

Bandura, A. (1986). *Social foundations of thought and action: A social cognitive theory.* Englewood Cliffs, NJ: Prentice Hall.

Beck, A. T., & Freeman, A. (1990). *Cognitive therapy of personality disorders.* New York: Guilford.

Berman, M. E., Kavoussi, R. J., & Coccaro, E. F. (1997). Neurotransmitter correlates of human aggression. In D. M. Stoff, J. Breiling, & J. D. Maser (Eds.), *Handbook of antisocial behavior* (pp. 305-315). New York: Wiley.

Blackburn, R., & Fawcett, D. (1999). The antisocial personality questionnaire: An inventory for assessing personality deviation in offender populations. *European Journal of Psychological Assessment, 15,* 14-24.

Boye, M. W., & Jones, J. W. (1997). Organizational culture and employee counterproductivity. In R. A. Giacalone & J. Greenberg (Eds.), *Antisocial behavior in organizations* (pp. 172-184). Thousand Oaks, CA: Sage.

Brain, P. F., & Susman, E. J. (1997). Hormonal aspects of aggression and violence. In D. M. Stoff, J. Breiling, & J. D. Maser (Eds.), *Handbook of antisocial behavior* (pp. 314-323). New York: Wiley.

Carey, G., & Goldman, D. (1997). The genetics of antisocial behavior. In D. M. Stoff, J. Breiling, & J. D. Maser (Eds.), *Handbook of antisocial behavior* (pp. 243-253). New York: Wiley.

Cleckley, H. (1976). *The mask of sanity* (5th ed.). St. Louis, MO: Mosby.

Cloninger, C. R., Bayon, C., & Przybeck, T. R. (1997). Epidemiology and Axis I comorbidity of antisocial personality. In D. M. Stoff, J. Breiling, & J. D. Maser (Eds.), *Handbook of antisocial behavior* (pp. 12-21). New York: Wiley.

Coccaro, E. F., Kavoussi, R. J., & McNamee, B. (2000). Central neurotransmitter function in criminal aggression. In D. H. Fishbein (Ed.), *The science, treatment, and prevention of antisocial behaviors* (pp. 6-16). Kingston, NJ: Civic Research Institute.

Cooke, D. J. (1998). Cross-cultural' aspects of psychopathy. In T. Millon, E. Simonsen, M. Birket-Smith, & R. D. Davis (Eds.), *Psychopathy: Antisocial, criminal, and violent behavior* (pp. 260-276). New York: Guilford.

Dahl, A. A. (1998). Psychopathy and psychiatric comorbidity. In T. Millon, E. Simonsen, M. Birket-Smith, & R. D. Davis (Eds.), *Psychopathy: Antisocial, criminal, and violent behavior* (pp. 291-303). New York: Guilford.

Fishbein, D. H. (Ed.). (2000). *The science, treatment, and prevention of antisocial behaviors.* Kingston, NJ: Civic Research Institute.

Gacono, C. B. (2000). *The clinical and forensic assessment of psychopathy: A practitioner's guide.* Mahwah, NJ: Lawrence Erlbaum.

Giacalone, R. A., & Greenberg, J. (Eds.). (1997). *Antisocial behavior in organizations.* Thousand Oaks, CA: Sage.

Giancola, P. R. (2000). Neurological functioning and antisocial behavior— Implications for etiology and prevention. In D. H. Fishbein (Ed.), *The science, treatment, and prevention of antisocial behaviors.* Kingston, NJ: Civic Research Institute.

Hare, R. D. (1991). *Manual for the Hare Psychopathy Checklist—Revised.* Toronto, ON: Multi-Health Systems.

Hare, R. D. (1998). Psychopaths and their nature: Implications for the mental health and criminal justice systems. In T. Millon, E. Simonsen, M. Birket-Smith, & R. D. Davis (Eds.), *Psychopathy: Antisocial, criminal, and violent behavior* (pp. 188-212). New York: Guilford.

Hare, R. D. (1999). *Without conscience: The disturbing world of the psychopaths among us.* New York: Guilford.

Hare, R. D., & Hervé, H. (1999). *The Hare P-Scan.* Toronto, ON: Multi-Health Systems.

Harris, G. T., Rice, M. E., & Quinsey, V. L. (1994). Psychopathy as a taxon: Evidence that psychopaths are a discrete class. *Journal of Consulting and Clinical Psychology, 62,* 387-397.

Hart, S. D., Cox, D. N., & Hare, R. D. (1995). *Manual for the screening version of the Hare Psychopathy Checklist—Revised (PCL-R:SV).* Toronto, ON: Multi-Health Systems.

Hart, S. D., & Hare, R. D. (1997). Psychopathy: Assessment and association with criminal conduct. In D. M. Stoff, J. Breiling, & J. D. Maser (Eds.), *Handbook of antisocial behavior* (pp. 22-35). New York: Wiley.

Hogan, J., & Hogan, R. (1989). How to measure employee unreliability. *Journal of Applied Psychology, 74,* 273-279.

Karper, L. P., & Krystal, J. H. (1997). Pharmacotherapy for violent behavior. In D. M. Stoff, J. Breiling, & J. D. Maser (Eds.), *Handbook of antisocial behavior* (pp. 436-444). New York: Wiley.

Kessler, R. C., McGonagle, K. A., Zhao, S., Nelson, C. B., Hughes, M., Eshleman, S., Wittchen, H., & Kendler, K. (1994). Lifetime and 12-month prevalence of

DSM-III-R psychiatric disorders in the United States: Results from the National Comorbidity Study. *Archives of General Psychiatry, 51,* 8-19.

Lilienfeld, S. O., & Andrews, B. P. (1996). Development and preliminary validation of a self-report measure of psychopathic personality traits in noncriminal populations. *Journal of Personality Assessment, 66,* 488-524.

Lilienfeld, S. O., Purcell, C., & Jones-Alexander, J. (1997). Assessment of antisocial behavior in adults. In D. M. Stoff, J. Breiling, & J. D. Maser (Eds.), *Handbook of antisocial behavior* (pp. 60-74). New York: Wiley.

Loeber, R., & Farrington, D. P. (1997). Strategies and yields of longitudinal studies on antisocial behavior. In D. M. Stoff, J. Breiling, & J. D. Maser (Eds.), *Handbook of antisocial behavior* (pp. 125-139). New York: Wiley.

Lynam, D. R. (1996). Early identification of chronic offenders: Who is the fledgling psychopath? *Psychological Bulletin, 120,* 209-234.

McGuffin, P., & Thapar, A. (1998). Genetics and antisocial personality disorder. In T. Millon, E. Simonsen, M. Birket-Smith, & R. D. Davis (Eds.), *Psychopathy: Antisocial, criminal, and violent behavior* (pp. 215-230). New York: Guilford.

Mealey, L. (1995). The sociobiology of sociopathy: An integrated evolutionary model. *Behavioral and Brain Sciences, 18,* 523-599.

Millon, T., Simonsen, E., Birket-Smith, M., & Davis, R. D. (1998). *Psychopathy: Antisocial, criminal, and violent behavior.* New York: Guilford.

Moffitt, T. E. (1993). Adolescence-limited and life-course-persistent antisocial behavior: A developmental taxonomy. *Psychological Review, 100,* 674-701.

O'Connor, B. P., & Dyce, J. A. (2001). Personality disorders. In M. Hersen & V. B. Van Hasselt (Eds.), *Advanced abnormal psychology* (pp. 399-417). New York: Kluwer Academic/Plenum.

Ogloff, J., Wong, S., & Greenwood, A. (1990). Treating criminal psychopaths in a therapeutic community program. *Behavioral Sciences and the Law, 8,* 81-90.

Ones, D. S., & Viswesvaran, C. (1998). Integrity testing in organizations. In R. W. Griffin, A. O'Leary-Kelly, & J. M. Collins (Eds.), *Dysfunctional behavior in organizations: Non-violent dysfunctional behavior* (pp. 243-276). Stamford, CT: JAI.

Pajer, K. A. (1998). What happens to "bad" girls? A review of the adult outcomes of antisocial adolescent girls. *American Journal of Psychiatry, 155,* 862-870.

Raine, A. (1997). Antisocial behavior and psychophysiology: A biosocial perspective and a prefrontal dysfunction hypothesis. In D. M. Stoff, J. Breiling, & J. D. Maser (Eds.), *Handbook of antisocial behavior* (pp. 289-304). New York: Wiley.

Rice, M. E., & Harris, G. T. (1997). The treatment of adult offenders. In D. M. Stoff, J. Breiling, & J. D. Maser (Eds.), *Handbook of antisocial behavior* (pp. 425-435). New York: Wiley.

Robins, L. N., & Regier, D. (1991). *Psychiatric disorders in America: The Epidemiologic Catchment Area study.* New York: Free Press.

Shaw, D. S., & Winslow, E. B. (1997). Precursors and correlates of antisocial behavior from infancy to preschool. In D. M. Stoff, J. Breiling, & J. D. Maser (Eds.), *Handbook of antisocial behavior* (pp. 148-158). New York: Wiley.

Siever, L. J. (1998). Neurobiology in psychopathy. In T. Millon, E. Simonsen, M. Birket-Smith, & R. D. Davis (Eds.), *Psychopathy: Antisocial, criminal, and violent behavior* (pp. 231-246). New York: Guilford.

Sperry, L. (1995). *Handbook of diagnosis and treatment of the* DSM-IV *personality disorders.* New York: Brunner/Mazel.

Stoff, D. M., Breiling, J., & Maser, J. D. (1997). *Handbook of antisocial behavior.* New York: Wiley.

Thornberry, T. P., & Krohn, M. D. (1997). Peers, drug use, and delinquency. In D. M. Stoff, J. Breiling, & J. D. Maser (Eds.), *Handbook of antisocial behavior* (pp. 218-233). New York: Wiley.

Van Velzen, C. J. M., & Emmelkamp, P. M. G. (1996). The assessment of personality disorders: Implications for cognitive and behavior therapy. *Behavior Research and Therapy, 34,* 655-668.

Von Knorring, L., & Ekselius, L. (1998). Psychopharmacological treatment and impulsivity. In T. Millon, E. Simonsen, M. Birket-Smith, & R. D. Davis (Eds.), *Psychopathy: Antisocial, criminal, and violent behavior* (pp. 359-371). New York: Guilford.

Widiger, T. A., & Sanderson, C. J. (1997). Personality disorders. In A. Tasman, J. Kay, & J. A. Lieberman (Eds.), *Psychiatry* (Vol. 2, pp. 1291-1317). Philadelphia: W. B. Saunders.

Widom, C. S. (1997). Child abuse, neglect, and witnessing violence. In D. M. Stoff, J. Breiling, & J. D. Maser (Eds.), *Handbook of antisocial behavior* (pp. 159-170). New York: Wiley.

CHAPTER 14

Borderline Personality Disorder

Brian C. Goff

DESCRIPTION OF THE DISORDER

Borderline personality disorder (BPD) is an Axis II personality disorder characterized by a pervasive inability to regulate emotions as well as behaviors associated with those emotions. The *DSM-IV* (American Psychiatric Association [APA], 1994) describes BPD as "a pervasive pattern of instability of interpersonal relationships, self-image, and affects, and marked impulsivity beginning by early adulthood and present in a variety of contexts"(p. 654). Five of nine diagnostic criteria must be met in order for a person to be diagnosed with the disorder:

1. Frantic attempts to avoid real or imagined abandonment

2. Unstable and intense relationships alternating between idealization and devaluation

3. Markedly unstable self-image or sense of self (e.g., feeling like one embodies evil or does not exist)

4. Potentially self-damaging impulsive behavior in at least two areas, such as binge eating, sex, drinking, or spending

5. Suicidal or parasuicidal (i.e., self-mutilating) behavior

6. Affective instability and reactivity of mood lasting a few hours to a few days

7. Chronic feelings of emptiness

8. Inappropriate and uncontrollable anger (subjectively experienced or outbursts)

9. Transient, stress-related paranoid ideation or dissociative symptoms

Linehan (1993a, chap. 1) reorganized the *DSM-IV* diagnostic criteria into five spheres of dysregulation. The first and primary sphere is emotion dysregulation. Borderline individuals tend to be emotionally labile and experience episodic depression, anxiety, and anger. The experience of anxiety and sadness is quite intense, even for those without comorbid anxiety or mood disorders (Comtois, Cowley, Dunner, & Roy-Byrne, 1999). Linehan (1993a) has likened the individual with BPD to an individual with third-degree burns covering his or her body. Analogous to the burn victim's experience of physical pain, the borderline individual's experience of emotional pain is characterized by extreme sensitivity to stimuli, intense reactions, and a slow return to baseline mood.

The second sphere, behavioral dysregulation, involves extreme and problematic impulsive behavior. Examples of behavioral dyscontrol include binge eating, substance abuse, impulsive spending, parasuicidal behavior (i.e., deliberate self-harm without the intent to die), and suicidal behavior. These behaviors typically function to regulate or cope with intense emotion, but generate chaos and ultimately more pain. Although all of these behaviors are self-damaging, occurrence of parasuicidal and suicidal behavior is most alarming and life threatening. Severity of parasuicidal behavior ranges from minor self-harm (e.g., superficial scratches) to accidental death. Cutting is the most common parasuicidal behavior. Other methods include burning, head banging, hitting oneself with a hammer or similar object, and ingesting harmful objects such as glass or pins. Parasuicide is a hallmark of BPD in that no other *DSM-IV* disorder lists it among the diagnostic criteria. Nearly 75% of borderline individuals engage in parasuicidal behavior (Clarkin, Widiger, Frances, Hurt, & Gilmore, 1983; Cowdry, Pickar, & Davies, 1985). Borderline individuals also engage in self-harm behavior with the intent to die. BPD is associated more closely with attempted and completed suicide than with any other mental disorder. Nearly 10% of all individuals diagnosed with BPD die by suicide (Frances, Fyer, & Clarkin, 1986). Rates of suicide and parasuicide in BPD decrease with age, with the highest risk period in young adulthood (Linehan, 1993a).

The third sphere, interpersonal dysregulation, encompasses a number of dysfunctional relationship patterns. Borderline individuals often have chaotic and conflictual relationships. Their assessment of others tends to swing from idealization to devaluation. Even with the most conflicted relationships, they are highly sensitive to criticism and fear rejection. To allay this fear, they may engage in extreme efforts to avoid abandonment.

The fourth sphere, cognitive dysregulation, is marked by dichotomous ("all-or-nothing") thinking and cognitive rigidity. In states of intense emotion, concentration and problem solving may be severely impaired. Paranoid ideation and dissociative behavior, ranging from trancelike states to complete dissociation, are also common in this sphere of dysregulation.

The fifth sphere, self dysregulation, refers to identity instability and chronic feelings of emptiness. Individuals with BPD frequently report not knowing who they are or what they want. They commonly follow the lead of those around them and judge the validity of their own opinions and perceptions on the basis of reaction of others. Thus, their identity is so context specific that they have no stable sense of self.

EPIDEMIOLOGY

The prevalence rate of BPD is about 2% in the general population and about 10% in psychiatric outpatient populations (Widiger & Frances, 1989; Widiger & Weissman, 1991). In inpatient settings, prevalence rates jump to about 20% (Kroll, Sines, & Martin, 1981). Fifty percent of personality-disordered inpatients are diagnosed with BPD (Widiger & Weissman, 1991).

The most robust demographic feature of individuals with BPD is gender. Nearly 75% of individuals diagnosed with BPD are women (Swartz, Blazer, George, & Winfield, 1990; Widiger & Frances, 1989). Age is consistently negatively associated with greater prevalence and severity of BPD (Akhtar, Byrne, & Doghramji, 1986; Paris, Brown, & Nowlis, 1987; Swartz et al., 1990). BPD is seen more commonly among Caucasians (Akhtar et al., 1986; Linehan, Kanter, & Comtois, 1999). Findings as to socioeconomic status are mixed; some showed BPD associated with lower SES (Swartz et al., 1990), whereas others found BPD to be associated with higher SES and advanced education (Taub, 1996).

Comorbidity of Axis I disorders with BPD is high. Individuals with BPD are commonly diagnosed with major depressive disorder, bipolar disorder, anxiety disorders (especially posttraumatic stress disorder), substance abuse disorders, and bulimia (see Linehan et al., 1999, for a review). Gender-specific patterns of comorbidity have been found, with males tending to show higher rates of comorbid substance-related disorders and females tending to show higher rates of eating disorders (Zanarini et al., 1998a). Complexity is the most notable feature of the Axis I diagnostic picture for individuals with BPD. In discriminating borderline individuals from those with other personality disorders, a complex pattern of comorbidity has been shown to have both predictive power (i.e., sensitivity) and discriminant power (i.e., specificity) (Zanarini, Gunderson, & Frankenburg, 1989). Zimmerman and Mattia (1999) found that approximately 70% of their BPD sample received a diagnosis of three or more current Axis I disorders, and nearly 50% were diagnosed with four or more current Axis I disorders.

Zanarini et al. (1998b) compared borderline individuals and other personality-disordered individuals on their rates of comorbid Axis II pathology. Rates of paranoid, avoidant, and dependent personality disorders were considerably higher among those with BPD than among those with other Axis II disorders. In contrast, Becker and colleagues (Becker, Grilo, Edell, & McGlashan, 2000) found that only other cluster-B personality disorders (histrionic PD and narcissistic PD) were significantly comorbid with BPD.

In summary, the prototypic borderline personality-disordered individual would be a young Caucasian woman with a history of psychiatric hospitalization. She would be diagnosed with at least three Axis I disorders, one of which would be a mood disorder or anxiety disorder. She would also present with characteristics of other personality disorders in addition to BPD.

ASSESSMENT

The diagnostic assessment of BPD is complicated by a number of factors. First, without longitudinal observation, the data available to the diagnostician come through two primary sources—snapshot observation and self-report information. Unfortunately, at-the-moment data available to an observer may not be characteristic of the individual's behavior and/or affect. Likewise, self-report data may be unreliable due to the reporter's memory and interpretation of his or her own behavior and affect state. Furthermore, a cross-sectional sample of BPD-related behavior may be difficult to distinguish from various Axis I syndromes (Skodol & Oldham, 1991). It is recommended that, whenever possible, diagnoses be based on longitudinal observation; unfortunately, such data are usually hard to obtain.

High rates of comorbidity also complicate the diagnostic picture. Typically, borderline individuals carry a cluster of comorbid disorders, all with unique characteristics (Zimmerman & Mattia, 1999). The relationship of comorbid Axis I disorders to BPD is varied, ranging from emotion-regulating behavior (e.g., alcohol abuse), to consequence (e.g., a depressive episode secondary to relationship turmoil), to an overlap of criterion sets (e.g., dysthymia). Thus, it is important to assess both presence and possible function of behaviors corresponding to comorbid conditions.

Another complication arises from the diagnostic criteria for BPD itself. The number of *DSM-IV* criteria for BPD (9) is almost double the minimum number required for the diagnosis (5), allowing for numerous behavioral presentations of the disorder. Therefore, a diagnostically homogeneous group of individuals could be behaviorally heterogeneous (Comtois, Levensky, & Linehan, 1999). This fact restricts the assumptions that can be drawn about an individual when all that is known is that the person carries a diagnosis of BPD. For an assessment to be useful, it should be behaviorally (i.e., phenomenologically) focused as well as categorically (i.e., diagnostically) focused.

Information germane to assessment clarity should be gathered from a number of sources, including the individual, his or her prior psychiatric records, concurrent providers, and significant others. Information can be gathered in an unstructured or semistructured format (e.g., PAS) (Tyrer, 1988). Collateral sources provide essential data regarding the chronicity and pervasiveness of problem behaviors.

Research supports the use of self-report inventories such as PDQ-R (Hyler, Oldham, Kellman, & Doidge, 1992) and PIQ II (Widiger, 1987) as diagnostic screening tools for BPD (e.g., Patrick, Links, van Reekum, & Mitton, 1995). Those endorsing BPD symptomatology on a self-report screening can be assessed more thoroughly using one of a number of semistructured interviews developed to assess personality disorders, such as DIB-R (Zanarini,

Gunderson, Frankenburg, & Chauncey, 1989), IPDE (Loranger, 1995), or SCID-II (First, Spitzer, Gibbons, Williams, & Benjamin, 1996). Assessment of comorbid Axis I conditions can be accomplished through a clinical interview following the *DSM-IV* (APA, 1994) or a semistructured interview such as the SCID (First, Spitzer, Gibbons, & Williams, 1995) or the CIDI (Wittchen, Kessler, Zhao, & Abelson, 1995), the latter of which requires little training to administer.

Behavioral observation can provide insight into the individual's cognitive style (e.g., dichotomous thinking, rigidity, self invalidation); sensitivity; and reactivity of affect, judgment, and insight. However, individuals with BPD may experience greater psychiatric disturbance than is evident in their behavioral presentation (Edell, Joy, & Yehuda, 1990). Therefore, it is useful to inquire beyond clinical observation and diagnostic assessment by gathering information concerning concomitant problems such as disruptive affective states (e.g., Brief Symptom Inventory) (Derogatis & Spencer, 1982), maladaptive cognitive patterns, and interpersonal and occupational functioning (e.g., Outcome Questionnaire – 45) (Lambert & Hill, 1994). It is also essential to take a detailed relationship history and assess for identity instability.

Given the relationship between BPD and suicidal behavior, it is imperative to take a thorough history of all prior suicidal and parasuicidal behaviors—including detailed contextual information and a detailed history of related hospitalizations—in order to assess short- and long-term risk. Included in this assessment is an inquiry into suicide-related behavior, such as suicidal ideation; communications of suicidality; expectancies and beliefs regarding suicide; and suicide-related affect (e.g., apathy, depression) and cognition (e.g., hopelessness). A detailed discussion of risk assessment for suicide is beyond the scope of this chapter. See Bongar (1992) for a thorough discussion of suicide risk factors, and Davis, Gunderson, and Myers (1999) for a discussion of suicide risk factors in chronically suicidal borderline individuals.

CLINICAL PICTURE
CASE DESCRIPTION

Amy[1,2] is a single, 32-year-old Caucasian female. She experiences her emotional world as a roller coaster, sometimes running smoothly and sometimes thrashing her about. Amy often feels "hijacked" by her emotions, feeling as though she is "along for the ride" wherever her emotions take her. Her most troubling emotions are sadness, anxiety, and shame. She has struggled with depression since her teenage years and is now typically melancholic. Superimposed on her melancholy are brief bouts of "paralyzing" depression, sometimes relegating her to bed for days. She is troubled by attacks of anxiety during which she cannot sleep, feels sick to her stomach, and becomes immobilized by her worries and second guessing. She regularly doubts her emotional reaction to situations and her interpretations of events, frequently questioning whether she is thinking and feeling "the right way." When criticized, she is initially angry, but her anger is quickly replaced by shame concerning the focus of criticism. She is hesitant to state preferences or offer opinions without first feeling that they will be well received.

In the face of intense distress, Amy finds relief by cutting herself. Amy does not remember ever reading about or being exposed to self-harm. At age 16, following a fight with her mother, Amy felt an urge to cut herself while shaving. She pressed down on the safety razor, slid it sideways along her thigh, and felt a sense of emotional relief. Since then, the frequency of her cutting has vacillated over the years, ranging from monthly to several times a week. For Amy, antecedents to cutting involve high levels of agitation or self-loathing, and cutting brings a sense of calm or emotional relief. She typically uses razor blades and cuts on her upper thigh in order to conceal scars. Her wounds usually require nothing more than adhesive bandages or gauze and tape; however, she has cut deeper because "the superficial cuts weren't enough" and has required stitches.

Amy has a history of multiple suicide attempts. She was 19 and a sophomore in college at the time of her first suicide attempt. She ingested 25 pills of her antidepressant medication following a fight with her boyfriend. She took the pills and then told her roommate, who drove her to a local hospital where she was admitted and stayed for 4 days. Since that time, she has made six other suicide attempts (all by overdose), ranging in lethality from requiring no medical intervention to being in intensive care for 3 days. She has been hospitalized five times following suicide attempts. Her most recent attempt was 3 months ago following an argument with her boyfriend in which he was talking about ending the relationship. She was alone in her apartment when she ingested a bottle of over-the-counter sleeping pills with a bottle of wine. Her boyfriend, feeling unsettled about how their phone conversation had ended, tried to call her back later that evening. When she did not answer, he drove over to her apartment and found her unconscious. She was medically treated in intensive care for a day and then transferred to inpatient psychiatry for 6 days.

History

Amy's biological parents are divorced and live in the same city in which she resides.

She maintains amicable but emotionally distant relationships with them and her two older sisters. She gives a history of an uneventful childhood up until age 14, when her parents divorced. Amy attempted to play the role of peacemaker between her parents and felt a sense of responsibility for her parents' divorce despite their efforts to explain otherwise. She lived with both of her parents alternately until age 18, when she left for college.

During Amy's teenage years, her mother was quite depressed and became competitive about the amount of time Amy spent with her as compared with her ex-husband. She accused Amy frequently of loving her father more than her. Although merely executing the joint custody arrangement, Amy's mother would accuse Amy of being selfish, saying "I wouldn't be so depressed if I had you all to myself." Amy felt that she could not keep both of her parents happy and yet needed to try.

During her grade school years, Amy's academic performance was unremarkable. By early high school, she began to struggle under the stress of her parents' divorce. Her father told her frequently that she was smarter than her grades reflected, and that if she "wanted to amount to anything," she had to do better. Amy began to fear tests and dislike school, yet was always clear in her own mind that she would go to college because it was expected of her. As her school performance declined, Amy became less social and had few friends. Her friendships and relationships with boyfriends were intense and short-lived, often "burning them out" with her problems. After graduation, Amy went to community college for 2 years and transferred to a nursing program, where she received her degree.

At the time of her parents' divorce, Amy went to counseling briefly because of her poor academic performance. She was diagnosed with clinical depression and prescribed an antidepressant, which she interpreted as additional evidence that she was the problem in the family. After a brief time, she terminated therapy, believing the therapist did not understand. She continued on her antidepressant medication under the management of her primary care physician. Amy did not see another therapist until her senior year in high school, when her mother noticed a recent cut on her leg that Amy could not convincingly explain away as she had on a few occasions over the prior year. Grudgingly, she saw a therapist and was diagnosed with major depression and generalized anxiety disorder. She terminated prematurely with this therapist because Amy felt that the therapy was a "waste of time." Amy had little interest in speaking to therapists because, in her mind, they could not make her a better person and so could not help. In all, Amy has worked with four therapists, none of whom she believes helped.

Apart from those who initiate contact with her, Amy rarely socializes, believing that she will ultimately be rejected once people get to know her. With the few friends she has, she subordinates her own desires and opinions and follows their lead as to activities. When a relationship becomes conflicted, Amy will often "sense" that rejection and abandonment are inevitable and opt to end that relationship. Amy's problems with emotion regulation negatively affect her relationships with others. She has difficulty regulating her emotional intensity, identifying her own feelings accurately, and interpreting nonverbal expressions of emotions in others (problems common to individuals with BPD) (Levine, Marziali, & Hood, 1997). Each of these difficulties impairs Amy's interpersonal functioning in kind.

She has been in an intimate relationship with a man for about 4 months that she describes as "shaky." They have nearly broken up three times; she feels the future of the relationship is tenuous. She complains that he is emotionally distant and minimizes her emotions. At times, he becomes frustrated by what he sees as her "neediness" and pulls away. She subsequently worries that he is going to abandon her, apologizes for being "needy," and invalidates her own emotions. Her self-harm behavior is disturbing to him as well, but he believes that this behavior is rare because she keeps her self-harm hidden from him unless it requires medical attention, and then he ends up noticing. Of her self-harm, he has commented to her, "I don't understand why you don't just stop doing it. It doesn't make any sense."

Employment

Amy is currently employed as a nurse in a nursing home facility. She has worked at her current facility for 9 months and in the nursing field for 5 years. This is her fourth placement in 5 years. With each of her prior employers, she began the job with a sense of having a fresh start (and of "waiting for the other shoe to drop"). Inevitably, some kind of interpersonal tension developed that would "swing" her perception of the person involved and, ultimately, her perception of the place of employment. She began to simultaneously devalue her job site and fear that they were losing favor with her, and she began to fear being fired. In combination with outside stressors, Amy's fear of being fired, her dread of interpersonal tension (secondary to impaired interpersonal problem-solving skills), and her polarized negative feelings about her workplace led to exacerbations in parasuicidal behavior, frequent absenteeism due to "paralyzing" anxiety, and increased suicidal behavior. At two of her jobs, she went on medical leave secondary to psychiatric hospitalizations for suicide attempts. With all three of her prior jobs, she exhausted all her vacation days and sick days on missing work due to emotional lability. She was fired from two of her jobs for missing work too frequently; the other job she quit, believing she would inevitably be fired for the same reason.

In her current position, her supervisor evaluates her work as typically above average. Notably, Amy is seen as conscientious, skilled at forming good rapport with patients, and technically skilled. When there are criticisms in her review, she feels her supervisor has glimpsed her "true nature" and has seen that she is not good enough. Although achievement is important to Amy, the imagined interpersonal consequences of failure (e.g., rejection by others, being seen as a failure) are most disconcerting to her. Amy's supervisor also notes that she has frequently called in to work "too upset to come in."

Amy's mood at work is unpredictable, making it difficult for coworkers to know what to expect from her in terms of her affect and level of performance. At times, it seems to other staff that Amy is "somewhere else" and has difficulty concentrating. Sometimes, she misunderstands that a particular task is her responsibility. On other occasions, she will work much slower than usual and appear as though "in a fog."

Amy's supervisor has received comments from coworkers that they feel they "walk on eggshells" around Amy. They perceive her as "hypersensitive," insecure, and unstable (Carroll, Hoenigmann-Stovall, King, Wienhold, & Whitehead, 1998). They feel that she reacts to criticism or joking around too seriously and becomes either defensive or ashamed; consequently, most are careful not to joke around with Amy (Bond, Paris, & Zweig-Frank, 1994). Amy ends up oscillating between feeling "picked on" and "left out."

In the first 6 months of working at the nursing home, Amy missed a week of work secondary to a psychiatric hospitalization after a suicide attempt. Upon return, her coworkers' sense of needing to walk on eggshells increased as curiosity spread about Amy's "breakdown." Although no one knew details or even about the suicide attempt, Amy feared that somehow everyone knew. Not wanting to be treated like a mental patient, she did not confide in anyone at work about what had happened. She is uncomfortable about her supervisor, the human resource department, knowing about her psychiatric problems and feels that if they knew "all of it," they would fire her. As it is, she believes that her "mental patient behavior" has given management ample reason to want to get rid of her.

Despite her problems at work, Amy enjoys being a nurse. When she is performing well at work, her feelings of worthlessness temporarily remit. Although she has overdosed on her own prescribed medication, she has never abused or taken medications accessible to her through her work duties because she opines that would violate a trust the nursing home has placed in her.

PRECIPITATING CONDITIONS

Biosocial Model of BPD

Linehan (1993a, chap. 2) has posited a biosocial model of borderline personality disorder. This model suggests that BPD develops out of the transaction between an emotionally dysregulated individual and what is termed an "invalidating environment." An emotionally dysregulated individual is one whose autonomic nervous system reacts intensely to relatively low levels of stress and is slow to return to baseline. Furthermore, the emotionally

dysregulated individual has impaired emotion modulation abilities; these include the ability to inhibit inappropriate reactions to strong affect, regulate physiological arousal associated with affect, sustain attention in the presence of strong affect, and work toward non-mood-dependent goals (Gottman & Katz, 1990). Emotion dysregulation is theorized to be biologically based and may be due to factors such as genetics, intrauterine abnormalities, or early childhood trauma that leaves biological marks (Figueroa & Silk, 1997).

An invalidating environment, postulated to be the contributing environmental factor, is described as one that trivializes, ignores, or punishes the individual's private experiences (i.e., thoughts, feelings, and perceptions of events). This invalidation communicates to the individual that his or her private experiences are incorrect, inappropriate, and unimportant. Invalidation occurs on a continuum from well-intentioned statements that are experienced as invalidating (e.g., "Why are you so upset?" "It's not that bad.") to physical and sexual abuse. Invalidating environments tend to oversimplify the ease with which problems are solved, so that when an individual encounters obstacles to achieving desired ends, he or she is, in essence, told to "just do it." Thus, the individual never learns to tolerate distress and solve difficulties. Over time, the individual learns to self-invalidate and trust others' reactions to them as indications of how to think and feel.

Individual and environmental conditions are hypothesized to continually influence and transform one another, over time, resulting in the individual becoming more emotionally reactive and behaviorally dysregulated, and the environment becoming more invalidating. For instance, an individual with extreme emotional vulnerability is likely to draw out more and more invalidating behavior from his or her environment. Approached another way, it may be that extreme levels of either contributing factor may offset lower levels in the other factor. For example, an individual raised in a severely invalidating environment may only need initially mild levels of emotion vulnerability to manifest borderline behavior patterns. In brief, the two factors are both influential on the other and compensatory for the other.

Exacerbating Conditions

Within the framework of BPD, a chronic and pervasive disorder, precipitating conditions refer to conditions that tend to exacerbate symptomatology, such as extreme emotional displays, impulsive behaviors, dissociative behavior, and parasuicidal behavior. Creating an inventory of common precipitating conditions for emotional intensity and related problematic behavior in borderline individuals is difficult for a variety of reasons. Given the borderline individual's emotional sensitivity and reactivity, he or she is more likely to respond to minor stressors than are other people, and is likely to have more extreme responses. Furthermore, the specific natures of antecedents that increase symptomatology are idiosyncratic from person to person; what one individual reacts to, another may not. Additionally, the context in which stressors occur requires (yet rarely receives) as much attention as the stressor itself. This means that a stressor that seriously affects an individual at one point in time may not at another because of an altered context. One such contextual domain is health; poor diet, use of mood-altering drugs, and sleep disturbances (to name a few health-related factors) moderate the impact of stress on the individual.

Despite these difficulties, one loosely generalizable precipitating condition that applies to borderline individuals is the impact of interpersonal problems (e.g., Figueroa & Silk, 1997; Labonte & Paris, 1993; Whewell, Ryman, Bonanno, & Heather, 2000). Two of the nine *DSM-IV* (APA, 1994) criteria for BPD are interpersonally oriented. Common problematic interpersonal themes include rejection, abandonment, criticism, and messages of invalidation. Many borderline individuals are especially sensitive to achievement-oriented events, such as failed expectations, poor performance reviews, and criticism of work product. These events can cut to the heart of core beliefs of worthlessness just as interpersonal events can resonate with core beliefs of unlovability. Whereas some may experience these achievement-oriented events as such, others may experience the sting of these events through interpersonal pathways. For example, the more serious impact of being demoted at work may be the impression it gives to others. Because interpersonal sequelae can arise from both achievement and interpersonal events (whereas achievement sequelae are typically limited to achievement events), those who are significantly vulnerable to interpersonal events (like individuals with BPD) are doubly vulnerable to negative events (Goff, 1998).

COURSE AND PROGNOSIS

Borderline personality disorder emerges in the late teens and early 20s. It is a chronic disorder, presenting symptoms for many years. Chronicity studies (e.g., Links, Heslegrave, & van Reekum, 1998) suggest diagnostic stability rates of between 50% and 70% at 7 years' follow-up, with the higher stability rates belonging to the most severe. Level of functioning remains relatively stable as well (e.g., psychiatric hospitalization rates) (Dahl, 1986), with the exception of parasuicidal behavior, which decreases with age.

The prognosis for individuals with BPD has been generally poor. Nearly all individuals with BPD have received outpatient psychiatric treatment (Perry, Herman, van der Kolk, & Hoke, 1990). Unfortunately, such individuals tend to respond poorly or decompensate in outpatient therapy. Their treatment tends to be anything but smooth. They often terminate prematurely, or their therapist burns out and terminates (Linehan, Cochran, Mar, Levensky, & Comtois, 2000). Treatment is undermined by pervasive noncompliance in keeping appointments, completing therapy assignments, and taking medications as prescribed. Lengthy hospitalizations and worsening of comorbid disorders often fragment the therapeutic process. Borderline personality disorder is also associated with worse outcomes in the treatment of comorbid Axis I disorders, such as major depression, substance abuse, bulimia, and PTSD (see Linehan & Heard, 1999, for a review).

Brief improvements are seen with psychiatric hospitalizations for crisis stabilization; however, improvements are attributable to the temporary separation of the individual from the stressor. The relief provided by the hospitalization is transitory because the individual then returns to his or her natural environment no more capable of tolerating distress or problem solving. Although some of these capabilities can be taught in inpatient settings, they often are not. Time constraints, competing institutional demands, staff training issues, and heterogeneous inpatient populations make inpatient units problematic settings for enhancing patient capabilities. What skills patients are taught are often poorly generalized to their natural environment. Furthermore, crisis-stabilizing hospitalizations can be iatrogenic, in that the temporary relief associated with hospitalization reinforces the behaviors linked to admission—typically parasuicidal or suicidal behavior.

In contrast to the plethora of discouraging results of standard treatments, a newer treatment, Dialectical Behavior Therapy (DBT), has provided hope. Numerous studies (see Koerner & Dimeff, 2000, for a review) have demonstrated the association between DBT and decreases in parasuicidal behavior, psychiatric hospitalization, anger, suicidal ideation, depression, hopelessness, and dissociation, and with increases in client retention, overall level of functioning, and overall social adjustment.

Referral Suggestions

When possible, referral to a DBT program or DBT-informed therapist is recommended. Referring entities may do well to suggest that an individual obtain assistance for specific problematic behavior rather than for a diagnosis. Diagnostic labeling often triggers reactions of defensiveness and denial, whereas observation-based descriptions of behavior elicit less negative responses. Individuals are often referred to the Portland DBT Program (a private-practice outpatient clinic specializing in DBT) for problems such as depression, anxiety, anger, emotional sensitivity, cutting impulsivity, and problems relating to others. Although my colleagues and I discuss with clients their diagnoses, we begin the discussion with problematic experiences (e.g., emotional and behavioral dysregulation) rather than diagnosis. We do this for pragmatic and clinical reasons, and to avoid becoming entangled with the deprecative reputation of the diagnosis. By the time the discussion moves to diagnosis, the diagnosis is seen as descriptive and sometimes experienced as validating—that others have similar problems.

RECOMMENDED DATA-BASED TREATMENTS

Brief Description

Developed by Dr. Marsha Linehan and her colleagues at the University of Washington, DBT is an empirically validated cognitive-behavioral treatment for borderline personality disorder (Linehan, 1993a, 1993b).[3] DBT is a behavioral treatment drawing heavily from an area of applied behavior analysis called self-management. Self-management of behavior is a process by which clients learn how to define problems behaviorally, monitor these behaviors in context, analyze the information according to models of learning, and develop analysis-based solutions. In DBT, problems are defined, analyzed, and solved in a collaborative fashion. Cause is not inferred based on personality traits, drive states, or self-object structures, but is hypothesized according to operant, respondent, and observational learning models. Solutions usually fall into one of four categories: skills training, cognitive restructuring, exposure techniques, or contingency management. Change-based therapy with borderline individuals often recapitulates their earlier invalidating environment and results in escalated and extreme responses by client and therapist alike. Thus, in DBT, behavior therapy is balanced with acceptance therapy and housed in a framework that is "dialectical" in nature.

An area of classical philosophy, dialectics promotes synthesizing opposing perspectives or positions. A dialectical perspective calls for a shift from a "black or white" stance to one that is "black and white." Dialectics continually searches for what is left out. Rather than asking for a surrender of an initial stance, it calls for the recognition of the truth in the opposing stance. In the therapy context, dialectical harmony is achieved by continually balancing treatment strategies (e.g., focusing on change and acceptance, treating the client and his or her environment) and client experiences (e.g., synthesizing pure emotion with reason, drawing from logic and intuition).

The core acceptance strategy in DBT is validation. The essence of validation is to communicate to clients that their responses are real and that they make sense and are understandable within their current or historical context. Validation is not used simply to make clients feel better, but is applied strategically to (a) provide a balance to the push for change, (b) reinforce clinical progress, (c) teach self-validation, and (d) strengthen the therapeutic relationship. Mindfulness is the core acceptance skill taught in DBT. Drawn from certain Eastern meditation practices, mindfulness is defined as observing one's internal experience (i.e., thoughts, feelings, images, and physical sensations) and external behaviors (i.e., overt actions) in context in the present moment. The quality of this experience is nonjudgmental; no attempt is made to judge the experience as good or bad, or to control or change the experience. In short, mindfulness is about focusing on one thing in the moment and accepting that moment without reservation with a willingness to do what is needed in order to respond effectively.

Treatment Stages

DBT provides a stage-based hierarchical structure around which to organize the treatment of multiproblem clients. Each stage corresponds to specific treatment targets. The pretreatment stage of DBT corresponds to "getting ready" targets: assessment, orientation to treatment, and establishing initial commitment to participate in therapy. Pretreatment is followed by

Stage 1, where treatment hierarchically targets (a) suicidal and parasuicidal behaviors; (b) therapy-interfering behaviors; and (c) behaviors that severely interfere with a reasonable quality of life (e.g., nonlethal impulsive behaviors, severely dysfunctional relationship behaviors). Stage 2 targets reduction of posttraumatic stress response patterns. Treatment in this stage typically involves changing clients' emotional responses to trauma-related cues, and modifying their perceptions and beliefs regarding the trauma. Stage 3 targets increasing self-respect, as well as working on other issues and problems with which the client may desire help, such as improving relationship quality or resolving career-related problems. The passage from one stage to the next occurs in order, but is not always smooth and continual. For instance, clients in Stage 2 often slip back to problems associated with Stage 1 (or even pretreatment) for a brief time.

Multimodal Treatment

Clients in DBT participate in two primary modes of therapy: individual therapy and skills training group. The chief function of individual therapy is to motivate the individual to use his or her most skillful behavior. To that end, individual therapists provide telephone consultation between sessions as needed to assist the individual in generalizing skills to his or her natural environment. With both the individual therapy and telephone consultation, emotional, cognitive, and environmental obstacles for skillfulness are assessed and treated. Obstacles to optimal skillfulness are treated through (a) manipulating consequences of behavior to change contingencies that promote dysfunctional over functional behavior, (b) exposure to reduce emotions and avoidant behaviors that prevent effective

action, or (c) cognitive modification to change distorted or extreme thinking. In dialectical tension with motivating clients to be optimally skillful is the task of accepting and validating problem-solving complexity and emotional pain (see Linehan, 1993a, for a detailed description of individual therapy strategies, including problem-solving strategies, validation strategies, and stylistic strategies).

Whereas individual therapy and telephone consultation improve client motivation, group skills training improves client capabilities. Training occurs in four primary skill sets: mindfulness, distress tolerance, emotion regulation, and interpersonal effectiveness (Linehan, 1993b). Mindfulness skills increase capabilities for nonjudgmental, in-the-moment awareness. The purpose of distress tolerance is to manage distress in ways that do not make matters worse. Emotion regulation involves increasing mindfulness to emotions and learning to increase and decrease various emotional states. Interpersonal effectiveness skills include increasing mindfulness to relationships, maintaining relationships, and building self-respect in interpersonal situations. Skills training is accomplished primarily through didactic strategies such as lecture, discussion, in-group practice, and homework assignments.

A final treatment modality is the therapist consultation group. Although the client is not physically present for this mode of treatment, it remains a central aspect of DBT. The consultation group targets therapists' own motivation and capabilities for doing effective therapy. It is, in essence, "therapy for the therapists." The team reinforces the therapist for doing effective therapy, because client-based reinforcers may be associated with the therapist acting ineffectively. For instance, a client may be pleased with the therapist for deviating from the session agenda. Metaphorically, if a client were in a fiery pit, the team would want to reinforce providing a ladder (i.e., a way out of misery), whereas client-based reinforcement may be contingent on the therapist providing a bucket of water to cool the client's feet (i.e., immediate but temporary relief) (Linehan, 1993a).

Time Element

Implementation of DBT requires attendance at weekly individual therapy and concurrent weekly skills training group; length of treatment varies. Original protocols called for an initial 1-year commitment to therapy (Linehan, 1993a, p. 112). Logistics-motivated modifications have produced protocols of varying lengths. For instance, in the Portland DBT Program (described more in Kim & Goff, 2000), the initial commitment and length of the skills training group is 6 months. Although the skills training group imposes a fixed-length structure, clients vary in the amount of pretreatment needed prior to entering the group to obtain initial commitment, and in the amount of post-skills training therapy needed. During this 6-month to 1-year period, serious behavioral dyscontrol (e.g., suicide attempts and other self-harm behavior) is often significantly reduced, sometimes even eliminated, and behavioral skills are implemented on a more regular basis. Complaints related to mood and relationships generally continue. Therapy is often necessary beyond 6 months to continue work on abiding Stage 1 problems and to refine and strengthen newly acquired skills. To this end, clients in our program are offered the opportunity to enter a "Phase 2 group." The purpose of this group is to refine skill knowledge and reinforce skillful behavior. Whereas the initial 6-month skills training group meets weekly for 2 hours

and requires concurrent individual therapy, Phase 2 groups meet weekly for 90 minutes and individual therapy is adjunctive. Clients make commitments to Phase 2 groups in 3-month intervals.

Termination from treatment is often difficult for individuals with BPD, and thus services are slowly tapered over time. In this way, problems that arise secondary to decreased services can be addressed while clients are still active in therapy. In our experience, we have found that clients have an easier time reducing individual therapy if they remain in a skills training group during the process.

Side Effects of Treatment

As with most psychosocial treatments, symptomatology may worsen before improving. Parasuicidal behavior and other problematic impulsive behaviors function to regulate emotion. As clients work to reduce these problematic behaviors, they lose their short-term benefit unless alternate methods of emotion regulation and distress tolerance are already in place. Furthermore, resisting the urge to engage in impulsive behavior is intensely difficult and can itself increase an individual's emotional distress. Conversely, the individual is spared the deleterious effects of these behaviors if they are skillfully resisted. In essence, tolerating distress, including the distress of intense urges, does not reduce pain, it simply prevents the pain from becoming worse.

With mixed results, pharmacotherapy commonly augments psychotherapy for borderline individuals. The disorder per se is not targeted, but rather areas of dysfunction, including emotional lability (antidepressants and anxiolytics); behavioral dyscontrol (mood stabilizers and anticonvulsants); and cognitive dysregulation, such as transient psychotic symptoms or dissociation (antipsychotics). More so than for others, these drugs produce nonspecific and even paradoxical effects for borderline individuals (see Dimeff, McDavid, & Linehan, 1999, for a review). Complicating the matter is the tendency for borderline individuals to be taking multiple-drug regimens, increasing side effects and negative drug interactions. Common work-relevant side effects relate primarily to central nervous system functioning: diminished attention and concentration, drowsiness, insomnia, headache, cognitive slowing, and fatigue. Benzodiazepines should be avoided because they intensify behavioral dyscontrol and are highly addictive.

Workplace Accommodations

DBT calls for few workplace accommodations for the treatment of borderline individuals. Allowing some form of brief, self-initiated removal from stressful stimuli would assist individuals in applying emotion regulation skills. Emotionally dysregulated, borderline individuals find it exceedingly hard to focus on the present moment and act skillfully. Mindfulness skills are taught in DBT that promote a sense of "groundedness" or "centeredness," characterized by present-minded thought and effectiveness-oriented action. Briefly stepping out of a stressful setting may be conducive to becoming mindful. In effect, it is "taking a breather." Additional accommodations may include early release a few days a week in order to attend therapy (especially for skills training group, where the meeting time of the group is less flexible), and having available a private setting where the individual could access urgent telephone consultation if needed.

DBT encourages, and actually teaches, environments to be validating of the difficulties and needs of borderline individuals (Kim & Goff, 2000). Indeed, making an accommodation is essentially functional validation; it communicates through action that the need is valid, like getting someone a glass of water when the person is thirsty. Dialectically, a basic tenet of DBT asserts that clients need to function better regardless of their situation or physical setting. A related tenet says that clients may not have caused their problems, but they must solve them anyway. On one hand, making no allowance for modifications may invalidate the individual's struggle and hinder success. Overmodifying may invalidate the individual's capabilities and communicate that he or she is fragile. The trick is to validate the realness of the individual's problem without invalidating his or her capabilities and strengths. When made, modifications should function to facilitate, yet still require, skillful behavior on the part of the individual.

The synthesis about accommodations lies in DBT's approach of consulting with the client rather than intervening directly in his or her environment. This consultation-to-the-client approach channels solutions through the client. Clients are coached to present their requests in a manner that does not damage their self-respect or the affected relationship. Obstacles of having accommodations made would be solved with the client, and at the same time, the client would be coached to tolerate the distress of the situation.

MAINTENANCE OF GAINS/RELAPSE PREVENTION

Even with good outcome data, DBT is not a panacea for clients with borderline personality disorder. Even while in treatment, clients advance and regress over an indeterminable period. Although this is understandable in light of the disorder's chronic nature, it highlights the need for thoughtful strategies of preserving clinical change.

One such set of strategies concerns methods of continuing therapy. Involvement in an ongoing DBT skills training group (such as a Phase 2 group described earlier), allowance for occasional "booster" sessions after formal therapy has ended, and even participation in Internet-based therapeutic discussion groups are all methods of extending treatment. One specific example is an Internet group whose members are all graduates of DBT programs. The group shares insights about and experiences of using DBT skills, and provides peer-based encouragement and instruction to act skillfully.

Dialectically, a second set of strategies concerns the process of ending therapy. Termination from therapy, if possible, should occur only after clients complete Stage 2 of therapy, where behaviors associated with posttraumatic stress are treated. The work of Stage 2 often precipitates relapses of Stage 1 behavior; therefore, this work is best done in a context where the lapse into prior behavior can be treated quickly. Additionally, as suggested earlier, gradually tapering services encourages the development of self-management skills and greater independence from the therapeutic relationship. Finally, development of adequate social support in the client's natural environment (and the skills necessary to access the support) should be a criterion for termination.

To further assist maintenance of client gains and prevention of relapse, we have added a self-management skills unit (Kim & Goff, 1999) to the units taught in standard DBT to formalize the teaching of relapse prevention strategies. The unit borrows heavily from Marlatt and Gordon's (1985) work in the area of relapse prevention. Clients are taught about relapse cycles and how to use other DBT skills to short-circuit the cycle. They are also taught to analyze behaviors according to learning principles and to make changes in antecedents and consequences in order to shape behavior.

Workplace Strategies

A maxim of behavioral psychology is that behaviors that are reinforced are more likely to occur. As supervisors note a welcome change in behavior, they should reinforce it through acknowledgement or praise. Note that reinforcements are idiosyncratic; some individuals do not experience praise as reinforcing but instead see praise as "the bar of expectation being raised" and experience subsequent anxiety. Also, it is important that reinforcing comments or responses not sound patronizing. A related suggestion is to validate (i.e., acknowledge nonjudgmentally) the individual's report of emotion and the difficulty of changing behavior. Supervisors should not assume they know how to help, but rather ask the individual if there is something they can do to help. In addition to providing content as to what would be helpful, the individual is communicating to what extent he or she wants the supervisor to be involved. Supervisors are encouraged to be patient, to the extent that business needs allow, recognizing that when learning new behavior, practice is needed before the new behavior comes naturally. They should be mindful of the fact that the BPD employee is interacting with his or her environment, and they are encouraged to consider whether the workplace is or is not validating.

For the most part, these suggestions most likely parallel basic management strategies for increasing productivity and job satisfaction. For individuals with BPD, departures from this style of management are more likely to be distressing and ultimately contribute to a loss of treatment gains.

SUMMARY

Borderline personality disorder is character-ized by dysregulated (i.e., reactive and sen-sitive) affect, impulsive behavior (including suicidal and parasuicidal behavior), chaotic relationships, black-or-white thinking, and a transient sense of self. Its diverse pre-sentation and typically complex pattern of comorbidity complicate diagnostic assess-ment and the prediction of workplace diffi-culties. Common work-relevant problems include frequent hospitalizations, emotional dysregulation and paranoia at work, inter-personal problems with coworkers or supervisors, and absences resulting from impulsive behavior.

There have been few data about effective treatments for BPD until recently. DBT is an empirically validated cognitive-behavioral therapy for borderline personal-ity disorder. Grounded in both behavioral theory and Eastern meditative traditions, it emphasizes change and acceptance. This dialectic addresses simultaneously the two fundamental problems for borderline individuals: (a) They need to increase their capabilities in a variety of domains, and (b) they feel fatally flawed and struggle with accepting themselves and their problems.

DBT is composed of individual therapy, skills training group, and telephone consul-tation. Each treatment modality functions interdependently with the others to increase clients' capabilities, increase their motiva-tion to change, and help generalize these new behaviors to their natural environ-ment. Additionally, DBT's treatment team approach enhances therapists' skills and motivation to implement the treatment. Supervisors in the workplace are invited to function as part of this treatment team. They can validate the individual's efforts and reinforce his or her changes in behav-ior. In managing the BPD employee, super-visors should assume a stance of flexibility (making accommodations that validate the individual's needs) and benevolent inflexi-bility (requiring skillfulness that validates the individual's strengths and capabilities).

NOTES

1. The case of Amy is fictional. She is a composite of various clients who have been seen at the Portland DBT Program, PC. Portland, Oregon. E-mail: info@port-landdbt.com. Website: www.portlanddbt.com. Phone: (503) 231-7854.

2. This case description illustrates common difficulties associated with BPD; however, another combination of the diagnostic criteria would paint a different pic-ture. As mentioned earlier, the experiences of those with BPD are varied. Not all of the criteria for borderline personality disorder are illustrated in this description, because that, too, would not be representative of the typical phenomenology of indi-viduals with BPD.

3. The information presented in this section is based primarily on Marsha M. Linehan's extensive writing on DBT. Readers are advised to consult her text on the subject (Linehan, 1993a) and the companion skills training manual (Linehan, 1993b) for a more thorough understanding of the model. For more information on training in DBT, contact the Behavioral Technology Transfer Group at (206) 675-8588.

REFERENCES

Akhtar, S., Byrne, J. P., & Doghramji, K. (1986). The demographic profile of borderline personality disorder. *Journal of Clinical Psychiatry, 47,* 196-198.

American Psychiatric Association. (1994). *Diagnostic and statistical manual of mental disorders* (4th ed.). Washington, DC: Author.

Becker, D. F., Grilo, C. M., Edell, W. S., & McGlashan, T. H. (2000). Comorbidity of borderline personality disorder with other personality disorders in hospitalized adolescents and adults. *American Journal of Psychiatry, 157,* 2011-2016.

Bond, M., Paris, J., & Zweig-Frank, H. (1994). Defense styles and borderline personality disorder. *Journal of Personality Disorders, 8,* 28-31.

Bongar, B. M. (1992). *Suicide: Guidelines for assessment, management, and treatment.* New York: Oxford University Press.

Carroll, L., Hoenigmann-Stovall, N., King, A., Wienhold, J., & Whitehead, G. (1998). Interpersonal consequences of narcissistic and borderline personality disorders. *Journal of Social and Clinical Psychology, 17,* 38-49.

Clarkin, J. F., Widiger, T. A., Frances, A., Hurt, S. W., & Gilmore, M. (1983). Prototypic typology and the borderline personality disorder. *Journal of Abnormal Psychology, 92,* 263-275.

Comtois, K. A., Cowley, D. S., Dunner, D. L., & Roy-Byrne, P. P. (1999). Relationship between borderline personality disorder and Axis I diagnosis in severity of depression and anxiety. *Journal of Clinical Psychiatry, 60,* 752-758.

Comtois, K. A., Levensky, E. R., & Linehan, M. M. (1999). Behavior therapy. In M. Hersen & A. S. Bellack (Eds.), *Handbook of comparative interventions for adult disorders* (2nd ed., pp. 555-583). New York: Wiley.

Cowdry, R. W., Pickar, D., & Davies, R. (1985). Symptoms and EEG findings in the borderline syndrome. *International Journal of Psychiatry in Medicine, 15,* 201-211.

Dahl, A. A. (1986). Prognosis of the borderline disorders. *Psychopathology, 19,* 68-79.

Davis, T., Gunderson, J. G., & Myers, M. (1999). Borderline personality disorder. In D. G. Jacobs (Ed.), *The Harvard Medical School guide to suicide assessment and intervention* (pp. 311-331). San Francisco: Jossey-Bass.

Derogatis, L. R., & Spencer, P. M. (1982). *Brief Symptom Inventory: Administration, scoring, and procedures manual.* Baltimore: Clinical Psychometric Research.

Dimeff, L. A., McDavid, J., & Linehan, M. M. (1999). Pharmacotherapy for borderline personality disorder: A review of the literature and recommendations for treatment. *Journal of Clinical Psychology in Medical Settings, 6,* 113-138.

Edell, W. S., Joy, S. P., & Yehuda, R. (1990). Discordance between self-report and observed psychopathology in borderline patients. *Journal of Personality Disorders, 4,* 381-390.

Figueroa, E., & Silk, K. R. (1997). Biological implications of childhood sexual abuse in borderline personality disorder. *Journal of Personality Disorders, 11,* 71-92.

First, M. B., Spitzer, R. L., Gibbons, M., & Williams, J. B. W. (1995). *Structured Clinical Interview for Axis I DSM-IV Disorders—Patient Edition (SCID-I/P).* New York: Biometrics Research Department, New York State Psychiatric Institute.

First, M. B., Spitzer, R. L., Gibbons, M., Williams, J. B. W., & Benjamin, L. (1996). *User's guide for the Structured Clinical Interview for DSM-IV Axis II personality disorders (SCID-II).* New York: Biometrics Research Department, New York State Psychiatric Institute.

Frances, A., Fyer, M., & Clarkin, J. F. (1986). Personality and suicide. *Annals of the New York Academy of Science, 482,* 281-293.

Goff, B. (1998). Self-esteem lability as a vulnerability for depression within the context of diathesis-stress models of depression (Doctoral dissertation, University of Oregon, 1998). *Dissertation Abstracts International, 59*(7-B), 3691.

Gottman, J. M., & Katz, L. F. (1990). Effects of marital discord on young children's peer interactions and health. *Developmental Psychology, 25,* 373-381.

Hyler, S. E., Oldham, J. M., Kellman, H. D., & Doidge, N. (1992). Validity of the Personality Diagnostic Questionnaire—Revised: A replication in an outpatient sample. *Comprehensive Psychiatry, 33,* 73-77.

Kim, S., & Goff, B. (1999). *Self-management and relapse prevention skills training unit.* (Available from the Portland Dialectical Behavior Therapy Program, 6126 SE Milwaukie Avenue, Portland, OR 97202)

Kim, S., & Goff, B. (2000). Borderline personality disorder. In M. Hersen & M. Biaggio (Eds.), *Effective brief treatment for adults: A clinician's guide.* New York: Academic Press.

Koerner, K., & Dimeff, L. A. (2000). Further data on dialectical behavior therapy. *Clinical Psychology: Science and Practice, 7,* 104-112.

Kroll, L. J., Sines, L. K., & Martin, K. (1981). Borderline personality disorder: Construct validity of the concept. *Archives of General Psychiatry, 39,* 60-63.

Labonte, E., & Paris, J. (1993). Life events in borderline personality disorder. *Canadian Journal of Psychiatry, 38,* 638-640.

Lambert, M. J., & Hill, C. (1994). Assessing psychotherapy outcomes and processes. In A. E. Bergin & S. L. Garfield (Eds.), *Handbook of psychotherapy and behavior change* (4th ed., pp. 72-113). New York: Wiley.

Levine, D., Marziali, E., & Hood, J. (1997). Emotion processing in borderline personality disorder. *Journal of Nervous and Mental Disease, 185,* 240-246.

Linehan, M. M. (1993a). *Cognitive-behavioral treatment of borderline personality disorder.* New York: Guilford.

Linehan, M. M. (1993b). *Skills training manual for treating borderline personality disorder.* New York: Guilford.

Linehan, M. M., Cochran, B. N., Mar, C. M., Levensky, E. R., & Comtois, K. A. (2000). Therapeutic burnout among borderline personality disordered clients and their therapists: Development and evaluation of two adaptations of the Maslach Burnout Inventory. *Cognitive and Behavioral Practice, 7,* 329-337.

Linehan, M. M., & Heard, H. (1999). Borderline personality disorder: Costs, course, and treatment outcomes. In N. Miller & K. Magruder (Eds.), *The cost-effectiveness of psychotherapy: A guide for practitioners, researchers and policy makers* (pp. 291-305). New York: Oxford University Press.

Linehan, M. M., Kanter, J. W., & Comtois, K. A. (1999). Dialectical behavior therapy for borderline personality disorder: Efficacy, specificity, and cost effectiveness. In D. S. Janowsky (Ed.), *Psychotherapy: Indications and outcomes* (pp. 93-118). Washington, DC: American Psychiatric Press.

Links, P. S., Heslegrave, R., & van Reekum, R. (1998). Prospective follow-up study of borderline personality disorder: Prognosis, prediction outcome, and Axis II comorbidity. *Canadian Journal of Psychiatry, 43,* 265-270.

Loranger, A. W. (1995). *International Personality Disorder Examination (IPDE) manual.* White Plains, NY: Cornell Medical Center.

Marlatt, G. A., & Gordon, J. R. (Eds.). (1985). *Relapse prevention: Maintenance strategies in the treatment of addictive behaviors.* New York: Guilford.

Paris, J., Brown, R., & Nowlis, D. (1987). Long-term follow-up of borderline patients in a general hospital. *Comparative Behavior, 5,* 140-144.

Patrick, J., Links, P., van Reekum, R., & Mitton, J. E. (1995). Using the PDQ-R scale as a brief screening measure in the differential diagnosis of personality disorder. *Journal of Personality Disorders, 9,* 266-274.

Perry, J. C., Herman, J. L., van der Kolk, B. A., & Hoke, L. A. (1990). Psychotherapy and psychological trauma in borderline personality disorder. *Psychiatric Annals, 20,* 33-43.

Skodol, A. E., & Oldham, J. M. (1991). Assessment and diagnosis of borderline personality disorder. *Hospital and Community Psychiatry, 42,* 1021-1028.

Swartz, M., Blazer, D., George, L., & Winfield, I. (1990). Estimating the prevalence of borderline personality disorder in the community. *Journal of Personality Disorders, 4,* 257-272.

Taub, J. M. (1996). Sociodemography of borderline personality disorder (PD): A comparison with Axis II PDS and psychiatric symptom disorders convergent validation. *International Journal of Neuroscience, 88,* 27-52.

Tyrer, P. (1988). Personality Assessment Schedule (PAS). In P. Tyrer & J. Alexander (Eds.), *Personality disorders: Diagnosis, management, and course* (pp. 43-62). London: Wright/Butterworth Scientific.

Whewell, P., Ryman, A., Bonanno, D., & Heather, N. (2000). Does the ICD 10 classification accurately describe subtypes of borderline personality disorder? *British Journal of Medical Psychology, 73,* 483-494.

Widiger, T. A. (1987). *Personality Interview Questionnaire II (PIQ II).* White Plains, NY: Cornell Medical Center, Westchester Division.

Widiger, T. A., & Frances, A. J. (1989). Epidemiology, diagnosis, and comorbidity of borderline personality disorder. In A. Tasman, R. E. Hales, & A. J. Frances (Eds.), *American Psychiatric Press Review of Psychiatry, Vol. 8* (pp. 8-24). Washington, DC: American Psychiatric Press.

Widiger, T. A., & Weissman, M. M. (1991). Epidemiology of borderline personality disorder. *Hospital & Community Psychiatry, 42,* 1015-1021.

Wittchen, H. U., Kessler, R. C., Zhao, S., & Abelson, J. (1995). Reliability and clinical validity of UM-CIDI *DSM-III-R. Journal of Psychiatric Research, 29,* 95-110.

Zanarini, M. C., Frankenburg, F. R., Dubo, E. D., Sickel, A. E., Trikha, A., Levin, A., & Reynolds, V. (1998a). Axis I comorbidity of borderline personality disorder. *American Journal of Psychiatry, 155,* 1733-1739.

Zanarini, M. C., Frankenburg, F. R., Dubo, E. D., Sickel, A. E., Trikha, A., Levin, A., & Reynolds, V. (1998b). Axis II comorbidity of borderline personality disorder. *Comprehensive Psychiatry, 39,* 296-302.

Zanarini, M. C., Gunderson, J. G., & Frankenburg, F. R. (1989). Axis I phenomenology of borderline personality disorder. *Comprehensive Psychiatry, 30,* 149-156.

Zanarini, M. C., Gunderson, J. G., Frankenburg, F. R., & Chauncey, D. L. (1989). The revised diagnostic interview for borderlines: Discriminating borderline personality disorder from other Axis II disorders. *Journal of Personality Disorders, 3,* 10-18.

Zimmerman, M., & Mattia, J. I. (1999). Axis I diagnostic comorbidity and borderline personality disorder. *Comprehensive Psychiatry, 40,* 245-252.

CHAPTER 15

Eating Disorders

DAVID H. GLEAVES
ANTONIO CEPEDA-BENITO

DESCRIPTION OF
THE EATING DISORDERS

Eating disorders are characterized by gross disturbances in eating behavior as well as extreme and distorted concerns about body shape and weight. The *Diagnostic and Statistical Manual of Mental Disorders—Fourth Edition* (*DSM-IV*) (American Psychiatric Association [APA], 1994) distinguishes between three major types of eating disorders: Anorexia Nervosa (AN), Bulimia Nervosa (BN), and Eating Disorder Not Otherwise Specified (EDNOS). The latter category refers to cases that satisfy some but not all the criteria required for the diagnosis of either AN or BN. Binge-eating Disorder (BED) is a more recently recognized disorder that technically falls into the EDNOS category.

Anorexia Nervosa

The most salient characteristic of AN patients is their "refusal to maintain a minimally normal body weight" (APA, 1994, p. 539), with the minimum weight threshold set at 85% of the person's expected weight for his or her age and height. These individuals lose weight (or fail to gain weight during puberty) because of intentional restriction of food intake (dieting, fasting); caloric expenditure (excessive exercising); or purging behaviors (self-induced vomiting, and misuse of laxatives, diuretics, or enemas) (Walsh & Garner, 1997).

Individuals with AN have an intense fear of gaining weight and becoming fat (APA, 1994). Paradoxically, this fear seems to increase as the person loses weight (Walsh & Garner, 1997). Individuals with AN may experience their bodies in a distorted way, feeling fat and chronically dissatisfied with their body shape. They monitor their own weight and body size religiously, and experience intense shame, disillusion, and frustration if they discover they have gained weight. Conversely, weight losses are experienced as important achievements and exemplars of self-discipline. That is, weight and body shape exert a disproportional influence on the self-esteem of individuals with AN (APA, 1994; Schlundt & Johnson, 1990; Walsh & Garner, 1997).

Poor nutrition alters the balance of hormones that regulate the menstrual cycle. Thus, postmenarcheal women with AN may experience amenorrhea. In young, anorexic adolescents, the onset of menstruation is sometimes postponed (APA, 1994). Starvation can also bring about metabolic, cardiovascular, neurological, gastrointestinal, and dermatological alterations, as well as many other medical complications (Cassell & Gleaves, 2000).

The *DSM-IV* distinguishes between two types of AN: Restricting Type and Binge-Eating/Purging Type. Restricting anorexics do not engage in binge eating and purging, whereas Binge-Eating/Purging anorexics do. Excessive dieting and exercising are not unique to either type of anorexia (APA, 1994). Walsh and Garner (1997) note that Restricting Type anorexics tend to be more obsessive and socially isolated than do Binge-Eating/Purging anorexics.

In addition to the eating and body image-related psychopathology of AN, several additional psychological problems are often present, including depression, anxiety, obsessive compulsive behavior, posttraumatic stress disorder, and substance use (Fornari et al., 1992; Gleaves, May, & Eberenz, 1998; Herzog, Keller, Sacks, Yeh, & Lavori, 1992; Holderness, Brooks-Gunn, & Warren, 1994). Interpersonal and family problems (Steiger, Liquornik, Chapman, & Hussain, 1991) and personality disorders (Gartner, Marcus, Halmi, & Loranger, 1989) are also common.

Bulimia Nervosa

The most defining characteristic of BN is the presence of repeated binge episodes followed by inappropriate compensatory responses (excessive exercise, purging) to prevent weight gains (APA, 1994). *DSM-IV* defines a binge as "eating in a discrete period of time an amount of food that is definitely larger than most individuals would eat under similar circumstances" (APA, 1994, p. 545). Walsh (1993) noted that some bulimics describe binges not so much as episodes of excessive eating but as eating with a sense of lack of control, even to the extent of dissociation. Moreover, research findings indicate that there is great variability in the amount of food that is consumed across binge episodes (Rossiter & Agras, 1990). Binges are often triggered by the intense hunger felt after dieting, dysphoric mood states, stress, feelings and thoughts associated with body image, and food cravings (APA, 1994; Cepeda-Benito, Gleaves, Williams, & Erath, 2000; Garfinkel, 1990; Schlundt & Johnson, 1990; Walsh & Garner, 1997).

About 80% of bulimic individuals resort to self-induced vomiting to compensate for binge eating (Schlundt & Johnson, 1990). Other purging methods include inappropriate use of laxatives, diuretics, enemas, and metabolism-altering drugs (Schlundt & Johnson, 1990). Bulimic individuals also resort to fasting or excessive exercising to "undo" bingeing episodes (Walsh & Garner, 1997). Thus, the *DSM-IV* classifies BN into Purging Type and Nonpurging Type according to the presence or absence of regular use of purging behaviors, respectively. It is generally accepted that BN Purging Type is associated with more pathology than is BN Nonpurging Type (e.g., Willmuth, Leitenberg, Rosen, & Cado, 1988).

As with AN, people with BN also frequently exhibit a variety of additional psychopathologies, including depression, anxiety, substance abuse (Braun, Sunday, & Halmi, 1994), and personality disorders (Braun et al., 1994; Herzog et al., 1992; Holderness et al., 1994).

Binge-eating Disorder

BED is a recent addition to the eating disorders category, although it is not currently accepted as a formal diagnosis in the *DSM-IV*. The core feature of BED is the presence of recurrent binge eating (as seen with BN), but with the absence of the compensatory behaviors that occur with BN. People with BED may not be as restrictive in their eating as people with BN, and a large percentage of individuals are obese. Furthermore, for many people with BED, dieting seems to follow rather than precede their binge eating (Spurrell, Wilfley, Tanofsky, & Brownell, 1997). Because of their obese status, people with BED are often very dissatisfied with their bodies; however, the body image distortion sometimes seen among people with AN or BN may not occur with BED (Johnson, Tsoh, & Varnado, 1996).

Some researchers (e.g., Hay & Fairburn, 1998) have conceptualized BED as being less severe than BN. However, the range and frequency of comorbid psychopathology for BED is similar to that with BN. Futhermore, mortality rates for BED may actually be higher than with BN because of the associated obesity (Agras, 2001).

EPIDEMIOLOGY

Stunkard (1993) noted that medical conditions characterized by refusals to eat that lead to starvation and amenorrhea are not a modern phenomenon. However, Stunkard also noted that symptoms of excessive preoccupation with body weight (Bruch, 1966) and fear of becoming fat (Crisp, 1967) emerged and developed within the past 50 years. Russell (1995) shares Stunkard's view and adds that manifestation or expression of AN probably changed throughout history in tune with sociocultural transformations.

Similarly, BN was not identified as a syndrome or variant of AN until 1979 (Russell, 1979).

Sociocultural variables are so influential in eating disorders that most investigators share Russell's (1995) opinion that AN and BN are two syndromes that cannot be understood outside of a sociocultural context. For example, in modern occidental culture, thinness in women has become a symbol of competence, success, discipline, and beauty. At the same time, obesity is equated with laziness, self-indulgence, and lack of discipline. Thus, findings that women are overly preoccupied with attaining thinness, that prevalence of eating disorders has exploded in the past 30 years, that eating disorders are found almost exclusively in girls and women, and that females with AN tend to be successful and perfectionistic are most likely consequences of the Occident's modern values and fashions (Garner & Fairburn, 1988; Lucas, Beard, O'Fallon, & Kurland, 1991; Stunkard, 1993).

Epidemiological studies indicate that most anorexics are girls and women (90% to 95%), and that in most cases, onset of the disorder occurs at some time in adolescence (between 12 and 20 years of age). It is estimated that the lifetime prevalence of AN in girls and women is around 1.6% (Walters & Kendler, 1995). However, many cases of EDNOS do not meet all the criteria for the diagnosis of AN but share many of the AN symptoms. According to Walters and Kendler, the cumulative prevalence of women with AN and women with severe AN symptoms is 3.7%.

Boys and men also develop AN, but at a much lower rate than girls and women. It is possible that prevalence of AN in men is higher than it seems to be but not readily recognized because of its reputation as a female disorder. There is some evidence indicating that males who become anorexic do so at an earlier age than females. Another marked difference between male and female anorexics is that males tend to be obese prior to dieting (Andersen & Holman, 1997). Most cases of BN are also girls and women (90% to 95%). Estimates of the lifetime prevalence of BN for girls and women range between 1% and 3% (APA, 1994; Fairburn & Beglin, 1990). However, studies of BN among female college students have reported prevalence rates in the 6% to 8% range (Schlundt & Johnson, 1990), and as high as 12.5% and 18.5% (Garfinkel et al., 1995; Pope, Hudson, Yurgelun-Todd, & Hudson, 1984). BN prevalence rates are considerably lower in women over 25 years of age. Bushnell, Wells, Hornblow, Oakley-Browne, and Joyce (1990) reported prevalence rates of BN in the 0.04% to 2% range in women between the ages of 25 and 44.

Males with BN usually have a later disorder onset than do women. A subgroup of men with a higher risk of developing BN are athletes who need to maintain their weight below specific thresholds (e.g., wrestlers, runners) or for whom physical appearance and body shape is particularly important (e.g., body builders) (Carlat, Camargo, & Herzog, 1997). Homosexuality and bisexuality also seem to be risk factors for BN in males, because prevalence of homosexuality and bisexuality is higher in men with BN than in the general population (10% versus 43%) (Carlat et al., 1997).

Investigators had often reported that eating disorders, specifically AN, were more common among females of middle to high social classes (e.g., Crisp, Palmer, & Kalucy, 1976). However, more recent studies also show that eating disorder cases can be found across all social classes (Turón, Homs, González, & Salvador, 1997). García-Camba (2001) affirms that absence of differences in prevalence of eating disorders across social strata does not indicate that sociocultural factors do not play a role in the etiology of eating disorders. This author speculated that modern society's emphasis on thinness as a symbol of attractiveness and success reaches all social classes.

Less is known about the epidemiology of BED. We do know that among people seeking treatment for weight-related problems, reported binge eating is very common. The estimated prevalence of the disorder may be between 2% and 5% of the general population (Johnson et al., 1996). The gender distribution is also apparently much different from other eating disorders (EDs); BED may be at least as common among men as women.

ASSESSMENT

Clinical evaluations of patients with eating disorders should include (a) a medical examination, (b) an evaluation of the person's personality and overall mental health, and (c) a detailed analysis of the presenting eating disorder symptomatology and related psychological processes. Personality inventories and measures of depression, anxiety disorders, and chemical dependence can be useful in detecting comorbid pathology that may interfere with the treatment and recovery of patients with eating disorders.

Eating Disorder Instruments

Several interviews and multidimensional, self-report questionnaires measure maladaptive behaviors, cognitive distortions, and comorbid psychopathology often associated with EDs. We will describe some of the most commonly used instruments.

The Eating Disorder Inventory-2 (EDI-2) (Garner, 1991) consists of 64 items that yield eight clinical subscales and 27 additional items that generate three provisional scales. Three of the eight clinical scales measure attitudes and behaviors concerning eating, weight, and body shape: Drive for Thinness, Bulimia, and Body Dissatisfaction. The other five clinical scales assess psychological constructs clinically relevant to eating disorders: Ineffectiveness, Perfectionism, Interpersonal Distrust, Maturity Fears, and Interoceptive Awareness. The three new constructs that form the provisional scales of the EDI-2 are Ascetism, Impulse Regulation, and Social Insecurity. The EDI-2 reliably is sensitive to changes in the course of the disorder, and reliably discriminates between different types of eating disorders, and between clinical and nonclinical populations (Garner, 1991). The multidimensional nature of the EDI-2 and its psychometric properties make this tool suitable for diagnostic purposes, treatment planning, and monitoring of treatment progress. However, whereas researchers continue to report good psychometric properties for the original eight scales, properties for the three newer scales have been called into question (Eberenz & Gleaves, 1994).

The Eating Attitudes Test (EAT-26) (Garner, Olmstead, & Polivy, 1983) was designed to measure the broad range of symptoms characteristic of AN: preoccupation with bulimia, concerns about body image and drive for thinness, purgative behaviors, dieting practices, slow eating, secret eating, and perceived social pressure to gain weight. Although the EAT has been shown to discriminate quite well between anorexic patients and controls, it is most useful as a screening device and as a complementary aid to other diagnostic tools.

The Bulimic Investigatory Test, Edinburgh (BITE) (Henderson & Freeman, 1987) is a 33-item questionnaire designed to identify the presence of bulimic symptoms and assess their intensity. It can be used as a screening tool for the detection of eating disorders in the general population, as a measure of the severity of symptomatology in eating disorder patients, and as a treatment outcome measure.

Evaluation of Body Image

Body image is so central to eating disorders that it is advisable to assess both the affective component of body image (dissatisfaction) and the perceptual component of body image (distortion). Body image can be assessed with self-rated questionnaires and visual aids that can range in sophistication from merely asking a patient to draw a picture of what she looks like and how she would like to look, to computerized tasks that require the patient to augment and reduce different body parts of a human figure projected on a screen.

The Body Shape Questionnaire (BSQ) (Cooper, Taylor, Cooper, & Fairburn, 1987) is a 34-item questionnaire that assesses satisfaction and anxiety levels associated with different body parts. This test discriminates between bulimic and normal populations, although there can be considerable overlap between bulimic patients and female college students (e.g., Raich, Deus, Muñoz, Perez, & Requena, 1991).

The Body Image Assessment (BIA) (Williamson, Davis, Bennett, Goreczny, & Gleaves, 1989) consists of nine silhouettes ranging in size from very thin to very fat. The silhouettes are randomly presented in separate cards, and the participant selects the images that best represent his or her current body size and ideal body size. The difference in size between the two images measures the level of dissatisfaction. Williamson, Cubic, and Gleaves (1993) found that when compared with same-size controls, eating disorder patients chose a larger current body size and smaller ideal body size.

Family Assessment

Despite theories that attempt to tie etiology of eating disorders to parenting practices and family dynamics, most evidence is anecdotal, and there are no empirically sound findings revealing that specific family patterns significantly contribute to development of eating disorders. Nevertheless, AN and BN in the family most likely threaten the stability and the day-to-day living in the family (Sevillano Fernández, 2001). The Family Environment Scale (FES) (Moos & Moos, 1981) is a 90-item, 10-scale measure. The FES allows for an assessment and description of interpersonal family relations with regard to levels of conflict, cohesion, and emotional expressiveness. The instrument also evaluates how family life encourages or hinders personal growth of the individual family members in the areas of autonomy, self-actualization, intellect and culture, morality and religiosity, and socialization/recreation. Finally, the FES provides information about family structure and organization, as well as the level of control that family members exert over each other.

Assessment of Comorbid Problems

Because of the common presence of a variety of additional psychopathologies, a comprehensive psychological and social history assessment should be regarded as a must. At the very least, an evaluation should screen for mood, substance use, and/or personality disorders. In some instances, posttraumatic stress disorder or a dissociative disorder is present, and the eating disorder may not respond to treatment until the posttraumatic condition is addressed first (Gleaves & Eberenz, 1994).

CLINICAL PICTURE AND WORKPLACE IMPACT

Hsu (1990) argued that economic productivity was one of the areas spared by the eating disorders. This conclusion was based on the finding that, across several studies of AN, the majority of patients, even some of the severely emaciated anorexics, do remain fully or partially employed (Hsu, 1990). This finding does not, however, indicate that the disorders do not affect the workplace environment. In many ways, they can and do, although the degree and type of impact is most likely quite variable, depending on which disorder is present, its level of severity, and the degree of comorbid psychopathology. The following case descriptions illustrate what may typically be seen in the workplace and the varying degrees to which an eating disorder may affect or be affected by the work environment.

Case 1: Anorexia Nervosa

Elizabeth is 33 years old and single, and she has been diagnosed as having AN, Restricting Subtype. She has struggled with eating problems since late adolescence and has been hospitalized once for a period of several weeks. Her weight fluctuates somewhat but is generally 20% to 25% below her expected weight. She does not view her low weight as a problem, although she realizes that other people typically do. She also experiences chronic severe depression and takes antidepressant medication. When she takes it regularly, it leads to a mild improvement in her depression but does not affect her eating disorder per se.

In terms of her job performance, Elizabeth is intelligent, perfectionistic, and achievement oriented. Succeeding in her career and doing well at her job are high priorities for her. Furthermore, her academic background is exceptional, and her work skills have never been a question. However, when her weight is at its lowest and her eating most restrictive, she experiences a variety of physical and cognitive deficits, including dizziness (due to low blood pressure) and difficulty concentrating. Her job performance is impaired during these times.

Elizabeth's workplace social life is also impaired. She does not eat at all at work or around coworkers; she avoids any eating-related social activities. She also has virtually no friends among her coworkers and does not completely confide in the few friends that she does have. Many coworkers recognize her probable eating disorder, but because they do not know her well or understand the problem, they do not feel comfortable approaching her to discuss the problem.

Case 2: Bulimia Nervosa

Sara is a 22-year-old recent college graduate who has struggled with BN for the past 4 years. Typically, she engages in large binge episodes during the evening. During a binge, she may engage in self-induced vomiting three to four times. Both her bingeing and purging are done in secret and only rarely at work. However, her coworkers are aware that she appears to be (and reports being) chronically on a diet. She usually brings her lunch to work and either eats very restrictively or skips lunch completely and exercises on her lunch break. Although her diets vary, she has strict rules about which foods are forbidden. If events at work lead her to eat these foods, she feels she has broken her dietary restraint, and she experiences strong urges to continue eating and/or to purge. After overeating at work, if she feels she is able to self-induce vomiting without getting caught, she will do so; if not, she will take several prescription-strength laxatives. Sara recognizes that her binge eating feels out of control. However, she does not see her rigid eating style as problematic and views her purging as a solution to the problem with bingeing.

Sara is socially active and routinely goes out with coworkers after work. She has not disclosed the fact that she has an eating disorder to her coworkers, nor is it noticeable to those around her. She is of normal weight and is viewed by her coworkers as physically fit and attractive. She also does not avoid eating during the evenings as she does during the day because she knows she will have the opportunity to purge. Drinking alcohol in particular will often lead to disinhibition and binge eating. Because Sara frequently drinks to excess, coworkers may begin to worry about a possible drinking problem before they suspect a eating disorder.

Case 3: Binge-eating Disorder

Carl is a 38-year-old single male with BED. He reports a history of "compulsive eating" dating back at least to high school. His weight has been quite erratic most of his adult life. He describes dieting but mainly as a response to the weight problems caused by his overeating. He feels that his eating is closely tied to his moods, with a tendency to eat when in a negative mood. Currently, Carl engages in large binge eating episodes on a daily basis, but always in the evenings after coming home from work. As his bingeing has increased, he has given up on most social activities and spends much of his evening time alone.

Other than his obese status, his eating-related problems generally are not recognizable to his coworkers. He is somewhat socially avoidant and particularly avoids food-related workplace social events (e.g., social lunches, parties). In an effort to conceal his eating problems, as well as to control them, he eats very sparingly at work. The severity of his binge eating fluctuates with the degree of work-related stress.

Commentary

Although we continue to emphasize the degree of variability among people with eating disorders, the preceding case examples may illustrate many characteristic features of each disorder. AN, if not so severe that the employee is simply unable to work, may affect both the employee and his or her coworkers. The employee's job performance may suffer because of the cognitive and emotional effects of the self-induced starvation, and social activities may be negatively affected secondary to the avoidance of food-related activities or secondary to a comorbid personality disorder. The eating-related problems may, in some cases, be easily recognized by fellow employees. It is even possible that the employee's eating problem may become a source of conflict among fellow employees, if several recognize a need for possible intervention but none is clear on the best approach.

In contrast, BN appears to be a clandestine disorder. People with the disorder are typically of average weight and, because of the shame associated with the disorder, may not disclose to others that a problem exists. Only in the more severe cases are physiological and/or cognitive deficits likely to affect a person's work performance. However, the various types of comorbid psychopathology may have more substantive work-related impact (see chapters 7, 14, and 18 of this volume for a discussion of depression, borderline personality disorder, and substance use, respectively—three problems that may co-occur with BN).

As with AN, BED may be recognizable by coworkers but not because of the disorder per se; rather, simply because of the commonly occurring obesity. Binge eating disorder most likely has the least workplace impact of the three disorders. However, the constant preoccupation with food as well as time spent planning and engaging in eating binges may markedly affect quality of life, reducing social relationships and leaving little time for other interests (Agras, 2001). Recurrent bingeing may even cause financial problems for the afflicted individual because of the money spent on food (a problem that may occur with BN as well as BED).

PRECIPITATING CONDITIONS, INCLUDING WORKPLACE STRESSORS

Sociocultural pressures to be thin are believed to play a major role in the etiology and maintenance of eating disorders, particularly AN and BN. Although these pressures may come from the media, family members, or peers, they may also come from the work environment. Whenever an occupation carries with it pressures to be thin, the risk of its contributing to eating disorders exists. In a recent survey of men and women admitted to an eating disorder treatment program, 37% of the men and 13% of the women reported being "in an occupation or athletic team in which control of weight is important for good performance" (Braun, Sunday, Haung, & Halmi, 1999, p. 419). Emphasis on appearance and/or low body weight may or may not be explicit. Some relatively obvious examples where there is explicit emphasis on body weight and/or physical appearance include acting; modeling; professional dancing; and many types of professional athletics (jockeying, professional tennis). However, any work environment in which hiring, promotion, and other work-related decisions are affected by physical appearance should be viewed as not only discriminatory, but also potentially contributing to the incidence of eating problems. Workplace competition has been suggested as associated with the "cult of slimming" (Offer, 2001), and sexual harassment has also been found to be associated with eating disorder symptomatology (Harned, 2000), with the authors of the study concluding that disordered eating may function as a way of coping with negative emotions created by sexual harassment.

In addition to specific body or weight-related stressors (such as sexual harassment or pressures to lose weight), general workplace stress may also play a role in maintaining eating-related problems. We know that occupational stress contributes to a wide variety of work-related psychological disorders (e.g., Sauter, Murphy, & Hurrell, 1990). For many people with eating disorders, bingeing and/or restrictive eating may occur in response to stress. Such disordered eating may be conceptualized as a form of maladaptive coping. Although the link between eating and substance use disorders is probably overstated, both disorders may be quite similar in terms of how they are used as mechanisms for coping with a stressful environment.

COURSE AND PROGNOSIS

Although anorexia and BN are similar disorders in many ways, their course and prognosis vary considerably. Anorexia may be a severely debilitating condition. Mortality rates are actually higher for anorexia than for any other psychiatric disorder (Sullivan, 1995), with a rate of approximately 5.6% per decade. Approximately half of the deaths are due to suicide, with the others caused by physical complications of the disorder. Many people with AN may need to be hospitalized. This may be a direct result of the eating disorder, a related physical problem, or suicidality or other self-injurious behavior.

For BN, the course and prognosis are more favorable. Medical complications generally are not life-threatening, and suicide rates are much lower than those for anorexia. Follow-up studies suggest that after 10 years, only 10% of individuals continue to experience the full syndrome, and 60% may be in full or partial remission of the eating disorder. However, 30% to 50% may still have a diagnosable eating disorder (Agras, 2001).

Less is currently known about the long-term course of BED; however, the prognosis is probably better than that for either AN or BN. In one study, at the 5-year follow-up, 15% of people with BED still had a diagnosable eating disorder, and only 9% continued to have BED (Fairburn, Cooper, Doll, Norman, & O'Connor, 2000).

People with BN and BED are generally receptive to recommendations for treatment because they feel that their eating problems are out of control (although they may not necessarily be compliant with specific treatment once it has begun). In contrast, people with AN may be more resistant to the idea of treatment in general, often because they do not view their restrictive eating as problematic. Consequently, referral strategies may require the involvement of family members in cases of severe anorexia.

Because of the negative impact of eating disorders, particularly if they become chronic, many working in the field have argued that early identification and intervention are needed to improve the course of the disorders. Although this suggestion is intuitively logical, a recent review of the outcome literature concluded that there was no consistent evidence that early intervention necessarily implied better long-term outcome (Reas, Schoemaker, Zipfel, & Williamson, 2001).

RECOMMENDED DATA-BASED TREATMENTS

The Continuum of Care

We now have a fairly large database regarding treatment of eating disorders, particularly AN and BN. One can now make somewhat informed decisions regarding not only the type of treatment (i.e., psychological versus pharmacological), but also the level of intensity. Based on the recognition that people with EDs may vary significantly with regard to their level of functioning and their treatment needs, a "stepped-care" approach (e.g., Fairburn & Peveler, 1990; Garner & Needleman, 1996) has been developed for treatment in which empirically or logically derived interventions are ordered into levels or steps based on their intrusiveness, cost, and probability of success. Initially, patients may be provided with a lowest step intervention, one that is least costly and intrusive. However, this intervention may not have the highest probability of success; thus, the next step up may be necessary either alone or in combination with the previous step (Garner & Needleman, 1996). There may also be many instances in which certain critical information necessitates the immediate choice of a higher level of treatment. The obvious situation here is if the person is in acute danger, because of either an extreme medical condition (as with severe anorexia) or a high risk of suicide. Various stepped-care decision

trees have been described in the treatment literature (see Agras, 1993; Fairburn & Peveler, 1990; Fairburn, Agras, & Wilson, 1992; Garner & Needleman, 1996). A general description of the typical levels of treatment follows.

Hospitalization (Inpatient Treatment). When the employee is in acute medical or psychiatric danger, hospitalization may be needed. Typically, the primary goals are (a) management of medical problems, (b) weight restoration (in acute anorexia), (c) interruption of potentially out-of-control bingeing and vomiting (in bulimia or anorexia nervosa), (d) management of comorbid psychological problems (e.g., depression or substance abuse), (e) disentanglement from a family system that may be making progress difficult, and (f) preparation for successful outpatient treatment. The last goal is critical. A great deal of change (e.g., weight gain or reduction in bingeing and purging) can be achieved in a relatively short period of inpatient treatment. However, without proper follow-up, all of these gains may be short-lived.

Residential Treatment. Some health professionals may not be aware that a group of treatment programs, identified as residential treatment facilities, is a small but sometimes important step down from hospitalization. Residential treatment programs do not offer the medical support available for the patient in a severely compromised medical condition, but they do offer 24-hour treatment for the severe anorexic or bulimic individual who cannot benefit from less intense treatment. Being able to eat all meals with treatment staff while also being observed after meals to prevent purging may help quickly normalize previously out-of-control behavior. The patient is also able to participate in therapy as intensely as with hospitalization but at a lower cost.

Day Treatment. One step down from residential treatment, the day program may function either as a follow-up to residential or inpatient treatment, or as an alternative for the severe patient who may still be able to benefit from something less than the most intense treatment. As the name implies, patients receive treatment during the day but do not remain in the facility overnight. Such an approach is less expensive, is generally less disruptive to a person's life, and, depending on his or her work schedule, may allow for continued work. These programs may also vary in intensity, with some requiring daily attendance and others requiring only 2 or 3 days per week.

Outpatient Psychotherapy. If the client's medical condition is not critical, and/or if his or her psychosocial functioning is not severely impaired by the disorder, outpatient treatment may be the optimal referral choice. This treatment may be individual or group therapy and may be based on a variety of approaches. Cognitive-behavioral and interpersonal (see below) therapies have received the most empirical support. As with the programs described above, outpatient treatment may vary considerably in level of intensity. Fairly typical would be group or individual therapy twice per week. However, many agencies now have what they call intensive outpatient programs that may meet as often as every night during the week. With outpatient eating disorder treatments in general, attention needs to be given to possible signs that a treatment of more intensity is needed. If weight gain cannot be initiated for the anorexic patient, or if bingeing and purging are not controlled, outpatient treatment may be determined to be inadequate.

Psychoeducation. Although outpatient therapies, particularly cognitive-behavioral therapy, do contain a psychoeducational component, another category of interventions may be regarded as strictly psycho-educational. One such program was examined by Olmsted et al. (1991) and compared with individual cognitive-behavioral treatment. The psychoeducational program included information on regulating body weight, normalizing eating, and reducing bingeing and purging. It also included information challenging societal standards of thinness for women. For the less severe patients, this program was as effective as more intense treatment. In general, although these educational interventions are quite variable, it does appear that many people with less severe psychopathology benefit from the information they contain.

Self-Help. Finally, use of self-help manuals, or "bibliotherapy," has become increasing popular in recent years, and there is increasing evidence that it can be effective for a variety of psychological problems (Pantalon, Lebetkin, & Fishman, 1995). Numerous self-help manuals for eating disorders exist (e.g., Weiss, Katzman, & Wolchick, 1988), and there is some empirical support for their use for both BN (Cooper, Coker, & Fleming, 1994) and BED (Carter & Fairburn, 1998). We cannot envision self-help being a recommended treatment for AN, although self-help manuals could certainly supplement additional treatments. Continued empirical research on their effectiveness is needed, but self-help manuals empirically supported per se or otherwise based on empirically supported treatments (e.g., Fairburn, 1995) may be considered as low level interventions for people with milder, less severe eating disorders.

Types of Treatment Approaches

Above, we described the range of treatment modalities available for eating disorder referrals. Here, we discuss briefly the different treatment approaches (i.e., pharmacotherapy vs. various types of psychotherapy) that may occur across most of the modalities.

Pharmacological Treatments. Use of psychotropic interventions may occur with most of the modalities discussed above, or use of medications may be the only intervention. With AN, a variety of drugs have been tried, but no medication has been shown to treat the anorexia per se (Johnson et al., 1996; Peterson & Mitchell, 1999). Medications such as antidepressants are usually aimed at treating the comorbid psychopathology and should not be considered specific treatments for the AN. In contrast, several types of antidepressants have been found to be effective in reducing the bingeing and purging associated with BN or the bingeing with BED (Johnson et al., 1996; Peterson & Mitchell, 1999). The selective serotonin reuptake inhibitors (e.g., fluoxetine) may be the drugs of choice for BN; the data are less clear for BED (Peterson & Mitchell, 1999). A significant limitation of pharmacological interventions is that their effectiveness may be temporary. That is, relapse may occur when the drugs are discontinued, and there is a lack of evidence that the drugs remain effective over extended periods of time, even while use continues (Walsh, 1991). Dropout rates may also be higher than with psychological interventions.

Psychological Treatments. With AN, very few controlled outcome studies exist, largely because of the ethical problems associated with putting people who are physically at risk in a "no treatment" or wait-list control group. In one of the few existing studies (Crisp et al., 1991), 90 anorexics were assigned to one of four treatment conditions: two outpatient, one inpatient, and one assessment only (no treatment). All three treatments were highly successful, whereas the control group was largely unimproved. At a 2-year follow-up (Gowers, Norton, Halek, & Crisp, 1994), 12 of 20 patients assigned to the outpatient individual and family treatment were classified as "well" or nearly well. Perhaps the most important finding was that outpatient therapy could be as effective as inpatient therapy. However, the main problem with this set of studies is that the treatments described were very comprehensive, making it difficult to identify the active ingredient(s).

Data are clearer for BN because numerous controlled and/or comparative outcome studies have now been conducted. Treatments that have received the most empirical research are cognitive-behavioral therapy (CBT) and interpersonal psychotherapy (IPT). The basic CBT approach has since been validated in several controlled outcome studies, and as Lewandowski, Gebing, Anthony, & O'Brien (1997) concluded, "Overall, results suggest that the use of a cognitive-behavioral therapy will result in favorable treatment outcomes" (p. 703). CBT also seems to have superiority over purely behavioral treatment. IPT (Weisman & Markowitz, 1994) helps clients identify and resolve current interpersonal relationship problems, but it does not address eating behaviors or attitudes directly. Several studies have supported its effectiveness with BN. One study directly compared IPT and CBT, and although cognitive-behavior therapy appeared superior at posttreatment, the differences had disappeared at the 1-year follow-up (Fairburn, Jones, Peveler, Hope, & O'Connor, 1993). Fairburn et al. (1995) also followed the above-mentioned group, along with researchers from another study, and found that even after 6 years, the people in the cognitive-behavioral and interpersonal psychotherapy conditions had maintained their gains, and the two treatments appeared to be equally effective. However, Fairburn (1997) cautioned that, in contrast with the vast body of research supporting CBT, the evidence supporting IPT is modest. He recommended that it not be considered as a first-choice treatment and perhaps should be used for those people who either fail to respond to CBT or are unwilling to engage in the therapy.

With BED, most of the treatments have been derived from the treatment for BN (both cognitive-behavior therapy and interpersonal therapy), and the effects on binge eating may be somewhat similar. However, with BED, there is an added problem of obesity, and treatment of binge eating alone does not result in significant weight loss (Johnson et al., 1996). There is somewhat of a controversy regarding if and/or how obesity associated with BED should be treated. Agras (1993) has suggested that weight loss should become a focus of treatment only after treatment for the binge eating. However, results of a study by Porzelius, Houston, Smith, Arfken, and Fisher (1995) suggest that concurrent treatment of binge eating and obesity may be possible, but that matching between binge eating severity and type of treatment may be critical.

Family Therapy. Because of the role the family may play in both the etiology and maintenance of eating disorders, family therapy is often recommended as an adjunctive or even primary form of treatment (Minuchin, Rosman, & Baker, 1978). When dealing with adolescents still living with parents, such a recommendation could be easily justified, even if only for practical purposes. Given the current focus on the workplace, where the employee is typically an adult who is likely to be living independently, family therapy may not need to be a standard recommendation. However, with adults, there may be a tendency to underestimate the degree to which family pathology may affect an eating disorder. Furthermore, there may be more than family-of-origin conflict (i.e., current marital problems may exacerbate an existing eating disorder). Family therapy may be available with most steps in the continuum of care described above and is likely to be a standard part of most inpatient and/or residential treatment programs.

Time Element

The length of treatment will vary depending on the type and severity of the eating disorder and which of the above-described "steps" is viewed as necessary. In general, treatment for AN is more time intensive than for either BN or BED. For the latter two, the typical length of treatment from controlled outcome studies is 12 to 20 sessions delivered over approximately 3 months. Thus, although real-world treatments may not necessarily be delivered in such a specific packaged form, substantial improvement may occur in this relatively brief period of time. As noted above, AN may be a chronic condition. Hospitalizations are typically as brief as possible but need to be followed with appropriate outpatient treatment.

Work-Related Side Effects

Possible work-related side effects of ED treatment are minimal relative to treatments for many other psychiatric problems. Side effects would also vary depending on the type of treatment. With pharmacological treatments, the newer antidepressant medications generally have many fewer side effects than do the tricyclics, but may include nausea, vomiting, insomnia, nervousness, and, occasionally, sexual and urinary difficulties. There are no known work-related untoward side effects of psychological treatments for eating disorders.

Workplace Accommodations

Perhaps the most significant workplace accommodation may simply be the ability to have time off for treatment. The amount of time necessary here will obviously depend on the intensity of the treatment. Outpatient psychological treatment for BN may be two appointments per week for a period of several weeks. These may occur in the evening, which would not affect the employee's work schedule. With AN and a need for hospitalization, the employee may need an extended leave from work. If an employee is involved in a day treatment program, a flexible work schedule may allow the person to continue working and receive treatment at the same time.

Maintenance of Gains/Relapse Prevention

Employers can work to improve maintenance of treatment gains by encouraging employees to continue with prescribed treatments and by attempting to create a work environment that shapes healthy eating patterns (Campbell et al., 2000; Poulter & Torrance, 1993). Although they have not been tested explicitly as an eating disorder treatment follow-up, wellness programs for employees that are aimed at improving dietary and exercise habits may be helpful, not only for the employee recovering from an eating disorder but for all employees. However, the focus should be on healthy eating and lifestyle rather than weight loss per se. It is also important that the workplace does not contribute to and/or promote disordered eating behavior. A work environment that mirrors Western society's emphasis on thinness and physical beauty, where obesity is a target of discrimination, is likely to be problematic for the recovering eating-disordered individual. It may seem an unrealistic goal to suggest that various workplaces attempt to disconnect themselves from themes so common in our society in general. However, any degree of movement in that direction may have a meaningful effect on the lives of employees struggling with eating-related disorders.

SUMMARY

Eating disorders are potentially severe and chronic conditions associated with a wealth of physical and/or additional psychological problems. AN in particular has the highest mortality rate of any psychological disorder. The impact on workplace behavior may be quite variable, although it will, in general, be much greater with AN than with BN or BED. The impact of associated psychological problems (e.g., substance abuse, depression, personality disorders) may be as great as that of the eating disorder per se. Current psychological and pharmacological treatments are effective for BN and BED. AN represents more of a treatment challenge. However, long-term follow-up studies suggest that even a majority of anorexics are able to maintain employment.

REFERENCES

Agras, W. S. (1993). Short-term psychological treatments for binge eating. In C. G. Fairburn & G. T. Wilson (Eds.), *Binge eating: Nature, assessment, and treatment* (pp. 50-76). New York: Guilford.

Agras, W. S. (2001). The consequences and costs of the eating disorders. *Psychiatric Clinics of North America, 24,* 371-379.

American Psychiatric Association. (1994). *Diagnostic and statistical manual of mental disorders* (4th ed.). Washington, DC: Author.

Andersen, A. E., & Holman, J. E. (1997). Males with eating disorders: Challenges for treatment and research. *Psychopharmacology Bulletin, 33*(3), 391-397.

Braun, D. L., Sunday, S. R., & Halmi, K. A. (1994). Psychiatric comorbidity in patients with eating disorders. *Psychological Medicine, 24,* 859-867.

Braun, D. L., Sunday, S. R., Haung, A., & Halmi, K. A. (1999). More males seek treatment for eating disorders. *International Journal of Eating Disorders, 25,* 415-424.

Bruch, H. (1966). Anorexia nervosa and its differential diagnosis. *Journal of Nervous and Mental Disease, 141,* 555-566.

Bushnell, J. A., Wells, J. E., Hornblow, A. R., Oakley-Browne, M. A., & Joyce, P. (1990). Prevalence of three bulimia syndromes in the general population. *Psychological Medicine, 20,* 671-680.

Campbell, M. K., Tessaro, I., Devellis, B., Benedict, S., Kelsey, K., Belton, L., & Henriquez Roldan, C. (2000). Tailoring and targeting a workplace health promotion program to address multiple health behaviors among blue-collar women. *American Journal of Health Promotion, 14,* 306-313.

Cassell, D. K., & Gleaves, D. H. (2000). *The encyclopedia of obesity and eating disorders* (2nd ed.). New York: Facts On Life.

Carlat, D. J., Camargo, C. A., & Herzog, D. B. (1997). Eating disorders in males: A report on 135 patients. *American Journal of Psychiatry, 154,* 1127-1132.

Carter, J. C., & Fairburn, C. G. (1998). Cognitive-behavioral self-help for binge eating disorder: A controlled effectiveness study. *Journal of Consulting and Clinical Psychology, 66,* 616-623.

Cepeda-Benito, A., Gleaves, D. H., Williams, T. L., & Erath, S. A. (2000). The development and validation of the State and Trait Food-Cravings Questionnaires. *Behavior Therapy, 31,* 151-173.

Cooper, P. J., Coker, S., & Fleming, C. (1994). Self-help for bulimia nervosa: A preliminary report. *International Journal of Eating Disorders, 16,* 401-404.

Cooper, P. J., Taylor, M. J., Cooper, Z., & Fairburn, C. G. (1987). The development and validation of the Body Shape Questionnaire. *International Journal of Eating Disorders, 6,* 485-494.

Crisp, A. H. (1967). Clinical aspects of anorexia nervosa. *Proceedings of the Nutrition Society, 26,* R32.

Crisp, A. H., Norton, K., Gowers, S., Halek, C., Bowyer, C., Yeldham, D., Levett, G., & Bhat, A. (1991). A controlled study of the effects of therapies aimed at adolescent and family psychopathology in anorexia nervosa. *British Journal of Psychiatry, 159,* 325-333.

Crisp, A. H., Palmer, R. L., & Kalucy, R. S. (1976). How common is anorexia nervosa? A prevalence study. *British Journal of Psychiatry, 128,* 549-554.

Eberenz, K. P., & Gleaves, D. H. (1994). An examination of the internal consistency and factor structure of the Eating Disorder Inventory-2 in a clinical sample. *International Journal of Eating Disorders, 16,* 371-379.

Fairburn, C. G. (1995). *Overcoming binge eating*. New York: Guilford.

Fairburn, C. G. (1997). Interpersonal psychotherapy for bulimia nervosa. In D. M. Garner & P. E. Garfinkel (Eds.), *Handbook of treatment for eating disorders* (2nd ed., pp. 278-294). New York: Guilford.

Fairburn, C. G., Agras, W. S., & Wilson, G. T. (1992). The research on the treatment of bulimia nervosa: Practical and theoretical implications. In G. H. Anderson & S. H. Kennedy (Eds.), *Biology of feast and famine*. San Diego, CA: Academic Press.

Fairburn, C. G., & Beglin, S. J. (1990). Studies of the epidemiology of bulimia nervosa. *American Journal of Psychiatry, 147*, 401-408.

Fairburn, C. G., Cooper, Z., Doll, H. A., Norman, P., & O'Connor, M. (2000). The natural course of bulimia nervosa and binge-eating disorder in young women. *Archives of General Psychiatry, 57*, 659-665.

Fairburn, C. G., Jones, R., Peveler, R. C., Hope, R. A., & O'Connor, M. (1993). Psychotherapy and bulimia nervosa: Longer-term effects of interpersonal psychotherapy, behavior therapy, and cognitive behavior therapy. *Archives of General Psychiatry, 50*, 419-428.

Fairburn, C. G., Norman, P. A., Welch, S. L., O'Connor, M. E., Doll, H. A., & Peveler, R. C. (1995). A prospective study of outcome in bulimia nervosa and the long-term effects of three psychological treatments. *Archives of General Psychiatry, 52*, 304-312.

Fairburn, C. G., & Peveler, R. C. (1990). Bulimia nervosa and a stepped care approach to management. *Gut, 31*, 1220-1222.

Fornari, V., Kaplan, M., Sandberg, D. E., Mathews, M., Skolnick, N., & Katz, J. L. (1992). Depressive and anxiety disorders in anorexia nervosa and bulimia nervosa. *International Journal of Eating Disorders, 12*, 21-29.

García-Camba, E. (2001). Trastornos de la comida alimentaria en el momento actual [Current issues in eating disorders]. In E. García-Camba (Ed.), *Avances en trastornos de la conducta alimentaria: Anorexia nerviosa, bulimia nerviosa, obesidad [Advances in eating disorders: Anorexia nervosa, bulimia nervosa, obesity]* (pp. 3-30). Madrid, Spain: Masson.

Garfinkel, P. E. (1990). Anorexia nervosa and bulimia nervosa: What knowledge of diagnosis and pathogenesis has taught about treatment. In R. J. McMahon & R. D. V. Peters (Eds.), *Behavior disorders of adolescence: Research, intervention, and policy in clinical and school settings* (pp. 99-110). New York: Plenum.

Garfinkel, P. E., Lin, E., Goering, P., Spegg, C., Goldbloom D. S., Kennedy, S., Kaplan, A. S., & Woodside, D. B. (1995). Bulimia nervosa in a Canadian community sample: Prevalence and comparison of subgroups. *American Journal of Psychiatry, 152*, 1052-1058.

Garner, D. M. (1991). *Eating Disorders Inventory-2*. Odessa, FL: Psychological Assessment Resources.

Garner, D. M., & Fairburn, C. G. (1988). Relationship between anorexia nervosa and bulimia nervosa: Diagnostic implications. In D. M. Garner & P. E. Garfinkel (Eds.), *Diagnostic issues in anorexia nervosa and bulimia nervosa: Brunner/Mazel eating disorders monograph series, No. 2* (pp. 56-79). Philadelphia: Brunner/Mazel.

Garner, D. M., & Needleman, L. D. (1996). Stepped-care and decision-tree models for treating eating disorders. In J. K. Thompson (Ed.), *Body image, eating disorders and obesity: An integrative guide to assessment and treatment* (pp. 225-252). Washington, DC: American Psychological Association.

Garner, D. M., Olmstead, M. P., & Polivy, J. (1983). Development and validation of a multidimensional eating disorder inventory for anorexia nervosa and bulimia. *International Journal of Eating Disorders, 2*, 15-34.

Gartner, A. F., Marcus, R. N., Halmi, K., & Loranger, A. W. (1989). *DSM-III-R* personality disorders in patients with eating disorders. *American Journal of Psychiatry, 146,* 1585-1591.

Gleaves, D. H., & Eberenz, K. P. (1994). Sexual abuse histories among treatment-resistant bulimia nervosa patients. *International Journal of Eating Disorders, 15,* 227-231.

Gleaves, D. H., May, M. C., & Eberenz, K. P. (1998). Scope and significance of posttraumatic symptomatology among women with eating disorders. *International Journal of Eating Disorders, 24,* 147-156.

Gowers, S., Norton, K., Halek, C., & Crisp, A. H. (1994). Outcome of outpatient psychotherapy in a random allocation treatment study of anorexia nervosa. *International Journal of Eating Disorders, 15,* 165-177.

Harned, M. S. (2000). Harassed bodies—An examination of the relationships among women's experiences of sexual harassment, body image, and eating disturbances. *Psychology of Women Quarterly, 24,* 336-348.

Hay, P., & Fairburn, C. (1998). The validity of the *DSM-IV* scheme for classifying bulimic eating disorders. *International Journal of Eating Disorders, 23,* 7-15.

Henderson, M., & Freeman, C. P. (1987). A self-rating scale for bulimia: The "BITE." *British Journal of Psychiatry, 150,* 18-24.

Herzog, D. B., Keller, M. B., Sacks, N. R., Yeh, C. J., & Lavori, P. W. (1992). Psychiatric comorbidity in treatment-seeking anorexics and bulimics. *Journal of the American Academy of Child and Adolescent Psychiatry, 31,* 810-818.

Holderness, C. C., Brooks-Gunn, J., & Warren, M. P. (1994). Co-morbidity of eating disorders and substance abuse: Review of the literature. *International Journal of Eating Disorders, 16,* 1-34.

Hsu, L. K. G. (1990). *Eating disorders.* New York: Guilford.

Johnson, W. G., Tsoh, J. Y., & Varnado, P. J. (1996). Eating disorders: Efficacy of pharmacological and psychological interventions. *Clinical Psychology Review, 16,* 457-478.

Lewandowski, L. M., Gebing, T. A., Anthony, J. L., & O'Brien, W. H. (1997). Meta-analysis of cognitive-behavioral treatment studies for bulimia. *Clinical Psychology Review, 17,* 703-718.

Lucas, A. R., Beard, C. M., O'Fallon, W. M., & Kurland, L. T. (1991). 50-year trends in the incidence of anorexia nervosa in Rochester, MN: A population-based study. *American Journal of Psychiatry, 148,* 917-922.

Minuchin, S., Rosman, B. L., & Baker, L. (1978). *Psychosomatic families: Anorexia nervosa in context.* Cambridge, MA: Harvard University Press.

Moos, R. H., & Moos, R. (1981). *Family Environment Scale manual.* Palo Alto, CA: Consulting Psychologists Press.

Offer, A. (2001). Body weight and self-control in the United States and Britain since the 1950s. *Social History of Medicine, 14,* 79-106.

Olmsted, M. P., Davis, R., Garner, D. M., Rockert, W., Irvine, M. J., & Eagle, M. (1991). Efficacy of a brief group psychoeducational intervention for bulimia nervosa. *Behaviour Research and Therapy, 29,* 71-83.

Pantalon, M. V., Lebetkin, B. S., & Fishman, S. T. (1995). Use and effectiveness of self-help books in the practice of cognitive and behavioral therapy. *Cognitive and Behavioral Practice, 2,* 213-228.

Peterson, C. B., & Mitchell, J. E. (1999). Psychosocial and pharmacological treatment of eating disorders: A review of research findings. *Journal of Clinical Psychology, 55,* 685-697.

Pope, H. G., Hudson, J. I., Yurgelun-Todd, D., & Hudson, M. S. (1984). Prevalence of anorexia nervosa and bulimia in three student populations. *International Journal of Eating Disorders, 3,* 45-51.

Porzelius, L. K., Houston, C., Smith, M., Arfken, C., & Fisher, E. (1995). Comparison of a standard behavioral weight loss treatment and a binge eating weight loss treatment. *Behavior Therapy, 26,* 119-134.

Poulter, J., & Torrance, I. (1993). Food and health at work—A review—The cost and benefits of a policy approach. *Journal of Human Nutrition and Dietetics, 6,* 89-100.

Raich, R. M., Deus, J., Muñoz, M. J., Perez, O., & Requena, A. (1991). Estudio de las actitudes alimentarias en una muestra de adolescentes [Study of eating attitudes in a sample of adolescents]. *Revista de Psiquiatria de la Facultad de Medicina de Barcelona, 18,* 305-315.

Reas, D. L., Schoemaker, C., Zipfel, S., & Williamson, D. A. (2001). Prognostic value of duration of illness and early intervention in bulimia nervosa: A systematic review of the outcome literature. *International Journal of Eating Disorders, 30,* 1-10.

Rossiter, E. M., & Agras, W. S. (1990). An empirical test of the *DSM-III-R* definition of binge. *International Journal of Eating Disorders, 9,* 513-518.

Russell, G. (1979). Bulimia nervosa: An ominous variant of anorexia nervosa. *Psychological Medicine, 9,* 429-448.

Russell, G. F. M. (1995). Anorexia nervosa through time. In G. I. Szmukler, C. Dare, & J. Treasure (Eds.), *Handbook of eating disorders: Theory, treatment and research* (pp. 5-17). New York: Wiley.

Sauter, S. L., Murphy, L. R., & Hurrell, J. J. (1990). Prevention of work-related psychological disorders. *American Psychologist, 45,* 1146-1158.

Schlundt, D. G., & Johnson, W. G. (1990). *Eating disorders: Assessment and treatment.* Needham Heights, MA: Allyn & Bacon.

Sevillano Fernández, J. P. (2001). Evaluación y motivación en los trastornos de la conducta alimentaria [Assessment and motivation in eating disorders]. In E. García-Camba (Ed.), *Avances en trastornos de la conducta alimentaria: Anorexia nerviosa, bulimia nerviosa, obesidad [Advances in eating disorders: Anorexia nervosa, bulimia nervosa, obesity]* (pp. 75-92). Madrid, Spain: Masson.

Spurrell, E. B., Wilfley, D. E., Tanofsky, M. B., & Brownell, K. D. (1997). Age of onset for binge eating: Are there different pathways to binge eating? *International Journal of Eating Disorders, 21,* 55-65.

Steiger, H., Liquornik, K., Chapman, J., & Hussain, N. (1991). Personality and family disturbances in eating-disorder patients: Comparison of "restrictors" and "bingers" to normal controls. *International Journal of Eating Disorders, 10,* 501-513.

Stunkard, A. J. (1993). A history of binge eating. In C. G. Fairburn & G. T. Wilson (Eds.), *Binge eating: Nature, assessment, and treatment* (pp. 15-34). New York: Guilford.

Sullivan, P. F. (1995). Mortality in anorexia nervosa. *American Journal of Psychiatry, 152,* 1073-1074.

Turón, J. V., Homs, J. P., González, A., & Salvador, M. A. (1997). Nuestra experiencia hospitalaria en el tratamiento de la bulimia nerviosa [Our experience treating bulimia nervosa in hospitalized patients]. *Revista del Departamento de Psiquiatria de la Facultad de Medicina de Barcelona, 14,* 118-121.

Walsh, B. T. (1991). Psychopharmacologic treatment of bulimia nervosa. *Journal of Clinical Psychiatry, 52*(Suppl. 10), S34-S38.

Walsh, B. T. (1993). Binge eating in bulimia nervosa. In C. G. Fairburn & G. T. Wilson (Eds.), *Binge eating: Nature, assessment, and treatment* (pp. 37-49). New York: Guilford.

Walsh, B. T., & Garner, D. M. (1997). Diagnostic issues. In D. M. Garner & P. E. Garfinkel (Eds.), *Handbook of treatment for eating disorders* (2nd ed., pp. 25-33). New York: Guilford.

Walters, E. E., & Kendler, K. S. (1995). Anorexia nervosa and anorexic-like syndromes in a population-based female twin sample. *American Journal of Psychiatry, 152,* 64-71.

Weisman, M. M., & Markowitz, J. C. (1994). Interpersonal psychotherapy: Current status. *Archives of General Psychiatry, 51,* 599-606.

Weiss, K., Katzman, M., & Wolchick, S. (1988). *You can't have your cake and eat it too: A program for controlling bulimia.* New York: Pergamon.

Williamson, D. A., Cubic, B. A., & Gleaves, D. H. (1993) Equivalence of body image disturbances in anorexia and bulimia nervosa. *Journal of Abnormal Psychology, 102,* 177-180.

Williamson, D. A., Davis, C. J., Bennett, S. M., Goreczny, A. J., & Gleaves, D. H. (1989). Development of a simple procedure for assessing body image disturbances. *Behavioral Assessment, 11,* 433-446.

Willmuth, M. E., Leitenberg, H., Rosen, J. C., & Cado, S. (1988). A comparison of purging and nonpurging normal weight bulimics. *International Journal of Eating Disorders, 7,* 825-835.

CHAPTER 16

Traumatic Brain Injury in the Workplace

CHARLES J. GOLDEN

DESCRIPTION OF THE DISORDER

Traumatic brain injury (TBI), also referred to as Head Injury or Acquired Brain Injury, is a dysfunction of the brain that results from a physical force outside of the individual that causes an alteration in the way the brain functions at a structural, biochemical, or behavioral level. These changes result in a diminished or altered state of consciousness, disturbances of behavior, problems in specific cognitive tasks, or emotional problems such as irritability or depression. The most common mechanism for TBI is to hit the skull with a large force that is transmitted through the skull to the brain itself, causing lasting or temporary damage (Golden, Zillmer, & Spiers, 1992).

Symptoms may include a wide range of problems that differ in both intensity and duration, depending on the injury and the individual. These deficits can include short-term memory loss; long-term memory loss; slowed ability to process information; trouble concentrating or paying attention over sustained periods of time; difficulty keeping up with a conversation; word-finding problems; problems in understanding language; loss of a second (acquired) language; spatial disorientation; driving difficulties; impulsivity; inflexibility; time disorientation; organizational problems; impaired judgment; problems doing more than one thing at a time; seizures; muscle spasticity; double vision; impaired visual fields; loss of smell or taste; slow or slurred speech; headaches or migraines; fatigue; lack of initiating activities; difficulty in completing tasks without reminders; increased anxiety; depression and mood swings; denial of deficits; impulsive behavior; lack of insight; agitation; egocentricity (inability to see how behaviors affect others); explosive behavior; erratic behavior; sensory losses; inability to deal with novel or new material; and impairment in reading, writing, or arithmetic.

In all cases of TBI, there is a physical alteration of the brain. However, such alteration may not be evident on standard neurological tests (CT scan, MRI, X rays, physical examination). In other cases, TBI is accompanied by other serious injuries (back injuries, chest injuries, broken bones, respiratory problems) that may cause the TBI to be missed. Although TBI is due to a physical change in the brain, the head does not need to hit an object for a TBI to occur. It can be caused by sudden acceleration or deceleration (such as an accident in which a car hits a wall, but the head does not hit any part of the car).

Most cases of TBI are classified as concussions. In such cases, there is either no loss of consciousness, or a loss of consciousness that typically lasts less than 30 minutes. The symptoms from a concussion may last only minutes, but can stretch in some individuals for up to 3 months. More serious cases of TBI are labeled as contusions. In such cases, bruising or bleeding occurs in the brain itself. Deficits from contusions may be permanent, although in many cases, the brain "reorganizes" so that long-term symptoms are not apparent. More serious contusions, which produce definite evidence of focal injuries in a specific area of the brain, are often called lacerations.

In milder head injuries, problems may arise from what has been labeled a diffuse axonal injury (DAI). DAI occurs when there is a sudden change in the acceleration of the brain, usually from sudden stops. In such cases, the rate of slowing is different for the cortex (outside of the brain) than for the deep structures within the brain. This difference in rates causes the cortex to pull away from the deeper structures, causing stretching of the axons that connect these structures. The stretching causes the axons to break or tear. Because axons are responsible for communication between different areas of the brain, such breaks or tears cause impairment, resulting in problems in attention, focusing, emotions, and cognitive skills. DAI may occur whether or not there is a physical blow to the head.

Other conditions can also result in complications of TBI. The most common occurs when the skull is fractured. In such cases, a piece of the skull or a foreign object (such as a bullet) may pierce the brain itself, causing destruction of brain tissue. Interestingly, in some cases where the skull is fractured but the brain is not pierced, the overall injury may be less because the fractured skull absorbs the impact of the injury to a greater degree than when the skull is intact. In cases when the skull is penetrated, veins and arteries within the brain may be torn, causing the release of blood into the brain. In other cases, the force of a blow may cause a weak spot in an artery or vein to rupture, again resulting in the release of blood into brain tissue. Blood is toxic to the brain, so such cases result in destruction of brain tissue.

Another major complication is edema, or swelling, which is the result of the blow to the brain, much as swelling occurs when an ankle or knee is injured. However, unlike swelling in the knee or ankle, swelling in the brain occurs within a contained vessel (the skull). Thus, the swelling causes pressure to build up in the brain. Such pressure may compress the brain tissue, causing injury to brain cells called neurons. In other cases, the build-up of pressure may cause arteries that provide blood to the brain to close off, much as flow in a hose is cut off if enough pressure is applied to the hose. This results in either hypoxia, the loss of adequate oxygenation to the brain cells, or anoxia, the complete loss of oxygen to the neurons. Either condition can lead to neuronal injury or death, depending on how long the condition persists and how serious it is. It is not unusual to see cases of TBI where the person seems normal at first, but later lapses into a coma because of pressure in the brain.

EPIDEMIOLOGY

An estimated 5.3 million Americans—a little more than 2% of the U.S. population—currently live with disabilities resulting from brain injury. These individuals, however, may not be aware of their condition, may be in denial about their condition, or may fail to report their condition. About 1 million people in the United States are treated for TBI and released from hospital emergency rooms every year. In many cases, they are released the same day without recognition of the long-term seriousness of their condition, thus returning to work too early and without awareness of the safety and functional impact of their disability.

Each year, 80,000 Americans experience the onset of long-term disability following TBI. Motor vehicle crashes are the leading cause of brain injury and account for 50% of all TBIs. Crashes involving smaller cars and motorcycles are typically most serious. Younger people, especially males, are most likely to get a head injury from a motor vehicle accident, but the impact of such injuries is often more serious in the elderly. Falls are the second leading cause of TBIs and are most common among the elderly. The overall risk of TBI is highest among adolescents, young adults, and those older than 65.

Individuals may appear to recover from an initial brain injury. However, such individuals are much more likely to have a second injury. After two brain injuries, the risk for a third injury is eight times greater than normal. The cost of traumatic brain injury in the United States is estimated to be $48.3 billion annually. Hospitalization accounts for $31.7 billion, and fatal brain injuries cost the nation $16.6 billion each year, resulting in substantially higher costs for medical insurance. The cost to the workplace in terms of lost days, impaired level of work, additional accidents, poor decisions and judgment, and shoddy work has never been calculated but is probably in the billions as well.

All employees, no matter what their age, gender, or background is, are at risk for head trauma. Such accidents may occur in the workplace (especially falls and accidents by employees who drive as part of the job) but often occur outside of the workplace as well. The outcome of TBI cases will depend on how quickly help is provided to the victim. Complications such as edema develop over time, so effective early treatment may prevent otherwise serious long-term problems.

ASSESSMENT

The assessment of TBI is a difficult and complex process. This arises from several factors: Symptoms are not always evident in casual interaction with the client, neurological tests are relatively insensitive to mild and moderate instances of brain injury, and patients may be unable or unwilling to report the symptoms that they have because of either a lack of awareness (called neglect) or a need to appear strong and not complain about "minor" symptoms (seen more often in young men.) Although cases of mild or moderate injury are more difficult to identify, these are the individuals who are most likely to return to work and cause problems in the workplace.

Initial Evaluation

The first phase of assessment after an accident is the emergency room or doctor's office. However, in many cases (the exact number is unknown), the patient does not go to the hospital because he or she fails to recognize the symptoms. Symptoms may appear evident to others (especially in the workplace, where more stressful demands are placed on the individual), but their etiology will not. The symptoms may be mistaken for a wide variety of other physical and emotional disorders, including stress, fatigue, lack of rest, depression, anxiety, lack of motivation, anger, goofing off, personal problems, and boredom. In the workplace, employees showing sudden changes in personality or work habits should be interviewed to determine if a TBI has occurred, and referred for more detailed evaluation if the possibility exists.

When the client goes to an ER or doctor's office, the client will usually receive a mental status examination (either formally or informally). Such examinations are designed to pick up more serious alterations in consciousness and cognitive functions and may miss milder symptoms that can later affect the workplace. If the doctor feels that the client shows symptoms of a concussion or contusion, the client may be referred for a CT scan or MRI.

These tests allow the radiologist to "see" the structure of the soft tissue of the brain. They may identify the presence of edema, lacerations, or bleeding in the brain that would then be treated medically. However, again, milder disorders will likely be missed by these tests. In addition, because edema or bleeding may build up over time, they might be missed as well because they have not yet developed to a level adequate for identification. Because of the emphasis on health care cost containment, these tests are not done as often as may be needed because they are relatively expensive.

Other tests that may be ordered initially include the EEG. The EEG is a measure of the brain's electrical activity. It is most useful in detecting the presence of a seizure disorder but is often of limited usefulness in cases of TBI. The EEG's usefulness is limited because it may come back normal if the seizure disorder is subtle or deep in the brain, the client does not have a seizure during the test, or the seizure disorder has not yet developed. Seizures may develop any time after a TBI, with most developing within the first 5 years.

In some cases, neuropsychological assessment may be employed during this initial phase of evaluation. However, whether such assessment takes place is heavily dependent on hospital policies (e.g., medical school or university-based hospitals are more likely to do such exams routinely) and insurance reimbursement policies. Neuropsychological testing differs from neurological testing in that it focuses on the behavioral and cognitive effects of the injury. Thus, it may pick up more subtle problems depending on the length and depth of the examination. Such exams are typically screening exams at this point, taking 1 to 2 hours and looking for the most frequent and obvious sequelae of TBI.

These tests will pick up more serious cases of brain injury, which will be referred for appropriate treatment. This will include medical treatment, medications, and rehabilitation as necessary. Again, because of attempts to control medical costs, the length of this treatment on an inpatient basis is much more limited than it was a decade ago, resulting in the release of many clients long before they are ready to return to work. Such clients will usually get recommendations for follow-up outpatient care, but they may not always attend such treatments because of cost.

Second Phase. The second phase of assessment occurs when the client is released to return to the workplace or chooses to return to the workplace. Initially, the employer should observe the returning employee; employees will return before they are fully recovered because of lack of insight, denial, lack of awareness, a desire to return to work, a fear of losing their job, or other pressure from an employer. Observation of the employee, which should focus on changes in the employee's work abilities and performance, can be more accurate and useful than any neurological or neuropsychological test (Sachs & Redd, 1993).

Observations should be done by a supervisor familiar with the individual's level of performance. It is often helpful to ease an employee with a previously diagnosed TBI back to work. Ideally, this should consist initially of fewer hours and lower stress levels (such as reducing the amount of work expected within a specific time period). Hours and level of work expected can be increased as the client shows that he or she can handle the current level until the individual can return to a normal work schedule or a level is found at which the individual is unable to function effectively.

If the client cannot return to work because of cognitive or emotional reasons, further neurological and neuropsychological evaluations are indicated. (It should be noted that in many cases of suspected TBI, there also may be ancillary physical injuries that can cause pain, slowness, emotional reactivity, and poor performance and that are not related in any way to head injury.) Neurological evaluation should focus on the development of seizures or secondary complications of TBI that could be evolving. Neuropsychological evaluation should focus on a comprehensive evaluation of the client's cognitive and emotional status.

Neuropsychological evaluations after return to work need to be more comprehensive than the screening exams that may have taken place earlier. Such exams need to evaluate all major areas of neuropsychological dysfunction: motor skills, tactile skills, proprioceptive skills, nonverbal auditory

functions, visual-spatial skills, language skills, memory skills, intellectual skills, achievement, emotional status, and executive skills. An examination may take between 4 and 8 hours depending on the tests employed and the overall speed of the client. The focus of the examination is to identify those factors that are responsible for the individual's workplace and personal problems. This, in turn, can lead to specific recommendations for rehabilitation or modifications to the job to enable the person to perform more effectively (Sbordone & Guilmette, 1999).

Third Phase. Once an individual has been identified as having problems due to a TBI, ongoing evaluation at work should monitor progress. Individuals may continue to improve their skills, because of both the passage of time and the natural recovery of such injuries (with return to maximum improvement taking from 3 to 24 months), as well as the effects of practice and rehabilitation. Individuals should be reevaluated periodically (in 6 to 12 months) until maximum recovery is reached. Neuropsychological evaluation should focus on the areas of weakness identified in the previous evaluation. Medical evaluation should continue to monitor the onset of seizures or other complications. Once maximum recovery has been reached, reevaluation is no longer necessary, and permanent changes can be made (if necessary) in the individual's work demands.

CLINICAL PICTURE

The impact of head injury may vary from extremely subtle signs to complete coma to death. Individuals may present with a variety of symptoms in intelligence, motor function, visual-spatial skills, auditory skills, language skills, reading, writing, arithmetic, memory, or intelligence, as well as impairment in any or all of the five basic sensory modalities (touch, smell, taste, hearing, or vision). Thus, we could describe a nearly infinite number of possible functional problems that may be observed. Rather than trying to do this impossible task, this section will focus on several common presentations of head injury that are most likely to cause problems in the workplace.

Case 1. RN was injured on the job when he fell from a telephone pole, where he was repairing a line. Initially, he was out of work because of his physical injuries, but was released for return when he had essentially recovered. On the job, he was found to be inconsistent: He did many tasks, even complex ones, as well as he did before, but he lost track of time, forgot instructions, had difficulties dealing with emergencies on his own, had problems when faced with complex problem solving, and was irritable with his supervisor. He was eventually fired before he came in for evaluation (with an attorney at that point).

This is a not-uncommon presentation, even after a person has seemingly recovered from a known accident. The individual may do tasks that he or she did previously without any problems, especially if the task was routine or overlearned and did not require special or unusual problem solving. However, memory for new procedures or instructions from supervisors that were easily remembered at one time are now forgotten, especially if they are complex or the worker needs to remember them over an extended period of time. Other symptoms commonly include irritability when corrected, often either out of frustration or the failure of the worker to even realize he or she has forgotten something. Such workers may conclude that they are being "picked on," which will lead to attitudinal problems that can interfere with work as well as other employees.

Problems following through on tasks may also appear in these clients. They may become less attentive to safety rules and less aware of their own errors. The speed at which they complete work when unsupervised may decrease because of a heightened tendency to be distracted and to go off on a tangent. This will occur even when the worker appears to be perfectly normal in his or her motor and verbal skills, leading others to expect fully normal performance.

Case 2. RR was injured in an automobile accident. Although he was initially in a coma, he seemed to recover quickly and to reach his full normal behavior. When he returned to work, however, he began jobs well but never finished them. Interpersonally, he was unable to get along with others, taking offense at seemingly innocuous comments and events. His verbal and motor skills appeared intact. He became belligerent with supervisors, claiming he knew how to do the job better than they did. He refused to acknowledge any errors in his work and blamed them on others when pressed.

RR illustrates several important symptoms. First, a worker may have a lack of insight as to his or her own problems. In some cases, because workers are verbally intact, they may be able to state what problems they have had, but this verbal awareness has no impact on their behavior, nor do they understand that their problems require them to ask for or accept help from others. This may be seen in grandiose statements that they are doing things perfectly, which can lead to serious problems.

This may be accompanied as well by a high degree of egocentricity. Such individuals act more like children—they attend to their own needs and wants but are unable to recognize the impact of their behavior on others. As a result, they quickly alienate other workers, who find them selfish and often offensive. Like a child, they may over-interpret events and behaviors, leading to more discord. They may get into frequent arguments and affect morale around them. Others may interpret their behavior as obnoxious or arrogant instead of recognizing the presence of a brain injury.

Case 3. GB was injured when the door of a dump truck was caught by the wind and hit him in the head. He was unconscious for a short period of time and appeared to recover. He returned to work, where he received several injuries while working with engines and other machinery that were part of his job. He was referred for evaluation because of the seriousness of the accidents.

On evaluation, GB was found to have difficulties in two areas. First, he was unable to process information coming to his brain from his arms and legs that told him where his arms and legs were located. Thus, he did well when he could watch himself while performing a task, but he was unable to do tasks when his vision was obstructed in any way, as was often the case when he worked with his machines. Thus, his accidents were due to him thinking his hands were in one place physically, when, in fact, they were several inches over, causing him to injure, smash, or catch his hands without realizing he was doing so.

In addition, he had trouble with three-dimensional localization in space. Prior to the injury, he was very good at visually imagining how the parts of a machine interacted with one another. He still could do this with machines he had previously known well, but was unable to do it with new machines with which he was not familiar. When working with a new automobile engine, for example, he tended to work as if it was laid out in the same way as an engine he had previously known, leading to errors in his work as well as general inefficiency and slowness. He proved unable to learn any new visual-spatial material adequately, which restricted his job performance considerably.

Case 4. WJC was injured in a work accident in which he slammed face-first from a motor scooter into a wall. He seemed to have only mild injuries and to have been unconscious only a short time. He took a week off from work because of bruises on his face, but returned the next week. His ability to do his job was unimpaired, but he developed widespread emotional problems. He became suspicious of everyone at work, got into arguments, showed large mood changes, complained that people smelled bad and were trying to poison him, lost his temper easily, and was unable to explain his outbursts in any reasonable way.

This worker suffered from injuries to the very front of the brain, in the orbital frontal area right above the eyes, a frequent result of "front face on" accidents. Although he had a loss of his sense of smell, he frequently smelled ugly things that were not there. This accounted for his accusations that people smelled bad and that his food smelled bad, which led to his conclusion that he was being poisoned. The bad smells were the result of a subtle seizure disorder that caused smell hallucinations (which are almost always hallucinations of noxious smells).

The second aspect of his problem was changes in personality, leading to mood changes, temper outbursts, and other signs of aggression, as well as symptoms of depression and anxiety. In some cases, these mood changes are sudden, also reflecting epileptic seizures, which cause mood and emotional changes, rather than overt motor symptoms, which are generally more familiar to others. Individuals with these problems do not recognize the source of their emotional changes, so they blame them on people and events around them.

PRECIPITATING CONDITIONS

TBI may occur on the job or off. The most common causes are motor vehicle accidents and falls. TBI is avoidable (unlike many of the other mental health disorders) by ensuring that employees follow safety regulations, drive carefully, use seatbelts, and avoid unnecessary dangerous situations.

COURSE AND PROGNOSIS

Moderate and Severe Injuries

The course and prognosis of TBI depend on the severity of the injury but are difficult to predict, even for medical professionals. In the case of severe and moderate head injuries, referral for medical care is obvious and generally immediate. Such individuals may be unconscious anywhere from 1 hour to a year or more. When such injuries occur on the job, it is necessary to get workers to medical care as soon as possible.

Prognosis for such conditions varies considerably. Generally, it will take a worker from 3 months to 2 years to reach maximal recovery. In some cases, residual symptoms will be very serious and obvious to anyone who comes into contact with the worker. In other cases, the residual is less obvious and follows the types of symptoms outlined in the Clinical Picture section previously.

Once 1 to 2 years have passed, individuals may continue to show some behavioral improvement, but their physiological improvement will have reached a maximum. A worker has likely reached maximum improvement when there is a 3-month period with no significant improvement in the person's condition. Such individuals can still improve their behavior with specific rehabilitation interventions, although progress may be slow.

If a worker returns to work after a serious injury, it is important that an employer work with the physicians, psychologists, and other rehabilitation specialists to ensure that the employer understands the full nature of the employee's limitations. Whereas the system is able to suggest limitations on lifting and similar physical issues, communication about psychological, behavioral, emotional, and cognitive problems requires more effort as well as a better understanding of how the employee's limitations may affect a specific job. In most cases, a detailed assessment of the worker's job is necessary so that problems can be avoided before they occur.

Anticipation of these problems is important because problems upon return to work can quickly mushroom into crises with TBI survivors. Although the head injury itself does not get worse with time, adaptation to a significant head injury is difficult for the TBI survivor. Survivors must learn to live with permanent disabilities that restrict them in many aspects of their lives and have a major impact on how others see them and relate to them. Although some of this adjustment occurs outside of work with the worker's family, the impact of such problems will be seen in the worker's attitude and performance on the job.

Furthermore, workers may develop depression, anxiety, and other psychological disorders in response to their losses, which may follow a pattern similar to that seen in grief reactions. These disorders can lead to further deterioration in the client's functional skills, which may, in turn, prevent the client from working at his or her maximum or from working at all, even though he or she is physically and cognitively able to do so.

If deficits are found in emotional functioning, the worker should be referred to a psychiatrist or psychologist familiar with the effects of TBI. A failure to see that the problem arises from the client's head injury can result in the administration of medications that cause serious side effects (such as fatigue) in the TBI survivor, causing further impairment at work and home. If problems are found in cognitive skills, referral to a neuropsychologist to further evaluate or help develop alternate strategies at work is appropriate. If the worker shows signs of seizures, referral to a neurologist who works with TBI clients is essential. Neurological evaluation may also be necessary in cases where motor problems or headaches are a major issue, which can lead to referrals to physical therapists, occupational therapists, and speech therapists, as well as other rehabilitation specialists.

The employer should focus on maintaining the job situation in such a way as to allow the TBI survivor to find success at work and to assume as much responsibility for his or her work as possible. Although the TBI survivor may need additional help or special accommodations, the employer (and others) must avoid infantilizing the survivor so that everything is done for him or her. In such cases, clients may lose all motivation to do things for themselves, becoming chronically impaired because they cannot take responsibility for themselves. In other cases, the blows to their self-esteem and self-image from excessive support may lead to depression and further decline in day-to-day functioning.

Mild TBI

Although the principles of treatment for mild TBI are much the same as for moderate and severe TBI, the identification of this disorder is not as easy and may put more pressures and demands on the employer. Many cases of mild TBI do not go to the emergency room or the doctor. The worker, the worker's family, or the employer may not see the injury as serious because there is little or no loss of consciousness. However, the length of time a person loses consciousness is only weakly related to the severity of the real injury or, more importantly, to the severity of any lasting, ongoing symptoms.

In addition, after a mild head injury, individuals may seem perfectly OK. They may be able to carry on a conversation without difficulty. They may indicate a desire not to be seen by a doctor or any other treating personnel. There may not even be any evidence that they have hit their head, although, as previously noted, a TBI can occur from rapid deceleration and not be related to a physical blow to the head.

Even when a client with a mild TBI goes to a hospital ER, he or she may get little treatment. The client is conscious and appears to be OK. Although he or she may be checked for bleeding within the brain, such tests are often normal even when there is an injury. Many of the cognitive and emotional injuries that occur cannot be seen on standard CT or MRI tests, but only on tests of brain metabolism such as Positron Emission Topography (PET), Single Positron Emission Computed Topography (SPECT), or other similar measures. Even an EEG may fail to notice a developing seizure disorder. In most cases, the individual is sent home the same day with little treatment, if any.

As a consequence, if there are problems, it is often the employer or the family who notices them first. Families are often slow to do this because of denial and an unwillingness to suggest that a family member has a serious problem. Thus, the first obvious signs of the disorder often happen in the workplace.

In most cases, the effects of a mild head injury will disappear within 3 to 6 months and in as little time as a single day. It is likely that less than 10% of all mild head injuries will cause permanent, irreversible damage. Therefore, how the worker is handled during this initial period is paramount because mishandling can lead to chronic emotional problems that mask as a continuing brain injury.

Such problems arise when workers return to work too early and find themselves unable to cope with job demands. In executives and other white-collar employees, this may appear as an inability to organize work, apparent forgetfulness, problems in dealing with emergencies, problems working with others, errors in judgment, inflexibility, apparent lack of caring about accuracy or quality of work, defensiveness, and denial that anything is wrong. In blue-collar workers, these same symptoms will appear along with slowness in manual tasks, quick fatigue, and clumsiness.

It should be noted parenthetically that all of these problems could be exacerbated and complicated by secondary injuries unrelated to the head injury. Because most cases of TBI arise from falls and motor vehicle accidents, the worker may also have injuries to the back and neck, headaches, broken bones, bruises, and other problems that interact with the worker's cognitive and emotional problems. In some cases, however, secondary injuries mask the cognitive problems so that they are not noticed until the secondary injuries have abated. In other cases, the secondary injuries prevent the worker from returning to work until after the cognitive and emotional problems have cleared up.

When a worker returns to work too early, the first impulse is to ask him or her to not return to work. Although this makes sense, it is not always the most effective and useful strategy. In consultation with the worker and the worker's physician and neuropsychologist, the employer should explore whether a modified work schedule (less time) or modified responsibilities or both would allow the worker to return to work in a way that is safe and helpful to the employer and the employee. Generally, employees with only minor deficits are better off keeping busy as much as they are able. This allows them to retain their sense of self (which is often defined by one's work) and self-esteem while not pushing them too hard.

On the other hand, too much work that leads to frustration and emotional outbursts or failure is detrimental to the worker as well. This can lead to long-term emotional consequences (depression, anxiety, anger), which can carry over well past the cessation of the physiological symptoms and mimic symptoms of brain injury. Thus, the ideal solution is a careful balance between too much and too little work, keeping the employee actively and usefully employed while not pushing him or her too far. This is the emotional and cognitive equivalent of "lifting" and "bending" restrictions that are commonly seen in other physical injuries.

In cases where these secondary problems can be avoided, the worker will most often return to normal within a 6-month period or less. As the worker improves, he or she can be given additional responsibilities and time until he or she is able to work full-time without restrictions. In a small number of cases, however, deficits will be permanent and will require permanent modification to hours or responsibilities. Such deficits are usually minor, with their importance dependent on the employee's specific responsibilities. A job analysis done with the worker's neuro-psychologist is again important in making these determinations.

RECOMMENDED DATA-BASED TREATMENTS

Medication

Many patients with TBI are given medications (Perna, Bordini, & Newman, 2001; Zasler, 1997). These medications fall into several classes: seizure medication, pain medication, medication for fatigue or alertness, and medication for psychiatric symptoms. Medication monitoring is important because the damaged brain may not react to these drugs as expected from models based on normal individuals (Bleecker & Hansen, 1994).

Time Element

Medications are often started at the time of injury and may be added as symptoms become clear. Physicians may prescribe seizure medication as a prophylaxis even in the absence of any overt seizures. Such medication may be continued for 3 to 12 months depending on the physician's judgment if no seizures occur. If they do occur, treatment may be for long periods of time depending on the course of the disorder.

Pain medications are a particularly challenging area. Some TBI patients complain of headaches that may or may not be related to the brain injury. In many cases, the pain is due to injuries to the neck, back, or scalp area rather than the brain itself. The length of time that the patient spends on the medication will be related to the persistence of the pain, which is often indeterminate.

Medications for arousal problems may be helpful in cases when the client shows low attentional abilities or excessive fatigue.

As with the other medications, time course is indeterminate. Medication for associated psychiatric symptoms typically will not begin unless the client or others complain of depression, anxiety, anger, or other psychiatric disorder. Time course is also indeterminate for these disorders.

Side Effects

Side effects are a major problem with each of these classes of medication in the workplace. It is important that the employer be aware of side effects and that this information be made available to the employee, his or her family, and his or her physician. (Unfortunately, this is rarely done in an organized and effective fashion.) The most common side effects of all of these medications are fatigue, loss of concentration and attention, memory problems, and slowness. It should be noted that each of these side effects is similar to the symptoms of the TBI itself. This should not be surprising, because the medication may impair the brain just as the TBI does, and the effects are in similar areas of the brain.

Clearly, these side effects will have an impact on work, much as the original symptoms do. In some cases, due to overreaction by the employee's brain, these symptoms may be worse than the TBI symptoms themselves. The employer should alert the physician to these effects because they may be modified or eliminated by changing doses of medication or changing the medication itself. The employer should be alert to signs of psychological or physical dependence on the medications as well, especially many of the pain medications.

Workplace Accommodations

The appropriate accommodations are similar to those for TBI itself—analysis and reduction of job responsibilities or time at work based on the individual's specific symptoms and job.

Physical and Occupational Therapy

In cases when the TBI is accompanied by motor deficits, either physical or occupational therapy or both may be necessary. Traditionally, physical therapy deals with gross motor impairment, whereas occupational therapy deals with fine motor impairment.

Time Element

These therapies typically start soon after the TBI and can last anywhere from 3 to 12 months (although longer periods of treatment are possible). The length of treatment depends on the severity and recovery rate of any motor impairment.

Side Effects

There are no serious side effects to these treatments except fatigue. In some cases, clients complain of pain afterwards as they are pushed to go beyond what is easy for them. These effects may impair work immediately after treatment if work has a significant motor component. This can be minimized by encouraging employees to go to therapy on days off and at the conclusion of the workday.

Workplace Accommodations

The major accommodation is providing time off for appointments. In some cases, employees will need to go three or more times a week. It is important that the employer make the process of attending therapy as easy as possible to avoid emotional conflicts and unnecessary anger.

Communication with the therapist on specific problems in this area will help the therapist focus on skills useful to the workplace.

Speech Therapy

Speech therapy deals with impairment in the understanding or expression of speech. Such therapy is needed only rarely in mild TBI, but is more common in moderate and severe TBI.

Time Element

This therapy typically starts soon after the TBI and can last anywhere from 3 to 12 months (although longer periods of treatment are possible). The length of treatment depends on the severity and recovery rate of any speech impairment.

Side Effects

There are no serious side effects to this treatment.

Workplace Accommodations

The major accommodation is providing time off for appointments. In some cases, employees will need to go three or more times a week. It is important that the employer make the process of attending therapy as easy as possible to avoid emotional conflicts and unnecessary anger. Communication with the therapist on specific problems in this area will help the therapist focus on skills useful to the workplace.

Cognitive Therapy

Cognitive therapy deals with changes in the worker's memory, concentration, attention, judgment, insight, reasoning, visual-spatial, achievement, and abstract skills.

This therapy may be given in conjunction with occupational or speech therapy, or may come from a separate cognitive therapist. It may be one-on-one or involve computerized training (Glisky, 1992; Glisky & Schacter, 1988; Kreutzer & Wehman, 1991; Wehman, 1991; Wehman, Kreutzer, Sale, & West, 1989).

Time Element

This therapy typically starts soon after the TBI and can last anywhere from 3 to 12 months (although longer periods of treatment are possible). The length of treatment depends on the severity and recovery rate of any cognitive impairment.

Side Effects

There are no serious side effects to this treatment.

Workplace Accommodations

The major accommodation is providing time off for appointments. In some cases, employees will need to go three or more times a week. It is important that the employer make the process of attending therapy as easy as possible to avoid emotional conflicts and unnecessary anger. Communication with the therapist on specific problems in this area will help the therapist focus on skills useful to the workplace. Gestures such as several days of paid sick leave, even after a mild injury, can have substantial returns.

Psychological Therapy

Psychological therapy addresses both the emotional impact of the organic injury as well as the adjustment of the client to the injury. This is particularly important because clients may develop anxiety, depression, anger, and paranoia toward the employer or insurance company as a reaction to his or her injury. Early therapy and monitoring can eliminate or at least reduce the seriousness of these symptoms.

Time Element

This therapy typically starts soon after the TBI and can last anywhere from 3 to 12 months (although longer periods of treatment are possible). The length of treatment depends on the severity and recovery rate of psychological problems.

Side Effects

There are no serious side effects to this treatment.

Workplace Accommodations

The major accommodation is providing time off for appointments. In some cases, employees will need to go one or more times a week. It is important that the employer make the process of attending therapy as easy as possible to avoid emotional conflicts and unnecessary anger. Communication with the therapist on specific problems in this area will help the therapist focus on skills useful to the workplace.

General Workplace Accommodations

An integral part of many treatments are accommodations by the workplace to the TBI. This allows the worker to return to productive work as early as possible and makes the employer look supportive of the injured worker, which is especially important in the many cases of TBI that occur because of work-related injuries or on the way to or from work. Inflexibility on the part of the employer will often result in anger that further deepens the client's condition and creates a sense of entitlement in him or her. Necessary workplace accommodations may include workplace modifications as well as the use of assistive devices (Bricout, 1999; Gale & Christie, 1987; Michaels & Risucci, 1993; Warren, 2000; West, 1995).

Time Element

These changes typically start soon after the TBI, when the worker is first cleared for part-time work, and can last anywhere from 3 to 12 months (although they may be permanent as well).

Side Effects

There are no serious side effects to these accommodations. Indeed, such accommodations work to avoid psychological complications.

Workplace Accommodations

The major accommodations are flexibility and creativity in working with the employee.

MAINTENANCE OF GAINS

Unlike many other mental health disorders, relapse is unlikely unless another TBI occurs, although those who have had one TBI generally are at higher risk for a second TBI. However, it is possible for the employer to make several errors that can cause regression in behavioral symptoms, and these errors should be discussed.

The foremost problem is that after finding a job that the employee is able to do after TBI (whether this is the employee's former job or a modified job), the employer switches the employee to another job either as a reward for good work or because of workplace demands. The most long-lasting symptom after TBI is difficulty in learning new material. Thus, switching the client to a similar job may result in some initial problems, but such problems can be worked out with patience or training.

However, switching the worker to an entirely new position may result in severe problems and even failure. Although the employer does not need to avoid all such attempts, nor is it advisable to not allow the worker to try a more difficult position, it is important to make it clear to the employee that he or she can return to his or her former (successful) job if the attempt fails. Flexibility becomes the key concept in working with TBI survivors. In those who do not have complete recovery, any new jobs may need to be modified in light of residual symptoms. Employers should monitor changes carefully, keeping in mind that recommendations from physicians or psychologists may not recognize the full extent of the client's problems in adapting to a new position or, on the other hand, may underestimate the potential of the client to learn new jobs.

A related problem is not listening to the worker's descriptions of problems. Patients with TBI are sometimes seen as "whiners" whose complaints are ignored unless solid medical evidence supports their complaints. Unfortunately, not all of the symptoms reported by TBI survivors are able to be documented in a medical or even neuropsychological examination with any certainty. Demanding such proof in all cases is neither fair nor accurate. The employer and the employer's insurance company need to work with the employee and physician to reach reasonable accommodations and requirements. Failure to do this leads to multiple problems that make what would have been relatively simple cases extremely complex and, in the long term, very costly in human and economic terms.

Finally, because workers who have had one TBI are more likely to have another, sending employees back to dangerous jobs after an injury may not be the most effective response, in terms of both the safety of the employee and the liability of the employer. In many cases, this may not be a problem, but careful consideration and consultation (involving the employee as well) must be included as part of the work assignment process. Failure to do so may lead to future, more serious problems.

SUMMARY

TBI is a significant challenge to the workplace. TBIs are common in work settings and outdoor work, primarily because of falls and motor vehicle accidents. However, although many TBI survivors may have residual symptoms, nearly all except the most severe cases remain employable on at least a part-time or modified job basis, with many able to return to their former positions without difficulty. Symptoms may include a wide range of problems that differ in both intensity and duration depending on the injury and the individual. The deficits from TBI can include short-term memory loss; long-term memory loss; slowed ability to process information; trouble concentrating or paying attention over sustained periods of time; difficulty keeping up with a conversation; word-finding problems; problems in understanding language; loss of a second (acquired) language; spatial disorientation; driving difficulties; impulsivity; inflexibility; time disorientation; organizational problems; impaired judgment; problems doing more than one thing at a time; seizures; muscle spasticity; double vision;

impaired visual fields; loss of smell or taste; slow or slurred speech; headaches or migraines; fatigue; a lack of initiating activities; difficulty in completing tasks without reminders; increased anxiety; depression and mood swings; denial of deficits; impulsive behavior; lack of insight; agitation; egocentricity (inability to see how behaviors affect others); explosive behavior; erratic behavior; sensory losses; inability to deal with novel or new material; and impairment in reading, writing, or arithmetic.

The symptoms of mild TBI may be more evident in the workplace than in the emergency room, so the employer may be the first to notice many of the effects of these injuries. In most cases, handling the worker carefully will allow him or her to complete recovery while maintaining a reasonable work schedule. Coordination of accommodations with the worker's physician and neuropsychologist is important so that the worker does not have emotional blow-ups, failure at work, or further injuries because of work demands. Most cases, when handled properly, will improve within a 6-month period or less. Therapies, which may need to be ongoing, can include physical therapy, occupational therapy, speech therapy, medication, seizure treatment, pain medication, psychotropic medication, cognitive therapy, psychological therapy, and workplace and job accommodations.

Unlike many other mental health disorders, relapse is unlikely unless another TBI occurs, although those who have had one TBI are generally at higher risk for a second TBI. However, employers can make several errors that can cause regression in behavioral symptoms, and these should be discussed. The foremost problem is that after finding a job that the employee is able to do after TBI (whether this is the employee's former job or a modified job), the employer switches the employee to another job, which puts stress on the worker's residual weaknesses. A related problem is not listening to the worker's descriptions of problems. Not all of the symptoms reported by TBI survivors are able to be documented in a medical or even neuropsychological examination with any certainty, so listening to the worker, as well as observing him or her, is essential. Finally, because workers who have had one TBI are more likely to have another, sending employees back to dangerous jobs after an injury may not be the most effective response. Careful consideration and consultation (involving the employee as well) must be included as part of the work assignment process.

REFERENCES

Bleecker, M. L., & Hansen, J. A. (1994). *Occupational neurology and clinical neurotoxicology.* Baltimore: Williams & Wilkins.

Bricout, J. C. (1999). The relationship between employers' perceived organizational context and their impressions of the employability of job applicants with either a severe psychiatric or physical disability. *Dissertation Abstracts International, 60*(1-A), 247.

Gale, A., & Christie, B. (1987). *Psychophysiology and the electronic workplace.* New York: Wiley.

Glisky, E. L. (1992). Computer-assisted instruction for patients with traumatic brain injury: Teaching of domain-specific knowledge. *Journal of Head Trauma Rehabilitation, 7*(3), 1-12.

Glisky, E. L., & Schacter, D. L. (1988). Acquisition of domain-specific knowledge in patients with organic memory disorders. *Journal of Learning Disabilities, 21*(6), 333-339, 351.

Golden, C. J., Zillmer, E., & Spiers, M. (1992). *Neuropsychological diagnosis and intervention.* Springfield, IL: Charles C Thomas.

Kreutzer, J. S., & Wehman, P. H. (1991). *Cognitive rehabilitation for persons with traumatic brain injury: A functional approach.* Baltimore: Paul H. Brookes.

Michaels, C. A., & Risucci, D. A. (1993). Employer and counselor perceptions of workplace accommodations for persons with traumatic brain injury. *Journal of Applied Rehabilitation Counseling, 24*(1), 38-46.

Perna, R. B., Bordini, E. J., & Newman, S. (2001). Pharmacological treatment considerations in brain injury. *Journal of Cognitive Rehabilitation, 19*(1), 4-7.

Sachs, P. R., & Redd, C. A. (1993). The Americans with Disabilities Act and individuals with neurological impairments. *Rehabilitation Psychology, 38*(2), 87-101.

Sbordone, R. J., & Guilmette, T. J. (1999). Ecological validity: Prediction of everyday and vocational functioning from neuropsychological test data. In J. J. Sweet (Ed.), *Forensic neuropsychology: Fundamentals and practice* (pp. 227-254). Lisse, Netherlands: Swets & Zeitlinger.

Warren, C. G. (2000). Use of assistive technology in vocational rehabilitation of persons with traumatic brain injury. In R. Fraser & D. Clemmons (Eds.), *Traumatic brain injury rehabilitation: Practical vocational, neuropsychological, and psychotherapy intervention* (pp. 129-160). Boca Raton, FL: CRC.

Wehman, P. H. (1991). Cognitive rehabilitation in the workplace. In J. Kreutzer & P. H. Wehman (Eds.), *Cognitive rehabilitation for persons with traumatic brain injury: A functional approach* (pp. 269-288). Baltimore: Paul H. Brookes.

Wehman, P., Kreutzer, J. S., Sale, P., & West, M. (1989). Cognitive impairment and remediation: Implications for employment following traumatic brain injury. *Journal of Head Trauma Rehabilitation, 4*(3), 66-75.

West, M. D. (1995). Aspects of the workplace and return to work for persons with brain injury in supported employment. *Brain Injury, 9*(3), 301-313.

Zasler, N. D. (1997). The role of medical rehabilitation in vocational reentry. *Journal of Head Trauma Rehabilitation, 12*(5), 42-56.

CHAPTER 17

Insomnia

CHRISTINA S. MCCRAE
H. HEITH DURRENCE
KENNETH L. LICHSTEIN

DESCRIPTION OF THE DISORDER

Insomnia poses significant health, safety, and economic burdens for both afflicted employees and their employers. Compared to good sleepers, employees who suffer from chronic insomnia have higher rates of tardiness, take more sick leave, visit health care practitioners more often, and exhibit decreased productivity and inhibited advancement. Insomniacs whose jobs require them to drive or operate machinery are at greater risk for on-the-job accidents. The potential impact of insomnia on the workplace is staggering when one considers that estimates of the number of individuals experiencing sleep problems ranges from 13% to 52% of the general population of developed countries. Fortunately, for employers and employees alike, effective and relatively inexpensive treatments are available. Sleep medications (both over-the-counter and prescription) are currently the most popular form of treatment. In this chapter, however, we discuss the reasons we

recommend psychological interventions over medication (e.g., better long-term relief of symptoms, more cost-effective in the long run). In our review of the impact of insomnia on the workplace, we place particular emphasis on work-related factors that may contribute to poor sleep as well as ways in which employers can facilitate appropriate diagnosis, treatment, and follow-up for employees plagued by poor sleep.

Although there is no consensus definition, most insomnia researchers and clinicians agree that insomnia is the inability to obtain adequate sleep because of retarded sleep onset, frequent arousals, and/or early-morning awakening (Bootzin & Nicassio, 1978). This definition may seem vague, but nonetheless encompasses two important elements. First, it rules out the occasional problems that even good sleepers may experience and instead emphasizes frequent and recurring difficulties in obtaining sufficient sleep. Second, by incorporating the word "adequate," it stresses the subjective nature of the problem. This is an important distinction, because insomnia is primarily a subjective phenomenon. People vary widely in the amount of sleep that they require to feel rested and perform well during the day, from as little as 3 hours (Jones & Oswald, 1968) to 12 or more hours. As a result, no objective definition of insomnia can be provided. Compounding this problem is the fact that there is no objective measure of biological sleep need. Thus, a subjective complaint of disturbed sleep or disrupted daily functioning because of poor sleep is required.

Generally, people with insomnia (PWI) are divided into groups based on the time of night they experience an inability to sleep. On the basis of this classification system, three major types of insomnia have been observed: (a) sleep onset insomnia, or difficulty in falling asleep; (b) sleep maintenance insomnia, or interrupted sleep characterized by frequent nighttime awakenings; and (c) terminal insomnia, or early-morning awakenings coupled with an inability to return to sleep. These symptoms may occur singly or in combination.

Insomnia is defined explicitly in three diagnostic systems. Because only one of these manuals is used regularly in the mental health field, we will restrict our discussion to this manual, the *Diagnostic and Statistical Manual of Mental Disorders, Fourth Edition* (*DSM-IV*) (American Psychiatric Association, 1994). The *DSM-IV* has a broad classification system that recognizes four main types of sleep disorders: sleep disorders related to another mental disorder, sleep disorders resulting from a general medical condition, substance-induced sleep disorders, and primary sleep disorders (which includes insomnia). The diagnostic features of insomnia in the *DSM-IV* include a persistent (i.e., for at least 1 month) complaint of difficulty initiating or maintaining sleep that causes significant distress and is associated with impaired social or occupational functioning.

EPIDEMIOLOGY

Insomnia is among the most frequent health complaints brought to the attention of health care providers (Morin, Culbert, & Schwartz, 1994). Depending upon the exact question and the time frame involved, sleep disorders in general are reported by 13% to 52% of community respondents (e.g., Bixler, Kales, Soldatos, Kales, & Healey, 1979; Gallup Organization, 1995; Karacan, Thornby, & Anch, 1976). Some of the variability in these estimates is due to the types of questions asked. Survey questions have included the following: "How often do you have trouble sleeping?" "Would you please look at this card and tell me if you have any of these sleep problems now?" "Has trouble falling asleep or trouble staying asleep bothered you in the past 12 months?" None of these surveys differentiated insomnia occurring once or twice a month from nightly or nearly nightly insomnia, nor did any of them assess the duration of the sleep difficulties. Two epidemiological surveys that addressed these issues suggest that 10% to 15% of adults complain of chronic insomnia (Ford & Kamerow, 1989; Mellinger, Balter, & Uhlenhuth, 1985).

Both being female and aging are associated with increased rates of reported sleep difficulty. Virtually all of the investigations cited above indicate that women are about 1.3 times more likely to report insomnia-like sleep problems than men, with the notable exception of 20- to 40-year-old women (no gender differences). Studies that include wide age ranges find that the elderly (defined here as greater than 65 years old) generally have an approximately 1.5 times higher prevalence rate of sleep disturbance than those less than 65 years old (Walsh & Ustun, 1999). Epidemiological studies specific to older adult populations provide consistent data, with frequent sleep complaints occurring in 43% to 50% of these samples (Blazer, Hayes, & Foley, 1995; Foley et al., 1995).

Insomnia has significant economic and social consequences. One recent study estimated that the direct cost of insomnia (defined as the cost of medical care or self-treatment borne by patients, organized health care providers, insurance providers, or the government) in the United States was $13.6 billion in 1995 (Walsh & Ustin, 1999). A separate study estimated the indirect costs associated with insomnia, including estimated monetary values for decreased productivity at work, health and property costs related to accidents, and medical costs associated with comorbid conditions, to be between $77.05 billion and $92.13 billion a year (Stoller, 1994).

Insomnia and the Workplace

Insomnia is not a benign problem because it can adversely affect a person's life by causing substantial psychosocial, occupational, health, and economic repercussions (Morin et al., 1994). These difficulties are the mechanism through which insomnia plays an important role in affecting the workplace and reducing workplace productivity. Individuals with chronic sleep disturbances experience more psychological distress, report greater impairments of daytime functioning, take more sick leave, are more preoccupied with somatic problems, and utilize health care resources more often than do good sleepers (Ford & Kamerow, 1989; Gallup Organization, 1995; Mellinger et al., 1985). In one study, 27% of a random community sample reported that their daytime functioning was negatively affected by poor sleep at least twice a week (Addison, Thorpy, Roehrs, & Roth, 1991). For those individuals in this sample who were dissatisfied with their sleep, this percentage increased to 70%. A Gallup study (Gallup Organization, 1995) found that PWI report poor performance at work, memory difficulties, concentration problems, and twice as many fatigue-related automobile accidents as compared to good sleepers. Perhaps the best study examining sleep disturbance's relationship to job performance was done with U.S. Navy personnel. In this longitudinal study, poor sleepers earned fewer promotions, remained at lower pay grades, and received fewer recommendations for reenlistment than did their good-sleeping peers (Johnson & Spinweber, 1983).

Although none of these chronic insomnia studies allows for a conclusion of causality, poor sleep and impaired daytime functioning are clearly related. More importantly to employers, daytime impairments discussed previously can negatively influence on-the-job performance by significantly reducing job productivity and by decreasing the number of workdays of their poor-sleeping employees. Indeed, a community survey of adults found that people reporting poor sleep at least seven nights a month (which represents minimal diagnostic criteria for insomnia) missed 5.2 more days of work per year than did people reporting good sleep (Schweitzer, Engelhardt, Hilliker, Muehlbach, & Walsh, 1992). These poor sleepers also estimated three times as many days of reduced productivity at work as those with no sleep difficulty. In summary, epidemiological evidence suggests that insomnia can have a profound effect on the workplace, reducing the ability of affected employees to maintain adequate productivity and safety on the job, while simultaneously impairing their overall quality of life.

ASSESSMENT

When a person complains of difficulty sleeping, a thorough investigation of this complaint is warranted. The key ingredient in conducting an assessment of sleep difficulties is to gather a sleep history. A detailed sleep history gives the interviewer insight into the nature, severity, and duration of the problem. We will discuss two methods of obtaining sleep information, with an emphasis on the subjective report of the individual, because this is crucial in the diagnosis of insomnia. These two methods are commonly used together and provide enough information for an adequate diagnosis when used appropriately.

Sleep Interview

Sleep interviews are a method of ascertaining the history of the sleep problem and are the most commonly used method of sleep assessment. A suggested format for a sleep history interview is presented in Table 17.1. This semistructured approach allows the interviewer to begin questioning on general issues, while providing more specific queries when necessary.

Several measures can be used to assist the sleep interview. For example, the Pittsburgh Sleep Quality Index (Buysse et al., 1991) can be used to screen for other sleep difficulties and to guide the sleep interview. This measure is a quick index (it takes approximately 10 minutes to complete) that gathers data on typical sleep during the previous month and includes several items that are helpful in screening out other sleep disorders.

Sleep Diaries

Sleep diaries are invaluable in the appraisal of sleep disturbance and the evaluation of treatment outcome. Whereas the sleep interview provides an essential retrospective overview, sleep diaries yield night-by-night information on perceptions of sleep pattern and quality, and may be obtained over many weeks. Thus, sleep diaries have become the staple of sleep assessment and have been used extensively both clinically and in research. These diaries typically assess a number of factors, including time to sleep onset, number and duration of nighttime awakenings, total sleep time, and perceived quality of sleep. Sleep diaries should be completed for a minimum of 2 weeks in order to ensure adequate stability of the sleep data (Wohlgemuth, Edinger, Fins, & Sullivan, 1999). An example of standard sleep diaries is presented in Figure 17.1.

Exclusion Criteria

To ensure that the sleep complaint is insomnia, several important exclusionary criteria should be addressed. Assessment criteria discussed previously assume that insomnia secondary to other problems has been excluded. Examples of secondary insomnia sources are a mental disorder (e.g., major depressive disorder, generalized anxiety disorder); a general medical condition (e.g., hyperthyroidism, cancer); the physiological effects of a substance (e.g., chemotherapy, abuse of drugs); or another sleep disorder (e.g., sleep apnea, periodic limb movement syndrome, narcolepsy).

Determining the primary or secondary status of an insomnia complaint has important implications for treatment and safety. For example, ruling out sleep apnea (a disorder characterized by excessive daytime sleepiness due to numerous nighttime awakenings) is crucial for people employed in occupations where severe daytime sleepiness is hazardous (e.g., truck drivers, crane

Table 17.1 Outline Plan for a Sleep History Assessment Comprising Content Areas and Suggested Interview Questions

Content Area	Prompt Question	Supplementary Questions
Presentation of the sleep complaint Pattern	Can you describe the pattern of your sleep on a typical night?	Time to fall asleep? Number and duration of wakenings? Time spent asleep? Nights per week like this?
Quality	How do you feel about the quality of your sleep?	Refreshing? Enjoyable? Restless?
Daytime effects	How does your night's sleep affect your day?	Tired? Sleepy? Poor concentration? Irritable? Particular times of day?
Development of the sleep complaint	Do you remember how this spell of poor sleep started?	Events and circumstances? Dates and times? Variation since then? Exacerbating factors? Alleviating factors? Degree of impact/intrusiveness?
Lifetime history of sleep complaints	Did you used to be a good sleeper?	Sleep in childhood? Sleep in adulthood? Nature of past episodes? Dates and times? Resolution of past episodes?
General health status and medical history	Have you generally kept in good health?	Illnesses? Chronic problems? Dates and times? Recent changes in health? Medications?
Psychopathology and history of psychological functioning	Are you the kind of person who usually copes well?	Psychological problems? Anxiety or depression? Dates and times? Resourceful person? Personality type?
Issues of differential diagnosis Sleep-related breathing disorder (SBD)	Are you a heavy snorer?	Interrupted breathing in sleep? Excessively sleepy in the day?
Periodic limb movements in sleep (PLMS) and restless legs syndrome(RLS)	Do your legs sometimes twitch or can't keep still?	Excessively sleepy in the day?
Circadian rhythm sleep disorders	Do you feel you want to sleep at the wrong time?	Too early? Too late?
Parasomnias	Do you sometimes act a bit strangely during your sleep?	Behavioral description? Time during night?
Narcolepsy	Do you sometimes just fall asleep without warning?	Times and places? Triggered by emotion? Poor sleep at night?
Current and previous treatments	Are you taking anything to help you sleep?	Now? In the past? Dates and times? What has worked? What have you tried yourself?

SLEEP QUESTIONNAIRE
Department of Psychology, The University of Memphis

NAME _____

Please answer the following questionnaire **WHEN YOU AWAKE IN THE MORNING.** Enter yesterday's day and date and provide the information to describe your sleep the night before. Definitions explaining each line of the questionnaire are given below.

EXAMPLE

		day 1	day 2	day 3	day 4	day 5	day 6	day 7
yesterday's day ⇒	TUES							
yesterday's date ⇒	10/14/97							
1. NAP (yesterday)	70							
2. BEDTIME (last night)	10:55							
3. TIME TO FALL ASLEEP	65							
4. # AWAKENINGS	4							
5. WAKE TIME (middle of night)	110							
6. FINAL WAKE-UP	6:05							
7. OUT OF BED	7:10							
8. QUALITY RATING	2							
9. MEDICATION (include amount & time)	Halcion 0.25 mg 10:40 pm							

ITEM DEFINITIONS

1. If you napped yesterday, enter total time napping in minutes.
2. What time did you enter bed for the purpose of going to sleep (not for reading or other activities)?
3. Counting from the time you wished to fall asleep, how many minutes did it take you to fall asleep?
4. How many times did you awaken during the night?
5. What is the total minutes you were awake during the middle of the night? This does <u>not include</u> time to fall asleep at the beginning of the night or awake time in bed before the final morning arising.
6. What time did you wake up for the last time this morning?
7. What time did you actually get out of bed this morning?
8. Pick <u>one</u> number below to indicate your overall QUALITY RATING or satisfaction with your sleep.
   1. very poor, **2.** poor, **3.** fair, **4.** good, **5.** excellent
9. List any sleep medication or alcohol taken at or near bedtime, and give the amount and time taken.

Figure 17.1   Example of a Standard Sleep Diary Incorporating Information on Sleep Pattern and Sleep Quality

operators, airline pilots). In order to screen for sleep apnea, it is important to determine if the person snores heavily, gasps for breath during the night, awakens with dry mouth, or has headaches upon arousal. If applicable, an interview of the person's bed partner is often helpful in answering these questions. Other key risk factors include obesity (larger people are more likely to have apnea), gender (males predominate), and age (older adults are more likely to have apnea). If an individual possesses several of these key risk factors, a referral should be made for polysomnographic sleep evaluation. For insomnia that is due to a medical condition, mental disorder, or substance abuse, a referral for treatment of this primary condition is warranted prior to treating the insomnia symptoms.

CLINICAL PICTURE

Typical functional losses include reports of poor work performance, memory problems, and impaired concentration (see our earlier section on Epidemiology for a more thorough discussion of these losses). The case study below provides a good example of the typical clinical presentation of insomnia and how it affects the workplace.

Case Description

John is a 35-year-old, married African American male who has been employed for 15 years in a shipping company. John's complaint is a familiar one. Despite his best efforts, which include avoiding naps during the day, limiting caffeine consumption in the afternoon, and reading nonstimulating material at bedtime, he cannot get to sleep in less than an hour. Approximately once a week, it takes John 3 or more hours to get to sleep.

John's job requires him to be constantly at peak performance. He regularly operates a forklift and a freight loader in performing his duties as shipping coordinator. The skills necessary to operate this equipment often require him to maintain concentration and attention for extended periods of time to maximize both productivity and personal safety. John has been worried about the potential consequences of his sleep difficulties at work for the past few months, because his insomnia problems have gotten worse during this time. John complains of having difficulty concentrating during the day, particularly when he does not drink enough coffee in the morning. Furthermore, he regularly feels fatigued and often lacks the energy necessary to move and load boxes in a timely manner. John's supervisor has commented on several occasions that his productivity is not where it used to be, and that he will have to formally discipline him if he cannot perform up to par.

In addition to his on-the-job difficulties, John has had to take several days off from work in the past few months. He calls in sick after nights when he is unable to get more than 2 or 3 hours of sleep, because he feels unable to perform with so little sleep. John was recently reprimanded for his frequent use of sick leave, and this formal reprimand will inhibit him from future upward mobility in the company.

In order to cope with his sleep onset difficulties, John has recently begun drinking one or two beers before bedtime and taking over-the-counter sleep medication to help him get to sleep. He is concerned about this, because he has used medication for only a short amount of time and has already had to increase the dose of the medication in order to get to sleep. His concerns notwithstanding, John is determined to get a good night's sleep and is willing to do whatever it takes to accomplish this goal. A recent car accident one morning after an insomnia night (he dozed off and ran a red light) prompted him to seek behavioral treatment for his insomnia difficulties.

PRECIPITATING CONDITIONS

Several different conditions may precipitate the onset of insomnia. Depression, for example, has been found to accompany insomnia in a number of investigations (e.g., Beutler, Thornby, & Karacan, 1978; Bonnet & Arand, 1995; Coursey, Buchsbaum, & Frankel, 1975) and is considered the number one cause of insomnia (Lichstein, 2000). Several studies examining mood in PWI found significant subclinical depression symptoms in comparison to people without insomnia (e.g., Chambers & Kim, 1993; Morin & Gramling, 1989). Ford and Kamerow (1989) gathered sleep and mood data from a random, longitudinal, community sample and determined that individuals with persistent insomnia had significantly higher rates of developing major depression. Given the nature of these data, it is not possible to determine causality. Thus, it is unclear whether depression causes insomnia or vice versa. Even without conclusive evidence, it is reasonable to conclude that either of these disorders can precipitate the other.

In a similar vein, previous epidemiological research found that the complaint of insomnia tends to accompany many symptoms that are consistent with anxiety (Bixler et al., 1979; Karacan et al., 1976; Mellinger et al., 1985). Ford and Kamerow (1989) also found increased rates of developing anxiety disorders in individuals with persistent insomnia. Overall, numerous studies examining mood in PWI have found consistently elevated depression and anxiety, albeit at a subclinical level. PWI are generally characterized by a clinical picture of a mildly depressed, neurotic, obsessively worrisome individual (e.g., Carskadon et al., 1976; Roth, Kramer, & Lutz, 1976). With this in mind, it is essential to examine the sleep of anyone presenting with either depression or anxiety symptoms.

Another potential cause of insomnia concerns people who have learned poor sleep habits. One part of this problem may be that the person never acquires a consistent sleep rhythm. PWI may inadvertently disrupt many bodily cycles, such as those involving temperature regulation and the functioning of the endocrine system, that require 24-hour synchronization. This concern is particularly important for those employees who work evening, night, or swing shifts. Careful monitoring of these individuals' sleep habits is warranted to determine if they are acquiring sufficient sleep in order to ensure adequate safety and productivity on the job.

As mentioned earlier, insomnia can arise from a number of secondary sources, such as psychiatric, medical, and substance abuse problems. The typical treatment for these cases is directed at removing the primary cause of the sleep disturbance. However, if the insomnia complaint has been present for at least a few months, a learned, behavioral component often aggravates these sleep difficulties. Because of their inability to sleep, people may associate the bedroom with frustration and arousal rather than with sleep. Similarly, because functioning with little sleep for long periods of time produces stress, obtaining adequate amounts of sleep may become a major preoccupation of these people. Thus, a vicious cycle can develop, where the more one needs to sleep, the less one is able to sleep. Behavioral components (i.e., primary insomnia) may develop even in insomnias secondary to medical, psychiatric, and substance abuse problems, and these behavioral components may then need aggressive treatment.

COURSE AND PROGNOSIS

Insomnia may be transient, chronic, or intermittent. Transient insomnia is often caused by stress, such as job- or family-related problems. It can also result from intense positive emotions related to a job promotion, an upcoming vacation, or a marriage proposal. As the name implies, it is typically brief, remitting within 3 months once either the stressor is removed or the individual adapts to it. In some cases (as mentioned above), insomnia that begins in response to a stressor develops a learned behavioral component and does not remit quickly. In other cases, the stressor is an enduring condition, such as a chronic illness or the death of someone close, resulting in sleep disturbance that has a longer course, persisting 6 months or longer. Chronic insomnia, however, is not always triggered by an identified stressor. Some individuals are particularly vulnerable to sleep disruption, experiencing insomnia beginning in childhood or adolescence and continuing through adulthood. Data from sleep clinic patients shows the average duration of chronic insomnia is 14 years (Stepanski et al., 1989). Intermittent insomnia is a form of chronic insomnia in which periods of good and poor sleep alternate. The precise pattern of alternation varies by individual. For some individuals, this pattern may alternate slowly (6 months of good sleep followed by 6 months of insomnia followed by 6 months of good sleep and so on). For others, the alternation may occur much more rapidly (2 weeks of good sleep followed by 6 weeks of insomnia followed by 3 weeks of good sleep).

Unlike transient insomnia, chronic and intermittent insomnia do not typically remit spontaneously; therefore, they are likely to have the greatest impact on the workplace. Fortunately, the prognosis for these more persistent forms of insomnia is good with treatment. Hauri (1991) estimates that sleep can be improved in 75% of cases by a skilled, well-informed clinician. As mentioned previously, individuals with persistent complaints of insomnia should be assessed thoroughly by a medical professional (including a polysomnographic evaluation when necessary) to rule out other potential causes of the sleep disturbance. If a sleep disorders center (SDC) is available, it can provide both evaluation and treatment. If an SDC is not available, a properly trained clinician can also provide such services. In fact, there are now several good books available for training nonspecialists (e.g., Espie, 1991; Hauri, 1991). Although treatment is most effective when administered by a trained professional (Morin et al., 1994), books such as Hauri and Linde's (1990) *No More Sleepless Nights* may also be used by employees who prefer a self-help approach.

TREATMENT

Pharmacological Treatment

Brief Description

Medications with sedative properties (hypnotics) are commonly used to treat insomnia. There are three main types of hypnotics: benzodiazepine receptor agonists (Dalmane, Ambien, Sonata); sedating antidepressants (Desyrel, Elavil); and antihistamines (Benadryl). Currently, benzodiazepines are the most frequently prescribed hypnotics. Newer, nonbenzodiazepine-type medications, such as zaleplon (Sonata) and zolpidem (Ambien), are rapidly gaining popularity because they have shorter half-lives than the older benzodiazepines and, as a result, are less likely to cause the severe side effects associated with benzodiazepine hypnotics (see below).

Time Element

Hypnotic medications provide short-term relief, but they have not been demonstrated to be effective beyond 6 weeks

(Morin & Kwentus, 1988). Sleep specialists (Buysse & Reynolds, 2000) recommend a 1-month trial followed by an attempt to taper and discontinue. Whether the newer hypnotics, such as zolpidem and zaleplon, will demonstrate better long-term relief than their predecessors remains to be demonstrated empirically. As a result of their time-limited efficacy, medications may be useful for individuals experiencing transient insomnia and individuals experiencing intermittent periods of poor sleep that last for only a few weeks. For chronic insomnia or intermittent insomnia involving more extended periods of poor sleep (i.e., greater than 1 month), medication is not the best form of treatment.

Side Effects

Hypnotics, particularly benzodiazepines, carry significant risk of side effects, including habituation and dependency (Langer, Mendelson, & Richardson, 1999). Rebound effects, which involve transient increases in sleep disturbance and anxiety following abrupt discontinuance of medication, are also common. Fortunately, rebound effects can be avoided in most cases by tapering the dosage of medication before stopping it. Daytime residual effects, which may affect work performance, include impaired psychomotor performance, impaired cognitive performance (particularly episodic memory), drowsiness, and anxiety. These residual effects have been associated with increased risk of falls and accidents (Langer et al., 1999). Because such events are rare occurrences, it is important to note that the clinical significance of these residual effects is unclear. In addition, many of the side effects mentioned may be less severe and/or absent for the newer, non-benzodiazepine-type medications (zolpidem and zaleplon).

Psychological Treatment

Brief Description

Psychological treatments target one or more of the behavioral habits that perpetuate poor sleep: somatic arousal, cognitive arousal, dysfunctional thoughts, and/or learned maladaptive sleep habits. See Table 17.2 for a brief description of the most common behavioral interventions.

Because of space limitations, we have decided to provide detailed coverage of only two of these interventions: sleep hygiene and stimulus control. A thorough description of all of the interventions described in Table 17.2 is available in a recently published book on insomnia (see Lichstein & Morin, 2000).

Sleep hygiene warrants closer attention because it can be learned quickly and administered easily. Typically, it is the first intervention that a treatment-seeking insomniac receives. Sleep hygiene consists of commonsense advice regarding five sleep-inhibiting behaviors (i.e., consuming a beverage containing caffeine before bed). When administering sleep hygiene, we have found it helpful to provide the individual with a handout listing the behaviors to be avoided and providing the rationale for each (see Figure 17.2). The rationale for each behavior is particularly important, because the individual will be more likely to comply with the instruction if he or she understands exactly how it will help improve sleep.

We also provide the individual with a log for monitoring treatment progress (see Figure 17.3). The use of a daily log is an essential part of many behavioral treatments because it helps to facilitate behavioral change. Although research has shown that sleep hygiene alone is not particularly effective, multicomponent treatments including sleep hygiene have been shown to be effective (Morin et al., 1994).

Table 17.2   Behavioral Interventions for Insomnia

Cognitive	(1)	Targets sleep maladaptive thoughts
	(2)	Therapist helps the patient to • Identify and challenge maladaptive beliefs (e.g., "I need 8 full hours of sleep every night in order to function.") • Replace these beliefs with adaptive ones (e.g., "Even if I do not sleep 8 full hours, I will still be able to function. I may feel a little tired, but almost everyone feels tired at work occasionally.")
Cognitive-behavioral	(1)	Targets sleep maladaptive thoughts and behaviors; combines cognitive therapy (described above) and one or more behavioral techniques (see examples below)
	(2)	Therapist helps the patient to • Identify sleep maladaptive thoughts and behaviors • Replace them with thoughts more conducive to sleep
Relaxation	(1)	Targets mental and/or physical arousal or tension
	(2)	Therapist teaches the patient one of several relaxation techniques: • Progressive muscle relaxation—different muscles are alternately tensed and relaxed; particular attention is paid to the way one's muscles feel when relaxed • Visual imagery—involves focusing on a mental image of a relaxing scene, object, or situation • Autogenic training—involves focusing on heaviness and warmth in one's arms and legs while repeating statements such as "My right arm feels heavy and warm."
Sleep hygiene[a]	(1)	Targets sleep-inhibiting behaviors
	(2)	Therapist instructs patient to avoid • Drinking caffeine or alcohol before bed • Smoking or exercising before bed • Napping
Sleep restriction	(1)	Limits/restricts the time allotted for sleep each night
	(2)	Therapist has the patient monitor sleep and determines allotted sleep time based on the amount of time the patient actually *sleeps* each night (time spent awake in bed trying to sleep is excluded)
	(3)	Goal is to regulate the sleep-wake cycle by tailoring the time spent in bed to the patient's true sleep need
Stimulus control[a]	(1)	Eliminates habits that cause the bed to become associated with wakefulness rather than sleep
	(2)	Therapist gives the patient a set of instructions intended to strengthen the association between the bed and sleep by • Reducing the amount of awake time spent in the bed and bedroom • Eliminating sleep-incompatible activities while in bed, such as eating, reading, watching television, paying bills, etc. (sex is the one exception to this rule)

a. Denotes interventions described in detail in this chapter.

Stimulus control also warrants special attention, because research has shown that it is the most effective single behavioral intervention (Morin et al., 1994). Stimulus control is based on the idea that insomnia is caused by the faulty association of the bed and bedroom with activities other than sleep (e.g., eating, watching TV, reading,

SLEEP HYGIENE INSTRUCTIONS
Department of Psychology, The University of Memphis

Following the instructions below increases the likelihood that you will sleep well.
Failing to follow any of these instructions may lead to sleep disruption.

(1) Avoid caffeine after noon: Caffeine is a stimulant that can lead to increased arousal
and difficulty falling and staying asleep. Some people are very sensitive to the effects
of caffeine, and use of caffeine after noon may disrupt sleep.

(2) Avoid exercise within 2 hours of bedtime: Exercising too close to bedtime may put
your body in an aroused state when you need to be relaxing. However, participation
in regular exercise that occurs earlier in the day may improve sleep.

(3) Avoid nicotine within 2 hours of bedtime: Nicotine, like caffeine, is a stimulant
that can make falling and staying asleep difficult.

(4) Avoid alcohol within 2 hours of bedtime: Although you may initially feel sleepy
after drinking alcohol, alcohol use near bedtime usually leads to more awake time
during the night.

(5) Avoid heavy meals within 2 hours of bedtime: Heavy meals close to bedtime put a
strain on your digestive system while you are trying to sleep. Heavy meals may
produce physical discomfort or metabolic changes that interfere with sleep.

Figure 17.2   Sleep Hygiene Handout, Including the Five Basic Instructions and the Rationale
For Each

worrying). The main goal of this intervention is to break sleep-incompatible associations and to strengthen the association of the bed and bedroom with sleep. Stimulus control consists of a set of six instructions. These instructions and the rationale for each are provided in Figure 17.4. As with sleep hygiene, a daily log can be used to monitor the individual's treatment progress.

Time Element

The number of treatment sessions varies depending on the severity and etiology of the insomnia as well as the individual's motivation and adherence to treatment. Typically, six to ten 1-hour sessions are needed; however, research has shown that such interventions can be administered effectively in as few as four 1-hour sessions (Lichstein, Wilson, & Johnson, 2000). Slight improvements in sleep can often be seen within a week of starting treatment. Significant improvement usually takes a little longer, but research has shown that such improvement is maintained up to 2 years following treatment (Morin et al., 1994).

SLEEP HYGIENE LOG
Department of Psychology, The University of Memphis

Name _____

Monitoring Use of Sleep Hygiene Instructions

We want to evaluate how many of the 5 sleep hygiene instructions you use. Please fill out the following table. Each column is a different day, and each row is a different instruction. Put the date in the top row and <u>check only those boxes</u> for instructions 1-6 to <u>show success</u>.

Today's date ⇒	1/12								
1. Did you avoid caffeine after noon?	✓								
2. Did you avoid exercise within 2 hours of bedtime?	✓								
3. Did you avoid nicotine within 2 hours of bedtime?	✓								
4. Did you avoid alcohol within 2 hours of bedtime?									
5. Did you avoid a heavy meal within 2 hours of bedtime?	✓								

In the above example, the individual complied with all stimulus control instructions except they did not avoid alcohol within 2 hours of bedtime (#4). They avoided caffeine after noon (1), avoided exercise within 2 hours of bedtime (2), avoided nicotine within 2 hours of bedtime (3), and avoided a heavy meal within 2 hours of bedtime (5).

Figure 17.3   Sleep Hygiene Log Used to Monitor Treatment Compliance

Side Effects

Although side effects have not been systematically studied for behavioral interventions, they are unlikely to cause any serious adverse effects. One exception to this is sleep restriction, which may induce additional sleep deprivation in individuals who are already experiencing significant daytime impairment.

Psychological Interventions Versus Medication

Both psychological and pharmacological interventions provide effective short-term treatment. However, hypnotic medications tend to lose their effectiveness over time and are not recommended for long-term maintenance (Buysse & Reynolds, 2000). This presents a problem, because insomnia is often chronic. Fortunately, psychological interventions have been shown to provide effective long-term management of insomnia (Morin et al., 1994). Another advantage of psychological interventions is that, unlike medication, they are not likely to cause unwanted adverse effects. Unfortunately, psychological interventions are underutilized. Although research has also shown that many insomniacs would prefer drug-free

STIMULUS CONTROL INSTRUCTIONS
Department of Psychology, The University of Memphis

Following the instructions below increases the likelihood that you will sleep well. Failing to follow any of these instructions may lead to sleep disruption.

(1) Don't use your bed or bedroom for anything (any time of the day) but sleep (or sex). Doing other things in bed is "misusing" the bed. Doing other things reinforces the notion that a variety of actions are appropriate in that setting (e.g., if you often watch television in bed, going to bed will become a cue to begin thinking about things related to what you have seen on television). If the bed is reserved for sleep alone, then climbing into bed will be a strong cue for you to fall asleep.

(2) Go to bed only when sleepy. Let your body tell you when it is tired. If you go to bed when you are sleepy, you are more likely to go to sleep right away, reinforcing the association between bed and sleep. If you are not sleepy, you might toss and turn, begin to think and get mentally and physically aroused. By establishing a fixed time for getting up and allowing your bedtime to vary, your body can determine how much sleep you do need to function well. Your body will let you know this by getting tired when it is time for you to go to bed.

(3) If you do not fall asleep within about 15-20 minutes, leave the bed and do something in another room. Go back to bed only when you feel sleepy again. Clock watching with regard to the 15-20 minute rule is not recommended. If you do not fall asleep within 20 minutes upon returning to bed, repeat this instruction as many times as needed. Although the idea of getting out of bed to promote better sleep might seem counterintuitive or strange, the reason for doing this is to strengthen the association of the bed and the bedroom with sleep. By getting out of bed when you have not fallen asleep after 15-20 minutes, you can promote this association.

(4) If you wake up during the night and do not fall back to sleep within 20 minutes, follow rule 3 again. New habits come only with repeated practice. When first beginning this treatment, it is common to have to get up many times each night before falling asleep.

(5) Use your alarm to leave bed at the same time every morning regardless of the amount of sleep obtained. This will help your body acquire a constant sleep rhythm. By varying the time you get up you are shifting your rhythm each day so that it is not in stable harmony with clock time.

(6) Avoid napping. Naps meet some of your sleep need and make it less likely that you will fall asleep quickly. By not napping, you also help to ensure that any sleep deprivation you feel from last night will increase your likelihood of falling asleep quickly tonight. If you must nap, do not nap past 3 pm. Napping throws your body rhythm off schedule and makes it more difficult for you to sleep at night.

Figure 17.4   Stimulus Control Handout Including the Six Instructions and the Rationale for Each treatment, pharmacological interventions are still used most frequently, with more than 7% of adults using hypnotic sleep medication each year (Mellinger et al., 1985). It is hoped that this trend will change as clinicians and other health care experts come to recognize the advantages of behavioral interventions. For example, although behavioral interventions may be more time-consuming initially than pharmacotherapy, they may prove more cost-effective in the long run.

WORKPLACE ACCOMMODATIONS

Workplace accommodations may include maintaining referral lists of clinicians trained to assess and treat insomnia; allowing the employee to take time from work for assessment and treatment; and providing sleep-related education (sleep hygiene information, and books such as Hauri and Linde's *No More Sleepless Nights*). Employer-sponsored health fairs are a good way to distribute such information.

For insomnia due to work-related stress, efforts should be directed at alleviating that stress if at all possible. For example, an employee experiencing conflict with a supervisor may receive help in resolving that conflict. Supervisors and managers should be educated about and sensitive to the effects of outside stressors on sleep (loss of a spouse, illness, upcoming marriage). If an employer sponsors an Employee Assistance Program, short-term counseling may be available to help the employee cope with such stressors.

Employees suffering from secondary insomnia should have adequate access to treatment for their primary condition (medical, psychiatric, or substance-related). Although allowing a sleep-deprived employee to take on-the-job naps or "power naps"

might have intuitive appeal, it is unclear whether napping is beneficial for individuals with insomnia. On one hand, daytime naps meet some of the individual's sleep needs and may interfere with nighttime sleep, perpetuating the insomnia. On the other hand, researchers have found that a short nap (less than 30 minutes) improved alertness in sleepy drivers (Horne & Reyner, 1996) and in college students with normal sleep-wake habits (Hayashi, Ito, & Hori, 1999; Hayashi, Watanabe, & Hori, 1999). Research (Della Rocco, Comperatore, Caldwell, & Cruz, 2000) has also shown both long (2 hours) and short (45 minutes) naps can improve performance on computer-based tasks in night shift workers. Unfortunately, these studies examined only good sleepers and night shift workers and, therefore, do not allow us to draw any conclusions regarding the benefits of naps on the work performance of individuals who do not sleep well and who work the day shift. Research on the effects of napping on the work performance of insomniacs is needed.

MAINTENANCE OF GAINS/RELAPSE PREVENTION

Monitoring an employee's job-related stress is one way of enhancing maintenance of gains and preventing relapse. Periodic education about sleep and sleep hygiene may also help, along with providing a supportive environment that encourages an employee to discuss job stressors and to seek appropriate health care when necessary. Ongoing access to appropriate health care and mental health care (beyond the initial assessment and diagnosis) is essential for employees experiencing secondary insomnia. Although gains made through behavioral interventions are typically well-maintained, some individuals may need to return to therapy periodically for "booster sessions." This is not uncommon for behavioral techniques. In such booster sessions, the clinician assesses what is currently going on with the employee, paying particular attention to reasons for relapse.

SUMMARY

Insomnia is a serious disorder that can negatively affect all aspects of an individual's life, including the workplace. Job-related negative effects include health and mental health problems, tardiness, absenteeism, accidents, and reduced productivity. In this chapter, we provided an overview of the impact of insomnia on the workplace and recommended referral strategies and on-the-job accommodations that may help to lessen this impact.

Diagnosis and assessment by a properly trained clinician is the first step to dealing with any type of sleep problem. Although a subjective complaint of poor sleep is central to an insomnia diagnosis, polysomnographic evaluation is often necessary because other sleep disorders (e.g., sleep apnea) may mimic the symptoms of insomnia. Insomnia can occur as a short-term problem in response to an easily identifiable stressor that may be positive or negative and may or may not be job-related (e.g., an upcoming promotion or the death of a spouse). In such situations, the insomnia often remits without treatment, but sleep medication may help to alleviate symptoms temporarily. More often, however, insomnia represents a chronic problem that can plague an individual for years. The precise pattern of chronic insomnia varies, with some individuals experiencing problems on a nearly nightly basis and others experiencing sleep difficulties intermittently over a

number of years. These more persistent forms of insomnia typically require treatment. We recommend psychological interventions over sleep medications in such cases. Medications can provide temporary relief, but tend to lose effectiveness after a month to 6 weeks of use. We prefer psychological interventions because they provide better long-term maintenance, are unlikely to cause any serious adverse effects, and are likely to be more cost-effective in the long run. When the insomnia is secondary to a medical or psychiatric illness or substance abuse problem, the primary condition should be treated aggressively. Concurrent treatment of the sleep problem, however, may also be helpful, because it is not uncommon for insomnia to develop a behavioral component in such situations.

One way employers can help reduce the negative effects of insomnia is by ensuring that employees have adequate access to appropriate professional services (see our suggestions for future research below). Employees with sleep complaints should be taken seriously and encouraged to seek help. By providing adequate health and mental health care benefits and offering on-the-job education about the effects and treatment of insomnia, employers can help ensure a safer and more productive workplace for all.

Future Research

Although a large amount of epidemiological research details the negative effects of insomnia on the workplace, no research has examined the effectiveness of workplace-based interventions for insomnia. Thus, development and evaluation of such workplace interventions is an area ripe for future investigation. For example, all of the psychological treatments described in this chapter could be administered in a group format and offered by a trained professional at the workplace. Research could examine not only whether the treated employees' sleep improved, but also whether they experienced lower rates of tardiness, took less sick leave, and exhibited increased productivity following treatment. If found effective, workplace-based group intervention would benefit employers and employees alike. For employers, it would be a cost-effective way of providing treatment for their poor-sleeping employees. For employees, it would make treatment easily accessible and provide them with a supportive environment in which they could discuss their sleep problems with fellow poor-sleeping employees. Group booster sessions could also be offered at the workplace in order to ensure the long-term maintenance of treatment gains.

Another form of intervention that merits future research is the effect of naps on the work performance of individuals with insomnia. Currently, there is no empirical evidence that addresses whether power naps are beneficial or detrimental for poor sleepers. Finally, future research may also examine the effect of on-the-job sleep education. It is possible that education about sleep hygiene and other sleep-related topics, such as stress management, may have a preventive effect, helping some employees to avoid developing sleep problems in the first place.

REFERENCES

Addison, R. G., Thorpy, M. J., Roehrs, T. A., & Roth, T. (1991). Sleep/wake complaints in the general population. *Sleep Research, 20,* 112.

American Psychiatric Association. (1994). *Diagnostic and statistical manual of mental disorders* (4th ed.). Washington, DC: Author.

Beutler, L. E., Thornby, J. I., & Karacan, I. (1978). Psychological variables in the diagnosis of insomnia. In R. L. Williams & I. Karacan (Eds.), *Sleep disorders: Diagnosis and treatment* (pp. 61-100). New York: Wiley.

Bixler, E. O., Kales, A., Soldatos, C. R., Kales, J. D., & Healey, S. (1979). Prevalence of sleep disorders in the Los Angeles metropolitan area. *American Journal of Psychiatry, 136,* 1257-1262.

Blazer, D. G., Hays, J. C., & Foley, D. J. (1995). Sleep complaints in older adults: A racial comparison. *Journal of Gerontology, 50,* M280-M284.

Bonnet, M. H., & Arand, D. L. (1995). 24-hour metabolic rate in insomniacs and matched normal sleepers. *Sleep, 18,* 581-588.

Bootzin, R. R., & Nicassio, P. M. (1978). Behavioral treatments for insomnia. In M. Hersen, R. Eisler, & P. Miller (Eds.), *Progress in behavior modification.* New York: Academic Press.

Buysse, D. J., & Reynolds, C. F. (2000). Pharmacologic treatment. In K. L. Lichstein & C. M. Morin (Eds.), *Treatment of late-life insomnia* (pp. 231-267). Thousand Oaks, CA: Sage.

Buysse, D. J., Reynolds, C. F., III, Monk, T. H., Hoch, C. C., Yeager, A. L., & Kupfer, D. J. (1991). Quantification of subjective sleep quality in healthy elderly men and women using the Pittsburgh Sleep Quality Index (PSQI). *Sleep, 14,* 331-338.

Carskadon, M. A., Dement, W. C., Mitler, M. M., Guilleminault, C., Zarcone, V. P., & Spiegel, R. (1976). Self-reports versus sleep laboratory findings in 122 drug-free subjects with complaints of chronic insomnia. *American Journal of Psychiatry, 133,* 1382-1388.

Chambers, M. J., & Kim, J. Y. (1993). The role of state-trait anxiety in insomnia and daytime restedness. *Behavioral Medicine, 19,* 42-46.

Coursey, R. D., Buchsbaum, M., & Frankel, B. L. (1975). Personality measures and evoked responses in chronic insomniacs. *Journal of Abnormal Psychology, 84,* 239-249.

Della Rocco, P. S., Comperatore, C., Caldwell, L., & Cruz, C. (2000). *The effects of napping on night shift performance* (FAA Office of Aviation Medicine Reports, pp. 1-33). Oklahoma City, OK: Federal Aviation Administration, Civil Aeromedical Institute.

Espie, C. A. (1991). *The psychological treatment of insomnia.* Chichester, UK: Wiley.

Foley, D. J., Monjan, A. A., Brown, S. L., Simonsick, E. M., Wallace, R. B., & Blazer, D. G. (1995). Sleep complaints among elderly persons: An epidemiologic study of three communities. *Sleep, 18,* 425-432.

Ford, D. E., & Kamerow, D. B. (1989). Epidemiologic study of sleep disturbances and psychiatric disorders: An opportunity for prevention? *Journal of the American Medical Association, 262,* 1479-1484.

Gallup Organization. (1995). *Sleep in America: 1995.* Princeton, NJ: Author.

Hauri, P. (1991). *Case studies in insomnia.* New York: Plenum.

Hauri, P., & Linde, S. (1990). *No more sleepless nights.* New York: Wiley.

Hayashi, M., Ito, S., & Hori, T. (1999). The effects of a 20-min nap at noon on sleepiness, performance and EEG activity. *International Journal of Psychophysiology, 32,* 173-180.

Hayashi, M., Watanabe, M., & Hori, T. (1999). The effects of a 20-min nap in the mid-afternoon on mood, performance, and EEG activity. *Clinical Neurophysiology, 110,* 272-279.

Horne, J. A., & Reyner, L. A. (1996). Counteracting driver sleepiness: Effects of napping, caffeine, and placebo. *Psychophysiology, 33,* 306-309.

Johnson, L. C., & Spinweber, C. L. (1983). Good and poor sleepers differ in Navy performance. *Military Medicine, 148,* 727-731.

Jones, H. S., & Oswald, I. (1968). Two cases of healthy insomnia. *Electroencephalography and Clinical Neurophysiology, 24,* 378-380.

Karacan, I., Thornby, J. I., & Anch, M. (1976). Prevalence of sleep disturbances in a primarily urban Florida county. *Social Science Medicine, 10,* 239-244.

Langer, S., Mendelson, W., & Richardson, G. (1999). Symptomatic treatment of insomnia. *Sleep, 22*(Suppl. 3), S437-S445.

Lichstein, K. L. (2000). Secondary insomnia. In K. L. Lichstein & C. M. Morin (Eds.), *Treatment of late-life insomnia* (pp. 297-319). Thousand Oaks, CA: Sage.

Lichstein, K. L., & Morin, C. M. (Eds.). (2000). *Treatment of late-life insomnia.* Thousand Oaks, CA: Sage.

Lichstein, K. L., Wilson, N. M., & Johnson, C. T. (2000). Psychological treatment of secondary insomnia. *Psychology and Aging, 15,* 232-240.

Mellinger, G. D., Balter, M. B., & Uhlenhuth, E. H. (1985). Insomnia and its treatment: Prevalence and correlates. *Archives of General Psychiatry, 42,* 225-232.

Morin, C. M., Culbert, J. P., & Schwartz, S. M. (1994). Nonpharmacological interventions for insomnia: A meta-analysis of treatment efficacy. *American Journal of Psychiatry, 151,* 1172-1180.

Morin, C. M., & Gramling, S. E. (1989). Sleep patterns and aging: Comparison of older adults with and without insomnia complaints. *Psychology and Aging, 4,* 290-294.

Morin, C. M., & Kwentus, J. A. (1988). Behavioral and pharmacological treatments for insomnia. *Annals of Behavioral Medicine, 10,* 91-100.

Roth, T., Kramer, M., & Lutz, T. (1976). The nature of insomnia: A descriptive summary of a sleep clinic population. *Comprehensive Psychiatry, 17,* 217-220.

Schweitzer, P. K., Engelhardt, C. L., Hilliker, N. A., Muehlbach, M. J., & Walsh, J. K. (1992). Consequences of reported poor sleep. *Sleep Research, 21,* 260.

Stepanski, E., Koshorek, G., Zorick, F., Glinn, M., Roehrs, T., & Roth, T. (1989). Characteristics of individuals who do or do not seek treatment for chronic insomnia. *Psychosomatics, 30,* 421-427.

Stoller, M. K. (1994). Economic effects of insomnia. *Clinical Therapeutics, 16,* 873-897.

Walsh, J., & Ustun, T. B. (1999). Prevalence and health consequences of insomnia. *Sleep, 22*(Suppl. 3), S427-S436.

Wohlgemuth, W. K., Edinger, J. D., Fins, A. I., & Sullivan, R. J. (1999). How many nights are enough? The short-term stability of sleep parameters in elderly insomniacs and normal sleepers. *Psychophysiology, 36,* 233-244.

Part IV

EFFECTS OF DISRUPTIVE BEHAVIOR AT WORK

CHAPTER 18

Alcohol and Drug Problem Management in the Workplace

PAUL M. ROMAN
SUZANNE C. BAKER

American culture has developed a mixed and muddled set of ideas about the meaning of psychoactive substances (Inciardi, 2002). As medications, certain psychoactive drugs have had dramatic effects in allowing people with psychoses to function in everyday life, and substances such as selective serotonin reuptake inhibitors (e.g., Prozac©) are widely accepted as a means to deal with the apparent national epidemic of depressive symptoms. At the other end of the spectrum, other psychoactive substances, such as heroin and crack cocaine, are viewed with fear and horror. Thus, intense stigma and social rejection are imposed upon their users.

Adding to the confusion is the fact that the majority of the American adult population uses alcohol, a legal psychoactive drug that is accepted amorphously as a "social lubricant" and is viewed only rarely as a medication. Delineating alcohol use, alcohol abuse, and alcoholism yields ambiguous distinctions at best; behaviors that are often objectively similar may be viewed by some as criminal deviance and by others as manifestation of illness (Roman, 1991). An indisputable conclusion, however, is that a significant proportion of people with alcohol or drug problems are stigmatized by their significant others.

Because a majority of the adults who use substances are employed, the workplace has long been faced with the challenge of what to do when alcohol or drug problems become evident among employees. Widely diffused contemporary rhetoric calls for drug-free workplaces, implying, more often than not, that people who are involved with drugs should not be employed. At the same time, however, this rhetoric offers unclear messages as to what should be done with people affected by the use of the legal drug, alcohol (Normand, Lempert & O'Brien, 1994).

If a majority attitude can be distilled from America's workplace leaders in the 21st century, it is that job applicants who use drugs should be denied employment,[1] and current employees with drug or alcohol problems should be given a chance to deal with their problems before being excluded from the workplace (Knudsen & Roman, 2001). When coupled, these strategies have a contradictory element. One policy embeds a notion of primary prevention wherein illegal drug users are precluded from being hired and thus contaminating the workplace with their disrespect for legal authority, questionable job performance, and/or inducement of co-workers to become users of illegal drugs. The second policy acknowledges that drug and alcohol problems are reversible or correctable, so that when these problems emerge among those already employed, the employees are the target of what can be called a human resource conservation policy. Viewing these human resource policies in this way rather than as corporate humanitarianism, it is clear that the policies may be based on avoiding loss of the organizational investments made in employees who may have "messed up" in one or more areas of their lives (Roman & Blum, 1999).

The focus of this chapter is the human resource conservation strategy, but the foregoing discussion offers an important context for understanding how employers implement this strategy and the extent to which they invest resources in it. The medicalized rhetoric of intervention and recovery is definitely affected by the "just say no" principle that implies individual control over the decision of whether to use psychoactive substances. The commitment of employers to saving the employment of substance-abusing employees is limited and may be accompanied by multiple contingencies.

DEVELOPMENT OF INTERVENTION STRATEGIES

Effective means to deal with employed people with alcohol problems have existed for nearly 60 years (Trice & Schonbrunn, 1981). However, diffusion of these techniques was very slow, either because employers did not perceive large-scale problems with alcohol abuse in their workforces, or because public relations concerns made them reluctant to admit such problems (Roman, 1981). The turning point occurred in the 1970s with the creation of the Employee Assistance Program (EAP) (Roman & Blum, 1985; Trice & Roman, 1972; Wrich, 1973).

This strategy was, in many ways, built upon the earlier industrial alcoholism programs, but it had much more of a human resource management flavor. It shifted the focus from employees with alcohol problems to employees with any kind of a personal problem that affected their work. Employers found this broad focus to be reasonable, and few would argue that they had no employees who brought personal troubles to the job. Subsequently, this broadened focus, along with the growth of treatment interventions for drug abuse, brought drugs other than alcohol under the aegis of EAPs as well.

As compared to programs that are broadly based in the community, workplace-based interventions have a variety of advantages in addressing substance abuse issues, as well as mental health, familial, legal, and financial problems affecting employees. Employees spend a great deal of time at work, offering ample opportunities for adverse changes in behavior to be observed and acted upon. Through both supervisory-subordinate and peer relationships, there are built-in opportunities for intervention. Both the employee and the employer have vested interests in maintaining the employment relationship; the employee needs a job and income, and the employer needs trained and committed people to produce goods and services.

Through linking health insurance coverage with employment, American workplaces have a further vested interest in ensuring that counseling and treatment are delivered to their insured employees in an efficient and effective manner, which includes early rather than delayed identification of problems. Finally, if employment continues, the employee who has received assistance can be monitored and receive aftercare in conjunction with employment, with both the employee and the employer again having vested interests in ensuring that the treatment "sticks."

THE SCOPE OF THE PROBLEM

Alcohol use, alcohol abuse, and alcoholism affect the workplace in myriad ways. It would be difficult to find human resource specialists who would dismiss the significance of these concerns. For decades, investigators have been estimating the massive financial losses to business and industry associated with patterns of employee drinking (e.g., Berry & Boland, 1977). Use of other drugs by employed and employable people has perhaps received more public attention, yet the impacts of these behaviors are likely much less than those created by alcohol. As we implied earlier, these impacts are also of a different order because of the moral and criminal dimensions associated with obtaining and using illegal drugs.

The serious presence of substance abuse problems in the workforce was recently documented in a 1997 national survey indicating that about 7.6% of the full-time employed workforce drinks heavily, and 7.7% uses illegal drugs (Zhang, Huang, & Brittingham, 1999). These two categories should not be regarded as equivalent in any respect, particularly because the data are based on self-report and the latter category,

by definition, includes a heterogeneous collection of behaviors. The comorbidity of these problems is high, because about a third of the heavy drinkers are illegal drug users, and about a third of the users of illegal drugs are also heavy drinkers. As compared to those using only illegal drugs or drinking heavily, the comorbids likely represent a higher risk of impaired work performance, and the likelihood of other deviant behaviors on the job is escalated.

Thus, there is ample reason to address workplace alcohol and drug issues. Although EAPs were originally an outgrowth of workplace alcohol programs, their rapid diffusion led to their use in a variety of different ways by their organizational sponsors. Because adoption has been voluntary, no enforced program standards exist that determine the structure and content of EAPs. Consequently, there is no reason to assume that an extant EAP includes an emphasis or even a sensitivity to alcohol and drug issues among the workforce, or that it is equipped to deal appropriately with these problems when they occur. Some EAPs consist only of telephone contact points, which are unlikely to provide the necessary mechanisms to manage a case of employee alcohol or drug dependence. But in many settings, EAP structures can incorporate extensive supports for alcohol and drug problem intervention. In this overview, we consider the elements that need to be in place if employee alcohol and drug problems are to be dealt with efficiently and effectively through EAPs or parallel programs.

MAKING AN EAP EFFECTIVE IN DEALING WITH ALCOHOL AND DRUG PROBLEMS

There is no firm basis of agreement as to what constitutes an appropriate EAP in terms of policy structure (or lack thereof), staffing, or scope of services. EAPs have multiple forms and different emphases, and it may be that their caseloads are determined largely by the workplace culture in which they operate. Because the vast majority of EAPs suggest that employees access services by self-referral (and sometimes suggesting only this possibility), the norms within the workplace affect the types of behavior that lead peers or supervisors to nudge employees toward sources of help. These norms often have a considerable effect on what employees themselves perceive as their own personal problems for which they should seek help. In the original design of EAPs in the 1970s, program staff were expected to alter workplace norms through supervisory training and employee education about specific personal problems. Recent national data indicate that this activity is least likely to occur in externally contracted EAP services (Steele, Schlenger, & Koritko, 2001), which have come to constitute the typical EAP structure, with the exception of major corporations.

A realistic observation is that different employers have different goals for EAPs, some of which include an emphasis on alcohol and drug problems and some of which do not. Settings vary, from those where an organizational leader has had personal experience with recovery from addiction to those where alcohol and drugs are simply not on the organization's cognitive map.

POLICY FUNDAMENTALS

For an EAP to address alcohol and drug problems effectively, a minimum of five components are essential:

1. The program's policy and philosophy should be based clearly on job performance. This distinguishes the EAP from a proactive clinical service that is available to assist employees and their families with whatever problems they might have.

2. The program is appropriately staffed to provide substance abuse services.

3. The program is directly and readily accessible to supervisors and employees.

4. Supervisors, employees, and union representatives are all aware of and supportive of the use of constructive confrontation as a strategy. This is a technique with proven effectiveness (Trice & Beyer, 1984) wherein recalcitrant employees are given an ultimatum that their poor performance will no longer be tolerated but that the organization is willing to support and facilitate their efforts to seek help.

5. Staff specialists are equipped and supported to link employees with appropriate resources for assistance, engage in case management through the treatment period, and implement long-term follow-up based in the workplace.

This list reflects a widely diffused core technology of EAPs that was designed to maximize EAP effectiveness in addressing alcohol and other substance abuse issues (Blum & Roman, 1989, 1995; Roman & Blum, 1985). These particular components have a foundation in empirical evidence vis-à-vis their impact on alcohol issues. However, across-the-board application of them to other problems is less clear-cut. For example, questions can be raised about the efficacy or even the danger of using a "get-tough" approach in the work context of a seriously depressed employee.

Supervisors should be fully trained regarding the organization's alcohol and drug problem intervention policy. It may be counterintuitive to suggest that the most effective way to identify and motivate an employee with an alcohol problem is to ignore the alcohol problem and focus upon other issues. This reflects the first policy fundamental, namely, that the employer's scope of legitimate interest in an employee's drinking centers on the effects of that drinking on work performance. This should be made clear in written policy statements that are distributed to all supervisors and employees.

Because supervisors should be trained to monitor employee performance and match performance with agreed-upon expectations, a pattern of deterioration in performance should be discernible. Well-trained supervisors will detect when this deterioration reflects problems with equipment, job design, or employee training. Documentation of problems with attendance and performance should be standard procedure for supervisors.

As it becomes clear that an employee has a documented performance problem that is not linked to job conditions, the supervisor should consider making a referral. In the case of an employee with an alcohol problem, it is likely that supervisors believe they know the cause of job problems. Because of excuses and other attempted negotiations that can occur relative to the documented performance decrements, supervisors should studiously avoid any discussion of alcohol problems with employees who are suspected of having such problems.

STAFFING FUNDAMENTALS

Generally speaking, help-seeking requires minimal social distance between those who need help and those who are equipped to provide it. Especially in dealing with ambiguous and stigmatic conditions such as alcohol and drug abuse, there must be a reasonable level of trust and confidence in the person who is expected to be the source of assistance. Thus, it is important for the workplace-based intervention service to have competent personnel actually based in the workplace. Familiarity with such an individual and confidence in that person's skills are likely prerequisites for many, if not most, supervisory referrals.

Such visibility and confidence will be enhanced by the active participation of EAP staff in supervisory training, as well as their ongoing presence in the workplace. Such participation includes the integration of EAP staff with the medical or human resources function in the organization, and staff should be knowledgeable about all aspects of workplace culture, regulations, and personnel policies. Many EAPs are staffed outside the host organization, with EAP personnel located elsewhere and occasionally or never coming on-site. Although such an arrangement may work well for self-referrals, especially where confidentiality is the primary concern, it is not ideal for supervisory access.

Access to a trusted expert usually precedes a successful referral of a subordinate with an alcohol problem. Workplace management should encourage such consultation prior to an attempt at a supervisory referral, and should discourage the attitude that the policy expects the supervisor to "go it alone." Consultation allows the EAP staff to encourage the supervisor to proceed with the referral and review the appropriate steps to ensure conformity with policy. At the same time, such consultation can be of great value in precluding inappropriate referrals.

A solid understanding of alcohol and drug problems is a prerequisite in staffing an EAP that will deal adequately and effectively with these issues in the employee population. Backgrounds in counseling or clinical psychology are not adequate in themselves because such training does not necessarily involve substance abuse issues. It is not essential for an EAP to have a fully trained and licensed clinician as the program operative, but rather one who is able to link effectively with a diagnostic resource. In a number of settings, especially those where there is joint operation of an EAP by management and labor, conflicts and confusion about individual rights are prevented by the use of diagnostic expertise altogether independent of the workplace.

CONSTRUCTIVE CONFRONTATION

A strategy with proven effectiveness in dealing with employees with substance abuse problems is constructive confrontation. This strategy is not used frequently, but it is vital for approaching employees who deny that anything needs to be done about either their behavior or their performance, or who repeatedly insist they can deal with things on their own. Constructive confrontation involves a meeting between the supervisor and the problem subordinate, with a representative of the union or employee association present if specified in the organizational policy. The meeting proceeds with presentation to the employee of documented evidence of performance decrements, coupled closely with assurances of the employer's willingness to suspend disciplinary steps and support help-seeking if the employee will follow prescribed steps to deal with the problem.

It is critical to underline that the responsibility for change rests completely with the employee, and that this is not a contractual agreement implying that employment will be maintained regardless of the outcome of help-seeking. The

alternatives of progressive discipline and possible dismissal on the grounds of the poor performance record are also outlined in this meeting. The combination of positive and negative elements in this meeting is critical, and it is essential that supervisors and managers be coached carefully by the EAP staff professional before attempting a constructive confrontation. By offering assistance as an immediate part of the process, the constructive element is emphasized. But at the same time, job jeopardy is suggested, indicating a distinct confrontational element. It is absolutely critical for the discussion to underline that the singular concern of the employer is the employee's job performance.

For obvious practical reasons, constructive confrontation typically occurs as a last resort, and it is clear that most supervisors would prefer not to become involved in such a meeting. From our own research, it is evident that nearly all self-referral actually involves informal discussions and persuasion by supervisors, possibly using the elements of constructive confrontation in an informal manner. Experience and research indicates that constructive confrontation works for those employees who are heavily invested in their jobs (Trice & Beyer, 1984). Early research suggested that job stability may be the center of a system of rationalizations that one's drinking and drug use were not problematic (Trice, 1962). Constructive confrontation undermines those rationalizations and, in Alcoholics Anonymous (AA) terms, may constitute a personal crisis that underlines that the individual has "hit bottom."

TREATMENT AND FOLLOW-UP

The key elements in the workplace's treatment role can be summarized as follows:

1. Assistance resources are selected on the basis of established effectiveness.

2. Linkage is made consistent with the employee's particular health insurance coverage.

3. Linkage is made consistent with the employee's job demands and career contingencies.

4. The staff specialist is directly involved in linkage and monitors compliance.

5. The staff specialist participates in reentry and involves the supervisor as appropriate.

6. The staff specialist engages in work-based supportive follow-up for 36 months or longer.

Core elements of EAPs are similar to the stated principles of contemporary managed care in terms of maximizing the efficiency and efficacy of treatment resources. Ironically, although EAPs clearly predate contemporary managed care, many in the EAP field feel considerable antagonism toward the latter because managed care has, in some instances, supplanted EAP functions. Most EAPs that were staffed internally by companies in the 1970s and 1980s were viewed as stewards of the employer's resources to deal with employee behavioral health problems, with an emphasis on substance abuse. In some instances, staff were not competent in managing these treatment dollars, whereas in other instances, the EAP simply did not keep good records about costs associated with treatment referrals. In these circumstances, those marketing managed care services easily made arguments in favor of the cost savings that employers would experience if they supplanted the EAP with a managed care contract that would more or less embed an EAP service.

A key step in the process is connecting the alcohol- or drug-abusing employee with the resource judged most appropriate for the employee's needs. This requires joint consideration of the employee's clinical condition; the differential effectiveness of available resources; the employee's particular benefits coverage; and job and career considerations that might be affected by where, when, and for how long the treatment occurs. In some instances, a guided referral to AA may be most appropriate, although this appears relatively rare today compared to the early days of industrial programming.

Another fundamental step in treatment planning and referral is that EAP staff members typically are in a position to monitor whether treatment recommendations are followed. They also may ascertain treatment progress, within the appropriate limits of confidentiality. Furthermore, the EAP can play vital roles in orchestrating the employee's reentry into the work setting with supervisors and peers if treatment has required a protracted absence.

Of greatest importance is the participation of the EAP in follow-up. Recovery from alcohol or drug problems is a gradual learning process with substantial risk of relapse. Experience has demonstrated efficacy of posttreatment follow-up by the EAP (Foote & Erfurt, 1991). Follow-up should be systematic and frequent, and it should occur for a relatively lengthy period. The "captive" nature of the workplace and work roles helps ensure that this can happen and it can be carried out in a cost-efficient manner. Such ease of access between professional and client within the work setting contrasts sharply with community-based attempts at follow-up. The integration of follow-up into the expectations of the EAP staff role is also a much better fit than are attempts to assign this role to treatment functionaries.

SHORTFALLS IN ALCOHOL
AND DRUG PROBLEM EMPHASIS

Given the widespread diffusion of EAPs and their potential for dealing with employee substance abuse problems, it may seem surprising that barriers to dealing with alcohol and drug problems are still evident. Some of these barriers are more or less obvious: inadequately written policies, or minimal efforts to diffuse policy content; EAP staff who lack alcohol and drug problem expertise; little access to or reliance on confrontation mechanisms; and concentration of program resources on case-finding and assessment rather than on case management and follow-up.

Additionally, in many instances, EAP staff are based in externally contracted organizations where supervisors are not likely to access assistance, highlighting the issue of social distance mentioned earlier. In many of these cases, EAP image is centered around self-referrals and is unlikely to generate early identification of employee alcohol and drug problems. Ironically, because of these emphases, EAP staff may maintain heavy caseloads as they deal with self-identified problems for which employees may be seeking convenient and low-cost assistance. Without good knowledge of quality control standards, employers may regard these caseload sizes as positive indicators of a high-quality service.

In fact, these concerns may be more problematic than they seem, for it may be difficult to introduce change among employers who believe they have already adopted an appropriate mechanism for dealing with employee alcohol and drug problems. This is a common consequence when a single program is used to mainstream several different behavioral health problems, each of which carries its own "issue baggage" and thus requires special attention.

Major potential for improving the efficacy of EAPs in dealing with alcohol problems may lie with the physician community. Especially in a managed care environment, physicians may have first-line data on the range of secondary impacts that alcohol problems can produce for the health status of adults and their dependents. Workplaces are, in turn, increasingly responsive to steps that will improve the efficiency of health care utilization. Because most primary care physicians and psychiatrists work primarily with employed people and their dependents, they are in a unique position to support and facilitate the efficacy of EAP efforts in identifying, confronting, and sustaining recovery efforts within the alcohol-problem population. In most communities, physicians are poorly trained in alcohol- and drug-related issues, and consequently, they handle these issues in several ineffective ways, such as trying to treat the problem themselves, using psychoactive drugs such as tranquilizers or antidepressants, or simply treating the consequences of the substance abuse to the patient's satisfaction.

CONCLUSION

Alcohol and drug problems are major issues in American society, and employers must deal with these issues within their workforces. Recent decades have seen efforts to mainstream the management of alcohol and drug problems into the health care system by defining them in medical terms and treating them as disease conditions. This has been partially successful, but considerable stigmatization continues to surround people who have chronic problems with the use of alcohol or drugs.

Apparent progress was made with the development of EAPs, and initially, it appeared that the management of substance abuse problems in the workplace could be dealt with effectively along with other problems that affected job performance and relationships in the workplace. As federal support for this programming effort was withdrawn during the 1980s, evidence began to accumulate that the potential for dealing constructively with employees' alcohol or drug dependence was being undermined by changes in EAP design and emphasis. These changes made EAPs responsive to a variety of other workplace issues that placed heavy demands on EAPs' time. Furthermore, EAPs became preoccupied with dealing with problems that employees presented through self-referrals. Both of these changes played into the general cultural themes surrounding alcohol and drug abuse, namely, ambivalence at best and stigmatization and avoidance at worst.

As this overview has indicated, EAPs have the potential for addressing alcohol and drug issues effectively through specific mechanisms of identification, referral, treatment, and follow-up. However, this will not happen unless the EAP is especially equipped to do so through its staffing and program operation. Many workplace decision makers are not informed about these possibilities and may simply assume that alcohol and drug problems are being dealt with through their EAPs, which are, in fact, unequipped to do so.

NOTE

1. Preemployment screening intended to eliminate job applicants, and screening of current employees intended to punish them or remove them from employment, are primarily legal and criminological concerns. Thus, they are beyond the scope of this chapter because their intentions are not therapeutic. Because of the legal ramifications involved in screening current employees for evidence of illegal drug use, readers are urged to consult information describing current regulations applicable to their own industries and locales and are discouraged from directly addressing any illegal drug use among employees without expert legal consultation. However, in this chapter, we will consider those instances where drug screening may be associated with therapeutic goals.

REFERENCES

Berry, R. E., & Boland, J. A. (1977). *The economic costs of alcohol abuse and alcoholism.* New York: Free Press.

Blum, T. C., & Roman, P. M. (1995). *Cost effectiveness and preventive impact of employee assistance programs* (Center for Substance Abuse Prevention Monograph No. 5). Washington, DC: Department of Health and Human Services.

Blum, T. C., & Roman, P. M. (1989). Employee Assistance Programs and human resources management. In K. M. Rowland & G. R. Ferris (Eds.), *Research in personnel and human resources management, Volume 7* (pp. 259-312). Greenwich, CT: JAI.

Foote, A., & Erfurt, J. C. (1991). Effects of EAP followup on prevention of relapse among substance abuse clients. *Journal of Studies on Alcohol, 52,* 241-248.

Inciardi, J. A. (2002). *The War on Drugs III: The continuing saga of the mysteries and miseries of intoxication, addiction, crime and public policy.* Boston: Allyn & Bacon.

Knudsen, H. K., & Roman, P. M. (2001, August). *Organizational responses to employee drug use: The case of drug testing.* Paper presented at the annual meeting of the American Sociological Association, Anaheim, CA.

Normand, J., Lempert, R. O., & O'Brien, C. P. (1994). *Under the influence: Drugs and the American work force.* Washington, DC: National Academy Press.

Roman, P. M. (1981). From employee alcoholism to employee assistance: An analysis of the de-emphasis on prevention and on alcoholism problems in work-based programs. *Journal of Studies on Alcohol, 42,* 244-272.

Roman, P. M. (1991). *Alcohol: The development of sociological perspectives on use and abuse.* New Brunswick, NJ: Rutgers University, Center of Alcohol Studies.

Roman, P. M., & Blum, T. C. (1985). The core technology of employee assistance programs. *ALMACAN: Magazine of the Association of Labor and Management Administrators and Consultants on Alcoholism, 15*(3), 8-19.

Roman, P. M., & Blum, T. C. (1999). Internalization and externalization as frames for understanding workplace deviance. In I. H. Simpson & R. L. Simpson (Eds.), *Research in the sociology of work: Deviance in the workplace* (pp. 139-164). Greenwich, CT: JAI.

Steele, P., Schlenger, W. S., & Koritko, L. (2001, September). *Factors characterizing a national sample of employee assistance programs.* Paper presented at the 3rd Annual Workplace and Managed Care Research Conference, Crystal City, VA.

Trice, H. M. (1962). The job behavior of problem drinkers. In D. Pittman & C. Snyder (Eds.), *Society, culture and drinking patterns* (pp. 562-579). New York: Wiley.

Trice, H. M., & Beyer, J. M. (1984). Work-related outcomes of constructive confrontation strategies in a job-based alcoholism program. *Journal of Studies on Alcohol, 45,* 393-404.

Trice, H. M., & Roman, P. M. (1972). *Spirits and demons at work: Alcohol and other drugs on the job.* Ithaca: Cornell University, New York State School of Industrial and Labor Relations.

Trice, H. M., & Schonbrunn, M. (1981). A history of job-based alcoholism programs, 1900-1955. *Journal of Drug Issues, 11,* 171-198.

Wrich, J. M. (1973). *The employee assistance program.* Center City, MN: Hazelden Foundation.

Zhang, Z., Huang, L. X., & Brittingham, A. M. (1999). *Worker drug use and workplace policies and programs: Results from the 1994 and 1997 National Household Survey on Drug Abuse.* Rockville, MD: Department of Health and Human Services, Substance Abuse and Mental Health Services Administration.

CHAPTER 19

Social Dysfunction in the Workplace

LINDSAY HAM
MELANIE VAN DYKE
DEBRA A. HOPE

I n the American workplace, the focus has shifted from an individualistic attitude to a more collaborative or team-oriented approach to compete in the global marketplace (Bolman & Deal, 1992). Therefore, team building has become a high priority in many businesses, yielding such benefits as increased performance, improved quality, higher levels of job satisfaction, and the utilization of creative forces within the organization (May & Schwoerer, 1994; Varney, 1989). Additionally, there has been increased attention to the mental health and skills deficits in employees, because these have been found to be related to productivity in the workplace (Carroll, 1996; Cartledge, 1989). Increasing productivity has become an important goal of organizations during the aggressive business environment (Shosh, 1996). This push for greater worker productivity highlights the value of employees and the value of their mental health (Shosh, 1996). The emphases on teamwork as well as employee mental health have led to an influx of interventions

for team building as well as a variety of workplace-related mental health programs (Bottom & Baloff, 1994; Carroll, 1996; Maples, 1992). In this environment, employee social dysfunction represents an important business and human problem.

Communication and interpersonal skills become increasingly important in the workplace as the team approach becomes more prevalent. Most team-building techniques focus on improving interpersonal relationships. Interpersonal skills such as trustworthiness, communication skills, manners, and personal appearance are critical for job acquisition and maintenance (Cartledge, 1989). On the other hand, difficulties in social interactions are common among those who seek mental health services in general, and have been associated with a variety of psychosocial problems, including schizophrenia, depression, social anxiety, many personality disorders, marital distress, aggression, and learning disabilities (Meier & Hope, 1998; Segrin, 1993). In the current business environment, such difficulties in social situations are not trivial because they may impair an individual's work performance and, consequently, the well-being of the business. In fact, social competence appears to be among the best predictors of occupational adjustment and vocational success for individuals with handicapping conditions (Cartledge, 1989; Foss, Bullis, & Vilhauer, 1984). Therefore, it is essential that professionals in human resources, management, and mental health be able to identify, assess, and intervene when social dysfunction affects the workplace.

Defining Social Dysfunction

First of all, the term *social dysfunction* must be explained because the concept refers to both social skills deficits and performance deficits. Both of these deficits can result in impaired interpersonal performance, although the treatment for each would be quite different. A social skills deficit is present if the individual does not possess the skills, or the behavioral repertoire, necessary for effective social interaction. A performance deficit is present when the individual possesses the necessary skills for successful social interactions, but is inhibited from performing adequately in certain situations, often because of anxiety. Social dysfunction (either a social skills or a performance deficit) is a recognized characteristic of numerous psychological disorders. For instance, social dysfunction may be seen in schizophrenia, substance abuse, major depressive disorder, social anxiety disorder, and many personality disorders (Hollin & Trower, 1986). Additionally, social dysfunction may be seen in marital distress and aggression, and in individuals with learning disabilities and/or mental handicaps (Hollin & Trower, 1986; Norton & Hope, 2001).

Social Skill. Although the global concept of social skills is well recognized and

frequently an important focus of assessment and treatment in mental health settings, no consistent, comprehensive definition of social skills has been identified (Kavale & Forness, 1996; Meier & Hope, 1998). However, according to Meier and Hope (1998), researchers and theorists tend to agree that

> social skill is comprised of a group of behaviors that enable[s] an individual to effectively engage in, maintain, and succeed in social interactions. These behaviors include the expression of both positive and negative emotions; facial expressions; the tone, volume, and speed of verbal expressions; posture; and appropriate content. (p. 235)

Furthermore, socially skilled behavior includes a complex combination of verbal and nonverbal responses that is very much sensitive to the context (Franklin, Jaycox, & Foa, 1999). Therefore, it is important to consider differences in the client's style and the client's cultural and environmental milieu in assessing and treating social skills (Bedell & Lennox, 1997; Franklin et al., 1999). Additionally, both excesses and deficiencies in behavior can be unskillful (e.g., excessive eye contact or a lack of eye contact can be unskillful) and must also be considered in the context. Table 19.1 summarizes many of the verbal and nonverbal behaviors associated with social skill, and also provides examples of social skill deficits.

Performance Deficits. Performance deficits often result from excessive anxiety. An individual may have the requisite skills, but something in the context triggers anxiety that then interferes with performance, possibly even resulting in behavioral avoidance. For example, a worker may communicate effectively with his or her immediate team members but is unable to participate

Table 19.1 Verbal and Nonverbal Behaviors Associated With Social Skills, Descriptions of Social Skills, and Examples of Social Skill Deficits

Verbal and Nonverbal Behaviors	Description of Social Skill	Example of Deficit
Eye contact/gaze	Looking directly at the other person's face while interacting	Staring too intently during conversation, not looking at the other person's face
Response duration	Directly answering questions with appropriate amount of detail	Overexplaining unnecessary details, giving insufficient or vague information
Speech latency	Responding to others' comments in a timely manner	Interrupting others, taking long pauses before speaking
Head movement/nods and gesturing	Appropriate nods and gestures that convey interest and reassurance	Excessive and/or distracting movement, nonresponsiveness to others' comments
Greetings	Appropriate salutation when approaching coworkers (e.g., "hello," "good morning")	Engaging in long conversations with coworkers, nonresponsive to seeing coworkers, may appear to be rude/aloof/unfriendly
Speech content	Appropriate content to setting (e.g., work-related topics at meetings, small talk in the breakroom)	Inappropriate content to setting (e.g., discussing personal details at meetings, avoiding small talk on breaks)
Facial expressions	Changing expressions with tone/content of conversation	Distracting facial expression (e.g., smiling when person is upset), lack of expression (e.g., not responding when person is upset)
Positive assertion: requests, compliments	Asking for help when needed, delegating tasks to others, giving appropriate compliments to coworkers	Not able to ask for help when needed, may appear to be unmotivated or incapable in work setting, not able to give compliments to coworkers, may appear to be rude/aloof/unfriendly
Negative assertion: refusals, confrontation	Turning down unreasonable requests, disagreeing with others and discussing alternatives	Not able to say "no" to unreasonable requests, may take on too much, not able to tell others when they disagree, may not speak up even when they have an important point to make or alternative to consider

when a manager joins the process. The manager may then underestimate the quality of the worker's contribution. Such performance deficits often result from social anxiety disorder (formerly called social phobia). Social anxiety disorder is defined as a person's fear of negative evaluation and concern that he or she will act in a way that will be humiliating or embarrassing when performing or interacting in social situations (American Psychiatric Association, 1994). Socially anxious individuals often avoid the situations they fear. Given that social anxiety disorder is the third most common psychiatric disorder, with a lifetime prevalence of 13.3% (Kessler et al., 1994), and that the majority of socially anxious individuals experience interference in occupational and academic settings (Turner, Beidel, Dancu, & Keyes, 1986), social anxiety likely has a significant impact on employee performance in many workplaces.

ASSESSMENT OF SOCIAL DYSFUNCTION

Training Managerial/Supervisory Personnel

Assessment of social dysfunction is relevant not only to those in mental health or human resource positions, but also to those in supervisory and managerial positions. Several studies have shown the importance of supervisor intervention in employees getting assistance for their problems. Supervisors are key people to whom workers go for assistance with both work and personal problems (Gerstein & Bayer, 1988; Hopkins, 1997; Rodgers & Rodgers, 1989), making them a key factor in whether or not workers use employee assistance programs (Gerstein & Bayer, 1988; Harley, 1991). The extent to which line supervisors are willing to identify and intervene with troubled workers is the most crucial factor in getting employees help (Gerstein & Bayer, 1988; Trice & Sonnenstuhl, 1988). According to Hopkins (1997), supervisor intervention with troubled workers was significantly influenced by being trained to identify and help troubled workers, being aware of workers' problems, and positive attitudes about help giving and seeking. Thus, it is important to train those in supervisory and managerial positions to identify and help troubled workers.

Intervening often involves referring to professional helping resources within the company or in the community. Given the role of gatekeeper to services, we will highlight some indicators of social dysfunction as they may manifest in the workplace.

Indications of Social Dysfunction. Several cues may alert a supervisor to a possible problem with social functioning that merits further assessment and possible intervention. These cues are similar to those used by mental health professionals to make this determination (Meier & Hope, 1998).

1. When interacting with the individual, the supervisor may develop a subjective impression that the employee's interpersonal behavior is inappropriate or awkward. For example, the employee may frequently interrupt the supervisor, make too little or too much eye contact, self-disclose excessively, speak only if asked a direct question, or display overly aggressive or unassertive behavior. It is important not to weigh one or two interactions too heavily. A referral is appropriate only if a persistent pattern of dysfunctional behavior develops.

2. The supervisor may notice that interactions with others are awkward or problematic. This could include any of the behaviors described above, as well as avoidance of interactions (e.g., choosing individual job assignments or always lunching alone). Avoidance or poor social skills may appear to be rudeness or aloofness to other employees (e.g., failure to say "good morning" to others).

3. An individual who has difficulties with assertiveness initially may be identified as not getting work completed, when the problem is that the employee cannot say "no" to excessive amounts of work or does not ask for help when warranted.

4. The employee may miss work frequently to avoid feared situations in the

workplace, such as calling in sick on the day of an important meeting. Lack of assertiveness in an employee's personal life may result in commitments that interfere with work attendance or performance (e.g., taking frequent calls from a troubled friend during work hours because of an inability to be assertive with the friend).

Clinical Assessment

Assessment of social dysfunction is essential in providing the proper intervention for such troubled employees. First, the assessment is often important in diagnosis and case formulation, and it aids in determining whether the deficits in social performance are attributable to a social skills deficit or a performance deficit. Furthermore, assessment will aid in planning treatment and possibly determining the need for a referral to a community mental health professional. Most individuals with social skills deficits do not seek help for their social skills, and they are often unaware that improvements in social skills may positively affect their occupational as well as overall functioning. Therefore, it is important to conduct further assessment if any of the cues mentioned previously have been noted, because the individual may not request help with his or her social functioning.

Clinical Interview. The first step in assessing social skills is a targeted clinical interview, in order to identify situations in which the individual experiences difficulty. The interview should begin with a history of the individual's social activity and functioning in order to understand how his or her social functioning has changed over time, as well as the extent and chronicity of interpersonal difficulties. These can help to sort out whether basic social skills were ever a part of a person's repertoire, or have been

developed and are inhibited by social anxiety. The next step in the interview should be to develop a detailed description of the social situations that the individual finds problematic. During this portion of the clinical interview, it is important that the clinician inquire about problems in work situations. Although the focus is on work-related performance, it may also be important to listen for whether these problems occur in other aspects of the person's life, such as at home, in public places, in recreational settings, and in dating. Additionally, the individual should be asked specifically whether she or he has difficulties with positive assertion, negative assertion, and conversations.

At this point, some problem areas should be identified. For each problem area, the individual should be asked to describe in detail the last time she or he engaged in that situation. From a detailed description, a clinician can develop an understanding of the individual's perceptions of events. In some cases, a significant other, coworker, or supervisor may be able to provide a more objective assessment of any problems. Often, one aspect of poor social skill is an inability to judge one's own performance adequately (e.g., Alden & Wallace, 1995).

Behavioral Observation. Behavioral observation provides a more complete understanding of the individual's social functioning than the clinical interview and is essential to a comprehensive assessment of social dysfunction. Data from behavioral observation assessments often guide treatment decisions (Bellack, Hersen, & Turner, 1979), and therefore must be designed carefully for accurate assessment data. Designing a behavioral observation assessment requires decisions regarding the settings in which observation will occur; the observational format; instructions given to the individual; level of measurement; and, if applicable, the confederate's behavior (Franklin et al., 1999; Meier & Hope, 1998). Ideally, the assessment would occur through naturalistic observation. For example, an employee assistance provider may be able to visit the work site unobtrusively. However, naturalistic observation can be difficult in many situations because of both ethical and practical concerns. Therefore, analogue observations are more commonly employed (Haynes & O'Brien, 2000; Norton & Hope, 2001).

Analogue observations, or role-plays, are those in which the individual being assessed engages in a staged interaction with another person, typically the clinician, a confederate, another member of the group in a group therapy setting, or a significant other (Norton & Hope, 2001; Trower, 1995). Typical scenarios include introducing oneself, giving and receiving compliments, refusing requests, and expressing positive and negative feelings. However, in the work setting, role-plays of work situations, such as interacting with coworkers, customers, and supervisors, may be important in assessing social functioning. The individual should be instructed to behave as he or she typically would in the simulated social interaction (Norton & Hope, 2001). The client is presented with the role-play scene, followed by a prompt to begin the role-play. The client responds to the prompt and the interaction proceeds. However, there may be a single prompt or an extended interaction, depending on the client's level of functioning as well as the type of problematic situation.

In setting up the role-play, consideration should be given to maximizing the external validity of the assessment (Franklin et al., 1999; Norton & Hope, 2001). The clinician should take into consideration the effects of environmental stimuli, the setting, and confederate characteristics on the individual's behavior. Including relevant props may make the situation more realistic. Some research has found that the role-play situation may elicit more skillful behavior than typically observed, and thus consideration of the external validity is essential (Bellack et al., 1979; Gorecki, Dickson, Anderson, & Jones, 1981). The clinician may ask the individual whether his or her behavior was typical of his or her behavior in natural settings, and may redesign the role-play if the behavior was atypical. Additionally, role-play partners should be given instructions for the situation, because their behavior will affect the individual's responses.

Role-plays may be either idiographically determined or standardized. Idiographic role-plays are beneficial in that the difficulties experienced are often idiosyncratic, and therefore may be more appropriate to the specific situational and personal characteristics of the individual than standardized role-plays. Research suggests that idiographic role-plays may increase the external validity of the assessment compared to standardized role-plays (Chiauzzi, Heimberg, Becker, & Gansler, 1985; Torgrud & Holborn, 1992). Information from the clinical interview will help in designing role-plays that are relevant to the individual's problems and likely to elicit the target behaviors. Standardized assessments are advantageous because they are already prepared, are relatively easy to use, and have demonstrated reliability and validity.

Three standard assessments appear to have good psychometric qualities and situations relevant to the workplace. The first assessment, the Behavioral Assertiveness Test-Revised (BAT-R) (Eisler, Hersen, Miller, & Blanchard, 1975), contains 32 standardized situations that are role-played with male and female confederates. Half of the situations involve positive assertion skills (e.g., giving praise), and the other half involve negative assertion skills (e.g., refusal skills). Additionally, half of the scenes involve role-playing an interaction with a familiar individual (e.g., boss, significant other), and the other half involve interacting with an unfamiliar individual (e.g., waiter/waitress). The role-plays are to be videotaped and later coded for several behavioral components (e.g., duration of eye contact, response latency, praise) and for overall assertiveness. The second assessment, the Assessment of Interpersonal Problem-Solving Skills (AIPSS) (Donahoe et al., 1990), contains 14 videotaped interactions (1 orientation interaction, 10 involving interpersonal problems, 3 scenes with no identifiable interpersonal problems). The client is asked to identify with a specific actor in the video segment; answer questions about each scene to assess receiving, processing, and sending skills; and role-play responses. Again, these role-plays are videotaped and later coded by trained observers using the scoring manual. Finally, the Idiographic Role-Play Test (IRP) (Kern, 1991) represents a compromise between the extremes of standardized and idiographic role-plays, in which there are six general assertion situation types from which the individual is asked to recall six examples of each type recently experienced. After obtaining detail about the situations, these are role-played with a partner using any props available. Again, the role-plays are videotaped for later coding.

After the role-play has been performed, the next task is to determine the client's performance in the interaction. The typical ratings used to quantify the performance are *molar, molecular,* and *self-ratings.* Molar ratings refer to those that judge the global characteristics of the performance, such as skillfulness, appropriateness, and effectiveness (e.g., Bellack, 1983; Hope, Heimberg, &

Bruch, 1995). Molecular ratings refer to those that quantify specific behaviors, such as eye contact, response duration, speech latency, head movement/nods, gesturing, facial expressions, requests, compliments, and refusals (e.g., Bellack et al., 1979; Trower, Bryant, Argyle, & Marzillier, 1978). Self-ratings may be subjective impressions of either specific components of social skill or the overall performance, with the top rating being anchored with the descriptor "as well as the average person would do" to avoid possible unattainable standards of perfection. However, self-ratings may be inaccurate in that clients have been found to be poor judges of the quality of their own performance (Alden & Wallace, 1995; Hope et al., 1995). Any discrepancy noted between self and observer ratings will likely make useful fodder for intervention. Therefore, some type of observer rating should be included along with self-ratings.

Self-Monitoring. Self-monitoring may aid in understanding the frequency of problematic situations in the natural environment as well as the client's subjective impression of the events. Furthermore, self-monitoring can be used to monitor change over time and enables the individual to be more involved in his or her own treatment. Self-monitoring is typically assigned as homework in which the client is instructed to be alert to certain problematic situations. A typical self-monitoring form includes the date and time of the interaction, a brief description of the interaction, the outcome, cognitions regarding the event, and a rating of the subjective impression of the client's performance on a 0 to 100 scale. However, because of the nature of self-monitoring, the clinician must consider the influence of reactivity, memory, and attention in the client's self-monitoring. For instance, the client's behavior may actually change as a result of the self-monitoring, and therefore give an inaccurate portrayal of the behavior (Masters, Burish, Hollon, & Rimm, 1987). Individuals may also selectively attend to either positive or negative aspects of the behavior being monitored. Poor memory may also contribute to missing data. Difficulties with memory and attention may be particularly important with individuals having mental handicaps.

Self-Report. Many self-report questionnaires have been developed to assess components of social dysfunction, with most focusing on assertion skills and social anxiety. Questionnaires have the advantage of being efficient, relatively nonthreatening, and standardized. However, it is important to consider reading ability before administrating such questionnaires, because research has shown that social skills deficits are common to individuals with learning disabilities (Cartledge, 1989; Kavale & Forness, 1996). Some of the more commonly used and well-researched self-report questionnaires assessing social skills that may be relevant to the workplace will be described in the following paragraphs.

The Rathus Assertiveness Schedule (RAS) (Rathus, 1973) is a 30-item questionnaire in which the items are rated on a scale from +3 ("Very characteristic of me, extremely descriptive") to -3 ("Very uncharacteristic of me, extremely non-descriptive"). The RAS includes items that describe actions and beliefs related to assertive situations (e.g., "Most people seem to me more aggressive and assertive than I am," "I enjoy starting conversations with new acquaintances and strangers"). The RAS has been shown to have good validity, in that the normative sample had significant correlations with observer ratings of assertiveness. A revised version of the RAS

(Simple RAS) (McCormick, 1984) was created for use with individuals with poor reading skills, which correlates with the original RAS at 0.90. The Assertion Inventory (AI) (Gambrill & Richey, 1975) is a 40-item measure in which the number of items circled indicates assertion situations in which the individual has difficulty. Based on scores on a discomfort scale, the individual is characterized as "unassertive," "assertive," "anxious performer," or "doesn't care." A study by Pitcher and Meilke (1980) provides support for the concurrent validity of the AI, as individuals classified as high, moderate, or low assertion were differentiated in role-plays. The RAS and AI cover situations dealing with assertion that apply to a broad adult population, with the Simple RAS being appropriate for both adults and adolescents.

The Assertion Self-Statement Test-Revised (ASST-R) (Heimberg, Chiauzzi, Becker, & Madrazo-Peterson, 1983) is a 24-item questionnaire consisting of items rated on a scale from 1 ("hardly ever had the thought") to 5 ("often had the thought"). This instrument assesses the frequency with which the individual responds to assertive interactions with positive thinking (e.g., "I was thinking that I could benefit by expressing myself") or negative thinking (e.g., "I was thinking that I would become embarrassed if I let my feelings be known"). Negative self-statement scores on the ASST-R were found to discriminate among participants who were classified as either low or high in assertion based on Wolpe-Lazarus Assertiveness Schedule (WLAS) (Wolpe & Lazarus, 1966) scores (Heimberg et al., 1983). The ASST-R is an appropriate measure when the assessor is interested in the client's cognitive processes.

Several commonly used self-report questionnaires to assess social anxiety are relevant to the workplace, including the

Brief Fear of Negative Evaluation (BFNE) (Leary, 1983b) and the Social Phobia Anxiety Inventory (SPAI) (Turner, Beidel, Dancu, & Stanley, 1989). The BFNE is a 12-item self-report measure designed to measure the core construct of social anxiety, fear of negative evaluation by others. The BFNE correlated very highly (.96) (Leary, 1983a) with the original 30-item Fear of Negative Evaluation Scale (FNE) (Watson & Friend, 1969). Additionally, the BFNE was found to have high internal consistency, test-retest reliability, and convergent validity (Leary, 1983a). Individuals who scored high on the FNE tended to be more socially anxious and more concerned with social approval than did those with low scores on the FNE (Leary, 1983b; Watson & Friend, 1969). The SPAI is a 45-item measure of social anxiety that has established reliability and validity (Turner et al., 1989). The SPAI has high test-retest validity and good internal consistency, and it is able to differentiate socially anxious individuals from normal controls as well as from individuals presenting with other anxiety disorders (Beidel, Turner, Stanley, & Dancu, 1989; Turner et al., 1989). The measure includes both somatic and performance items.

Treatment Indicators

Becker, Heimberg, and Bellack (1987) noted some guidelines about who is and is not likely to benefit from social skills treatment. Negative treatment indicators include opposing the connection between interpersonal behavior and personal difficulties; not allowing the therapist to control the pace and strategy of treatment; refusing to attempt homework assignments; and rigid, maladaptive cognitive styles. Positive treatment indicators include having interpersonal difficulties in the areas of positive or negative assertion, accepting the idea that he or she must change his or her behavior to improve, and having supportive people readily available in the environment.

TREATMENT OF SOCIAL DYSFUNCTION IN THE WORKPLACE

Social Skills Training

When the assessment has revealed a social skills deficit, then a social skills training approach is indicated. Social skills training is an empirically based approach to treatment with more than 100 published evaluations of social skills training and six comprehensive critical reviews, demonstrating the effectiveness of this approach (Bedell & Lennox, 1997). Although social skills training has been described in many manuals as well as videotapes, the following components are generally included: instruction, rehearsal, feedback, and homework (Bedell & Lennox, 1997; Trower, 1995). A group format is another possible treatment option in which role-plays and feedback can be done among the group members.

Components of Social Skills Training

Instruction. This component involves identifying a particular problem skill or skills theme and describing this theme's function in social interactions (Bedell & Lennox, 1997; Trower, 1995). Each skill theme or "skill concept" may be broken down into a sequence of behavioral elements to help the client understand what needs to be done. The instruction phase is important in teaching many of the cognitive aspects of improved social skills as well as setting the standards for performance and feedback. These skill themes or concepts provide the standards by which the client may decide what behavior is appropriate in a given situation and then organize and guide the performance (Bedell & Lennox, 1997).

The clinician should first define behavior by giving an operational definition of the skill being performed and its major components, possibly by differentiating the skill from other behaviors. Later in the process, the clinician may help the client to organize the information in the environment and to attend to relevant information in social interactions. Bedell and Lennox (1997) describe the following five recommendations that can be given to clients to help in understanding the wishes and/or feelings of others:

1. Listen to verbal information the other person provides about his or her want(s) and feelings(s).

2. Observe the behavioral cues provided by the other person.

3. Be aware of situational cues.

4. Imagine what you would want or feel if you were the other person.

5. Remember past experiences with the other person. How did the other person feel and what did the person want in prior similar situations? (p. 19)

The clinician may also guide behavior by providing templates for the client to use in social situations, such as phrases to use as well as appropriate situations in which to use particular social behaviors.

Modeling appropriate behavior for the client may be a component of the instructional phase of social skills training. Learning by observing others may be an efficient method of acquiring these social skills, because the client can observe the entire social interaction carried out in its entirety and can judge its effectiveness. However, many argue that modeling should not be a part of social skills training because that may inhibit the client from performing in his or her own way, and it may also be demoralizing to see someone perform successfully in social situations (Trower, 1995). These concerns may be overcome by choosing good modeling strategies. According to Trower (1995), the best method for modeling is to have a model who is similar to the client in age, gender, and socioeconomic status and who exhibits coping rather than mastery performance. These factors may help the client to associate himself or herself with the model and encourage emulation. The clinician also may model appropriate behavior if necessary. Self-modeling can be an effective intervention if there are carefully selected, repeated observations of the client on videotape showing only the *desired* behaviors (Dowrick & Dove, 1980). Not only does this method result in a model who is matched on all attributes, but also may enhance the individual's self-efficacy by being able to view himself or herself performing successfully (Clark & Kehle, 1992; Kehle & Gonzales, 1991).

Rehearsal. A core component of social skills training is rehearsal or "supervised practice." The client role-plays situations with a role-play partner (often the clinician), with each successive attempt approximating more closely the final desired effect. Imaginal role-plays may be conducted prior to the live role-plays for some clients. The role-plays should start with easy situations, broken into smaller components for more impaired individuals. The initial role-plays may involve merely saying "hello" or shaking hands, and later build up to more difficult situations. There should be many role-plays within a session, with feedback between each role-play.

Feedback. Feedback, coaching, and reinforcement are also important components of social skills training. During the rehearsal process, the client should obtain information on his or her performance so that he or she can improve. It is important to emphasize positive reinforcement in feedback. The clinician should comment first on a positive aspect of the individual's performance and then provide a specific recommendation for change. Both the positive feedback and the suggestion for improvement should be specific. For instance, in a role-play with a coworker that does something that displeases the client, the clinician would say, "I liked the way you looked directly at me as you spoke. Do the role-play again, this time also talking about how you are upset." Feedback can be given by having the client examine his or her own behavior, or it can come from the clinician or other role-players. It may include audio- or videotape replay of the role-play (Liberman, DeRisi, & Mueser, 1989).

Homework. Homework assignments are intended to help the client implement the new skills in the problem situations in the natural environment without the supervision, supportive guidance, or assurance of a positive response. Homework assignments should be graduated, beginning with situations that have a high probability of successful performance and positive outcome, and building up to those that are more difficult and problematic.

Overview of Typical Social Skills Training Intervention. Social skills training centers around the problem areas identified during the assessment. In a typical session, an initial role-play to assess baseline skills in a specific targeted situation is performed prior to the instruction phase. These ideographic deficits are then targeted in the session. However, social skills training may also be conducted with groups of six to eight individuals with common problems (Trower, 1995). Once the problem area(s) have been established, the instruction phase begins. Typically, role-plays begin with a specific goal that the client is trying to accomplish, such as saying "hello" or refusing an unwanted request to work overtime. It may be necessary to break the role-play into specific steps in appropriate behavior, including verbal and nonverbal. Feedback is given following each role-play, and role-plays should be repeated as needed. Homework assignments should be incorporated into the training when appropriate skills have been acquired, and they should be reviewed in subsequent therapy sessions. Self-monitoring may be introduced so that the client can learn to observe his or her own behavior and provide himself or herself feedback in the natural environment. The following is an example of a training package for a common core problem of basic conversation skill deficit (Trower, 1995; Trower, Bryant, & Argyle, 1978):

Session 1. This is an introductory training exercise that involves practicing a brief, five-point conversation. (Turn to the person next to you, greet the individual, ask a couple of questions, answer any questions, and close the conversation with a farewell.)

Session 2. This session deals with observational skills and includes exercises and guidance on obtaining information about situations and other people.

Session 3. The third session includes listening skills such as verbal and nonverbal reflections, minimal encouragements such as head nods and "mm-hmms," listener commentary, and questions.

Session 4. This session covers speaking skills with guidance on things to talk about, how to gain experience and knowledge, and how to remember information. Advice is also given on self-disclosure and the nonverbal accompaniments of speech.

Session 5. The fifth session involves meshing skills, including the continuity of conversation themes, the timing of utterances, and cues for managing speaking turns.

Session 6. This session deals with mainly nonverbal expression of interpersonal attitudes, primarily warmth and assertiveness.

Session 7. This session focuses on everyday social routines, such as greeting and parting; giving compliments, praise, and other types of support; apologizing; excusing; and saving face. This session also incorporates assertive routines such as insisting on rights and refusing.

Session 8. This session moves on to problem-solving skills, including choosing alternative responses and deciding on general strategies of behavior.

Session 9. This session involves giving some general guidance on the rules that apply to particular situations in the natural environment. This may be adapted to work situations, such as meetings, socializing at break times, and communicating with others when working on projects.

Social Skills Training for Individuals With Severe and Persistent Mental Illness

Liberman et al. (1989) have developed a social skills training program for individuals with severe and persistent mental illness based on a three-stage model of social interaction similar to the basis of other training programs. It is recommended that clients be stabilized on medication before beginning social skills training. Stage 1 is *receiving,* which includes those skills necessary for accurate perception of social information from others. Stage 2 is *processing,* including the steps necessary for choosing the most effective skills for the situation. Stage 3 is *sending,* which is the actual behavioral skills involved in the social transaction. This training program includes modules in Medication Self-Management, Conversation Skills, Friendship and Dating Skills, Recreation for Leisure, Symptom Self-Management, and Grooming and Self-Care, each divided into specific skill areas that are further subdivided into components. This social skills training program may be particularly applicable to vocational rehabilitation settings, as well as for workplace counseling for any setting that employs individuals with severe and persistent mental illness or other severely impaired individuals. Liberman and colleagues (1989) give a detailed outline of the procedures of the training sessions.

Assertiveness Training

Aspects of assertiveness training may be included in the overall social skills training, or they may become a separate training program. Assertive behavior is differentiated from both submissive and aggressive behavior, and may be beneficial for individuals on either extreme of this continuum (Bedell & Lennox, 1997; Gambrill, 1995). Therefore, assertiveness training can be used for a wide range of problems, from explosive behavior and delinquency to depressed individuals and individuals with disabilities (Gambrill, 1995). Just as the term *social skills* is difficult to define, so is *assertion*. However, Wolpe (1958) used *assertion* to refer to the expression of both negative and positive feelings in social situations. Descriptions of assertive behavior typically include the importance of directness, clarity, and respect (Rakos, 1991). Typical behaviors that are emphasized in assertiveness training are refusing requests, responding to criticism, asking someone to change his or her behavior, disagreeing with others, apologizing, ending interactions, asking favors, and complimenting others (Gambrill, 1995).

The procedures typically used in assertiveness training are those described for general social skills training (instruction, rehearsal, feedback, homework), with a focus on assertiveness. The duration of assertiveness training is typically 7 to 12 weekly sessions (Gambrill, 1995). Some self-help books make useful adjuncts to treatment, including *Your Perfect Right* (Alberti & Emmons, 1970) and *The Assertive Option* (Jakubowski & Lange, 1978).

Problem-Solving Skills

Problem-solving skills training may be incorporated into social skills training and is intended to enable people to identify effective ways of coping with problems of everyday life, including the workplace (Bedell & Lennox, 1997). This training often begins with teaching the importance of taking a problem-solving stance, and barriers and resistance to problem solving are identified and modified. The client must be able to view problems as being under some degree of personal control. Once this orientation to problem solving has been established, there are generally five steps to problem solving (Nezu & Nezu, 1989, 2001):

1. Identify the problem (goal + obstacle = problem).

2. Generate alternative solutions (brainstorming to maximize possible problem solutions, including both feasible and nonfeasible).

3. Evaluate possible solutions (comparing and judging the possible solutions, creating a list of pros and cons).

4. Make a decision and implement a solution.

5. Evaluate whether the chosen solution was effective.

Job Coaches

The use of job coaches may be beneficial in reinforcing behaviors learned in social skills training in the work setting and in establishing a link between the training and natural settings, promoting behavior maintenance and generalization. Cartledge (1989) suggests that job coaches provide critical assistance to workers with disabilities, as this population has success with skill acquisition but not substantial skill maintenance or transfer. Therefore, the use of job coaches may be necessary for those who have marked social skill deficits. Job coaches may help the worker by reinforcing behaviors learned in social skills training in the work setting, establishing reinforcing contingency plans in the work setting, and prompting the worker to use self-control procedures. The job coach may use reinforcements such as compliments or prizes for appropriate behavior. For instance, when working on assertiveness skills, a client may receive verbal praise (e.g., "good job") from his or her job coach for asking for help on a difficult task. The job coach is needed until a successful adjustment from in-session to the work setting has been achieved.

Social Skills Training as a Workplace-Wide Intervention

Although there appears to be little research in workplace-wide social skills training interventions, there have been some studies in classroom and schoolwide intervention for children and adolescents (Merrell & Gimpel, 1998). Based on the research in education, it seems that the best method for employing a social skills training intervention in the workplace would involve two phases. The first would involve an in-service phase that would include the entire workforce, possibly broken down into smaller groups depending on the number of employees. This may involve some basic training in communication, assertion, and/or problem-solving skills, as well as some self-report measures to help in identifying those with more severe difficulties. Specific modules relevant to the particular work setting, such as conflict resolution, may be part of this first phase. The second phase would involve supplementing this with small group training for those with the most social difficulties. This procedure may benefit as a method to both increase workers' interpersonal skills and identify those in need of further treatment.

ANXIETY MANAGEMENT

If it is determined through assessment that there are performance deficits due to anxiety, then treatment for the social anxiety is indicated. Performance deficits may occur with or without social skills deficits. Cognitive-behavioral therapy for social anxiety disorder has been found to be efficacious in reducing the symptoms and disability associated with social anxiety disorder (Hope & Heimberg, 1993; Turk, Fresco, & Heimberg, 1999). Cognitive-behavioral treatments for social anxiety disorder may use an individual

(Hope, Heimberg, Juster, & Turk, 2000) or group (Turk, Heimberg, & Hope, 2001) format. These treatments generally consist of psychoeducation about social anxiety, coping skills such as cognitive restructuring or relaxation, exposure to feared situations, and relapse prevention.

Components of Treatment for Social Anxiety

Psychoeducation. This component involves being given a cognitive-behavioral explanation of social anxiety as a learned response, initiating self-monitoring, and constructing a fear and avoidance hierarchy. The fear and avoidance hierarchy is a rank-ordered ideographic list of feared situations (Hope et al., 2000; Turk et al., 1999). The psychoeducational component is the primary focus in the initial sessions.

Coping. Coping consists primarily of cognitive restructuring, based on the idea that the core of the problems of social anxiety are dysfunctional thoughts regarding negative evaluation (Trower, 1995; Rapee & Heimberg, 1997; Turk et al., 1999). Cognitive restructuring typically involves training in the skills of identification, analysis, and disputation of problematic cognitions through structured exercises (Hope et al., 2000). Preparatory cognitive restructuring exercises are completed prior to the exposure exercises described below.

Relaxation training (Jacobsen, 1938; Ost, 1987) may also be used as a coping mechanism. After gaining basic proficiency in relaxing, the client is assisted in using relaxation to cope with anxiety during exposures to feared situations as described below.

Exposure. Exposure may be imaginal, role-played, or in vivo in format, depending upon the nature of the feared situation and the severity of the fear. Using the fear and avoidance hierarchy as a guide, the clinician gradually encourages the client to enter feared situations using his or her coping skills. Exposure is graduated, starting with less threatening situations (perhaps in a less threatening format) and working up to harder situations. Beginning exposures involve simulated situations within the therapy sessions (role-played exposure), eventually leading to exposures outside the therapy session (in vivo exposure). In the individual format, office staff and professional colleagues may supplement the therapist during role-plays. The in vivo exposures generally are assigned as homework. Imaginal exposure may be conducted prior to engaging in the in vivo and role-play situations if needed.

Throughout the exposure (typically every 1 to 2 minutes), the clinician records the client's level of anxiety using the Subjective Units of Discomfort Scale (SUDS) (Wolpe & Lazarus, 1966). SUDS ranges from 0 (no anxiety) to 100 (the most anxiety the client has experienced or can imagine experiencing). Using the SUDS ratings as a guide, the therapist ends the exposure when the client's anxiety decreases (or at least plateaus), typically 5 to 10 minutes. After completing the exposure exercise, the clinician and the client process the performance (i.e., goals, coping, etc.).

Relapse Prevention. Relapse prevention in cognitive-behavioral treatment for social anxiety disorder involves evaluating progress and ensuring that the client will continue to pursue treatment goals and use cognitive restructuring skills after treatment has been terminated (Hope et al., 2000).

Impediments to Treatment

Becker et al. (1987) noted some common problems.

Too Little Practice of New Skill. The clinician should determine when the client is ready to learn a new skill by looking for improved performance (i.e., shorter response latencies and reduced anxiety about the new skill). Overpractice is helpful to the client, in that the strength of a behavior or a thought is related to the frequency of its use. Therefore, overtraining is not usually a problem unless the therapist moves so slowly that the client gets bored. If clients are unable to learn new skills, the therapist could use several aids to promote the use of the skill. For instance, if the client forgets the skill components, the therapist could post a list behind his or her chair that is in the client's visual field (Becker et al., 1987).

Reliance on the Client as the Sole Source of Information. Understanding the client's work environment may shed light on the presenting issues. It may be helpful to get information from the employer, particularly if they are the referral source (Becker et al., 1987).

Suicidal Ideation Requires Immediate Treatment and Close Monitoring. During the initial evaluation, it is important to assess thoughts of suicide, check for a formulated plan, ask about previous attempts, and ask about friends or family members who have thought about or made an attempt (Becker et al., 1987).

CONCLUSION

The assessment and treatment of social dysfunction (either social skills deficits or performance deficits) have become important aspects of the workplace. The current workplace environment places an emphasis on team building; thus, employees need adequate social skills to be productive workers. This chapter first focused on techniques for assessing social dysfunction, including the clinical interview, behavioral observation, self-monitoring, and self-report. Next, the primary treatments for social dysfunction—social skills training and anxiety management—

were discussed. It is important to train mental health professionals in the workplace and supervisory/managerial staff in identifying possible social dysfunction. In addition, mental health professionals should be aware of the treatment for social dysfunction.

REFERENCES

Alberti, R. E., & Emmons, M. L. (1970). *Your perfect right.* San Luis Obispo, CA: Impact.

Alden, L. E., & Wallace, S. T. (1995). Social phobia and social appraisal in successful and unsuccessful social interactions. *Behaviour Research and Therapy, 33,* 497-505.

American Psychiatric Association. (1994). *Diagnostic and statistical manual of mental disorders* (4th ed.). Washington, DC: Author.

Becker, R. E., Heimberg, R. G., & Bellack, A. S. (1987). *Social skills training treatment for depression.* New York: Pergamon.

Bedell, J. R., & Lennox, S. S. (1997). *Handbook for communication and problem-solving skills training.* New York: Wiley.

Beidel, D. C., Turner, S. M., Stanley, M. A., & Dancu, C. V. (1989). The Social Phobia and Anxiety Inventory: Concurrent and external validity. *Behavior Therapy, 20*(3), 417-427.

Bellack, A. S. (1983). Recurrent problems in the behavioral assessment of social skill. *Behaviour Research and Therapy, 21,* 29-41.

Bellack, A. S., Hersen, M., & Turner, S. M. (1979). The relationship of role playing and knowledge of appropriate behavior to assertion in the natural environment. *Journal of Consulting and Clinical Psychology, 47,* 670-678.

Bolman, L. G., & Deal, T. E. (1992). What makes a team work? *Organizational Dynamics, 21*(2), 34-44.

Bottom, W. P., & Baloff, N. (1994). A diagnostic model for team building with an illustrative application. *Human Resource Development Quarterly, 5*(4), 317-336.

Carroll, M. (1996). *Workplace counselling.* London: Sage.

Cartledge, G. (1989). Social skills and vocational success for workers with learning disabilities. *Rehabilitation Counseling Bulletin, 33*(1), 74-79.

Chiauzzi, E. J., Heimberg, R. G., Becker, R. E., & Gansler, D. (1985). Personalized versus standard role plays in the assessment of depressed patients' social skill. *Journal of Psychopathology and Behavioral Assessment, 7,* 121-133.

Clark, E., & Kehle, T. J. (1992). Evaluation of the parameters of self-modeling interventions. *School Psychology Review, 21*(2), 246-254.

Donahoe, C. P., Carter, M. J., Bloem, W. D., Hirsch, G. L., Laasi, N., & Wallace, C. J. (1990). Assessment of interpersonal problem-solving skills. *Psychiatry, 53,* 329-339.

Dowrick, P. W., & Dove, C. (1980). The use of self-modeling to improve the swimming performance of spina bifida children. *Journal of Applied Behavior Analysis, 13,* 1156-1158.

Eisler, R. M., Hersen, M., Miller, P. M., & Blanchard, E. (1975). Situational determinants of assertive behaviors. *Journal of Consulting and Clinical Psychology, 43,* 330-340.

Foss, G., Bullis, M., & Vilhauer, D. (1984). Assessment and training of job-related social competence for mentally retarded adolescents and adults. In A. Halpern & M. Fuhrer (Eds.), *Functional assessment in rehabilitation* (pp. 145-158). Baltimore: Brookes.

Franklin, M. E., Jaycox, L. H., & Foa, E. B. (1999). Social skills training. In M. Hersen & A. S. Bellack (Eds.), *Handbook of comparative interventions for adult disorders*. New York: Wiley.

Gambrill, E. (1995). Assertion skills training. In W. O'Donohue & L. Krasner (Eds.), *Handbook of psychological skills training* (pp. 81-118). Boston: Allyn & Bacon.

Gambrill, E. D., & Richey, C. A. (1975). An assertion inventory for use in assessment and research. *Behavior Therapy, 6*, 550-561.

Gerstein, L., & Bayer, G. (1988). Employee assistance programs: A systematic investigation of their use. *Journal of Counseling and Development, 66*, 294-297.

Gorecki, P. R., Dickson, A. L., Anderson, H. N., & Jones, G. E. (1981). Relationship between contrived in vivo and role-play assertive behavior. *Journal of Clinical Psychology, 37*, 104-107.

Harley, D. A. (1991). Impaired job performance and worksite trigger incidents: Factors influencing supervisory EAP referrals. *Employee Assistance Quarterly, 6*(3), 51-70.

Haynes, S. N., & O'Brien, W. H. (2000). *Principles and practice of behavioral assessment*. New York: Plenum/Kluwer.

Heimberg, R. G., Chiauzzi, E. J., Becker, R. E., & Madrazo-Peterson, R. (1983). Cognitive mediation of assertive behavior: An analysis of the self-statement patterns of college students, psychiatric patients, and normal adults. *Cognitive Therapy and Research, 7*, 455-464.

Hollin, C. R., & Trower, P. (Eds.). (1986). *Handbook of social skills training* (Vol. 2). Oxford, UK: Pergamon.

Hope, D. A., & Heimberg, R. G. (1993). Social phobia and social anxiety. In D. H. Barlow (Ed.), *Clinical handbook of psychological disorders: A step-by-step treatment manual* (pp. 99-136). New York: Guilford.

Hope, D. A., Heimberg, R. G., & Bruch, M. A. (1995). Dismantling cognitive-behavioral group therapy for social phobia. *Behaviour Research and Therapy, 33*, 637-650.

Hope, D. A., Heimberg, R. G., Juster, H., & Turk, C. (2000). *Managing social anxiety: A cognitive-behavioral approach*. San Antonio, TX: Psychological Corporation.

Hopkins, K. M. (1997). Influences on formal and informal supervisor intervention with troubled workers. *Employee Assistance Quarterly, 13*(1), 33-54.

Jacobsen, E. (1938). *Progressive relaxation*. Chicago: University of Chicago Press.

Jakubowski, P., & Lange, A. J. (1978). *The assertive option*. Champaign, IL: Research Press.

Kavale, K. A., & Forness, S. R. (1996). Social skills deficits and learning disabilities: A meta-analysis. *Journal of Learning Disabilities, 29*(3), 226-237.

Kehle, T. J., & Gonzales, F. (1991). Self-modeling for emotional and social concerns of childhood. In P. W. Dowrick (Ed.), *A practical guide to video in the behavioral sciences* (pp. 211-252). New York: Wiley.

Kern, J. M. (1991). An evaluation of a novel role-play methodology: The standardized idiographic approach. *Behavior Therapy, 22*, 13-29.

Kessler, R. C., McGonagle, K. A., Zhao, S., Nelson, C. B., Hughes, M., Eshleman, S., Wittchen, H. U., & Kendler, K. S. (1994). Lifetime and 12-month prevalence of *DSM-III-R*: Psychiatric disorders in the United States. *Archives of General Psychiatry, 51*, 8-19.

Leary, M. R. (1983a). A brief version of the Fear of Negative Evaluation Scale. *Personality and Social Psychological Bulletin, 9,* 371-375.

Leary, M. R. (1983b). Social anxiousness: The construct and its measurement. *Journal of Personality Assessment, 47,* 66-75.

Liberman, R. P., DeRisi, W. J., & Mueser, K. T. (1989). *Social skills training for psychiatric patients.* New York: Pergamon.

Maples, M. F. (1992). STEAMWORK: An effective approach to team building. *Journal for Specialists in Group Work, 17*(3), 144-150.

Masters, J. C., Burish, T. G., Hollon, S. D., & Rimm, D. C. (1987). *Behavior therapy: Techniques and empirical findings* (3rd ed.). New York: Harcourt Brace Jovanovich.

May, D. R., & Schwoerer, C. E. (1994). Developing effective work teams: Guidelines for fostering work team efficacy. *Organization Development Journal, 12*(3), 29-39.

McCormick, I. A. (1984). A simple version of the Rathus Assertiveness Schedule. *Behavioral Assessment, 7,* 95-99.

Meier, V. J., & Hope, D. A. (1998). Assessment of social skills. In A. S. Bellack & M. Hersen (Eds.), *Behavioral assessment: A practical handbook* (4th ed.). Needham Heights, MA: Allyn & Bacon.

Merrell, K. W., & Gimpel, G. A. (1998). *Social skills of children and adolescents: Conceptualization, assessment, treatment.* Mahwah, NJ: Lawrence Erlbaum.

Nezu, A. M., & Nezu, C. M. (1989). Unipolar depression. In A. M. Nezu & C. M. Nezu (Eds.), *Clinical decision making in behavior therapy: A problem-solving perspective* (pp. 117-156). Champaign, IL: Research Press.

Nezu, A. M., & Nezu, C. M. (2001). Problem solving therapy. *Journal of Psychotherapy Integration, 11*(2), 187-205.

Norton, P. J., & Hope, D. A. (2001). Analogue observational methods in the assessment of social functioning in adults. *Psychological Assessment, 13,* 59-72.

Ost, L. G. (1987). Applied relaxation: Description of a coping technique and review of controlled studies. *Behaviour Research and Therapy, 26,* 13-22.

Pitcher, S. W., & Meilke, S. (1980). The topography of assertive behavior in positive and negative situations. *Behavior Therapy, 11,* 532-547.

Rakos, R. F. (1991). *Assertive behavior: Theory, research and training.* New York: Routledge.

Rapee, R. M., & Heimberg, R. G. (1997). A cognitive-behavioral model of anxiety in social phobia. *Behaviour Research and Therapy, 35*(8), 741-756.

Rathus, S. A. (1973). A 30-item schedule for assessing assertive behavior. *Behavior Therapy, 4,* 398-406.

Rodgers, F., & Rodgers, C. (1989, November-December). Business and the facts of family life. *Harvard Business Review,* pp. 320-327.

Segrin, C. (1993). Social skills deficits and psychosocial problems: Antecedent, concomitant, or consequent? *Journal of Social and Clinical Psychology, 12*(3), 336-353.

Shosh, M. (1996). Counseling in business and industry. In W. J. Weikel & A. J. Palm (Eds.), *Foundations of mental health counseling* (pp. 242-247). Springfield, IL: Charles C Thomas.

Torgrud, L. J., & Holborn, S. W. (1992). Developing externally valid role-play for assessment of social skills: A behavioral analytic perspective. *Behavioral Assessment, 14,* 245-277.

Trice, H. M., & Sonnenstuhl, W. J. (1988). Drinking behavior and risk factors related to the work place: Implications for research and prevention. *Journal of Applied Behavioral Science, 24,* 327-346.

Trower, P. (1995). Adult social skills: State of the art and future directions. In W. O'Donohue & L. Krasner (Eds.), *Handbook of psychological skills training* (pp. 54-80). Boston: Allyn & Bacon.

Trower, P., Bryant, B. M., & Argyle, M. (1978). *Social skills and mental health.* London: Methuen.

Trower, P., Bryant, B., Argyle, M., & Marzillier, J. (1978). *Social skills and mental health.* Pittsburgh, PA: University of Pittsburgh Press.

Turk, C. L., Fresco, D. M., & Heimberg, R. G. (1999). Cognitive behavior therapy. In M. Hersen & A. S. Bellack (Eds.), *Handbook of comparative interventions for adult disorders* (pp. 287-316). New York: Wiley.

Turk, C. L., Heimberg, R. G., & Hope, D. A. (2001). Social anxiety disorder. In D. H. Barlow (Ed.), *Clinical handbook of psychological disorders: A step-by-step treatment manual* (pp. 114-153). New York: Guilford.

Turner, S. M., Beidel, D. C., Dancu, C. V., & Keyes, D. J. (1986). Psychopathology of social phobia and comparison to avoidant personality disorder. *Journal of Abnormal Psychology, 95,* 389-394.

Turner, S. M., Beidel, D. C., Dancu, C. V., & Stanley, M. A. (1989). An empirically derived inventory to measure social fears and anxiety: The Social Phobia and Anxiety Inventory. *Psychological Assessment, 1*(1), 35-40.

Varney, G. H. (1989). *Building productive teams: An action guide and resource book.* San Francisco: Jossey-Bass.

Watson, D., & Friend, R. (1969). Measurement of social-evaluative anxiety. *Journal of Consulting and Clinical Psychology, 33,* 448-457.

Wolpe, J. (1958). *Psychotherapy by reciprocal inhibition.* Stanford, CA: Stanford University Press.

Wolpe, J., & Lazarus, A. A. (1966). *Behavior therapy techniques: A guide to the treatment for neuroses.* New York: Pergamon.

CHAPTER 20

Anger, Hostility, and Violence in the Workplace

JOHN L. MCNULTY
ROBERT HOGAN
CHRISTOPHER R. BORDEAUX

"Employee Kills 4, Then Self at Factory," "Latest in Workplace Slayings," "Gunman Downs Four in Washington." The steady and unavoidable drumbeat of headlines testifies to the fact that violence in the workplace, almost unknown before the 1970s, is changing the way employers screen, hire, retain, support, and fire employees. Around 2 million Americans suffer workplace violence each year (Warchol, 1998)—a figure that is likely an underestimate because more than half of all victimizations occurring at work are not reported to the authorities (Bachman, 1994). An estimated 8% of all rapes, 7% of all robberies, and 16% of all assaults occur at work. Overall, one out of every six violent crimes experienced by U.S. residents age 12 or older happens at work.

Workplace homicide is the fastest-growing form of murder in the United States (Anfuso, 1994). In 2000, the latest year for which occupational fatality data are available, the Bureau of Labor Statistics

(2000) recorded 674 workplace homicides. Homicide is the third leading cause of death at work for all workers and the second leading cause of death at work for women. Warchol (1998) reported that between 1992 and 1996, 396,000 aggravated assaults, 51,000 rapes and sexual assaults, 84,000 robberies, and 1,000 homicides were committed in the workplace. Although the latest data from the Bureau of Labor Statistics show that the number of workplace homicides has begun to decline from a high of 1,080 in 1994, there is no reason to suspect that the downward trend will continue without increased preventive action on the part of state and governmental agencies, employers, and employees.

Not all violence in the workplace stems from employer or employee relations. When violence is associated with criminal behavior, terrorist acts, hate crimes, or stalkers harming an estranged partner, the workplace simply provides a setting. This chapter focuses on aggressive acts perpetrated by employees against other employees or the organization. We offer a particular vantage point, socioanalytic theory (Hogan, 1982), for understanding workplace aggression. We begin by summarizing the effects of workplace aggression on organizations and their employees. We then review various definitions of aggression and provide an overview of current research perspectives. Next, we provide a theoretical synthesis of the trends and finish with some comments on how to assess workplace violence-related risk factors.

EFFECTS OF WORKPLACE VIOLENCE

Aside from the strictly human tragedies caused by workplace violence, such incidents have a substantial financial impact on organizations themselves. Six out of 10 incidents of workplace violence occur in private companies (Bachman, 1994). These incidents are costly in terms of lawsuits, lost productivity and employee effects, coping activities, and what has been termed "damage control." The National Safe Workplace Institute (NSWI) has calculated that a single episode of workplace violence will cost a company an average of $250,000 in lost work time and legal expenses (Anfuso, 1994). Employees lose almost 2 million days of work each year as a result of workplace violence, for an average of 3.5 days per crime. Such missed work results in more than $55 million in lost wages annually, not including sick days and annual leave (Bachman, 1994).

The Workplace Violence Research Institute (WVRI) (Mattman, 2001) reports that multiple lawsuits are filed against an employer each time a violent incident results in deaths or injuries. Negligent hiring and retention generally cause litigation following acts of violence by employees, and are the basis for subsequent suits. Several recent awards in such cases exceeded $3 million.

It is hard to accurately estimate losses in productivity, but decreases of as much as 80% for 2 weeks after an incident have been reported. Lost productivity is caused by the absence of the injured worker, work interruptions brought on by formal investigations, facility damages, decreased efficiency and productivity because of posttraumatic stress, and employees seeking counseling.

Coping skills that people use to deal with life's everyday stressors are inadequate to deal with the changes and emotional reactions experienced after workplace violence. Barnett-Queen and Bergmann (1990) identified three general types of consequences that follow work-related trauma: (a) *reexperiencing* consequences—feeling the incident is happening again, intrusive thoughts about the event, fear of another incident, and nightmares; (b) *withdrawal* consequences—attempts not to feel emotions connected to the incident, including overworking or not coming back to work, depression, avoidance of reminders of the incident, withdrawal from family and friends, and self-medicating with alcohol or drugs; and (c) *other* consequences—anger, irritability, sleep problems, and concentration difficulties.

Secondary victimization may occur if nonvictims in an organization (a) deny that the event occurred, (b) discount the magnitude of the incident, (c) blame the victim(s), (d) stigmatize the victim(s) (e.g., ridicule symptoms by suggesting they are malingered), and (e) deny assistance.

The WVRI (Mattman, 2001) study also reported dramatic increases in employee turnover and drops in employee morale after violent events, leading to increased training costs and productivity decreases. For example, Mattman (2001) suggests that employees may feel betrayed when workplace violence occurs because they feel that their employer did not provide a safe work environment.

A second WVRI (Kaufer & Mattman, 2001) study estimated that $36 billion is lost each year because of workplace violence of all sorts. In 1994, the WVRI interviewed more than 600 professionals across a variety of disciplines, including human resources, legal counsel, employee assistance, risk management, and line operations. Public and private sectors were represented, as well as small, medium, and large organizations. Results were compared to the annual statistics developed by Northwestern National Life, the Bureau of Justice Statistics, the Bureau of Labor Statistics, and the American Management Association. When the WVRI repeated the study using a different group of organizations in 1996, the figure "fell" to $35.4 billion.

DEFINITIONS OF WORKPLACE AGGRESSION

Although physical assaults are the most visible form of workplace violence, they are by no means the only form. Indeed, Bulatao and VandenBos (1996) suggest that the process of defining workplace violence is a research topic in itself. A narrow definition focuses on physical assaults and threats of assault. A broader definition includes all destructive acts, even lapses in etiquette. For example, Folger and Baron (1996) define workplace violence as any behavior intended to harm current or previous coworkers or their organization, from physical assaults to withholding information. Others often distinguish between hostile aggression (acts intended to hurt someone or destroy something) and instrumental aggression (acts designed to attain particular

goals or objectives). Most research has ignored instrumental aggression—behavior directed toward gaining status, power, or material or financial resources that is often couched in the language of organizational politics (Folger & Baron, 1996). Furthermore, behavior that could be construed as instrumental aggression may not be recognized as such given the ease with which instrumental, or hostile, intent can be concealed.

Buss (1961) categorized forms of aggression along three dimensions: physical versus verbal aggression, active (inflicting harm through performance of an action) versus passive (withholding some action) aggression, and direct (harm aimed expressly at an intended target) versus indirect (harm caused through an intermediary or by attacking something the target values) aggression. Most research focuses on active, physical aggression, whether directly or indirectly expressed. Passive physical aggression (e.g., not providing needed resources, cutting off coworkers during work-related conversation or meetings, showing up late for meetings, deliberately making a coworker look bad) and passive verbal aggression (e.g., not returning phone calls, refusing requests, "silent" acknowledgment of false rumors) are rarely, if ever, considered when trying to understand workplace aggression.

Robinson and Bennett (1995) developed a typology of deviant workplace behavior using multidimensional scaling techniques. They found four categories based on the seriousness or harmfulness of the behavior and whether the organization or employees were the targets of the behavior. The first category, property deviance, included sabotaging equipment and stealing from the company. The second category, production deviance, included less harmful acts, such as intentionally working slow or wasting resources. Political deviance, the third category, was characterized by favoritism, gossiping about coworkers, and blaming coworkers. The final category, personal aggression, included sexual harassment, verbal abuse, and behavior that endangered coworkers.

In short, physical assaults constitute a relatively small proportion of what may be construed as aggression in the workplace. Although costs associated with violent acts are staggering, they also may reflect only a portion of what employers actually may lose through lost productivity alone when other forms of aggression are considered.

RESEARCH ON THE CAUSES OF WORKPLACE AGGRESSION

Early theories focused on instinctual bases for aggression (e.g., Freud, 1920/1959). Lorenz (1966) argued that aggression is the result of evolutionary pressures to survive, control resources, and gain access to mates; aggression generally serves instrumental purposes, but will erupt *in vacuo* when the pressure for its expression becomes too great.

Dollard, Doob, Miller, Mowrer, and Sears (1939) proposed a frustration-aggression hypothesis, arguing that aggressive behaviors result from thwarted efforts to reduce aversive stimulation. Subsequent research finds that frustration is indeed linked to organizational sabotage and interpersonal aggression (Spector, 1975), as well as verbal aggression against supervisors (Day & Hamblin, 1964). Frustrating changes, such as downsizing and layoffs, are also associated with workplace aggression (Baron & Neuman, 1996).

Bandura's (1973) social learning theory focuses on conditions in the environment, not inside individuals, that predispose a person to violence. Most important here is one's learning history—the degree to which a person has been rewarded for violent behavior—and related environmental contingencies—conditions that make violence seem appropriate.

In contemporary psychology, there are a number of cognitive models of aggression, including perceptions of organizational injustice (Greenberg & Alge, 1998; Greenberg & Barling, 1999). When organizational procedures and policies (procedural justice), or the outcomes of these policies (distributive justice), are seen as inequitable, employees may try to restore their sense of justice by engaging in aggressive behavior (Barling, 1996). Employees may feel that rewards are distributed in a partisan or irrational manner, or that they are distributed in an inconsiderate or discourteous manner (interpersonal justice), further aggravating the situation (Folger & Baron, 1996).

Martinko and Zellars's (1998) cognitive appraisal model of workplace aggression and violence focuses on the relations between organizational trigger mechanisms (e.g., terminations, layoffs); emotional arousal; and the causal attributions employees make toward coworkers, supervisors, or the organization more generally. Their model also recognizes the moderating influence of individual differences variables such as negative affectivity, emotional susceptibility, and impulsivity. Douglas and Martinko (2001) studied the links between certain individual differences variables and the frequency of actual or potentially harmful acts by employees. They found significant main effects for trait anger, favorable attitudes toward revenge, the belief that others are responsible for negative workplace outcomes, and exposure to aggressive cultures. Furthermore, the relation between trait anger and aggressive acts was moderated by individual self-control. Overall, trait anger, self-control, and their interaction accounted for 44% of the variance in aggressive act frequency beyond demographic characteristics alone.

Descriptive research (Resnick & Kausch, 1995) has identified a number of risk factors associated with aggressive behavior in general. Past violence, including actual and threatened assaults, is strongly related to subsequent violence. The demographic predictors of violence are age (late teens and early 20s), gender (male), low socioeconomic status, and low IQ. Several mental health risk factors also have been identified. People with certain mental disorders (schizophrenia, mania, bipolar disorder, major depression, obsessive-compulsive disorder, panic disorder, and phobia); symptoms (persecutory delusions, command hallucinations); and organic brain dysfunction are more likely to commit aggressive acts than is the general population. Substance abuse is also related to aggression, as are antisocial or borderline personality disorders.

SOCIOANALYTIC THEORY AND WORKPLACE AGGRESSION

Although we know a great deal about specific and proximal predictors of workplace aggression, we think these findings should be placed in a larger conceptual context in order to organize and interpret the particular findings. One such perspective is socioanalytic theory (Hogan, 1982), which is an effort to synthesize the best insights of psychoanalysis and symbolic interactionism (i.e., Sigmund Freud and George Herbert Mead, or John Bowlby and Erving Goffman). These seemingly disparate traditions—Viennese psychiatry and University of Chicago sociology—share several common emphases, the most important of which are (a) a commitment to evolutionary theory as the basis for understanding social behavior; (b) the belief that much social behavior is unconsciously motivated; (c) the view that overt social behavior is a text to be interpreted, that public actions carry symbolic meaning; and (d) that the source of unconscious motivation, and that which is expressed symbolically, is a set of core values—for Freud, one's superego, and for Mead, one's identity.

Drawing on two generalizations from sociology—that people always live in groups and that every group has a status hierarchy—socioanalytic theory assumes that two broad motive patterns drive the dynamics of everyday life, including one's occupational strivings: a need to be accepted and appreciated (or to avoid being criticized and rejected) and a need for status, power, and the control of resources (or to avoid losing them). Social life and occupational life are organized in terms of a continuous series of interactions (or interpersonal transactions) during which people try to gain acceptance and power (or defend against their loss); the interactions themselves are organized in terms of the core values of the participants (the values determine in what interactions one will join, what role one is willing to play in the interaction, and how one will play the role). Biology makes interaction inevitable and universal; individual temperament (which comes from biology) and individual values (which come from culture and personal experience) give our interactions their personal and idiosyncratic flavor.

The foregoing is a brief sketch of our assumptions about human nature. When these assumptions are combined with a few additional observations about aggression, we have a general model for interpreting workplace violence.

Based on our general view of human nature, we propose seven generalizations about aggression. The first is that, as Freud, Lorenz, and many (mostly European) writers suggest, people are aggressive by nature. Social scientists tend to assume that people are generally benevolent; violent people are made that way by inauspicious social circumstances. Along with Freud, we believe that the capacity for genocide, homicide, fratricide, rape, and cannibalism is latent within all of us. In the introduction to his translation of *Beowulf,* the Nobel Prize-winning Irish poet Seamus Heaney (2000) notes that part of the importance of *Beowulf* is the insight it gives us into the life and culture of 8th-century England (and, by extension, preindustrial society in general). It was a society that was

> honor-bound and blood-stained, presided over by the laws of the blood-feud, where the kin of a person slain are bound to exact a price for the death, either by slaying the killer or by receiving satisfaction in the form of . . . a legally fixed compensation. The claustrophobic and doom-laden atmosphere . . . gives the reader an intense intimation of what [life was like for these people]. All conceive of themselves as . . . in thrall to a code of loyalty and bravery, bound to seek glory in the eye of the warrior world. The little nations are grouped around their lord, the greater nations spoil for war and menace the little ones, a lord dies, defenselessness ensues, the enemy strikes, vengeance for the dead becomes an ethic for the living, bloodshed begets further bloodshed, the wheel turns, the generations tread and tread. (pp xii-xiv)

In reading this, one thinks immediately of recent events in Afghanistan, rural Albania, and the Middle East. "Homo homini lupus" (man is a wolf to man), said the Latin poet Terrance. So it has been, and so it always will be.

Second, it is important to distinguish between violence that is socially approved and violence that is socially disapproved. This distinction makes clear that genocide is in the eye of the beholder. When the Russian army entered Berlin and Vienna in 1944, it began perpetrating terrible atrocities on the German citizens. British journalist George Orwell dared to report these atrocities and was pilloried by British and American society—because the Russians had been on our side in the war against Germany. Recently in Afghanistan, the forces of the Northern Alliance—working with the U.S. Army—treated its Taliban prisoners with ferocious cruelty with virtually no comment in the "free press." Our second point is that we stigmatize the violence we do not like and ignore the violence that suits our purposes.

Our third point is that, although the human propensity to violence is innate, there are important individual differences in this capacity—some people are more aggressive than others (Lykken, 1995). When parents and society intervene properly in the rearing of aggressive children, the children often grow up to become heroes. The U.S. Special Forces, small teams of two to four men who worked alongside the Northern Alliance in Afghanistan in pursuit of the Taliban, are routinely characterized in the press as the most deadly people on earth—deadly to their targets, heroes to the American public. On the other hand, if parents and society do not intervene properly in the rearing of aggressive children, these children become adults whose aggressive tendencies are not socially sanctioned.

Our fourth point is that, broadly speaking, most aggression is instrumental and is designed to achieve a purpose. The purpose is plain to see in the interactions of preschoolers. Some preschoolers (the aggressive ones) use aggression to get their way, which usually means taking the toy that they want. But the aggressive behavior also raises their status in the play group. As they get older, the aggressive kids separate into two groups. The first group continues its snatch-and-grab tactics, which is antisocial aggression, and this behavior begins to alienate the group from the rest of the children. Members of the second group approach a child who has the toy that they want, propose sharing the toy, and then appropriate it for themselves, which is socialized aggression. The toyless child usually does not care because he or she is now playing with the high-status child (cf. Hawley & Little, 1999). Once again, aggression serves instrumental purposes: It allows one to achieve one's immediate purpose, but it may also promote status and popularity. When people behave aggressively, others are watching and evaluating them. The aggressive behavior makes a statement to that audience about the actor's identity—I am a tough or dangerous person, and one not to be trifled with. Academic deans and marine drill sergeants know this as well as convicts in prison.

Our fifth point is that, in the larger social context, aggression often works, and passivity leads to subjugation and defeat. The payoff for aggression at the corporate level is obvious—successful organizations pursue aggressive strategies and behave aggressively toward their competitors, seeking actively to put them out of business. The same is true for countries and cultural groups. Consider the respective fates of the Maoris of New Zealand and the aborigines of Australia. The former are/were quite aggressive and fought their white colonizers furiously, thereby preserving their status in contemporary New Zealand society. The latter were passive and paid a terrible price.

Our sixth point concerns the little-noticed fact that there are important social class differences in the expression and tolerance of aggression. For example, in the middle class, there are few sanctions against verbal abuse, but strong sanctions against physical violence—it is okay to insult people but unacceptable to strike them. In the working class, there are sanctions against verbal abuse, but few sanctions against physical violence—if you are insulted verbally, you either retaliate or lose status. This strongly suggests that the study of workplace violence is, in reality, the study of working-class violence.

Finally, then, if the study of workplace violence is the study of working-class violence, then the dynamics of workplace violence are straightforward: There are predisposing factors and triggering factors. In terms of predisposing factors, although most normal people have the capacity for aggression, some people are more aggressive than others. In the group of naturally aggressive people, the predisposing factors include being young, male, and working class. Within that group, some people are more likely to perceive insults and betrayal than others—this is reflected in the paranoid personality. Paranoid people—people with a low threshold for perceiving insults—from a working-class background believe violence is the correct response to an insult. Within this class of people, some are more impulsive than others, and they are the people most at risk to engage in workplace violence.

On one hand, this analysis is consistent with the findings of Douglas and Martinko (2001). On the other hand, our data, based on a sample of 140 prison inmates convicted of crimes of violence, show that they are working-class males with elevated scores for the paranoid and borderline personality disorders (cf. Hogan & Hogan, 1997). Such people are impulsive and hypervigilant for signs of mistreatment, and they feel honor bound to retaliate when they are mistreated, usually by means of physical violence.

In summary, antisocial violence in general and workplace violence in particular are a function of (a) an aggressive temperament (Lykken, 1995); (b) a particular identity (I am a person who is not to be insulted); (c) low self-control; (d) a readiness to perceive insults (paranoid personality); and (e) a belief in violence as a legitimate response to insult. This analysis works as well for the perpetrators of the attack on the World Trade Center as it does for ordinary thugs and the occasional violent employee.

MANAGING WORKPLACE AGGRESSION

Several techniques and strategies are available to identify people at risk for workplace aggression and to prevent such acts from occurring. We highlight some of these methods here, focusing primarily on preemployment screening and risk assessment. For the interested reader, several recent edited works explore prevention techniques in depth (e.g., Griffin, O'Leary, & Collins, 1998; VandenBos & Bulatao, 1996).

Preemployment Screening

In a recent survey of organization prevention practices (Bush & O'Shea, 1996), 95% of the respondents used some type of preemployment screening to identify potentially violent employees. Such screening is designed to identify the individual (vs. workplace) mental health risk factors mentioned earlier in this chapter. However, obtaining information about these mental health risk factors is constrained by various state and federal statutes and the Americans with Disabilities Act. This legislation is designed to protect the privacy rights of the individual and to prevent employment discrimination against qualified individuals with disabilities, including some forms of mental illness that are related to increased incidence of aggressive behavior. Information provided by various background checks (e.g., job references, criminal background, credit history) may be used for hiring purposes provided such information is shown to be relevant to performance in the job the potential employee is seeking. If such background information cannot be obtained, techniques can be used during a screening interview that may prove helpful. For example, job candidates may be asked to describe situations in which they felt they were treated unfairly, or in which a supervisor had done something that made them angry. Interviewers can develop hypothetical scenarios, asking the job candidates about how they would react in similar situations. However, information gathered with these techniques must be used with caution. Concerns over their reliability and validity in the context of employment decisions must be addressed.

Testing and Assessment

Bush and O'Shea (1996) conclude that there is no reliable and valid test that predicts violent behavior. However, individual testing does serve a valuable role in the assessment of aggression-related risk factors. In fact, assessment is best suited for identifying the presence or absence of risk factors. In our view, the two factors most likely to result in workplace violence are (a) employees who are working class, overly sensitive to signs of mistreatment (paranoid), and impulsive; and (b) abusive and incompetent managers. Excellent methods are available for identifying violence-prone employees and incompetent managers, methods that do not rely on psychiatric screening (cf. Hogan, 1991). These include recently developed and well-validated inventories of normal personality based on the Five-Factor Model and inventories of dysfunctional interpersonal characteristics.

Assessing Employee Risk Factors. As noted earlier, several personality characteristics, psychiatric diagnoses, and symptoms of mental illness are related to increased incidence of aggressive behavior. Many personality tests and tests of general mental health are highly reliable and valid predictors of those risk factors. However, in preemployment situations, privacy law may restrict the use of such tests. For example, Mossman (1995) reported that using certain items from the Minnesota Multiphasic Personality Inventory and the California Psychological Inventory for preemployment screening violates job candidates' privacy rights. Another issue concerns how test information is integrated into an overall assessment of aggression risk. Test information should be evaluated in the context of information provided from other sources (e.g., background checks, interviews with the employee or job candidate and knowledgeable others) in order to evaluate the presence or absence of aggression risk factors. Data from all available sources should be integrated carefully by an expert qualified in the interpretation of such data and who is qualified to render an opinion concerning the employee's or job candidate's status.

Assessing Organizational Risk Factors

Although testing and assessment can be useful in identifying aggression risk factors, predicting future violence is extraordinarily difficult. As indicated earlier, many of the risk factors associated with aggressive behavior are situational or organizational. Martinko and Zellars (1998) identify a number of such factors, including widespread job losses, few job opportunities, lower pay and fewer benefits, and authoritarian management styles. High levels of frustrating events, terminations, and layoffs, and even minor frustrations such as disciplinary reprimands, may trigger violent behaviors. These authors suggest that organizations may consciously or unconsciously reinforce aggression through authoritarian management practices, rigid rules and procedures, adverse physical conditions, and inflexible personnel policies. Employees may feel victimized by treatment from organizational officials (Folger & Skarlicki, 1998), such as not receiving fair compensation for relative contributions; perceived inequitable distribution of rewards, or an arbitrary rationale for that distribution; and inconsiderate or discourteous treatment by management (Folger & Baron, 1996).

Organizations can monitor each of these potential risk factors in a variety of ways. For example, many organizations form threat assessment teams to identify safety needs, monitor violent activities, evaluate potential threats when they occur, and plan appropriate courses of action (Bush & O'Shea, 1996). Such teams may also conduct workshops on stress management, effective communication, and conflict resolution, providing employees with tools to improve the accuracy of employee communication exchanges and reduce the possibility of conflict in stressful situations. Members of the team often come from different areas within the organization (e.g., human resources, attorneys, security or law enforcement) in order to bring a variety of perspectives to bear on aggression-related issues.

Organizational climate surveys provide a mechanism for assessing employee perceptions of the work environment. James and McIntyre (1996) identify several organizational attributes important to the individual's perception and interpretation of the organization's psychological climate: role stress and lack of harmony; leadership facilitation and support; job challenge and autonomy; and work group cooperation, friendliness, and warmth. Each of these "climate variables" can be easily related to the various risk factors associated with workplace aggression. Periodic surveys of these variables can identify employee perceptions of, for example, organizational injustice and job stress, and where in the organization problems exist that could lead to employee aggression.

Finally, performance evaluation systems can be broadened to include assessment of the leadership and communication styles employed by management. Information from various sources (subordinates, peers, and supervisors), such as that obtained from 360° performance reviews, can identify potential problem behaviors and perceptions of others that could trigger aggression. Workplace violence is almost always unacceptable, but the management practices of many organizations also may make it inevitable.

REFERENCES

Anfuso, D. (1994). Deflecting workplace violence. *Personnel Journal, 73,* 66-77.

Bachman, R. (1994). *National crime victimization survey: Violence and theft in the workplace* (Tech. Rep. No. NCJ-148199). Washington, DC: U.S. Department of Justice.

Bandura, A. (1973). *Aggression: A social learning analysis.* Englewood Cliffs, NJ: Prentice Hall.

Barling, J. (1996). The prediction, experience, and consequences of workplace violence. In G. R. VandenBos & E. Q. Bulatao (Eds.), *Violence on the job: Identifying risks and developing solutions* (pp. 29-49). Washington, DC: American Psychological Association.

Barnett-Queen, T., & Bergmann, L. H. (1990, July). Response to traumatic event crucial in preventing lasting consequences. *Occupational Health & Safety,* pp. 53-55.

Baron, R. A., & Neuman, J. L. (1996). Workplace violence and workplace aggression: Evidence on their relative frequency and potential causes. *Aggressive Behavior, 22,* 161-173.

Bulatao, E. Q., & VandenBos, G. R. (1996). Workplace violence: Its scope and the issues. In G. R. VandenBos & E. Q. Bulatao (Eds.), *Violence on the job: Identifying risks and developing solutions* (pp. 1-23). Washington, DC: American Psychological Association.

Bureau of Labor Statistics. (2000). *National census of fatal occupational injuries, 2000.* Washington, DC: Author.

Bush, D. F., & O'Shea, P. G. (1996). Workplace violence: Comparative use of prevention practices and policies. In G. R. VandenBos & E. Q. Bulatao (Eds.), *Violence on the job: Identifying risks and developing solutions* (pp. 283-297). Washington, DC: American Psychological Association.

Buss, A. H. (1961). *The psychology of aggression.* New York: Wiley.

Day, R. C., & Hamblin, R. L. (1964). Some effects of close and punitive styles of supervision. *American Journal of Sociology, 69,* 499-510.

Dollard, J., Doob, L. W., Miller, N. E., Mowrer, O. H., & Sears, R. R. (1939). *Frustration and aggression*. New Haven, CT: Yale University Press.

Douglas, S. C., & Martinko, M. J. (2001). Exploring the role of individual differences in the prediction of workplace aggression. *Journal of Applied Psychology, 86*, 547-559.

Folger, R., & Baron, R. A. (1996). Violence and hostility at work: A model of reactions to perceived injustice. In G. R. VandenBos & E. Q. Bulatao (Eds.), *Violence on the job: Identifying risks and developing solutions* (pp. 51-85). Washington, DC: American Psychological Association.

Folger, R., & Skarlicki, D. P. (1998). A popcorn metaphor for employee aggression. In R. W. Griffin, A. O'Leary, & J. M. Collins (Eds.), *Dysfunctional behavior in organizations (Vol. 23, Part A): Violent and deviant behavior in organizations* (pp. 43-81). Stamford, CT: JAI.

Freud, S. (1959). *Beyond the pleasure principle*. New York: Bantam. (Original work published 1920)

Greenberg, J., & Alge, B. J. (1998). Aggressive reactions to workplace injustice. In R. W. Griffin, A. O'Leary, & J. M. Collins (Eds.), *Dysfunctional behavior in organizations (Vol. 23, Part A): Violent and deviant behavior in organizations* (pp. 83-117). Stamford, CT: JAI.

Greenberg, L., & Barling, J. (1999). Predicting employee aggression against coworkers, subordinates, and supervisors: The roles of person behaviors and perceived workplace factors. *Journal of Organizational Behavior, 20*, 897-913.

Griffin, R. W., O'Leary, A., & Collins, J. M. (Eds.). (1998). *Dysfunctional behavior in organizations (Vol. 23, Part A): Violent and deviant behavior in organizations*. Stamford, CT: JAI.

Hawley, P. H., & Little, T. D. (1999). On winning some and losing some: A social relations approach to social dominance in toddlers. *Merrill-Palmer Quarterly, 45*, 185-214.

Heaney, S. (2000). *Beowulf*. New York: Farrar Straus and Giroux.

Hogan, R. (1982). A socioanalytic theory of personality. In M. Paige & R. Dienstbier (Eds.), *Nebraska symposium on motivation* (pp. 55-89). Lincoln: University of Nebraska Press.

Hogan, R. (1991). Personality and personality assessment. In M. D. Dunnette & L. Hough (Eds.), *Handbook of industrial and organizational psychology* (2nd ed., pp. 873-919). Chicago: Rand McNally.

Hogan, R., & Hogan, J. (1997). *Hogan development survey manual*. Tulsa, OK: Hogan Assessment Systems.

James, L. R., & McIntyre, M. D. (1996). Perceptions of organizational climate. In K. R. Murphy (Ed.), *Individual differences and behavior in organizations* (pp. 416-450). San Francisco: Jossey-Bass.

Kaufer, S., & Mattman, J. W. (2001). *The cost of workplace violence to American business* [Electronic version]. Palm Springs, CA: Workplace Violence Research Institute.

Lorenz, K. (1966). *On aggression*. New York: Plenum.

Lykken, D. T. (1995). *The antisocial personalities*. Hillsdale, NJ: Lawrence Erlbaum.

Martinko, J. J., & Zellars, K. L. (1998). Toward a theory of workplace violence and aggression: A cognitive appraisal perspective. In R. W. Griffin, A. O'Leary, & J. M. Collins (Eds.), *Dysfunctional behavior in organizations (Vol. 23, Part A): Violent and deviant behavior in organizations* (pp. 1-42). Stamford, CT: JAI.

Mattman, J. W. (2001). *Preventing violence in the workplace* [Electronic version]. Palm Springs, CA: Workplace Violence Research Institute.

Mossman, D. (1995). Violence prediction, workplace violence, and the mental health expert. *Consulting Psychology Journal: Practice and Research, 47*, 223-233.

Resnick, P. J., & Kausch, O. (1995). Violence in the workplace: Role of the consultant. *Consulting Psychology Journal: Practice and Research, 47*, 213-222.

Robinson, S. L., & Bennett, R. J. (1995). A typology of deviant workplace behaviors: A multidimensional scaling study. *Academy of Management Journal, 38*, 555-572.

Spector, P. E. (1975). Relationships of organizational frustration with reported behavioral reactions of employees. *Journal of Applied Psychology, 60*, 635-637.

VandenBos, G. R., & Bulatao, E. Q. (Eds.). (1996). *Violence on the job: Identifying risks and developing solutions.* Washington, DC: American Psychological Association.

Warchol, G. (1998). *National crime victimization survey: Workplace violence, 1992-96* (Tech. Rep. No. NCJ-168634). Washington, DC: U.S. Department of Justice.

CHAPTER 21

Harassment and Discrimination in the Workplace

Tahira M. Probst
Donna J. Johns

The Fourteenth Amendment of the U.S. Constitution guarantees all citizens equal protection under the law. The Civil Rights Act of 1964 extended the scope of the 14th Amendment by prohibiting discrimination in employment settings based on an individual's race, religion, national origin, sex, or color. Its passage makes it illegal for employers to use those factors when making hiring, firing, salary, or promotion decisions in their organizations. Since then, 11 states and the District of Columbia have expanded these workplace rights to include sexual orientation. However, despite these landmark legislative acts and numerous court rulings that uphold these laws, harassment and discrimination due to race, gender, and sexual orientation are still distressingly common occurrences at work.

Sixty percent of professional and 25% of blue-collar African-Americans report being discriminated against at work (Fernandez, 1998). African-Americans working in white-majority organizations report twice as much employment discrimination than do African-Americans working in a more diverse setting (Seltzer & Thompson, 1985). Perhaps more sobering is the increasing number of Whites (59%) who indicate they believe African-Americans would file undeserved charges of discrimination if they lost their jobs—up from 56% in 1972 (Fernandez, 1998). Unfortunately, discrimination based on race is not the only form of workplace harassment that occurs.

Although sexual harassment is a recognized problem within U.S. organizations, researchers estimate that more than 50% of women will be sexually harassed sometime

AUTHORS' NOTE: The authors wish to thank Nicole Nelson for helpful comments on an earlier draft of the chapter. Correspondence concerning this chapter should be addressed to Tahira M. Probst, Department of Psychology, Washington State University, 14204 NE Salmon Creek Avenue, Vancouver, WA 98686-9600. Electronic mail should be sent to probst@vancouver.wsu.edu.

during their work career (Gutek, 1985). Despite all efforts, the glass ceiling effect and wage disparities continue to be barriers to organizational success for many women and minorities. Women make up 46% of the workforce but only 0.5% of all directors and CEOs of the largest 1,000 U.S. companies (Fierman, 1990). In addition, women and minorities are believed to gain entrance into organizations via a loosening of the standards, yet they are held to higher standards for promotion than are men and receive fewer promotions, even after accounting for other relevant factors (Biernat & Kobrynowicz, 1997; Olson & Becker, 1983).

Sexual minorities in the workplace are perhaps the most vulnerable to workplace discrimination and harassment because there is, as yet, no federal law that extends basic civil rights protection to that group. Although some cities, states, and individual organizations have expanded these rights to cover sexual orientation, homophobic attitudes are still prevalent. In a survey of 191 Alaskan employers, Green and Brause (1989) reported that 18% of respondents said they would fire homosexual employees, 27% would not hire homosexuals, and 26% indicated they would not promote known homosexual employees. A national survey of sexual minority employees found that up to 68% of gay men and 58% of lesbian women had experienced discrimination at work due to their sexual orientation (Badgett, Donnelly, & Kibbe, 1992).

The costs of such racial, gender, and sexual minority discrimination and harassment can be measured in several ways. One can examine the legal costs to organizations that ensue when employees initiate discrimination lawsuits. Statistics indicate that this is a high cost. Sexual harassment costs the typical Fortune 500 company $6.7 million per year, excluding the actual cost of litigation (Wagner, 1992). Approximately 30,000 cases of racial discrimination are investigated by the Equal Employment Opportunity Commission (EEOC) each year, with monetary benefits to plaintiffs exceeding $60 million yearly (EEOC, 2001b). These numbers, of course, do not reflect the litigation costs to organizations in defending themselves from such lawsuits.

The most important costs of racial, gender, and sexual orientation discrimination and harassment, however, cannot be easily quantified with simple numbers and statistics. These are the psychological, physical, and mental health outcomes of discrimination and harassment experienced not only by the victim, but also by others in the organization. The damage done to targets of employment discrimination and to unwitting bystanders in the organizations may be more hidden, but they also may be more costly to the overall well-being of the organization.

The purpose of this chapter is to detail the psychological, physical, and mental health consequences of racial, gender, and sexual orientation harassment in the workplace. In particular, we are interested in exploring not only the direct effects on the victims of harassment, but also the extent to which the experience and witnessing of employment discrimination and harassment might affect other organizational employees. Finally, this chapter also seeks to assess the existence and effectiveness of interventions aimed at deterring or preventing the incidence of such discrimination.

In order to address each of these issues, we will examine the types of discrimination and harassment experienced due to race, gender, and sexual minority status. In addition, we will summarize research detailing the psychological, physical, and mental health effects on targeted employees and organizational bystanders. Finally, for each group, we will discuss the prevalence and effectiveness of legal and organizational interventions aimed at reducing the incidence and negative effects of workplace discrimination and harassment.

RACE-BASED EMPLOYMENT DISCRIMINATION AND HARASSMENT

Race-based discrimination occurs when employment decisions are made on the basis of race or have a disparate impact on members of a particular racial group. Statistics bear out that whereas many Americans believe equal opportunity exists and affirmative action programs are obsolete (cf. Initiative 200 in Washington State and Proposition 109 in California), minorities do not, in fact, have equal *outcomes* in the workplace. In 1999, African-American men earned 76 cents for every dollar that a white man earned (Bureau of Labor Statistics, 2001; Grossman, 2000). There are many reasons for this disparity other than race-based discrimination; however, it is significant that this statistic has remained unchanged since 1979. According to Cox (1994), African-Americans are less likely to be promoted and more likely to plateau at lower job levels than are their white counterparts. Finally, an overwhelming majority (89%) of African-Americans believe that they have to be better performers than whites to get ahead (Fernandez, 1998; Grossman, 2000). Again, this number is essentially unchanged since the early 1970s.

Whereas the disparities that exist in the workplace with respect to hiring, salary, and promotion opportunities may have long-term economic consequences for minorities, day-to-day racial harassment experienced by minorities may take a greater psychological and physical health toll. Racial harassment is a form of race discrimination that includes racial jokes, ethnic slurs, offensive or derogatory comments, or other verbal or physical conduct based on an individual's race or color (EEOC, 2001a). Such actions can create an intimidating, hostile, or offensive working environment, and they can interfere with the individual's work performance. According to the EEOC, racial harassment complaints are increasing nationwide, and racial harassment charges filed with EEOC have more than doubled over the past decade. Nearly 29,000 new charges were filed against employers for race-based discrimination in 2000 alone (EEOC, 2001b).

Numbers alone, however, cannot convey the true workplace environment that some minorities face. In a press release describing the settlement that the EEOC made with the Larson Automotive Group in Tacoma, Washington, for subjecting a class of African-American employees to persistent racial harassment, a clearer picture of the kinds of behaviors and attitudes that racial minorities face emerges.

> According to the suit, the owner of the company and other managers allegedly referred to African-American workers as "boy" and "nigger" on a regular basis. The racially hostile work environment was perpetuated through racially derogatory cartoons, jokes, and slurs that occurred over a prolonged period. (EEOC, 2001a)

Aversive Racism: Contemporary Racial Discrimination

Although these forms of overt harassment, known as *dominative racism,* (Kovel, 1970) do exist, some researchers have concluded that modern forms of racism are more subtle, indirect, and insidious (Gaertner & Dovidio, 2000a; Pettigrew &

Martin, 1987). According to Gaertner, Dovidio, and colleagues (Dovidio & Gaertner, 2000; Dovidio, Gaertner, Anastasio, & Sanitioso, 1992; Dovidio, Gaertner, & Bachman, 2001; Gaertner & Dovidio, 2000a), contemporary racism, known as *aversive racism,* stems from (a) the current cultural emphasis on fairness, justice, and equality; and (b) the historically racist culture of the United States. Aversive racists will not discriminate against minorities in situations where normative appropriate behavior is clear and unambiguous, because this would violate their egalitarian self-image (Dovidio et al., 1992). However, when the norms prescribing behavior are unclear or ambiguous, or if the person can justify a negative response on the basis of some factor other than race, negative behavior toward the racial minority will ensue.

Several studies of aversive racism have clear implications for racial minorities in the workplace. Dovidio, Mann, and Gaertner (1989) conducted a study asking participants to evaluate black and white people on 7-point scales. When the scales were anchored with 1 = *bad* to 7 = *good,* there was no evidence for bias in the evaluative ratings of the black and white people. Dovidio et al. suggest that this is due to the fact that a biased response (e.g., "bad") is obvious in this situation. However, when the rating scale anchors were positive, ranging from 1 = *not at all good* to 7 = *extremely good,* thereby eliminating the negative connotation of the lower end ratings, differences were found such that whites were evaluated more positively than were blacks. The results of this study indicate that racial bias might have a negative impact on the performance appraisal process of racial minorities.

A second study indicates aversive racism might also play a role in the hiring process. Kline and Dovidio (1982) asked students to make college admission decisions for black and white applicants based on application packets that clearly divided applicants into poor, moderate, and strong candidates. Whereas there was no admission discrimination shown for the clearly poor black and white candidates, white candidates rated as "moderate" and "strong" were admitted more often than black applicants with identical qualifications. These findings were replicated nearly 20 years later using an organizational selection context (see Dovidio & Gaertner, 2000). The results from these studies seem to support opinion research where blacks report that they need to be better qualified than whites to gain entrance to an organization (Cox, 1994).

Yet a third study by Hitt, Zikmund, and Pickens (1982) showed the potential impact of aversive racism in employment decision-making processes. The researchers sent out résumés to the personnel directors of 200 U.S. corporations, half identifying the applicant as black and half with no identifying information. The identification of race resulted in more responses to the submitted résumé than when race was not identified. Notably, however, there were fewer positive responses to the black applicants than to the unidentified applicants. Again, using the aversive racism framework, overt bias is avoided because the personnel directors responded more frequently to the black applicants; however, subtle racism is evidenced by the fewer positive responses.

Effects of Dominative and Aversive Racism on Employees

Whether overt or subtle, racial discrimination and harassment appear to take a heavy toll on the psychological and physical health-related outcomes of targeted employees (Erlich & Larcom, 1992; Frone, Russell, & Cooper, 1990; K. James, 1994;

S. A. James, 1985). Erlich and Larcom (1992) found that race-based verbal and physical harassment on the job was related to higher levels of psychological and physical disorders among targeted racial minorities. Notably, racial minorities who had experienced verbal or physical harassment that was *not* race based did not report the same elevated levels of psychological and physical disorders.

Physical Health Outcomes. In a study examining the causes of "John Henryism" (prolonged, high-effort coping with difficult psychosocial stressors) among African-Americans, S. A. James (1985) found that African-American perceptions of workplace prejudice and discrimination predicted self-reported health problems with high blood pressure—the leading cause of disability and premature death among African-Americans. However, researchers (e.g., Watson, Pennebaker, & Folger, 1986) have argued that self-reported health outcomes may not be valid. Furthermore, reliance on such measures weakens the internal validity of many studies that rely on such self-reports. To counter such arguments, K. James (1994) directly measured the blood pressure of 89 working minority volunteers from four different organizations. As was found by S. A. James (1985), this study found that workplace prejudice and discrimination scores were significantly positively related to actual blood pressure levels.

Psychological Outcomes. In addition to affecting the physical health of targeted employees, racial harassment and discrimination can also have negative effects on job-related stress, self-esteem, and other psychological health outcomes. In a study of workplace discrimination among African-Americans, Frone et al. (1990) found that reported discrimination was significantly

related to increases in work distress, depression, and physiological symptoms. In a study of Chinese students in Canada, Pak, Dion, and Dion (1991) found that the experience of discrimination was related to higher levels of stress and lower levels of self-esteem.

An additional interesting finding from the Pak et al. (1991) study is that Chinese respondents who experienced discrimination had more positive attitudes toward the Chinese compared to other groups than did Chinese respondents who had not been harassed. In addition, not only is discrimination related to increased affiliation with one's own group, but it is also related to decreased affiliation with one's supervisors. James, Lovato, and Khoo (1994) found that minorities exposed to workplace prejudice perceived a greater distance between their values and the values of their supervisors. Thus, harassment has the dual outcomes of heightened identification and solidarity with one's own group and decreased identification with the outgroup. These dual outcomes, of course, can create additional difficulties for organizations trying to reduce racial discrimination by breaking down ingroup-outgroup barriers.

Effects on Majority Group Members. Although there appears to be substantial evidence for the adverse effects of race-based discrimination and harassment on the targets of such harassment, research also shows that majority group member employees are adversely affected as well by working in a racially hostile environment. In a study of Hispanic employees at a large southwestern state university, Gutierres, Saenz, and Green (1994) found that Hispanic workers experienced increased levels of job-related tension and an increase in reported physical health problems when working in work groups with high levels of reported racial discrimination (e.g., being excluded from informal networks, having to work harder to get ahead, and being placed in dead-end jobs). Interestingly, white employees in these same racially hostile work groups also had higher levels of stress than did white employees in non-hostile work groups. Thus, although more research needs to be conducted in this area, these results suggest that the effects of racial discrimination and harassment extend beyond the direct targets of such discrimination and harassment.

Organizational Interventions

In order to combat workplace racial discrimination and harassment, one must know the cause of such discrimination and harassment. Many research studies have shown that being a numerical minority in the workplace is one of the best predictors of negative stressful outcomes at work. Solo status (being the only one or one of a few people of a given race in a larger, majority-dominated work group) has been shown to lead to extreme evaluations and a higher incidence of stereotyping by majority group members (Gutierres et al., 1994). Saenz and colleagues (Lord & Saenz, 1985; Saenz, 1994; Saenz & Lord, 1989) showed that such disproportionate representation can also result in performance deficits on memory and problem-solving tasks completed by the minority group members.

Affirmative Action. The studies on disproportionate representation suggest that one organizational remedy would be to increase the representation of minorities in the organization by actively recruiting minority group members through programs such as affirmative action. Research has shown that increasing the numbers of minorities into all levels of the organizational

hierarchy can have beneficial effects for minority employees. In a study of black, Hispanic, and white subordinates and supervisors, Ford (1980) showed that black subordinates of black supervisors experienced significantly higher levels of supervisor satisfaction and lower levels of job-related stress than did blacks who were supervised by whites. Additionally, minority subordinates felt that minority supervisors were more supportive of them than were white supervisors.

Although affirmative action may be useful in increasing minority participation in organizations, there are several problems with taking this approach as a primary mechanism for reducing racial discrimination and harassment in the workplace. According to Pettigrew and Martin (1987), racial minorities face a triple jeopardy in the workplace. Not only are they subjected to negative racial stereotypes, which is exacerbated by their solo roles within the organization, but they also play the token role in many organizations with affirmative action programs. Tokenism is the belief by white coworkers that minority employees are incompetent merely because they received their jobs through affirmative action (Pettigrew & Martin, 1987). In other words, the employee was hired by the organization to "serve as the token minority as a gesture toward diversity," rather than because of the employee's job-related skills and abilities. As a way to counter this triple jeopardy, Pettigrew and Martin (1987) suggest that organizations who hire minorities through affirmative action programs should "make a special effort to circulate information about the competency and personal characteristics of all new hires—both black and white . . . [including] specific skills, accomplishments, and interests" (p. 66). This information might then partially offset the assumption of incompetence and perception of dissimilarity between the minority and majority group members.

Diversity Training Programs. Aside from reducing the disproportionate representation of minorities through affirmative action programs, perhaps the most common organizational approach to reducing intergroup conflict, racial discrimination, and harassment is the use of diversity training programs. More than 50% of U.S. corporations now have a diversity training initiative in place, and many of the companies that do not have a program currently plan to implement one shortly (Gordon, 1995).

According to the Society for Human Resource Management (2001), more than 80% of top-level executives believe that diversity training is important for their organizations. However, would-be diversity trainers need to be aware of the pitfalls that can befall even the best intentioned organizations. According to Pettigrew and Martin (1987), diversity training programs are extremely difficult to design, difficult to deliver, and difficult to evaluate. Training is difficult to design because diversity training programs can often appear to be perpetuating stereotypes, rather than eliminating them (Cox & Beale, 1997). Reports of "diversity training programs . . . exploding in their sponsors' faces" (Gordon, 1995, p. 25) indicate that there can be a backlash from these training initiatives. Diversity training can be difficult to deliver because of a denial of personal prejudice by majority group members and an avoidance of situations (such as diversity training) where evidence to the contrary may surface. This is often manifested by a resistance to diversity training on the part of majority group members (Kovel, 1970; Pettigrew & Martin, 1987). Finally, diversity training is difficult to evaluate because of the difficulty

involved in monitoring the behavior and attitudes that are supposed to change as a result of the training.

Recategorization. Perhaps the best approach to facilitating racial harmony within an organization is based on Allport's (1954) intergroup contact hypothesis and described by Gaertner and Dovidio (2000b) in their book on the Common Ingroup Identity Model. According to Allport (1954), ingroup-outgroup interactions can be facilitated by encouraging common goals for the two groups and fostering a sense of intergroup interdependence. Changing the categorization from "ingroup" and "outgroup" (e.g., white and black) to one group that has a common identity (e.g., all members of the same organization) can redirect employee cognitive and motivational forces away from ingroup favoritism toward the reduction of bias (Gaertner & Dovidio, 2000b). One possible organizational intervention, then, according to Pettigrew and Martin (1987), would be to reorganize jobs, tasks, and work group assignments to maximize the interdependence of majority group members and minority employees (see Hackman & Oldham, 1976; Sherif, 1966) and emphasize healthier outgroups with which the new common group can compete (e.g., Microsoft employees competing in solidarity against Apple employees).

Conclusions

Despite decades of legislative progress and the civil rights movement, racial and ethnic minorities face levels of racial discrimination and harassment that are still all too high. According to a 1996 survey of minority employment in the federal government, the U.S. Merit Systems Protection Board (USMSPB) found that 55% of African-Americans, 21% of Asian-Americans,

28% of Hispanics, and 19% of Native Americans felt that they were subject to "flagrant or obviously discriminatory practices" in their place of work (USMSPB, 1996). In contrast, only 4% of white respondents believed that minorities were subject to racial discrimination in the federal government. Taken together, these statistics go a long way toward explaining why the majority of ethnic and racial minority respondents in this sample also felt that little would be done by management to stop the harassment.

The consequences of racial and ethnic harassment can be severe. Research described above suggests that harassment and discrimination are related to high blood pressure and other physical health problems, low self-esteem, an increase in job-related stress, depression, and lower job satisfaction among the victims of harassment. In addition, these effects appear to generalize to nonminority employees in racially hostile work groups (Gutierres et al., 1994).

Organizational interventions aimed at reducing workplace discrimination and harassment have focused largely on (a) increasing the numbers of minorities in the organization through affirmative action programs, and (b) instituting diversity awareness training programs. Both of these remedies have shown little success in reducing the prevalence of racial discrimination at work. On the other hand, the use of recategorization by fostering a common ingroup identity appears to have promise as a method of reducing ingroup-outgroup bias. Although the technique of recategorization appears to be solidly founded in theory, and laboratory empirical research is supportive, experimental research needs to be conducted in organizational settings to generalize these results to the workplace.

GENDER-BASED HARASSMENT AND DISCRIMINATION

Researchers have proposed that women not only face many of the same stressors that men face in the workplace, but are also vulnerable to additional stressors as a direct result of their entry into traditionally male-dominated and patriarchal organizations (Jick & Mitz, 1985; Keita & Hurrell, 1994; Nelson & Hitt, 1992). Not surprisingly, Trocki and Orioli (1994) found that working women report more physical, emotional, and behavioral symptoms of stress than do working men. The purpose of this section of the chapter is to explore the effects of three such stressors faced by working women in today's organizations: the experience of sexual harassment, the hidden barrier of the glass ceiling, and the widespread prevalence of the working mother stereotype.

Sexual Harassment

Definition and Prevalence. Sexual harassment is a form of sex discrimination involving "unwelcome sexual advances, requests for sexual favors, and other verbal or physical conduct of a sexual nature . . . when submission to or rejection of this conduct explicitly or implicitly affects an individual's employment, unreasonably interferes with an individual's work performance or creates an intimidating, hostile or offensive work environment" (EEOC, 1997). According to some estimates, 50% of all working women will be sexually harassed at some point during their career (Gutek, 1985).

Certain organizations are more likely to have higher incidence rates of sexual harassment, just as certain women are more likely to be targets of sexual harassment. Research indicates that organizations with lenient management norms (Hulin, 1993; Pryor, LaVite, & Stoller, 1993), weak or nonexistent sexual harassment policies (Hesson-McInnes & Fitzgerald, 1997), and cultures tolerant of sexual harassment (Fitzgerald, Hulin, & Drasgow, 1994) are more likely to have higher rates of sexual harassment than are organizations with strict policies, severe consequences, and cultures that are intolerant of harassment. In addition, women working in traditionally male-dominated occupations or in jobs where there are few women are at greater risk of being sexually harassed than are those working in a more gender-balanced work setting (Fitzgerald et al., 1994).

Effects on the Victim of Harassment. Numerous studies have detailed the adverse effects of sexual harassment on the victims. These outcomes can be categorized into job-related outcomes, psychological outcomes, and health outcomes (Fitzgerald et al., 1994). Job-related outcomes for victims of harassment have been shown to include job loss (Coles, 1986; Gutek, 1985), higher rates of absenteeism (USMSPB, 1987), decreased job satisfaction (Baker, 1989; Fitzgerald, Drasgow, Hulin, Gelfand, & Magley, 1997; Gruber, 1992), increased turnover intentions (Fitzgerald et al., 1997; Schneider, Swan, & Fitzgerald, 1997), lower productivity (USMSPB, 1987), and reduced organizational commitment (Schneider et al., 1997). Psychological consequences of sexual harassment are numerous as well. Studies have shown sexual harassment to be related to increased anxiety, depression, a higher risk for posttraumatic stress disorder (Schneider & Swan, 1994), lower self-confidence (Benson & Thompson, 1982), and reduced self-esteem (Gruber & Bjorn, 1982). Finally, sexual harassment takes a toll on the physical health of the victims as well, increasing the

incidence of alcohol abuse (Richman, Flaherty, & Rospenda, 1996) and such psychosomatic disorders as headaches, gastrointestinal disturbance, and sleep disruption (Fitzgerald et al., 1994; Fitzgerald et al., 1997).

Although the consequences of sexual harassment are numerous and negative, perhaps the most distressing research finding is the evidence that assertive coping strategies exacerbate the negative effects of sexual harassment. In other words, women who respond most assertively to sexual harassment experience even more negative outcomes than do women who respond less assertively (Hesson-McInnes & Fitzgerald, 1997).

Research on Bystander Stress and Ambient Sexual Harassment. More recently, researchers have begun to examine the indirect effects of sexual harassment on members of the organization other than those who are the direct targets. There have been two lines of research on this topic. The first examines the effects of "ambient sexual harassment"—indirect exposure to sexual harassment in a work group as measured by the frequency of sexually harassing behaviors experienced by others in a woman's work group (Glomb et al., 1997). The second examines the effects of bystander stress—stress associated with an awareness of the harassment of one's coworkers (Schneider, 1995, 1996). Both of these lines of research suggest that the effects of sexual harassment reach beyond the direct victims of sexual harassment.

Glomb et al. (1997) developed a model of ambient sexual harassment to study the consequences of indirect exposure to sexual harassment, that is, being in a work group where sexually harassing behaviors occur, even if the respondent is not a direct target of the harassment. Using structural equation modeling, Glomb et al. found that ambient sexual harassment had a significant negative relationship with job satisfaction (standardized path coefficient = −.35, $p < .05$) and a significant positive relationship with psychological conditions (standardized path coefficient = .26, $p < .05$). Ambient sexual harassment was also indirectly related to physical health conditions via its effect on psychological health (standardized path coefficient = .60, $p < .05$). Notably, these effects were demonstrated even after accounting for any personal experience with sexual harassment that the respondent may have had. Thus, indirect exposure to sexual harassment appears to have an adverse effect on employee levels of job satisfaction, psychological health, and physical health.

Researchers have also begun to assess the outcomes of bystander stress, that is, the stress associated with observing or hearing about a coworker being sexually harassed (Schneider, 1995, 1996). Whereas ambient sexual harassment is a group-level variable, bystander stress is a self-report measure of perceived stress. Schneider's research suggests that women who experience bystander stress report less supervisor and coworker satisfaction, lower levels of life satisfaction, and higher levels of psychological distress than do others in the organization who do not report bystander stress.

These studies indicate that the effects of sexual harassment are more pervasive than originally thought. Not only do the direct targets of sexual harassment experience lower job satisfaction and higher levels of psychological and physical health problems, but also women in work groups with high levels of ambient sexual harassment and women who report experiencing bystander stress appear to have similar outcomes as well. Although compelling, these studies are limited in that they generalize only to other women in the organization. Studies have yet to assess the effects of such indirect exposure to sexual harassment on men in the organization.

Effectiveness of Sexual Harassment Training. Given the negative job-related, psychological, and physical health outcomes associated with sexual harassment, it is important to determine whether current organizational interventions are effective in preventing the occurrence of sexually harassing behaviors. Although there are many different possible organizational interventions, ranging from one-on-one rehabilitation counseling with sexual harassers (Salisbury & Jaffe, 1996) to modifying the organizational climate (e.g., organizational tolerance for sexual harassment) (Hulin, Fitzgerald, & Drasgow, 1996), organizations have relied primarily on corporatewide sexual harassment awareness training (Perry, Kulik, & Schmidtke, 1998) to stem the incidence of sexual harassment.

The primary purpose of sexual harassment awareness training is to increase the trainee's level of knowledge regarding what does and does not constitute sexual harassment. Studies have generally shown that sexual harassment training does appear to increase participants' ability to label sexual harassment correctly and to distinguish the severity of the harassment (Beauvais, 1986; Blakely, Blakely, & Moorman, 1998; Perry et al., 1998; Wilkerson, 1999). In addition, awareness training appears to reduce the actual level of inappropriate behavior by men who had been previously identified as having a high propensity to harass (Perry et al., 1998). Unfortunately, the beneficial effects of sexual harassment training in the Perry et al. study did not influence participants' long-term attitudes regarding their propensity to harass others. In addition, some studies have shown that brief training interventions may have the unwanted effect of increasing the tendency to *perceive* sexual harassment, but not increasing the expertise to correctly *identify* sexual harassment (Moyer & Nath, 1998).

In conclusion, organizational interventions have focused primarily on raising corporate awareness regarding what constitutes sexual harassment. Most studies have shown these interventions to be effective in raising awareness and expertise, with few studies assessing the effectiveness of these programs on actually reducing the incidence of sexual harassment in the organization. Therefore, future studies on the validity of sexual harassment training should begin to focus more on results measures (i.e., whether sexual harassment actually declines) and less on learning outcomes (i.e., whether participants can correctly identify sexual-harassing behaviors).

Although sexual harassment is clearly the most egregious form of abuse that a woman can face in the workplace, other forms of gender-based discrimination and harassment exist that are arguably more prevalent and have negative psychological and physical health outcomes as well. The next section of this chapter will discuss three such forms: the glass ceiling, wage discrimination, and working mother stereotypes.

The Glass Ceiling and Wage Disparity

Definition and Prevalence. Women make up 46% of the workforce but only 0.5% of all directors and CEOs of Fortune 1000 corporations (Fierman, 1990). On average, a woman earns 76 cents for every dollar her male counterpart earns (Bowler, 1999). Recent evidence suggests this wage disparity may be diminishing, particularly for younger full-time workers (Employment Policy Foundation, 2000). Whereas this may be good news for new entrants into the

workforce, the disparity has not diminished for employees who entered with a wage gap upon hiring (Marini & Fan, 1997; Morgan, 1998). Finally, studies show that women are promoted less often than men, even after accounting for such job-related factors as measured abilities (Olson & Becker, 1983), formal education, and childhood socialization (Cannings, 1988). Statistics such as these indicate that despite all efforts, the glass ceiling effect and wage disparities continue to be barriers to organizational success for many women and minorities.

Although they do not involve *overt* discrimination or harassment, the glass ceiling and its accompanying inequity—wage disparity—are pervasive organizational phenomena that have detrimental consequences for affected employees and their organizations. *Glass ceiling* (Davidson & Cooper, 1992; Morrison, White, & Van Velsor, 1987) is the term used to describe the artificial barriers based on attitudinal or organizational bias that prevent qualified individuals from advancing upward in their organization into management-level positions. The glass ceiling is so named because of the invisible nature of the barrier that determines the level to which women and minorities can rise in an organization. According to Davies-Netzley (1998), women in corporate settings who have the skills and drive for advancement are particularly vulnerable to the effects of the glass ceiling, often failing to advance because of a lack of peer support and unavailable mentoring. Thus, whereas wage disparity refers to the *outcomes* of gender-based discrimination in the workplace, the glass ceiling effect refers more to the *process* by which this gender-based discrimination occurs.

Since the 1980s, a steady stream of research has focused on the various underlying causes of the glass ceiling effect. Some of the proposed explanations for the continuing presence of the glass ceiling are individual differences in job selection, differential education and training, gender role socialization, stereotypes, and personal values and prejudices (Trentham & Larwood, 1998). Although research indicates that some of the gender gap may be attributed to gender differences in education, experience, job skills, and career choices, a significant proportion of the variability remains unaccounted for and may be ascribed to "unequal pay for equal work" (Silverman, 1997). Tomaskovic-Devey and Skaggs (1999) tested the hypothesis that women and minorities earn lower wages because they have lower productivity. They concluded that wage discrepancies are not a function of differences in productivity, but rather are most likely due to the social closure of women and minorities from desirable positions. Although the debate over the true causes for the glass ceiling effect will continue, the one consistent research finding across studies indicates that, in general, all employee groups except heterosexual Caucasian men may have diminished opportunities to advance in the workplace (Maume, 1999; McDonald & Hite, 1998; Morgan, 1998).

Effects of the Glass Ceiling on Women. The psychological consequences of the glass ceiling effect and the wage disparity are numerous. Research has shown that the glass ceiling effect can lead to job-related stress and apathy, which, in turn, can pave the way to reduced task performance (Konrad & Cannings, 1997). This can create a downward cycle, whereby upper-level management may then feel justified in the continuation of employment discrimination based on gender and minority status (Trentham & Larwood, 1998).

Another common source of job stress for women and minorities seeking to break through the glass ceiling stems from the overcompensating activities undertaken by the individuals to prove they are good enough, qualified enough, and capable enough for advancement to upper-level management (Kanter, 1977). Not only can these overcompensating activities lead to job stress, they are also capable of leading to feelings and symptoms of burnout. If outward signs of burnout are manifested by the worker, further reductions in job proficiency may result. Therefore, the glass ceiling may function not only as an advancement barrier, but also as a catalyst to career suicide, whereby no matter what the individual does, the actions will be viewed by the corporate decision makers as less than desirable and counterproductive for the company.

Organizational Effects. According to Ohlott, Ruderman, and McCauley (1994), the glass ceiling perpetuates subtle forms of discrimination where women and minorities have fewer opportunities to partake in developmental experiences. These reduced opportunities leave the organization in a vulnerable position in today's global climate, where diversity is considered a corporate asset. Although the glass ceiling helps maintain the power structure status quo for the company, it also serves to reduce the talent pool from which future corporate leaders will emerge.

A related outcome of the glass ceiling phenomenon is a reduction in organizational flexibility (Cox, 1994). An organization must be flexible in order to adapt quickly to the ever-changing demands of the business world. In today's highly competitive global marketplace, lack of organizational flexibility may well be disastrous. Research has shown that women and minorities have greater cognitive flexibility than do Caucasian men. For example, Rotter and

O'Connell (1982) showed that women have a higher tolerance for ambiguity than do men, which is related to cognitive complexity and the ability to excel in performing ambiguous tasks (Shaffer, Hendrick, Regula, & Freconna, 1973). According to Cox (1994), organizations that do not embrace women and minorities into upper levels of the organizational hierarchy tend to be more narrow-thinking, rigid, and inflexible than organizations that actively advance employees from such populations.

Interventions to Combat the Glass Ceiling Effect. Unfortunately, there are few empirical studies of organizational interventions to reduce the subtle discrimination of the glass ceiling effect. In addition, legal interventions such as the Equal Pay Act of 1963 are limited in their effectiveness and do not address the underlying causes of the glass ceiling and wage disparity effects. Although the wage gap has narrowed from 59% to 74% since the passage of the Equal Pay Act, the rate of improvement stands at less than half a penny per year. Finally, although the Equal Pay Act of 1963 was instituted for the express purpose of outlawing wage discrimination, some researchers have argued that it has served to perpetuate and reinforce the existing disparities (see Kalantari, 1995; Pincus & Shaw, 1998).

Working Mother Stereotypes

The civilian workforce is expected to increase by 26 million people between 1990 and 2005 (U.S. Department of Labor, 1992), and although women account for 62% of the increase, many working women are treated as former mothers, current mothers, or potential mothers (Hochschild, 1997). The working mother stereotype assumes that working mothers are inherently less reliable because of their responsibilities as mothers. Not only is it expected that a working mother will be unreliable in her work attendance and punctuality, but her performance is suspect because it is assumed that she can never fully divorce her thought processes from her role as a mother (Sokoloff, 1980).

Effects of the Working Mother Stereotype. The impact of the working mother stereotype is generally negative and threefold (Kennelly, 1999). First, the working mother stereotype allows the employer to view the woman in a negative light and assumes she has a weak commitment to the organization, thereby reducing the likelihood of pay raises and advancement opportunities. Second, research on the so-called confirmatory bias suggests that people tend to seek out and remember information that reinforces their original assumptions (Snyder & Cantor, 1979; Snyder & Swann, 1978). Therefore, an initial belief that women with children are poorer performers than women without children may result in less-than-deserved performance reviews, which, in turn, can have a negative impact on pay raises and advancement opportunities. Finally, if an employer assumes that all working mothers are overburdened by the responsibilities of motherhood with few personal assets for use in the workplace, this can have a detrimental effect on a woman's chances for corporate advancement. Working women are often relegated to the "mommy track" (Schwartz, 1989), requiring them to postpone their career track until child-rearing responsibilities are complete.

Besides diminished pay and lack of career advancement opportunities, it has been suggested that women with high career orientations and young children are more likely to be dissatisfied with their lives than are young mothers with low career orientations or high family orientations (Faver, 1982). Empirical research indicates that working mothers do suffer from the stress that accompanies role overload, in which the working mother is expected to juggle occupational demands with family demands (Beck, 1984; Duxbury & Higgins, 1994).

As a result of this role stress, many working mothers choose to reduce their work hours (Konrad & Cannings, 1997) or partake in job sharing or other such flexible work arrangements (Lee & Duxbury, 1998). Although these forms of occupational innovations can be beneficial to help the mother reduce her role conflict stress, they serve to further the organization's view of the reduced commitment of the working mother.

Conclusions

Many forms of gender-based discrimination and harassment occur at work, ranging from sexual harassment to the glass ceiling and working mother stereotypes. Although the antecedents for these organizational phenomena differ, the consequences are largely the same: increased job-related stress, decreased job satisfaction, increased turnover intentions, decreased organizational commitment, and increased physical and psychological health complaints. The resulting costs to an average organization employing 10,000 employees has been calculated conservatively by Cox (1994) to be more than $6.2 million annually. Despite the high cost of gender-based discrimination and harassment to working women and their employing organizations, these phenomena are still all too common.

DISCRIMINATION AND HARASSMENT OF SEXUAL MINORITIES AT WORK

In this last section, we turn our focus to the experiences of sexual minorities (gays, lesbians, and bisexuals) in the workplace. A discussion of the experiences of sexual minorities in the workplace was reserved for last because of the significantly different legal and social environments facing sexual minorities compared to women and racial minorities in today's work settings. First, there are major federal, state, and local civil rights laws protecting women and racial minorities against workplace discrimination and harassment. Although some states, cities, and corporations have extended basic civil rights to sexual minorities, no such federal protection currently exists. Second, far less social stigma is attached to bias and prejudice targeting homosexuals than to that targeting women or racial minorities. Although overwhelming numbers of individuals in the United States would proclaim themselves to be free of racial or gender-based prejudice, 59% of Americans in a recent Gallup poll felt free to express their belief that homosexuality is morally wrong (Yang, 1998). Thus, sexual minorities face not only a workplace environment that is openly disapproving (Waldo, 1999), but also a work environment where there are few legal protections against harassment and discrimination.

Finally, whereas race and gender are primary dimensions of diversity (Cox, 1994) in that they are generally visible to the observer, sexual orientation is an invisible characteristic of a person's identity and cannot be perceived accurately via visual identification. With the invisible nature of one's sexual orientation comes an added stressor for sexual minorities at work in that they are faced with a catch-22 situation. Sexual minorities can conceal their orientation from their coworkers and supervisors and avoid workplace discrimination, yet they risk psychological and physical strain in doing so (Ellis & Riggle, 1995; Probst & Johns, 2000). Alternatively, they can be open about their identity at work, but also be open to overt discrimination and harassment that may result from revealing their identity. Statistics suggest that the vast majority of sexual minorities choose the former option over the latter, and with good reason (Digh, 1999; Levine & Leonard, 1984).

Discrimination is viewed by gays, lesbians, and bisexuals (GLBs) as widely pervasive (Croteau, 1996). Between 25% and 66% of respondents in 11 different studies reported experiencing workplace discrimination because of their sexual orientation (Croteau, 1996). More importantly, higher levels of discrimination were reported among those who were more open about their sexual orientation. The perception of discrimination was supported in a recent survey of Fortune 500 CEOs, in which 66% of CEOs indicated they would hesitate to give a management job to a known homosexual person (Kovach, 1995; Digh, 1999). Empirical evidence also appears to support these findings. In a study of gay and lesbian law students seeking internships after graduation, half sent résumés with "Active in Gay People's Alliance" listed under their extracurricular activities, whereas half did not. Those résumés that self-identified as gay generated significantly fewer interview offers than did identical résumés that were not labeled (Adam, 1981). Finally, D'Augelli (1992) found that 77% of lesbian and gay undergraduates at a large university campus had been verbally harassed because of their orientation; 27% had been threatened

with physical violence; and 3% had been punched, hit, kicked, or beaten. Given that fellow students eventually become fellow coworkers, it is not surprising that the vast majority of sexual minorities choose to conceal their homosexuality at work for fear of reprisals (Digh, 1999; Levine & Leonard, 1984).

Workplace Heterosexism: Defining Discrimination Against Sexual Minorities

Although many terms can be used to describe negative social attitudes toward sexual minorities, many researchers (e.g., Herek, 1992; Waldo, 1999) argue that the most appropriate term for discrimination against sexual minorities in the workplace is *workplace heterosexism*. Heterosexism is "an ideological system that denies, denigrates, and stigmatizes any non-heterosexual form of behavior, identity, relationship or community" (Herek, 1992, p. 89). Therefore, workplace heterosexism refers to indirect and direct harassment and discrimination experienced by sexual minorities at work. Direct workplace heterosexism includes those forms of organizational discrimination that are explicit in nature (e.g., direct gay bashing and/or slurs and organizational policies explicitly excluding sexual minorities), whereas indirect workplace heterosexism refers to implicit organizational events that stigmatize nonheterosexual orientations (e.g., coworkers making offensive jokes about sexual minorities) (Waldo, 1999).

Effects of Workplace Heterosexism

Although different in nature, both forms of workplace heterosexism have been found to be related to adverse outcomes among sexual minorities. Meyer (1995) found that experiencing prejudicial events—such as being subjected to "gay," "fag," and "dyke" jokes or being excluded from social events— was significantly associated with negative mental health outcomes. Waldo (1999) found that both direct and indirect forms of heterosexism were associated with decreased job satisfaction (path coefficient = −.43), increased physical health conditions (.13), and higher levels of psychological distress (.33). It is interesting to note that these strong effects were found even after accounting for the effects of other general job stressors.

Waldo (1999) found that GLB workers face a host of adverse outcomes regardless of whether they choose to remain closeted or come out. However, Ellis and Riggle (1995) found that there are advantages and disadvantages associated with coming out to coworkers. In their study of homosexuals in Indianapolis and San Francisco, gays and lesbians who were "totally open" (i.e., out to their bosses and coworkers) were more satisfied with their coworkers than were those who were less open. However, those who were more closeted were more satisfied with their pay, and, in fact, did earn significantly more than those who were completely open in the workplace.

Finally, in a research study similar to the Erlich and Larcom (1992) study of race-based versus non-race-based discrimination, Herek, Cogan, and Gillis (1996) found that GLB men and women subjected to antigay crimes exhibited more depression symptoms than did those who had suffered non-bias-related crimes. Thus, being targeted solely because of one's sexual orientation appears to have a more detrimental impact than if one had been targeted randomly.

Organizational Effects of Workplace Heterosexism

Unfortunately, we could not find any research assessing the indirect effects of workplace heterosexism on heterosexual employees in work groups that are hostile toward sexual minorities. Based on research on ambient sexual harassment, bystander stress, and the diffusion of effects found for racial discrimination, one might speculate that there would be adverse effects associated with working in an environment that is hostile toward sexual minorities.

It is clear, however, that there is a high price to pay for workplace harassment and discrimination targeted at sexual minorities. Given estimates that suggest sexual minorities account for 10% of the population (Digh, 1999), it is not surprising that researchers estimate that the decline in productivity associated with working in an environment that is hostile toward gays, lesbians, and bisexuals results in $1.4 billion in lost organizational output each year (Caudron, 1995).

Interventions to Alleviate Workplace Heterosexism

Legal Interventions (or Lack Thereof). Although persistent efforts have been made to pass some form of federal nondiscrimination legislation aimed at protecting sexual minorities, at this point in time, the Employment Non-Discrimination Act (ENDA) is not yet law. Given that research indicates that heterosexuals greatly underestimate the level of discrimination that sexual minorities experience (Van Den Bergh, 1999), this is perhaps not surprising. However, 84% of voters polled by *Newsweek* in 1996, and 83% of the general population sampled in 1998, supported equal rights and protection in employment for gays and lesbians in the workplace (Digh, 1999). Therefore, it would appear that there is support for some form of federal protection.

At this point, 11 states and the District of Columbia have state laws protecting sexual minorities. Initial research suggests that sexual minorities working in these states report that their organizations have more policies supportive of sexual minorities than do the organizations of GLB workers in nonprotected states (Probst & Johns, 2000). In addition, they report being more committed to their organizations, having fewer intentions to quit working for their companies, and having marginally significant higher levels of pay satisfaction. However, there are no differences in the extent to which GLB employees choose to come out at work, nor are there differences in reported levels of workplace heterosexism.

Organizational Interventions. The data presented in the previous section make it clear that for the time being, sexual minorities cannot rely on legislation to prevent harassment and discrimination against sexual minorities at work. However, many organizations, including 75% of Fortune 1000 companies, are unilaterally beginning to include sexual orientation in their nondiscrimination statements (Digh, 1999). Yet another study conducted by the Society for Human Resource Management found that 63% of firms state that they have policies prohibiting discrimination based on sexual orientation, but in reality, only 38% have those policies in writing (Digh, 1999).

Regardless of whether organizations have policies in writing, evidence seems to indicate that it is the perceived effectiveness of such policies that is associated with employee outcomes rather than the sheer

number or absence/presence of such policies. Just because a policy is on the books does not mean the organizational climate is any different. Bill Therrien, Vice President of Human Resources for Prudential in Newark, New Jersey, says, "Even with our statement of non-discrimination, people have told me they don't think this is a safe place. Simply because a corporate office comes out with a policy doesn't dictate the way the whole organization will be. The fear remains" (quoted in Caudron, 1995, p. 52).

Empirical research appears to confirm this anecdotal evidence. In our study of 178 homosexuals from 25 different states (Probst & Johns, 2000), we examined the effectiveness of organizational policies aimed at protecting sexual minorities in reducing the incidence of workplace discrimination and harassment. Independent variables assessed included the number of organizational policies aimed at sexual minority inclusion and protection as well as the perceived effectiveness and organizational support for such policies. Dependent variables assessed included experiences of workplace heterosexism, job satisfaction, organizational commitment, turnover intentions, mental health outcomes, perceived job security, and being out at work.

The consistent finding across all the variables was that the sheer number of organizational policies was unrelated to employee outcomes. Rather, it was the perceived effectiveness of the policies that strongly predicted sexual minority employee outcomes. Sexual minorities who perceived their organizations' policies to be effective reported higher levels of organizational commitment, increased feelings of job security, fewer health-related conditions, lower turnover intentions, lower psychological distress, being "out" at work to a greater extent, higher levels of job satisfaction, and fewer experiences of indirect and direct workplace heterosexism than did employees who perceived their organizational policies to be ineffective or to lack support. In each analysis, the number of policies was a non-significant predictor of employee outcomes.

The implications from this study are clear. Organizations not only need to develop effective policies of inclusion, but they also need to strongly communicate their support of these policies. Merely having the policies on the books will not do the trick. However, the results of this study also indicate that organizations that are willing to make the effort to enforce such policies will reap the benefits in lower employee turnover, fewer absences due to illness, higher organizational commitment, and greater job satisfaction. Given the costs cited above associated with lost productivity due to working in a hostile work environment, these benefits are clearly worth the effort an organization would make toward effective antidiscrimination policies.

SUMMARY AND DIRECTIONS FOR FUTURE RESEARCH

Despite civil rights legislation, the rising popularity of diversity and sexual harassment training programs, and the increasing number of companies supportive of the rights of sexual minorities, workplace discrimination and harassment remain overly prevalent. Research conducted over the past few decades has clearly detailed the negative outcomes that result from such harassment and discrimination: decreased self-esteem, increased physical and mental health problems, increased turnover, decreased job satisfaction, increased depression, increased job stress, and lower productivity, to name a few. In addition, initial research appears to suggest that the effects of discrimination and harassment are not confined to the victims, but rather are diffused throughout the hostile work environment.

Although it is abundantly clear that multiple negative effects are associated with workplace discrimination and harassment, significant research still needs to be conducted. First, more research needs to be conducted on intervention effectiveness. Too many organizations implement diversity training programs, conduct sexual harassment awareness sessions, or institute new organizational policies without conducting the necessary follow-up research to assess the effectiveness of the program in reducing organizational levels of harassment and discrimination. Second, although the topics of racial discrimination, gender-based discrimination, and workplace heterosexism were treated separately in this chapter, research needs to assess the extent to which being a "multiple minority" (i.e., being a member of multiple minority groups) significantly increases the risk of being the target of one or more forms of workplace discrimination or harassment. Finally, research has shown that an organization's tolerance for sexual harassment is one of the best predictors of women experiencing sexual harassment in an organization. Research needs to extend this work by looking at an organization's overall diversity climate as a predictor of multiple forms of workplace harassment and discrimination. Like an organization's tolerance for sexual harassment, an organization's tolerance or acceptance of diversity may be the best predictor of the workplace experiences of minorities. Finally, the results of such research could then inform and suggest organizational interventions aimed at reducing workplace discrimination and harassment.

REFERENCES

Adam, B. D. (1981). Stigma and employability: Discrimination by sex and sexual orientation in the Ontario legal profession. *Canadian Review of Sociology and Anthropology, 18*, 216-221.

Allport, G. W. (1954). *The nature of prejudice.* Reading, MA: Addison-Wesley.

Badgett, L., Donnelly, C., & Kibbe, J. (1992). *Pervasive patterns of discrimination against lesbians and gay men: Evidence from surveys across the United States.* Washington, DC: National Gay & Lesbian Task Force Policy Institute.

Baker, N. L. (1989). *Sexual harassment and job satisfaction in traditional and non-traditional industrial occupations.* Unpublished doctoral dissertation, California School of Professional Psychology, Los Angeles.

Beauvais, K. (1986). Workshops to combat sexual harassment: A case study of changing attitudes. *Signs, 12,* 130-145.

Beck, J. (1984). Problems encountered by the single working mother. *Ergonomics, 27,* 577-584.

Benson, D. J., & Thompson, G. E. (1982). Sexual harassment on a university campus: The confluence of authority relations, sexual interest and gender stratification. *Social Problems, 29,* 236-251.

Biernat, M., & Kobrynowicz, D. (1997). Gender- and race-based standards of competence: Lower minimum standards but higher ability standards for devalued groups. *Journal of Personality and Social Psychology, 72,* 544-557.

Blakely, G. L., Blakely, E. H., & Moorman, R. H. (1998). The effects of training on perceptions of sexual harassment allegations. *Journal of Applied Social Psychology, 28,* 71-83.

Bowler, M. (1999). Women's earnings: An overview. *Monthly Labor Review, 122,* 13-21.

Bureau of Labor Statistics. (2001). Median weekly earnings of full-time wage and salary workers by selected characteristics. Retrieved from ftp://ftp.bls.gov/pub/special.requests/lf/aat37.txt

Cannings, K. (1988). Managerial promotion: The effects of socialization, specialization, and gender. *Industrial and Labor Relations Review, 42,* 77-88.

Caudron, S. (1995). Open the corporate closet to sexual orientation issues. *Personnel Journal, 74*(8), 42-55.

Coles, F. S. (1986). Forced to quit: Sexual harassment complaints and agency response. *Sex Roles, 14,* 81-95.

Cox, T. (1994). *Cultural diversity in organizations: Theory, research, and practice.* San Francisco: Berrett-Koehler.

Cox, T., & Beale, R. L. (1997). *Developing competency to manage diversity: Readings, cases, and activities.* San Francisco: Berrett-Koehler.

Croteau, J. M. (1996). Research on the work experiences of lesbian, gay, and bisexual people: An integrative review of methodology and findings. *Journal of Vocational Behavior, 48,* 195-209.

D'Augelli, A. R. (1992). Lesbian and gay male undergraduates' experiences of harassment and fear on a campus. *Journal of Interpersonal Violence, 7,* 383-395.

Davidson, M. J., & Cooper, C. L. (1992). *Shattering the glass ceiling: The woman manager.* London: Chapman.

Davies-Netzley, S. A. (1998). Women above the glass ceiling: The perceptions of corporate mobility and strategies for success. *Gender & Society, 12,* 339-355.

Digh, P. (1999). In and out of the corporate closet. *Mosaics, 5*(4), 1, 5-7.

Dovidio, J. F., & Gaertner, S. L. (2000). Aversive racism and selection decisions: 1989 and 1999. *Psychological Science, 11,* 315-319.

Dovidio, J., Gaertner, S., Anastasio, P., & Sanitioso, R. (1992). Cognitive and motivational bases of bias: Implications of aversive racism for attitudes toward Hispanics. In S. Knouse & P. Rosenfeld (Eds.), *Hispanics in the workplace* (pp. 75-106). Newbury Park, CA: Sage.

Dovidio, J. F., Gaertner, S. L., & Bachman, B. A. (2001). Racial bias in organizations: The role of group processes in its causes and cures. In M. E. Turner (Ed.), *Groups at work: Theory and research* (pp. 415-444). Mahwah, NJ: Lawrence Erlbaum.

Dovidio, J. F., Mann, J., & Gaertner, S. L. (1989). Resistance to affirmative action: The implications of aversive racism. In F. Blanchard & F. Crosby (Eds.), *Affirmative action in perspective* (pp. 81-102). New York: Springer-Verlag.

Duxbury, L., & Higgins, C. (1994). Interference between work and family: A status report on dual-career and dual-earner mothers and fathers. *Employee Assistance Quarterly, 9,* 55-80.

Ellis, A. L., & Riggle, E. D. B. (1995). The relation of job satisfaction and degree of openness about one's sexual orientation for lesbians and gay men. *Journal of Homosexuality, 30,* 75-85.

Employment Policy Foundation. (2000, September). Redefining the income gap. *Training, 37,* 38.

Equal Employment Opportunity Commission. (1997). Facts about sexual harassment. Retrieved from http://www.eeoc.gov/facts/fs-sex.html

Equal Employment Opportunity Commission. (2001a). EEOC settles racial harassment suit against car dealership. Retrieved from http://www.eeoc.gov/press/1-31-01.html

Equal Employment Opportunity Commission. (2001b). Race-based charges: FY 1992 through FY 2000. Retrieved from http://www.eeoc.gov/stats/race.html

Erlich, H. J., & Larcom, B. E. K. (1992, November). *The effects of prejudice and ethnoviolence on workers' health.* Paper presented at the 2nd American Psychological Association and National Institute for Occupational and Safety Health Conference on Work, Stress, and Health, Washington, DC.

Faver, C. A. (1982). Achievement orientation, attainment values, and women's employment. *Journal of Vocational Behavior, 20,* 67-80.

Fernandez, J. P. (1998). *Race, gender, and rhetoric.* New York: McGraw-Hill.

Fierman, J. (1990, July 30). Why women still don't hit the top. *Fortune,* pp. 40-42, 46, 50, 54, 58, 62.

Fitzgerald, L. F., Drasgow, F., Hulin, C. L., Gelfand, M. J., & Magley, V. J. (1997). Antecedents and consequences of sexual harassment in organizations: A test of an integrated model. *Journal of Applied Psychology, 82,* 578-589.

Fitzgerald, L. F., Hulin, C. L., & Drasgow, F. (1994). The antecedents and consequences of sexual harassment in organizations: An integrated model. In G. P. Keita & J. J. Hurrell (Eds.), *Job stress in a changing workforce: Investigating gender, diversity, and family issues* (pp. 55-73). Washington, DC: American Psychological Association.

Ford, D. L. (1980). Work, job satisfaction, and employee well-being: An exploratory study of minority professionals. *Journal of Social and Behavioral Sciences, 26,* 70-75.

Frone, M. R., Russell, M., & Cooper, M. L. (1990, August). *Occupational stressors, psychosocial resources, and psychological distress: A comparison of Black and White workers.* Paper presented at the annual meeting of the Academy of Management, San Francisco.

Gaertner, S. L., & Dovidio, J. F. (2000a). The aversive form of racism. In C. Stangor (Ed.), *Stereotypes and prejudice: Essential readings*. Philadelphia: Psychology Press/Taylor & Francis.

Gaertner, S. L., & Dovidio, J. F. (2000b). *Reducing intergroup bias: The common ingroup identity model*. Philadelphia: Psychology Press/Taylor & Francis.

Glomb, T. M., Richman, W. L., Hulin, C. L., Drasgow, F., Schneider, K. T., & Fitzgerald, L. F. (1997). Ambient sexual harassment: An integrated model of antecedents and consequences. *Organizational Behavior & Human Decision Processes, 71,* 309-328.

Gordon, J. (1995). Different from what? *Training, 32*(5), 25-34.

Gruber, J. E. (1992, March). *The sexual harassment experiences of women in non-traditional jobs: Results from cross-national research*. Proceedings of Sex and Power Issues in the Workplace. Bellevue, WA: Conference on Sex and Power Issues in the Workplace.

Gruber, J. E., & Bjorn, L. (1982). Blue-collar blues: The sexual harassment of women autoworkers. *Work and Occupations, 9,* 271-298.

Grossman, R. J. (2000). Race in the workplace. *HR Magazine, 45*(3), 41-45.

Gutek, B. (1985). *Sex and the workplace*. San Francisco: Jossey-Bass.

Green, M. S., & Brause, J. K. (1989). *Identity reports: Sexual orientation bias in Alaska*. Anchorage, AK: Identity Incorporated.

Gutierres, S. E., Saenz, D. S., & Green, B. L. (1994). Job stress and health outcomes among white and Hispanic employees: A test of the person-environment fit model. In G. P. Keita & J. J. Hurrell (Eds.), *Job stress in a changing workforce: Investigating gender, diversity, and family issues* (pp. 107-126). Washington, DC: American Psychological Association.

Hackman, R., & Oldham, G. R. (1976). Motivation through the design of work. *Organizational Behavior and Human Performance, 16,* 250-279.

Herek, G. M. (1992). The social context of hate crimes: Notes on cultural hetero-sexism. In G. M. Herek & K. T. Berrill (Eds.), *Hate crimes: Confronting violence against lesbians and gay men* (pp. 89-104). Newbury Park, CA: Sage.

Herek, G. M., Cogan, J. C., & Gillis, J. R. (1996, July). *Psychological correlates of hate crimes victimization among gay men, lesbians, and bisexuals*. Paper presented at the annual meeting of the American Psychological Association, San Francisco.

Hesson-McInnis, M. S., & Fitzgerald, L. F. (1997). Sexual harassment: A preliminary test of an integrative model. *Journal of Applied Social Psychology, 27,* 877-901.

Hitt, M. A., Zikmund, W. G., & Pickens, B. A. (1982). Discrimination in industrial employment: An investigation of race and sex bias among professionals. *Work and Occupations, 9,* 217-231.

Hochschild, A. R. (1997). *Time bind: When work becomes home and home becomes work*. New York: Henry Holt.

Hulin, C. L. (1993, May). *A framework for the study of sexual harassment in organi-zations: Climate, stressors, and patterned responses*. Paper presented at the annual meeting of the Society for Industrial/Organizational Psychology, San Francisco.

Hulin, C. L., Fitzgerald, L. F., & Drasgow, F. (1996). Organizational influences on sexual harassment. In M. S. Stockdale (Ed.), *Sexual harassment in the workplace: Perspectives, frontiers, and response strategies* (pp. 127-150). Thousand Oaks, CA: Sage.

James, K. (1994). Social identity, work stress, and minority workers' health. In G. P. Keita & J. J. Hurrell (Eds.), *Job stress in a changing workforce: Investigating gender, diversity, and family issues* (pp. 127-146). Washington, DC: American Psychological Association.

James, K., Lovato, C., & Khoo, G. (1994). Social identity correlates of minority workers' health. *Academy of Management Journal, 37*, 383-396.

James, S. A. (1985). Psychosocial and environmental factors in Black hypertension. In W. D. Hall, E. Saunders, & N. B. Shulman (Eds.), *Hypertension in Blacks: Epidemiology, pathophysiology, and treatment* (pp. 132-143). Chicago: Year Book Medical Publications.

Jick, T. D., & Mitz, L. F. (1985). Sex differences in work stress. *Academy of Management Review, 10*, 408-420.

Kalantari, B. (1995). Dynamics of job evaluation and the dilemma of wage disparity. *Journal of Business Ethics, 14*, 397-406.

Kanter, R. M. (1977). *Men and women of the corporation.* New York: Basic Books.

Keita, G. P., & Hurrell, J. J. (1994). *Job stress in a changing workforce: Investigating gender, diversity, and family issues.* Washington, DC: American Psychological Association.

Kennelly, I. (1999). That single-mother element: How white employers typify Black women. *Gender & Society, 13*, 168-192.

Kline, B. B., & Dovidio, J. F. (1982, April). *Effects of race, sex, and qualifications in predictions of a college applicant's performance.* Paper presented at the annual meeting of the Eastern Psychological Association, Baltimore.

Konrad, A. M., & Cannings, K. (1997). The effects of gender role congruence and statistical discrimination on managerial advancement. *Human Relations, 50,* 1305-1328.

Kovach, K. A. (1995, August). ENDA promises to ban employment discrimination for gays. *Personnel Journal, 8,* 48-49.

Kovel, J. (1970). *White racism: A psychological history.* New York: Pantheon.

Lee, C. M., & Duxbury, L. (1998). Employed parents' support from partners, employers and friends. *Journal of Social Psychology, 138*, 303-322.

Levine, M., & Leonard, R. (1984). Discrimination against lesbians in the workplace. *Signs: Journal of Women in Culture & Society, 9*, 700-710.

Lord, C. G., & Saenz, D. S. (1985). Memory deficits and memory surfeits: Differential cognitive consequences of tokenism for tokens and observers. *Journal of Personality and Social Psychology, 49*, 918-926.

Marini, M. M., & Fan, P. L. (1997). The gender gap in earnings at career entry. *American Sociological Review, 62*, 588-604.

Maume, D. J. (1999). Glass ceiling and glass escalators: Occupational segregation and race and sex differences in managerial promotions. *Work and Occupations, 26*, 483-509.

McDonald, K. S., & Hite, L. M. (1998). Exploring the glass ceiling: An exploration of gender differences in management-development experiences. *Journal of Management Education, 22*, 242-254.

Meyer, I. (1995). Minority stress and mental health in gay men. *Journal of Health Sciences and Social Behavior, 36*, 38-56.

Morgan, L. A. (1998). Glass ceiling effect or cohort effect? A longitudinal study of the gender earnings gap for engineers, 1982 to 1989. *American Sociological Review, 63*, 479-483.

Morrison, A. M., White, R. P., & Van Velsor, E. (1987). *Breaking the glass ceiling.* Reading, MA: Addison-Wesley.

Moyer, R. S., & Nath, A. (1998). Some effects of brief training interventions on perceptions of sexual harassment. *Journal of Applied Social Psychology, 28*, 333-356.

Nelson, D. L., & Hitt, M. A. (1992). Employed women and stress: Implications for enhancing women's mental health in the workplace. In J. C. Quick,

L. R. Murphy, & J. J. Hurrell, Jr. (Eds.), *Stress and well-being at work: Assessments and interventions for occupational mental health* (pp. 164-177). Washington, DC: American Psychological Association.

Ohlott, P. J., Ruderman, M. N., & McCauley, C. D. (1994). Gender differences in managers' developmental job experiences. *Academy of Management Journal, 37,* 46-67.

Olson, C. A., & Becker, B. E. (1983). Sex discrimination in the promotion process. *Industrial and Labor Relations Review, 36,* 624-641.

Pak, A. W., Dion, K. L., & Dion, K. K. (1991). Social-psychological correlates of experienced discrimination: Test of the double jeopardy hypothesis. *International Journal of Intercultural Relations, 15,* 243-254.

Perry, E. L., Kulik, C. T., & Schmidtke, J. M. (1998). Individual differences in the effectiveness of sexual harassment awareness training. *Journal of Applied Social Psychology, 28,* 698-723.

Pettigrew, T., & Martin, J. (1987). Shaping the organizational context for Black American inclusion. *Journal of Social Issues, 43*(1), 41-78.

Pincus, L., & Shaw, B. (1998). Comparable worth: An economic and ethical analysis. *Journal of Business Ethics, 17,* 455-470.

Probst, T. M., & Johns, D. (2000, April). *Assessing the effects of organizational policies on the experiences of sexual minorities in the workplace.* Paper presented at the annual meeting of the Western Psychological Association, Portland, OR.

Pryor, J. B., LaVite, C. M., & Stoller, L. M. (1993). A social psychological analysis of sexual harassment: The person/situation interaction. *Journal of Vocational Behavior, 42,* 68-83.

Richman, J. A., Flaherty, J. A., & Rospenda, K. M. (1996). Perceived workplace harassment experiences and problem drinking among physicians: Broadening the stress/alienation paradigm. *Addiction, 91,* 391-403.

Rotter, N. G., & O'Connell, A. N. (1982). The relationships among sex-role orientation, cognitive complexity and tolerance for ambiguity. *Sex Roles, 8,* 1209-1220.

Saenz, D. S. (1994). Token-status and problem solving capability deficits: Detrimental effects of distinctiveness and performance monitoring. *Social Cognition, 12,* 61-74.

Saenz, D. S., & Lord, C. G. (1989). Reversing roles: A cognitive strategy for undoing memory deficits associated with token status. *Journal of Personality and Social Psychology, 56,* 698-708.

Salisbury, J., & Jaffe, F. (1996). Individual training of sexual harassers. In M. Pauldi (Ed.), *Sexual harassment on college campuses: Abusing the ivory power* (pp. 141-152). Albany: State University of New York Press.

Schneider, K. T. (1995). *Bystander stress: The effect of organizational tolerance of sexual harassment on victims' co-workers.* Unpublished doctoral dissertation, University of Illinois, Urbana-Champaign.

Schneider, K. T. (1996, August). *Bystander stress: The effect of organizational tolerance of sexual harassment on victims' co-workers.* Paper presented at the annual meeting of the American Psychological Association, Toronto.

Schneider, K. T., & Swan, S. (1994, April). *Job-related, psychological, and health-related outcomes of sexual harassment.* Paper presented at the 9th annual conference of the Society for Industrial/Organizational Psychology, Nashville, TN.

Schneider, K. T., Swan, S., & Fitzgerald, L. F. (1997). Job-related and psychological effects of sexual harassment in the workplace: Empirical evidence from two organizations. *Journal of Applied Psychology, 82,* 401-415.

Schwartz, F. N. (1989). Management women and the new facts of life. *Harvard Business Review, 67,* 65-96.

Seltzer, R., & Thompson, E. (1985). *Attitudes towards discrimination and affirmative action for minorities and women* (Research Reports, 143). Washington, DC: Howard University, Institute for Urban Affairs and Research.

Shaffer, D., Hendrick, C., Regula, R., & Freconna, J. (1973). Interactive effects of ambiguity tolerance and task effort on dissonance reduction. *Journal of Personality, 41*, 224-233.

Sherif, M. (1966). *In common predicament*. Boston: Houghton-Mifflin.

Silverman, E. R. (1997, April 14). NSF employment study confirms issues facing women, minorities. *The Scientist, 11*, 1.

Society for Human Resource Management. (2001). *Impact of diversity initiatives on the bottom line*. Alexandria, VA: Author.

Snyder, M., & Cantor, N. (1979). Testing hypotheses about other people: The use of historical knowledge. *Journal of Experimental Social Psychology, 15*, 330-342.

Snyder, M., & Swann, W. B. (1978). Hypothesis-testing processes in social interaction. *Journal of Personality & Social Psychology, 36*, 1202-1212.

Sokoloff, N. J. (1980). *Between money and love: The dialectics of women's home and market work*. New York: Praeger.

Tomaskovic-Devey, D., & Skaggs, S. (1999). An establishment-level test of the statistical discrimination hypothesis. *Work and Occupations, 26*, 422-445.

Trentham, S., & Larwood, L. (1998). Gender discrimination and the workplace: An examination of rational bias theory. *Sex Roles, 38*, 1-28.

Trocki, K. F., & Orioli, E. M. (1994). Gender differences in stress symptoms, stress-producing contexts, and coping strategies. In G. P. Keita & J. J. Hurrell (Eds.), *Job stress in a changing workforce: Investigating gender, diversity, and family issues* (pp. 7-22). Washington, DC: American Psychological Association.

U.S. Department of Labor, Women's Bureau. (1992). *Women workers outlook to 2005*. Washington, DC: Author.

U.S. Merit Systems Protection Board. (1987). *Sexual harassment of federal workers: An update*. Washington, DC: Government Printing Office.

U.S. Merit Systems Protection Board. (1996). *Fair and equitable treatment: A progress report on minority employment in the federal government*. Washington, DC: Government Printing Office.

Van Den Bergh, N. (1999). Workplace problems and needs for lesbian and gay male employees: Implications for EAPS. *Employee Assistance Quarterly, 15*(1), 21-60.

Wagner, E. J. (1992). *Sexual harassment in the workplace: How to prevent, investigate, and resolve problems in your workplace*. New York: AMACOM.

Waldo, C. R. (1999). Working in a majority context: A structural model of heterosexism as minority stress in the workplace. *Journal of Counseling Psychology, 46*, 218-232.

Watson, D., Pennebaker, J. W., & Folger, R. (1986). Beyond negative affectivity: Measuring stress and satisfaction in the workplace. *Journal of Organizational Behavior Management, 8*, 141-157.

Wilkerson, J. M. (1999). The impact of job level and prior training on sexual harassment labeling and remedy choice. *Journal of Applied Social Psychology, 29*, 1605-1623.

Yang, A. (1998). *From wrong to rights: Public opinion on gay and lesbian Americans moves towards equality*. Washington, DC: National Gay and Lesbian Task Force.

CHAPTER 22

Absenteeism and Mental Health

GARY JOHNS

bsenteeism is the failure to report for scheduled work. Although individual incidents of absence are innocuous, the aggregated impact of absence on the North American economy alone is at least $40 billion (Dalton & Wimbush, 1998; Rhodes & Steers, 1990). Furthermore, there is reason to believe that absenteeism is becoming even more of a concern to organizations. This is because global competition and the pace of environmental change have put an increased premium on speed, quality, service, and teamwork, factors that are especially vulnerable to the lack of coordination prompted by elevated absenteeism (Harrison, Johns, & Martocchio, 2000).

Perhaps the most important reason for those with interests in mental health to be informed about absenteeism is the negative consequences that the behavior can have for individuals. For the reasons cited above, absenteeism is viewed negatively by employers. However, research also shows that absenteeism is associated with or predictive of other (often) counterproductive behaviors, including lateness (Koslowsky, Sagie, Krausz, & Singer, 1997), reduced personal productivity (Bycio, 1992), and turnover (Mitra, Jenkins, & Gupta, 1992). As a specific example, Tharenou (1993) found that elevated absence among apprentice electricians preceded lower course grades, lower performance appraisals, and lower job satisfaction. Thus, absenteeism is both a precursor of and a result of poor work adjustment. A salient consequence of all of this is that the behavior is a common cause of workplace conflict, occasionally between employees (Barker, 1993) and frequently between management and employees (Moore, Nichol, & McHugh, 1992). The upshot of this is that attendance management and excessive absenteeism are among the most common subjects of contention in labor arbitration cases.

It is anticipated that readers' interests in absenteeism might stem from a variety of

AUTHOR'S NOTE: Preparation of this chapter was supported by grant 00-ER-0506 from Quebec's Fonds pour la Formation de Chercheurs et l'Aide à la Recherche and grant 410-99-1491 from the Social Sciences and Humanities Research Council of Canada.

circumstances. Thus, I have tried to cater broadly to (a) individual clinicians whose clients might be experiencing work problems, (b) organizational consultants and practitioners who might be interested in the more systemic aspects of attendance management, and (c) mental health researchers who might wish to incorporate absenteeism into their research but lack familiarity with the variable. Given this breadth, referencing is illustrative rather than exhaustive. Recent comprehensive reviews of the absenteeism literature can be found in Johns (1997) and Harrison and Martocchio (1998).

SOME BASIC FACTS ABOUT ABSENTEEISM

Like any variable of clinical and scientific interest, there is some general accumulated knowledge about absenteeism that is useful to be aware of, whether one's interests lie in counseling absentees, managing attendance, or researching absence.

• *Absenteeism is actually a complex set of behaviors masquerading as a unitary phenomenon.* Perhaps the most important general research finding of the past two decades is that absence has many causes, and the propensity for such causes can vary widely among individuals. In effect, this means that absenteeism has different meanings for different individuals (Johns & Nicholson, 1982), a fact that has been confirmed by both daily diary studies (Hackett, Bycio, & Guion, 1989) and experimental policy-capturing studies (Martocchio & Judge, 1994) revealing substantial differences in absence causation profiles between people. Thus, absences and absentees should not be typecast in terms of cause. Some indirect proof of the multiple causes of absence can be inferred from the wide

variety of disciplines that have studied absence, including psychology, sociology, economics, medicine, management, nursing, law, public health, and industrial relations.

• *Psychological processes figure prominently in absence causation.* Although absenteeism has a wide variety of causes, many of these causes are mediated or moderated by more proximal psychological influence. For example, economists have often demonstrated a negative relationship between wages and absenteeism (e.g., Drago & Wooden, 1992). However, such associations can be tempered by individual differences in the value of nonwork time (Youngblood, 1984) or equity motives (e.g., Geurts, Schaufeli, & Rutte, 1999). Similarly, as detailed below, there are strong indications of a psychological basis for many ostensible medical causes of absence.

• *Much absenteeism is under the individual's control.* Attendance is obviously susceptible to random events such as the car failing to start on a work morning. However, the salience of such examples should not obscure the substantial voluntary component to much absenteeism. Haccoun and Dupont (1987) reported that 72% of their sample of hospital employees admitted not being ill when claiming a sick day. Dalton and Mesch's (1991) sample of communication workers attributed only 41% of their days missed to illness. Event history analyses of individuals' attendance records discount random or habitual models of attendance and point to the "strategic scheduling" of absence (e.g., using available sick days before a temporal deadline) (Fichman, 1989; Harrison & Hulin, 1989). Between-person studies show that rational decision models predict absenteeism (Harrison, 1995; Martocchio, 1992). In summary, it can be concluded that a good proportion of absence from work is potentially avoidable (Dalton & Wimbush, 1998).

• *Most people are absent very little; a few people are absent a lot.* Absence is a low base rate behavior. In North America, time lost rates due to absenteeism vary from around 2% to 6% depending on industry, occupation, and region (Bureau of Labor Statistics, 1999; Statistics Canada, 1995). In a given population or sample, the absenteeism of individuals is almost never normally distributed. Rather, absence distributions are truncated by zero occurrences on the low end and positively skewed, with relatively few employees contributing relatively much absenteeism. Because it is a low base rate behavior, the aggregate costs of absenteeism are often unappreciated, and the behavior often receives little attention until some dramatic event occurs, such as disrupted production due to understaffing. When this occurs, solutions to absenteeism are often ad hoc, not well considered, and disconnected from other human resources initiatives. In addition, because a high rate of absence is unusual, its occurrence invites negative dispositional attributions concerning its cause. In the process, the absence behavior of the average employee is often ignored, untouched by the attendance management system in place.

• *Absenteeism tends to be viewed as mildly deviant behavior.* Despite the fact that absence has a wide variety of causes, it tends to be viewed by observers as mildly deviant behavior. That is, it tends to be seen as violating implicit workplace norms concerning regularity of attendance in exchange for wages or salary (Robinson & Bennett, 1995). At minimum, absence is seen as unfairly damaging the financial interests of the employing organization. A more extreme view, in line with the attributional scenario described above, is that high absentees are disloyal malingerers. Johns (1994a, 1994b, 1997) reviews the evidence that supports the pervasiveness of deviant attributions concerning absence, including negative stereotyping of absentees, guilt feelings about absence, and underreporting of the behavior.

• *People are self-serving regarding their own attendance records.* The popular view of absenteeism as mildly deviant behavior motivates people to view their own attendance records and those of others in a self-serving manner. Specifically, people have a marked tendency to underreport their own actual absenteeism (Johns, 1994b). For example, Johns (1994a) found that utility company employees self-reported missing 3.3 days a year, whereas their actual mean absence was 7.1 days. In addition to underestimating their own absenteeism, people have a decided tendency to see their own attendance records as superior to those of their work group and occupational peers (Harrison & Shaffer, 1994; Johns, 1994a; Johns & Xie, 1998). For example, Johns (1994a) found that 87% of his sample claimed to be absent less than average. A lack of accurate awareness of one's own absence record is not conducive to self-regulation of attendance—why improve one's own attendance when it is already excellent and superior to that of others? This logic contributes to the conflict over attendance that was described earlier.

• *It can be useful to distinguish between absence frequency and time lost.* Organizational personnel files often code absences as to their type and cause, and large organizations tend to employ a bewildering array of such codes. In fact, these codes are seldom useful for understanding absence because many of them are little-used, and those that are used contain unverifiable attributions of cause. Thus, absence scholars have come to rely on measures of time lost and frequency to express absence. Time lost is simply the total number of days missed due to absence over some time period, such as a month or a year. Frequency of absence comprises the number of absence *episodes* over a similar time period, regardless of the length of each episode. Thus, 3 days in a row counts as one episode. Both measures can be expressed as rates in order to account for variations in work days scheduled, and, as implied earlier, both measures are positively skewed at the individual level of analysis.

Organizations tend to be interested in time lost because of its direct financial impact. However, a joint consideration of both time lost and frequency can have great diagnostic value, because there is evidence suggesting that frequency may be more likely to reflect voluntariness (Chadwick Jones, Nicholson, & Brown, 1982; Hackett & Guion, 1985). Thus, from a systemic point of view, work units in which high time lost is accompanied by high frequency may be most suitable for intervention. Also, from a workflow or teamwork standpoint, frequent short absences may be more disruptive than a few longer episodes. For purposes of individual diagnosis and counseling, the subtle patterning of absence may prove informative. For instance, frequent absences adjacent to weekends or holidays may signal voluntary "vacation planning." Likewise, frequent Monday absences may signal weekend substance abuse.

• *There are known demographic correlates of absenteeism.* Meta-analytic research has firmly established demographic correlates of absenteeism, although the exact reasons for these associations are poorly understood. Women tend to be absent more than men (Côté & Haccoun, 1991), even in the rare case of job equivalence (e.g., Kivimäki, Sutinen, et al., 2001). Johns (1997) provides an extensive discussion of the possible reasons for this, finding relatively little direct evidence for domestic demands but stronger evidence for stress and physical and mental health concerns. Older employees tend to be absent less than younger employees, particularly with regard to frequency of absence. However, this finding pertains only to men, as women tend not to exhibit an age-absence association (Hackett, 1990).

SOME CAUSES OF ABSENTEEISM

In this section, I review some of the causes of absenteeism that are particularly pertinent to those with interests in mental health.

Job Satisfaction, Fairness, and Support

Job satisfaction, an important component of general life satisfaction, is a prominent contributor to mental health. The idea that attitudes toward the job might affect attendance perhaps constitutes the oldest scientific model of absence causation, and it is still dominant among industrial-organizational psychologists. The essence of this model is that absenteeism is assumed to be a manifestation of withdrawal from dissatisfying aspects of the job. Over the years, enough research has accumulated to spawn at least five meta-analyses of the relationship between job satisfaction and absenteeism. Hackett (1989) dissects the differences among them and presents corrected population correlations from his own definitive data set. As such, the following conclusions seem warranted:

- The strongest corrected attitudinal correlates of absenteeism are overall job satisfaction ($r = -.23$ with time lost) and satisfaction with the content of the work itself ($r = -.21$ with frequency of absence).
- Satisfaction with pay, promotions, supervision, and coworkers exhibits much smaller correlations with absence.
- There are probable moderators of the connection between job satisfaction and absence.

The tendency for satisfaction with the work itself to predict absenteeism is probably responsible for the well-documented tendency for people who hold higher occupational status to have better attendance records (e.g., Bureau of Labor Statistics, 1999). Surprisingly, there has been little research into moderators of the satisfaction-absence relationship to examine when or for whom dissatisfaction is prone to be converted into absenteeism. Hackett (1989) found a stronger relationship in samples with a larger proportion of women, suggesting that women may be more prone than men to withdraw from dissatisfying work. Drago and Wooden (1992) found that work group dynamics interacted with satisfaction such that group cohesion magnified the positive effects of satisfaction and the negative effects of dissatisfaction on attendance. More research of this nature would be welcome, especially regarding potential personality moderators.

It may seem counterintuitive that satisfaction with factors such as pay, supervision, and coworkers is not especially predictive of absence. However, there are growing indicators that a more specific focus on organizational fairness and support sheds light on withdrawal via absenteeism. Such factors are captured imperfectly in work facet satisfaction measures.

Lewicki, Poland, Minton, and Sheppard (1997) studied "time theft," the self-reported proclivity to falsely call in sick, convert anticipated lateness into absence, and concoct stories to justify absence. In a large bank credit card processing division, they found that a number of fairness variables were more highly related to time theft than was overall job satisfaction, including general and supervisory fairness, as well as systemic and procedural justice. Similarly, Colquitt, Conlon, Wesson, Porter, and Ng (2001) meta-analyzed the relationships between justice dimensions and a withdrawal composite that included absence and turnover. Both distributive and procedural justice exhibited substantial negative correlations with withdrawal, and further analyses particularly implicated distributive justice. This finding squares with Dutch research showing a clear connection between workplace inequity and absenteeism (Geurts et al., 1999; van Dierendonck, Schaufeli, & Buunk, 1998; Van Yperen, Hagedoorn, & Geurts, 1996). It also corresponds to research revealing increased absenteeism following failure to achieve promotion (Schwarzwald, Koslowsky, & Shalit, 1992) and decreased absence following promotion (Lam & Schaubroeck, 2000). It is unlikely that such findings simply reflect passive withdrawal from dissatisfaction. Rather, as Johns and Nicholson (1982) predicted, "Absence might be usefully viewed as an attempt to fulfill or modify a series of implicit social contracts between the worker and the employing organization" (p. 153). The temporary withdrawal of labor is one way to balance the equity equation, especially when paid sick days are available for consumption.

Fairness and justice connote support for the dignity and rights of employees. This raises a question as to whether broader forms of organizational support can counter absenteeism. Such support involves employee perceptions that the organization is concerned with their well-being and willing to help them. Eisenberger, Armeli, Rexwinkel, Lynch, and Rhoades (2001) found that perceived organizational support was positively associated with supervisory ratings of attendance and giving advance notice of absenteeism. Other research shows a clear connection in the expected direction between perceived organizational support and records-based absence data (Eisenberger, Fasolo, & Davis-LaMastro, 1990; Eisenberger, Huntington, Hutchison, & Sowa, 1986). It should be noted that the exact details of such support may be important. Thompson, Beauvais, and Lyness (1999) found that, when available, "absence autonomy" was the most commonly used benefit out of 16 such benefits.

To summarize, unfavorable attitudes toward the job, and especially toward the content of the work, are predictive of absenteeism. However, there is growing evidence that issues of workplace fairness and support may be especially critical determinants of attendance patterns.

Personality

The idea that personality might have an important impact on work behavior has a long but undistinguished history. However, serious interest has been rekindled with the advent of the five-factor model of personality and much stronger theory that predicts which personality constructs might be related to which specific work behaviors.

The possibility of a relationship between personality and absenteeism suggests that the behavior should exhibit temporal and cross-situational consistency. A meta-analysis by Farrell and Stamm (1988) concluded that absence history correlated .71 with current time lost and .65 with current frequency. Rentsch and Steel (1998)

found that frequency of absence in Year 1 correlated .59 to .53 with absence exhibited 4 to 6 years later. Cross-situational absence consistency has also been demonstrated, both in the school-to-work transition (Brenner, 1968) and following substantial job design changes (Ivancevich, 1985). Harrison and Price (in press) measured self-reported absence across 11 different social settings (e.g., work, classes, medical appointments, religious services, parties) where attendance might be more or less expected. The resulting Setting × Setting matrix yielded a coefficient alpha of .62, which is within the (lower) bounds of acceptable internal consistency for a psychological construct.

The above evidence provides some indirect support for the folk concept of absence proneness. However, proneness is a hollow, circular construct in that it is often both inferred from and used as an explanation for elevated absenteeism. What is needed, then, is one or more theoretical mechanisms that might link personality to absenteeism. Likely candidates include integrity, job satisfaction, affect, and cognition (Johns, 2001).

Integrity. Integrity is a rather vague construct centered around honesty in the workplace and the proclivity of individuals to engage in organizationally counterproductive behaviors such as theft and absenteeism. Over the years, psychologists have developed selection tests to tap the integrity construct. Overt integrity tests measure attitudes toward honesty and generally have been validated against theft. Personality-based tests tend to center around subtraits of the Big Five dimension of conscientiousness, and they have been used successfully to predict broader composites of counterproductivity (Ones, Viswesvaran, & Schmidt, 1993). In a meta-analysis focusing specifically on absenteeism, Ones,

Viswesvaran, and Schmidt (1992) reported a corrected correlation of .33 between personality-based integrity and absence, higher integrity resulting in lower absence. More recently, conventional personality measures of conscientiousness have also been shown to exhibit significant negative correlations with absence (Conte & Jacobs, 1999; Hattrup, O'Connell, & Wingate, 1998; Judge, Martocchio, & Thoreson, 1997).

Job Satisfaction. Traditionally, job satisfaction has been considered to be influenced by situational factors such as compensation, job design, and human relations practices. However, in recent years, increasing attention has been directed toward a possible dispositional substrate to satisfaction. Research has shown that a broad personality construct called *core self-evaluations* is reliably related to job satisfaction (Judge & Bono, 2001). In this research, more satisfied individuals reported higher self-esteem and self-efficacy, exhibited higher internal control, and were lower in neuroticism. Both achieving interesting work and viewing one's job as complex and challenging have been implicated in the association between personality and job satisfaction. It will be recalled that satisfaction with the content of the work is the best facet predictor of absence. Thus, it is certainly feasible that some variance in absence is due to personality, mediated by satisfaction. In fact, job satisfaction has been shown to mediate the relationship between personality characteristics and propensity to quit, a withdrawal variable often associated with absenteeism (Day, Bedeian, & Conte, 1998).

Affect. Beyond job satisfaction, there is growing evidence that mood at work, indexed by affectivity, is associated with absenteeism. In particular, four studies report lower absence among those higher in positive affect (George, 1989; Iverson &

Deery, 2001; Iverson, Olekalns, & Erwin, 1998; Pelled & Xin 1999). Martocchio and Jimeno (in press) offer an interesting theory of how affect may mediate the relationship between other personality characteristics and absenteeism, which they frame as a mood-regulatory behavior.

Cognition. It is possible that certain personality characteristics influence attendance via their impact on cognitions about one's capacity to get to work. For example, Judge and Martocchio (1996) determined that people with low work ethic, external locus of control, and excuse-making tendencies were more likely to attribute absenteeism to external, environmental causes rather than internal causes. Mirroring the finding that external academic locus of control prompts absenteeism from college classes (Trice & Hackburt, 1989), Johns (1994c) reported that external health locus of control was associated with work absence. All of these findings correspond with evidence that self-efficacy for attendance is associated with reduced absence (Frayne & Latham, 1987; Johns, 1994c; Salgado & Moscoso, 2000).

Health and Stress

A number of variables in the domain of health and stress have been investigated as to their potential for absence causation.

Depression. Affective disorders, including depression and neurosis, have been implicated consistently in the occurrence of absenteeism (e.g., Kessler & Frank, 1997; Moncrieff & Pomerleau, 2000; Stansfeld et al., 1995). Furthermore, it is possible that some reports of common minor illnesses, which are the most usual self-reported cause of absence, are, in fact, disguising depression. Among a host of illness-related and environmental constraints on attendance, Johns and Xie (1998) found that employees were least likely to endorse the legitimacy of depression. The specter of depression also runs through the other health-related causes of absence to be discussed below. This is due to its association with negative health-related behaviors (e.g., smoking and drinking), its covariation with chronic pain, and its counterindication for coping with stress.

Substance Use. A large number of studies have reported elevated absence from work among smokers (e.g., North et al., 1993; Parkes, 1987). The most common interpretation of these results reflects the susceptibility of smokers to physical illness. However, a psychological component cannot be ruled out because of the existence of a reciprocal connection between smoking and depression (Windle & Windle, 2001).

Much research finds a positive association between problem drinking patterns and absenteeism, whereas volume consumed per se has less of a relationship (e.g., Marmot, North, Feeney, & Head, 1993, Upmark, Möller, & Romelsjö, 1999; Webb et al., 1994). Several studies reveal that abstainers are at greater risk of absenteeism than are moderate consumers (Upmark et al., 1999; Vasse, Nijhuis, & Kok, 1998; Webb et al., 1994). Vasse et al. opine that abstainers might lack the stress-coping facility that moderate consumption can provide. Alternatively, some might have medical conditions that prompt both abstention and absenteeism.

Pain. Martocchio, Harrison, and Berkson (2000) present a meta-analysis of the relationship between lower back pain and absence and evaluate the efficacy of various interventions. Their most striking finding is that back pain is related much more strongly to frequency of absenteeism

than to total time lost. It will be recalled that frequency is often thought to be a better indicator of voluntarism. Furthermore, "back schools" that provide support and instruction to sufferers were the least effective of four back pain interventions in reducing absence. Exercise and reduced bed rest were the most effective (if least validating) interventions, ironic in light of growing evidence that fear-avoidance regarding work and physical exercise is a robust predictor of absenteeism among back pain sufferers (Linton & Halldén, 1998; Waddell, Newton, Henderson, Somerville, & Main, 1993).

Much research has implicated migraine headaches as a cause of absence. Furthermore, women are more likely to experience migraines than men and more likely to absent themselves in response to migraine symptoms (Breslau & Davis, 1993; de Lissovoy & Lazarus, 1994; Lipton, Steward, & Von Korff, 1994). The well-established connection between chronic pain and depression (Banks & Kerns, 1996), and the tendency for women to suffer more from depression than men (Culbertson, 1997), suggest that migraine pain and resulting depression are partly responsible for elevated absenteeism among women.

Stress. Work stress is the perceived failure to cope with job demands, a perception that is often expressed as anxiety or tension. Stressors are environmental characteristics that may stimulate feelings of stress. There is research evidence (reviewed by Johns, 1997) that both stress and stressors, usually measured via questionnaires, are associated with elevated absence. However, both null findings and counterintuitive signs suggest that the stress-absence connection is a complicated one. This complication stems from the fact that several implicit and potentially contradictory models underlie the connection, a point generally ignored in the typical research study in this domain. These include a medical model, an escape model, an off-job stress model, and a restorative model.

Regarding the *medical model*, stress is implicated in infectious disease, pregnancy complications, and cardiovascular disease (Adler & Matthews, 1994). The infectious disease connection is especially well established, in that stress is associated with depressed immune system functioning as well as related diseases such as upper respiratory problems (Cohen & Herbert, 1996). All of this having been said, there is a paucity of research that explicitly and *independently* measures stress, physical illness, and absenteeism in the same study.

In the *escape model*, absenteeism is framed as a means of simply removing oneself from stressful organizational conditions. Medical mediation may or may not be implied. By far, stress-provoking job designs and role relationships have been studied the most. Smulders and Nijhuis (1999) provide a concise review of this work, noting that high job demands, low control, and role complications sometimes have been associated with elevated absence, but at the same time finding many null and some reversed-sign associations. Their own research, for example, revealed a negative relationship between job demands and absence, echoing the observation of "presenteeism" (showing up at work sick) among hard-to-replace caregivers and teachers (Aronsson, Gustafsson, & Dallner, 2000). Research on organizational restructuring and downsizing is interesting in regard to absenteeism: Should the stress of downsizing stimulate escape via absenteeism or attendance due to fear of job loss? Two studies have reported an increase in long-term absence spells and a reduction in short spells (Kivimäki, Vahtera, Griffiths, Cox, & Thomson, 2001; Stansfeld, Head, & Ferrie, 1999). Although it is possible to interpret these results as being due to a stress-sickness connection, it is just as possible that people are most careful to legitimate their absences when the threat of restructuring is occurring. It bears emphasizing that poor job design has been implicated as a mediator in studies examining the impact of downsizing and restructuring on absenteeism.

The *off-job stress model* posits that nonwork demands can cause stressful role conflict that results in absenteeism. Although this topic has not been studied very much, research does show that family-work conflict mediates the relationship between elder care responsibilities and self-reported absenteeism (e.g., Gignac, Kelloway, & Gottlieb, 1996).

Finally, the *restorative model* advances the idea that absenteeism may be a more positive, proactive reaction to stress, rather than passive escape or medical surrender. Although there is almost no research probing this idea, it would account for some of the anomalies in stress-absence research, because it implies that absence can sometimes reduce stress. In a daily diary study of nurses, Hackett and Bycio (1996) found no evidence for stress reduction but instead interpreted their results in maintenance terms. That is, absenteeism prevented an increase in stress and tiredness. More research of this nature is encouraged.

Social Influence

Historically, absenteeism has been viewed as an index of the adjustment of individuals to their workplace, with little attention paid to the social context in which such adjustment was occurring. However, in the past 20 years, there has been a growing awareness of the impact of social context on absence behavior (Johns, 1997). Interest in the social approach to absenteeism began with a simple but compelling observation: There is great variation in absence rates across social units such as work groups within the same department, departments within the same organization, and organizations within the same industry, as well as between industries, occupations, and even nations (see Johns, 1997). In many cases, these differences are so striking as to defy interpretation in terms of individual-level variables such as health, demographics, or job satisfaction. For example, in the 2 fiscal years spanning 1991 to 1993, Transport Canada reported absence rates among air traffic controllers that ranged from 11.78 shifts missed per employee in Toronto to 21.01 missed in Edmonton, Alberta (Rowan, 1993). Kaiser (1998) assembled absence rates from various nations. In 1992, time lost rates varied from 1.6% in Japan to 2.9% in the United States to 11.6% in Sweden.

What accounts for such striking differences? One answer for which there is growing evidence is *absence cultures* (Chadwick-Jones et al., 1982; Johns & Nicholson, 1982; Nicholson & Johns, 1985). Absence cultures consist of "shared understandings about absence legitimacy . . . and the established 'custom and practice' of employee absence behavior and its control" (Johns & Nicholson, 1982, p. 136). A key dimension of absence cultures concerns norms. Earlier, it was explained that people have some tendency to underestimate their own absenteeism and to see their attendance records as superior to those of others. Nevertheless, there is substantial evidence that perceived expectations about how much absence is normal or typical influence individual and group attendance behavior (e.g., Gellatly, 1995; Gellatly & Luchak, 1998; Harrison, 1995; Xie & Johns, 2000). In addition, there is reason to expect that norms also reflect the perceived

legitimacy of various causes of absence (Harvey & Nicholson, 1999; Johns & Xie, 1998) and (cross-nationally) beliefs about the role of state support for sickness benefits.

Although the absence culture concept could apply to any of several levels of analysis above the individual (e.g., department, organization), extant evidence particularly implicates the work group or team level. For instance, group cohesiveness generally promotes lower absenteeism, and both the task and social aspects of cohesiveness have been implicated (Johns, 1997). However, cohesion may actually stimulate absenteeism when job dissatisfaction is low (Drago & Wooden, 1992) or when collusion to take days off occurs (cf. Xie & Johns, 2000). Perhaps the best evidence for the existence of absence cultures is cross-level research showing that absenteeism or beliefs about absenteeism aggregated to the work group level account for variance in the absenteeism of individual group members (Gellatly & Luchak, 1998; Johns, 1994c; Markham & McKee, 1995; Martocchio, 1994; Mathieu & Kohler, 1990; Xie & Johns, 2000).

The fact that absenteeism appears to be under considerable social control has a number of important implications. For one thing, the substantial variation in absence across defined social units suggests that although the behavior is under social control, there is no natural level of absence that might be called universally high or low. Thus, the absenteeism of individuals must always be interpreted in light of local and occupational standards. Absenteeism that is considered low in one context (e.g., in Sweden or in the shipping department) might be considered high in another context (e.g., in Japan or in the research lab).

As noted above, formal work groups or teams seem to be a particular nexus for the development of absence cultures. Although norms frequently emerge in such groups to regulate attendance, there is no guarantee as to their direction. This especially may be the case with self-managed teams, those that, by design, lack conventional hierarchical supervision. Harrison et al. (2000) provide several theoretical reasons why self-management might be expected to reduce absenteeism. They then review the small amount of extant evidence suggesting that, if anything, self-management might actually increase absence. At least two factors might be responsible, both of which may be heightened under self-management. One is collusion among team members to take days off, as inferred by Xie and Johns (2000) and observed directly by Edwards and Scullion (1982). Another is stress-producing conflict within self-managed teams. Kivimäki, Sutinen, et al. (2001) found that poor teamwork climate was a robust predictor of absenteeism among Finnish hospital physicians. Barker (1993) showed that absenteeism itself is often a source of conflict in self-managed teams, in that failure to "pull one's weight" leads to feelings of inequity.

The social dynamics underlying absence also have implications in the context of workplace diversity (Harrison et al., 2000), particularly in the domain of teamwork. For instance, it was established earlier that women tend to be absent more than men and that younger men are absent more than older men. Thus, the North American trend toward more diverse work groups could result in considerable conflict when task interdependence is high and normative consensus about absence levels and legitimate reasons for absence fails to emerge. For example, Perry, Kulik, and Zhou (1999) determined that age differences between grounds workers and their higher level supervisors were associated with increased employee absence. In particular, cultural diversity may have implications for normative conflict regarding absenteeism, although we have almost no research on this. However, substantial cross-national differences in absence rates may reflect normative differences in expectations regarding appropriate standards of attendance. Such differences may, in turn, stem from cross-cultural differences in work centrality, time orientation, gender role differentiation, or economic orientation (Addae & Johns, in press; Kaiser, 1998). Johns and Xie (1998) found that Canadians were more likely than Chinese to endorse depression, stress, and illness as reasons for absence. On the other hand, one might expect that employees from more collective cultures, such as China and Mexico, would be more likely to endorse absenteeism to care for an extended family member than would those from more individualistic cultures.

MANAGING ABSENCE AND ATTENDANCE

I conclude the chapter with a few observations about managing absence and attendance (for an alternative book-length treatment, see Rhodes & Steers, 1990). To me, it makes sense for organizations to pursue a policy of "managed attendance" (Harrison et al., 2000). Such a general policy emphasizes accountability for good attendance while avoiding the draconian perils of trying to absolutely minimize absence. The net result is an absence culture that meets speed, quality, and service requirements while avoiding "presenteeism." Two basic principles apply: First, all employees should be exposed to conditions that encourage reasonable attendance, not just high absentees. Next, the wide range of meanings or causes of absence should be catered to, suggesting a multipronged approach.

To begin at the beginning, it is unwise to hire people who have a propensity for absenteeism. Access to past attendance records is a good but rare screening device, but the records have to be used so as to avoid adverse impact due to gender. Integrity tests have been shown to be valid predictors of absenteeism (Ones et al., 1992), and they avoid adverse impact. Also, certain recruiting sources have been shown to minimize absence, including, in the case of nurses, school referrals and ads in professional journals (Griffeth, Hom, Fink, & Cohen, 1997). Once hired, employees should not be exposed to human resources policies that reward absence. Research clearly demonstrates that liberal sick day policies and lax absence controls result in higher absenteeism (e.g., Dalton & Mesch, 1991; Drago & Wooden, 1992). On the other hand, policies and practices that encourage attendance are advisable. For example, flextime systems that allow for some discretion in when people arrive at and leave work clearly combat absence (Baltes, Briggs, Huff, Wright, & Neuman, 1999). Such systems cater to child care and elder care demands and prevent the conversion of anticipated lateness into absence. They also connote organizational support for employees.

In the workplace itself, the basic antidote for absence is good job design that provides reasonable levels of skill variety, task significance, autonomy, and feedback (Hackman & Oldham, 1980). Both the stress and the job satisfaction literatures suggest this. Particular care should be taken in situations of restructuring and downsizing to avoid job design by default. Two of the most common errors are assigning employees extra tasks for which they are untrained and reducing employee control or autonomy over how work is accomplished. The other key factor is fair treatment. As noted earlier, attendance patterns are especially sensitive to inequity and injustice. In contemporary organizations, intense competition and rapidly changing conditions often force organizations to make changes that may be perceived by employees as violating existing psychological contracts. In such situations, caring and informative explanations for the changes should be provided. Such accounts have been shown to prevent stock theft during a pay-cut period (Greenberg, 1990), and there is every reason to believe that they should counter time theft in the form of absenteeism.

Employee assistance programs that help workers deal with stress, substance abuse, and so on have a good record of absence reduction (Unckless, Mathieu, & Kelley, 1998), probably in part because they concentrate on those with especially high absence rates. For less troubled but still much-absent individuals, self-management training has been shown to reduce absenteeism (Frayne & Latham, 1987). Such training focuses on setting attendance goals and on systematically anticipating and overcoming obstacles to good attendance. A low-cost alternative that appears to improve attendance among those with average absence records is the Absence Feedback Intervention (Gaudine & Saks, 2001). This intervention, which supplies employees with regular feedback about their own absence record and the average for their work unit, is predicated on my research showing that people underestimate their own absence levels and see themselves as superior to their peers (Johns, 1994a, 1994b; Johns & Xie, 1998).

The fact that absenteeism is quite susceptible to social influence suggests harnessing this influence to manage attendance. There is virtually no research on this, although Majchrzak (1987) reported a successful intervention in which team leaders communicated and clarified attendance policies. Harrison et al. (2000) suggested that self-managed teams might be authorized to set collective attendance goals, develop their own flexible attendance policies (e.g., a member can occasionally work from home), and even pool sick days.

Actors and observers often harbor rather different attributions about the causes of absence, and absence is often the subject of labor arbitration. For these reasons, some firms have found it useful to institute "no-fault" absenteeism management systems that essentially grant employees a fixed number of days off without need for explanation, after which termination will occur (Moore et al., 1992). When they work properly, such systems can preclude much of the tension that can surround absence, especially that between employees and their direct managers. However, such systems may be at odds with the provisions of the Americans with Disabilities Act or the Family and Medical Leave Act, both of which may excuse certain types of absences (ADA, 2001).

To conclude, from a mental health perspective, much absenteeism is both a cause of and a result of poor work adjustment. However, causal factors have been pretty well mapped, and corresponding interventions offer much promise for managing attendance, to the benefit of both the individual and the organization.

REFERENCES

ADA, FMLA, and absentee policies: Proceed with caution. (2001, June). *HR Focus, 78*, 2.

Addae, H. M., & Johns, G. (in press). National culture and perceptions of absence legitimacy. In M. Koslowsky & M. Krausz (Eds.), *Voluntary employee withdrawal and inattendance—A current perspective*. New York: Plenum.

Adler, N., & Matthews, K. (1994). Health psychology: Why do some people get sick and some stay well? *Annual Review of Psychology, 45*, 229-259.

Aronsson, G., Gustafsson, K., & Dallner, M. (2000). Sick but yet at work: An empirical study of sickness presenteeism. *Journal of Epidemiology and Community Health, 54*, 502-509.

Baltes, B. B., Briggs, T. E., Huff, J. W., Wright, J. A., & Neuman, G. A. (1999). Flexible and compressed workweek schedules: A meta-analysis of their effects on work-related criteria. *Journal of Applied Psychology, 84*, 496-513.

Banks, S. M., & Kerns, R. D. (1996). Explaining high rates of depression in chronic pain: A diathesis-stress framework. *Psychological Bulletin, 119*, 95-110.

Barker, J. R. (1993). Tightening the iron cage: Concertive control in self-managing teams. *Administrative Science Quarterly, 38*, 408-437.

Brenner, M. H. (1968). Use of high school data to predict work performance. *Journal of Applied Psychology, 52*, 29-30.

Breslau, N., & Davis, G. C. (1993). Migraine, physical health and psychiatric disorder: A prospective epidemiological study in young adults. *Journal of Psychiatric Research, 27*, 211-221.

Bureau of Labor Statistics. (1999). Absences from work of employed full-time wage and salary workers by occupation and industry. *Employment and Earnings, 46*(1), 224.

Bycio, P. (1992). Job performance and absenteeism: A review and meta-analysis. *Human Relations, 45*, 193-220.

Chadwick-Jones, J. K., Nicholson, N., & Brown, C. (1982). *Social psychology of absenteeism*. New York: Praeger.

Cohen, S., & Herbert, T. B. (1996). Health psychology: Psychological factors and physical disease from the perspective of human psychoneuroimmunology. *Annual Review of Psychology, 47,* 113-142.

Colquitt, J. A., Conlon, D. E., Wesson, M. J., Porter, C. O. L. H., & Ng, K. Y. (2001). Justice at the millennium: A meta-analytic review of 25 years of justice research. *Journal of Applied Psychology, 86,* 425-445.

Conte, J. M., & Jacobs, R. R. (1999, May). *Temporal and personality predictors of absence and lateness.* Paper presented at the annual convention of the Society for Industrial and Organizational Psychology, Atlanta.

Côté, D., & Haccoun, R. R. (1991). L'absentéisme des femmes et des hommes: Une méta-analyse. *Canadian Journal of Administrative Sciences, 8,* 130-139.

Culbertson, F. M. (1997). Depression and gender: An international review. *American Psychologist, 52,* 25-34.

Dalton, D. R., & Mesch, D. J. (1991). On the extent and reduction of avoidable absenteeism: An assessment of absence policy provisions. *Journal of Applied Psychology, 76,* 810-817.

Dalton, D. R., & Wimbush, J. C. (1998). Absence does not make the heart grow fonder. In R. W. Griffin, A. O'Leary-Kelly, & J. M. Collins (Eds.), *Dysfunctional behavior in organizations: Non-violent dysfunctional behavior* (pp. 197-246). Stamford, CT: JAI.

Day, D. V., Bedeian, A. G., & Conte, J. M. (1998). Personality as predictor of work-related outcomes: Test of a mediated latent structural model. *Journal of Applied Social Psychology, 28,* 2068-2088.

de Lissovoy, G., & Lazarus, S. S. (1994). The economic cost of migraine: Present state of knowledge. *Neurology, 44*(Suppl. 4), S56-S62.

Drago, R., & Wooden, M. (1992). The determinants of labor absence: Economic factors and workgroup norms across countries. *Industrial and Labor Relations Review, 45,* 764-778.

Edwards, P. K., & Scullion, H. (1982). *The social organization of industrial conflict: Control and resistance in the workplace.* Oxford, UK: Basil Blackwell.

Eisenberger, R., Armeli, S., Rexwinkel, B., Lynch, P. D., & Rhoades, L. (2001). Reciprocation of perceived organizational support. *Journal of Applied Psychology, 86,* 42-51.

Eisenberger, R., Fasolo, P., & Davis-LaMastro, V. (1990). Perceived organizational support and employee diligence, commitment, and innovation. *Journal of Applied Psychology, 75,* 51-59.

Eisenberger, R., Huntington, R., Hutchison, S., & Sowa, D. (1986). Perceived organizational support. *Journal of Applied Psychology, 71,* 500-507.

Farrell, D., & Stamm, C. L. (1988). Meta-analysis of the correlates of employee absence. *Human Relations, 41,* 211-227.

Fichman, M. (1989). Attendance makes the heart grow fonder: A hazard rate approach to modeling attendance. *Journal of Applied Psychology, 74,* 325-335.

Frayne, C. A., & Latham, G. P. (1987). Application of social learning theory to employee self-management of attendance. *Journal of Applied Psychology, 72,* 387-392.

Gaudine, A. P., & Saks, A. M. (2001). Effects of an absenteeism feedback intervention on employee absence behavior. *Journal of Organizational Behavior, 22,* 15-29.

Gellatly, I. R. (1995). Individual and group determinants of employee absenteeism: Test of a causal model. *Journal of Organizational Behavior, 16,* 469-485.

Gellatly, I. R., & Luchak, A. A. (1998). Personal and organizational determinants of perceived absence norms. *Human Relations, 51,* 1085-1102.

George, J. M. (1989). Mood and absence. *Journal of Applied Psychology, 74,* 317-324.

Geurts, S., Schaufeli, W. B., & Rutte, C. G. (1999). Absenteeism, turnover intention and inequity in the employment relationship. *Work & Stress, 13,* 253-267.

Gignac, M. A. M., Kelloway, E. K., & Gottlieb, B. H. (1996). The impact of caregiving on employment: A mediational model of work-family conflict. *Canadian Journal on Aging, 15,* 525-542.

Greenberg, J. (1990). Employee theft as a reaction to underpayment inequity: The hidden cost of pay cuts. *Journal of Applied Psychology, 75,* 561-568.

Griffeth, R. W., Hom, P. W., Fink, L. S., & Cohen, D. J. (1997). Comparative tests of multivariate models of recruiting source effects. *Journal of Management, 23,* 19-36.

Haccoun, R. R., & Dupont, S. (1987). Absence research: A critique of previous approaches and an example for a new direction. *Canadian Journal of Administrative Sciences, 4,* 143-156.

Hackett, R. D. (1989). Work attitudes and employee absenteeism: A synthesis of the literature. *Journal of Occupational Psychology, 62,* 235-248.

Hackett, R. D. (1990). Age, tenure, and employee absenteeism. *Human Relations, 43,* 610-619.

Hackett, R. D., & Bycio, P. (1996). An evaluation of employee absenteeism as a coping mechanism among hospital nurses. *Journal of Occupational and Organizational Psychology, 69,* 327-338.

Hackett, R. D., Bycio, P., & Guion, R. M. (1989). Absenteeism among hospital nurses: An idiographic-longitudinal analysis. *Academy of Management Journal, 32,* 424-453.

Hackett, R. D., & Guion, R. M. (1985). A reevaluation of the absenteeism-job satisfaction relationship. *Organizational Behavior and Human Decision Processes, 35,* 340-381.

Hackman, J. R., & Oldham, G. R. (1980). *Work redesign.* Reading, MA: Addison-Wesley.

Harrison, D. A. (1995). Volunteer motivation and attendance decisions: Competitive theory testing in multiple samples from a homeless shelter. *Journal of Applied Psychology, 80,* 371-385.

Harrison, D. A., & Hulin, C. L. (1989). Investigations of absenteeism: Using event history models to study the absence-taking process. *Journal of Applied Psychology, 74,* 300-316.

Harrison, D. A., Johns, G., & Martocchio, J. J. (2000). Changes in technology, teamwork, and diversity: New directions for a new century of absenteeism research. *Research in Personnel and Human Resources Management, 18,* 43-91.

Harrison, D. A., & Martocchio, J. J. (1998). A time for absenteeism: A 20-year review of origins, offshoots, and outcomes. *Journal of Management, 24,* 305-350.

Harrison, D. A., & Price, K. H. (in press). Context and consistency in absenteeism: Studying social and dispositional influences across multiple settings. *Human Resource Management Review.*

Harrison, D. A., & Shaffer, M. A. (1994). Comparative examinations of self-reports and perceived absenteeism norms: Wading through Lake Wobegon. *Journal of Applied Psychology, 79,* 240-251.

Harvey, J., & Nicholson, N. (1999). Minor illness as a legitimate reason for absence. *Journal of Organizational Behavior, 20,* 979-993.

Hattrup, K., O'Connell, M. S., & Wingate, P. H. (1998). Prediction of multidimensional criteria: Distinguishing task and contextual performance. *Human Performance, 11,* 305-319.

Ivancevich, J. M. (1985). Predicting absenteeism from prior absence and work attitudes. *Academy of Management Journal, 28,* 219-228.

Iverson, R. D., & Deery, S. J. (2001). Understanding the "personological" basis of employee withdrawal: The influence of affective disposition on employee tardiness, early departure, and absenteeism. *Journal of Applied Psychology, 86*, 856-866.

Iverson, R. D., Olekalns, M., & Erwin, P. J. (1998). Affectivity, organizational stressors, and absenteeism: A causal model of burnout and its consequences. *Journal of Vocational Behavior, 52*, 1-23.

Johns, G. (1994a). Absenteeism estimates by employees and managers: Divergent perspectives and self-serving perceptions. *Journal of Applied Psychology, 79*, 229-239.

Johns, G. (1994b). How often were you absent? A review of the use of self-reported absence data. *Journal of Applied Psychology, 79*, 574-591.

Johns, G. (1994c, July). *Medical, ethical, and cultural constraints on work absence and attendance.* Presentation at the International Congress of Applied Psychology, Madrid.

Johns, G. (1997). Contemporary research on absence from work: Correlates, causes and consequences. *International Review of Industrial and Organizational Psychology, 12*, 115-174.

Johns, G. (2001). The psychology of lateness, absenteeism, and turnover. In N. Anderson, D. S. Ones, H. K. Sinangil, & C. Viswesvaran (Eds.), *Handbook of industrial, work & organizational psychology* (Vol. 2, pp. 232-252). London: Sage.

Johns, G., & Nicholson, N. (1982). The meanings of absence: New strategies for theory and research. *Research in Organizational Behavior, 4*, 127-172.

Johns, G., & Xie, J. L. (1998). Perceptions of absence from work: People's Republic of China versus Canada. *Journal of Applied Psychology, 83*, 515-530.

Judge, T. A., & Bono, J. E. (2001). Relationship of core self-evaluation traits—self-esteem, generalized self-efficacy, locus of control, and emotional stability—with job satisfaction and job performance: A meta-analysis. *Journal of Applied Psychology, 86*, 80-92.

Judge, T. A., & Martocchio, J. J. (1996). Dispositional influences on attributions concerning absenteeism. *Journal of Management, 22*, 837-861.

Judge, T. A., Martocchio, J. J., & Thoresen, C. J. (1997). Five-factor model of personality and employee absence. *Journal of Applied Psychology, 82*, 745-755.

Kaiser, C. P. (1998). Dimensions of culture, distributive principles, and decommodification: Implications for employee absence behavior. *Journal of Socio-Economics, 27*, 551-564.

Kessler, R. C., & Frank, R. G. (1997). The impact of psychiatric disorders on work loss days. *Psychological Medicine, 27*, 861-873.

Kivimäki, M., Sutinen, R., Elovainio, M., Vahtera, J., Räsänen, K., Töyry, S., Ferrie, J. E., & Firth-Couzens, J. (2001). Sickness absence in hospital physicians: 2 year follow up study on determinants. *Occupational and Environmental Medicine, 58*, 361-366.

Kivimäki, M., Vahtera, J., Griffiths, A., Cox, T., & Thomson, L. (2001). Sickness absence and organizational downsizing. In R. D. Burke & C. L. Cooper (Eds.), *The organization in crisis: Downsizing, restructuring, and privatization* (pp. 78-94). Oxford, UK: Basil Blackwell.

Koslowsky, M., Sagie, A., Krausz, M., & Singer, A. D. (1997). Correlates of employee lateness: Some theoretical considerations. *Journal of Applied Psychology, 82*, 79-88.

Lam, S. S. K., & Schaubroeck, J. (2000). The role of locus of control in reactions to being promoted and being passed over: A quasi experiment. *Academy of Management Journal, 43*, 66-78.

Lewicki, R. J., Poland, T., Minton, J. W., & Sheppard, B. H. (1997). Dishonesty as deviance: A typology of workplace dishonesty and contributing factors. *Research on Negotiations in Organizations, 6,* 53-86.

Linton, S. J., & Halldén, K. (1998). Can we screen for problematic back pain? A screening questionnaire for predicting outcome in acute and subacute back pain. *The Clinical Journal of Pain, 14,* 209-215.

Lipton, R. B., Steward, W. F., & Von Korff, M. (1994). The burden of migraine: A review of cost to society. *PharmacoEconomics, 6,* 215-221.

Majchrzak, A. (1987). Effects of management policies on unauthorized absence behavior. *Journal of Applied Behavioral Science, 23,* 501-523.

Markham, S. E., & McKee, G. H. (1995). Group absence behavior and standards: A multilevel analysis. *Academy of Management Journal, 38,* 1174-1190.

Marmot, M. G., North, F., Feeney, A., & Head, J. (1993). Alcohol consumption and sickness absence: From the Whitehall II study. *Addiction, 88,* 369-382.

Martocchio, J. J. (1992). The financial cost of absence decisions. *Journal of Management, 18,* 133-152.

Martocchio, J. J. (1994). The effects of absence culture on individual absence. *Human Relations, 47,* 243-262.

Martocchio, J. J., Harrison, D. A., & Berkson, H. (2000). Connections between lower back pain, interventions, and absence from work: A time-based meta-analysis. *Personnel Psychology, 53,* 595-624.

Martocchio, J. J., & Jimeno, D. I. (in press). Employee absenteeism as an affective event. *Human Resource Management Review.*

Martocchio, J. J., & Judge, T. A. (1994). A policy-capturing approach to individuals' decisions to be absent. *Organizational Behavior and Human Decision Processes, 57,* 358-386.

Mathieu, J. E., & Kohler, S. S. (1990). A cross-level examination of group absence influences on individual absence. *Journal of Applied Psychology, 75,* 217-220.

Mitra, A., Jenkins, G. D., Jr., & Gupta, N. (1992). A meta-analytic review of the relationship between absence and turnover. *Journal of Applied Psychology, 77,* 879-889.

Moncrieff, J., & Pomerleau, J. (2000). Trends in sickness benefits in Great Britain and the contribution of mental disorders. *Journal of Public Health Medicine, 22,* 59-67.

Moore, M. L., Nichol, V. W., & McHugh, P. P. (1992). Review of no-fault absenteeism cases taken to arbitration, 1980-1989: A rights and responsibilities analysis. *Employee Responsibilities and Rights Journal, 5,* 29-48.

Nicholson, N., & Johns, G. (1985). The absence culture and the psychological contract—Who's in control of absence? *Academy of Management Review, 10,* 397-407.

North, F., Syme, S. L., Feeney, A., Head, J., Shipley, M., & Marmot, M. G. (1993). Explaining socio-economic differences in sickness absence: The Whitehall II study. *British Medical Journal, 306,* 361-366.

Ones, D. S., Viswesvaran, C., & Schmidt, F. L. (1992, August). *Personality characteristics and absence taking behavior: The case of integrity.* Paper presented at the annual meeting of the Academy of Management, Las Vegas, NV.

Ones, D. S., Viswesvaran, C., & Schmidt, F. L. (1993). Comprehensive meta-analysis of integrity test validities: Findings and implications for personnel selection and theories of job performance. *Journal of Applied Psychology, 78,* 679-703.

Parkes, K. R. (1987). Relative weight, smoking, and mental health as predictors of sickness and absence from work. *Journal of Applied Psychology, 72,* 275-286.

Pelled, L. H., & Xin, K. R. (1999). Down and out: An investigation of the relationship between mood and employee withdrawal behavior. *Journal of Management, 25*, 75-89.

Perry, E. L., Kulik, C. T., & Zhou, J. (1999). A closer look at the effects of subordinate-supervisor age differences. *Journal of Organizational Behavior, 20*, 341-357.

Rentsch, J. R., & Steel, R. P. (1998). Testing the durability of job characteristics as predictors of absenteeism over a six-year period. *Personnel Psychology, 51*, 165-190.

Rhodes, S. R., & Steers, R. M. (1990). *Managing employee absenteeism.* Reading, MA: Addison-Wesley.

Robinson, S. L., & Bennett, R. J. (1995). A typology of deviant workplace behaviors: A multidimensional scaling study. *Academy of Management Journal, 38*, 555-572.

Rowan, G. (1993, December 20). High overtime criticized in audit. *The Globe and Mail,* pp. A1-A2.

Salgado, J. F., & Moscoso, S. (2000). Autoeficacia y criterios organizacionales de desempeño. *Apuntes de Psicología, 18*, 179-191.

Schwarzwald, J., Koslowsky, M., & Shalit, B. (1992). A field study of employees' attitudes and behaviors after promotion decisions. *Journal of Applied Psychology, 77*, 511-514.

Smulders, P. G. W., & Nijhuis, F. J. N. (1999). The job demands-job control model and absence behaviour: Results of a 3-year longitudinal study. *Work & Stress, 13*, 115-131.

Stansfeld, S., Feeney, A., Head, J., Canner, R., North, F., & Marmot, M. (1995). Sickness absence for psychiatric illness: The Whitehall II study. *Social Science and Medicine, 40*, 189-197.

Stansfeld, S., Head, J., & Ferrie, J. (1999). Short-term disability, sickness absence, and social gradients in the Whitehall II study. *International Journal of Law and Psychiatry, 22*, 425-439.

Statistics Canada. (1995). *Work absence rates, 1977 to 1994* (Labour and Household Surveys Division Catalogue No. 71-535, No. 7). Ottawa: Author.

Tharenou, P. (1993). A test of reciprocal causality for absenteeism. *Journal of Organizational Behavior, 14*, 269-290.

Thompson, C. A., Beauvais, L. L., & Lyness, K. S. (1999). When work-family benefits are not enough: The influence of work-family culture on benefit utilization, organizational attachment, and work-family conflict. *Journal of Vocational Behavior, 54*, 392-415.

Trice, A. D., & Hackburt, L. (1989). Academic locus of control, type A behavior, and college absenteeism. *Psychological Reports, 65*, 337-338.

Unckless, A. L., Mathieu, J. E., & Kelley, P. L. (1998, August). *The relative effectiveness of absence interventions: A meta-analysis.* Paper presented at the annual meeting of the Academy of Management, San Diego.

Upmark, M., Möller, J., & Romelsjö, A. (1999). Longitudinal, population-based study of self reported alcohol habits, high levels of sickness absence, and disability pensions. *Journal of Epidemiology and Community Health, 53*, 223-229.

van Dierendonck, D., Schaufeli, W. B., & Buunk, B. P. (1998). The evaluation of an individual burnout intervention program: The role of inequity and social support. *Journal of Applied Psychology, 83*, 392-407.

Van Yperen, N. W., Hagedoorn, M., & Geurts, S. A. E. (1996). Intent to leave and absenteeism as reactions to perceived inequity: The role of psychological and social constraints. *Journal of Occupational and Organizational Psychology, 69*, 367-372.

Vasse, R. M., Nijhuis, F. J. N., & Kok, G. (1998). Associations between work stress, alcohol consumption, and sickness absence. *Addiction, 93*, 231-241.

Waddell, G., Newton, M., Henderson, I., Somerville, D., & Main, C. J. (1993). A fear-avoidance beliefs questionnaire (FABQ) and the role of fear-avoidance beliefs in chronic low back pain and disability. *Pain, 52,* 157-168.

Webb, G. R., Redman, S., Hennrikus, D. J., Kelman, G. R., Gibberd, R. W., & Sanson-Fisher, R. W. (1994). The relationships between high-risk and problem drinking and the occurrence of work injuries and related absences. *Journal of Studies on Alcohol, 55,* 434-446.

Windle, M., & Windle, R. C. (2001). Depressive symptoms and cigarette smoking among middle adolescents: Prospective associations and intrapersonal and interpersonal influences. *Journal of Consulting and Clinical Psychology, 69,* 215-226.

Xie, J. L., & Johns, G. (2000). Interactive effects of absence culture salience and group cohesiveness: A multi-level and cross-level analysis of work absenteeism in the Chinese context. *Journal of Occupational and Organizational Psychology, 73,* 31-52.

Youngblood, S. A. (1984). Work, nonwork, and withdrawal. *Journal of Applied Psychology, 69,* 106-117.

CHAPTER 23

Passive-Aggressive Behavior in the Workplace

JOHN F. BINNING
EDWIN E. WAGNER

When President Clinton's staffers removed all of the Ws from White House keyboards, was this passive-aggressive? When the door of your new car is scratched with a key in the company parking lot, is this a result of passive-aggression? Are computer hackers who create destructive viruses being passive-aggressive? If you arrive at your local Whammy Burger at 10:30 a.m. and the manager refuses to serve you breakfast because the lunch menu takes effect at 10:30, is this passive-aggression? Is it passive-aggression when a coworker surreptitiously removes one of your documents from the office printer, or spreads false rumors about you? In a July 11, 2001, syndication of *Dear Abby,* a cashier reported "purposely forgetting" to bag an item or "accidentally" overcharging those customers who are so "rude" as to carry on a cell phone conversation during checkout. Is this passive-aggression?

The answers to questions like these are not readily apparent. In fact, even trained professionals can be confused about the construct of passive-aggression. For example, in a national news story, a mother drowned her five children. During an interview on a network news program about this tragic situation, a psychologist, while suggesting that the mother was angry with the father for pressuring her to have more children than she wanted, described her behavior as passive-aggressive. Seemingly, he was trying to highlight the misdirected expression of the aggression—anger toward the husband enacted through violence toward the children. Clearly, the mother's actions were aggressive—but they were not passive! In fact, none of the situations described above involves passive-aggression in its traditional clinical form.

Passive-aggression is a common but generally misunderstood form of counterproductive work behavior. By their very nature, passive-aggressive individuals can be some of the most difficult employees to manage effectively. Passive expressions of aggression can be particularly destructive to work organizations because such expressions rely on obstructionism that strikes at the sine qua non of organized human activity (i.e., efficient coordination of employee activities). Passive-aggression undermines the organization's functioning by stealthily "dis-integrating" employees' interactions and wreaking havoc on smooth operations. There is evidence that passive-aggression is especially destructive to interpersonal relationships, may be increasing in frequency, and often is managed ineffectively (cf. Daw, 2001; Podesta & Sanderson, 1999). In fact, some regard passive-aggression as "the strategy of the 90s" (Gaines, 1996, p. 14), in large part because of the unprecedented incidence of corporate downsizing (Cascio, 1993) that creates anxiety, hostility, and distrust of management coupled with heightened fear of job loss and diminished opportunities to express dissent. In addition to the destructive potential of passive-aggression, there is some evidence that individuals prone to passive expressions of aggression also are more likely to exhibit active aggression and antisocial acts (Berman, Fallon, & Coccaro, 1998).

An employee can exhibit passive-aggressive behavior occasionally, or it can constitute the primary way of dealing with one's work responsibilities. In the latter case, passive-aggression can represent a clinically significant disorder of personality described by the American Psychiatric Association's *Diagnostic and Statistical Manual of Mental Disorders* (*DSM-IV*) (American Psychiatric Association [APA], 1994). Based on the premise that passive-aggression is not a clearly understood psychological construct, our goals in the remainder of this chapter include clarifying the behavioral domain of passive-aggression, distinguishing it from other forms of aggressive behavior, providing guidance on how to identify passive-aggression in the workplace, describing how situational conditions can spawn passive-aggressive behavior, discussing some of the consequences of passive-aggression, and suggesting ways to manage passive-aggressive behavior in order to mitigate its destructive effects on organizational functioning.

A BRIEF HISTORY OF PASSIVE-AGGRESSION AS A CONSTRUCT

The term *passive-aggressive* was first coined in a 1945 military technical bulletin to describe a particular reaction to military stress manifested by passive opposition, inadequate responses, obstructionism, and general resistance to external demands (Wetzler & Morey, 1999). As such, it is the only Axis II personality disorder described in the various editions of the *DSM* to originate solely from observations of work behavior. Furthermore, current conceptualizations specifically note that these oppositional tendencies occur most frequently in work situations (*DSM-IV*). It is important to add, however, that the opposition and resistance exhibited by the passive-aggressive (PA) employee are accomplished under the guise of superficial compliance made possible by considerable skill in deflecting accountability, externalizing blame, and garnering "valid" excuses for lapses in effective performance.

While seemingly oxymoronic, the term appropriately describes a psychological construct often conceptualized as being rooted in emotional conflict—conflict between anger and fear, or assertiveness and inhibition. A common view is to regard a passive-aggressive response as deriving from conflict between dependency, which is resented, and autonomy, which is feared. The "aggressive" component refers to feelings of anger and hostility toward authority accompanied by fear or anxiety about being autonomous, resulting in passivity. Passive-aggressive employees presumably have learned that it is safer to assuage their disagreements with authority via covert means, rather than to assert themselves in a more direct way. According to Wetzler and Morey (1999), passive-aggressive individuals are unwilling to fulfill expectations, but their resistance is expressed indirectly. Passive-aggressive behavior appears to be innocent and innocuous, and the hostile motivation for the behavior is concealed. The "crime" is one of omission, rather than commission.

Passive-aggression has been conceptualized from a variety of theoretical perspectives, including psychodynamic, psychoanalytic, cognitive-behavioral, social learning, interpersonal, and biological (McCann, 1988). The passive expression of aggression may result from formative experiences involving being victimized; being hurt, bullied, or rejected; and feeling helpless, coupled with the active discouragement of open expressions of negative emotions. Thus, this developmental combination may engender passive coping in reaction to feelings of frustration, fear, anger, hostility, and resentment. While the etiology of passive-aggressive behavior is interesting and clinically significant (cf. Cole, 1984), the focus of this chapter will be on the clear delineation of the construct and on strategies for managing the behavior in work settings.

Defining the construct domain for passive-aggression is a daunting task, given its checkered taxonomic history (Millon, 1993; Wetzler & Morey, 1999). It entered the civilian clinical nomenclature when it was included in the *DSM-I* (APA, 1952) to describe a particular personality type that was disruptive to interpersonal relationships.

With each revision, there was considerable discussion about its independence from other personality disorders, culminating in its being relegated (and potentially renamed Negativistic Personality Disorder) to an appendix in the *DSM-IV* concerned with clinical categories requiring "further study." Wetzler and Morey (1999) have argued forcefully for the reinclusion of the PA Personality Disorder as a full-fledged personality disorder in future *DSMs*, and they make the interesting point that its clinical utility may actually have been eroded by careless use of the term in the vernacular as a designation for anyone whose resistiveness engenders frustration in others. This points up the importance of distinguishing between employees who show an inveterate pattern of passive-aggressive behavior and those who, on occasion, may exhibit specific, counterproductive work behaviors that are covert and passive.

Despite the taxonomic controversies, there is considerable evidence that passive-aggressive behavior is common (Neuman & Baron, 1998; Podesta & Sanderson, 1999; Wetzler & Morey, 1999), but underresearched (Blashfield & Intoccia, 2000; Fossati et al., 2000; Sprock & Hunsucker, 1998). In their call for systematic research on workplace aggression, Neuman and Baron (1997) stated that future research must include "a focus on behaviors that are primarily verbal, passive, and indirect" (p. 41). Although they do not specifically refer to it as such, they appear to be describing passive-aggressive behavior. In its current clinical incarnation, PA Personality Disorder is defined in the *DSM-IV* by the following diagnostic criteria:

> A pervasive pattern of negativistic attitudes and passive resistance to demands for adequate performance, beginning by early adulthood and present in a variety of

contexts, as indicated by four (or more) of the following: (1) passively resists fulfilling routine social and occupational tasks; (2) complains of being misunderstood and unappreciated by others is sullen and argumentative; (3) unreasonably criticizes and scorns authority; (4) expresses envy and resentment toward those apparently more fortunate; (5) voices exaggerated and persistent complaints of personal misfortune; and (6) alternates between hostile defiance and contrition. (APA, 1994, p. 734)

In the next section, we will present a framework for distinguishing passive-aggressive behavior from other classes of aggressive behavior.

A FRAMEWORK FOR DISTINGUISHING AGGRESSIVE BEHAVIORS

Aggressive behavior is intended to express hostility and inflict harm that can be either physical or psychological. Expressions of aggression can take many different forms, and these emanate from the interaction of social, situational, and personal factors. Several taxonomic frameworks for delineating aggressive behaviors have been proposed. A classic framework for organizing these varied forms of aggressive behavior was offered by Buss (1961). This three-dimensional framework distinguished between active/passive, direct/indirect, and verbal/physical forms of aggressive behavior. Mantell (1994) proposed a framework for delineating forms of workplace violence that distinguished between covert, overt, and dangerous behaviors. Robinson and Bennett (1995) proposed a framework to delineate various forms of deviant work behavior, including production deviance, property deviance, political deviance, and personal aggression. The first two include behaviors

focused primarily on the organization, whereas the other two are focused on other people in the organization. Neuman and Baron (1998) presented an empirically derived framework that included three dimensions: expressions of hostility, obstructionism, and overt aggression. Finally, Fox and Spector (1999) presented a four-category framework of counterproductive work behaviors that included minor and serious deviance directed at other people or the organization. There are several points of convergence as well as divergence in these frameworks. One point of convergence is that each framework includes passive-aggressive behaviors, but in each case, passive-aggressive behaviors fall into multiple dimensions. Therefore, taxonomically speaking, each framework is limited in its ability to clearly delineate passive-aggressive behavior from other types of aggressive or counterproductive work behaviors.

We propose an amalgamation of these frameworks that we believe is particularly useful for delineating passive-aggression from other forms of aggressive behavior, especially in the workplace. This three-dimensional framework is illustrated in Figure 23.1. To elaborate, behavioral expressions of aggression can be active or passive, overt or covert, and direct or indirect. Active expressions of aggression involve *initiating or instigating* actions intended to harm a person or organizational entity. Passive expressions of aggression involve *withholding* actions with the intention of harming someone or an organizational entity. Overt expressions of aggression are done blatantly, "out in the open," and with relatively less concern for whether the target can identify the perpetrator. Covert expressions of aggression are intended to inflict harm, while concealing from the target the identity or intent of the perpetrator. The direct versus indirect

	ACTIVE	**PASSIVE**
DIRECT/ **INDIRECT**	↓ *Initiating* ↓ *Instigating* ↓ *Prompting*	↓ *Obstinate* ↓ *Inert* ↓ *Unreceptive*

	ACTIVE	**PASSIVE**
OVERT → *Blatant* → *Obvious* → *Unconcealed*	**QUADRANT 1** **ASSAULTING OTHERS** ▪ *Harassing* ▪ *Attacking* ▪ *Assailing*	**QUADRANT 2** **REFUSING TO PERFORM** ▪ *Repudiating* ▪ *Rebuffing* ▪ *Rejecting*
COVERT → *Secret* → *Clandestine* → *Anonymous*	**QUADRANT 3** **SABOTAGING OTHERS** ▪ *Destructive* ▪ *Incapacitating* ▪ *Debilitating*	**QUADRANT 4** **FAILING TO PERFORM** ▪ *Malingering* ▪ *Lethargic* ▪ *Indolent*

Figure 23.1   Typology of Aggressive Behaviors

dimension refers to whether the aggressive behavior is perpetrated directly at the intended target or whether a third party is in some way involved, either as coperpetrator or as covictim.

When mapped in terms of these three dimensions, passive-aggressive behavior can be recognized as passive and covert. This is described in Quadrant 4 in Figure 23.1. A hallmark of passive-aggressive behavior is the withholding of actions in circumstances where such restraint is both harmful to another and difficult to attribute directly to the passive-aggressor. Especially in the workplace, where accountability for behavior often is formalized, the covert nature of passive-aggressive behavior is particularly distinguishing because it shields the passive-aggressive employee from punitive sanctions for his or her passive recalcitrance. Finally, passive-aggression can be either direct or indirect. In other words, the passive withholding of action, in a manner designed to covertly conceal one's insubordination, can be perpetrated by either withholding action to directly harm the target, or involving a third party to indirectly harm the target (e.g., failing to deny false rumors about the target's spouse, or forgetting to tell a coworker about a client's call for assistance).

Referring back to the opening paragraph of this chapter, all of the scenarios described fall outside of Quadrant 4. The episodes involving the altered keyboards, scratched car, computer hacking, purloined document, false rumors, and disgruntled cashier fall into Quadrant 3 because they involve initiating some action, despite the fact that they were enacted covertly to conceal the perpetrators' identity or aggressive intent. Alternatively, if the false rumors were spread in a blatant manner with no regard for concealing the perpetrator's identity, this could easily qualify as Quadrant 1 behavior. The drowning incident involves

Quadrant 1 behavior, despite its ostensible indirectness. More generally, incidents of workplace violence that receive so much media attention (e.g., disgruntled ex-employees shooting coworkers) are examples of Quadrant 1 behavior. Finally, the manager of Whammy Burger behaved passively, but did so in an overt way with no attempt to hide his identity, which qualifies as Quadrant 2 behavior. It is reasonable to suggest that his aggressive intent was hidden covertly behind the organization's policy about the breakfast cut-off. In this case, the behavior could qualify as Quadrant 4 behavior; however, the relative overtness of the manager's behavior is more openly repudiating than is commonly found with passive-aggression. To summarize, some of the scenarios were covert, and some were presumably indirect in their focus, but none involved the deliberate but covert withholding of action that results in harm—a necessary condition to qualify as Quadrant 4 passive-aggression. Clinicians may argue about whether such behaviors are conscious or unconscious, but clearly, three elements are involved: (a) There is a lack of appropriate behavior manifested as a passive withholding of action, (b) the aggressive intent is hidden, and (c) organizational efficiency is degraded. As we will discuss later, the chronicity of such behavior defines the PA personality.

PASSIVE-AGGRESSIVE BEHAVIOR VERSUS PASSIVE-AGGRESSIVE PERSONALITY

Each person develops a characteristic way of perceiving, feeling, thinking, behaving, and interacting with others in the course of his or her daily activities. This characteristic mode of meeting social and vocational demands can result in smooth and effective navigation through life, or it can lead to problematic, dysfunctional, and even harmful consequences for both the individual and those associated with him or her. Personality psychologists and psychiatrists have advanced myriad conceptualizations of how people successfully and unsuccessfully meet life's demands, and this has led to a variety of theories of "normal" personality as well as pathological functioning. Opinions vary considerably about whether disorders of personality represent qualitatively distinct clinical syndromes, or whether they are better viewed as maladaptive variations of behavioral regularities exhibited by "normal" people (cf. Axelrod, Widiger, Trull, & Corbitt, 1997). This debate is an important one, but not central to the goal of this chapter. Our focus is on problematic patterns of behavior that are best described as passive-aggressive. These patterns of behavior can be exhibited chronically, representing seemingly intractable, self-defeating ways of behaving, and thus qualify as a clinically significant personality disorder. On the other hand, they can occur in a more acute or situation-specific way that may not reach a diagnostic clinical threshold, but can nevertheless cause significant disruptions to workplace functioning.

As mentioned earlier, *passive-aggressive* is a clinical term that nevertheless originated within the world of work. Although anyone can exhibit this class of behaviors, individuals with PA Personality Disorder can be expected to exhibit these behaviors frequently, consistently, and inflexibly, resulting in maladaptivity and distress (Widiger, 1998). In a later section, we will describe the situational factors that are conducive to the instigation of passive-aggressive behaviors, but it is important to realize that employees with PA Personality Disorder will consistently exhibit passive-aggressive behaviors independently of these situational forces.

This makes management of their passive-aggression much more challenging than if it occurs infrequently or only under specific and identifiable circumstances.

IDENTIFYING THE PASSIVE-AGGRESSIVE PERSONALITY

Behaviors in the workplace that are both passive and covert (i.e., Quadrant 4) could be evinced by almost any employee under circumstances conducive to expressing retaliatory hostility in a manner that is indirect and not readily detectable. Under such conditions, the behavior is usually conscious and deliberate. For example, a salesperson who is compelled to wait on too many customers might discourage purchases by not volunteering relevant product information to promote a sale. Conversely, a coworker may habitually take a message and "forget" to relay it to the intended recipient, thus disrupting an important information flow. A coworker who consistently avoids interactions with certain others through absence, silence, and avoidance, thus creating work inefficiency, also may be exhibiting chronic passive-aggression. As a first clue, it is important to look for a general pattern of passivity. The employee who approaches many or most work situations with a passive, "It doesn't matter to me" style, or who is overly conciliatory and seldom asserts a strong personal opinion, may be demonstrating passive-aggressive behavior. This also commonly covaries with exhortations about feeling misunderstood or unappreciated. Other indications that an employee may prefer passive-aggressive strategies include the excessive generalizing and stereotyping of authority figures in a contemptuous way (Waddell, 1992).

Nearly everyone exhibits passive-aggressive behaviors occasionally, such as neglecting to return a sensitive phone call or procrastinating before responding to someone's request. Such behaviors, of course, can be more a result of low conscientiousness than hidden hostility, but the behavior manifested by the bona fide passive-aggressive personality is frequent and consistent. The critical feature of the PA employee's behavior, as it manifests in the workplace, is chronicity. That is, the PA employee is compelled to exhibit covert and passive hostility regardless of the work environment. This creates a problematic situation because proactive supervisors and managers may mistakenly apply customary work-based solutions in an attempt to resolve PA employee issues, resulting in frustration and wasted time and energy. Consequently, the key to dealing with PA employees is, first and foremost, identification. It is crucial, in attempting to manage a PA employee, to avoid confusing the genuine personality disorder with employees who are passive-aggressive only occasionally and/or are reacting to work conditions that might reasonably be expected to elicit such behaviors.

Frequency studies and descriptions of the PA personality vary depending on which of the five editions of the *DSM* are used to model the disorder. Millon (1993) has acknowledged the high incidence of the PA personality diagnosis compared to other personality disorders, and Clay, Hultquist, and Quinn (1994) assert that "passive-aggressive tendencies are more likely to be exhibited in the workplace than any other setting" (p. 41). Reports of the base rate for PA personalities in clinical samples have varied between 2% and 10% (Fossati et al., 2000). In one study of "healthy" volunteers and another of nonclinical university students, PA personality diagnoses were the most common of the Axis II disorders (Berman et al., 1998; Stern, Kim, Trull,

Scarpa, & Pilkonis, 2000). Studies of workplace aggression have shown that passive-aggression is significantly more prevalent than active aggression (Baron & Neuman, 1996). Finally, a sample of managers reported that passive forms of aggression significantly outnumbered active forms of aggression following the receipt of negative feedback (Geddes & Baron, 1997). Therefore, it is reasonable to assume that managers are likely to be confronted with problems attributable to the PA employee.

Passive-aggressive personalities have been described as argumentative, complaining, critical, dawdling, defiant, destructive, helpless, immature, inadequate, inefficient, irritable, negative, obstructionist, pouting, procrastinating, resistive, sullen, stubborn, and sulking. Other descriptors include overly conforming, passing the buck, playing dumb, stalling, stonewalling, and scapegoating (Ashforth & Lee, 1990). Although any of the above may apply to the individual case, clearly, a more concise, nuclear definition of the PA employee's behavior pattern would be helpful in identifying the disorder. Accordingly, along with the current *DSM-IV* criteria presented earlier, we recommend the more recent definition supplied by Wetzler and Morey (1999), which focuses on the unwillingness to fulfill expectations: "Passive-aggressive individuals are obstructionists who try to frustrate and block progress, taking on more and more responsibilities until their life is nothing but unfinished business. . . . They are masters of mixed messages and nonspecific suggestions" (p. 57). "Unwillingness" implies an ingrained attitude, "expectations" ties the behavior directly to the work setting, and "unfinished business" suggests unacceptable behavior that is both covert and passive. Thus, our own analysis of the PA employee as exhibiting chronic Quadrant 4 behavior is consistent with current definitions.

Examining and contrasting Quadrants 1 and 4 in Figure 23.1 can help elucidate the behavior of the PA employee. An isolated, overt, and active expression of hostility, such as smashing a piece of machinery in a fit of rage, is just the opposite of the habitual, covert, and passive manifestation of anger evinced by the PA employee, such as failing to service the equipment properly. For the sake of completeness, another dimension could be added to Figure 23.1 indicating whether a behavior was rare or habitual. Such a paradigm would provide a more comprehensive classification of hostile behaviors in the workplace; but inasmuch as overt, active displays of anger would hardly be tolerated to the point of becoming frequent, expanding the simpler eight-cell table to accommodate frequency seems unnecessary. Managers simply should keep in mind that the PA personality will demonstrate chronic Quadrant 4 behavior.

Some of the descriptors commonly applied to PA employees, such as "conflicted," "ambivalent," and "helpless," are clinical terms that most managers cannot be expected to assimilate in attempting to identify the PA employee. Similarly, whether the PA employee's behavior is unconsciously motivated is not a workplace issue. Moreover, although the PA employee inevitably induces frustration in coworkers and supervisors, interpersonal difficulties are earmarks of other clinical syndromes as well and cannot be considered definitive. The position taken here, based on workplace utility, is that in attempting to identify the PA employee, the manager should document that the employee's inefficient behavior is not due to a lack of ability, but rather, to chronic acts of hostility that are both covert and passive.

PASSIVE-AGGRESSION VERSUS COVERT, ACTIVE AGGRESSION

It is not uncommon for people to confuse passive-aggression with other covert forms of aggression. As discussed earlier, in its traditional clinical form, passive-aggression involves withholding positive behavior, rather than actively exhibiting negative behavior in response to a situation. Confusion can arise when acts of aggression are surreptitiously perpetrated, because part of the motivation may be the same. Passive-aggression is intended to be covert in that the perpetrator is motivated to conceal the aggression from others. Active, but covert, aggression is different in that the perpetrator is motivated to conceal his or her identity, but not the aggressive act. This distinction is portrayed in Figure 23.1 contrasting Quadrants 3 and 4. Spreading malicious rumors, corrupting a coworker's hard drive, and stealing or damaging property is intended to be covert, but usually is an active expression of aggression (generally labeled sabotage), and therefore belongs in Quadrant 3. Passive, overt forms of aggression also can be confused with passive-aggression (Quadrant 2 vs. Quadrant 4). Both forms of aggression involve obstinance and resistance, but Quadrant 2 behaviors are exhibited with little concern for concealing the intent. A sit-down strike, a deliberate work slowdown, or a flat rejection of a request is a relatively passive response to some provocation, but it is more overt than passive-aggression.

SITUATIONAL DETERMINANTS OF PASSIVE-AGGRESSIVE BEHAVIOR

A variety of situational factors are likely to foster passive reactions to feelings of anger and hostility. Any situation where frustrating or threatening events occur (e.g., virtually any workplace), combined with the perceived likelihood of being punished or sanctioned for aggressive behavior, is conducive to passive-aggression. Fox and Spector (1999) found strong relationships between situational constraints on performance and incidence of a variety of passive-aggressive behaviors, such as ignoring one's boss, working slowly despite a need for productivity, and being purposely tardy for work. They also found negative relationships between beliefs about the likelihood of being punished and the incidence of passive-aggressive behaviors. Geddes and Baron (1997) pointed out that passive forms of aggression are more likely than active aggression when there is an expectation of continued contact with the victim, or the presence of potential witnesses is greater.

Passive-aggression can occur anywhere individuals misconstrue a personal relationship as a struggle in which they have relatively less power, leaving them vulnerable to punitive sanctions or retaliation. Thus, it is not uncommon that "coworkers and bosses are functionally transformed into master sergeants and dictators" (Wetzler & Morey, 1999, p. 57). The formal authority and legitimate power vested in managers is an integral part of the fuel mix for passive-aggression. Therefore, any group or organization with hierarchical power differentials will likely engender some passive-aggressive behavior.

Supervisor characteristics can create conditions conducive to passive-aggressive behavior. For example, a capable subordinate assigned to a less competent or overly controlling supervisor can experience significant frustration and potential for conflict. One way to oppose authority in this situation is to exhibit forms of passive-aggression

(Lowman, 1993). Supervisors who rely primarily on autocratic, dominating, and aggressive styles will more likely evoke passive-aggression. On the other hand, laissez-faire leaders, by not enforcing accountability for performance, can enable the PA employee to mistreat coworkers. An additional consideration is authoritative behavior that is perceived to be inappropriate or unfair (Podesta & Sanderson, 1999). In fact, "a growing body of evidence suggests that individuals' perceptions that they have been treated unfairly often play a key role in workplace aggression" (Neuman & Baron, 1998, p. 412). Interpersonal justice and informational justice are important for creating a work environment that deemphasizes "brute" authority and replaces it with a more participatory style of supervision (Neuman & Baron, 1997).

All organizations require coordination of members' activities, and this coordination implies control. Coordination can derive either from standardized policies and procedures or from direct supervision (Mintzberg, 1989). Any organization that is more heavily reliant on direct supervisory control (e.g., a bureaucratic or mechanistic organization) is more likely to promote a culture emphasizing authoritative control. As implied above, this environment is more likely to evoke the frustration and hostility that fuels the potential for passive-aggressive behavior. Organizations structured in a mechanistic or bureaucratic way are most likely to engender not only passive-aggression, but also other covert forms of more active aggression, such as sabotage (Quadrant 3). For example, the term *Lordstown Syndrome* was coined to describe the deliberate sabotage of a General Motors assembly line (Rothschild, 1973). The sabotaging of automobiles on the production line was thought to be a manifestation of widespread worker dissatisfaction and anger about work conditions devoid of opportunities for personal autonomy and growth.

Jobs for which there are few standard operating procedures or well-defined standards of performance are fertile ground for passive-aggressive behavior. These types of jobs are increasingly prevalent (Mintzberg, 1989), as flatter and more organic organizational structures evolve to accommodate the rapid change that is occurring in most industries. Latitude and autonomy in how to perform one's job can provide a "discretionary screen" behind which the PA employee can hide. Similarly, any work setting where job security is emphasized (e.g., strong labor union, academic tenure, or a notable Title VII litigation history) can free the PA employee to obstruct smooth functioning with relative impunity.

An organization's culture and climate include shared perceptions and norms about appropriate ways of dealing with frustration, anger, and job dissatisfaction. Some organizations are more tolerant of overt expressions of aggression, whereas others have zero tolerance for such expressions. In the former case, employees in aggression-tolerant or contentious cultures can actually believe that certain forms of aggression are job-related and appropriate because "everyone does it." This can include active and passive expressions of aggression. In the latter culture, one can expect more frequent passive expressions of aggression, because the more active and overt forms would be punished. More generally, organizations can expect less counterproductive passive-aggression when cultural values and management behavior emphasize fairness, accountability for performance, employee trust and empowerment, safety, and security (Boye & Jones, 1997).

CONSEQUENCES OF PASSIVE-AGGRESSION IN THE WORKPLACE

In the best case, the PA employee merely slows work processes. In the worst case, he or she paralyzes workflows, and this can cause critical financial and psychological consequences when real time constraints and deadlines are looming. Moreover, these consequences are difficult to forecast because PA employees can be intermittent in their passive expressions of aggression. They can time their lethargy to cause maximal disruption of others' work lives. Although the PA employee can have systemic negative effects for an organization, it might be helpful to briefly address the consequences of passive-aggression for likely targets in an organization.

Consequences for Coworkers

Passive-aggressive employees are a negative interpersonal force in the workplace. They verbalize discontent and may breed contempt for authority. They have volatile interpersonal relationships with coworkers, and they can bring issues of fairness and intraorganizational equity to the fore. For example, a PA employee who routinely fails to attend meetings on time, is frequently tardy or absent, or who never volunteers for special duties can be instrumental in shaping the norms of an organization's or unit's culture. This can cause coworkers to either diminish their contributions to the organization or perceive inequity in their relationship with the organization. Recall that perceptions of unfairness and inequity can fuel further aggression, so that a passive-aggressive contagion can arise. The potential for these workplace disruptions is exacerbated by the fact that the majority of passive-aggressive behaviors in the workplace are directed against coworkers rather than supervisors or subordinates (Baron & Neuman, 1998).

Consequences for Supervisors

The supervisor of a PA employee can be seduced into dysfunctional "micromanaging," playing a cat-and-mouse game centered on catching the PA employee in an act of dereliction, while being presented with myriad excuses and explanations for each occurrence that often pass the "smell test." This can be a momentous drain on a supervisor's time and energy. Managers can be drawn into the "easier to do it myself" trap that, in effect, rewards PA employees for their subversions and adds job demands to an already hectic agenda. Monitoring and sanctioning the PA employee can be effective for alleviating problems, but one procedural misstep can result in the PA employee filing a grievance or otherwise calling into question the propriety of the supervisor's management skills. Therefore, chronic passive-aggression can cause some supervisors to actually insulate the PA employee from normal job demands similar to the coddling of a difficult child. The trap here is that it is perceived as easier to placate rather than confront the resistance. This also can lead to coworker perceptions of inequity because of unequal workloads.

Consequences for the Organization

The obstructions and work slowdowns orchestrated by the PA employee are obvious drains on any organization, but more pernicious implications of passive-aggression exist. As organizations become increasingly organic and unstructured to cope with rapid change, they are increasingly interested in fostering employees' tendencies to identify situations requiring one to go above and beyond the call of duty or to perform nonroutine tasks that are outside a formal job description. Thus, organizations are increasingly interested in promoting a total quality management philosophy that depends on voluntary and informal contributions. This voluntary performance of organization-enhancing tasks is often labeled organizational citizenship (Van Dyne, Graham, & Dienesch, 1994). Passive-aggressiveness may take a significant toll on the incidence of organizational citizenship or extrarole behaviors. Because of the inherently discretionary nature of these types of behaviors, employee hostility can be directed toward *not* exhibiting these behaviors, with little concern on the employees' part for being held specifically accountable. For example, if an employee is walking toward the lunchroom and notices a malfunctioning piece of equipment (e.g., laser printer out of paper, or hydraulic arm leaking fluid), there is considerable latitude in how to behave. A passive-aggressive act would be to deliberately ignore the defect and proceed to lunch. If questioned later about the situation, the employee can easily claim that he or she had not observed the problem, or even that he or she is not responsible for the equipment's maintenance. The intentional withholding of informal contributions, in the aggregate, can be quite costly to an organization.

MANAGING THE PASSIVE-AGGRESSIVE PERSONALITY IN THE WORKPLACE

Prior to official inclusion in the *DSM-I*, the characterological structure of individuals who were later to be named passive-aggressive was discussed in the psychoanalytical literature, and it was acknowledged that such patients are difficult to treat. Today, although there are no reported outcome studies for PA employees seen for psychotherapy, the consensus is that treatment is arduous, and that even after many sessions, major personality changes cannot be anticipated. Therefore, most health maintenance organizations would be reluctant to sanction long-term psychotherapy for a PA employee, and furthermore, PA employees could be expected to resist such referrals and/or engage disingenuously in a therapeutic relationship as yet another expression of passive-aggressiveness. For these reasons, recommendations for dealing with the PA employee in the workplace have focused on developing on-the-job coping strategies for supervisors and managers rather than advocating referrals to a psychologist or psychiatrist (Connor, 1991).

In common with the psychiatric literature, there is consensus on how to deal with PA employees, but no corroborating empirical research. These workplace recommendations possess face validity inasmuch as they are based on what is known about the PA employee vis-à-vis the constraints imposed by a work environment. However, it must be acknowledged that without hard data, there is no assurance concerning the efficacy of the advice tendered.

Recommendations concerning the management of the PA employee can be organized into six areas: identification, documentation, presentation, remediation, verification, and evaluation. These recommended procedures are presented as sequential steps, but they overlap, and, depending upon the specific circumstances, short-circuiting can reasonably occur. For example, without proper documentation, it may be impossible to conduct remediation; or if the employee rejects the presentation, it may be advisable to jump ahead to the evaluation phase and consider termination of employment.

Identification. Identification has been treated in an earlier section, but its importance cannot be overemphasized, and many authors devote the lion's share of their advice to identifying the PA employee. To iterate, the position offered here is that managers are not clinicians and should eschew psychodynamic conceptualizations in favor of a work-oriented approach that focuses on the PA employee's efficiency-reducing pattern of hostile behavior.

Documentation. Documenting the PA employee's negative work performance is important for two reasons. First, should the employee choose to challenge punitive actions taken by the supervisor, necessary back-up material would be available to justify organizational decisions. Passive-aggressive personalities are not loath to pursue legal channels to establish their "innocence," and because their behavior is covert, they take refuge behind protective rules and regulations.

Second, a typical passive-aggressive tactic is to deny guilt, and without documentation, a manager may find it impossible to move the employee into the presentation phase. The literature is rife with anecdotes about well-intentioned managers being driven to distraction by employees who smile sweetly, adopt a hurt expression, and refuse to recognize that they have done anything wrong, thus providing the manager with a good example of passive-aggressive behavior, but avoiding a resolution of the problem.

Documentation should be objective and specific, referring to behaviors, incidents, and the consequences for management and the broader organization. The PA employee has to be shown that there is a substantial record of misbehavior that cannot be evaded. This "disconfirmation" of the PA employee's beliefs and perceptions is an important part of motivating change

(McIlduff & Coghlan, 2000), and it may require some challenging of negative behaviors, thoughts, and restrictive attitudes. Logs showing that a passive-aggressive secretary consistently types fewer letters than other office pool personnel or repair invoices indicating that the lathe of a passive-aggressive machinist has a higher-than-average rate of malfunctioning are examples of the type of record keeping that will pin down the PA employee.

It is at the documentation phase that it is likely to dawn on managers that PA employees exact a heavy toll on their time and energy. This is best viewed as part of the job of being a manager. Supervisors may feel that they have better things to do, but they must get used to the idea that dealing effectively with PA employees is time-consuming and energy draining.

Presentation. Once the PA employee's misbehavior has been documented appropriately, the manager can proceed to the next stage—presenting the information in a manner that is most likely to be accepted and to lead to constructive change. The watchwords are "objectivity" and "minimization of perceived threat." The manager's demeanor should be unemotional, and documentation should be presented in a straightforward manner, based on facts as opposed to rumors or innuendos. As far as possible, a confrontational atmosphere should be avoided, and the employee should not be blamed for the behaviors. The feedback should be perceived as considerate in tone, timely, and focused on constructive goals for change (Geddes & Baron, 1997). Getting an employee to agree that there is a need for performance improvement is considered by some to be the Achilles' heel of management coaching (Phillips, 1998), and passive-aggressive personalities are adept at shirking

responsibility, thereby arousing ire in their supervisors (Trimpey & Davidson, 1994). If a manager gets angry, the PA employee has won a victory. The manager should present the facts calmly, avoid recriminations, and, it is hoped, persuade the employee to accept the next phase—remediation. It may be helpful to pay close attention to the employee's reactions, his or her perception of the situation, and expressed opinions about any proposed remediation. It is particularly helpful to create "psychological safety" to mitigate defensive resistance as much as possible (McIlduff & Coghlan, 2000). If presentation fails and the employee adamantly refuses to accept responsibility for subpar performance, the manager has the option of going directly to the evaluation phase. Not all negotiations are successful, and the manager, having done his or her best, should prepare to deal more punitively with the intractable employee.

Remediation. It is not necessary for the employee to admit wrongdoing. As long as he or she is willing to accept the facts as presented and modify behavior accordingly, it is possible to move to the remedial phase. In remediation, it is best to deal with a narrow set of behaviors that is job relevant and can be monitored closely. It is likely that the PA employee has evinced an array of passive-aggressive behaviors that have irritated others and reduced efficiency, but they cannot all be attacked at once. Furthermore, it is advisable to spell out task requirements in excruciating detail. Passive-aggressive personalities are masters at doing only what they are told and, by not displaying initiative, subtly sabotaging the attainment of work objectives. The employee undergoing remediation should understand fully what is expected and how successful performance will be measured.

Verification. Some authorities recommend a written contract as part of the verification process. Such agreements, if undertaken, should (probably) be executed with the formal participation of an HR representative to prevent the PA employee from personally interpreting the contract in a uniquely idiosyncratic way. In order for verification to be effective, an objective monitoring system must be set up that indicates clearly whether commitments are being met (Wormald, 1997). Logs, checklists, tally sheets, and the like are preferable. Times and durations of coffee breaks, number of nondefective units built, and frequency of customer complaints are examples of verifications that are both objective and job-related. Obviously, specific individuals must be assigned to monitor the verification process, providing another illustration of how PA employees drain off resources that could otherwise be used more productively.

Evaluation. Ideally, evaluation should take place after the employee has complied successfully with the verification process. At that point, a decision can be made about whether to attempt to alter another set of behaviors. If so, presentation and verification should be reinstituted. This step should not be taken lightly. Having survived one hurdle, a PA employee could easily become querulous and sulky, claiming victimization if subjected to another round of monitoring. If the initial behavioral modification is sufficient for at least minimal job performance, it may be prudent to rest content with what has been achieved.

Evaluation can be conducted at any point in the employee's career. In fact, inasmuch as a PA employee will always find ways to express hostility indirectly, the manager must be consistently vigilant. Evaluation also furnishes opportunities for innovative solutions. For example, an employee with a history of disruptive interpersonal relationships could be considered for transfer to a job where he or she can function in relative isolation. Presentation should precede any contemplated workplace change, however, and performance verification of any new tasks is advisable.

The PA employee poses a challenge to the manager's equanimity, patience, and creativity as well as his or her time and energy. Success is never guaranteed; nevertheless, it is possible to modify the PA employee's behavior so that his or her performance is at least acceptable. The supervisor of a PA employee is advised to (a) remain objective and maintain an emotional distance from the employee; (b) lower expectations; (c) accept infringements on one's time and energy; and (d) focus on achieving circumscribed, realistic, job-relevant behavior modifications.

SUMMARY AND CONCLUSIONS

Passive-aggressive behavior in the workplace represents harmful expressions of hostility that are both passive (i.e., withholding of a more positive action) and covert (i.e., concealed behind a façade of innocence). Workers who believe that they are being treated unfairly may deliberately and consciously express retaliatory PA behaviors. Such reactions are apt to be provoked by authoritarian and/or bureaucratic work environments. On the other hand, either consciously or unconsciously, the PA personality displays a chronic pattern of PA behavior regardless of the circumstances. Therefore, it is essential to differentiate between PA behaviors that may, in part, reflect structural problems in the organization and those mainly attributable to the personality of the PA employee.

If a PA employee has been identified properly, the manager should attempt to deal objectively and nonaccusingly with the poor work performance. It is important to maintain relevant, job-related records in order to document derelict past performance and, it is hoped, substantiate subsequent improvement. The manager should not try to galvanize a PA personality into becoming an enthusiastic, proactive employee but should instead strive to bring about discrete and measurable behavioral changes indicative of tolerable work performance.

REFERENCES

American Psychiatric Association. (1952). *Diagnostic and statistical manual of mental disorders.* Washington, DC: Author.

American Psychiatric Association. (1994). *Diagnostic and statistical manual of mental disorders* (4th ed.). Washington, DC: Author.

Ashforth, B., & Lee, R. (1990). Defensive behavior in organizations: A preliminary model. *Human Relations, 43,* 621-648.

Axelrod, S. R., Widiger, T. A., Trull, T. J., & Corbitt, E. M. (1997). Relations of five-factor model antagonism facets with personality disorder symptomatology. *Journal of Personality Assessment, 69,* 297-313.

Baron, R. A., & Neuman, J. H. (1996). Workplace violence and workplace aggression: Evidence on their relative frequency and potential causes. *Aggressive Behavior, 22,* 161-173.

Baron, R. A., & Neuman, J. H. (1998). Workplace aggression—The iceberg beneath the tip of workplace violence: Evidence of its forms, frequency, and targets. *Public Administration Quarterly, 21,* 446-464.

Berman, M. E., Fallon, A. E., & Coccaro, E. F. (1998). The relationship between personality psychopathology and aggressive behavior in research volunteers. *Journal of Abnormal Psychology, 107,* 651-658.

Blashfield, R. K., & Intoccia, V. (2000). Growth of the literature on the topic of personality disorders. *American Journal of Psychiatry, 157,* 472-473.

Boye, M. W., & Jones, J. W. (1997). Organizational culture and employee counterproductivity. In R. A. Giacalone & J. Greenberg (Eds.), *Antisocial behavior in organizations.* Thousand Oaks, CA: Sage.

Buss, A. H. (1961). *The psychology of aggression.* New York: Wiley.

Cascio, W. F. (1993). Downsizing: What do we know? What have we learned? *Academy of Management Executive, 7,* 95-104.

Clay, J. A., Hultquist, C. M., & Quinn, R. A. (1994, Spring). Who's managing whom? *Public Manager,* pp. 41-43.

Cole, M. (1984). How to make a person passive-aggressive or the power struggle game. *Transactional Analysis Journal, 14,* 191-194.

Connor, J. C. (1991, November). Managing passive-aggressive people. *HRMagazine,* pp. 74-78.

Daw, J. (2001). Road rage, air rage, and now "desk rage." *Monitor on Psychology, 32,* 52-54.

Fossati, A., Maffei, C., Bagnato, M., Donati, D., Donini, M., Fiorilli, M., & Novella, L. (2000). A psychometric study of *DSM-IV* passive-aggressive (negativistic) personality disorder criteria. *Journal of Personality Disorders, 14,* 72-83.

Fox, S., & Spector, P. E. (1999). A model of work frustration-aggression. *Journal of Organizational Behavior, 20,* 915-931.

Gaines, L. (1996, March/April). Surviving those passive-aggressive employees. *Executive Female,* pp. 13-16.

Geddes, D., & Baron, R. A. (1997). Workplace aggression as a consequence of negative performance feedback. *Management Communication Quarterly, 10,* 433-454.

Lowman, R. L. (1993). *Counseling and psychotherapy of work dysfunctions.* Washington, DC: American Psychological Association.

Mantell, M. (1994). *Ticking bombs: Defusing violence in the workplace.* Burr Ridge, IL: Irwin.

McCann, J. T. (1988). Passive-aggressive personality disorder: A review. *Journal of Personality Disorders, 2,* 170-179.

McIlduff, E., & Coghlan, D. (2000). Understanding and contending with passive-aggressive behavior in teams and organizations. *Journal of Managerial Psychology, 15,* 716-736.

Millon, T. (1993). Negativistic (passive-aggressive) personality disorder. *Journal of Personality Disorders, 7,* 78-85.

Mintzberg, H. (1989). *Mintzberg on management.* New York: Free Press.

Neuman, J. H., & Baron, R. A. (1997). Aggression in the workplace. In R. A. Giacalone & J. Greenberg (Eds.), *Antisocial behavior in organizations.* Thousand Oaks, CA: Sage.

Neuman, J. H., & Baron, R. A. (1998). Workplace violence and workplace aggression: Evidence concerning specific forms, potential causes, and preferred targets. *Journal of Management, 24,* 391-419.

Phillips, K. R. (1998, March). The Achilles' heel of coaching. *Training and Development,* pp. 41-44.

Podesta, C., & Sanderson, V. (1999). *Life would be easy if it weren't for other people.* Thousand Oaks, CA: Corwin.

Robinson, S. L., & Bennett, R. J. (1995). A typology of deviant workplace behaviors: A multidimensional scaling study. *Academy of Management Journal, 38,* 555-572.

Rothschild, E. (1973). *Paradise lost: The decline of the auto-industrial age.* New York: Random House.

Sprock, J., & Hunsucker, L. (1998). Symptoms of prototypic patients with passive-aggressive personality disorder: *DSM-IIIR* versus *DSM-IV* negativistic. *Comprehensive Psychiatry, 39,* 287-295.

Stern, B. L., Kim, Y., Trull, T. J., Scarpa, A., & Pilkonis, P. (2000). Inventory of Interpersonal Problems personality disorder scales: Operating characteristics and confirmatory factor analysis in nonclinical samples. *Journal of Personality Assessment, 74,* 459-471.

Trimpey, M., & Davidson, S. (1994). Chaos, perfectionism, and sabotage: Personality disorders in the workplace. *Issues in Mental Health Nursing, 15,* 27-36.

Van Dyne, L., Graham, J. W., & Dienesch, R. M. (1994). Organizational citizenship behavior: Construct redefinition, measurement, and validation. *Academy of Management Journal, 37,* 765-802.

Waddell, J. R. (1992, March). Rebel without a job. *Supervision,* pp. 3-5.

Wetzler, S., & Morey, L. C. (1999). Passive-aggressive personality disorder: The demise of a syndrome. *Psychiatry, 62,* 49-59.

Widiger, T. A. (1998). Personality disorders. In D. F. Barone, M. Hersen, & V. B. Van Hasselt (Eds.), *Advanced personality.* New York: Plenum.

Wormald, K. (1997). Back stabbers. *Office Systems, 14,* 30-32.

Part V

ORGANIZATIONAL PRACTICE AND MENTAL HEALTH

Dysfunctional Behavior in the Workplace and Organizational Design, Climate, and Culture

DANIEL J. SVYANTEK
LINDA L. BROWN

The organizational behavior literature has shown a disproportionate emphasis on desirable phenomena (such as improved productivity or organizational citizenship behaviors) as topics of research (Robinson & Bennett, 1995). However, dysfunctional employee behavior may be responsible for millions, if not billions, of dollars in losses to organizations and is potentially dangerous to employees within the organization (Robinson & Bennett, 1995).

These concerns have led to a growth in research on dysfunctional behavior in the workplace (Griffin, O'Leary-Kelly, & Collins, 1998). Much of this research has focused on how individual differences in employees relate to dysfunctional behavior. Griffin et al. (1998), for example, have developed a model of the dynamics of dysfunctional behavior in organizations that is concerned with individual differences and

individual pathologies as antecedents of behavior. This model, however, also includes organizational characteristics (e.g., norms, culture, reward, and control systems) as potential influences on employee behavior in general. A clearer understanding of how organization-level variables affect dysfunctional behavior in the workplace is needed.

Explaining complex human behavior requires consideration of person-by-situation interactions (Mischel, 1996). The context in which an individual resides is seen as interacting with that individual to produce behavior. Here, the organizational context is of interest. The behaviors exhibited in a situation have an adaptive function (Morris, 1988). The degree to which behavior is adaptive, however, is defined relative to the situation. Therefore, the context and individuals within it must be considered together in understanding a behavior (whether it be positive or dysfunctional).

This chapter proposes that integration of concepts derived from organizational theory will aid understanding of why dysfunctional behavior occurs. *Organizational theory* may be defined as the study of (a) how organizations structure themselves and function internally, and (b) how organizations are affected by the environment in which they operate (Morgan, 1998). This chapter is concerned with how organizations structure themselves and function internally. The chapter will investigate how organizations define the context in which workplace behavior, including that which is pathological and disruptive, occurs, and how the organizational context can support dysfunctional behavior.

ORGANIZATIONAL CONTEXTS AND EMPLOYEE BEHAVIOR

Four primary organization-level variables help define the context of workplace behavior: organizational structure, organizational culture, organizational climate, and organizational design. *Organizational structure* refers to the formal system of task and authority relationships within an organization (Morgan, 1998). This variable is often defined as the "organizational chart," although it should be recognized that power relationships, political structures, and so on are often not reflected in an organizational chart. Organizational structure is concerned with how organizational members coordinate their actions and use resources to achieve organizational goals. *Organizational culture* may be defined as a set of shared values and norms, held by employees, that guides employees' interactions with peers, management, and clients/customers (Morgan, 1998). *Organizational climate* is more behaviorally oriented in that climates for safety or service, for example, may be

found in the workplace (Schneider, 2000). These climates represent the specific patterns of interactions and behaviors that support safety or service in the organization. *Organizational design* is the process through which an organization's administration manages organizational structure, culture, and climate to control the activities necessary to meet the organization's goals (Morgan, 1998).

Taken together, these variables help define the context in which workplace behavior occurs. Organizational culture is proposed as the antecedent, causal element for organizational structure, climate, and design. A major reason for formation of organizational culture is the creation of social order (Trice & Beyer, 1993). Organizational culture allows recurrent behavior patterns among people to develop within organizations. These patterns form the basis of predictable interactions within an organization. Therefore, the remainder of this chapter will focus on how organizational culture affects other organization-level variables and dysfunctional behavior in the workplace.

Organizational Culture: The Primary Antecedent of Behavior in Organizations

Organizational culture provides employees with contextual information. Namenwirth and Weber (1987) propose that culture serves four purposes for any social group. These purposes define (a) what it means to be a member of the group, (b) social and economic justice within the group, (c) how the elements of the group are organized to produce a socially "good" group, and (d) how the group makes the materials or services it was formed to produce.

Namenwirth and Weber's (1987) first three purposes are linked closely to how a social group integrates individual members in the social system. These three purposes provide group members with information on what the valued behaviors are within a social situation. The last purpose of the cultural system is concerned with adaptation of the social group to its external environment. The integration and adaptation functions of the culture may not be directly related (Svyantek, 1997; Svyantek & Brown, 2000). Organizational cultures may be (a) integrated in a satisfying manner for employees, and productive; (b) integrated in a satisfying manner for employees, and nonproductive; (c) integrated in a nonsatisfying manner for employees, and productive; or (d) integrated in a nonsatisfying manner for employees, and nonproductive. We propose that, for purposes of predicting dysfunctional behavior within an organization, that the integration function is most critical. Therefore, the focus of this chapter is on the first three purposes and the internal functioning of the organization.

Organizational culture has been defined in a variety of ways. Deal and Kennedy (1982) view culture as the dominant values espoused by an organization. Organizational culture has been defined as the philosophy that guides organizational policy (Ouchi, 1981; Pascale & Athos, 1981). These definitions tap into parts of the essence of organizational culture, yet none of them captures the full picture of organizational culture because none provides a multidimensional, multilevel definition of organizational culture (Nahavandi & Malekzadeh, 1988).

Schein's (1985) model of the three levels of organizational culture is a multidimensional, multilevel definition of culture. First, the most superficial or visible level of culture is artifacts and creations: These represent the physical and social environment of the social situation. The second level of culture is values, norms, and attitudes, or a sense of what "ought to be." Finally, at the deepest level lie the unconscious assumptions held uniformly by all members of the culture. It is these unconscious assumptions that make up the true culture of an organization. Therefore, organizational culture is the antecedent of other organization-level variables.

Schein (1985) proposed that organizational founder(s) are the primary source(s) of the values that define organizational culture. These values, in turn, are the primary guides for the later development of organizational structure, climate, and design as the organization matures. Organizational culture, once established by the founder(s), is maintained over time through organizational socialization practices to assimilate newcomers into the organization. Therefore, organizational culture may be highly resistant to change and "frozen" in the sense that the assumptions and beliefs established by the founder(s) are maintained, although change may be required to improve organizational effectiveness. Organizational culture may be so embedded in the people, processes, and relationships that change is resisted even as the organizational culture ceases to be relevant in a changing environment (Schein, 1985).

For example, Moch and Bartunek (1990) provide an extensive case study of an organizational culture change effort that was designed to institute a more participative working style in an organization with an existing autocratic working style. This effort failed. Employee cognitive frameworks defining organizational culture were found to be resistant to change on a deep level. Surface elements related to them could be changed slightly as long as the changes did not violate beliefs held at the deep level. Attempts at deep-level change were strongly, and successfully, resisted by organizational members. Therefore, organizational culture both maintains itself across time and influences the behavior of individuals within an organization. The mechanisms by which this maintenance and influence occur are described in the next two sections.

Maintenance of Organizational Culture Across Time

The maintenance of organizational culture across time is an interaction process between individual employees and the values that define an organizational culture. Buss (1987) presented a model of individual-social situation interaction that shows how cultural value systems may develop and maintain themselves. Buss proposes that people make selections about their social environment daily. Selection involves the active seeking of some social situations and the avoidance of others by individuals. Selection points are seen as decision nodes: They direct individuals down one "path" of the social environment and preempt other paths. The selection of paths to follow is hypothesized to be based primarily on personality characteristics of individuals. Therefore, some personality types will actively select a particular social environment. Other personality types will avoid the same environment.

Buss's (1987) model is akin to two organizational behavior concepts: person-organization fit and the Attraction-Selection-Attrition (ASA) model. Person-organization fit has been defined as "the congruence between patterns of organizational values and patterns of individual values, defined here as what an individual values in an organization, such as being team-oriented or innovative" (Chatman, 1991, p. 459). The emphasis here is on the match of an individual's values, when considered along with the value system in a specific organizational context, and the potential effects that that match (or lack of match) has on that individual's subsequent behavior and attitudes.

Person-organization fit has been shown to be related to a number of organizational variables, including (a) job choice decisions by organizational applicants (Cable & Judge, 1996); (b) organizational attraction of applicants (Judge & Cable, 1997); (c) selection decisions made by recruitment interviewers (Cable & Judge, 1997); (d) employee job satisfaction, job tenure, and career success (Bretz & Judge, 1994); and (e) employee's level of task and organizational citizenship performance (Goodman & Svyantek, 1999).

The process by which person-organization fit may come to maintain an organizational climate across time is illustrated in the ASA model (Schneider, 1987a, 1987b; Schneider, Goldstein, & Smith, 1995). Schneider (1987b) proposed that "attributes of people, not the nature of the external environment, or organizational technology, or organizational structure, are the fundamental determinants of organizational behavior" (i.e., "the people make the place") (p. 437). The ASA framework is a mechanism for explaining homogeneity of organizational-level variables such as organizational culture and organizational climate. Schneider (1987a) stated that such homogeneity is due to three main processes. First, it occurs because people are attracted to places that they prefer (Attraction). Second, homogeneity results from people being selected into settings to which they are perceived to be compatible (Selection). Organizations tend to select certain individuals who appear to fit with those already there. Third, if people manage to enter an environment that is not a fit for them, they will tend to leave it (Attrition). Therefore, as Schneider (1987b) proposes, the people make the place. This model has been supported empirically. For example, Schein and Diamonte (1988) found a relationship between three different personality variables and organizational characteristics. People who rated themselves as high on a personality characteristic were more likely to be attracted to an organization that was described as reflecting that characteristic. Similarly, it was found that organizational climate information and personality variables interact in a recruitment situation (Furlong & Svyantek, 1998). Personality variables were found to prime individuals to perceive and select organizational climates in which they have a high probability of succeeding.

Schneider's ASA framework indicates that particular kinds of people are attracted to certain settings, and those who fit are not as likely to leave the organization. Thus, the ASA framework suggests there will be a restriction in range of individual differences in organizations (i.e., as compared with the general population). This restriction of range results in an organization of people who will also be similar in behavior, experiences, orientations, feelings, and reactions, and it creates a relatively homogeneous group of individuals. Such homogeneity, in turn, helps maintain the organizational culture across time.

The Influence of Organizational Culture on Work Behavior

Organizational culture affects behaviors within an organization. Organizational culture defines a *strong situation* (Mischel, 1977) for individuals residing within it. A strong situation provides people with generally accepted rules and guidelines for appropriate behavior. The rules that are present in strong situations constrain people from acting in a manner inconsistent with accepted conduct and behavior. Organizations develop values and norms to set parameters on the behaviors exhibited within an organization.

For example, organizations possess norms and values as to proper decision-making practices (Ott, 1989). These have been shown to affect choice of decision-making strategies through the creation of organizational decision-making styles (Svyantek, Jones, & Rozelle, 1991; Svyantek & Kolz, 1996). Such a collection of norms and values can be labeled an organizational decision climate. The policies and practices of an organization supporting such styles are hypothesized to create a specific decision-making climate for that organization.

The effects of organizational climate are particularly strong when the individual is motivated to adapt (Showers & Cantor, 1985). The ability to recognize and correctly adapt to the reality of organizational life is a critical component of career success (Sathe, 1985) where managers are motivated to understand the behaviors that are supported in their environment (Hannaway, 1989). Managers rely heavily on the information they receive from their social structure to infer behaviors that are appropriate, and they use this information to balance organizational goals and their personal career interests when making a decision (Hannaway, 1989; Svyantek et al., 1991; Svyantek & Kolz, 1996). They must, in effect, analyze and interpret their organization's decision-making climate, and use these interpretations to guide their decision behavior. This maximizes individual rewards and minimizes individual punishments for the decision maker. Thus, appropriateness of a decision will be contingent upon the organizational culture within which the decision maker operates.

Constraints on the accepted range of behaviors within an organization create multiple organizational climates supporting responses for organizational criteria (e.g., customer service or decision making). These constraints are created by, and reflect, the values and assumptions that comprise an organizational culture.

How Organizational Culture Influences Organizational Behavior

Organizational culture and organizational climate are closely related constructs that are linked both conceptually and practically (Schneider, 2000). The value of organizational culture and organizational climate is their ability to explain behaviors and relationships among people who share some sort of common experience or situation (Payne, 2000). There are two primary distinctions between the two constructs. First, individuals studying organizational culture have emphasized the use of qualitative research methods, whereas individuals studying organizational climate have conducted their research primarily with quantitative research tools (Payne, 2000; Schneider, 2000). Second, organizational culture research is conducted on a deeper level (e.g., underlying values held by the group) than is organizational climate research (e.g., the observed behaviors of members of a group) (Schein, 2000).

Schneider (2000) provided a framework for reconciling organizational culture and organizational climate. Organizational climate, according to Schneider, represents the descriptions of things that happen to employees of an organization. Organizational climate is behaviorally oriented, in that climates for safety or service, for example, may be found in the workplace. These climates represent the patterns of interactions and behaviors that support safety or service in the organization. Therefore, organizational climate is a description of what occurs within the organization. However, when employees are questioned on why these patterns exist, deeper levels of insight are found. The question of why is answered with stories and myths that describe life in the organization, and this defines organizational culture. Thus, organizational culture is an antecedent of constructs such as organizational climate and organizational design (Cooke & Szumal, 2000).

This framework serves as the basis for our model of how organizational culture affects employee behavior. The model is presented in Figure 24.1. At the extreme left is the founder(s). As noted by Schein (1985), the founder is the primary antecedent of organizational culture. The behavioral manifestations of the founder's personality traits form the basis for the values and assumptions that form organizational culture. These values and assumptions represent a deeper level of the organizational context. Over time, values and assumptions defining organizational culture become translated into organizational structure and organizational climate. Typically, the organization will have only one structure, but, as the figure shows, multiple climates may exist for important behaviors or goals in the organization. Organizational structure and organizational climate represent more surface-level variables: These variables are what are observable by the newcomer to an organization. The fit between the values and assumptions underlying these surface variables and the personality traits of a newcomer helps determine the outcome of the ASA model. The organizational structure and organizational climate then support different behavior, which may be functional or dysfunctional.

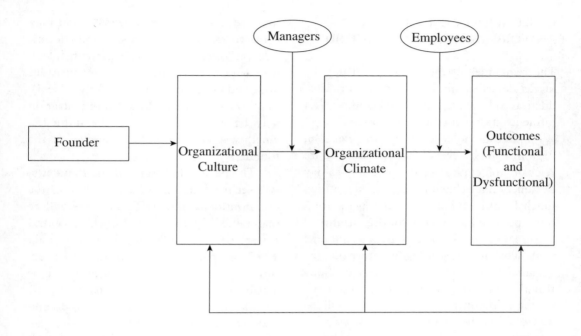

Figure 24.1   A Model of the Relationship Between Organizational Culture, Organizational Climate, and Dysfunctional Behaviour in the Workplace

The effects of the organizational context variables are influenced by the individuals in the organization. Managers have a more direct influence on the translation of organizational culture values into surface-level variables. This is illustrated by the solid line between the managers and the linkage of organizational culture and the surface variables. The degree and direction of this influence will be affected by the managers' individual differences (e.g., personality). Employees are seen as having a more direct influence on the translation of the surface variables (organizational structure and organizational climate) into behavioral outcomes: This is illustrated by the solid line between the employees and the linkage of organizational culture and the surface variables. The degree and direction of this influence will be affected by the employees' individual differences (e.g., personality), their degree of person-organization fit, and their perceptions of the implementation of policies within the organization.

Finally, there is a reciprocal relationship between behavioral outcomes, organizational climate, and organizational culture. Therefore, although organizational culture may cause organizational climate, changing the patterns of behaviors and interactions defined by organizational climate (or organizational structure) through an organizational design process may lead to changes in organizational culture (Schneider, 2000). This possibility is indicated by the feedback loops from organizational climate and organizational design to organizational culture in Figure 24.1. In addition, the nature of behavioral outcomes seen in the organization provides feedback on the degree to which organizational culture and the surface variables are supporting functional or dysfunctional organizational behaviors.

DYSFUNCTIONAL BEHAVIORS AND ORGANIZATIONAL CULTURE

The remainder of the chapter will use the model described above to provide an introduction to how organizational contexts can influence dysfunctional behaviors.

Extreme violence is a rare event in organizations; these events are more relevant for clinical study. The day-to-day dysfunctional behaviors (e.g., taking a long lunch break) exhibited by employees are a more predictable function of organizational culture. Figure 24.1 will be used as a model framework for integrating literature on how organizational culture may affect dysfunctional behavior in organizations. Each of the components of the model will be addressed in the following discussion.

Organizational Culture and the Founder

The founder(s) of an organization are critical in the formation of the organizational culture. The founder(s), however, may have personality traits that lead to dysfunctional behaviors in an organization.

Leaders in an organization set the example or tone for its culture, climate, and structure (Bass, 1998; Kets de Vries, 1979; Kets de Vries & Miller, 1991). This is particularly true for the founder(s) of an organization (Schein, 1985). Kets de Vries (1991) focuses on the psychological makeup of leaders and executives and their impact on their organizations and their subordinates. He has found situations where followers have an unhealthy dependency upon a leader who has lost touch with reality, and the followers come to share in this delusion (Kets de Vries, 1979). Kets de Vries (1993) notes that entrepreneurial ventures can be particularly prone to this dysfunction. Employees joining a newly

founded, entrepreneurial organization may come to experience distrust of others outside the organization, feelings of helplessness and secretiveness, and inconsistent policy administration (Kets de Vries, 1993). Employees in a newly founded organization may be very vulnerable to the influence, whether it be positive or negative, of the founder.

The personality traits of the founder(s) will set the tone for the initial state of the organizational culture. This culture will be maintained by the ASA model. A central feature of the ASA model (Schneider et al., 1995) is that the goals, processes, structures, and culture of an organization can be attributed to the characteristics of its founder(s) and early leaders. These organizational attributes persist over time, even after the founder and his or her cohorts are gone, and perpetuate early behaviors that formed the culture and the organizational processes that maintain the culture. This is particularly true of so-called strong cultures in which particular and identifiable values and behaviors (often attributable to its founder[s]) are accepted almost unconditionally throughout the organization (Schneider, Brief, & Guzzo, 1996). In this way, organizations will attract or develop leaders over time who will maintain the established organizational culture, whether that culture fosters functional or dysfunctional behavior.

Dysfunctional Organizational Cultures

One of the primary purposes of organizational culture is the creation of a predictable pattern of behavior within an organization through providing employees with a common value system. This value system may be based largely on the traits of the original founders of the organization (Schein, 1985). A key thing to remember is that these value systems will form within a specific organization. The shape that a value system takes in different organizations will vary immensely.

General patterns of value systems have been identified. For example, Cooke and Szumal (2000) proposed that three general types of organizational culture exist. Cultures may be (a) *constructive,* where the cultural value systems are characterized by norms of achievement, self-actualization, humanism, and affiliation; (b) *passive-defensive,* where the cultural value systems are characterized by norms of approval, convention, dependency, and avoidance; or (c) *aggressive-defensive,* where the cultural value systems are characterized by norms of opposition, power, competition, and perfectionism. Frost (1985) proposed that the organizations supporting dysfunctional behaviors could be classified as *neurotic, psychotic,* or *sociopathic.* Neurotic organizations are characterized by anxiety and avoidance behaviors, which are related to an inability to manage stress effectively and a fear of failure. Psychotic organizations are characterized by paranoia and distortions of reality. Sociopathic organizations are marked by a lack of ethics and an unwillingness to follow normal standards of conduct.

Therefore, organizational cultures may exist that support dysfunctional behaviors by organizational members to greater or lesser degrees. Although the constructive culture may be seen as the ideal system for governing a workplace, it is not the only value system that exists. There are many dysfunctional organizational cultures. This implies that these value systems are related primarily to how employees are treated in the organization (not to how the organization interacts with its environment), because these dysfunctional cultures are perpetuated across time.

From Organizational Culture to Organizational Climate

It is necessary to understand how organizational cultures may influence the performance of dysfunctional behaviors by employees. One way in which organizational culture may affect performance is through the creation of an organizational structure and climate that support patterns of dysfunctional behavior.

The surface manifestations of organizational culture are important indicators of the value system. Core organizational processes (e.g., organizational structure and climate) are determinants of the behaviors that are rewarded and punished within an organization. Organizational climates that foster aggression in an organization may be developed (Sperry, 1998). These climates support patterns of role conflict, role ambiguity, role overload, and ingroup/outgroup formation.

Similarly, Robinson and O'Leary-Kelly (1998) showed that an antisocial organizational climate can be created. They showed that organizational practices promoted antisocial behavior in individual employees. Moreover, results of this study support the ASA model. The effects of the antisocial climate increased in strength the longer an individual remained in the antisocial climate. In addition, the antisocial climate was found to be more satisfying for employees who exhibited more antisocial personality traits than it was for those who did not exhibit the same pattern of personality traits.

Specific organizational practices that support dysfunctional behavior have been identified. For example, O'Leary-Kelly, Griffin, and Glew (1996) proposed that aggression in an organization may be supported through the observation of aggressive behaviors within an organization that are rewarded rather than punished.

Sperry (1998) proposed that organizations may cultivate inappropriate workplace aggression based on organizational practices of an emphasis on increased productivity standards, support of competitiveness among employees, development of strong hierarchies, role conflict, and a lack of controls for retarding inappropriate aggression. Giacalone, Riordan, and Rosenfeld (1997) linked employee sabotage to a number of factors, including the organization's history of sabotage and how management has reacted to acts of sabotage in the past (i.e., ignored or punished this behavior). Vredenburgh and Brender (1998) posit that certain organizational conditions support the abuse of interpersonal power by individuals in an organization. They believe that highly ambiguous decision making and a climate of secrecy contribute to the abuse of power. Allowing managers wide personal latitude (rather than establishing organizational policies) for controlling resources can also help to create a climate where interpersonal abuse of power may flourish.

Organizational practices may be formed to legitimize dysfunctional behavior. Robinson and Kraatz (1998) showed that neutralization strategies are used by employees to legitimize or neutralize their deviant actions. This is done by some organizational member(s) constructing a perception (in other members of the organization) that there is a congruency between organizational values and norms and the observed dysfunctional behavior. Neutralization strategies may include the use of such tactics as rationalization, excuses, outright rejection or redefinition of norms, or simple concealment of the dysfunctional behavior. In all cases, the outcome of successful neutralization is organizational acceptance of the deviance. Robinson and Kraatz hypothesize that organizational factors—including weak norms, a focus on short-term relationships,

decentralization, low standardization, and little overall employee direction or monitoring—all serve to promote neutralization strategies.

Organizational culture values (deep) and organizational practices (surface) exist that may foster dysfunctional behavior in organizations. The next section looks at potential dysfunctional behavioral outcomes.

Dysfunctional Behavioral Outcomes

Dysfunctional behaviors have varied definitions. We will focus on those behaviors that are potentially harmful to individuals or the organization itself.

Robinson and Bennett (1995) have defined a typology with four types of dysfunctional work behaviors. They proposed that two dimensions may be used to define dysfunctional behaviors: the seriousness or harmfulness of the dysfunctional acts, and the degree to which the dysfunctional behaviors are harmful to individuals within the organization or are directed at the organizations. These two dimensions define the four types of dysfunctional behavior. *Production deviance* consists of acts that are less serious and are directed at the organization. Examples of these include leaving early, taking excessive breaks, intentionally working slow, and wasting organizational resources. *Property deviance* consists of acts that are more serious but still directed at the organization. Examples of these acts include sabotaging equipment, accepting kickbacks, lying about the number of hours worked, and stealing from the company. *Political deviance* consists of acts of influence and are directed at individuals in the organization. Examples of these acts include showing favoritism, gossiping about coworkers, blaming coworkers, and competing excessively against others in the organization. *Personal aggression* consists of acts that attack individuals in the organization. Examples of these acts include sexual harassment, verbal abuse, stealing from co-workers, and endangering co-workers by employees.

It is necessary to define the target of dysfunctional behaviors. Targets of dysfunctional behavior may be (a) internal or external to the organization, and (b) specific or nonspecific (O'Leary-Kelly et al., 1996). The choice of a specific target may be based on the target's aversive treatment of the individual exhibiting the dysfunctional behavior. Choice of nonspecific targets seems to be related more to factors in the general organizational context. In addition, dysfunctional behavior against different classes of targets may have different antecedents. One study showed that individual differences (e.g., history of aggression and amount of alcohol consumed) predicts aggression by employees against coworkers (Greenberg & Barling, 1999). Aggressive behavior against a supervisor in the same study, however, was predicted by two perceived workplace factors (procedural justice and workplace surveillance). Neither class of factors (individual differences or perceived workplace factors) predicted aggression against a subordinate.

Managerial Individual Differences and Dysfunctional Behavior

Managers have a major influence on the translation of the values of the organizational culture into more concrete organizational practices. The effects of dysfunctional managerial behavior influence organizational climate and behavioral outcomes. Sperry (1998) described three types of dysfunctional managers. First, there are toxic supervisors, who create hostile work environments for employees. Second, there are violent supervisors, who use threats and intimidation to control others in the organization. Finally, there are colluding supervisors, who act with others in secret to gain something at the expense of others. There appear to be four primary ways in which these types of managerial behavior may result in problematic organizational practices.

First, dysfunctional managerial behaviors may reflect a lack of fit between a manager and the organization (Sperry, 1996). However, given the ASA model's predictions, it is likely that behaviors that reflect a lack of fit eventually will lead to the manager leaving the organization. Second, dysfunctional managerial behaviors may be the result of a negative interaction between the manager and the organization (Sperry, 1996). Here, the manager's reactions likely will be caused by a similar process described for employees in the next section. Third, this behavior may be the result of a managerial fit with the behaviors supported by the organization. In this case, the behaviors will continue because they are rewarded by the organization. Finally, in some cases, the behaviors may simply reflect dysfunctional personality traits within the manager (Kets de Vries & Miller, 1991). Dysfunctional managerial individual difference variables include antisocial personality disorders (Babiak, 1995, 2000); individual alienation from the needs of the organization (Conger, 1990; Maccoby, 2000); and individual predispositions, such as biological loadings for addiction (Sperry, 1996).

Authoritarian personality traits also contribute to dysfunctional managerial behavior and lead to dysfunctional organizational practices. Ashforth (1994) studied another negative attribute found in managers, called *petty tyranny*. Petty tyranny is characterized by authoritarian managers whose behaviors (a) abuse their position of authority; and (b) fail to show consideration to subordinates by exhibiting behaviors such as severe and public criticism of others, taking credit for others' work, blaming others for their own mistakes, emotionality, and micromanagement. Ashforth believes petty tyranny is an outcome of interactions between a leader's individual personality characteristics and situational factors allowing, or supporting, this type of behavior in the workplace. Petty tyrants are seen as contributing to employee mental heath problems such as low self-esteem; poor work performance; reactance; and more general feelings of frustration, stress, and helplessness. The result of petty tyranny is probably an increased probability of dysfunctional behavior among subordinates. Other outcomes can also reinforce the continued debasement of the manager's followers and their contributions to the workplace.

A major contributing factor to behaviors such as petty tyranny appears to be organizational values about their use. Organizations without clear, unambiguous sanctions against such behavior may be manipulated by individual managers for personal gain.

The lack of clear, unambiguous norms about behaviors in an organization allows the personality trait of aberrant self-promotion to have free rein (Gustafson, 2000; Gustafson & Ritzer, 1995). Aberrant self-promotion is "a narcissistic personality configuration in combination with antisocial behavior" (Gustafson & Ritzer, 1995, p. 147). Gustafson (2000) found that scores of aberrant self-promoters (ASPs) reflect a difference in *degree*, rather than in the type of pathology. These individuals are thought to occur in 5% of the general population. She goes on to describe ASPs as having personality characteristics of "exploitativeness, entitlement, grandiosity, superficial charm and lack of empathy or guilt" (Gustafson, 2000, p. 299). They also possess high self-esteem and low concern for socially

desirable responding, and they demonstrate a great deal of antisocial behavior. She suggests that ASP-type leaders impair the mental health of their followers and can cause the failure of the organization if left to operate unchecked. ASP leaders do so by lying, mismanaging organizational resources, subverting or ignoring organizational policy in their own self-interests, threatening or bullying others who try to limit their power, and refusing to accept responsibility for their own mistakes and shortcomings. Babiak (1995, 2000), in his case study of psychopaths in organizations, hypothesizes that they are drawn to leadership positions where they have power over others, where their positions do not require detail-oriented work, where they can manipulate others, and where they have the opportunity to earn more income than nonmanagement employees. The work environments that attract these types of leaders tend to be those in the midst of "rapid chaotic change," in which old rules are broken, risks are taken, more flexibility is available, and there is opportunity for excitement. All of these organizational factors can serve to cover up a psychopath's deviant behavior of manipulation and abuse of others for personal gain.

When a situation is ambiguous, clear criteria or guidelines are not available to help resolve the ambiguity. Here, individual differences in managerial behavior, not organizational culture, may determine the formation of new organizational practices. These practices may reflect the interests of the manager, not those of the organization. This, in turn, may lead to dysfunctional behaviors among employees.

Employees and Dysfunctional Behavior

One reason that organizational climate remains a potent influence on employee behavior is that the policies, processes, and structures that come to support a behavior are used as indicators of what management values. Siehl, Ledford, Silverman, and Fay (1988) proposed that employee perceptions of company practices are used to infer organizational values. It is possible for management to behave in ways counter to the company's espoused values, and this incongruence could then, in turn, affect employee behaviors, beliefs, and attitudes. Schneider (2000) similarly describes one potent source of organizational culture as the beliefs that employees in an organization hold about what management of the organization values. These inferences are drawn based on their observations of surface-level practices (organizational structure and organizational climate).

Organizational culture has been defined as the deep level of values, beliefs, and assumptions shared by the members of an organization. These assumptions guide the behavior of employees who reside in the organization. This results in patterns of behavior that are likely to be consistent and predictable across time and situations. The direction and kind of employee behavior that will be seen is based largely on employees' perceptions of the first three of Namenwirth and Weber's (1987) purposes of organizational culture (Svyantek, 1997; Svyantek & Brown, 2000). Employees' behaviors are guided by their perceptions of (a) what it means to be part of the organization, (b) how social and economic justice are defined in the organization, and (c) how the organization produces a socially defined "good" organization.

Boye and Jones (1997), in their study of antisocial behavior in organizations and how culture affected the behavior, found that dishonest or unethical management behavior influenced subordinates to behave in ways that were counterproductive to the organization. These counterproductive or deviant behaviors included stealing, manipulating company pay records, slowing the work pace, and doing sloppy work. The unethical, dishonest management behavior was, perhaps, accepted in that particular organizational culture as part of its standard of integrity, therefore providing a behavioral and ethical model for employees to follow on the job.

The above discussion describes scenarios of employee dysfunctional behavior that fit the accepted norms of the organization. However, dysfunctional behavior may be the result of a lack of fit with the accepted norms of an organization. Two primary organizational perceptions appear to influence the degree to which dysfunctional behaviors are performed by employees in this situation. These are employee perceptions of the justice climate in the organization, and their own level of power in the organization.

Employees' perception (or lack of perception) of a climate of justice in an organization is a major influence on their performance of dysfunctional behaviors. Organizational justice provides a framework for looking at how employees perceive the fairness of outcomes in terms of the fair distribution of resources in an organization and the fairness of the organizational procedures. Folger and Skarlicki (1998) propose that perceived organizational injustice (perceived lack of fair treatment or outcomes) is important in predicting employee aggression and retaliation. They believe that when an employee perceives that an accepted organizational norm has been violated by someone higher up, a valued rule of conduct has been broken and the violation is considered to be unjust. Such perception of injustice can lead to the employee feeling a need for revenge or retribution toward the organization, which can then lead to aggressive behavior on his or her part. Mudrack, Mason, and Stepanski's (1999) research compared individuals' perceptions of fairness in organizations and found that the work context, not individual differences, determined the individual perceptions of fairness. In other words, perception of fairness may not be a stable attitude, but rather an individual attitude that changes depending on the organizational context.

Tepper (2000) looked at the partial mediating effects of organizational justice on the consequences of abusive supervision in a field study. He found that perceived abusive supervision is considered to be a source of interactional injustice that could lead to employees being more likely to quit their jobs. Employees who did not quit (low job mobility) associated the abusive supervision with lower job and life satisfaction, lower normative and affective commitment, more work/family conflict, and more psychological distress. Interestingly, perceived low job mobility did not act as a mediator or moderator in the relationships between perceived justice and the other dependent variables. Tepper also found that abusive supervision might not be considered deviant if it conforms to the organization's policies and norms, supporting the vital role of culture in determining appropriate behavior.

Bennett (1998) found that an employee's perceived lack of control or powerlessness over his or her work environment can be a cause of workplace deviance and dysfunctional behavior. Deviant behavior often took form as interpersonally directed deviance, such as the use of obscenities at work, loss of one's temper, and even assaults and violence on the job. The deviant behavior that the employee exhibits as a result of the perceived loss or lack of control serves to give the employee a sense that he or she has (re)gained control, and can indeed somehow affect his or her work environment. Bennett goes on to say that deviance can also act as an outlet for employee frustration stemming from the perceived loss or lack of control.

CONCLUSIONS AND RECOMMENDATIONS

This chapter has provided a framework for integrating organizational context variables, such as organizational culture, into the study of dysfunctional behavior in the workplace. We offer tentative conclusions about the nature of the relationship between dysfunctional behavior and the organizational context. In addition, we believe that upon recognizing an increase in dysfunctional behavior, organizational management is faced with a decision. It may (a) ignore the increase in the dysfunctional behavior(s) and hope the behavior goes away, or (b) take action to decrease the dysfunctional behavior. Therefore, we also provide a discussion of a process for altering organizational cultures to decrease dysfunctional behavior.

The Performance of Dysfunctional Behaviors in Organizations

First, when considering organizational culture as a context for dysfunctional behavior, the important cultural values are those related to how employees are treated in the workplace (Svyantek, 1997; Svyantek & Brown, 2000). These cultural values are translated by the management of an organization into observable practices (e.g., organizational climate or organizational structure) that define important behaviors and create a vision of the social order in the organization (Trice & Beyer, 1993).

Second, organizational cultures (and the associated observable organizational practices) have the potential for supporting either functional or dysfunctional behaviors. For example, Cooke and Szumal (2000) proposed that three general types of organizational culture exist. It is likely that the degree of dysfunctional behavior will vary across constructive, passive-defensive, and aggressive-defensive cultures. Therefore, types of dysfunctional behavior found in organizations should be different across cultural types. For example, organizations with constructive cultures are probably more likely to observe fewer dysfunctional behaviors directed at individuals who violate organizational norms in the workplace. This is the political deviance behavior described by Robinson and Bennett (1995). Constructive cultures should experience the least amount of consistent dysfunctional behaviors. Dysfunctional behaviors here may also be more under the control of individual variables (e.g., personal history of violence) (Greenberg & Barling, 1999) than organizational variables. Passive-defensive and aggressive-defensive cultures, however, are more likely to have dysfunctional behaviors in them. It is likely that the target of the dysfunctional behavior will be the organization in both cases, with less serious incidents being seen in the passive-defensive culture (e.g., production deviance behaviors) (Robinson & Bennett, 1995) and more serious incidents in the aggressive-defensive culture (e.g., property deviance behaviors) (Robinson & Bennett, 1995).

Third, an interactional perspective is necessary for understanding dysfunctional behavior in the workplace. Serious dysfunctional behaviors directed at individuals (e.g., personal deviance behaviors) (Robinson & Bennett, 1995), for example, may be most likely to occur in organizations without strong cultural values against such behaviors. These behaviors, however, will be performed only by individuals with some personality disorder, such as the authoritarian personality who becomes the petty tyrant (Ashforth, 1994) or the aberrant self-promoter (Gustafson, 2000). Dysfunctional behavior by an employee is voluntary (Robinson & Bennett, 1995). It violates significant organizational norms and, in doing so, threatens the well-being of an organization, its members, or both. Employee deviance is voluntary because employees either lack the motivation to conform to normative expectations or become motivated to violate these expectations. It is likely that motivation to violate the expectations will be dependent on the individual in the situation (e.g., the aberrant self-promoter is more likely to violate expectations if no sanctions are perceived) (Gustafson, 2000).

Fourth, person-organization fit is thus a critical variable in understanding the relationship between organizational culture and dysfunctional behavior. Not all individuals are equally suited to all organizations. The performance of dysfunctional behavior may be a matter of misfit between the individual and the situation and not just a set of individual and/or organizational variables considered in isolation from each other. For example, Sperry (1996) proposes that good fit is related to higher job performance, higher job satisfaction, increased self-esteem, and less stress for employees. Dysfunctional responses to poor fit, however, include increased stress, burnout, cynicism, role ambiguity, and role conflict among employees. As noted above, indications of poor fit are not necessarily deficits of either the person or the organization. Rather, *misfit* is the issue.

Fifth, the target of dysfunctional behavior will be dependent on organizational and individual factors. Organizations will be the target of the dysfunctional behavior when employees are reacting to consistent organizational practices that they do not like. Individuals are more likely to be the target when an individual is seen as being responsible for the organizational practice that employees do not like. The factors influencing the choice of a target may differ across levels of the organizational hierarchy as well. For example, Greenberg and Barling (1999) showed that individual differences (e.g., history of aggression and amount of alcohol consumed) predict aggression by employees against peers, whereas aggressive behavior against a supervisor in the same study was predicted by two perceived workplace factors (procedural justice and workplace surveillance). No consistent pattern of factors (individual differences or perceived workplace factors) predicted aggression against a subordinate. The choice of a subordinate as a target is likely to be a combination of individual differences (e.g., perceived vulnerability of the target) and workplace factors (e.g., perceived organizational sanctions for the behavior).

Sixth, consistent with the interactional model, individual differences will play a part in dysfunctional behaviors exhibited by managers and employees. It is proposed that the exhibition of dysfunctional behaviors will be affected by personality differences among employees and employee differences in the perception of organizational justice and power in the organization. As the severity of a personality disorder increases or the perceptions of justice and power diverge from the average perception in the organization, the more severe will be the dysfunctional behavior performed. Individual differences may be the proper locus of study for the more extreme, violent dysfunctional behaviors exhibited in the workplace.

Finally, the performance of dysfunctional behaviors by employees is an important source of feedback for organizations. Organizations seeing an increase in employee dysfunctional behavior should use this information to plan organizational change efforts.

Decreasing Dysfunctional Behaviors in Organizations

Remedies for the performance of dysfunctional behaviors in the workplace may come from two primary classes of antecedent causes—the individual employees performing the dysfunctional behaviors and organizational factors that influence the performance of the dysfunctional behaviors. The primary focus of change efforts, to date, has been on interventions designed to alter employee behavior. For example, Burke and Richardsen (1993) looked at the use of organizational- versus individual-level interventions to reduce stress and burnout on the job. In their review of research, they found that little research had been conducted on changing the work environment to reduce the effects of employee burnout. The emphasis is on changing the employee rather than the organization.

The primary focus of this viewpoint may be characterized as a human resource approach to decreasing dysfunctional behavior in the workplace. For example, instead of changing the organizational culture, organizations can seek to increase the fit of individuals to the organization (Gustafson & Mumford, 1995; Schneider et al., 1995). This means that the recruiting, selection, and promotion processes should be designed to attract people who fit the organization's culture as well as screen out those who are potentially harmful to the organization and its employees. If the organizational culture values competitive behavior, then individuals with personal high needs for achievement might be selected. A potential limitation of this approach is the danger that only like-minded individuals will be employed, when some diversity of approach and thinking could benefit the organization by keeping it more competitive and avoiding groupthink. It is worth noting, and perhaps obvious, that in selection and promotion, it is important that the organization attempt to screen out potentially dysfunctional employees. This is especially important for leadership positions, and particularly in organizations in the midst of change or turmoil, because it is in these positions and periods that the most damage to individual mental health and organizational effectiveness can be done (Babiak, 2000; Gustafson & Ritzer, 1995; Kets de Vries & Miller, 1985). Effective recruitment, selection, and promotions processes involve well-trained individuals from various functions in the organization. Job descriptions should be constructed carefully so that they accurately reflect the requirements for the position. Interviewers should be trained to look for evidence of dysfunction, such as lying, inconsistency in responses, and overly aggressive behaviors, as well as skills, abilities, and past experience of a candidate. Reference checks should also be conducted to confirm the candidate's background and search for any problem work behaviors in their past.

We have shown that there is a relationship between organizational culture and dysfunctional behavior. This approach to decreasing dysfunctional behavior has its roots in organizational development. Organizational development approaches to change traditionally have taken a more context-specific approach to changing organizational practices for purposes of increasing organizational effectiveness. We propose that a similar approach is appropriate for decreasing many of the day-to-day dysfunctional behaviors noted earlier.

Organizational cultures define a strong situation (Mischel, 1977) for employees. Altering the organization at the deep level (organizational culture) or surface level (e.g., organizational structure or organizational climate) is an appropriate strategy to use. This is particularly true for organizations facing a general rise in dysfunctional behavior among employees (e.g., extending the time spent on breaks) as opposed to situations where only a few employees are responsible for the dysfunctional behavior (e.g., the exhibition of violent behavior in the workplace). By altering the situation, it is likely that the level of dysfunctional behavior exhibited by employees within the organization will decrease. For example, it may be necessary to alter organizational characteristics that prompt (e.g., observations of aggression in the workplace) and support (e.g., incentive inducements) aggressive behavior if an organization wishes to decrease the level of aggression in an organization (O'Leary et al., 1996).

The research process for understanding how to change organizational cultures to decrease dysfunctional behavior is a context-specific approach. The emphasis is on understanding the history of the organization and the processes that created the organizational practices that support dysfunctional behavior. The researcher's role becomes clinical in nature (Schein, 2000) when analyzing the influence of organizational culture. Qualitative research methods become an important tool for the researcher.

The organizational intervention process becomes a clinical process according to Schein and Kets de Vries (Quick & Gavin, 2000). This process, aimed at consulting in complex organizations, involves tailoring the intervention at the specific level or system of the organization and using not only organizational development interventions, but also traditional clinical or counseling therapy when it is appropriate for individuals requiring intervention. The interventions should be collaborative efforts in problem solving between organizations, employees, and change agents.

The basic model we propose for changing an organization to decrease dysfunctional behavior is similar to that used traditionally to change organizations in order to increase behaviors related to organizational effectiveness. This model is based on Lewin's (1958) model of change and the action research model.

Lewin's (1958) model involves three steps. The first step is *unfreezing* the current state of the system. During this step, the need for change is recognized by the members of an organization, and initial steps are taken toward that change. The second step is *movement*. This step involves intervening in the organization to change a behavior or process to a new level. Finally, the third step is *refreezing*. During this step, the change began in the movement step is institutionalized by altering other practices of the organization to support the change in the desired behavior. The action research model is a process of (a) diagnosis of the causes of a problem, (b) feedback of the diagnostic information to an organizational client, (c) planning of an intervention to address the problem, (d) implementation of the intervention, and (e) evaluation of the effects of the intervention on the problem (Burke, 1982). This process repeats itself as necessary.

Therefore, upon recognizing an increase in dysfunctional behavior, the first step in the change process is to conduct a diagnosis of the antecedent causes of such dysfunctional behavior. Diagnosis defines the causes of the dysfunctional behavior. Organizational management should realize that the problem probably will not lie with the employees. It is as likely that the problem is the result of organizational factors as employee factors. The organization must be willing to take action to change organizational practices, sanction organizational managers, or do whatever is necessary if organizational factors (e.g., culture, climate, or structure) are implicated in the causes of dysfunctional behavior. This diagnosis should represent an attempt to gather the reasons why a problem is occurring.

Underlying causes of consistent patterns of dysfunctional behavior (e.g., employee sabotage) will probably be at a deep level (e.g., in the organizational culture). The question becomes whether the organization should plan to intervene at this level when trying to eliminate dysfunctional behavior.

We believe that the intervention should not be at the deep level. Rather, the organization should intervene at the surface level (e.g., organizational structure or the organizational climate defining the situational elements that influence the performance of dysfunctional behaviors). Schneider (2000) proposed that a reciprocal relationship exists between organizational climate and organizational culture. This reciprocal relationship is illustrated in Figure 24.1. Organizational culture leads to the development of regular practices in the workplace, which then define organizational climate. However, changes in the practices defining organizational climate can lead to changes in organizational culture. The model of change we are advocating is one in which the behavioral practices supporting dysfunctional behaviors are to be changed first. The change in values defining the organizational culture may occur at a later time, but as long as the behavior changes, the organizational goals will have been reached.

Therefore, a complete diagnosis will provide information on both why a dysfunctional behavior occurs and what observable organizational practices support this dysfunctional behavior. Intervention will occur on the observed organizational practices level. For example, sexual harassment is a dysfunctional behavior that has an individual as a target and is very serious in its potential repercussions for the victim, perpetrator, and the organization in which it occurs. Training sessions used to decrease sexual harassment, while providing persuasive information on why this is a bad behavior, get their primary impact from an explanation of the sanctions that will be imposed on the perpetrator(s) of such behavior in the organization. It is likely that fear of these sanctions, at least initially, is the primary reason why a potential perpetrator may not perform an act of sexual harassment. Such change in organizational practice decreases the performance of a dysfunctional behavior. Change in the cultural value system of the organization may occur with time as newcomers, who see only the newly imposed sanctions for such behavior in their tenure in the organization, incorporate the reasons why sexual harassment is a dysfunctional behavior in their perceptions of the organizational culture.

There are many potential ways of altering organizational practices to decrease the performance of dysfunctional behavior. Kets de Vries and Miller (1985) and Kets de Vries (1989) advocated establishing organizational safeguards to protect employees against dysfunctional leaders. These involve creation of human resource policies (e.g., against sexual harassment or discrimination against minorities) that clearly define acceptable behaviors. Violations of these policies are a clear indication of inappropriate behavior. Internal structures can also act as barriers to results of dysfunctional behavior by individuals in positions of power in the organization. An organization

should be structured so as to distribute power less centrally, in order to involve more people in the development of strategy, problem solving and decision making, and regular operation of the organization (Kets de Vries & Miller, 1985). Checks and balances can be put in place, such as audit functions and reward and budgeting systems that prevent or at least make it difficult for such leaders (and followers) to abuse the systems and other individuals. These functions not only reflect good operating processes and procedures, but also can be used by individuals to draw inferences about the values of the organizational culture. Such formal structural practices may be used to prevent individuals who are working only to serve their own personal interests from causing much damage.

The Organizational Golden Rule

We believe that the organizational context (organizational culture, organizational climate, and organizational structure) in which employees work has a profound impact on their mental health and the performance of dysfunctional behaviors in an organization. This impact occurs because the organizational context provides information on (a) the value placed by the organization on its employees, and (b) the degree to which there is justice in the organization.

Boye and Jones (1997) believe that managers should create a work environment that demonstrates that the organization appreciates employees and rewards them for productive behavior. They propose that managers model desired behavior, values, and ethics. Employees should be treated with trust, respect, and dignity, and they should be compensated fairly to communicate the value that the organization places in them. As a final managerial policy, dysfunctional behavior must be dealt with through the use of policies and consistent discipline of unacceptable behavior.

Respect for others, as a cultural value of the organization, is a starting point for decreasing dysfunctional behavior in organizations. When this norm is breached, workplace incivility occurs (Andersson & Pearson, 1999). Workplace incivility—a lack of "politeness and regard for others . . . within workplace norms for respect" (Andersson & Pearson, 1999, p. 454)—leads to antisocial behavior, which may escalate to aggression and then to violence in organizations. If, however, the organization's culture is one of high-minded values where norm violations and incivility are not accepted or are punished, dysfunctional behavior in the workplace may be less frequent than in a cultural context where norms are weak and unfair, inconsistent treatment is ignored, and incivility is allowed.

The organizational practices necessary to show this respect need not be costly. For example, one local organization used its policies to demonstrate how people were to be treated and valued within the organization. This organization had an unwritten but widely known policy that demonstrated the respect that the organization had for its employees. This policy stated that if there were to be any layoffs resulting from foreseeable business conditions, it was the responsibility of management to be aware of and plan for them some months in advance. This was especially crucial in the year's fourth quarter and the beginning of the first quarter of the following year, right around the Christmas and New Year's holidays. The policy was that no layoffs were to occur after November 1 until February 1. The culture of the company was to keep employment as stable as possible so that employees could plan for their holidays and not find themselves unable to pay the bills that those holidays generated. Other organizations took a different tack and notified employees of layoffs planned for late in the year (especially in the situation of a merger or acquisition) so as to help them budget for the holidays accordingly.

This policy required senior management to do a little extra work: The dividends of this work, however, were the employees' perceptions that they were valued by the organization. Establishing mutual respect between employees and the organization is an obvious starting point. Therefore, the Golden Rule of "Do unto others as you would have them do unto you" is as appropriate for organizational contexts as it is for any social situation. In this way, appropriate cultural norms will be established to discourage dysfunctional behavior.

REFERENCES

Andersson, L. M., & Pearson, C. M. (1999). Tit for tat? The spiraling effect of incivility in the workplace. *Academy of Management Review, 24*(3), 452-471.

Ashforth, B. E. (1994). Petty tyranny in organizations. *Human Relations, 47,* 755-778.

Babiak, P. (1995). When psychopaths go to work: A case study of an industrial psychopath. *Applied Psychology: An International Review, 44*(2), 171-188.

Babiak, P. (2000). Psychopathic manipulation at work. In C. B. Gacono (Ed.), *The clinical and forensic assessment of psychopathy: A practitioner's guide* (pp. 287-311). Mahwah, NJ: Lawrence Erlbaum.

Bass, B. M. (1998). *Transformational leadership*. Mahwah, NJ: Lawrence Erlbaum.

Bennett, R. J. (1998). Perceived powerlessness as a cause of employee deviance. In R. W. Griffin, A. O'Leary-Kelly, & J. M. Collins (Eds.), *Dysfunctional behavior in organizations: Violent and deviant behavior* (pp. 221-239). Stamford, CT: JAI.

Boye, M. W., & Jones, J. W. (1997). Organizational culture and employee counter-productivity. In R. A. Giacalone & J. Greenberg (Eds.), *Antisocial behavior in organizations* (pp. 172-184). Thousand Oaks, CA: Sage.

Bretz, R. D., & Judge, T. A. (1994). Person-organization fit and the theory of work adjustment: Implications for satisfaction, tenure, and career success. *Journal of Vocational Behavior, 44,* 32-54.

Burke, R. F., & Richardsen, A. M. (1993). Psychological burnout in organizations. In R. T. Golembiewski (Ed.), *Handbook of organizational behavior* (pp. 263-298). New York: Marcel Dekker.

Burke, W. W. (1982). *Organization development: Principles and practices*. Boston: Little, Brown.

Buss, D. M. (1987). Selection, evocation, and manipulation. *Journal of Personality and Social Psychology, 53,* 1214-1221.

Cable, D. M., & Judge, T. A. (1996). Person-organization fit, job choice decisions, and organizational entry. *Organizational Behavior and Human Decision Processes, 67,* 294-311.

Cable, D. M., & Judge, T. A. (1997). Interviewers' perceptions of person-organization fit and organizational selection decisions. *Journal of Applied Psychology, 82,* 546-561.

Chatman, J. A. (1991). Matching people and organizations: Selection and socialization in public accounting firms. *Administrative Science Quarterly, 36,* 459-484.

Conger, J. A. (1990). The dark side of leadership. *Organizational Dynamics, 19*(2), 44-55.

Cooke, R. A., & Szumal, J. L. (2000). Using the Organizational Culture Inventory to understand the operating cultures of organizations. In N. M. Ashkanasy, C. P. M. Wilderon, & M. F. Peterson (Eds.), *Handbook of organizational culture and climate* (pp. 147-162). Thousand Oaks, CA: Sage.

Deal, T. E., & Kennedy, A. A. (1982). *Corporate cultures*. Reading, MA: Addison-Wesley.

Folger, R., & Skarlicki, D. (1998). A popcorn metaphor for employee aggression. In R. W. Griffin, A. O'Leary-Kelly, & J. M. Collins (Eds.), *Dysfunctional behavior in organizations: Violent and deviant behavior* (pp. 43-81). Stamford, CT: JAI.

Frost, T. F. (1985). The sick organization: Part 1: Neurotic, psychotic, sociopathic. *Personnel, 62,* 40-44.

Furlong, M. A., & Svyantek, D. J. (1998). The relationship between organizational climate and personality: A contextualist perspective. *Journal of Psychology and Behavioral Sciences, 12,* 43-53.

Giacalone, R. A., Riordan, C. A., & Rosenfeld, P. (1997). Employee sabotage: Toward a practitioner-scholar understanding. In R. A. Giacalone & J. Greenberg (Eds.), *Antisocial behavior in organizations* (pp. 109-129). Thousand Oaks, CA: Sage.

Goodman, S. A., & Svyantek, D. J. (1999). Person-organization fit and contextual performance: Do shared values matter? *Journal of Vocational Behavior, 55,* 254-275.

Greenberg, L., & Barling, J. (1999). Predicting employee aggression against coworkers, subordinates and supervisors: The roles of person behaviors and workplace factors. *Journal of Organizational Behavior, 20,* 897-913.

Griffin, R. W., O'Leary-Kelly, A., & Collins, J. (1998). Dysfunctional work behaviors in organizations. In C. L. Cooper & D. M. Rousseau (Eds.), *Trends in organizational behavior* (Vol. 5, pp. 65-82). Greenwich, CT: JAI.

Gustafson, S. B. (2000). Personality and organizational destructiveness: Fact, fiction and fable. In L. R. Bergman & R. B. Carins (Eds.), *Developmental science and the holistic approach* (pp. 299-313). Mahwah, NJ: Lawrence Erlbaum.

Gustafson, S. B., & Mumford, M. D. (1995). Personal style and person-environment fit: A pattern approach. *Journal of Vocational Behavior, 46*(2), 163-188.

Gustafson, S. B., & Ritzer, D. R. (1995). The dark side of normal: A psychopathy-linked pattern called self-promotion. *European Journal of Personality, 9*(3), 147-183.

Hannaway, J. (1989). *Managers managing: The workings of an administrative system.* New York: Oxford University Press.

Judge, T. A., & Cable, D. M. (1997). Applicant personality, organizational culture and organizational attraction. *Personnel Psychology, 50,* 359-394.

Kets de Vries, M. F. R. (1979). Managers can drive their subordinates mad. *Harvard Business Review, 57*(4), 125-134.

Kets de Vries, M. F. R. (1989). Leaders who self-destruct: The causes and cures. *Organizational Dynamics, 17*(4), 4-17.

Kets de Vries, M. F. R. (Ed.). (1991). *Organizations on the coach: Clinical perspectives on organizational behavior and change.* San Francisco: Jossey-Bass.

Kets de Vries, M. F. R. (1993). Doing a Maxwell: Or why not to identify with the aggressor. *European Management Journal, 11*(2), 169-174.

Kets de Vries, M. F. R., & Miller, D. (1985). Narcissism and leadership: An object relations perspective. *Human Relations, 38*(6), 583-601.

Kets de Vries, M. F. R., & Miller, D. (1991). Leadership styles and organizational cultures: The shaping of neurotic organizations. In M. F. R. Kets de Vries (Ed.), *Organizations on the couch: Clinical perspectives on organizational behavior and change* (pp. 243-263). San Francisco: Jossey-Bass.

Lewin, K. (1958). Group decision and social change. In E. E. Maccoby, T. M. Newcomb, & E. L. Hartley (Eds.), *Readings in social psychology* (pp. 197-211). New York: Holt, Rinehart & Winston.

Maccoby, M. (2000). Narcissistic leaders: The incredible pros, the inevitable cons. *Harvard Business Review, 78*(1), 68-77.

Mischel, W. (1977). The interaction of person and situation. In D. Magnusson & N. S. Endler (Eds.), *Personality at the crossroads: Current issues in interactional psychology.* Hillsdale, NJ: Lawrence Erlbaum.

Mischel, W. (1996). *Personality and assessment.* Mahwah, NJ: Lawrence Erlbaum.

Moch, M. K., & Bartunek, J. M. (1990). *Creating alternative realities at work: The quality of work life experiment at FoodCom.* New York: Harper Business.

Morgan, G. R. (1998). *Organizational theory* (2nd ed.). Reading, MA: Addison-Wesley.

Morris, E. K. (1988). Contextualism: The world view of behavior analysis. *Journal of Experimental Child Psychology, 46,* 289-323.

Mudrack, P. E., Mason, E. S., & Stepanski, K. M. (1999). Equity sensitivity and business ethics. *Journal of Occupational & Organizational Psychology, 72*(4), 539-560.

Nahavandi, A., & Malekzadeh, A. (1988). Acculturation in mergers and acquisitions. *Academy of Management Review, 13,* 79-90.

Namenwirth, J. Z., & Weber, R. P. (1987). *Dynamics of culture.* Boston: Allen & Unwin.

O'Leary-Kelly, A. M., Griffin, R., & Glew, D. J. (1996). Organization-motivated aggression: A research framework. *Academy of Management Review, 21,* 225-253.

Ott, J. S. (1989). *The organizational culture perspective.* Pacific Grove, CA: Brooks/Cole.

Ouchi, W. G. (1981). *Theory Z*. Reading, MA: Addison-Wesley.

Pascale, R. T., & Athos, A. G. (1981). *The art of Japanese management*. New York: Simon & Schuster.

Payne, R. L. (2000). Climate and culture: How close can they get? In N. M. Ashkanasy, C. P. M. Wilderon, & M. F. Peterson (Eds.), *Handbook of organizational culture and climate* (pp. 163-176). Thousand Oaks, CA: Sage.

Quick, J. C., & Gavin, J. H. (2000). The next frontier: Edgar Schein on organizational therapy (Interview). *Academy of Management Executive, 14*(1), 31-44.

Robinson, S. L., & Bennett, R. J. (1995). A typology of deviant workplace behaviors: A multidimensional scaling study. *Academy of Management Journal, 38*, 555-572.

Robinson, S. L., & Kraatz, M. S. (1998). Constructing the reality of normative behavior: The use of neutralization strategies by organizational deviants. In R. W. Griffin, A. O'Leary-Kelly, & J. M. Collins (Eds.), *Dysfunctional behavior in organizations: Violent and deviant behavior* (pp. 203-220). Stamford, CT: JAI.

Robinson, S. L., & O'Leary-Kelly, A. M. (1998). Monkey see, monkey do: The influence of work groups on the antisocial behavior of employees. *Academy of Management Journal, 41*(6), 658-672.

Sathe, V. (1985). *Culture and related corporate realities*. Homewood, IL: Irwin.

Schein, E. (2000). Response to Manfred Kets de Vries' commentary. *Academy of Management Review, 14*(1), 48.

Schein, E. H. (1985). *Organizational culture and leadership*. San Francisco: Jossey-Bass.

Schein, V. E., & Diamonte, T. (1988). Organizational attraction and the person-environment fit. *Psychological Reports, 62*, 167-173.

Schneider, B. (1987a). E=f(P,B): The road to a radical approach to person-environment fit. *Journal of Vocational Behavior, 31*, 353-361.

Schneider, B. (1987b). The people make the place. *Personnel Psychology, 40*, 437-453.

Schneider, B. (2000). The psychological life of organizations. In N. M. Ashkanasy, C. P. M. Wilderon, & M. F. Peterson (Eds.), *Handbook of organizational culture and climate* (pp. xvii-xxi). Thousand Oaks, CA: Sage.

Schneider, B., Brief, A. P., & Guzzo, R. A. (1996). Creating a climate and culture for sustainable organizational change. *Organizational Dynamics, 24*(4), 7-9.

Schneider, B., Goldstein, H. W., & Smith, D. B. (1995). The ASA framework: An update. *Personnel Psychology, 48*, 747-773.

Showers, C., & Cantor, N. (1985). Social cognitions: A look at motivated strategies. *Annual Review of Psychology, 36*, 275-305.

Siehl, C., Ledford, G., Silverman, R., & Fay, P. (1988). Preventing culture clashes from botching a merger. *Mergers and Acquisitions, 22*, 51-57.

Sperry, L. (1996). *Corporate therapy and consulting*. Philadelphia: Brunner/Mazel.

Sperry, L. (1998). Organizations that foster inappropriate aggression. *Psychiatric Annals, 28*, 279-284.

Svyantek, D. J. (1997). Order out of chaos: Non-linear systems and organizational change. *Current Topics in Management, 2*, 167-188.

Svyantek, D. J., & Brown, L. L. (2000). A complex systems approach to organizations. *Current Directions in Psychological Science, 9*(2), 69-74.

Svyantek, D. J., Jones, A. P., & Rozelle, R. (1991). The relative influence of organizational decision frames on decision making. *Advances in Information Processing in Organizations, 4*, 127-145.

Svyantek, D. J., & Kolz, A. R. (1996). The effects of organizational frames and problem ambiguity on decision-making. *Journal of Business and Psychology, 11*(2), 131-150.

Tepper, B. J. (2000). Consequences of abusive supervision. *Academy of Management Journal, 43*(2), 178-190.

Trice, H. M., & Beyer, J. M. (1993). *The cultures of organizations*. Englewood Cliffs, NJ: Prentice-Hall.

Vredenburgh, D., & Brender, Y. (1998). The hierarchical abuse of power in work organizations. *Journal of Business Ethics, 17*(1), 1337-1347.

CHAPTER 25

An Application Model Relating the Essential Functions of a Job to Mental Disabilities[1]

Steven F. Cronshaw
Brenda L. Kenyon

THE LEGISLATIVE BACKGROUND TO IDENTIFYING ESSENTIAL FUNCTIONS AND ACCOMMODATING THE MENTALLY DISABLED

To begin this chapter, we discuss the major legislative impetus for helping individuals with mental disabilities function effectively in the workplace. The Americans with Disabilities Act (ADA) of 1991 protects disabled workers from discriminatory practices by employers and requires these employers to provide reasonable accommodations to disabled people short of undue hardship. The ADA states, however, that the worker must be able to perform the essential functions of the position. Therefore, much revolves around properly

defining what these essential functions are and how these relate to mental disabilities. Subsequent clarification by the Equal Employment Opportunity Commission presents four factors that should be considered when determining whether a job function is essential (State of Minnesota, n.d.):

1. The employees in the position concerned must be required to actually perform the function.

2. The position exists to perform the function.

3. There are a limited number of employees who can share the function.

4. The function is central to a highly specialized position.

AUTHORS' NOTE: This chapter is dedicated to Kenton with the hope that its contents may, in some small way, help him in his transition to the world of work.

Additional evidence that a job function is essential includes the following:

i. The employer's judgment as to which functions are essential;

ii. Written job descriptions prepared before advertising or interviewing applicants for the job;

iii. The amount of time spent on the job performing the function;

iv. The consequences of not requiring the incumbent to perform the function;

v. The terms of a collective bargaining agreement;

vi. The work experience of past incumbents in the job; and/or

vii. The current work experience of incumbents in similar jobs. (p. 121)

The specification of essential functions becomes important to the proper application of the ADA, inasmuch as "the employer is not obligated to remove essential functions from a job as a reasonable accommodation" (State of Minnesota, n.d.). In Figure 25.1, we summarize the major steps in our integrated model intended for use by a multidisciplinary team to analyze and relate essential job functions to the provision of reasonable accommodations for mentally disabled individuals.

AN APPLICATION MODEL RELATING ESSENTIAL JOB FUNCTIONS TO INDIVIDUAL ASSESSMENT AND ACCOMMODATION

In this section of our chapter, we introduce an integrated model that brings together the systems concerns of the human resources professional with the individually based clinical concerns of the mental health professional. The model is pictorially represented in Figure 25.1. It consists of four phases: three phases of data collection (Job Analysis, Workplace Assessment, and Clinical Assessment) and a final phase of identifying and providing Workplace Accommodation. The assessment model is broken down into a series of stages represented by the boxes in Figure 25.1. The solidly outlined boxes are activities carried out primarily by the human resources manager, with the assistance of the worker where this is appropriate. The boxes outlined in broken lines contain activities carried out primarily by the mental health practitioner, with the involvement of the client as appropriate. The box outlined by the dotted line (i.e., Stage 8 of Identifying Workplace Accommodations) is an activity requiring the extensive involvement of the human resources manager, the mental health professional, and the worker/client.[3] Key points of contact within the application model are indicated by arrows. As will be seen, the application model in fact assumes that there will be extensive, ongoing contact and discussion between stakeholders to the individual accommodation (management, mental health professional, and worker/client). We will now discuss each of the stages in the applications model in more detail, beginning with the identification of essential job functions.

1. *Job Analysis: Identify Essential Job Functions.* We use Functional Job Analysis, or FJA (Fine & Cronshaw, 1999), as our job analysis methodology of choice to illustrate the identification of essential job functions, although we recognize that other job analysis methods are available that can address the provisions of the ADA (e.g., the DACUM method) (see Ohio State University, 2000). The output, which,

Data Collection and Integration

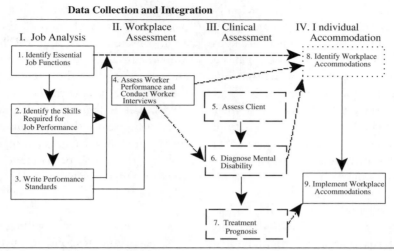

Figure 25.1   Stages in the Application Model Relating Essential Job Functions to Individual Assessment and Accomodation

within FJA, is analogous to an essential function, is a set of activities directed by the worker toward achieving organizational objectives. Each output consists of one or more tasks where a task is defined in the FJA system as "an action or action sequence group through time, designed to contribute a specified end result to the accomplishment of an objective, and for which functional levels and orientation can be reliably assigned"[4] (Fine & Cronshaw, 1999, p. 49). Tasks are the fundamental unit of work and, as such, along with outputs, provide the operational focus on the work needed to apply the ADA in a careful, systematic, and informed manner.

An example at this point will help to clarify the application of FJA to identifying essential functions of the job. A task under the output of Servicing Customer Accounts for the job of Franchise Manager within a large cleaning and maintenance company is as follows (Evans, 1994):

Phone/visit customers at existing accounts, discussing concerns and representing franchise interests, drawing, listening, interpersonal, and problem solving skills and knowledge of customers' needs, job order requirements, and capabilities of cleaning crew and equipment, in order to assess customer satisfaction with cleaning services and maintain business relationship.

The task, as for the other tasks under this output, requires the worker to exercise skills in getting the work done to standards required by the franchise owners. Standards that were applied by the franchise owners to the performance of their individual managers on this task included the following:

- The manager actively seeks performance feedback from the customer.
- The manager develops and maintains a rapport with the customer.
- The manager is diplomatic and tactful in all of his or her dealings with customers.

When the tasks under this output are laid out in this detail, it is readily appreciated that the output—which contains several such tasks—is an "essential function" within the meaning of the ADA because (a) the tasks under the output are actually performed; (b) the Franchise Manager position exists to ensure that customers are kept happy and return to the franchise for more work (otherwise, the franchise will go out of business); (c) other workers on staff at that location (i.e., the cleaners and their supervisors) would not share the function; and (d) the function requires interpersonal skills that are not necessarily possessed by other employees on the job site (i.e., cleaners and supervisors). In the next two sections, we will explore further the importance of identifying the skills and performance standards that apply to individual tasks comprising essential functions. As well, we will consider the matter of mental disability and how this concept can be properly understood and located within the job reference points provided by FJA.

2. *Job Analysis: Identify the Skills Required for Job Performance.* As will be seen, the concept of skill is central to working within the ADA to accommodate and integrate workers with mental disabilities into the workplace.[5] For organizations, skill has come to refer to the broad set of competencies—mental, interpersonal, physical, and adaptive—that the worker provides voluntarily to the organization in exchange for paid remuneration. Skills, and the worker's willingness to exercise those skills on behalf of the organization, are central to managers' thinking about what labor can and should bring to their productive enterprise.[6] In the FJA system, worker skills are of three types (the definitions of all three skills are taken from Fine & Cronshaw, 1999).

Adaptive skills are competencies that enable people to manage themselves in relation to the demands of conformity and/or change in particular situations. They are acquired in the course of life experience, particularly early childhood, on practically a subconscious level, and are displayed by individuals as they exercise responsibility and effort, and as they generally relate to the context of the work (Fine & Cronshaw, 1999). Let us return to the performance standards previously given under the task for the Franchise Manager. To perform that task to the three performance standards given, the manager will require at least three adaptive skills:

- He or she must be willing and able to listen and respond to customer complaints/concerns.
- He or she must be willing and able to exercise control over negative emotions invoked by critical comments by customers about the work completed.
- He or she must be willing and able to maintain a professional demeanor at all times with customers.

Although the adaptive skills are described in worker-oriented and not clinical language, the reader will probably note close parallels and immediate points of connection with the behavioral symptomatology used by mental health professionals in their clinical diagnoses. For example, consider some *Diagnostic and Statistical Manual of Mental Disorders (DSM-IV-TR)* (American Psychiatric Association [APA], 2000) criteria for a Major Depressive Episode:

(1) depressed mood most of the day, nearly every day, as indicated by either subjective report (e.g., feels sad or empty) or observation made by others (e.g., appears tearful). . . .

(2) markedly diminished interest or pleasure in all, or almost all, activities most of the day, nearly every day. . . .

(4) diminished ability to think or concentrate, or indecisiveness, nearly every day (either by subjective account or as observed by others). (p. 356)

There is little doubt that the individual undergoing a Major Depressive Episode would be impaired in exercising the adaptive skills listed above for the Franchise Manager task, even if he or she performs well on the task when not affected by the disorder.

If the adaptive skills required by the job are specified by a job analysis before the clinical diagnosis (e.g., depression), hypotheses can be generated easily about which adaptive skills in the workplace should be affected by the disability. These hypotheses can be tested further for their applicability to the individual when management conducts performance appraisals that assess worker application of adaptive skills on the job (see Step 4 under the Workplace Assessment stage in Figure 25.1). This is one of at least three points (as illustrated by connecting dashed arrows in Figure 25.1) where managers and mental health professionals can pool their expertise in jointly testing hypotheses about the type of disability and its effects in the workplace. The result of testing these hypotheses, and answering the questions they raise, will certainly contribute to a more targeted and successful mental health intervention. It is useful to note that adaptive skills often will generalize across several tasks under the same output (essential function) and as such provide wide coverage of an individual's adaptive functioning within the workplace. Mental disorders often function to suppress the expression of adaptive skill (e.g., the depression example above). Conversely, the use of adaptive skills sometimes can offset the negative effects of a mental disability on job performance. A pivotal question is whether the

mental disability is sufficiently pervasive in its effects to overwhelm the adaptive skills normally brought by the person as a positive contribution to the workplace.

Functional skills are competencies that enable people to appropriately process Things, Data, and People (TDP) on simple to complex levels, drawing on their physical, mental, and interpersonal resources. They are acquired from early infancy as people exercise their potential through relating to Things, Data, and People in their immediate environment, and they are sharpened in later experiences through school, in play, in volunteer work, and in pursuit of hobbies (Fine & Cronshaw, 1999). FJA presents three scales on which tasks and jobs are assessed for their standing on functional skills. These scales reflect the complexity of worker involvement with Things (at four levels), Data (at six levels), and People (at eight levels). As well, the relative extent of involvement of the task or job in Things, Data, and People can be assessed by measures of Functional Orientation. Rather than go through a detailed explanation of Functional Skills (which would take more space than we have here), we will give the TDP Complexity and Orientation ratings for the previously presented task for the Franchise Manager and refer the reader to Fine and Cronshaw (1999) for further information on the detailed definition of Functional Skills.

TDP Functional Ratings for Franchise Manager Task (phone/visit customers)

Complexity Scale	Orientation Scale
Things: Handling (Level 1A)	Things: 5%
Data: Analyzing (Level 4)	Data: 35%
People: Consulting (Level 4)	People: 60%

The results show that this task within the essential function of Servicing Customer

Accounts requires (in greatest measure) a People involvement (of 60%) at medium level of People complexity and requires (in lesser measure) a Data involvement at medium level of complexity. When we also draw in the related performance standards for this task, it is easy to see that mental disorders compromising the worker's capability for dealing sympathetically and sensitively with people (e.g., Asperger's Syndrome[7]) will have a negative impact on the performance of this task. Because the function (output) of Servicing Customer Accounts is essential, the mental health professional and manager might well conclude that voluntary treatment of a mental disorder is the first step,[8] but if the treatment is not effective, it would impose an undue burden on the employer to provide an individual accommodation by redesigning this function or, because it is part of an essential function, exempting the worker from performing it.

Specific Content Skills are competencies that enable people to perform a specific job to predetermined standards using specific equipment, technology, and procedures and relying on functional skills. Specific Content Skills are learned on the job; during training in vocational, technical, trade, or professional schools; or as part of focused self-study (Fine & Cronshaw, 1999). A Specific Content Skill for the task given for the Franchise Manager is the knowledge of crew organization and equipment used by staff to clean customers' premises. These skills, although necessary for job performance, are built on top of the skill base provided by functional and adaptive skills. In providing for mental health in the workplace, it is important not to focus an inordinate amount of attention on Specific Content Skills—the adaptive and functional skills provide a richer and more informative basis for developing and testing hypotheses

about the impact of mental disability in the workplace and possibilities for individual accommodation.

3. *Job Analysis: Write Performance Standards.* Performance standards provide the most immediate, but emotionally charged, reference points whereby the manager becomes connected to the process illustrated in Figure 25.1. As well, the workers have an important stake in these standards and use them through their workday to guide and direct their activities. When essential functions become compromised by a mental disability, it is the worker's standing on the related performance standards (especially if performing at an unsatisfactory level) that will signal management that a serious problem exists that must be resolved in a timely manner. Therefore, the complete and careful wording of the performance standards becomes crucial to the application model in Figure 25.1. An extended treatment of performance standards is well beyond the aegis of this chapter, but additional information, including how to properly word performance standards, can be found in Fine and Cronshaw (1999).

TASKS, SKILLS, AND PERFORMANCE STANDARDS PROVIDE REFERENCE POINTS BY WHICH TO FULLY DEFINE ESSENTIAL FUNCTIONS FOR ADA PURPOSES

Under the ADA, the mentally disabled worker may ask that nonessential job functions be waived as a reasonable accommodation. Conversely, management can require the worker to perform the essential functions of the position if reasonable accommodations (to the point of undue hardship for the employer) have been made to allow the disabled worker to perform those essential functions. Therefore, the sorting of essential from nonessential functions becomes pivotal to the proper application of the ADA. For analytic purposes, these essential functions (outputs) can understood from three interrelated and complementary perspectives:

• *Tasks Performed Under the Output (i.e., the Function).* In FJA, the tasks are worded in purely descriptive language. They provide an objective statement of in which actions the worker engages and what gets done as a result of those actions. If the FJA is done properly, there should be little or no disagreement among the stakeholders—disabled worker, manager, and mental health professional—over what the worker does (actions) and what gets done (results). In other words, this reference point is fixed by the FJA system, and so, once that system is understood and followed, carefully written tasks provide a common understanding among stakeholders as to what is actually done, and what gets done, by the job holder.

• *Skills, or Competencies, That Workers Bring to Performing the Tasks.* Again, this reference point is fixed through the definitions and scaling offered by the FJA system. However, difficult questions will still arise around how the mental disability suppresses or inhibits the expression of skills, whether the work-related impairment results in temporary or permanent skill deficits, and so on.

• *Performance Standards Applying to Tasks or Groupings of Tasks Under Outputs (Functions).* Performance standards, which can be either descriptive or numerical, are worded in evaluative language (Fine & Cronshaw, 1999). They communicate the performance expectations that management has of the workers and

that the workers have of themselves. Stakeholders will often disagree over the performance standards that do, or should, apply to a given job. When this happens, the stakeholders—management, worker/client, and clinician—must come to a common understanding of performance standards that apply to the job. In effect, this reference point will remain indeterminate until it is agreed on through discussion and consensus by the stakeholders. If the performance standards are left indeterminate (i.e., they are not fixed by the stakeholders), the FJA reference system, or any other system, will be incomplete as a basis for determining the likely effects of the mental disability on job functioning and for identifying individual accommodations needed to bring the individual to a satisfactory level of job performance.

The use of job analysis to establish the three sets of reference points (tasks, skills, and performance standards) within essential functions addresses the questions of what the disabled worker must do, what he or she must get done within the work system, the competencies that he or she must bring to the situation, and the performance standards that must be met. Once the stakeholders identify the task and skill reference points, and agree on the performance standards that apply, the job analysis phase in Figure 25.1 is complete.

Job analysis identifies the essential functions performed by the worker and provides other job information needed to design individual accommodations under the ADA. Job analysis provides the required information about the job side of the job-worker situation; however, information about the worker and his or her current fit to, and success in, the job is also required. It is to the assessment of the worker that we now turn in the second phase of the application model in Figure 25.1.

4. *Workplace Assessment: Assess Worker Performance and Conduct Worker Interviews.* If individual accommodations are to be provided to the mutual satisfaction of the worker and the employer, the worker's present contribution in the workplace must be identified with respect to tasks performed, skills used, and performance standards met. For example, it should be determined whether the individual is impaired in many, or only a few, areas of job performance and whether performance in these areas is only slightly impaired or is wholly unsatisfactory. In addition, the individual's perspective on these workplace demands and challenges is needed to better understand his or her unique style of responding to the workplace. We amplify on these two needs below.

• *Assess Worker Performance From the Management Perspective.* Performance appraisal takes the performance standards identified by management in partnership with the worker and places them within an instrument or process that can be used to assess worker performance periodically. The worker's performance is most often rated by his or her supervisor(s), but ratings may also be obtained from peers or even subordinates.[9] At its best, performance appraisal can and should provide many data to help in diagnosing the mental problem and identifying needed individual accommodations (see dotted line in Figure 25.1). Unfortunately, performance appraisals too often use either uselessly broad trait descriptors (e.g., "motivated," "conscientious") or narrow technical capabilities (e.g., ratings of knowledge of equipment operation to assess performance of individual workers). Where careful and detailed assessments on performance standards related to adaptive and functional skills are provided through regular performance appraisal, they comprise information

that can be very useful in identifying the mental disorder and providing individual accommodations. Peers and supervisors at the work site can be interviewed to obtain information augmenting formal performance appraisal. These interviews can provide additional insights to the client/worker's strengths and areas of difficulty.

• *Conduct Interviews to Get the Worker's Perspective.* A thorough assessment should also include exploration of the client's experience of the workplace. For individuals experiencing mental disorders, the workplace can be a source of support and stability or, conversely, a source of stress and dissatisfaction. It is extremely important to determine which dynamic is operating. Information about which aspects of the job are perceived as rewarding, stressful, challenging, overwhelming, or potentially helpful to the individual should be collected through the interview. This information can help determine which aspects of the job, if changed or maintained, are likely to be beneficial or detrimental to the individual.

At this juncture, the job analysis and workplace assessment phases of the application model in Figure 25.1 have been completed.[10] Most of the work in these two phases has been done by management or their representatives in the human resources department, although the clinician should receive regular communications on (and agree with) the work being done and may observe work being done in the first two phases. In Phase 3, the emphasis shifts to the clinician to assess his or her client and provide the remaining information needed for the identification and provision of individual accommodations.

5. *Clinical Assessment: Assess Client.* The clinical assessment information collected will depend on the diagnostic questions

asked. Diagnostic questions might include the following:

- Is the client/worker in fact suffering from a mental disorder/problem?
- If so, does this disorder or problem affect job performance? Or are its effects limited only to other areas of life functioning (an unlikely finding in most cases)?
- How does the problem or disorder manifest itself on the job? In other words, which performance standards are affected for which essential functions?
- Is the disorder or problem short-term and treatable, or is it long-term, chronic, and not amenable to treatment?
- What skills and strengths does the individual bring to the job that serve to offset the impact of the problem?

The mental health professional should reach consensus on the diagnostic questions with management before undertaking his or her psychological assessment. It is important that any job information used in this discussion be focused only on the essential functions of the job.

Generally, the psychological assessment is conducted by one or more mental health professionals away from the work site, often at the offices of the mental health professional, and it uses assessments (including both standardized tests and "soft" methods such as the clinical interview). The assessment data provide information about the nature of the client's problem; specific cognitive, emotional, or functional deficits that might affect performance in the workplace; and information about the potential protective or contributing factors inside and outside the workplace. Typically, the individual assessment provides at least the following data:

- The client's current thinking
- Problem-solving, memory, attention, and concentration skills
- Stress tolerance and impulse control
- Emotional stability and interpersonal relations
- Coping capacity and endurance

As can be seen, the psychological assessment will cover many of the areas of functional and adaptive skills identified in the job analysis phase of Figure 25.1.

The clinical assessment should provide a specific description of the primary psychological problem and its manifestation. For example, anxiety is manifest in many different ways (e.g., avoidance of the job situation, a tendency toward perfectionism in performing job tasks). Understanding how the predominant features of the mental disorder manifest themselves for a specific individual across the essential functions within the given job-worker situation will be crucial in planning accommodations.

6. *Clinical Assessment: Diagnose Mental Disability.* An accurate diagnosis of the mental disorder and its etiology by the mental health practitioner is necessary if both accommodation and treatment of the individual are to be successful (i.e., result in higher motivation and productivity, lower work stress, higher life satisfaction, and greater opportunities for advancement). However, the mental health practitioner is not the only source of diagnostic information. Although the use of individual mental health assessments (e.g., ability testing, personality inventories, clinical interviews) comprise a major input to diagnosis of the mental disability, diagnostic information can, and should, be contributed from the management side as well. As shown previously, management can present performance appraisal information that, if

focused on functional and adaptive skills, augments and fills out the profile of the client/worker as he or she acts and reacts in the workplace environment. The mental health professional and manager should discuss together the strengths and limitations of each data source and integrate their data so as to best answer the diagnostic questions.

As part of the diagnosis, the mental health professional will be asked (or at least *should* be asked) to render opinions on questions such as the following: To what extent is the client's disorder a result of an unhealthy work environment, and to what extent is it attributable to attitudes, skills, predispositions, or pathologies that the client carries with him or her? To what extent is the client's dysfunctional behavior the result of an interaction between personal factors and work-related causes? Which of the performance standards applying to this worker will be affected by the disorder, and which ones will be unaffected? Which worker skills are compromised by the disorder, and which ones are left intact? Is it possible for the worker to use intact skills to compensate for skills affected by the disorder? If so, which skills are involved? Such questions will require the mental health professional to be knowledgeable in the basic job analysis terminology and concepts introduced earlier in this chapter and to seek the assistance of the manager and client in mapping clinical symptoms and categories onto work-related outcomes.

Because the mental health approach is diagnostically driven (e.g., see the listing of disorders and their diagnostic criteria in the *DSM-IV*), recommendations by the mental health practitioner will tend to categorize the individual in terms of general criteria of the disorder. These recommendations do not address skills, often pivotal, by which the

individual can make a positive contribution to the workplace, nor do they address unique aspects of the individual's functioning that may moderate the impact of the problem at work or at home. For example, while it is a general finding that individuals with depression all suffer significant fatigue, there are large individual differences in the expression and management of this symptom. Some depressed people may ask their employer for a shortened workday to preserve sufficient energy to function the next day, not to mention in other aspects of their lives. This is particularly important for individuals with families or dependents. Other people, who live alone, might find work an important distraction from depression, preferring to expend their limited energy at work and using their after-work hours to rest. Still others might find that some particular aspect of the job, such as the satisfaction of completing a task or the social contact at work, contributes to well-being despite the fatigue. For these individuals, a standard workday might be appropriate, but altering the job to include more circumscribed tasks or team-based work would be beneficial. The mix of clinical assessment information and job-based assessments will prove to be useful in tailoring individual accommodations to the unique circumstances and needs of the client/worker and the employer.

It is a complex matter to integrate the available information—from both the workplace assessment and the clinical assessment—in answering the diagnostic questions. It will be at this time that a listening stance of mutual respect between mental health professionals and managers is especially important. The goal is to reach an informed consensus on what problem or disorder is affecting the client/worker, what essential job functions are affected, and the etiology by which the problem or disorder affects significant aspects of the individual's work and personal life. Integration and interpretation will likely involve testing provisional hypotheses about the type, etiology, and effects of the disorder/problem. Some of these hypotheses may have to be set aside if the assessment data do not support them. Consequently, this hypothesis-testing process will require give-and-take from all parties to the application model.

7. *Clinical Assessment: Treatment Prognosis.* Once a mental health problem is identified, the client usually works with a mental health practitioner to learn strategies for coping with or reducing symptoms and to explore life changes to ensure continued well-being. The treatment prognosis that results will have an effect on the type of individual accommodation offered to the worker. A poor prognosis for recovery across the life domains, including work, may indicate that the worker has limited potential for performing in his or her existing position, and that reclassification of the individual to a new job, sometimes at a lower salary or classification level, may be necessary. In extreme cases, especially those presenting a safety risk to the worker, peers, or general public, the worker may have to be outplaced. Obviously, the onus will be on the employer to present the objective evidence needed to justify these management actions, especially in the latter instance. Where the prognosis is good for a complete or even partial recovery, individual accommodations will often be easier and more palatable to both worker and management.

After the completion of Step 7 in the application model, information has been collected and integrated that is needed to identify and implement individual accommodations for the essential functions of the job. It is to this fourth and final phase of the application model in Figure 25.1 that we now turn.

8. *Individual Accommodation: Identify Workplace Accommodations.* The psychological assessment data from Stage 3, combined with the information obtained through the job analysis and worker assessment in the workplace in Stages 1 and 2, should form the database from which necessary, appropriate, and effective accommodations are derived. When it comes to identifying accommodations for the mentally disabled individual, we believe it is fair to say that each stakeholder owns a different piece of the puzzle and can bring a complementary perspective to the problem. The mental health professional brings an understanding of the etiology of the disorder and general ideas about how it can be accommodated in the work setting. The manager, assisted by the job analysis and other information available to management, is in the best position to assess the practicality and feasibility of the workplace accommodation and to suggest alternate means for providing the accommodation. The worker/client brings the intimate knowledge of which workplace adjustments are most likely to work for him or her, which can reduce stress and discomfort while contributing to improved productivity.

The best solution to the individual accommodation will result from a creative synthesis of ideas from all the stakeholders. Two examples will help to illustrate the need to make individual accommodations responsive to both client and employer needs:

- Reducing concentration demands for a person with chronic depression (who has not responded well to drug treatment and psychotherapy) might work in a retail sales job, where demands are lower and public safety is not at issue, but not in air traffic control, where the worker must monitor instruments continuously and carefully, with the potential for catastrophic accident if his or her attention lapses.

- Reducing interpersonal contact for a person with a social phobia might work well for a software engineer, who can do most of the work alone, but not for a nurse, for whom social contact and a caring attitude are integral to the job.

In other words, a cooperative approach between mental health professional and manager is needed if the unique circumstances of the individual are to be best aligned with the essential functions of the job to achieve practical and effective individual accommodations of mental health problems.

9. *Individual Accommodation: Implement Workplace Accommodations.* The manager will have to be the driving force behind the implementation of any workplace accommodations. If the accommodation is to be put in place in a timely and effective fashion, it is vital that the manager fully buy into the accommodation and the reasoning behind putting it in place. This is especially true in the case of mental health disabilities (e.g., chronic depression, mental retardation, autism) that will require difficult and costly accommodations on the part of the employer. Top management support for ADA initiatives is also necessary if these are to be resourced adequately. The nature of the individual accommodations put in place will depend on the type of disability, availability of resources, and other factors specific to the individual case.

Accommodation is best carried out through the joint efforts of the client, mental health professionals, managers in the organization (especially in human resources), and other interested parties having expertise in workplace mental problems (e.g., consultants). Often, accommodation will have to be offered in a coordinated manner (e.g., the depressed worker may be given additional sick leave from work in order to participate in a treatment regimen developed by the mental health professional). Other chapters in this book discuss individual accommodations that are suited to particular types of disability.

CRITICAL ISSUES IN ACCOMMODATING MENTAL DISABILITIES IN THE WORKPLACE: THE MULTIDISCIPLINARY TEAM AND ITS PROCESS

We have presented an application model that focuses attention on bringing the technical and professional expertise of managers and mental health professionals, as well as the help of the client, to bear on the problem of individual accommodation. However, technical skills are not enough. Much needs to be done to set up the positive and productive group process needed to ensure that all parties to the application model contribute to effective problem solving and that they are enthusiastically committed to the resulting individual accommodations. In the remainder of the chapter, we will look more closely at this multidisciplinary team and the processes that it must put into place to get the most out of the application model.

The Multidisciplinary Team. As already shown, the parties to a mental health intervention in the workplace will have differing stakes in it. The client, the person experiencing the mental health problem, will usually have a highly personal stake in long-term employment. Employment provides him or her with access to financial resources, opportunities for social interaction, and possibilities for future career and personal growth. Sometimes, the workplace provides valuable opportunities and support at a time of peril and distress. At other times, the client will see the workplace as a contributor to his or her problems and mental distress. The mental health professional relies on the client for much of his or her information and most often will advocate for, or at least work toward, a resolution meeting client needs. Employers will come to mental health interventions from a fundamentally different perspective. Human resources (HR) managers, representing the employer's interests, view their primary role as bringing the right workers and skills into the product or service mix in order to ensure efficient and effective production. This is not to say that HR managers are uncaring of workers—but when all is said and done, the HR manager is primarily responsible to the organization, and not to each and every one of the individuals who comprise it. The employer will tend to view workers as a means to its desired ends (e.g., increased production, higher profits) and not as ends in themselves. The client and the mental health professional, on the other hand, will advocate for the individual as the ultimate end to be served in any mental health intervention. These fundamental differences in underlying interests must be understood, and a positive collaborative arrangement worked out between the parties, if the mental health intervention is to be efficient and effective.

The success of the intervention depends to a considerable extent on the process health of the multidisciplinary team that carries it out. Thus, creating an effective team requires careful attention to how the team is composed. The team will often draw on the skills of the client/worker; human resources manager; clinical specialist (psychologist, psychiatrist, psychiatric social worker); and possibly others (e.g., a specialist in particular disability or a representative from a community mental health group). When in doubt as to the team composition, it should be more, rather than less, inclusive of ancillary professionals and community-based resource people. The complexity of the issues involved in individual accommodation makes it advisable to seek additional help where this can be found.

ESTABLISHING AND MAINTAINING A HEALTH TEAM PROCESS

In addition to getting the right team composition, attention must be paid to setting the process conditions by which these players can work effectively as a multidisciplinary team. The goal is not only to bring together professional skills when and as needed, but also to create synergies between the players whereby new and innovative solutions are found and tried. Therefore, careful attention to a healthy and productive group process will be vital to achieving the best outcomes for the worker/client and the organization.

Schwarz (1994) makes many valuable suggestions about how positive group processes and outcomes can be better achieved. He recommends that groups follow 16 ground rules for effectiveness. We discuss a few of these below and relate them to our application model. We leave it to the reader to consult Schwarz's book as a valuable resource for improving the effectiveness of the multidisciplinary team.

Schwarz's (1994) first ground rule for effective groups is for group members to test their assumptions and inferences with each other. This advice is germane to present discussion because managers and mental health professionals operate from fundamentally different orientations.[11] Managers have a pragmatic, skills-oriented perspective when it comes to defining the disabled worker's roles and responsibilities, and this can be referred to as the *managerial approach*. Mental health professionals take a client advocacy, problem-centered perspective that can be called the *mental health approach*. Because these two approaches have a tendency to come into conflict unless the relationship between managers and mental health professionals is managed carefully, we now describe these two approaches in greater detail, as well as the advantages and limitations of each for understanding and dealing with workers' mental disabilities. With these differences understood, managers and mental health professionals can work together in a more informed manner to provide accommodation and treatment under the ADA.

The managerial approach to dealing with mental problems in the workplace will start first with what the job requires of the worker in terms of the tasks he or she must perform, the skills that he or she must bring to the workplace, and the performance standards the worker must meet to hold up his or her end of the employment contract. The manager's primary concern is that the disabled person works efficiently and effectively to meet the organization's objectives. In this regard, mental health professionals sometimes fail to fully appreciate that the manager is held responsible for results; low productivity, from whatever cause, will result in lower evaluations of the manager's performance and, in turn, put the manager's job and career in jeopardy. Managers will be aware of, and often sympathetic to, the disabled worker's trials and tribulations, but will be most interested in hearing from the mental health professional about how quickly the worker can be brought to

a highly productive status within the organization and how long that status will be maintained. When providing this information to management, the mental health professional is well advised to use the type of terminology and concepts that we presented under the occupational analysis section of this chapter: "With accommodation and treatment, here are the skills the worker brings to the employer . . ."; "Let's work together to identify ways of accommodating and treating the worker that will allow him or her to consistently meet your organization's performance standards within an acceptable period of time"; and so on. Paradoxically, the concepts of job analysis, and the information collected in that phase of the intervention, provide a vocabulary, a working language, that the mental health professional can use to make his or her activities on behalf of the disabled worker more recognized and acceptable to management while simultaneously pursuing his or her desired outcome of client improvement toward sustained mental health.

The mental health approach to dealing with mental problems in the workplace focuses on the type of problem facing the client, using the common characteristics of a disorder (e.g., depression) to generate strategies for accommodating the individual in the workplace and treating him or her. Because the mental health professional is working toward the improved mental health status of the client who has been diagnosed with a problem, he or she typically will show less concern for the essential functions of the job and the worker's performance in those functions. Managers should be prepared for this and recognize that, although this attitude may be somewhat perplexing to them, it is an expression of the mental health professional's legitimate role as a specialist in clinical diagnosis and treatment, and not an attempt to undermine the pragmatic, bottom-line interests of the manager. Where improvements in job performance can be obtained through treatment and accommodation, the mental health professional likely will consider this as a fulfillment of his or her mandate of achieving improved mental health for the client across the full range of his or her functioning, both on the job and off. (Managers will reverse this means-ends ordering and view improved mental health as the means of achieving the ultimate end of employee productivity.)

Schwarz (1994) emphasizes that team members focus on interests, not on positions. This is advice well taken. The clinical psychologist focuses on an interest when he or she says, "I want see that the client improves in all areas of life functioning and is satisfied with the outcome," but on a position when she says, "I must be given at least a year to treat this client." Statement in terms of interests, rather than a hard-and-fast position, allows all parties some "elbow room" in communicating their wishes and expectations, and in working to a consensus incorporating solutions that (ideally) meet everyone's interests. It is easy to see here that a conflict could result when the mental health professional and manager adopt firm but opposing positions to be defended, thereby undermining cooperative relations and consensus among the stakeholders.

Another recommendation is that groups jointly design ways to test disagreements and solutions (Schwarz, 1994). Earlier in this chapter, we discussed ways in which managers and mental health professionals can contribute data to assist in the diagnosis of a disorder/problem, its treatment, and its accommodation in the workplace. This approach leads naturally toward application of Schwarz's suggestion for the joint testing of disagreements and solutions. It is especially valuable to have a complete set of diagnostic information from both the individual assessments done by the mental health professional (e.g., ability tests, clinical interviews) and the job assessments conducted by management (e.g., task banks, performance appraisal results) available to all stakeholders to mental health intervention. If the mental health professional and the manager disagree on how the mental problem will manifest itself on the job, each should make a case and justify its validity by drawing on available data. Solutions emerging from this process are more likely to be based on the best facts available and to be valid and acceptable to both parties.

Schwarz (1994) recommends that groups be ready to discuss undiscussable issues. For our multidisciplinary team, these undiscussable issues are likely to be in the area of professional "turf protection," or fears of career gain/loss if the outcome of the intervention is perceived to go against one party or the other. These issues should be made discussable within the group in the service of a better intervention, even if they require a level of disclosure that many professionals and managers find uncomfortable. As well, process problems within the group (e.g., tendencies of a group member to withhold information) should be made discussable.

Perhaps Schwarz's (1994) most valuable advice is that the group should make decisions by consensus. Consensus decision making ensures that all sides to the application model have been heard and have offered their perspectives and skills. Team members also will be more committed to implementing solutions (in this case, individual accommodations) that have been arrived at by consensus. Consensus decision making is the litmus test that not only has a healthy group process been followed, but also the optimal solution has been reached and all stakeholders are committed to seeing the individual accommodation put in place.

Table 25.1   Hypothesized Relationship of Occupational Skill Types to *DSM-IV* Classification of Mental Disorders for Disabilities Most Likely to Be Encountered in Job Settings

Disorder from DSM-IV	Type(s) of Occupational Skill Most Proximal to Etiologies of Mental Disorder			
	Things	*Data*	*People*	*Adaptive*
Mental retardation	X			
Learning disorder	X			
Motor skills disorder	X			
Communication disorder	X	X		
Pervasive developmental disorders	X	X	X	X
Attention-deficit and disruptive behavior disorders			X	
Substance-related disorders			X	
Mood disorders – depression; Bipolar disorder		X		X
Anxiety disorders		X	X	X
Impulse-control disorders			X	
Personality disorders			X	X

CONCLUSION

This chapter begins with the definition of essential functions under the ADA and proposes a methodology for identifying those essential functions. However, we do not stop there. We discuss a theory of work and a methodology for measuring crucial work variables (i.e., the Functional Job Analysis, or FJA system) that relates those essential functions to the fundamentals of what the mentally disabled worker/client does in the job and what he or she gets done. We believe that an understanding of these deeper and richer connections is necessary for the most effective and informed individual accommodations. The application model proposed here, using the identification of essential functions as a starting point, is intended to guide application of the FJA theory and methodology toward achieving the best outcomes for the mentally disabled worker and the employer alike.

This chapter can only hint at broader and deeper questions that require sustained theoretical and research attention. Some questions needing further exploration include the following: Where do mental disabilities stand conceptually and practically relative to workplace skills? Does having some mental disabilities imply a lack of skill, as if skill and problem are at opposite ends of an underlying continuum? Does having certain other mental disabilities cause impairments that serve to inhibit or mask the expression of an underlying skill? If the mental disability is removed or ameliorated, will the previously underused, suppressed, or masked skill then express itself fully on the job? How can we predict when this will, or will not, happen? Much depends on our answers to these questions, yet the questions do not admit to easy or superficial analysis.[12] Considerable work remains to be done in integrating the respective HRM and mental health literatures if we are to find satisfactory answers to them. As a beginning to this work, we present in Table 25.1 some obvious connections between the FJA skills discussed above and mental disorders as classified in the *DSM-IV*. The Xs within this cross-classification indicate where substantial similarities are found between the way that FJA skills deficits are manifested behaviorally on the job and descriptions of behavioral symptoms of mental disorders from the *DSM-IV*. These connections suggest the need for a closer examination of the etiology of mental disability and the expression of these disabilities in the workplace. Further study of these issues should lead to a better understanding of mental disability in the workplace, as well as to the development of practical measures to treat and accommodate these disabilities.

NOTES

1. Much of the thinking in this chapter comes from our struggles as professionals from very different professional training and orientations to come together in assisting clients who are dealing with mental health issues in the workplace. The first author, Steven Cronshaw, is trained as an industrial/organizational psychologist, with a systems-level perspective on organizational functioning and the individual's place in that system. The second author, Brenda Kenyon, is trained as a clinical psychologist with a primary focus on the assessment and treatment of individuals with mental health concerns. In coming together on mental health interventions in the workplace, we have been surprised at the extent to which we differ in basic assumptions and viewpoints that we bring to the problem. These differences have required much discussion and careful listening to reach a common basis of understanding, but there has been much learning on both sides as we have worked together. In reflecting on our experiences, we have developed an application model that we believe the reader will find helpful for merging diverse professional and managerial expertise around mental health issues in the workplace. So far, we have tried out only some of the process recommendations we make in this chapter, but we believe all of them to be sound based on the relevant literature as well as our personal extrapolations into the roles and techniques presented here.

2. In Canada, legislation under the Canadian Human Rights Act requires employers in the federal jurisdiction to undertake similar measures to accommodate people with mental disabilities.

3. We will refer to the disabled individual as the "worker" where management carries out its activities within the application model and as the "client" when the mental health professional has a primary involvement.

4. We will return to the matter of functional level and orientation later in this chapter.

5. The term *disability* in the ADA is defined, with respect to an individual, as "(A) a physical or mental impairment that substantially limits one or more of the major life activities of such individual; (B) a record of such an impairment; or (C) being regarded as having such an impairment." This chapter, of course, focuses on mental, and not physical, impairments.

6. Many managers will assume that the word *disability* invariably translates into a lack of, or a deficit in, job-related skills. This is, of course, the type of stereotyping that the ADA and other legislation for the disabled are trying to combat. If we are to avoid contributing to this problem, we must be clear about how both terms—*skill* and *disability*—are defined.

7. Diagnostic criteria for Asperger's Syndrome given in the *DSM-IV* include impairments in social interaction such as failure to read nonverbal cues and lack of social or emotional reciprocity.

8. Asperger's Syndrome is a problem at the higher end of the spectrum of Pervasive Developmental Disorders, often referred to as autism (Schopler, Mesibov, & Kunce, 1998). These disorders are chronic and persistent. Prognosis for treatment is usually poor. The only viable option may be to reclassify the individual into a job better suiting his or her skills and minimizing the effect of the disability. The job would have to minimize the demands on interpersonal and change management skills with which autistic people have the most difficulty (reclassification can be a useful, and necessary, individual accommodation where no other options are available).

9. One variant on this process is to have the worker rate him- or herself on the performance standards in the performance appraisal and compare the results to ratings from supervisors, peers, and/or subordinates. Areas of disagreement between the worker and supervisor, in particular, may highlight areas of performance that will have to be discussed and reconciled if workplace accommodations are to be made to best effect.

10. We assume that the mental health professional and client are kept involved with the first two phases by making suggestions and offering observations, even though management provides most of the expertise and person hours.

11. The differing interests and perspectives of the manager and mental health professional in mental health intervention in the workplace is reflected in the specialized professional vocabularies they use. For example, managers will often refer to the affected individual as a "worker" or "employee"; the mental health professional will refer to the same person as a "client" or "patient."

12. It is possible to identify some mental disabilities (e.g., mental retardation) that have associated with them permanent deficits in certain job skills and other mental disabilities of a more transitory kind (e.g., state depression) that might only temporarily suppress or mask the expression of job skills. But where, for example, does impulse-control disorder fall in this scheme? Is it a problem, a deficit in adaptive skills, or both?

REFERENCES

American Psychiatric Association. (2000). *Diagnostic and statistical manual of mental disorders* (4th ed., text revision). Washington, DC: Author.

Evans, C. R. (1994). *Rating source differences and performance appraisal policies: Performance is in the "I" of the beholder.* Unpublished doctoral dissertation, University of Guelph, Guelph, Ontario, Canada.

Fine, S. A., & Cronshaw, S. F. (1999). *Functional job analysis: A foundation for human resources management.* Mahwah, NJ: Lawrence Erlbaum.

Ohio State University. (2000). *DACUM process.* Columbus, OH: Center on Education and Training for Employment. Retrieved from http://www.dacum.com/ohio/

Schopler, E., Mesibov, G. B., & Kunce, L. J. (Eds.). (1998). *Asperger syndrome or high-functioning autism?* New York: Plenum.

Schwarz, R. M. (1994). *The skilled facilitator: Practical wisdom for developing effective groups.* San Francisco: Jossey-Bass.

State of Minnesota. (n.d.). *Title 1: ADA reference guide. Topic 6: Essential job functions.* Department of Employee Relations, Office of Diversity and Equal Opportunity. Retrieved from http://www.doer.state.mn.us/odeo-ada/images/pdf-file/title1.pdf

CHAPTER 26

Job Accommodations for Mental Health Disabilities

Lois E. Tetrick
Leah P. Toney

Employment is a source of self-worth, meaning, and well-being for all people. Being excluded from productive work leads to social stigmatization and devaluation, as well as poor individual health (Mechanic, 1998). The Americans with Disabilities Act (ADA) of 1990 prohibits employment discrimination against qualified people with disabilities, in an attempt to provide disabled people with equal opportunities to experience the benefits of productive employment, participate fully in society, and live independently (Wasserbauer, 1997). The mandate requires employers with 15 or more employees to accommodate individuals with physical or mental health disabilities who can perform the essential functions of the job with some accommodations. Mental health disability is often more stigmatizing than physical disability. Because mental illnesses are usually manifest through an individual's behavior, they call for accommodations that are different from those for physical disabilities.

The goal of this chapter is to aid human resource professionals and service providers in understanding the components of the ADA, barriers to effective compliance, and development of accommodations for individuals with mental health disabilities.

COMPONENTS OF THE AMERICANS WITH DISABILITIES ACT

The ADA has three primary components: criteria for "persons with disabilities," the definition of "qualified individual with a disability," and the concept of "reasonable accommodation" (Kaufmann, 1993).

Definition of Disability

The foundational concept for disability rights in general is that disability is the result of an interaction between the individual's impairments and environmental factors (Pope & Tarlov, 1991, as cited in

Mechanic, 1998). Thus, individuals with impairments can participate in society to the extent that the environment is structured so as to not impose obstacles to participation. The ADA does not offer a specific definition of physical or mental impairment. Rather, it offers a three-faceted test for disability. The ADA covers qualified individuals who (a) have a physical or mental impairment that substantially limits one or more of their major life activities; (b) have a record of such an impairment; or (c) are regarded as having such an impairment, whether or not they have any major functional limitations. This definition is particularly relevant to people with mental health disabilities because it addresses both the functional limitations arising from manifestations of the disability, and the social consequences of stigma common to people with a history of psychiatric problems or treatment (Blanck & Pransky, 1999; Kaufmann, 1993).

By itself, a diagnosis of a mental health disability is not enough to demonstrate a substantial limitation in life functioning. Rather, the presence of a disability under the ADA is contingent upon the nature, severity, expected duration, and long-term effects of a specific individual's condition (Parry, 1993). Although the ADA originally protected individuals whose symptoms improve due to treatment such that major life activities are no longer impaired, the U.S. Supreme Court recently ruled in three cases that in determining whether a person has a disability under the ADA, any measures taken to control symptoms, such as medication or therapy, must be considered (Coleman, Cooney-Painter, & Moonga, 2000; Dalgin, 2001). It is likely that this issue of what degree of symptoms constitutes a disability will continue to be defined in the courts. Additionally, it is likely that future litigation will consider the extent to which an employer is responsible for accommodating individuals who are not seeking treatment. Furthermore, it is important to note that the ADA excludes some psychiatric conditions from protection, including compulsive gambling, kleptomania, pyromania, transvestism, transsexualism, pedophilia, exhibitionism, voyeurism, gender identity disorders not resulting from physical impairments, other sexual behavior disorders, and substance abuse disorders resulting from current use of illegal drugs (Wylonis, 1999). Although current users of illegal drugs are disqualified from protection under the ADA, individuals who are currently alcoholics or have a history of drug or alcohol abuse are covered (Shaw, MacGillis, & Dvorchik, 1994).

Definition of Qualified

To receive ADA protection, the person must be qualified for the job. The ADA defines a "qualified individual with a disability" as "an individual with a disability who, with or without reasonable accommodation, can perform the essential functions of the employment position that such individual holds or desires." In contrast to the Rehabilitation Act of 1973, the ADA requires that employers simultaneously determine whether a person is qualified and what accommodations might allow the person to perform the essential job functions (Miller, 1997). Essential job functions are tasks and responsibilities necessary to the successful performance of the job and, if not performed, change the fundamental nature of the job (Wasserbauer, 1997). The following criteria are used to assess the essential functions of a job: (a) Does the job exist to perform the function? (b) Which employees can perform the function? (c) What special skills are needed to perform the function? Essential job functions should then be documented in a written job description before a job is posted or candidates are interviewed. An important task especially relevant to accommodations for mental health disabilities is defining essential job functions related to emotional and psychosocial performance, and differentiating the essential functions from the marginal functions (Crist & Stoffel, 1992). It is critically important for employers to include all essential job functions, including psychosocial performance, in a written job description.

Definition of Reasonable Accommodations

Reasonable accommodations are changes in the work structure or work environment that allow an individual with a disability to compete equally with nondisabled people (Miller, 1997). Reasonable accommodations make it more likely that a disabled individual will apply for a job, achieve the same level of competence in job performance as a nondisabled person, and receive the same benefits from the job as nondisabled workers (Wasserbauer, 1997). Employers are required to accommodate an individual whether the disability is a condition that exists prior to employment or one that develops during employment (Crist & Stoffel, 1992).

Undue Hardship. Employers are not obligated to provide exceptionally burdensome accommodations that impose undue hardship to the organization. An accommodation that imposes undue hardship requires significant difficulty or expense when considered in light of the nature and cost of the accommodation needed and the overall operational, financial, and personnel resources of the facility. According to the ADA, undue hardship includes any action that is "excessively costly, extensive, substantial, or disruptive, or that would fundamentally alter the nature or operation of the business" (Miller, 1997). It is important to note that according to the EEOC (1997), disruption due to employees' fears, prejudices, or negative reactions to accommodation of the disabled individual do not constitute an undue hardship.

Threat. Although the media and the public often associate mental health disabilities with aggressive and unsafe behavior, most individuals with mental health disabilities do not pose a greater threat to the safety of employees than the general population (Monahan, 1992; Swanson, Holzer, Ganju, & Jono, 1990). Nevertheless, if an employee with a disability poses a direct threat to him- or herself and/or employees, he or she may be excluded from employment. Direct threat is defined by EEOC as significant risk of "substantial harm to the individual or others that cannot be eliminated or reduced by reasonable accommodation" (EEOC, 1997, p. 33). Employers should identify and document the specific behaviors that would constitute direct threat and include safety qualifications in the job description before the job is posted, in order to protect themselves in the case of discrimination claims (Crist & Stoffel, 1992; Mechanic, 1998). Direct threat assessments must be made on an individual basis, comparing the job qualifications to the person's abilities and limitations. In the case of *School Board of Nassau County v. Arline* (1987), the Supreme Court set the standard for the determination of direct threat, and the ADA adopted this analysis in its entirety (Miller, 1997). According to Miller (1997), the Court delineated three factors to consider when evaluating whether an individual's disability poses a direct threat: (a) the nature, duration, and severity of the risk; (b) the probability of harm; and

(c) whether the employer could reasonably accommodate the employee's disability. To exclude an individual from a job on the basis of direct threat, the employer must obtain objective evidence that an applicant or employee has recently demonstrated specific behavior that threatened or caused injury or harm, and that reasonable accommodation cannot eliminate this risk (Crist & Stoffel, 1992; Miller, 1997). The perception that the individual could commit harmful or threatening acts in the future is not considered direct threat (Crist & Stoffel, 1992).

BARRIERS TO COMPLIANCE WITH THE ADA

The ADA was implemented in 1992, and the findings are mixed as to how well employers are doing in accommodating people with disabilities (Schall, 1998). Bruyere, Brown, and Mank (1997) reported that a 1994 Harris poll found that 2 out of 10 people with disabilities had still encountered physical barriers, 3 out of 10 reported being discriminated against, and 4 out of 10 felt that employers did not acknowledge their ability to work full-time. However, a 1995 Harris poll of employers found that 81% of the participants said there had been a substantial increase in accommodations for people with disabilities. It has been argued that this latter finding may reflect what people report more than what has actually happened (see Schall, 1998). Nevertheless, none of these surveys has specifically addressed accommodations for employees with mental health disabilities, although Pardeck (1997) reported that in the first 14 months that the ADA was in effect, most complaints were for hidden disabilities, which would include most mental illness claims. Mental illness is the second

most common charge of discrimination filed with the EEOC under the ADA (Scheid, 1998). Therefore, it seems reasonable that the general business community remains guarded about the feasibility of making accommodations for people with mental health disabilities. This hesitancy may stem from two sources: concerns about compliance with the ADA and the effect of reasonable accommodations on organizational functioning, and concerns about people with mental health disabilities.

Concerns About Compliance With the ADA

The ADA has been criticized as being too ambiguous (Moore & Crimando, 1995). It does not offer concrete guidelines regarding whether a particular disability necessarily constitutes a disability covered by the ADA as noted above. Also, there are no explicit guidelines as to whether a particular accommodation is or is not appropriate for a particular disability, or even what constitutes an undue hardship on an organization in making an accommodation. In fact, Pollet (1995) concluded, based on her review of the cases, that it was not possible to specify definitive rules. Essentially, each individual's request for accommodation under the ADA needs to be handled on a case-by-case basis. This reflects a change in prior human resources thinking based on the EEOC whereby an organization is expected to treat people the same or at least equally. The ambiguity resulting from specific guidelines also increased organizations' concerns about litigation under the ADA and the costs inherent in such litigation (Moore & Crimando, 1995).

In addition to the costs of litigation, employers were concerned about the costs of accommodations (Moore & Crimando, 1995). The cost of accommodating employees with mental illnesses is low; the Job Accommodation Network reported that the cost of more than two thirds of the accommodations for individuals with physical or mental health disabilities is less than $500 (Zuckerman, 1993). In fact, Roessler and Sumner (1997), in their study of accommodations for people with chronic illnesses, reported that many accommodations did not have any direct cost, and only about 30% of accommodations cost more than $1,000. The employers surveyed by Scheid (1998) reported that making accommodations for people with mental illness was not costly. Although these concerns may not have disappeared, the available data suggest that most accommodations for physical and mental disabilities are not costly (Berry & Meyer, 1995).

Concerns About Hiring People With Mental Illness

The literature indicates that many people, including employers and managers, experience discomfort being around people with disabilities (Berry & Meyer, 1995; Boyle, 1997). This discomfort is greater when the disability is not visible externally, with the greatest stigma being associated with mental illness (Mechanic, 1998). The stereotype of people with mental illness is that they are "unpredictable, irrational, slow, stupid, and unreliable" (Scheid, 1998, p. 314). Furthermore, mental illness is often believed to be associated with violence (Scheid, 1998); however, as Mechanic (1998) points out, people with mental illness are not more dangerous than others, except possibly when they are in a psychotic phase of serious mental illness or when substance abuse is involved. This characterization is not consistent with many organizational cultures (Boyle, 1997; Harlan & Robert, 1998; Kirsh, 2000; Pati & Bailey, 1995).

Overcoming these negative stereotypes and attitudes toward individuals with mental health disabilities has been the subject of several studies. The literature suggests that first, organizations need a policy on compliance with the ADA (Diksa & Rogers, 1996; Scheid, 1998). Managers and supervisors need to be informed about the ADA, the organization's policy regarding accommodation for people with mental disabilities, and what mental illnesses are and what they are not (Thakker & Solomon, 1999). Finally, employers need to coordinate various workplace systems and programs such as employee assistance programs, wellness programs, coaching and mentoring, and training programs to create an organizational culture that is supportive of employees with mental health disabilities (Kirsh, 2000; Unger, 1999).

Another concern with making accommodations for people with mental health disabilities may stem from the type of accommodations needed. Accommodations for people with physical disabilities are usually accomplished by changing the physical environment (e.g., adjusting furniture so as to accommodate wheelchairs). Accommodations for people with mental health disabilities are not as straightforward because the disability is usually manifested in behaviors, therefore requiring behavioral accommodations (Kaufmann, 1993). According to the ADA, such accommodations might include job restructuring; part-time or modified work schedules; reassignment to a vacant position; acquisition or modification of equipment or devices; appropriate adjustment or modification of examinations, training materials, or policies; and provision of qualified readers or interpreters and other, similar accommodations for people with disabilities. These accommodations are often viewed by managers and coworkers as inconsistent with the behaviors of a "good employee," which adds to the stigma of having a mental illness (Boyle, 1997; Mechanic, 1998).

Employee Self-Advocacy and Self-Identification

Although the ADA has the potential to help millions of Americans succeed in the workplace, people with mental health disabilities must understand their rights under the ADA, identify barriers and accommodation strategies, initiate requests with the employer for reasonable accommodations, and implement accommodations collaboratively with their employers in order to benefit from the legislation (Roessler & Rumrill, 1995). Studies have shown that individuals with psychiatric conditions often do not know about their rights, and those who are well-informed do not always feel confident in discussing arrangements for job accommodations with an employer (Granger, 2000; Granger & Gill, 2000). Additionally, there has been increasing interest in the literature regarding how an individual with a mental health disability determines whether to request an accommodation, what information to disclose, and who to involve in the planning of accommodations (Baldridge & Veiga, 2001; Granger, 2000; Granger & Gill, 2000; Koch, 2000). Although involving coworkers and other members of the organization can be helpful to increase understanding of the need for accommodation and to garner support, the probability of disclosure depends greatly on characteristics of the work environment as well as individuals' beliefs (see Baldridge & Veiga, 2001, for a review). Furthermore, disclosure may be embarrassing to the individual and result in negative coworker attitudes and stigmatization (Granger, 2000). The EEOC (1997) has published a special guidance book on the

decision-making process concerning employment of people with psychiatric disabilities, but the key is disseminating this information to individuals who need it.

Granger and Gill (2000) discuss the importance of mental health consumers' acquiring career-building skills in order to advocate for themselves instead of relying on job coaches and other mental health professionals. Mental health professionals as well as human resource professionals should not only make books and resources on the ADA available, but also teach skills via role-play, group discussions, and in vivo skill application instead of having a job coach make arrangements for the individual. For example, the Work Experience Survey (WES) (Roessler & Gottcent, 1994) is a structured interview that can be used by mental health professionals to facilitate consumers' identification of barriers to job performance and potential reasonable accommodations. Roessler and Gottcent (1994) suggest that use of the WES allows employees to limit the intrusiveness of the accommodation process and enhance their sense of control over the process and its outcomes. Mental health consumers should seek out skills and knowledge involving the ADA, job searches, disclosure strategies, analysis of the essential functions of a job, assessment of the need for specific job accommodations, negotiation skills, conflict resolution, and analysis of a workplace culture (Granger & Gill, 2000; Koch, 2000).

Furthermore, it is important for employees to develop social support relationships at work, and they may also want to consider joining an employment peer support group for support and information outside of the workplace. Human resource professionals should provide employees with a reference library of books, Web sites, and contact information for such support groups, and make it possible for employees to access the information anonymously (such as on the organization's Web site). Of course, for employees to use this resource, the human resources department will need to advertise it so that employees know it is available. One potential way to disseminate such information is to include it as a note on pay stubs. (A list of resource books and Web sites appears in the appendix at the end of this chapter.)

DEVELOPING ACCOMMODATIONS

The ADA and the process of developing accommodations can be viewed from a mediation perspective in the framework of alternative dispute resolution (ADR), as observed by Blanck, Andersen, Wallach, and Tenney (1994). Blanck and his colleagues demonstrated how ADR could be used to ensure equality of job opportunity by presenting eight crucial decision points in the accommodation process: address the disability, get the facts, identify reasonable accommodations, assess the need for expertise, assess cost factors and potential undue hardship, initiate a problem-solving dialogue, develop an accommodation plan, and evaluate the accommodation plan.

The authors suggest that the first step in developing accommodations is identifying and/or addressing the disability. An employer is not required to accommodate a disability until the employee identifies him- or herself as having a disability and needing reasonable accommodation. Second, employers should gather facts about whether the employee's condition qualifies as a disability under the ADA, in what ways the disability limits the employee's work, and whether the employee can perform the essential functions of the job with or without reasonable accommodation (Blanck et al., 1994). Employers can ask for medical

documentation of the disability (Dalgin, 2001). After facts have been gathered about the disability and the employee's particular challenges, an assessment of threat should be made, that is, whether or not the employee's disability poses a direct threat to him- or herself or coworkers under the ADA. Next, the employer should identify essential job functions by reviewing the employee's written job description. According to Blanck and colleagues (1994), the next task is to identify the type and scope of potential reasonable accommodations, and whether the costs of any accommodations would cause undue hardship to the employer.

Gates, Akabas, and Oran-Sabia (1998) point out that it is imperative that all key players participate in the development of accommodations. If a consultant or job coach is to be used, according to ADR, he or she should function as a neutral problem solver by finding solutions that work for both parties (Blanck et al., 1994). The consultant or job coach should provide a list of accommodations that are agreeable to the employee, and the employer should select those it is willing to implement and provide a business-related reason for rejecting any potential accommodations, and initiate a formal dialogue with the employee. During this meeting, the employer and employee, together with the consultant, should develop an accommodation plan and establish a time line for the implementation of short- and long-term reasonable accommodations. The support of the employee's supervisor also has been shown to be critical to successful return to work and maintenance of employees with mental health conditions (Akabas, 1994; Gates, 1993; Gates, Akabas, & Kantrowitz, 1996). However, if the employee's supervisor does not feel that he or she has the authority to implement accommodations, the individual with such authority, as well as other relevant coworkers and/or representatives from the employee assistance program, should be involved in accommodation planning (Gates et al., 1998). Nevertheless, consent from the employee must be obtained to include additional coworkers in any discussion of the employee's condition so that his or her confidentiality is maintained (Mechanic, 1998).

Blanck et al. (1994) suggest putting the plan in writing as a "road map" and signing it to make the plan specific, thorough, tangible, and substantiated. Plans for accommodations should include an open-door policy that empowers the employee and employer to modify the plan when necessary. Finally, Blanck and colleagues (1994) point out the need to evaluate the accommodation plan periodically. With the episodic nature of many mental illnesses, accommodations may have to be modified to match the individual's ability to perform various job responsibilities. The most important characteristics of the development and evaluation of accommodations are collaboration, flexibility, and documentation.

Theoretical Frameworks for Developing Accommodations

There appear to be two frequently used theoretical approaches for developing accommodations for people with mental health disabilities: behavioral analysis and self-efficacy.

Behavior Analysis. Using a behavior analysis framework, Hantula and Reilly (1996) stated that behavior is a function of the environment; therefore, there are no disabled people, only particular environments that are either enabling or disabling of a behavior. They proposed that it is the interaction between an individual and the individual's environment that determines whether or not a person has a "disability." This approach purports that work performance is predominantly a function of the environment in which it occurs (Hantula & Reilly, 1996; Komaki, 1981-1982). Hantula and Reilly explained that the goal of reasonable accommodation, then, is to arrange the environment so that the probability of the occurrence of essential job-related behaviors is increased. This framework is useful when developing accommodations because it encourages the practitioner or employee to consider the specific situation at hand and how to best construct the environment to maximize important job behaviors, instead of choosing an accommodation from a published list. Because the primary causal factors of behavior in the workplace are the social reinforcement contingencies, the majority of accommodations for mental health disabilities will involve a permanent and ongoing change in management style and technique instead of a one-time engineering or mechanical change, as is frequently done to accommodate individuals with physical disabilities (Hantula & Reilly, 1996; Mancuso, 1990; Wyld, 1997).

This behavioral analysis approach, also referred to as the performance management approach, is rooted in behavior analysis in organizations and "seeks to systematically identify and reinforce successful work behavior, as well as the work environments which occasion it" (Hantula & Reilly, 1996, p. 114). Performance management has been shown to be highly effective in increasing a wide variety of positive work behaviors (O'Hara, Johnson, & Beehr, 1985). Thus, performance management can be used as a foundation from which to design, implement, and evaluate reasonable work accommodations for people with mental health disabilities.

Self-Efficacy. In a similar vein, Crist and Stoffel (1992) use Bandura's (1977) theory on self-efficacy as a basis for understanding the purpose of the ADA, returning individuals to work roles. The authors describe employability as a match between work-related skills, one's beliefs regarding job-related competence, and the job itself. *Self-efficacy* is the term Bandura (1977) used to refer to an individual's judgment about his or her own skills or abilities to perform a task or succeed in a particular situation, and perceived self-efficacy has been found to predict subsequent behavior better than performance skills (Bandura, 1982). Crist and Stoffel (1992) cite Bandura's four sources of self-efficacy judgments (emotional arousal, verbal or social persuasion, vicarious experience, and performance accomplishments). Performance accomplishments appear to have the strongest effect on behavior. Thus, from a self-efficacy point of view, the purpose of reasonable accommodation is to give employees the opportunity to experience performance accomplishments. These experiences, in turn, will increase self-efficacy and lead to the successful performance of essential job-related behaviors.

Types of Accommodations

Both the ADA and the literature on job accommodations provide many examples of reasonable accommodations for mental health illness that consider the fact that mental health disabilities present recurrent functional challenges to employees. Mancuso (1990) categorized these potential challenges as follows: (a) duration of concentration, (b) screening out of environmental stimuli, (c) maintenance of stamina throughout the workday, (d) management of time pressure and deadlines, (e) initiation of personal contact, (f) a focus on multiple tasks simultaneously, (g) response to negative feedback, and (h) physical and emotional side effects of psychotropic medications. Accommodations are likely to target aspects of the work environment that would ameliorate these difficulties. Crist and Stoffel (1992) developed a thorough list of potential reasonable accommodations for each of Mancuso's (1990) functional limitation categories. (Readers are referred to Crist and Stoffel for all of the specific accommodations.) Those accommodations listed in the literature typically involve flexibility with work schedules and the work environment, job duty modification, emotional support, effective supervision, and coworker education. Some potential examples are as follows: flexible scheduling that allows time off for therapy followed by incremental increases in job responsibility; restructuring of office space (Blanck et al., 1994) or testing space (Zuriff, 1997), such as providing a private space, purchasing room dividers, and allowing employees to work from home; modification of training or testing materials and methods, including extension of time limits and provision of readers (Nester, 1993); increased supervision, including goal setting along with positive feedback (Mancuso, 1990); reassignment to a vacant position and/or part-time status (Kaufmann, 1993); auxillary aids and services, such as a job coaches and/or readers; and redelegation or restructuring of job assignments. Because some individuals with mental health disabilities have difficulty with social skills and social interaction, it is possible that accommodations might include time off for social skills training or inclusion of feedback and guidance regarding appropriate job-related social interaction skills. Employers are encouraged to be creative and collaborate with the employee to develop individualized accommodations.

On-Site Emotional Support. Parrish (1991) surveyed employers of individuals with psychiatric disabilities, most of whom were providing peer and other support services through NIMH Community Support Program. She reported that many respondents found emotional supports helpful, such as identifying coworkers willing to provide support on the job, making employee assistance programs available, providing on-site crisis intervention programs, and allowing telephone calls for support during work hours. Blanck and colleagues (1994) discussed the use of peer support for 6 weeks to accommodate a sales employee with bipolar disorder. The firm sent a coworker of the employee's choice to accompany him on out-of-town national sales campaigns. This accommodation decreased the stress of travel and irregular schedules for the employee, and assured the company that the employee's interactions with customers would continue to be positive and productive. Gates and colleagues (1998) also emphasized the importance of coworker support for successful return to work and maintenance of workers with mental health conditions. They used House's (1981) categorization of social support at work (emotional, instrumental, informational, and feedback support) to develop a mapping technique that identifies those individuals at work who are likely to offer support and those who are in need of training and education to ensure successful return to work after leave for psychiatric treatment.

A job coach is also an on-site source of support for an employee (Finkle, 1995). A job coach typically determines the type and quality of duties expected from the employee, reads or completes a performance contract for the employee, monitors the employee as he or she performs job duties, and then makes accommodation recommendations. Granger (2000), in a study of 20 focus groups with people with psychiatric disabilities, found that in general, those individuals with job coaches reported that the most valued support in getting job accommodations was their job coach or job developer. However, Parrish (1991) recommended that employers encourage the use of on-site supports, but that they should not promote continued use of these supports any longer than necessary because of the stigmatization that can occur when such visible, on-site supports are used.

Effective Supervision. Employees with mental health disabilities may often be accommodated through the use of increased and more effective supervision. Hantula and Reilly (1996) define effective supervision as "supervisory and management practices or systems which maximize individual performance and protect the dignity of the individual" (p. 114). Accommodations that increase effective supervision are likely to be beneficial for all employees, not just those with disabilities (Bruyere et al., 1997; Carling, 1993; Hantula & Reilly, 1996). Leadership research across industries has shown that supervisory monitoring of employee behavior and implementation of consequences (predominantly positive reinforcement) is associated with higher productivity in terms of individual performance (Brewer & Ridgway, 1998; Kirby & Davis, 1998; Komaki, 1986; Komaki, Collins, & Penn, 1982; Larson & Callahan, 1990) and team performance (Komaki, Desselles, & Bowman, 1989; Rasker, Post, & Schraagen, 2000). Not only should increased monitoring and reinforcement increase the performance of employees with mental health disabilities (Mancuso, 1990), but monitoring and reinforcement should communicate clear and unambiguous performance standards. Czajka and DeNisi (1988) found that specified performance standards eliminated the perception of employees with disabilities as members of an outgroup needing special favors, and resulted in individuals with disabilities receiving performance ratings comparable to those of nondisabled individuals. Thus, it appears that good management practices such as clear performance goals, regular monitoring and feedback, and positive reinforcement should be included as important aspects of an accommodation plan.

Employment Testing Accommodations. The ADA also covers accommodations in selection and promotion procedures involving tests. As noted by Wyld (1997), EEOC advises employers to inform applicants or employees in advance of any employment tests that will be administered and to inquire as to whether any reasonable accommodation will be needed. Employers should allow participants with learning disabilities or visual problems to have extended time to complete exams and/or to have the chance to take tests in a quiet, isolated area. Additionally, Nester (1993) and others discuss the use of readers—individuals who read written test questions and response options orally to test takers—to accommodate employees or applicants with reading disabilities. Thus, ADA requires alterations to test administration practices in order to accommodate individuals. However, it is often feared that changing the format or conditions of administration can also affect the nature of what is being measured and the validity of the inferences made from test scores (Fischer, 1994). Thus, ADA's standard of reasonable accommodation may be in opposition to APA Division 5's recommendations for psychometric validation and standardization (Fischer, 1994). (For a more thorough discussion of the

measurement implications of the ADA, see Fischer, 1994.) The American Educational Research Association, the American Psychological Association, and the National Council on Measurement in Education (1999), in their *Standards for Educational and Psychological Testing,* offer guidelines on testing individuals with disabilities, including types of accommodations and suggestions for maintaining the validity of modified tests. Human resources professionals should consult this guide when deciding how to accommodate individuals with disabilities in a testing sitution.

CONCLUDING COMMENTS

Based on the available evidence, it appears that progress has been made in accommodating individuals with mental health disabilities into the work environment. However, evaluations of the effects of the accommodations are rare. A few empirical evaluations of supported employment and vocational rehabilitation programs have suggested the effectiveness of these programs (Block, 1992; Bozzer, Samson, & Anson, 1999; Bybee, Mowbray, & McCrohan, 1996; Rogers, Sciarappa, MacDonald-Wilson, & Danley, 1995), although several of these studies involved unemployed people or very small sample sizes. Therefore, these empirical evaluations have not provided information about the effectiveness of actual accommodations under long-term employment conditions. Future research and program evaluation efforts need to assess the effectiveness of reasonable accommodations based on individuals' mental illness and the work environment and job demands they face from both the individuals' and the organizations' perspectives.

APPENDIX

Addresses and Phone Numbers

American Bar Association, Commission on Mental and Physical Disability Law, 1800 M St., NW, 2nd Floor South, Washington, DC 20036, (202) 331-2240

Equal Employment Opportunity Commission, 1801 L. Street, NW, Washington, DC 20507, (202) 663-4900, (800) 669-4000

Department of Justice, Office on the Americans with Disabilities Act, Civil Rights Division, Box 66118, Washington, DC 20035-6118, (202) 514-0301

Job Accommodation Network, 918 Chestnut Ridge Road, Suite 1, PO Box 6080, Morgantown, WV 26506, (800) 526-7234

Books

Equal Employment Opportunity Commission. (1992). *A technical assistance manual on the employment provisions (Title I) of the Americans with Disabilities Act.* Washington, DC: Government Printing Office.

Equal Employment Opportunity Commission. (1997). *EEOC enforcement guidance: The Americans with Disabilities Act and psychiatric disabilities.* Washington, DC: Author.

Zuckerman, D., Debenham, K., & Moore, K. (1993). *The ADA & people with mental illness: A resource manual for employers.* Washington, DC: American Bar Association.

Bazelon Center for Mental Health Law. (1999). *Mental health consumers in the workplace: How the Americans with Disabilities Act protects you against employment discrimination* (2nd ed.). Philadelphia: Matrix Research Institute.

Web Sites

Equal Employment Opportunity Commission: http://www.eeoc.gov

Job Accommodation Network: http://janweb.icdi.wvu.edu

Disability Business Technical Assistance Centers: http://www.adata.org

Bazelon Center for Mental Health Law: http://www.bazelon.org

Matrix Research Institute: http://www.matrixresearch.org

REFERENCES

Akabas, S. H. (1994). Workplace responsiveness: Key employer characteristics in support of job maintenance for persons with mental illness. *Psychosocial Rehabilitation Journal, 17*(3), 91-102.

American Educational Research Association, American Psychological Association, & National Council on Measurement in Education. (1999). *Standards in educational and psychological testing.* Washington, DC: American Psychological Association.

Americans with Disabilities Act of 1990, 42 U.S.C.A. & 12101 et seq. (West 1993).

Baldridge, D. C., & Veiga, J. F. (2001). Toward a greater understanding of the willingness to request an accommodation: Can requesters' beliefs disable the Americans with Disabilities Act? *Academy of Management Review, 26*(1), 85-99.

Bandura, A. (1977). Self-efficacy: Toward a unifying theory of behavioral change. *Psychological Review, 84,* 191-215.

Bandura, A. (1982). Self-efficacy mechanism in human agency. *American Psychologist, 37,* 122-147.

Berry, J. O., & Meyer, J. A. (1995). Employing people with disabilities: Impact of attitude and situation. *Rehabilitation Psychology, 40,* 211-222.

Blanck, P. D., Andersen, J. H., Wallach, E. J., & Tenney, J. P. (1994). Implementing reasonable accommodations using ADR under the ADA: The case of a white-collar employee with bipolar mental illness. *Mental and Physical Disability Law Reporter, 18*(4), 458-464.

Blanck, P. D., & Pransky, G. (1999). Workers with disabilities. *Occupational Medicine: State of the Art Reviews, 14*(3), 581-593.

Block, L. (1992). The employment connection: The application of an individual supported employment program for persons with chronic mental health problems. *Canadian Journal of Community Mental Health, 11,* 79-89.

Boyle, M. A. (1997). Social barriers to successful reentry into mainstream organizational culture: Perceptions of people with disabilities. *Human Resource Development Quarterly, 8,* 259-268.

Bozzer, M., Samson, D., & Anson, J. (1999). An evaluation of a community based vocational rehabilitation program for adults with psychiatric disabilities. *Canadian Journal of Community Mental Health, 18,* 165-177.

Brewer, N., & Ridgway, R. (1998). Effects of supervisory monitoring on productivity and quality of performance. *Journal of Experimental Psychology: Applied, 4*(3), 211-277.

Bruyere, S. M., Brown, D. S., & Mank, D. M. (1997). Quality through equality: Total quality management applied to the implementation of Title I of the Americans with Disabilities Act of 1990. *Journal of Vocational Rehabilitaion, 9,* 253-266.

Bybee, D., Mowbray, C. T., & McCrohan, N.M. (1996). Towards zero exclusion in vocational opportunities for persons with psychiatric disabilities: Prediction of service receipt in a hybrid vocational/case management service program. *Psychiatric Rehabilitation Journal, 19,* 15-27.

Carling, P. J. (1993). Reasonable accommodations in the workplace for individuals with psychiatric disabilities. *Consulting Psychology Journal, 45*(2), 46-62.

Coleman, C. J., Cooney-Painter, D., & Moonga, S. K. (2000). Attention deficit/hyperactivity disorder in the workplace under the ADA in the wake of *Sutton* and its companions. *Employee Responsibilities and Rights Journal, 12*(2), 47-61.

Crist, P. A., & Stoffel, V. C. (1992). The Americans with Disabilities Act of 1990 and employees with mental impairments: Personal efficacy and the environment. *American Journal of Occupational Therapy, 46,* 434-443.

Czajka, J. M., & DeNisi, A. S. (1988). Effects of emotional disability and clear performance standards on performance ratings. *Academy of Management Journal, 31*(2), 394-404.

Dalgin, R. S. (2001). Impact of Title I of the Americans with Disabilities Act on people with psychiatric disabilities. *Journal of Applied Rehabilitation Counseling, 32*(1), 45-50.

Diksa, E., & Rogers, E. S. (1996). Employer concerns about hiring persons with psychiatric disability: Results of the Employer Attitude Questionnaire. *Rehabilitation Counseling Bulletin, 40,* 31-44.

Equal Employment Opportunity Commission. (1997). *EEOC enforcement guidance: The Americans with Disabilities Act and psychiatric disabilities.* Washington, DC: Author.

Finkle, A. L. (1995). Reasonable accommodation obligation: Some practical tips. *Employee Assistance Quarterly, 10*(3), 1-20.

Fischer, R. J. (1994). The Americans with Disabilities Act: Implications for measurement. *Educational Measurement: Issues and Practice, 13*(3), 17-37.

Gates, L. B. (1993). The role of the supervisor in successful adjustment to work with a disabling condition: Issues for disability policy and practice. *Journal of Occupational Rehabilitation, 3*(4), 179-190.

Gates, L. B., Akabas, S. H., & Kantrowitz, W. (1996). Supervisors' role in successful job maintenance: A target for rehabilitation counselor efforts. *Journal of Applied Rehabilitation Counseling, 27*(3), 60-66.

Gates, L. B., Akabas, S. H., & Oran-Sabia, V. (1998). Relationship accommodations involving the work group: Improving work prognosis for persons with mental health conditions. *Psychiatric Rehabilitation Journal, 21*(3), 264-271.

Granger, B. (2000). The role of psychiatric rehabilitation practitioners in assisting people in understanding how to best assert their ADA rights and arrange accommodations. *Psychiatric Rehabilitation Journal, 23*(3), 215-223.

Granger, B., & Gill, P. (2000). Strategies for assisting people with psychiatric disabilities to assert their ADA rights and arrange job accommodations. *Psychiatric Rehabilitation Skills, 4*(1), 120-135.

Hantula, D. A., & Reilly, N. A. (1996). Reasonable accommodation for employees with mental disabilities: A mandate for effective supervision? *Behavioral Sciences and the Law, 14*, 107-120.

Harlan, S. L., & Robert, P. M. (1998). The social construction of disability in organizations: Why employers resist reasonable accommodation. *Work and Occupations, 25*, 397-435.

House, J. S. (1981). *Work stress and social support*. Reading, MA: Addison-Wesley.

Kaufmann, C. L. (1993). Reasonable accommodations to mental health disabilities at work: Legal constructs and practical applications. *Journal of Psychiatry and Law, 21*(2), 153-174.

Kirby, S. L., & Davis, M. A. (1998). A study of escalating commitment in principal-agent relationships: Effects of monitoring and personal responsibility. *Journal of Applied Psychology, 83*(2), 206-217.

Kirsh, B. (2000). Factors associated with employment for mental health consumers. *Psychiatric Rehabilitation Journal, 24*, 13-21.

Koch, L. C. (2000). Assessment and planning in the Americans with Disabilities Act era: Strategies for consumer self-advocacy and employer collaboration. *Journal of Vocational Rehabilitation, 14*, 103-108.

Komaki, J. L. (1981-1982). Managerial effectiveness: Potential contributions of the behavioral approach. *Journal of Organizational Behavior Management, 3*(3), 71-83.

Komaki, J. L. (1986). Toward effective supervision: An operant analysis and comparison of managers at work. *Journal of Applied Psychology, 71*(2), 270-279.

Komaki, J. L., Collins, R. L., & Penn, P. (1982). The role of performance antecedents and consequences in work motivation. *Journal of Applied Psychology, 67*(3), 334-340.

Komaki, J. L., Desselles, M. L., & Bowman, E. (1989). Definitely not a breeze: Extending an operant model of effective supervision to teams. *Journal of Applied Psychology, 74*(3), 522-529.

Larson, J. R., & Callahan, C. (1990). Performance monitoring: How it affects work productivity. *Journal of Applied Psychology, 75*(5), 530-538.

Mancuso, L. (1990). Reasonable accommodations for workers with psychiatric disabilities. *Psychosocial Rehabilitation Journal, 14*(2), 3-19.

Mechanic, D. (1998). Cultural and organizational aspects of application of the Americans with Disabilities Act to persons with psychiatric disabilities. *Milbank Quarterly, 76*, 5-23.

Miller, S. P. (1997). Keeping the promise: The ADA and employment discrimination on the basis of psychiatric disability. *California Law Review, 85,* 701.

Monahan, J. (1992). Mental disorder and violent behavior: Perceptions and evidence. *American Psychologist, 47,* 511-521.

Moore, T. J., & Crimando, W. (1995). Attitudes toward Title I of the Americans with Disabilities Act. *Rehabilitation Counseling Bulletin, 38,* 232-247.

Nester, M. A. (1993). Psychometric testing and reasonable accommodation for persons with disabilities. *Rehabilitation Psychology, 38*(2), 75-85.

O'Hara, K., Johnson, C. M., & Beehr, T. A. (1985). Organizational behavior management in the private sector: A review of empirical research and recommendations for future investigation. *Academy of Management Review, 16,* 848-864.

Pardeck, J. T. (1997). Americans with Disabilities Act of 1990: Implications for human service agencies. *Clinical Supervisor, 15,* 147-161.

Parrish, J. (1991). *Reasonable accommodations for people with psychiatric disabilities.* Informal survey report. Rockville, MD: National Institute of Mental Health.

Parry, J. (1993). Mental disabilities under the ADA: A difficult path to follow. *Mental and Physical Disability Law Reporter, 17*(1), 100-112.

Pati, G., & Bailey, E. K. (1995). Empowering people with disabilities: Strategy and human resource issues in implementing the ADA. *Organizational Dynamics, 23*(3), 52-69.

Pollet, S. L. (1995, Spring). Mental illness in the workplace: The tension between productivity and reasonable accommodation. *Journal of Psychiatry & Law,* pp. 155-184.

Rasker, P. C., Post, W. M., & Schraagen, J. M. C. (2000). Effects of two types of intra-team feedback on developing a shared mental model in Command & Control teams. *Ergonomics, 43*(8), 1167-1189.

Roessler, R., & Gottcent, J. (1994). The Work Experience Survey: A reasonable accommodations/career development strategy. *Journal of Applied Rehabilitation Counseling, 25*(3), 16-21.

Roessler, R. T., & Rumrill, P. D. (1995). Promoting reasonable accommodations: An essential postemployment service. *Journal of Applied Rehabilitation Counseling, 26*(4), 1-7.

Roessler, R. T., & Sumner, G. (1997). Employer opinions about accommodating employees with chronic illness. *Journal of Applied Rehabilitation Counseling, 28,* 29-34.

Rogers, E. S., Sciarappa, K., MacDonald-Wilson, K., & Danley, K. (1995). A benefit-cost analysis of a supported employment model for persons with psychiatric disabilities. *Evaluation and Program Planning, 18,* 105-115.

Schall, C. M. (1998). The Americans with Disabilities Act: Are we keeping our promise? An analysis of the effect of the ADA on the employment of persons with disabilities. *Journal of Vocational Rehabilitation, 10*(3), 191-203.

Scheid, T. K. (1998). The Americans with Disabilities Act, mental disability, and employment practices. *Journal of Behavioral Health Services & Research, 25,* 312-324.

School Board of Nassau County v. Arline, 480 U.S. 273, 288 (1987).

Shaw, L. R., MacGillis, P. W., & Dvorchik, K. M. (1994). Alcoholism and the Americans with Disabilities Act: Obligations and accommodations. *Rehabilitation Counseling Bulletin, 38*(2), 108-123.

Swanson, J. W., Holzer, C. E., Ganju, V. K., & Jono, R. T. (1990). Violence and psychiatric disorder in the community: Evidence from the Epidemiologic Catchment Area surveys. *Hospital & Community Psychiatry, 41*(7), 761-770.

Thakker, D., & Solomon, P. (1999). Factors influencing managers' adherence to the Americans with Disabilities Act. *Administration and Policy in Mental Health, 26,* 213-219.

Unger, D. D. (1999). Workplace supports: A view from employers who have hired supported employees. *Focus on Autism and Other Developmental Disabilities, 14,* 167-179.

Wasserbauer, L. I. (1997). Mental illness and the Americans with Disabilities Act: Understanding the fundamentals. *Journal of Psychosocial Nursing, 35*(1), 22-26.

Wyld, D. C. (1997). Attention deficit/hyperactivity disorder in adults: Will this be the greatest challenge for employment discrimination law? *Employee Responsibilities and Rights Journal, 10,* 103-125.

Wylonis, L. (1999). Psychiatric disability, employment and the Americans with Disabilities Act. *Psychiatric Clinics of North America, 22*(1), 147-158.

Zuckerman, D. (1993). Reasonable accommodations for people with mental illness under the ADA. *Mental and Physical Disability Law Reporter, 17*(3), 311-320.

Zuriff, G. E. (1997). Accommodations for test anxiety under ADA? *Journal of the American Academy of Psychiatry and the Law, 25*(2), 197-206.

Author Index

Subject Index

About the Editors

Jay C. Thomas, PhD, ABPP, is an Associate Professor in the School of Professional Psychology, Pacific University, and is Director of the Counseling Psychology program. He spent several years in private practice as an industrial and organizational psychologist, largely in hiring and training workers and in performance management. His research interests lie in job stress, mental health in the workplace, and program evaluation. His PhD is in industrial and organizational psychology from the University of Akron. He is a Diplomate in Industrial and Organizational Psychology, awarded by the American Board of Professional Psychology, and is a licensed psychologist in Oregon.

Michel Hersen (PhD, ABPP, State University of New York at Buffalo, 1966) is Professor and Dean, School of Professional Psychology, Pacific University, Forest Grove, Oregon. He completed his postdoctoral training at the West Haven VA (Yale University School of Medicine Program). He is Past President of the Association for Advancement of Behavior Therapy. He has coauthored and coedited 134 books and has published 223 scientific journal articles. He is the coeditor of several psychological journals, including *Behavior Modification, Aggression and Violent Behavior: A Review Journal, Clinical Psychology Review, Journal of Anxiety Disorders, Journal of Family Violence, Journal of Clinical Geropsychology,* and *Journal of Developmental and Physical Disabilities.* He is also the editor-in-chief of a new journal titled *Clinical Case Studies,* which is totally devoted to description of clients and patients treated with psychotherapy, and he coedited the recently published 11-volume work titled *Comprehensive Clinical Psychology.* He has been the recipient of numerous grants from the National Institute of Mental Health, the Department of Education, the National Institute of Disabilities and Rehabilitation Research, and the March of Dimes Birth Defects Foundation. He is a Diplomate of the American Board of Professional Psychology, Fellow of the American Psychological Association, Distinguished Practitioner and Member of the National Academy of Practice in Psychology, and recipient of the Distinguished Career Achievement Award in 1996 from the American Board of Medical Psychotherapists and Psychodiagnosticians. Finally, at one point in his career, he was in full-time private practice, and on several occasions, he has had part-time private practices.

About the Contributors

Suzanne C. Baker is a doctoral student in sociology and a National Institute on Alcohol Abuse and Alcoholism research trainee at the Institute for Behavioral Research and Human Service Delivery at the University of Georgia. She obtained her undergraduate degree from Ohio University, where she graduated with honors in sociology. During her undergraduate training, she worked on a joint research project between sociology faculty and the Institute for Local Government Administration and Rural Development that examined the impact of welfare reform in rural Ohio. Following graduation, she served as the Domestic Policy Fellow for the Population Reference Bureau in Washington, D.C. She has conducted research in the areas of health, alcohol, and social demography. Her recent works have focused on workplace predictors of alcohol use, Employee Assistance Program utilization for employees with alcohol problems, and Hispanic immigrant self-employment within ethnic economic enclaves. Currently, she is working on a research project examining the influence of workplace culture and occupational attainment on depression among full-time workers in the U.S. labor force.

Kirsten N. Barr received a BSc from the University of British Columbia and an MA in experimental psychology from Lakehead University, and she is currently completing a PhD at Queen's University, where she studies forensic and evolutionary psychology. She rationalizes that as long as she is a student, the only way she can travel is to complete each degree in a different city.

Deborah R. Becker, MEd, CRC, is Assistant Research Professor of Community and Family Medicine and of Psychiatry, Dartmouth Medical School. She is a rehabilitation specialist and is the senior project director at the New Hampshire-Dartmouth Psychiatric Research Center. She has been Project Director for vocational, housing, and dual-diagnosis research studies. Along with Robert E. Drake, she has described and researched the Individual Placement and Support approach to supported employment. She provides consultation and training on vocational rehabilitation and program implementation. Ms. Becker has also worked in positions of direct service and administration in community support programs for people with severe mental illness.

Terry A. Beehr is currently Professor and Director of the PhD program in Industrial/Organizational Psychology at Central Michigan University. His PhD is in organizational psychology from the University of Michigan, and he previously held postgraduate appointments at the Institute for Social Research and Illinois

State University. He has conducted research on occupational stress, employee retirements, leadership, careers, and culture.

H. John Bernardin is University Research Professor in the College of Business at Florida Atlantic University in Boca Raton. He is the former director of doctoral studies in industrial/ organizational psychology at Virginia Tech. Dr. Bernardin is past editor of *Human Resource Management Review* and has served on the editorial board of numerous journals, including the *Academy of Management Review*. He is the author of six books and more than 100 articles related to human resource management. Dr. Bernardin received his PhD in industrial/ organizational psychology from Bowling Green State University.

John F. Binning is an Associate Professor of Industrial/Organizational Psychology at Illinois State University and president of The DeGarmo Group, Inc., a human resource consulting firm. He received his MA and PhD degrees from the University of Akron, and a BA in psychology from Butler University. Dr. Binning's research interests include psychological and administrative processes that affect the validity of selection decisions in assessment center and employment interview contexts. He is also developing a structured personality assessment system to measure job candidates' congruence with discomforting and stressful job demands, thus enhancing predictions of emotional exhaustion and assisting client organizations to better manage employee turnover. He has published his research findings in *Journal of Applied Psychology, Academy of Management Journal, Organizational Behavior and Human Performance,* and *Human Resource Management Journal.* For 20 years, he has consulted with organizational clients on projects such as selection system design and validation, EEO compliance, performance appraisal, training design and implementation, and managerial assessment and succession planning.

Christopher R. Bordeaux, MA, is a doctoral student at the University of Tulsa. He has authored and collaborated on several publications on job attitudes and their relevant outcomes. His current research focuses on the task and contextual performance outcomes of affective disposition, constituency commitment, and climate characteristics.

Krista Brockwood, Senior Research Associate at the Foundation for Accountability, received her MS in industrial/organizational psychology from Portland State University, where she is also pursuing a doctoral degree. During her graduate career, she served as both project manager and research assistant to Dr. Hammer for the duration of a 3-year study of dual-career couples in the sandwiched generation. More specifically, Ms. Brockwood has focused her research efforts on the accommodations people make to balance work and family. She has co-authored a number of national conference papers and has published a paper on work and family accommodations based on her master's thesis. Presently, Ms. Brockwood is with the Foundation of Accountability, a nonprofit research and consumer advocacy organization for healthcare quality in the United States.

Linda L. Brown received her MA in industrial and organizational psychology from the University of Akron. She is currently continuing her studies in the PhD program in industrial and organizational psychology at the University of Akron. Prior to attending graduate school, she was a human resource executive with more than 20 years of experience in such major corporations as Nestle, Bendix, and Kenworth Truck Company. Her research interests include organizational culture and change, power in organizations, and leadership.

Suzanne Caubet, BS, is a graduate assistant in the Department of Psychology at Portland State University. She received her BS in psychology from Portland State University and is currently earning an MS in applied psychology. She has worked on various research projects, including a longitudinal study of dual-earner couples in the sandwiched generation. She is specifically interested in measurement assessment, survey construction, and workforce development. Ms. Caubet is currently working with the Oregon Governor's Office of Education and Workforce Development researching strategies to increase work-force interest and participation in health care occupations.

Antonio Cepeda-Benito (PhD, Purdue University, 1994) is Associate Professor of Psychology at Texas A&M University in College Station. He is interested in the psychological processes involved in the formation, maintenance, and cessation of ingestive-compulsive behaviors. One of his areas of study involves the development and validation of measurement tools to assess eating-disorder and smoking related constructs and their role in the development, maintenance, and cessation of these disorders.

Scott F. Coffey (PhD, University of Mississippi, 1996) is Assistant Professor of Psychiatry in the Department of Psychiatry at the University at Buffalo, State University of New York, and is also Associate Research Scientist at the Research Institute on Addictions. In addition, he is the Clinical Director of the Mentally Ill Chemically Addicted Treatment Service at Buffalo General Hospital. Dr. Coffey has served as principal investigator and coinvestigator on several National Institutes of Health-supported grants and has published on the assessment, course, and treatment of posttraumatic stress disorder (PTSD), substance use disorders (SUD), and PTSD-SUD comorbidity.

Cari L. Colton is a doctoral candidate in the industrial/organizational psychology program at Portland State University. She has worked on various research projects, including a project focused on studying work and family issues among dual-earner couples in the sandwiched generation. Her specific research interests center around organizational factors, such as organizational culture and supervisor support, that may influence individuals' ability to manage work and family demands. Her dissertation research is focused on the distinction between formal and informal organizational support for work and family issues. She was also a contributing writer to the Lifescape project, a project for the dissemination of information to working families and employers, conducted by the Boston College Center for Work and Family. Ms. Colton has given several conference presentations in the area of work and family and has worked on several consulting projects with companies in the Portland, Oregon area.

Cary L. Cooper is currently BUPA Professor of Organizational Psychology and Health in the Manchester School of Management, as well as Deputy Vice Chancellor of the University of Manchester Institute of Science and Technology (UMIST). He is the author of more than 80 books (on occupational stress, women at work, and industrial and organizational psychology); has written more than 300 scholarly articles for academic journals; and is a frequent contributor to national newspapers, TV, and radio. Professor Cooper is an editor of the international scholarly *Blackwell Encyclopedia of Management* (a 12-volume set) and the editor of Who's Who in the Management Sciences. He has been an adviser to the World Health Organization, ILO.

Charles E. Drebing, PhD, is Assistant Professor of Psychiatry at the Boston University School of Medicine and a research psychologist in the VHA's New England Mental Illness Research Education and Clinical Center (MIRECC). His primary research interests focus on health services utilization and pathways to care, particularly in the areas of psychosocial rehabilitation, addictions treatment, and dementia care. He is co-author of a new book about problem gambling, *Don't Leave It To Chance.*

H. Heith Durrence is a doctoral candidate at the University of Memphis. He earned his master's degree in psychology from the University of Memphis in 1999 and is currently working as a research coordinator with AmGen pharmaceuticals investigating the effects of chemotherapy on quality of life. He also works in Professor Lichstein's behavioral medicine lab conducting clinical research on sleep disorders.

Andrea Fagiolini (MD, University of Pisa School of Medicine, Pisa, Italy) is an Assistant Professor of Psychiatry at the University of Pittsburgh School of Medicine. He joined the faculty in 1998, after completing his psychiatric residency at the University of Modena Medical School, Italy. He conducts research primarily on pharmacological treatment strategies for bipolar disorder and weight gain in patients treated with psychotropic medications. The results of his research have appeared in several international peer-reviewed research journals. In addition to conducting research, Dr. Fagiolini is a full-time psychiatrist at the Western Psychiatric Institute and Clinic, Pittsburgh, Pennsylvania. He is a member of the educational committee of the International Society of Bipolar Disorders and has received various awards of recognition from the City of Livorno Medical Society, the Institute for Research and Prevention of Depression and Anxiety, and the Italian Society of Psychopathology.

David M. Fresco is currently an assistant professor in the Department of Psychology at Kent State University. His research focuses on cognitive and personality styles (e.g., explanatory flexibility, explanatory style, optimism) associated with vulnerability to psychological and physical health concerns; the comorbidity of depression and anxiety—particularly the origins, etiology, and treatment of generalized anxiety disorder; and the development of treatments to promote resiliency to stress and to prevent anxiety, depression, and health concerns.

Edward S. Friedman, MD, is an assistant professor in the Department of Psychiatry at the University of Pittsburgh School of Medicine in Pittsburgh, Pennsylvania. He is medical director of the Depression Treatment and Research Program and Principal Investigator for the STEP-BD Program at Western Psychiatric Institute and Clinic, University of Pittsburgh Medical Center. He received his medical degree from the University of Pittsburgh School of Medicine. He served an internship in medicine and psychiatry, training in general and child psychiatry, and a residency in general psychiatry at Western Psychiatric Institute and Clinic. Dr. Friedman has presented on mood disorders, treatment-resistant depression, seasonal affective disorder, and psychotherapy, among other topics. He is a member of The Pittsburgh Psychiatric Society, The Allegheny County Medical Society, the International Society for Bipolar Disorders, and the American Psychiatric Society.

David H. Gleaves (PhD, Louisiana State University, 1993) is Associate Professor of Psychology at Texas A&M University in College Station. He co-authored *The Encyclopedia of Obesity and Eating Disorders* and has published 52 scientific journal articles. He is on the editorial board of several journals, including *Journal of Abnormal Psychology, Journal of Clinical Psychology, Eating Disorders: The Journal of Treatment and Prevention,* and *The Journal of Trauma and Dissociation.*

Brian C. Goff, PhD, is a licensed psychologist and assistant director of the Portland DBT Program, a private practice clinic specializing in dialectical behavior therapy. He received his doctorate from the clinical psychology program at the University of Oregon, where he studied cognitive and behavioral approaches to the treatment of depression and anxiety disorders and researched cognitive vulnerabilities to depression. He is a presenter and consultant for the Portland DBT Program, providing training and consultation to other mental health professionals and agencies on DBT and the treatment of multidiagnosed, difficult-to-treat individuals. He also oversees the program's research efforts. Dr. Goff has taught at the University of Oregon and Willamette University in the areas of research methodology, psychopathology, and clinical ethics. He holds an odd reverence for the game of golf, but does not play enough.

Charles J. Golden, PhD, is Professor of Clinical Psychology and Director of the Neuropsychology Assessment Center at Nova Southeastern University in Fort Lauderdale, Florida. He is a Fellow of the National Academy of Neuropsychologists and the American Psychological Association, and he is board certified in both clinical neuropsychology and clinical psychology. He is also a past president of the National Academy of Neuropsychologists. He has published more than 200 books, articles, and chapters.

Lindsay S. Ham is a clinical psychology doctoral student in the Department of Psychology at the University of Nebraska-Lincoln. She received her master's degree from the University of Nebraska-Lincoln in 1999. Her current research and clinical interests include social anxiety and drinking, alcohol expectancies and valuations, anxiety disorders, substance use disorders, and co-morbidity in anxiety and substance use disorders.

Leslie B. Hammer, Associate Professor, Department of Psychology, Portland State University, received her PhD in industrial/organizational psychology from Bowling Green State University. She has been studying work and family issues for more than 10 years. Her most recent work is based on a 3-year grant to study dual-earner couples in the sandwiched generation. Her research has focused on the stressors and rewards of coordinating work and family roles. She has written several articles on difficulties in managing work and family demands, and has given numerous presentations at national conferences in the area of work and family. Her work has also been noted in *Business Week* Online and *Time Magazine*. Dr. Hammer is also a codirector of a new occupational health psychology program being developed in the Department of Psychology at Portland State University.

Richard G. Heimberg is Professor and Director of the clinical psychology program at Temple University as well as Director of the Adult Anxiety Clinic. His interests include the psychopathology and treatment of anxiety disorders, especially social anxiety disorder and generalized anxiety disorder. He is the author of a new book, *Cognitive Behavioral Group Therapy for Social Phobia: Basic Mechanisms and Clinical Strategies,* and coeditor of the forthcoming book *Generalized Anxiety Disorder: Advances in Research and Practice.*

Jeffrey Hite received his MS in counseling psychology from Loyola College in Baltimore, Maryland, and is currently working toward completion of his doctorate in clinical psychology at Pacific University's School of Professional Psychology. His research interests include mental health in the workplace and the use of assessment feedback as a means of improving therapeutic outcome. Mr. Hite is currently working clinically with children and adolescents in an outpatient community mental health setting.

Robert Hogan received his PhD from the University of California at Berkeley and has been Professor of Psychology and Social Relations at Johns Hopkins University and McFarlin Professor and Chair of the Department of Psychology at the University of Tulsa. He is a past editor of the *Journal of Personality and Social Psychology* and is the author of 300 scholarly articles, chapters, and books. Dr. Hogan is also the author of the Hogan Personality Inventory and is widely credited with having pioneered the use of personality assessment to solve problems in organizations, including screening applicants for potentially antisocial behavior.

Debra A. Hope is Professor and Director of Clinical Training in the Department of Psychology at the University of Nebraska-Lincoln and Director of the UNL Anxiety Disorders Clinic. She received her doctorate in 1990 from the University at Albany-State University of New York. Her current research and clinical interests include social anxiety disorder, outcome and process of cognitive-behavioral treatments for anxiety disorders, and information processing models of psychopathology.

Donna J. Johns is currently a clinical psychology doctoral student at Pacific University in Forest Grove, Oregon. She has been active in research on diversity in the workplace and sexual minority issues. She currently has a manuscript in press looking at sexual minority identity formation.

Gary Johns is Professor of Management and the Concordia University Research Chair in Management in the John Molson School of Business at Concordia University in Montreal. His research interests include absenteeism from work, job design, organizational context, self-serving behavior, and research methodology.

Brenda L. Kenyon (Hons. BA, University of Waterloo; MA, University of Guelph; PhD, Concordia University, Montreal) is a clinical psychologist with expertise in the assessment, diagnosis, and treatment of psychological problems in children and adults. She has worked in hospital and educational settings, and maintains a private practice where she works with adults with mental health problems. Currently, Dr. Kenyon is the Director of the Centre for Psychological Services at the University of Guelph, where she provides psychological services to children, families, and adults; is involved in the training of graduate students in psychology; and teaches courses in the Department of Psychology.

Barbara A. Lee is Dean of the School of Management and Labor Relations, Rutgers University. An attorney, she has taught employment law and higher education law at Rutgers since 1982 and has served as department chair, associate dean, and associate provost prior to assuming the deanship. She is the author of numerous books and articles on employment law, higher education law, employment discrimination, and academic employment practices. She serves on the Executive Committee of the New Jersey Bar Association's Labor and Employment Law Section, and is a former member of the board of directors of the National Association of College and University Attorneys. She also serves as an expert witness for litigation involving employment discrimination and sexual harassment.

Kenneth L. Lichstein is Professor of Psychology at the University of Memphis. He earned his doctoral degree in clinical psychology from the University of Tennessee in 1976. Most of his career has been devoted to investigating methodological and clinical aspects of behavioral medicine, with an emphasis on sleep disorders. Professor Lichstein has published more than 80 journal articles and book chapters, as well as two books. He is the founding editor of *Behavioral Sleep Medicine*.

Brian P. Marx received his PhD in 1996 from the University of Mississippi and is currently an Assistant Professor of Psychology at Temple University. His current research interests are in risk factors for and responses to sexual victimization and emotion and psychopathology. His research has been published in *Journal of Consulting and Clinical Psychology, Experimental and Clinical Psychopharmacology,* and *Journal of Traumatic Stress.*

Christina S. McCrae is an Assistant Professor of Psychology at the University of Florida. She is a clinical geropsychologist who earned her doctoral degree from Washington University in St. Louis in 1999. Her research focuses on the behavioral treatment of sleep problems in the elderly. She is currently investigating home-administered treatment using peer counselors, telephone, and Web-based technology to treat insomnia in the caregivers of dementia patients.

Tracy McDonald is a doctoral student at Pacific University, School of Professional Psychology, in Forest Grove, Oregon. Her research interests include anxiety disorders, state of change, outcomes, CBT, and depression. Her clinical interests include Dialectical Behavior Therapy and working with multidiagnositic, difficult-to-treat clients.

John L. McNulty, PhD, is an Assistant Professor of Psychology at the University of Tulsa. He has authored several publications on personality assessment and individual differences in personality. Although much of Dr. McNulty's work focuses on clinical populations, he is also conducting research on the role of personality in the workplace and career success.

Kim T. Mueser, PhD, is a licensed clinical psychologist and a professor in the Departments of Psychiatry and Community and Family Medicine at Dartmouth Medical School in Hanover, New Hampshire. He received his PhD in clinical psychology from the University of Illinois at Chicago in 1984 and was on the faculty of the Psychiatry Department at the Medical College of Pennsylvania in Philadelphia until 1994, when he moved to Dartmouth Medical School. Dr. Mueser's clinical and research interests include the psychosocial treatment of severe mental illnesses, dual diagnosis, and posttraumatic stress disorder. He has published extensively and given numerous lectures and workshops on psychiatric rehabilitation. He is the co-author of several books, including *Social Skills Training for Psychiatric Patients* (1989), *Coping With Schizophrenia: A Guide for Families* (1994), *Social Skills Training for Schizophrenia: A Step-by-Step Guide* (1997), and *Behavioral Family Therapy for Psychiatric Disorders* (2nd ed., 1999).

Brian P. O'Connor received his PhD from the University of Victoria, Canada, in 1987. His interests are in normal and abnormal personality, interpersonal theory, and research methods. He sometimes suffers from the delusion that he is a hockey player.

Michael P. O'Driscoll is Professor of Psychology at the University of Waikato, Hamilton, New Zealand, where he teaches courses in organizational psychology. He has a PhD in psychology from Flinders University of South Australia. His primary research interests are in the fields of job-related stress and coping, and the interface between job experiences and people's lives off the job (especially family commitments and responsibilities), including conflict between job and family commitments. More generally, he is interested in work attitudes and behaviors, and the relationship between work and health. He has published empirical and conceptual articles on these and other topics in organizational and social psychology. He has served as an editorial consultant for several academic journals and is currently the editor of the *New Zealand Journal of Psychology*.

Walter Penk, PhD, ABPP, is the Chief of the Psychology/Vocational Rehabilitation Services (116B) at the Edith Rogers Memorial Veterans Hospital in Bedford, Massachusetts. He is Associate Director of the New England Mental Illness Research, Education, and Clinical Center. He serves on the adjunct faculties of Boston University School of Medicine (Clinical Associate Professor in Psychiatry) and Harvard Medical School (Lecturer in Psychiatry at Cambridge Hospital). He is a member of the Scientific Advisory Board for the National Vietnam Veterans Readjustment Study and he co-chairs the VA's Psychosocial Rehabilitation committee regarding Best Practices in managing persons with psychoses as well as substance abuse, major depression disorders, and PTSD. His clinical and research interests focus on integrating mental health services in the workplace, pursued through funding clinical research centering on PTSD studies for risk management of violence encountered in employment.

Tahira M. Probst is Assistant Professor of Psychology at Washington State University Vancouver. She received her PhD in industrial/organizational psychology in 1998 from the University of Illinois at Urbana-Champaign. Her current research interests include outcomes of workplace diversity, the relationship between employee job insecurity and workplace safety, and the cross-cultural effectiveness of human resource practices. Her research has appeared in the *Journal of Applied Psychology, Organizational Behavior and Human Decision Processes, Journal of Personality and Social Psychology,* and *Journal of Occupational Health Psychology*.

Paul M. Roman is Distinguished Research Professor of Sociology and has been Director of the Center for Research on Behavioral Health and Human Services Delivery, Institute for Behavioral Research, University of Georgia, since 1986. His research is focused on the sociological aspects of alcohol problems, with particular attention to the organization of treatment systems and to the workplace and the design of intervention efforts to deal with employees with substance abuse problems. His current research also focuses on the patterns of organizational structure associated with organizational innovation and change among substance abuse treatment providers. Other recent research has centered on referral patterns associated with different types of employee problems referred to employee assistance programs, national patterns of drinking and drug-related behaviors and attitudes among employed people, and the structural and process characteristics of EAPs.

Deborah A. Roth is Assistant Professor of Psychology in Psychiatry at the Center for the Treatment and Study of Anxiety at the University of Pennsylvania. She received her PhD in Personality/Abnormal Psychology from the University of Toronto in 1999 and completed a postdoctoral fellowship with Richard G. Heimberg, PhD, at Temple University. Dr. Roth's research interest focuses on the broad topic of interpersonal relationships in the anxiety disorders. She is interested in interpersonal factors that might contribute to the development of anxiety disorders, as well as the impairments in interpersonal functioning that are seen in people with these disorders. Dr. Roth is also interested in psychotherapy process and outcome and in training issues.

Russell K. Schutt, PhD (University of Illinois at Chicago), is Professor of Sociology at the University of Massachusetts Boston. He also has an adjunct appointment at the Harvard Medical School (Lecturer in Sociology in the Department of Psychiatry at the Massachusetts Mental Health Center), where he was a co-investigator on the Boston McKinney Project, a randomized trial of group and independent living for homeless mentally ill persons. His primary research interests and publications concern homelessness, mental health, organizational process, and legal practices, with a particular focus on the impact of the organization of services on satisfaction, cognitive functioning, housing stability, and other outcomes. He has authored, co-authored, and co-edited books on research methods, sociology of organizations, and homelessness and has produced training programs on question design, research methods, and services for homeless people.

Erin L. Scott is currently a doctoral student in the clinical psychology program at Temple University. Her interests include the role of panic attacks in anxiety disorders and the overlap between panic disorder and hypochondriasis.

Carlla S. Smith obtained her PhD in industrial-organizational psychology from Rice University and is currently Professor of Psychology at Bowling Green State University. Her research interests include occupational health and safety, the effects of shiftwork and alternative work schedules on worker health and well-being, and stress measurement. She coauthored (with Robert Dipboye and William Howell) a textbook on industrial-organizational psychology and a book on work stress (with Lorne Sulsky). She has presented and published research internationally and has consulted widely with organizations on work stress and shiftwork.

Lorne M. Sulsky received his PhD in industrial/organizational psychology in 1988 from Bowling Green State University. Since 1992, he has served as a faculty member at the University of Calgary. He has coauthored (with Carlla Smith) a book on the topic of work stress, and he has published and presented research in the areas of work stress and performance measurement. He frequently engages in applied projects, assisting organizations with stress management and performance improvement.

Valerie J. Sutherland, PhD, is a Chartered Occupational Psychologist and an Associate Fellow of the British Psychological Society now working as an independent consultant and lecturer in occupational psychology. Prior to this, she worked as a senior research fellow and lecturer in organizational psychology at the University of Manchester Institute of Science and Technology in the Manchester School of Management. Her research interests are in the fields of occupational stress, safety and quality improvement in the workplace, and management development. Recent activities include a stress audit for teachers, stress management workshops for senior managers in international business based in Germany and the United Kingdom, and safety improvement projects in the paper industry. Her recent publications include books, book chapters, and articles on the topic of stress and safety in the workplace.

Daniel J. Svyantek, PhD, received his degree in industrial/organizational psychology from the University of Houston in 1987. He is currently a faculty member in the Psychology Department of the University of Akron. He has consulted with several organizations on projects in the areas of problem solving, compensation systems, and implementing work teams and other organizational culture change projects. He is particularly interested in the development of new evaluation methods for organizational interventions and how the practical value of research is defined within organizations to create contextually specific definitions of intervention success.

Lois E. Tetrick is Professor of Industrial and Organizational Psychology at the University of Houston. She received her doctorate from Georgia Institute of Technology. She has served on the editorial boards of several journals and is currently an associate editor of the *Journal of Occupational Health Psychology.* Her research interests include occupational health and safety, organizational learning, the psychology of the employment relationship, and psychological contracts.

Michael E. Thase, MD, is Professor of Psychiatry at the University of Pittsburgh School of Medicine and the Western Psychiatric Institute and Clinic, and an active clinical investigator whose research focuses on the assessment and treatment of mood disorders, including the correlates of differential response to various treatments for depression. A 1979 graduate of the Ohio State University College of Medicine, Dr. Thase has directed the Depression Treatment and Research Program at the University of Pittsburgh since its inception in 1987 and is now the Chief of Adult Academic Psychiatry. A Fellow of the American Psychiatric Association, he has authored or coauthored more than 330 scientific articles and book chapters, as well as five books.

Leah P. Toney is a doctoral student in industrial and organizational psychology at the University of Houston. She received a master's degree in clinical psychology from Louisiana State University. Her research interests include employee health, work/life balance, and organizational change management.

Paula Truax (PhD, University of Washington, 1995) is Assistant Professor, School of Professional Psychology, Pacific University, Forest Grove, Oregon. She completed her internship and postdoctoral training at Wilford Hall Medical Center in San Antonio, Texas. She has authored and coauthored a number of scientific papers and book chapters on depression, effectiveness research, and behavioral case conceptualization. Her current research interests include effectiveness outcome research, clinical significance testing, depression, and anxiety disorder treatments.

Krista L. Uggerslev completed her MSc degree in industrial-organizational psychology at the University of Calgary in 2000. She has published and presented research in the area of performance appraisal and personnel selection. She has also been involved in a variety of applied consulting projects. Currently, she is working on her doctoral degree in industrial-organizational psychology.

Melanie M. VanDyke, M.A., is a doctoral candidate in the Clinical Psychology Training Program at the University of Nebraska-Lincoln. She is currently working as a psychology intern at the Missouri Health Sciences Consortium, completing rotations at the Truman Memorial Veterans Hospital and Mid-Missouri Mental Health Center. Her current research and clinical interests include cognitive-behavioral treatment of anxiety disorders, treatment process and outcome research, and the use of technology in providing clinical services.

Edward E. Wagner, a Professor Emeritus of the University of Akron, possesses ABPPs in both clinical and counseling psychology and is a Fellow of Division 12 (Clinical) of APA. He has published extensively in the field of assessment and psychodiagnostics and is the author of the Hand Test and The Logical Rorschach.